ELLEN TERRL

D1195253

BEST PRACTICES SERIES

Enterprise Systems Integration

Second Edition

THE AUERBACH
BEST PRACTICES SERIES

Broadband Networking
James Trulove, Editor
ISBN: 0-8493-9821-5

Business Continuity Planning
Ken Doughty, Editor
ISBN: 0-8493-0907-7

**The Complete Book
of Remote Access:
Connectivity and Security**
Victor Kasacavage, Editor
ISBN: 0-8493-1253-1

**Designing a Total
Data Solution:
Technology, Implementation,
and Deployment**
Roxanne E. Burkey and
Charles V. Breakfield, Editors
ISBN: 0-8493-0893-3

**High Performance Web
Databases: Design,
Development, and
Deployment**
Sanjiv Purba, Editor
ISBN: 0-8493-0882-8

**Making Supply Chain
Management Work**
James Ayers, Editor
ISBN: 0-8493-1273-6

**Financial Services
Information Systems**
Jessica Keyes, Editor
ISBN: 0-8493-9834-7

**Healthcare Information
Systems**
Phillip L. Davidson, Editor
ISBN: 0-8493-9963-7

**Multi-Operating System
Networking: Living with UNIX,
NetWare, and NT**
Raj Rajagopal, Editor
ISBN: 0-8493-9831-2

Network Design
Gilbert Held, Editor
ISBN: 0-8493-0859-3

Network Manager's Handbook
John Lusa, Editor
ISBN: 0-8493-9841-X

**New Directions in Internet
Management**
Sanjiv Purba, Editor
ISBN: 0-8493-1160-8

**New Directions in Project
Management**
Paul Tinnirello, Editor
ISBN: 0-8493-1190-X

**The Privacy Papers:
Technology and Consumer,
Employee, and Legislative
Actions**
Rebecca Herold, Editor
ISBN: 0-8493-1248-5

Web-to-Host Connectivity
Lisa Lindgren and Anura Gurugé,
Editors
ISBN: 0-8493-0835-6

**Winning the Outsourcing
Game: Making the Best Deals
and Making Them Work**
Janet Butler, Editor
ISBN: 0-8493-0875-5

AUERBACH PUBLICATIONS

www.auerbach-publications.com
TO ORDER: Call: 1-800-272-7737 • Fax: 1-800-374-3401
E-mail: orders@crcpress.com

BEST PRACTICES SERIES

Enterprise Systems Integration

Second Edition

Editor

JUDITH M. MYERSON

AUERBACH PUBLICATIONS

A CRC Press Company

Boca Raton   London   New York   Washington, D.C.

Library of Congress Cataloging-in-Publication Data

Enterprise systems integration / edited by Judith M. Myerson—2nd ed.
   p. cm. — (Best practices series)
Includes bibliographical references and index.
ISBN 0-8493-1149-7 (alk. paper)
   1. Information resources management. 2. Management information systems.
I. Myerson, Judith M. II. Best practices series (Boca Raton, Fla.)
T58.64.E68 2001
658.4′038—dc21
                            2001045195
                                CIP

Visit the Auerbach Publications Web site at www.auerbach-publications.com

© 2002 by CRC Press LLC
Auerbach is an imprint of CRC Press LLC

No claim to original U.S. Government works
International Standard Book Number 0-8493-1149-7
Library of Congress Card Number 2001045195
Printed in the United States of America 1 2 3 4 5 6 7 8 9 0
Printed on acid-free paper

Contributors

DAN ADLER, *Chief Technology Officer, Inventure America, New York, New York*

MARY AYALA-BUSH, *Principal, Computer Sciences Corporation, Waltham, Massachusetts*

JIM AYERS, *Principal, CGR Management Consultants, Playa del Rey, California*

CHARLES BANYAY, *Manager, Deloitte & Touche Consulting Group, Toronto, Ontario, Canada*

PETER M. BECK, *Consulting Engineer, SSDS Division, TCI, Fairfax, Virginia*

ALAN BENANDER, *Associate Professor, Computer and Information Science, Cleveland State University, Cleveland, Ohio*

BARBARA BENANDER, *Associate Professor, Computer and Information Science, Cleveland State University, Cleveland, Ohio*

PRASAD BINGI, *Department of Management and Marketing, Indiana University–Purdue University, Fort Wayne, Indiana*

MICHAEL BLANK, *Senior Engineer, WebMethods, Inc., Fairfax, Virginia*

JANET BUTLER, *Senior Editor, Auerbach Publications, Rancho de Taos, New Mexico*

KAZEM CHAHARBAGHI, *Faculty Member, Manufacturing Technology and Production Management, Cranfield University, Bedford, England*

BOSCO CHEUNG, *Senior Consultant, Deloitte & Touche Consulting Group, Toronto, Ontario, Canada*

TREVOR CLARKE, *Management Consultant, Deloitte Consulting, Toronto, Ontario, Canada*

MADISON CLOUTIER, *Vice President, Marketing, Tower Technology Corporation, Austin, Texas*

DALE COHEN, *Electronic Messaging Team Project Manager, R.R. Donnelley & Sons Company, Chicago, Illinois*

FRANK CULLEN, *Principal, Blackstone and Cullen, Atlanta, Georgia*

DAWNA TRAVIS DEWIRE, *President, Decision Tree Associates, and Faculty Member, Babson College, Babson Park, Massachusetts*

RICHARD T. DUÉ, *President, Thomsen Dué Associates, Ltd., Edmonton, Alberta, Canada*

ADAM FADLALLA, *Associate Professor, Computer and Information Science, Cleveland State University, Cleveland Ohio*

RAINER FEURER, *Research Student, Cranfield University, Bedford, England*

v

Contributors

DAN FOBES, *Software Architect, Yardley, Pennsylvania*
TYLER FRANK, *Doctoral Candidate, Manufacturing Management Program, University of Toledo, Toledo, Ohio*
IDO GILEADI, *Senior Manager, ICS, Deloitte Consulting, Toronto, Ontario, Canada*
JAYANTH K. GODLA, *PricewaterhouseCoopers LLP, Bloomfield Hills, Michigan*
HAL H. GREEN, *Director, Manufacturing Systems Division, SETPOINT, Inc. Houston, Texas*
GREGORY JAMES, *Manager, Knowledge Discovery Services, and D.B.A. Candidate, Cleveland State University, Cleveland Ohio*
SVEN JAMES, *President, CompuSven, Inc., Naples, Florida*
BILL JEFFERY, *Vice President, A.T. Kearney, Dallas, Texas*
RICHARD L. JENSON, *Associate Professor of Accounting, Utah State University, Logan, Utah*
I. RICHARD JOHNSON, *Professor of Accounting, Utah State University, Logan, Utah*
JOHN JORDAN, *Principal, Consulting and Systems Integration, Computer Sciences Corporation, Waltham, Massachusetts*
MARIE KARKANIAN, *Senior Manager, Deloitte Consulting, Toronto, Ontario, Canada*
GREG KILMARTIN, *Engineer, The Tolly Group, Point Pleasant, New Jersey*
KEITH G. KNIGHTSON, *Associate Director, Telecom Architect Program, Canadian Government Telecommunications Agency, Kanata, Ontario, Canada*
WALTER KUKETZ, *Consulting and Systems Integration, Computer Sciences Corporation, Waltham, Massachusetts*
POLLY PERRYMAN KUVER, *Consultant, Boston, Massachusetts*
CAROL L. LARSON,, *Technical Consultant, Beaverton, Oregon*
JAMES A. LARSON, *Senior Software Engineer, Intel Architecture Laboratory, Hillsboro, Oregon*
RICHARD J. LEWIS, JR., *eCom Connections and Miami University, Oxford, Ohio*
LISA M. LINDGREN, *Independent Consultant, High-Tech Marketing Specialist, Meredith, New Hampshire*
CONGHUA LI, *Manager, Deloitte Consulting, Toronto, Ontario, Canada*
CARMA MCCLURE, *Vice President of Research, Extended Intelligence, Chicago, Illinois*
MICHAEL A. MISCHE, *President, Synergy Consulting Group, Inc., Boalsburg, Pennsylvania*
JIM MORRISON, *Principal, A.T. Kearney, Dallas, Texas*
JOHN P. MURRAY, *Independent IT Consultant and Writer, Madison, Wisconsin*
JUDITH M. MYERSON, *System Architect/Engineer, Philadelphia, Pennsylvania*
DAVID NELSON, *Director of Marketing, Wingra Technologies, Madison, Wisconsin*
FRED NEUFELD, *National Data Warehouse System Engineer, Sun Microsystems, Canada*

SRINIVAS PADMANABHARAO, *Consultant, Deloitte Consulting, Ontario, Canada*
RAJAGOPAL PALANISWAMY, *Doctoral Candidate, Manufacturing Management Program, University of Toledo, Toledo, Ohio*
RALPH SPENCER POORE, *Chief Technology Officer, Privacy Infrastructure, Inc., Dallas, Texas*
T.M. RAJKUMAR, *Associate Professor, Department of Decision Sciences and Management Information Systems, Miami University, Oxford, Ohio*
MARTIN SCHLEIFF, *Technical Lead, Boeing Corp., Seattle, Washington*
MANEESH K. SHARMA, *Department of Accounting and Finance, Indiana University–Purdue University, Fort Wayne, Indiana*
ROSHAN L. SHARMA, *Principal, Telecom Network Service, Dallas, Texas*
ANTONIO SI, *Assistant Professor, Department of Computing, Hong Kong Polytechnic University, Hong Kong, China*
ROBERT L. SLOAN, *Business Information Systems Architect, Nylon Business Unit, E.I. du Pont de Nemours and Co., Charlotte, North Carolina*
DANIEL L. SPAR, *Consultant, Transarc Corp., Falls Church, Virginia*
BHAVANI THURAISINGHAM, *Lead Engineer, Center for Integrated Intelligence Systems, The MITRE Corporation, Bedford, Massachusetts*
DEBORAH TYROLER, *Director, Webstream and Interactive Services, International Communications, Inc., Framingham, Massachusetts*
JOHN R. VACCA, *Information Technology Specialist, Pomeroy, Ohio*
JOHN VAN DEN HOVEN, *Manager, Information Systems Planning, Noranda, Inc., Toronto, Ontario, Canada*
DAVID WADSWORTH, *IJava Evangelist, Sun Microsystems, Toronto, Ontario, Canada*
JOHN WARGIN, *Manager, Strategic Consulting and Business Alignment Practice, Hewlett-Packard, Germany*
MICHAEL WEBER, *Project Manager, Redesign and Implementation Processes and IT Support, Hewlett-Packard, Germany*
COLIN WYND, *Business Development Manager, Net Metrix Division, Hewlett-Packard, Colorado Springs, Colorado*
ELANA YELLIN, *Web Site Producer, International Communications, Inc., Framingham, Massachusetts*

Contents

Contents

Contents

Introduction

The wave of corporate mergers and growth of business on the Internet have boosted enterprise systems integration's profile in both IT and business. All these factors have contributed to enterprise integration's importance, but the marketplace conditions and changing regulations of today's global and highly competitive economy remain the major reasons why companies choose an integrated approach. Companies that can provide information needed or that can quickly devise and roll out new products and services are today's proven leading organizations. Integrated enterprise systems can provide information across all points in an organization and the unique way systems integration blends business practices and information technology. Doing so enables a company to rapidly meet the demands of a changing market.

The second edition of *Enterprise Systems Integration* brings together the perspectives, knowledge, and experience of more than 70 experts in the various areas that involve enterprise integration. Their expertise ranges from hands-on experience with technology and project management to the higher-level issues of business and management strategy. Each chapter examines an issue or technology relevant to today's enterprise. Collectively, these chapters span the range of enterprise computing and systems integration.

Business is a driving force behind the enterprise resource planning (ERP) systems that aim at integrating enterprise systems across functional departments. Translating business strategy and requirements, however, is not an easy task. The opening section of this book, "Integration Drivers," gives much-needed guidance in this area, particularly for those organizations that have encountered difficulties during the implementation process of ERP systems. The first two chapters explain how to manage IT in conjunction with business strategy and processes. The third chapter provides a framework for aligning ERP strategy with the overall business strategy.

The concept of an integrated enterprise began with the mainframe days. The big iron was the enterprise system by default, as no other technologies could match its processing capabilities. This was no longer true with the advent of client/server and networked desktop systems when they blurred the notion of a cohesive enterprise. In later years, the concept was revived with ERP packages, such as Baan, J.D. Edwards, Oracle, PeopleSoft, and SAP. All aim at overcoming problems associated with incompatible and nonuniform systems. For the past few years, these systems have been enhanced with E-business and E-commerce solutions over the Internet. More recent are the ERP application service providers (ASPs) that offer professional service to large and small organizations on a rental basis.

Specifically, Section VII, "Enterprise Resource Planning," explains what ERP is, how different it is from supply-chain management (SCM), and how to choose an ERP implementation strategy. It points out the role of host integration servers and what ASPs do. It discusses how to enhance manufacturing performance with ERP systems. This section also considers risk management skills needed in a packaged environment, external factors to ERP systems and critical issues impacting the implementation.

Remaining sections look at various architectural frameworks and technologies from an enterprise perspective. An important part of this perspective is to watch how technology works within the entire organization, and how each section covers integration into the overall enterprise.

- Enterprise architectures
- Enterprise networking
- Enabling technologies
- Enterprise messaging
- Component-based development
- Internet commerce
- Database servers in an integrated environment
- Project and systems management
- Data warehousing

Section III, "Enabling Technologies," focuses on the growing importance of CORBA, COM, Enterprise Java, and XML — all as middleware solutions. Data warehouses have been Java-enabled, and XML serves as a bridge with legacy systems. Also important are the use of FrontPage 2000 in Web-enabling databases, and the application servers to tie client/server and legacy systems. Section IV, on component-based development, briefly discusses the economics and domain engineering of system components, and gives an overview of Java on its role in server-side applications. Proper management of object libraries is vital to component-based development.

Section V, "Database Servers in an Integrated Environment," spans the range from design and architecture to management and integration in the enterprise. It stresses remote data subset synchronization as the key piece in any remote information technology, while providing a framework to support a wide range of database platforms. It shows how business rules are buried within a schema and application software, how to design a capacity design server, and how to use CORBA to integrate databases. Section VI, on data warehousing, provides a strategy and framework for development and application. It considers online data mining, building data warehouses with users, as well as administering and managing huge repositories of legacy data.

Integrated enterprise systems connect database and data warehousing servers across the enterprise network comprising the Internet, intranets, and extranets. As discussed in Section VIII, "Enterprise Networking," it is important to adequately plan, design, and optimize these networks. The larger the enterprise network becomes, the greater and more complex the network traffic problems will be. To minimize the risk of prolonged downtime, proper tools for troubleshooting, monitoring, and analyzing network problems must be available when needed.

Exchanging messages over the enterprise network facilitates messaging between users and applications. The architecture of an Oracle application, for example, is based on an asynchronous messaging model that allows applications as separate modules to send messages to one another based on their availability. Section IX, "Enterprise Messaging," briefly discusses messaging gateways, directory services, and migration tools. Also discussed are the jurisdictional issues in transmitting data across the borders of nations. Each nation has its own set of laws it may wish to enforce.

ERP profoundly affects the way in which organizations operate, and this is particularly true for E-commerce. The section on "Internet Commerce" covers Web-based testing and capacity planning and the use of XML and metrics in developing business-to-business commerce. As the transmissions become more global, implications of multilingual Web sites are significant in enterprisewide systems integration.

Once armed with the strategy and technologies, IT managers must successfully deploy ERP systems within budget and on time. In addition, they must be able to integrate them into the rest of the enterprise systems they rent or buy. The book concludes with a section on managing enterprise integration successfully. Each project has its own unique characteristics and enterprise systems integration is unlike any other systems development project. The three chapters in the section on "Project and Systems Management" look at what nine factors for project success are, how to salvage projects in trouble, and how to guarantee high uptime availability with service level management. The remaining chapters provide an overview of the systems integration life cycle and choosing a systems integrator.

New to the second edition of *Enterprise Systems Integration* are two appendices: ERP Vendors and ERP Resources. The number of ERP vendors has grown since the handbook's first edition. To widen the existing ERP customer base, some vendors also offer ASP hosting or professional service for the design, implementation, systems integration, and continuous operations management. Some large companies may opt for certain ASP applications to try them before acquiring them for integration into ERP systems. The second appendix looks at some ERP resources on the Web, and briefly discusses how useful collaborative commerce may be to multi-enterprises.

Enterprise computing has become a means for leveraging and optimizing individual performance, knowledge, and operational processes. Integration is the construct and infrastructure that provides these ends. It is also central to realizing strategic and financial objectives. This convergence of knowledge, technology, and human performance, which comprises today's enterprise, allows creative business process design. Thus, an organization can create new and innovative ways to service customers or to do business with suppliers and make itself a leader in its field. This capability relies on a successful strategy that integrates the enterprise. The second edition of *Enterprise Systems Integration* gives the business insight and the technological know-how to ensure a successful systems integration strategy.

Section I
Integration Drivers

Chapter 1
Defining Systems Integration

Michael A. Mische

Major system integration efforts are being performed in almost every organization, as the private and public sectors attempt to become more competitive. Some of the motivations to integrate clearly revolve around technological issues, the need to improve the results of technology investments, and cost reductions. Straddled with legacy technologies and systems that are inflexible and expensive to maintain, these organizations have only limited options. They must migrate to newer technologies.

The overwhelming reason to integrate is the need to become more competitive in an environment that is constantly changing and highly competitive. The competitive pressures facing organizations are enormous, and the consequences of failing to integrate and exploit technology to create competitive advantage are indisputable. The competitive landscape has changed dramatically, and companies can no longer depend on the traditional ways of competing to ensure their viability. For example, it is true that:

- A full 70 percent of the largest firms in 1955 no longer exist.
- As many as 10 percent of the 1980 *Fortune 500* have disappeared.
- Only three of the top ten companies in the world in 1972 remain in the top ten today.
- The average life expectancy of a large industrial company is 40 years.
- Employment and security are no longer mainstays of the economy. Companies have downsized and cut employment ranks significantly.
- Investors and Wall Street are demanding that companies take action by rewarding cost cutting and downsizing. For example, the day Sears announced it was discarding 50,000 jobs, its stock climbed nearly 4 percent.

New rules of competition are driving new ways of organizing. Companies can ill afford to continue to compete in the same way that they once did. At the forefront is technology and system integration. Technology and integrated business practices can neutralize the traditional advantages of size and location. Integrated processing solutions can allow a company to compete anywhere, at any time. Electronic commerce, knowledge-based systems, and the Internet know no size or constraints.

The integration of technologies with new organizational designs and business processes also supports the collaboration of workers regardless of where they are geographically located. Integration allows information and knowledge to be simultaneously shared by workers, business partners, and even collaborative competitors. Integration allows for concurrent work on a problem or project regardless of location, time zones, and the location of information. The creation of collaborative work environments also provides opportunities to develop and deploy new organizational designs that exploit technologies and human performance by melding knowledge and business processes. Core knowledge (i.e., knowledge that is essential to the process and the organization) becomes embedded in the process and available to all.

The need to integrate is also driven by new forms of business and partnerships. Groups of companies and workers not only share data and information, but also have exposure to their respective business partners' operations. For example, Toyota, long known as a creative user of technology, provides its suppliers and partners with advanced visibility into parts designs, engineering measures, and inventory levels. Wal-Mart and K-Mart provide suppliers with access and instant information related to item movement. A customer buys a coat at Wal-Mart and a data stream follows that tells the supplier the coat color, size, price, and where it was sold. The supplier, who is responsible for managing the inventory at that Wal-Mart location, immediately begins a replenishment process designed to restock the item in a day or less. The competitive advantage of integrating technology with human performance, knowledge, and organizational designs is powerful.

DEFINING SYSTEMS INTEGRATION

Determining the size and breadth of the integration industry and isolating what exactly is the process for integrating systems are extremely difficult to do with any level of precision. Much rhetoric is produced about system integration, but comparably less authoritative reference material exists on precisely what integration is or is not, and how to perform integration. No uniformly acknowledged definition describes system integration. The term *system integration* enjoys enormous popularity among vendors and consultants, all of whom have an undeniable vested interest in keeping the definition relatively ambiguous. As such, it has also come to mean just about anything, including outsourcing. Some of the largest vendors and consultants define *system integration* rhetorically; that is, integration depends on what the individual calls it and what he or she wants integrated. Undoubtedly, significant marketing advantage can be gained from the ambiguity.

Another definition, developed by an industry association of vendors, defines *integrator* as the point of integration for technology solutions delivery. This is hardly an effective definition, especially when considered in a contemporary context of new organizational designs and processes. In contrast, users tend to define *integration process* as a process that concentrates on features and functions. Many information management and technology professionals tend to view integration as more of a technical issue.

In an effort to add some structure to the industry, the Gartner Group has defined integration as a "large [more than $1 million], complex IS project that includes designing and/or building a customized architecture or application, as well as integrating it with new or existing hardware, packaged and custom software, and communications." This definition goes a long way toward creating a credible standard, but it still lacks a tangible quality. There is something limiting to imposing price as a defining component of integration, because too many factors influence the expenditures of an organization. There are too many ways of counting and classifying costs to use price as a differentiating criterion for defining system integration.

The Technological Definition of Systems Integration

Historically, system integration was confined to the technical aspects of hardware and the interconnectivity of computing components. Integration had a mechanical connotation and piecemeal quality: making different pieces of equipment work together. As the industry and knowledge evolved, integration began to include software, data, and communication. Today, system integration encompasses all of these. In a world that places premiums on cyber customers, cyber companies, virtual employees, telecommuting, and speed, integration has come to mean more than just technology. Systems integration involves a complete system of business processes, managerial practices, organizational interactions and structural alignments, and knowledge management. It is an all-inclusive process designed to create relatively seamless and highly agile processes and organizational structures that are aligned with the strategic and financial objectives of the enterprise. A clear economic and competitive value proposition is established between the need and objectives for systems integration and the performance of the enterprise.

Systems integration represents a progressive and iterative cycle of melding technologies, human performance, knowledge, and operational processes together. It is more a journey than a specific set-point project. Some organizations, such as Boeing, Wal-Mart, Merrill Lynch, Federal Express, and Chrysler, are very sophisticated and extremely advanced in their use of integration. For example, Boeing designed and tested the new 777 entirely online before building a prototype or model. Customers of the aircraft, such as United Airlines and Singapore Air, had direct links into the design of the plane. Mechanics, pilots, and engineers were trained on aircraft maintenance, flying characteristics, and design, long before the plane was built, through electronic models and knowledge delivery systems. The result was a super aircraft that employed integrated technologies and business processes; it was built in 40 percent less time than any other plane.

Chrysler has reduced the time it takes to design and build a new car by 40 percent through the integration of technologies, processes, new organizational structures, and human performance. System integration has become the primary vehicle for creating more agile and competitive organizations.

From a technological perspective, system integration is the melding of divergent and often incompatible technologies, applications, data, and communications into a uniform information technology architecture and functional working structure. The reality today is that integration involves many aspects of technology and organizational processes. What may be integration for one company may not be integration for another. For example, what may be defined and practiced as integration for Chrysler probably will be something entirely different for Volvo. Consequently, there may not be one single definition for integration that is appropriate for all situations and projects.

The States of Systems Integration

More appropriately, there are states of system integration. Each state of integration has its own unique definition, properties, aspects, and complexities. Each state also has a unique economic value proposition, and each can be applied to the specific situations of an organization. When considering what is or is not integration, it is important to distinguish what the state of integration is within an organization and what it can realistically achieve. An important dimension of defining integration is the point at which integration is being defined and the status of integration that the organization has achieved.

There are four states of system integration:

1. State 1: Interconnectivity
2. State 2: Interoperability
3. State 3: Semantic consistency
4. State 4: Convergent integration

Three of these are contingent on technology and its status; however, the fourth represents a convergence of technology and human performance, processes, and knowledge. It is the highest and most sophisticated state of integration.

State 1: Interconnectivity. This is the most elementary state of integration. It forms the foundation for all subsequent integration. Interconnectivity involves making various pieces of often disparate equipment and technologies work together. This includes the sharing of peripherals, the simple transferring of files, and the creation of common pathways between different components. The basic applications, functionality, and uses all remain fairly specific with respect to their technologies and users, with little or no integration at the functional levels.

State 2: Interoperability. Interoperability refers to the ability to make one application and technology function with another in a manner that exploits the capabilities of both. Most of the "integrated" vendor software offerings provide this level of integration, which usually updates and feeds other applications and interfaces with other databases. For the majority of organizations, interoperability is the state of their integration.

State 3: Semantic Consistency. Much effort and investment have been directed toward the implementation of database management systems and sophisticated management reporting systems. The trademark for this form of integration is the rationalization of data elements, terms, and meaning. The emphasis is on providing accessibility to data and minimizing the potential for errors in human interpretation through the creation of standard data definitions and formats. In achieving semantic integration, simply implementing database management systems is not enough; data must be rationalized and have significant meaning to the user.

State 4: Convergent Integration. This is the highest and most sophisticated form of the integration states. Systemic integration requires the presence of the first three states but involves much more than the integration of technologies, applications, and the rationalization of shared databases. Convergent integration involves the integration of technology with business processes, knowledge, and human performance. Systems integration is the enabler, the delivery vehicle for new organizational designs and processes. Convergent integration has seven prerequisite components:

1. Technology integration, which requires interconnectivity
2. Applications and software integration, which requires interoperability
3. Data and data repository integration, which requires semantic integration
4. Communications network integration, which requires interconnectivity, interoperability, and semantic integration
5. The design and integration of new business processes with new technical capabilities
6. The embedding of knowledge within new business processes and enabling technologies
7. The integration of human performance with new processes

In its most advanced state and form, convergent integration allows the organization to compete differently by providing the means to reconfigure itself and quickly adapt to changing opportunities.

Operationally, integrated systems have some distinguishing characteristics and share five essential attributes:

1. Functional and technical compatibility is provided.
2. The technologies used to process applications and data are relatively transparent to users. Integration can be achieved at any level and using any technology. The issue is selecting the best technology that optimizes several key criteria: user utility, technology longevity, adaptability and scalability, and speed of solution delivery.
3. Application systems, data, access paths to data, and graphical user interfaces (GUIs) are harmonized and standardized for the user (i.e., they look and work the same and are intuitive to a new user).
4. All enterprisewide data is rationalized; data means the same thing from system to system and application to application, and data is uniformly defined throughout the organization.
5. All enterprisewide applications and computing environments are scalable and portable to a variety of needs. That is, technologies and applications can be rapidly deployed and tailored for specific use in the organization. Essential application code and data structures are replaceable and reproducible, not constantly reinvented.

These five characteristics define the integration process and the integrated system. System integration is achieved when the processing environment, technologies, human performance, and business processes all function in a harmonious and congruent manner.

THE REALITIES AND MYTHS OF SYSTEMS INTEGRATION AND THE MARKETPLACE

With the lack of a clear definition and industry standards for integration, it is little wonder that there are a number of myths and misconceptions about system integration and systems integrators. Some of the more common myths surrounding system integration are discussed in the following sections.

Myth: Systems integration is a purely technical issue. The reality is that systems integration is a progressive process and is situational to the organization attempting to integrate. In some instances, system integration may be predominantly one of technology, but this is not necessarily so in all cases. Systems integration involves many other facets of the enterprise, including applications, data, communications, business processes, and how the organization deploys, manages, and effectively uses information technology to gain competitive advantage. Thus, there are various states of integration that are endemic to the organization, its technology, and its strategic objectives.

Myth: Systems integration drives organizational change and business process reengineering. The reality is that system integration may be an enabler for systemic change in the organization, but the business books are full of cases of integration projects that yielded little, if any, systemic change. Transactions may have been accelerated, but the basic ways in which the business performed, was managed, and was organized did not change. System integration can enable massive process and structural changes in the organization. To do so requires the organization to want to change and establish change as a priority.

Depending on the state of integration, system integration may or may not require business process reengineering. Systems integration can be the enabling agent of business process reengineering, but it alone is not reengineering. As the organization moves to a higher state of integration, reengineering and new organizational designs are almost always involved. Organizations that are in the fourth state of integration experience significant change.

Myth: Systems integration projects are driven by application development or the acquisition of third-party software, or both. The reality is that third-party software offerings, such as those provided by SAP-AG, Oracle, and Computer Associates, provide a catalyst for integration and are useful. However, in all cases, achieving a convergent state of integration involves far more than applications and technologies. What is required is systemic change in the way businesses are operated, organized, and managed to best leverage technology and human performance. Software alone can force some changes in the way an organization is managed and structured, but the organization must be led through the journey of change.

Myth: Systems integration projects can be performed without special project management competencies, such as change management or technical skills. The reality is that systems integration projects are large, complex, and risky. They demand a highly skilled and disciplined project team, dedicated leadership, and a formal methodology to provide guidelines for performance and behavior. Because of the size and complexity of these system integration efforts, they demand comprehensive project management techniques not only to track and report on the status of the project, but also to anticipate its needs and challenges.

Myth: Systems integrators and integration firms are unique and different. The reality is that there are a number of differences among systems integrators; however, for the most part they are subtle. Some integrators are very large; others are smaller. Organizations considering the use of an integrator have a large and varied selection from which to choose. The key to selecting an integrator is to understand the state of integration one is in, what state of integration the organization is trying to achieve, and matching the integrator to that state.

SUMMARY

The integration of systems has broad ramifications for the organization. In most situations, system integration involves more than technology; it involves the convergence of technology, processes, knowledge, and human performance. It is a systemic change in the ways organizations operate and are structured. To effectively integrate and optimize their use of technology and competitive performance, organizations attempting integration must transcend the normal boundaries of technology and address their fundamental business and organizational practices.

Integration is a progressive process, a constant evolution of technology, business processes, knowledge, and human capital. As demonstrated by such leaders as Boeing, Chrysler, Federal Express, and Wal-Mart, improved performance and financial returns can be generated through the integration of technologies and the leverage provided. More important, the competitive position of the organization can be vastly improved through convergent integration.

This chapter has provided an opening glance into the integration marketplace and some of the key issues regarding system integration. This chapter defined system integration, explored some of the major attributes and qualities of system integration, and discussed some of the more prevalent drivers for system integration. The remaining chapters of this book provide additional insights into the system integration process and a framework to follow to ensure a successful integration effort.

Chapter 2

Aligning Strategies, Processes, and Information Technology: A Case Study

Rainer Feurer
Kazem Chaharbaghi
Michael Weber
John Wargin

Process innovations and redesigns frequently must employ technology in order to achieve major improvements in performance. Information technology (IT) has become an enabler for newly designed processes by eliminating limitations of time, location, or organizational structure, or by providing a new basis for differentiation. This can only be achieved, however, when processes and IT are carefully aligned with the overall organization's objectives and interfunctional teamwork.

While there is general consensus among practitioners that business/IT alignment is necessary, the way to achieve it is often unclear. This is because business strategies are usually defined first and the operations and supporting strategies, including technologies, are then aligned. Such a sequential approach defines strategies, processes, and actions in light of the technologies available, as opposed to identifying technologies that drive the critical success factors.

A better approach is one in which strategies, processes, technologies, and actions are defined and aligned concurrently. The aim of this chapter

0-8493-1149-7/02/$0.00+$1.50
© 2002 by CRC Press LLC

is to present a business-alignment approach, one used and developed by Hewlett-Packard Co. (HP) for designing and implementing new business processes that are enabled and supported by new generations of information systems.

This approach has been practiced over several years, both internally and externally, generating a portfolio of best practices. The well-defined activities are closely linked and are applied by multifunctional teams for the purpose of business reengineering as well as redesigning core business processes. The whole approach is complemented by a strong focus on teamwork, specialized and objective-driven business units, and a commitment to quality and customer satisfaction.

FRAMEWORK FOR BUSINESS ALIGNMENT

Strategies are only effective when they are readily translated into actions. This implies that supporting ITs need to be highly responsive. Business processes should be continuously optimized through the application of relevant technologies and carried out by high-performance teams. Strategies must therefore be:

- Formulated by closely examining the role of technology as an enabling source
- Translated into actions through highly interactive processes that consider all current and future business factors

In the past, the design of business processes and IT applications was focused on achieving incremental benefits. Flexibility and ability to react to major changes were largely neglected. The business alignment framework in Exhibit 1 links any given strategy and its corresponding actions.

Linking Strategy and Actions

Strategies determine the critical success factors that in turn define the necessary business processes and their information needs. The availability, cost, and flexibility of different technologies may limit their selection; therefore, business processes must be translated into feasible application models while information requirements are translated into workable data models. In this way, the gap between the ideal and workable solutions can be minimized while ensuring a logical linkage between strategy and optimized actions.

The aim of such a framework is twofold:

1. To make process changes without being restricted by or limited to existing technology, applications, and suboptimal data structures
2. To make visible the impact of new technologies on processes, and vice versa

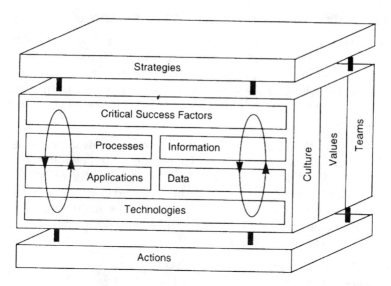

Exhibit 1. Business Alignment Framework

The business alignment framework takes into account the necessary process changes resulting from changes in the environment as well as potential advancements in technology. Because any change in strategy and technology potentially results in a change in the value system, culture, and team structures of the organization, it is vital to include these additional factors within the overall framework.

By employing this framework, HP has experienced a number of benefits, including:

- Optimization of all the business processes with the support of integrated technology, as opposed to suboptimization of individual processes and organization units with the support of fragmented technology
- Consistent focus on processes that maximize stakeholder value
- Common understanding of issues and future targets throughout the organization
- High level of transparency and flexibility to act and react to changes stemming from the competitive environment as well as improvements in technology
- High level of commitment from people throughout the organization

In this framework, target processes, technologies, and standards drive the selection of potential solutions. User participation forms an integral part of the framework and helps to ensure fast and effective implementation.

IMPLEMENTING THE BUSINESS ALIGNMENT FRAMEWORK

The business alignment framework is implemented by cross-functional teams that include members from different organizational and functional units. Team members are given a charter by senior-level management to initiate and implement major changes. To prevent tunnel vision, teams are sometimes supported by external consultants and a key role is assigned to management.

According to the structure of the framework, business processes and information requirements are defined in parallel with technology enablers and models, which are then linked throughout the alignment process. Objectives and measures are defined and reviewed in light of the intended overall strategy, which leads to adjustments and refinements of existing results. The approach used to develop the business alignment framework includes the following modules:

- Breakthrough objectives and process links
- Business models
- Technology enablers and models
- Solution mapping and selection
- Functional mapping

Breakthrough Objectives and Processes

The alignment process commences with the existing business strategy or strategic direction of the organization or organizational unit. Based on a strategy review, potential breakthrough objectives are defined. Breakthrough objectives create a distinct competitive differentiation in the eyes of the customer when implemented. This can be achieved through significant improvements in performance in the area of cost, introduction or distribution of new products, outsourcing of noncore activities, consolidation scenarios, or modification of supplier relationships.

After a comprehensive list of potential breakthrough objectives is defined, the most critical (usually two to five) objectives are selected. These objectives form the basis of critical success factors, which, in this sense, are all those factors that have to go right in order to achieve a breakthrough. In parallel, potential obstacles that prevent the achievement of the breakthroughs are identified. These may fall into different categories, including management practices, technology support, training, and goal conflicts between different stakeholders.

Innovative, Core, and Supportive Processes

The next step is formulating the key processes that have a major effect on achieving the breakthrough objectives. These processes basically support the critical success factors. Processes that support several critical success

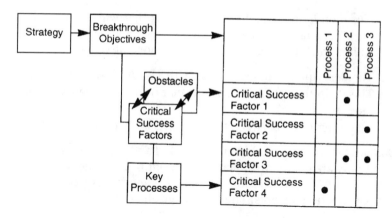

Exhibit 2.   Breakthrough Objectives, Critical Success Factors, and Key Processes

---

Exhibit 3.   Process Classification and Potential Impact

Major Processes	Process Classification	Process Impact			
		Cost	Quality	Speed	Flexibility
Manage Product and Parts Info	Core	X		X	X
Control Production	Innovative		X	X	X
Plan and Procure Material	Innovative	X	X	X	X
Manage Material Flow	Core–Innovative	X		X	X
Manufacturer Products	Core	X	X	X	X
Distribution	Core		X	X	X
Financial	Supportive				X

factors are classed as innovative processes. These usually involve multi-functional activities that directly create stakeholder value. They become the focus of business, process, and information models. Other process categories include supportive and core processes which, although important, do not result in differentiation in the eyes of the stakeholders because these processes usually correlate with only one or two critical success factors. Exhibit 2 shows diagrammatically the way in which breakthrough objectives and innovative processes are identified. Exhibit 3 illustrates the classification process used to determine innovative, core, and supportive processes based on their potential impact on cost, quality, speed, and flexibility.

Business Models

Business models are developed for describing innovative processes and their role within the overall organization. HP designs business models not only for facilitating communications and achieving consensus, but also as a basis for identifying enabling technologies that will allow the organization to achieve major improvements in performance or differentiation. This requires the following three equally important views:

1. The description of business activities or processes (process model)
2. The definition of business information requirements (information model)
3. The interaction between the business activities and information

Business models can yield highly adapted and flexible IT infrastructures that not only are geared to specific needs but provide benefit to the entire organization. At HP, the creation of business models is performed by several cross-functional teams. The advantages include:

- Users can be closely involved in the modeling process and committed to the definition of their processes from the very early stage.
- Well-defined models can be reused and adapted to other business areas and subsidiaries.
- Work of parallel teams is more efficient if supported by a common structure and hierarchical decomposition.

The business models developed take a tree-shaped form in which each global process can be described as a collection of activities and subprocesses. While global processes are modeled by top-level management or core teams, the more detailed representations are produced by specialist subteams. In developing and linking the models, inconsistencies, omissions, and misunderstandings are observed and corrected. In parallel to developing the process hierarchy, information models are developed.

Information Models

Information models aim to identify and describe business data objects (e.g., assets, orders, locations) together with their interrelationships. For example, an order combined with a location creates the data object called Shipment. Information modeling is therefore concerned with two major questions: What information does the business need? What interrelationship exists with other information?

To support this goal, data objects must be driven by business needs and defined in isolation from existing information systems and applications. This is in contrast to the approach used in the past in which data was designed and created for a specific application system that supported a single function from a limited perspective. This method leads to a high level of data redundancy and inconsistency. Information models, however, regard information as detached from existing or potential applications with the aim of improving the timeliness, completeness, and accuracy of shared information while decreasing redundancy.

There are two levels of information models. At the highest level of abstraction, the global information model identifies the 10 or 20 data objects or clusters that are critical for the implementation of breakthrough objectives. This model is primarily used for communication with senior-level management and setting a framework for detailed modeling performed by dedicated subteams.

The second type of model contains a more detailed explosion with approximately 100 to 200 data objects. This model is also used to validate the appropriate process models in the process hierarchy.

Although the process and information models are developed independent of any application systems, they help to determine where technology can play an enabling role, as discussed next.

Technology Enablers and Models

The impact of IT has several characteristics, the most important of which are:

- *Integrative.* IT supports coordination and integration between different activities and processes.
- *Direct.* IT is used to improve the sequence of activities and processes so that they can be carried out faster and in parallel. Furthermore, unnecessary intermediaries may be eliminated.
- *Information.* IT is used to capture process information for knowledge generation, process analysis, and decision making.

Standards

Technology can be a cost-effective enabler only if certain standards are defined and adhered to. It is therefore necessary to examine and define which technology elements, based on today's technology and standards as well as likely future trends, can be applied in the implementation of the business processes.

The selected standards should be seen not as a limiting factor but rather as a mechanism that improves exchangeability of technology, flexibility, cost effectiveness, and efficiency. The definition of standards, for example, in the area of IT may include such considerations as the design of the physical and logical network concepts including internal and external communications needs, operating systems, and databases, as well as the definition of potential hardware requirements and implementation outlines including outsourcing and multivendor scenarios.

Solution Mapping and Selection

Once the business models and the technology standards are defined, the next step is to select solutions that best support and enable the defined

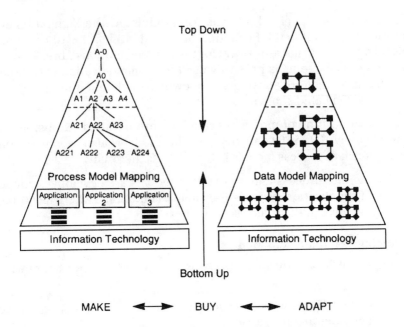

Exhibit 4. Mapping Potential Solutions to Processes and Information Requirements

business processes. This can be achieved by matching the defined process and information models to the process and data models of existing and potential newly developed solutions. This forms a top-down, bottom-up approach, as shown in Exhibit 4.

Using this approach, processes that can be enabled or supported by IT are combined into clusters of potential applications. These could include financial systems, manufacturing resource planning, production control, sales tracking, and customer databases. This clustering is performed at a very high level and, as such, does not yet include detailed functional requirements. In a parallel activity, key objectives for the selection of application solutions, together with importance ratings, are defined.

Based on the solution clusters and the selected objectives and weightings, a market analysis of existing application solutions is performed in which the top two to four candidates within each area are short-listed and then checked for their fit with the process and information models and adherence to agreed-on standards and core concepts. In addition, business fit is evaluated according to such criteria as vendor size, availability of localized application versions, and references.

The selection process is continued by translating the process models into detailed functionality requirements; it may also include prototyping of

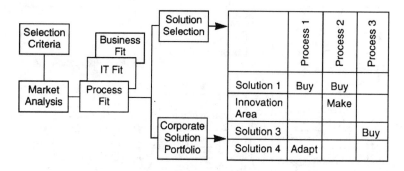

Exhibit 5. Solution Mapping and Selection

---

selected processes or parts of the process. This analysis is used to determine whether:

- The newly defined business processes can be supported or enabled by using standard applications.
- It is possible to modify and adapt existing application solutions.
- It is necessary to develop custom application solutions.

Developing a Corporate Solutions Portfolio

During this step, it is also possible to develop a corporate solutions portfolio of applications that can be shared across different organizational units or used for similar processes. Exhibit 5 illustrates the solution mapping and selection process.

Functional Mapping

Solutions and applications are selected on the basis of process and information models defined by teams of planners and users. Once a specific application is selected, it is possible to go back and really start the process of matching the key functions to the actual selected applications in order to determine the extent of application adaptation or process change required. This process is termed "functional mapping."

Functional mapping (Exhibit 6) is the beginning of the implementation process; however, it must still be regarded as part of the overall business alignment framework because modifications to and changes in business processes and solution adaptation are still possible.

The defined business processes are checked with users in terms of the detailed fit with specific business or process events and compared to the functionality of the selected solutions. In cases where a gap exists, two alternatives are examined:

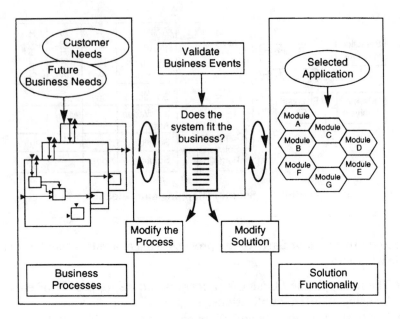

Exhibit 6. Functional Mapping

1. Modify the business process
2. Modify the application solution, which may involve minor changes such as report generation or major changes such as recoding specific software modules

In cases where the implementation of a breakthrough objective depends on the existence of a specific process, the decision will always be the modification of the application rather than sacrificing the process in the defined form. The process of functional mapping operates best if users can test to what extent the selected solution supports the newly defined processes; for this purpose, HP uses piloting centers and laboratories.

INDUSTRIAL APPLICATIONS

Two industrial applications demonstrate the potential of the business alignment framework. The first application reflects work carried out by HP for another organization in support of the construction of a transplant operation. This application illustrates the way in which the framework can be applied to a newly designed business and drive the selection of open-systems-based applications to significantly reduce IT costs. The second application is internal and demonstrates the way in which the framework can be applied to redefine existing operations. It incorporates additional considerations, such as finding a compromise between conflicting goals and objectives of different groups involved in the process of change.

Application to a Greenfield Operation

HP was selected to help a large multinational car manufacturer develop a new transplant operation in the U.S. This transplant was considered to be the first step in the redesign of the organization toward a worldwide network of factories and represented a "greenfield" operation; as such, it was not subject to existing technologies, processes, work methods, and support systems. The only constraints were the short implementation time frame (18 months), certain environmental conditions, and the network of suppliers, customers, and the parent company.

The first step involved the creation of teams, together with the identification and definition of the key project requirements based on strategic considerations of the overall organization, as well as internal and external benchmarks. The most important requirement was defined as achieving a premium on flexibility and adaptability in terms of new products or models, quantity, expandability, and "change of charter" (e.g., serving worldwide versus selected markets).

A balanced approach between using people and technology would allow the organization to adapt the transplant strategy or processes more rapidly with market requirements, while at the same time being more motivational to the transplant personnel. The aim was to commit flexible resources at the latest possible moment in the production process, thus saving additional money. Another requirement was that the factory and infrastructures should be driven by innovative processes, thus allowing the acquisition and transfer of new knowledge and best practices. Finally, the project aimed at establishing new levels and types of partnerships, thus recognizing the role of the transplant as part of a larger network. After identifying these and other key requirements, their significance and the competitive deficit of the organization were determined in the form of a gap analysis. The resulting focus pattern (Exhibit 7) drove the execution of the business alignment and was regularly used for control purposes.

The breakthroughs in the area of process innovation and technology enablers were defined using cross-functional teams from both organizations. The breakthroughs, together with some of the critical success factors for the project, are shown in Exhibit 8. The next step was to identify key processes that would have a major impact on achieving the objectives. High-level business models of the transplant and its environment were developed and subsequently translated into key processes. These key processes were segmented into innovative, core, and supportive processes in order to identify those that would have the strongest impact on overall transplant performance. These subprocesses were subsequently modeled by cross-functional teams in a hierarchical way, as previously described. Exhibit 9 is a simplified representation of the highest level (A0) process model that contains the four subprocesses.

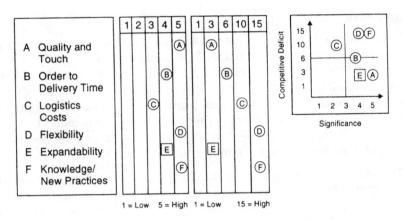

Exhibit 7. Project Goals, Significance, and Competitive Deficit

Exhibit 8. Breakthroughs and Critical Success Factors in the Area of Technology Enablers

Critical Success Factors / Information Technology Breakthroughs	Open systems	Global vendors and suppliers	High level of transparency on process structure and interrelationships with other processes	Multifunctional teamwork	Multiple vendors	Scalability of systems	Standard solutions wherever possible	Incorporation of members of existing plants
Integrated and standardized applications (cost efficiency, flexibility, no vendor dependency)	●	●			●	●	●	
Process, team driven design and execution of approach			●	●				●
IT cost/product at 50% of cost level in existing plants	●	●	●			●	●	
Modularity of systems (for flexibility)			●			●	●	●
Ability to transfer experience to other plants		●		●		●	●	●

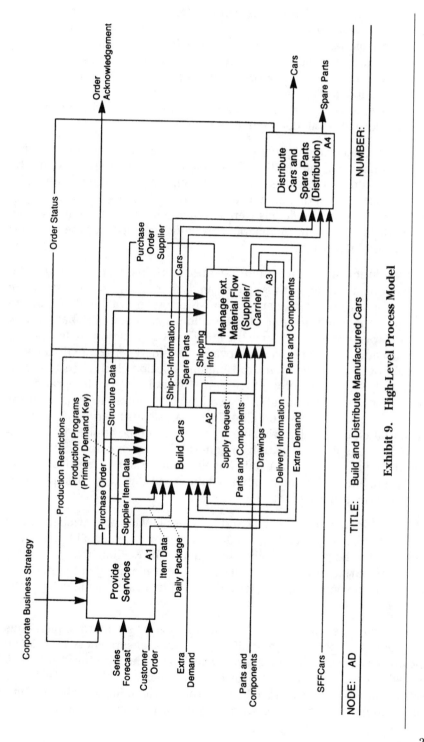

NODE: AD   TITLE: Build and Distribute Manufactured Cars   NUMBER:

Exhibit 9. High-Level Process Model

Each of the subprocesses was modeled and documented accordingly. While the top levels were modeled by a core team of planners, the subprocesses were modeled by dedicated and specialist subteams that included possible future users as well as experienced users of existing processes. This consistent modeling approach, supported by a computerized tool, made it possible to link the process models, rapidly and completely identify conflicts, and meet the required time frame. In parallel with the process models, information models were generated.

Using the hierarchical process models, structure and resource requirements for material, information, financial flows, and personnel could be defined. In addition, process report requirements, including manual and computerized methods and access to central systems, could be easily identified. The process models were applied in the specification of potential solutions by drawing up functional requirements lists for the activities within a certain process.

These functional requirements were then clustered into potential applications, together with a market analysis of commercially available applications. The potential applications were then evaluated in order to determine the extent to which they would satisfy the functional requirements. It was possible to reduce the number of applications to five potential final candidates. This was achieved by evaluating the functional fit of several potential applications for different solution clusters (e.g., bill-of-material, MRP, material flow) together with their level of integration. In the evaluation of functional fit, a level corresponding to 60 percent or above was considered acceptable. The analysis also served as a cross-check that commercially available solutions could be applied in the running of a transplant operation in general. If only one application had scored above 50 percent, it would have been necessary to reconsider the decision to aim for commercially available solutions in the first place, or to change the processes.

In addition to functional fit, IT and business fit were also evaluated. The overall fit of each application was determined by mapping all the applications with the help of a three-dimensional matrix. Exhibit 10 diagrammatically summarizes the process of application mapping and selection, together with some sample criteria used for the evaluation in each of the three dimensions.

The project resulted in the selection of several standard applications that would support highly optimized processes, ensure effectiveness and efficiency, and maintain a high level of flexibility. The structured approach with which the project was performed, together with the standard solutions used, made it possible to achieve the intended implementation time frame without compromising the quality of the project outcomes.

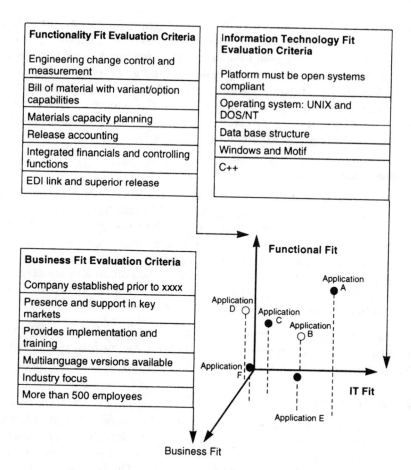

Exhibit 10.   Application Mapping and Selection

Application to an Existing Business

HP has used the business alignment framework to redesign its order fulfillment process. Although the application of the overall framework remained the same as in the previous example, two additional dimensions had to be addressed:

1. Because the business process already existed, it was necessary to evaluate the impact of potential changes.
2. Because the process spanned several business units and product groups (some of which had conflicting goals), it was necessary to decide where and how compromises could be achieved.

In this case, the greatest benefits could be achieved by concentrating on improving on-time delivery, speed of new product introduction, and price performance in a common way. Other group-specific factors were then dealt with independently by the different business units. This analysis also formed the basis for the definition of breakthrough objectives, such as 100 percent delivery on customer date and cost reduction of 30 to 40 percent for each group and business unit that would clearly improve the performance of the overall organization in terms of the selected business goals. Based on these and other breakthroughs, a new order fulfillment process was designed using an end-to-end perspective.

Strategy Impact

Because different groups had differing requirements, it was necessary to incorporate a vector called "strategy impact." Determining strategy impact was used to fine tune the overall process to the requirements of individual groups. It also made it possible to incorporate the changes arising from the competitive environment or product-specific marketing programs, and adjustments of inventory levels due to specific component shortages or trends. Exhibit 11 is a high-level view of the redesigned order fulfillment process together with the strategy impact vectors.

To ensure high levels of flexibility, the process models attempt to balance the use of human support and technology support; wherever no major improvements could be achieved, human support was favored.

Cost Justification

Because order fulfillment processes that had evolved through numerous continuous improvement efforts were already in place, it was necessary to justify the implementation costs of the newly defined processes, including the cost of the new IT systems and applications. The cost of nonalignment that represents the cost of tolerating nonvalue-adding activities had to be determined for comparison purposes. Here, different techniques were employed, including:

- Actually tracking a customer order from the moment of quotation to final delivery
- Measuring the time involved in handling exceptions
- Benchmarking with related and nonrelated industries
- Reexamining core competencies that, for example, resulted in subcontracting the whole postmanufacturing delivery activities
- Establishing common performance measures

When it was determined that the cost of nonalignment outweighed the cost of new process development and implementation, the core processes and relevant subprocesses were modeled and translated into functional requirements so that potential solutions could be selected or developed.

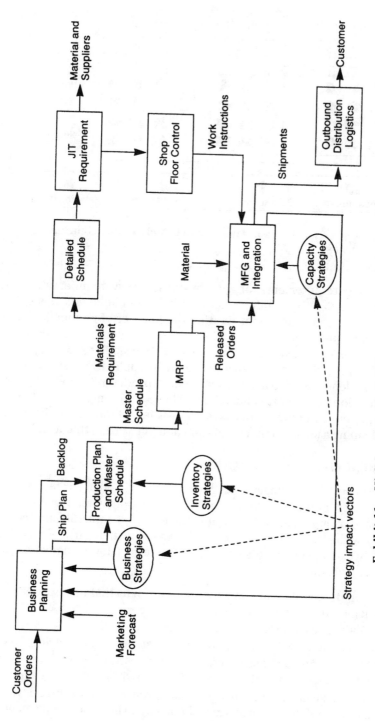

Exhibit 11. High-Level Order Fulfillment Process and Strategy Impact

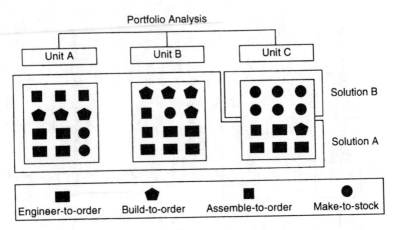

Exhibit 12. Application Selection Alternatives in Multibusiness Unit Environments

Because the requirements for each business unit were different, it was impossible to select one uniform application. A portfolio analysis determined the best compromise for limiting the number of application solutions for implementation. Exhibit 12 shows the outcome of the portfolio analysis. For example, business units A and B have similar product portfolios for which application solutions can easily be applied. For business unit C, solution A lends itself to a limited number of products. Therefore, a second application solution was necessary. These solution clusters allowed HP to implement the new processes using a few standard applications while redefining a speedy implementation and minimizing the overall cost.

RECOMMENDED COURSE OF ACTION

Information systems managers recognize the need to align strategies, people, processes, and technologies in dynamic business environments in which speed of implementation is critical. The two examples illustrate step by step how the framework can be applied to define new business models and modify existing ones. This structured framework for alignment allows the user organization to:

- Develop processes that focus on breakthroughs that make a clear difference in the eyes of customers
- Identify and use appropriate enabling technologies
- Achieve a high level of transparency and reduce redundancies
- Use standard applications based on open systems wherever possible in order to reduce cost and implementation time while ensuring integration
- Allow for flexibility so that changes arising from the competitive environment as well as advancements in technology can be rapidly implemented

Chapter 3

The Enterprise Resource Planning System as a Strategic Solution

Richard L. Jenson
I. Richard Johnson

A reader of the business press or an observer of organizations will notice three recurring themes being played out in highly competitive companies. These companies are:

- Focusing on core business processes that lead to customer satisfaction
- Tearing down functional boundaries that inhibit cooperation, fragment processes, and discourage communications
- Linking, integrating, and controlling processes with the use of powerful information technology, known as ERP systems

Proponents of various business process engineering approaches assert that the ineffectiveness of most organizational processes stems from a "division of labor" mentality held over from the industrial era where processes remain fragmented through overspecialization and spread across departmental boundaries. As a result, operations require more effort to coordinate, and it is often difficult to determine who is responsible for the entire process. Management interventions such as reengineering seek to eliminate process fragmentation, organize work around key business processes, and exploit the enabling technologies of modern information technology (IT) to link the core processes of the enterprise.

The emergence of IT as a process enabler and integrator also deserves emphasis. Traditionally, the role of IT has been viewed as merely *supporting* the enterprise. However, in observing the most successful companies in today's competitive corporate environment, it is clear that the role of IT has become much more dominant from both strategic and operational perspectives. Most modern organizations would have difficulty maintaining an identity apart from the IT infrastructure that controls their processes and facilitates communications and transactions with their trading partners. ERP systems have received considerable attention in the IT press and various practitioner journals over the last several years. Larger organizations are implementing information systems that link the supply chain of the organization using a shared database and tightly integrated business processes. The dominant enterprise systems integrator is SAP AG (Waldorf, Germany) with approximately 30 percent of the ERP market. Oracle, PeopleSoft, Baan (now wholly owned by Invensys plc, London, England), and J. D. Edwards round out the major players in this market.

The potential benefits of ERP solutions include greatly improved integration across functional departments, emphasis on core business processes, proven and reliable software and support, and overall enhanced competitiveness. In implementing a configurable off-the-shelf ERP solution, an organization can quickly upgrade its business processes to industry standards, taking advantage of the many years of business systems reengineering and integration experience of the major ERP vendors.

WHY ORGANIZATIONS ARE TURNING TO ERP

ERP system adoptions have accelerated over the past year. This can be attributed to several factors that are discussed in the following paragraphs:

- *Reengineering for Best Practice.* Because of emerging competitive pressures in their respective industries, companies are scrambling to make changes in their core processes that will both meet customer demand and slash logistics costs associated with meeting such demand. For example, SAP touts its R/3 enterprise software as having over 1,000 catalogued "best" business practices compiled within its reference model. According to SAP advocates, these practices have been refined over 25 years of experience over thousands of implementations. Rather than "reinventing the wheel," adopting organizations generally compare their existing practices to the R/3 reference model and then make the necessary changes to the old processes to accommodate the R/3 process implementation. Baan (Baan Company, N. V., The Netherlands) delivers a somewhat smaller predefined process set, but provides tools (such as the Dynamic Enterprise Modeler) that enable customers to match their specific business processes and their organization model with the integrated Baan IV application Suite or BaanERP software, both supported by iBaan Portal.

- *Globalization and Multicurrency Issues.* The global economy has fostered a business environment in which multinational operations are the rule rather than the exception. Obviously, many companies locate facilities abroad to exploit lower labor rates. Moreover, localization requirements often make it necessary for companies to maintain a manufacturing presence in the countries in which they sell. Clearly, globalization presents almost overwhelming challenges, ranging from cultural differences to multicurrency and value-added tax issues. ERP software has been designed with global organizations in mind and provides an integrated, centralized database that can accommodate distributed transaction processing across multiple currencies.
- *Existing Systems in Disarray.* The authors assert that the wave of ERP implementations is at least partly due to a pent-up demand for an off-the-shelf solution to the general disarray across very large systems. The move to distributed processing appeased some end users as personal work stations and local area networks allowed users to participate in low-end processing. Generally, mission-critical applications remained on the legacy systems while the perceived gaps were filled through end-user computing. The resulting complexity and loss of centralized control are now almost universally recognized, and the push for server-side processing and "thin clients" is evidence of the backlash. Many organizations see enterprise systems as a return to centralized control over business processes.
- *Integration and Discipline.* As Michael Hammer and James Champy emphasized in their bestseller *Reengineering the Corporation,*[1] a major cause of broken systems is process fragmentation. That is, organizational processes tend to be spread across functional boundaries. As a result, many individuals and multiple departments must interact to complete a transaction. Coordination becomes complex with no individual or department assuming responsibility for the whole process. Often, no one knows the status of a transaction, or worse, the transaction "falls through the cracks." In addition, data entry and databases are often duplicated as individuals and departments attempt to impose control on their portion of the transaction where none exists for the process as a whole. With ERP, organizations see opportunities to enforce a higher level of discipline as they link their processes and share their database.

THE BENEFITS OF ENTERPRISE SYSTEMS

Conventional wisdom says that no single system software company can be all things to all companies. This basic attitude set the stage for a blitzkrieg assault of North American companies by the German company SAP AG. The viability of enterprisewide software capable of managing information needs for the entire company was ludicrous. Only a few short years ago the concept was virtually unknown by the majority of corporate America. Times have changed. The list of companies that have either adopted or are in the process of adopting enterprise software is impressive and growing at an accelerating pace. A brief look at several companies that have made the switch and some of their experiences follow.

Data reported by SAP AG concerning the new Fujitsu SAP system reveal the following. Fujitsu was facing increasingly complex business processes with a series of aging mainframes and software that could no longer be upgraded. After a successful 10-month installation of SAP, they enjoyed the following benefits:

- 90 percent reduction of cycle time for quotation from 20 days to 2 days
- 60 to 85 percent improved on-time delivery
- 50 percent reduction for financial closing times from 10 to 5 days[2]

"Manufacturers' Services Ltd. in Concord, MA has grown dramatically through acquisitions in Europe, Asia, and the United States. It is using The Baan Company software as the glue that keeps it all together.[3]

General Motors selected SAP to enable common financial information and processes throughout the global corporation. The company expects the software to greatly reduce the cost and number of the many different financial systems currently employed throughout the world. Implementation of the new system is expected to be completed by the year 2002.

An interview with Boeing officials produced the following comment: "Baan forced us to look for ways to simplify our processes, and because the software is integrated, end users must now work together to solve problems within the internal supply chain."[4]

The incentive for adopting enterprise software varies greatly from company to company. One common thread, however, is the anticipated business improvement that will follow adoption. Roy Clothier, president of Pacific Coast Feather Company, explained the experience of his company as follows: "R/3 has all the tools we need to run our business," Clothier says. "We're already getting very satisfactory results — like reducing our inventory at the same time that we are improving our ability to service our customers — and we feel we're only scratching the surface of the benefits that are out there. Every day we find new ways to gain more value from R/3."[5]

The IBM Storage Products Company (part of IBM's Storage Systems Division) experienced the following success with its ERP system: 110 days after the system went into production, SPC recognized the following improvements: the time for checking customer credit upon receiving an order reduced from 15 to 20 minutes to instantaneously; responses to customer billing inquiries occurred in real time, versus 15 to 20 minutes; entering pricing data into the system took five minutes where it could take 80 days before; and shipping repair and replacement parts was done in three days, compared to as many as 44.[6]

Most companies adopting ERP software appear to be well satisfied. Not all companies, however, have enjoyed this same degree of satisfaction. One noted exception is FoxMeyer Health Corp. FoxMeyer expected the technology to cut cost, speed up inventory turnover, and increase the availability of useful information. Company spokesman Wade Hyde, however, sums up what FoxMeyer found, in the following comment: "The computer-integration problems we had were a significant factor leading to the bankruptcy filing."[7]

THE IMPLEMENTATION PROCESS

The IT press has focused significant attention on the trauma that often accompanies the implementation of ERP systems. Clearly, the introduction of an enterprise system is a nontrivial event in any organization. Given the scope of organizational change triggered by the typical implementation, it should not come as a surprise. Successful enterprise systems require a high degree of discipline from the organization. Consequently, organizations not accustomed to this level of discipline will struggle with such a comprehensive intervention. For example, an R/3 implementation forces the organization to examine all of its existing processes and compare them with the "best practices" incorporated within the package. In reconciling the differences (or "gaps"), the organization must generally reengineer its processes to fit R/3. Although it is theoretically possible to modify R/3 (make changes to the source code) to fit the existing organizational process, few experts would advise this approach. Current implementation wisdom emphasizes the need to leave the software in its "vanilla" state. The price to be paid for adding "chocolate chips" is higher implementation cost and increased difficulty of incorporating future software upgrades.

As is typical with any large-scale systems implementation, organizations adopting ERP use highly structured, phased methodologies. These projects are complex undertakings that must address issues such as process and task redesign, hardware, software, database administration, and software configuration. While such methodologies are beyond the scope of this chapter, a few of the major milestones are described as follows:

- *Form the Implementation Team.* While almost all organizations find it necessary to bring in outside ERP consulting expertise, the process requires a dedicated team of managers and other key employees that may convene for a period of months, perhaps years, to establish the plans, develop the objectives of the project, and manage the implementation process.

- *Blueprint the Current State.* The process typically begins with an assessment of the "current state" of organizational processes. The implementation teams will usually use process modeling techniques and software to document business events, the tasks that must be performed, the individuals and departments who perform them, the flow of information, and the linkages to other processes within the organization. From the current state, the team should identify existing weaknesses and opportunities to reengineer for best practice.

- *Gap Analysis.* With enhanced understanding and documentation of the current state, the implementation team can then compare the current state with the business processes and solutions the system provides. As a practical matter, the organization will almost always adopt the ERP process version. Therefore, the gap analysis reveals the major process discrepancies that will require significant changes to existing processes. Occasionally, the ERP product may not offer a corresponding process. In such cases, the organization may require a work-around solution.

- *Design, Scripting, and Configuration.* The design of new processes will generally evolve in an iterative fashion as the implementation team, assisted by key users, designs and documents the reengineered processes. The team prepares scripts of each of the redesigned processes to assist the user in navigating the system. The scripts will identify the steps within each process, the menu path the user must take, the system screens that will be accessed, explanations of the data fields that require input, and key decision points the user must address. The process designs will also drive the configuration of database tables that allow configuration of business objects such as data entry screens and reports.

- *Simulation, Testing, and Training.* As with any system implementation, extensive simulation and testing is required with the newly configured system prior to going "live." Testing takes place on a test "instance," a logically distinct version of the database. Experienced ERP integrators recommend that simulations be conducted by nondevelopment team members. Similarly, users new to the environment are trained using a "sandbox" instance prior to being introduced to the live production system.

- *Going Live.* The intense implementation process culminates in live activation of the actual production system. At this stage, master and transaction database files have been populated with genuine records. Basis administration has been established and technical support mechanisms are in place. Graphical user interfaces have been installed on the applicable work stations and users trained in their use. Assessment mechanisms must be implemented to assure the ongoing business integrity and to monitor basis systems performance.

THE CHALLENGES OF ERP IMPLEMENTATION

Obviously, many implementation problems relate to situations or processes that are unique to a particular company. The most frequent problem cited in the FoxMeyer experience described earlier was the inability of its enterprise software to handle the sheer volume of transactions required. In the Monsanto case, training its staff of some 18,000 employees to use the software after installation has turned out to be a significant problem. The lack of employees trained in the installation and use of ERP software is currently a global problem. With so much interest and movement toward such solutions in the past couple of years, there is a shortage of knowledgeable, experienced people to assist with the adoptions. Many, if not most, World Wide Web sites of ERP partners have a section dealing with systems-related employment opportunities.

CONCLUSION

Even though there appears to be a near stampede to adopt ERP systems worldwide, many significant questions linger. Not only are there the basic questions unique to potential adopters such as: Does the new system really fit the organizational needs? Does the organization have strategic business reasons for adopting the software? Do the cost of software implementation and the resulting disruptions of the business process outweigh the potential benefits that may be gained? Other broader questions can also be raised.

ERP solutions have been touted as "best practice" software. This claim is based on the long development period of a dynamic program. Given so many recent changes in the way the world does business, is it possible that this software incorporates all of these recent improvements? Does a company currently employing state-of-the-art business practices lose its competitive advantage by adopting standard practices used by all companies currently using ERP software?

These, along with many other questions, may be difficult to answer. Perhaps only time will provide clues into the wisdom of the global movement toward enterprise software. This much is currently known; many of the largest companies in the world are adopting the software and singing its praises. Improvements will undoubtedly be made as ERP vendors respond to the needs of the corporate world. The companies watching the show from the sidelines may be well advised to become part of the cast.

INTEGRATION DRIVERS

Notes

1. Hammer, Michael and Champy, James, *Reengineering the Corporation*. (New York: Harper-Business, 1993).
2. SAP America, 1998. SAP Consumer Products [online]. From Customer Successes, Fujitsu. Available from:
   http://www.sap.com/ [accessed April 28, 1998].
3. Melymuka, Kathleen, "An Expanding Universe," *Computerworld*, September 14, 1998, p. 56.
4. Baan Company, 1988. From Customers, The Boeing Company. Available from: http://www.baan.com/ [accessed September 22, 1998].
5. SAP America, 1998. SAP Consumer Products [online]. From Customer Successes, Pacific Coast Feather Company. Available from: http://www.sap.com/ [accessed April 28, 1998].
6. SAP America, 1998. SAP Consumer Products [online]. From Customer Successes, IBM Storage Products Company. Available from: http://www.sap.com/ [accessed April 28, 1998].
7. Hyde, Wade, "Technology (A Special Report): Working Together — When Things Go Wrong: FoxMeyer Drug Took a Huge High-Tech Gamble; It Didn't Work," *Wall Street Journal*, Eastern edition, November 18, 1996.

Section II
Enterprise Architectures

Chapter 4

Architecture Frameworks for Client/Server and Netcentric Computing

Accenture

At the heart of systems development, the use of architectures provides *insurance*: insurance against the complexities of development and maintenance, against the obsolescence of technologies, against the possibility that all the parts of a solution may not work together. Architectures are the master plans that ensure that the solution will work.

This notion implies that risk is involved, and that is so. In client/server and netcentric environments, a number of risks are generally present.

More Complex Development and Maintenance

A number of factors contribute to the complexity of client/server and netcentric solutions:

- Client/server applications incorporate sophisticated graphical user interfaces (GUIs). GUIs are usually event driven rather than hierarchical. They are interactive and require more complex logic than traditional terminal (e.g., 3270) style interfaces.
- Client/server and netcentric applications have to "cooperate" with other applications. Communication code must establish communication connections, ensure that messages are sent and received correctly, manage errors, and handle any required data translation. Care must be taken that programmers and designers have these skill sets.
- The skills required for development, installation, and support of netcentric systems may be difficult to find.

More Difficult Operations Support

Operations support for netcentric solutions is more difficult than for traditional systems. The increased complexity of operations support, including hardware and software configuration management, is directly related to the number and location of distributed nodes. If a system has 100 remote nodes, it is more difficult to ensure that they are at the same software and hardware versions than it is with two local nodes.

In addition, data backup/restore must now occur at multiple locations, and support for hardware, software, and communications problems must also be provided locally at multiple sites.

More Complex Data Security

When data are distributed, protecting that data becomes more difficult. Intelligent workstations are inherently less secure than minicomputers and mainframes. The effort required to maintain an equivalent level of data security, therefore, increases.

New Distributed Data Update and Refresh Strategies

Most client/server systems incorporate multiple copies of the same data. This requires logic to ensure that data values in each of those copies are consistent. For example, if a user working off server A wants to change a "balance due" field, how and when will this change be reflected on servers B and C?

Increased Susceptibility to Viruses and Malicious Users

Again, this risk is directly proportional to the number of nodes in a distributed system. Each workstation is a potential point of entry for a virus or a malicious hacker.

Higher Communications Loads

Netcentric applications must communicate with each other and with other applications, typically legacy systems. This is accomplished over communications networks. For a networked system to work well, accurate estimates of the amount of network traffic must be determined. This is often difficult because, as the knowledge and popularity of newly released applications increase, application use (and network traffic) increases. Applications designed with communication speeds in mind may, therefore, end up being "communications bound." In addition, there are not many tools available that model new age computing communication loads.

Missed Opportunities

Because netcentric systems are comprised of hardware and software that are continually being improved, it is often difficult to stop waiting for enhancements. Many development teams become paralyzed, waiting for the next release of some component that promises to facilitate the installation process or enhance the final product.

Lack of a Standard Operating Environment

There are many popular operating system and window manager options that can be used to develop workstation applications. The risk is in choosing a combination that ends up with little or no support in the long run and requires future migrations of applications and data.

Increased Complexity of User ID and Password Strategies

Because netcentric solutions require the use of multiple computers, user ID and password strategies become more complex. For example, a security system on one computer may require password changes more frequently than on another, or maximum and minimum password lengths may conflict on different systems. Even if these issues are not present, the maintenance of security information on multiple platforms is difficult.

THE BENEFITS OF ARCHITECTURES

The risks just discussed illustrate the need for architectures as crucial aspects of client/server and netcentric systems development. What is an architecture?

An architecture is a proven mechanism and an approach that can be used to isolate and mitigate the risks of delivering applications now and into the future.

According to the Gartner Group, an architecture is "a formal specification of how a computer solution will be organized." Gartner sets forth seven characteristics of a successful architecture:

1. Delimitation of the problem to be addressed
2. Decomposition of the solution to components with clearly assigned responsibilities
3. Definition of interfaces, formats, and protocols to be used between the components; these should be sufficiently clear and robust to permit asynchronous development and ongoing reimplementation of the components
4. Adequate documentation to permit compliance by implementers
5. An auditing mechanism that exercises the specified interfaces to verify that specified inputs to components yield specified results
6. An extendibility mechanism to enable response to changing requirements and technologies
7. Policies, practices, and organizational structures that facilitate adoption of the architecture

In the netcentric environment, an architecture is used to define how a system is structured and how the various components of the system interact. In a netcentric computing environment, there are more components and many more interactions that make an architecture even more important.

Organizations that have carefully implemented, delivered, and utilized these architectures have realized some of the following benefits:

1. *Better productivity and less "reinvention of the wheel."* Architectures can abstract common requirements and approaches from applications and can eliminate having to identify, analyze, and implement them for each application. This improves developer productivity and the quality of the final product.

2. *Consistent, reliable, high-quality applications.* The framework provided by an architecture encourages applications to be built in a consistent fashion or structure, to deliver consistent behavior, and to work with a consistent interface (both to users and other applications), resulting in a system easier to build, use, and maintain.

3. *Rapid delivery of business solutions.* By providing a consistent external interface, an architecture simplifies integration of applications and facilitates rapid delivery of new solutions. This is achieved through the use of standard architecture components, adherence to standards, and the availability of the necessary tools, techniques, and training.

4. *Reduced impact of changes to underlying products and tools.* Because an architecture incorporates "layers of isolation," new products and tools can be more easily integrated into a system. Changes in one element of the architecture are less likely to affect other architecture elements.

5. *Better integration of business applications within and between organization business units.* By providing consistency of architecture components within and across an organization, the opportunity to build applications that have a higher degree of integration is greater. This should facilitate the exchange of critical information across the company.

6. *Isolation of users and applications developers from the complexities of the underlying technologies.* By having a standard architecture that includes a standard set of tools with a consistent interface, users and developers are not required to know the details of the platform technologies (i.e., the operating system, database, and network). Additional technology components could be added in the future with minimal additional training for the users.

7. *A consistent, standard development framework.* An architecture provides a framework for analyzing the requirements of a system or application. It can help business applications developers by providing a

structure from which to work. In a netcentric environment, the requirements of a GUI, distributed data, and distributed processing contribute to the complexity of the solution. Moreover, these requirements have many interdependencies. Without an architecture to help structure the problem, it is easy for applications developers to become overwhelmed by technical issues and spend insufficient time on the business problems they are there to solve.

8. *A common background for IS personnel.* In addition to providing a common approach for building systems, an architecture provides a common means of describing systems and a common language. As a result, IS personnel are more easily interchanged and cross-trained, providing more flexibility in the management of the organization.

This chapter will move from a high-level description of an overall architecture — what is called an Enterprise Information Architecture — to a summary of the primary technical architectures discussed in this book: the execution, development, and operations architectures for client/server and netcentric computing solutions. More detail on each of these architectures — their services and subservices — is provided in subsequent chapters of Section II.

THE ENTERPRISE INFORMATION ARCHITECTURE (EIA)

What are the components of an effective architecture? The Enterprise Information Architecture (EIA) framework provides a starting point for understanding what is meant by the various architectures under consideration. The EIA framework contains seven layers (Exhibit 1).

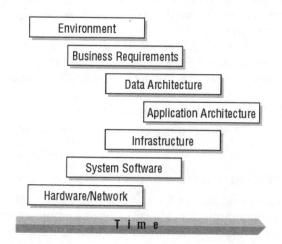

Exhibit 1.   Enterprise Information Architecture (EIA)

1. The *environment* layer includes those factors that influence the business requirements and technical layers. These factors may be either internal (e.g., profitability) or external (e.g., government regulation and market competition).
2. The *business requirements* layer addresses the business needs of the organization. Both the environment layer and the business requirements layer are mainly concerned with business-level processes, strategies, and directions. The layers below are mainly concerned with the information technology to support the business. The business requirements give key input and guidelines on how to define the lower layers. The link from business requirements to the information technology layers is crucial to a successful EIA.
3. The *data architecture* layer consists of a high-level data design that describes the structure of an enterprise's data needs in terms of entities and relationships between entities. The structure and relationships of data entities can be used to define the basic relationships of business functions and applications.
4. The *applications architecture* layer defines the applications that must exist to support the business functions and their relationships. It also addresses any issues about distributed data processing.
5. The *infrastructure* layer deals with those components of an architecture that can be used by multiple applications and that are developed and maintained within the enterprise. Usually, these common technical components help support the applications architecture. This layer also includes the infrastructure of the organization that manages the architecture definition and design and its technical components.
6. The *systems software* layer encompasses the software and standards obtained from and maintained by outside vendors (e.g., a database management system).
7. The *hardware/network* layer deals with central processing units, local area network (LAN), wide area networks, and other hardware and physical network components of the environment.

Redefining the Enterprise Information Architecture

For purposes of this volume, these components can be grouped into four categories of architecture (Exhibit 2).

Business Solutions Architecture

Because this chapter does not focus on business specifics, the top three levels can be grouped into a business solutions architecture. It is important to remember, however, that when it is time to decide what technical architecture to use, many of the answers are found by looking at the business solutions architecture. The decisions made for the application and

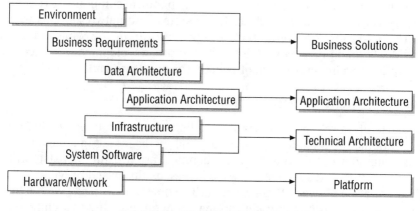

Exhibit 2. EIA Model Redefined

data architectures drive the requirements of the technical architecture and platform. At the same time, the constraints of the technical architecture and platform can also shape the application architecture and the business solutions that are possible.

Applications Architecture

The applications architecture layer can be defined here as those services that perform business functions on the computer. It represents the components that provide the automation support for a business function or activity in the business process (but does not include the platform and cross-application architecture). For example, a manufacturer's sales and marketing system application architecture could include sales tracking applications and the distributed data architecture to support both networked sales offices and mobile sales people.

Technical Architecture

The infrastructure and system software layers are combined to form the technical architecture. The technical architecture is where the buy decisions of the system software marketplace are combined with the build decisions for the needs of specific applications. We treat these as one architecture by incorporating these two concepts. The technical architecture is comprised of the execution, development, and operations architectures, which are discussed subsequently.

Platform Architecture

The final layer in the EIA model is the platform architecture layer. It is often described as "the things you can see." The netcentric platform architecture provides a framework for selecting the platform components required: the servers, workstations, operating systems, and networks. This framework represents the overall technology platform for the implementation and deployment of the execution architecture, development architecture, operations architecture, and, of course, the applications.

THE TECHNICAL ARCHITECTURE

Because of its relative importance in client/server and netcentric implementations, the technical architecture will be discussed in some detail in the remainder of this chapter. The technical architecture consists of the infrastructure and systems software layers, as discussed previously. The differentiation between them is primarily a question of "make versus buy," that is, a key decision for organizations intent on "building an architecture" is how much they want to build versus how much they can simply buy from preexisting sources. An organization can choose to build a great deal, thereby making the architecture very close to what it wants. That means that there is a great deal of logic being built by the shop.

Alternatively, the organization can choose to buy most of what it wants. To the extent that business or application demands make it necessary for the tools to be integrated, developers can then do simple assembly, or gluing together, of the pieces. The decision for most organizations depends on balancing demands. On the one hand, the organization has a large front-end commitment to build and an ongoing commitment to maintain an infrastructure architecture; on the other hand, the organization has a tool that is exactly what it wants.

Over the years there has been a tendency to buy rather than make. This is especially the case as the market matures with more technical entrants. It is practical for IS organizations to build technical architecture components only when essential. By purchasing rather than building, they can then more easily apply their strong skills in the applications architecture business.

Components of the Technical Architecture

The technical architecture layer can in turn be broken into three primary components: execution, development, and operations (Exhibit 3).

1. An *execution* architecture describes the components required when an application executes.
2. A *development* architecture describes the components required to create the execution architecture.
3. An *operations* architecture describes the components required to operate and manage the system.

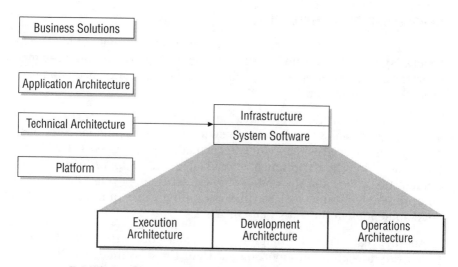

Exhibit 3. Three Components of a Technical Architecture

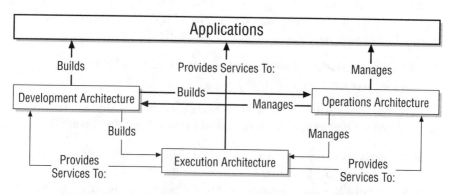

Exhibit 4. Relationships Among the Technical Architectures

These architectures must be flexible enough to accommodate a wide range of technologies, but they must also be structured enough to provide valuable guidelines and to ensure that interoperability is available where it is required. Exhibit 4 illustrates the relationships among the execution, development, and operations architectures.

The remainder of this chapter will provide an overview of these technical architectures. Because of its relative importance in the design and delivery of netcentric solutions, the execution architecture will be discussed last and in much more detail.

DEVELOPMENT ARCHITECTURE

The development environment is the production environment for one or several systems development projects as well as for the maintenance efforts. Thus, it requires the same attention as a similarly sized end-user execution environment.

The purpose of the development architecture is to support the tasks involved in the analysis, design, construction, and maintenance of business systems as well as the associated management processes. It is important to note that the environment should adequately support *all* the development tasks, not just the code/compile/test/debug cycle. Given this, a comprehensive framework for understanding the requirements of the development environment should be used.

Another reason for the comprehensive framework is that it is important to get the development environment right the first time. Changing the development environment when construction is fully staffed may entail serious disruptions and expensive loss of productivity.

Experience has shown that, within the same medium- to large-size project with the same people, moving from a poor to a good development environment, productivity can be improved by a factor of ten for many tasks. The improvements come in two categories:

1. The elimination of redundant and non-value-added tasks
2. The streamlining of useful tasks

While it seems intuitive that most tasks can be streamlined, the following list gives a few examples of redundant tasks that must be eliminated:

- Analysis to determine how to merge the uncoordinated changes applied by two programmers to the same module
- Reentry of the source code for and retesting of a module, which was accidentally deleted
- Recurring discussions about "what a design packet should contain" or "what constitutes good programming style in a particular context"
- Repeated design, coding, testing, and maintenance of very similar logic (e.g., error handling, date conversion and manipulation, main structure of a module)
- Searching for the manuals of a particular productivity tool to find information
- Remigration to system test of a cycle because the impact analysis for a change request was incomplete
- Requesting support from another team (e.g., environment support, information management) and waiting unnecessarily for a response

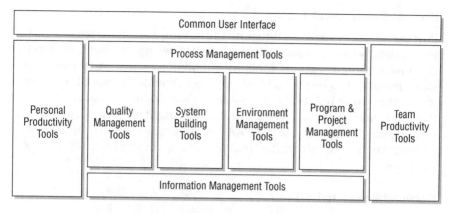

Exhibit 5. Development Architecture

On a smaller project, these problems can be solved using a brute force approach. This becomes very expensive as the project grows and, finally, impossible. A well-designed development environment becomes important as the project team reaches 20 to 30 people, and is absolutely critical with a project size of more than 50 people.

The investment needed to design, set up, and tune a comprehensive, good development and maintenance environment is typically several hundred man days. Numbers between 400 and 800 days are commonly seen, depending on the platforms, target environment complexity, amount of reuse, and size of the system being developed/maintained. This investment warrants the following considerations:

- *This effort is large enough to justify work that will make it more efficient.* Among the factors that affect the effort, reuse is the most apparent. These guidelines, together with the parallel project to instantiate the model, constitute a step toward greater reuse.
- *The effort is large enough to require a cost/benefit analysis.*

Exhibit 5 is the model used throughout this book to describe the development architecture. The components of the development architecture include the following.

Common User Interface Tools

Common user interface tools provide a common launching place for all the tools in the development environment to make it appear more integrated and consistent. This is the simplest level of integration, in that all the tools are presented to the developer via a single view of the entire environment. Tools that support the common user interface are known as "window managers," e.g., Microsoft Windows and Motif.

Process Management Tools

Process management tools integrate the development environment by providing tool-to-tool communication and workflow management. Tool-to-tool communication integrates tools by enabling information in the form of short messages to be passed from one tool to another. Workflow management integration builds the development methodology and process into the tool environment. Workflow management enforces the correct sequencing of tasks and tools. Process integration is often implemented through the use of integration frameworks or through custom coding of interfaces.

Personal Productivity Tools

Personal productivity tools are a collection of software applications that enhance the development environment for the individual developer. These applications are typically integrated suites of PC software that allow the developer to work on the workstation independent of the development server or mainframe to complete tasks such as analysis and documentation. These tools are basic office automation software and include spreadsheet software, word processing software, graphics software (e.g., drawing, diagramming, and presentation), and personal calendar software.

Quality Management Tools

Quality management is a management discipline that promotes a customer satisfaction focus and continuous improvement. Quality management tools support the planning and measurement of quality. These tools include quality function deployment tools, measurement and metrics tools, statistical process control tools, and continuous improvement tools.

System Building Tools

System building tools comprise the core of the development architecture and are used to design, build, and test the system. All the system building tools must be integrated and share development objects appropriately. These include:

- Analysis and design tools
- Reverse engineering tools
- Construction tools
- Testing tools
- Configuration management tools

Environment Management Tools

A netcentric development environment is complex and sophisticated. It supports many different functional and technical requirements (illustrated by the execution architecture), many different development teams, and tools from many different product vendors, and often must support projects in different stages of the development life cycle. These tools monitor performance, provide help desk support, manage and distribute changes to the development environment, administer the environment, and track and plan development environment capacity.

Environment management tools include

- Service management tools
- Systems management tools
- Managing change tools
- Service planning tools

Program and Project Management Tools

Program and project management are usually differentiated by the size of the effort; programs are typically composed of more than one project. Similarly, the program and project management tools are differentiated by the ability to support multiple projects, complex functions, and adequate performance when supporting multiple concurrent projects.

Program and project management tools provide many key features that assist project planners in planning, scheduling, tracking, and reporting on project segments, tasks, and milestones.

These tools include

- Planning tools
- Scheduling tools
- Tracking tools
- Reporting tools

Team Productivity Tools

Team productivity tools are used to make the work cell and project team more productive as a whole. Instead of the software residing on the individual's PC or workstation, these tools typically are LAN based and shared by the project members. These tools are focused on enhancing communication and information sharing.

These tools include:

- E-mail
- Teamware
- Publishing tools
- Group calendars
- Methodology browsing tools

Information Management

Information management of the development architecture is provided through an integrated development repository. At this level of integration, tools share a common repository of development objects, design documents, source code, and test plans and data. Ideally, the repository would be a single database with an all-encompassing information model. Practically, the repository must be built by integrating the repositories of the different development tools through interfaces. Tool vendors may also build part of the integrated repository by integrating specific products.

The repository includes:

- Folder management
- Repository management

OPERATIONS ARCHITECTURE

An operations architecture is a combination of tools, support services, procedures, and controls required to keep a production system running well. It differs from an execution architecture in that its primary users are systems administrators and production support personnel. Exhibit 6 shows the framework used throughout this book to illustrate the operations architecture. It depicts a set of tools supporting the execution and development architectures.

The major tool categories of the operations architecture include the following.

Software Distribution

Software distribution is the automated delivery to, and installation of, applications and systems software on servers and end-user devices (e.g., workstations, kiosks, etc.). This can be for an organization's internal computing environment as well as for its extended one, i.e., its business partners and customers. The architectural support required to support software distribution is largely driven by the number of workstations, servers, and geographic locations to be served.

Configuration and Asset Management

To manage a netcentric environment successfully, one must have a solid understanding of *what* is *where*, and one must maintain rigor in the change control procedures that govern modifications to the environment. Configuration and asset management information that may need to be tracked includes such details as product licensing information, warranty information, vendor names, logical and physical device information (such as total capacity and current utilization), product configuration tracking, software

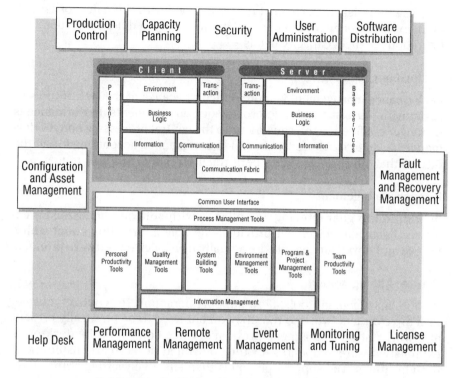

Exhibit 6. Operations Architecture Framework

and data version levels, network configuration parameters, physical location, and perhaps accounting information.

Fault Management and Recovery Management

The fault management services of an operations architecture assist in the diagnosis and correction of system faults. Faults may include network-, server-, workstation-, or even application-level faults. Fault diagnosis may require services for isolation; viewing of host, server, and workstation error logs; and determining the software and data versions and configurations of affected machines.

Capacity Planning

Capacity planning tools focus on components of an environment such as the network, physical space, and processing power to understand the need to change the capacity of those components based on organizational changes. The tools typically focus on components that are considered to be extremely sensitive to changes in computing resource usage. The tools may use historical management data combined with estimates for growth or changes to configuration to simulate the ability of different system configurations to meet capacity needs.

Performance Management

Performance management is more difficult because of the lack of tools to assist with performance in heterogeneous environments. Performance is no longer confined to the network or to the central processing unit. Performance needs to be viewed in an end-to-end manner, accounting for all the factors that affect the system's performance relative to a user request.

License Management

In addition to guaranteeing compliance with software licensing agreements, license management provides valuable information about which people and how many people are actually using a given software product.

Remote Management

Remote management tools allow support personnel to "control" a user's desktop over a network so that they do not need to be physically present at a workstation to diagnose problems. Once control of the desktop is established, screen updates for the controlled desktop are displayed at both locations. The support person is then effectively sitting at the workstation being controlled and can do necessary diagnostics.

Event Management

In addition to hardware devices, applications and systems software also generates events. Common event-handling mechanisms are required to provide information to management in a simple, consistent format, and to forward information on important events for management purposes.

Monitoring and Tuning

The number of devices and the geographic disparity of devices in a netcentric environment increase the effort required to monitor the system. The number of events generated in the system rises due to the increased complexity. Devices such as client machines, network components, and servers generate events on startup or failure to periodically report device status.

Security

The security concerns of netcentric environments have been widely publicized. Although requirements for netcentric security architectures are constantly evolving as new security breaches are discovered, there are many tool categories that can help provide reasonable levels of security.

User Administration

The netcentric environment introduces many new challenges to the task of user administration. The majority of these stem once again from the dramatically increased number of system components. Adding a user to the system may require adding a user to the network, one or more server operating systems, one or more database systems (so that the user can access data), an e-mail system, and an existing host-based system.

Production Control

Scheduling processes across a distributed environment can be quite complex, requiring significant management effort to ensure that the processes run smoothly. Many other day-to-day activities become more difficult in a distributed environment, including print management, file transfer and control, mass storage management, backup and restore, archiving, and system startup and shutdown.

Help Desk

As netcentric computing puts the operations help desk closer to the "end user" in terms of visibility and influence, the help desk will need to become integrated with the business processes being supported through netcentric. Unless the operations help desk is well integrated with the business process, there is risk that the user may be given information that is incorrect, forwarded to the wrong department, or otherwise mishandled. It is also important that the information collected by the help desk about a user be properly shared with other stakeholders in the business process.

EXECUTION ARCHITECTURE

The netcentric execution architecture framework identifies those common, run-time services required when an application executes in a netcentric environment. The services can be broken down into logical areas: presentation services, information services, communication services, communication fabric services, transaction services, environment services, base services, and business logic (Exhibit 7).

As shown in the exhibit, the netcentric execution architecture is best represented as an extension to a client/server execution architecture. The exhibit shows the logical representation of a requester and a provider, designated by the "client" and the "server." Although the figure shows only one "client" and one "server," a physical implementation of an execution architecture typically has many clients and many servers. Thus, the services described here can be located on one physical machine but most likely will span many physical machines, as shown in Exhibit 8.

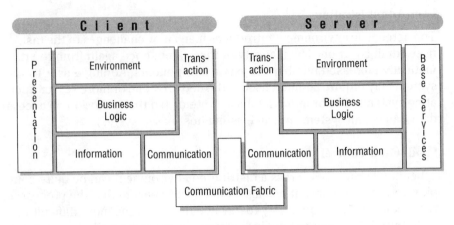

Exhibit 7.   Netcentric Execution Architecture

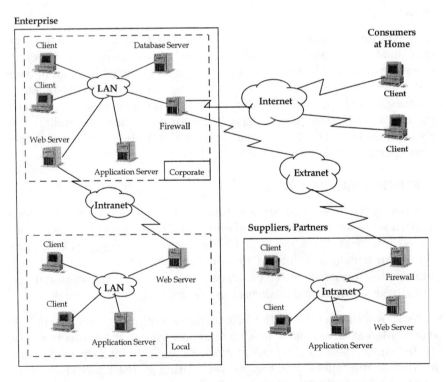

Exhibit 8.   Execution Architecture: Physical Picture

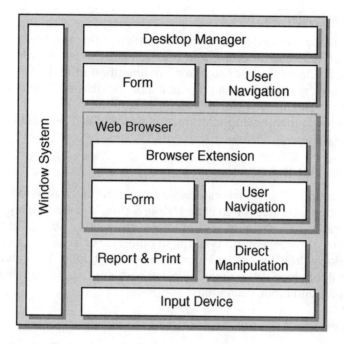

Exhibit 9. Presentation Services

This section provides an overview of the services and subservices within the execution architecture. More detailed information is provided in Section II.

PRESENTATION SERVICES

Presentation services (Exhibit 9) enable an application to manage the human–computer interface, including capturing user actions and generating resulting events, presenting data to the user, and assisting in the management of the dialog flow of processing. Typically, presentation services are required only by client workstations.

The major presentation services are:

- Desktop manager services
- Direct manipulation services
- Form services
- Input devices services
- Report and print services
- User navigation services
- Web browser services
- Window system services

Desktop Manager Services

Desktop manager services provide for implementing the "desktop metaphor," a style of user interface that tries to emulate the idea of a physical desktop. It allows the user to place documents on the desktop, launch applications by clicking on a graphical icon, or discard files by dragging them onto a picture of a wastebasket. Desktop manager services include facilities for launching applications and desktop utilities and managing their integration.

Direct Manipulation Services

Direct manipulation services enable applications to provide a direct manipulation interface (often called "drag & drop"). A direct manipulation interface allows users to manage multiple "application objects" by manipulating visual representations of those objects. For example, a user may sell stock by dragging "stock" icons out of a "portfolio" icon and onto a "trading floor" icon. Direct manipulation services can be further divided into display and input/validation.

Form Services

Form services enable applications to use fields to display and collect data. A field may be a traditional 3270-style field used to display or input textual data, or it may be a graphical field, such as a check box, a list box, or an image. Form services provide support for display, input/validation, mapping support, and field interaction management.

Input Devices

Input devices detect user input from a variety of input technologies, such as pen–based, voice recognition, touchscreen, mouse, and digital camera.

Report and Print Services

Report and print services support the creation and on-screen previewing of paper or photographic documents which contain screen data, application data, graphics, or images.

User Navigation Services

User navigation services provide a user with a way to access or navigate between functions within or across applications. Historically, this has been the role of a text-based menuing system that provides a list of applications or activities for the user to choose from. However, client/server technologies introduced new navigation metaphors. A common method for allowing a user to navigate within an application is to list available functions or information by means of a menu bar with associated pull-down menus or context-sensitive pop-up menus.

Web Browser Services

Web browser services allow users to view and interact with applications and documents made up of varying data types such as text, graphics, and audio. These services also provide support for navigation within and across documents no matter where they are located through the use of links embedded into the document content. Web browser services retain the link connection, i.e., document physical location, and mask the complexities of that connection from the user.

Web browser services can be further subdivided into:

- Browser extension services
- Form services
- User navigation services

Browser Extension Services

Browser extension services provide support for executing different types of applications from within a browser. These applications provide functionality that extend browser capabilities. The key browser extensions are plug-ins, helper/application viewers, Java applets, Active/X controls, and JavaBeans.

Form Services

Like form services outside the web browser, form services within the web browser enable applications to use fields to display and collect data. The only difference is the technology used to develop the forms. The most common type of forms within a browser is Hypertext Markup Language (HTML).

User Navigation Services

Like user navigation services outside the web browser, user navigation services within the web browser provide a user with a way to access or navigate between functions within or across applications. These user navigation services can be subdivided into three categories: hyperlink, customized menu, and virtual reality.

Window System

Typically part of the operating systems, window system services provide the base functionality for creating and managing a GUI: detecting user actions, manipulating windows on the display, and displaying information through windows and graphical controls.

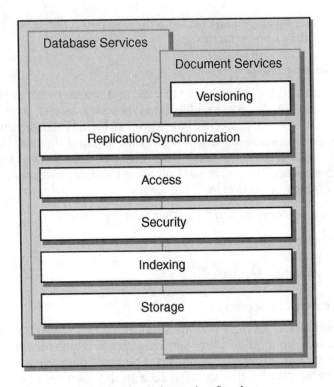

Exhibit 10. Information Services

INFORMATION SERVICES

Information services (Exhibit 10) manage information assets and enable applications to access and manipulate data stored locally or remotely from documents, databases, or external data sources. They minimize an application's dependence on physical storage and location within the network. Information services may also be used directly by the end user when ad hoc data and document access are integral to the application work task. Information Services are grouped into two primary categories:

- Database services
- Document services

Database Services

Database services are responsible for providing access to a local or remote database as well as maintaining integrity of the data within the database. These services also support the ability to store data on either a single physical platform or, in some cases, across multiple platforms. These services are typically provided by database management system (DBMS) vendors and accessed via embedded or call-level SQL variants and supersets. Depending upon the underlying storage model, non-SQL access methods may be used instead.

Database services include:

- Storage services
- Indexing services
- Security services
- Access services
- Replication/synchronization services

Storage Services

Storage services manage physical data storage. These services provide a mechanism for saving information so that data will live beyond program execution. Data are often stored in relational format (an RDBMS) but may also be stored in an object-oriented format (OODBMS) or other structures such as IMS and VSAM.

Indexing Services

Indexing services provide a mechanism for speeding up data retrieval. In relational databases, one or more fields can be used to construct the index. Therefore, when a user searches for a specific record rather than scanning the whole table sequentially, the index is used to find the location of that record faster.

Security Services

Security Services enforce access control to ensure that records are only visible or editable by authorized people for approved purposes. Most DBMSs provide access control at the database, table, or row levels to specific users and groups as well as concurrency control. They also provide execution control for such things as stored procedures and database functions.

Access Services

Access Services enable an application to retrieve data from a database as well as manipulate (insert, update, or delete) data in a database. SQL is the primary approach for accessing records in today's DBMSs.

Replication/Synchronization Services

Replication Services support an environment in which multiple copies of databases must be maintained. Synchronization Services perform the transactions required to make consistent information sources that are intended to mirror each other.

Document Services

Document services provide similar structure and control for documents that DBMSs apply to record-oriented data. A document is defined as a collection of objects of potentially different types (e.g., structured data, unstructured text, images, or multimedia) that a business user deals with. Regardless of the software used to create and maintain the component parts, all parts together constitute the document, which is managed as a single entity.

Document services include:

- Storage services
- Indexing services
- Security services
- Access services
- Replication/synchronization services
- Versioning services

Storage Services

Storage services manage the physical storage of documents. Generally, the documents are stored in a repository using one of the following methods: proprietary database, industry standard database, or industry standard database and file system.

Indexing Services

Locating documents and content within documents is a complex problem and involves several alternative methods. Most document management products provide index services that support searching document repositories by the methods of attribute search, full-text search, context search, or Boolean search.

Security Services

Documents should be accessed exclusively through the document management backbone. If a document is checked in, checked out, routed, viewed, annotated, archived, or printed, it should be done only by authorized users. Security services control access at the user, role, and group levels.

Access Services

Access services support document creation, deletion, maintenance, and retrieval. These services allow users to capture knowledge or content through the creation of unstructured information, such as documents.

Access Services also allow users to effectively retrieve documents they created, and documents that were created by others.

Versioning Services

These services maintain a historical record of the changes to a document over time. By maintaining this record, versioning services allow for the recreation of a document as it looked at any given point in time during its evolution.

COMMUNICATION SERVICES

Communication services enable an application to interact transparently with other applications regardless of whether they reside on the same computer or on a remote computer.

There are five primary communications services categories (Exhibit 11):

1. Core messaging services
2. Specialized messaging services
3. Communications security services
4. Virtual resource services
5. Directory services

Core Messaging Services

Broadly defined, messaging is sending information or commands between two or more recipients. Recipients may be computers, people, or processes within a computer. To send this message, a protocol (or in some cases, multiple protocols) is used that both the sender and receiver can understand. A protocol is a set of rules describing, in technical terms, how two end points should exchange information. Protocols exist at several levels during the exchange of information. Protocols facilitate transport of the message carrying the information. Both end points must recognize and observe the protocol. As an example, a common protocol in today's networks is the TCP/IP protocol.

Core messaging services can further be divided into the following services:

- *File Transfer Services.* File transfer services enable the copying and receiving of files or other large blocks of data between two resources.
- *Remote Procedure Call (RPC) Services.* RPCs are a type of protocol by which an application sends a request to a remote system to execute a designated procedure using supplied arguments and return the result.
- *Message-Oriented Services.* Message-oriented services refers to the process of distributing data and control through the exchange of records known as messages. Message-oriented services provide the

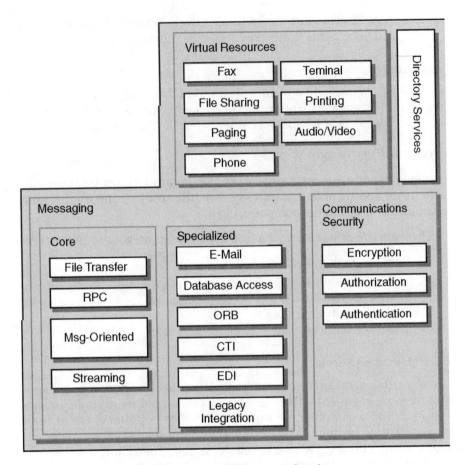

Exhibit 11. Communication Services

application developer with a set of simple verbs (e.g., connect, send, receive, and disconnect) that are used to exchange information with other distributed applications.

- *Streaming Services.* Streaming is the process of transferring time-sensitive data streams (e.g., video and/or audio) in real time. Streaming differs from the other types of core messaging services in that it delivers a continuous, one-way stream of data rather than the relatively short messages associated with RPC and message-oriented messaging, or the large, batch transfers associated with file transfer. Streaming may be used to deliver video, audio, and other real-time content across the Internet or within enterprise networks.

Specialized Messaging Services

Specialized messaging services extend the core messaging services to provide additional functionality. Specialized messaging services may extend core messaging services in the following general ways:

- Provide messaging among specialized systems by drawing upon basic messaging capabilities
- Define specialized message layouts
- Define specialized intersystem protocols
- Suggest ways in which messaging draws upon directory and security services to deliver a complete messaging environment

Specialized messaging services is comprised of the following subservices:

- *E-Mail Messaging.* E-mail messaging services reliably exchange messages using the store-and-forward messaging style. E-mail message systems traditionally include a rudimentary form of directory services.
- *Computer-Telephone Integration (CTI) Messaging.* CTI integrates computer systems and telephone systems to coordinate data and telephony activities. CTI messaging has two primary functions: device-specific communication and message mapping.
- *EDI (Electronic Data Interchange) Messaging.* EDI supports system-to-system messaging among business partners by defining standard message layouts. Companies typically use EDI to streamline commercial transactions within their supply chains.
- *Object Request Broker (ORB) Messaging.* ORB messaging enables objects to transparently make requests of and receive responses from other objects located locally or remotely. Objects communicate through an ORB. An ORB enables client objects to access server objects either locally or remotely over a network and invoke operations (i.e., functions and methods) on them.
- *Database Access Messaging.* Database messaging services (also known as database access middleware or DBAM) provide connectivity for clients to access databases throughout the enterprise.
- *Legacy Integration Messaging.* Legacy services provide gateways to mainframe legacy systems.

Communications Security Services

Communications security services control access to network-attached resources. Combining network security services with security services in other parts of the system architecture (e.g., application and database layers) results in robust security.

Communications security services are broken down into the following three categories:

1. *Encryption Services.* Encryption services encrypt data prior to network transfer to prevent unauthorized interception.
2. *Authorization Services.* When a user requests access to network resources, authorization services determines if the user has the appropriate permissions and either allows or disallows the access.
3. *Authentication Services.* Authentication services verify network access requests by validating that users are who they claim to be. For secure systems, one or more authentication mechanisms can be used to validate authorized users and to verify which functions and data they can access.

Virtual Resource Services

Virtual resource services proxy or mimic the capabilities of specialized, network-connected resources. This allows a generic network node to emulate a specialized physical device. In this way, network users can interface with a variety of specialized resources.

A common example of a virtual resource service is the capability to print to a network printer as if it were directly attached to a workstation.

Virtual resource services include:

- *Terminal Services.* Terminal services allow a client to connect to a nonlocal host via a network and to emulate the profile (e.g., the keyboard and screen characteristics) required by the host application.
- *Print Services.* Print services connect network workstations to shared printers.
- *File Sharing Services.* File sharing services allow users to view, manage, read, and write files that may be located on a variety of platforms in a variety of locations.
- *Phone Services.* Phone virtual resource services extend telephony capabilities to computer platforms.
- *Fax Services.* Fax services provide for the management of both inbound and outbound fax transmissions.
- *Audio/Video Services.* Audio/video services allow nodes to interact with multimedia data streams. These services may be implemented as audio only, video only, or combined audio/video.
- *Paging Services.* Paging virtual resource services provide the message formatting and display functionality that allows network nodes to interface with wireless paging systems.

Directory Services

Managing information about network resources involves a variety of processes ranging from simple name/address resolution to the logical integration of heterogeneous systems to create a common view of services, security, etc. This breadth of functionality is discussed as part of Directory Services.

Because of their ability to unify and manage distributed environments, Directory Services play a key role in locating and accessing resources in a network, including Internet/intranet architectures.

COMMUNICATIONS FABRIC SERVICES

As communications networks become increasingly complicated and inter-connected, the services provided by the network itself have by necessity increased as well. Clients and servers are rarely directly connected to one another but are commonly separated by a network of routers, servers, and firewalls, providing an ever-increasing number of network services such as address resolution, message routing, and security screening.

The communications fabric extends the client/server computing model by placing intelligence into the physical network, acknowledging the net-work as a sort of stand-alone system that provides intelligent shared net-work services. There is certainly overlap between services typically thought of as part of a client/server architecture and services increasingly provided by the network itself.

Communications Fabric Services is comprised of two subservices: Transport Services and Network Media Services (Exhibit 12).

Transport Services

Transport Services are responsible for establishing, maintaining, and ter-minating end-to-end communications between users and processes. Con-nection management provides transfer services that ensure the delivery of data from sender to receiver, which support the transferring of messages from a process running on one machine to a process running on another. In addition, connection management provides services that initiate a connec-tion, gracefully terminate a connection, and handle abrupt termination. These services take place for application before and after the data are for-matted for transport over the network.

Transport services include:

- *Message Transport Services.* These are responsible for the end-to-end delivery of messages. They can include functionalities such as end-to-end data transfer, connection control, reliable transfer, flow control, and multiplexing.
- *Packet Forwarding/Internetworking Services.* The Packet Forward-ing/Internetworking Service transfers data packets and manages the path that data take through the network. It includes functionalities

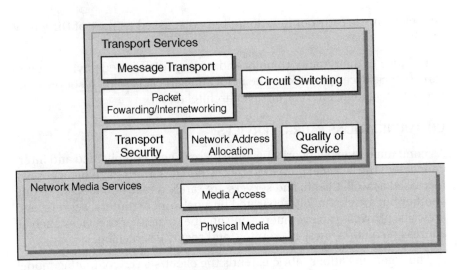

Exhibit 12.   Communications Fabric Services

such as fragmentation/reassembly, addressing, routing, switching, and multicasting.

- *Circuit Switching Services.* Where message transport services and packet forwarding/internetworking services support the transfer of packetized data, circuit switching services establish physical circuits for the transfer of such things as circuit-switched voice, fax, and video.
- *Transport Security Services.* Transport security services (within the transport services layer) perform encryption and filtering.
- *Network Address Allocation Services.* Network address allocation services manage the distribution of addresses to network nodes. This provides more flexibility compared to having all nodes assigned static addresses.
- *Quality of Service (QoS) Services.* QoS services deliver a defined network throughput for designated traffic by allocating dedicated bandwidth, prioritizing data traffic, etc.

Network Media Services

The network media layer provides the following capabilities:

- Final framing of data for interfacing with the physical network
- Receiving, interpreting, and acting on signals from the communications fabric
- Transferring data through the physical network

Network media services performs two primary service functions:

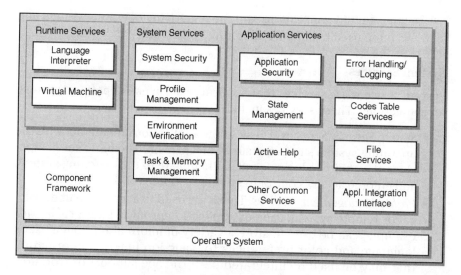

Exhibit 13. Environment Services

1. *Media Access Services.* Media access services manage the low-level transfer of data between network nodes. These services provide functions such as physical addressing, packet transfer, shared access, flow control, error recovery, and encryption.
2. *Physical Media Services.* The physical media includes both the physical connectors and the physical media (wired or wireless).

ENVIRONMENT SERVICES

Environment services provide miscellaneous application and system level services that do not deal directly with managing the user interface, communicating to other programs, or accessing data (Exhibit 13).

Runtime Services

Runtime services convert noncompiled computer languages into machine code during the execution of a program. Two subservices comprise runtime services: language interpreter and virtual machine.

1. *Language Interpreter Services.* Language interpreter services decompose a fourth generation or scripting language into machine code (executable code) at runtime.
2. *Virtual Machine Services.* Typically, a virtual machine is implemented in software on top of an operating system and is used to run applications. The virtual machine provides a layer of abstraction

between the applications and the underlying operating system and is often used to support operating system independence.

System Services

System services are services that applications can use to perform system-level functions. These services include:

- *System Security Services.* These allow applications to interact with the operating system's native security mechanism. The basic services include the ability to login, logoff, authenticate to the operating system, and enforce access control to system resources and executables.
- *Profile Management Services.* These are used to access and update local or remote system, user, or application profiles. User profiles, for example, can be used to store a variety of information from a user's language and color preferences to basic job function information that may be used by integrated performance support or workflow services.
- *Task and Memory Management Services.* These allow applications or other events to control individual computer tasks or processes and manage memory. They provide services for scheduling, starting, stopping, and restarting both client and server tasks (e.g., software agents).
- *Environment Verification Services.* These ensure functionality by monitoring, identifying, and validating environment integrity prior and during program execution. (e.g., free disk space, monitor resolution, and correct version).

Application Services

Application services are miscellaneous services that applications can use for common functions. These common functions can apply to one application or can be used across applications. They include:

- *Applications Security Services.* Besides system level security such as logging into the network, there are additional security services associated with specific applications, including user access services, data access services, and function access services.
- *Error Handling/Logging Services.* Error handling services support the handling of fatal and nonfatal hardware and software errors for an application. Logging services support the logging of informational, error, and warning messages.
- *State Management Services.* State management services enable information to be passed or shared among windows or web pages or across programs.

- *Codes Table Services.* Codes table services enable applications to utilize externally stored parameters and validation rules.
- *Active Help Services.* Active help services enable an application to provide assistance to a user for a specific task or set of tasks.
- *File Services.*
- *Application Integration Interface Services.* An application integration interface provides a method or gateway for passing context and control of information to an external application.
- *Other Common Services.* This is a catchall category for additional reusable routines useful across a set of applications (e.g., date routines, time zone conversions, and field validation routines).

Component Framework Services

Component framework services provide an infrastructure for building components so that they can communicate within an application and across applications, on the same machine or on multiple machines across a network, to work together. DCOM/COM+, NET and CORBA are among the leading component industry standards. These standards define how components should be built and how they should communicate.

Operating System Services

Operating system services are the underlying services such as multitasking, paging, memory allocation, etc., typically provided by today's modern operating systems. Where necessary, an additional layer or APIs may be provided to gain either operating system independence or a higher level of abstraction for application programmers.

TRANSACTION SERVICES

Transaction services provide the transaction integrity mechanism for the application. This allows all data activities within a single business event to be grouped as a single, logical unit of work.

In small- to moderate-scale environments of fewer than 150 simultaneous users on a single server, this service may be provided by the DBMS software with its restart/recovery and integrity capabilities. For larger client/server environments, an emerging class of software, referred to as "distributed online transaction managers," might be more applicable. These transaction managers provide sharing of server processes across a large community of users and can be more efficient than the DBMSs.

Transactions services include (Exhibit 14):

- TP monitor services
- Resource management services

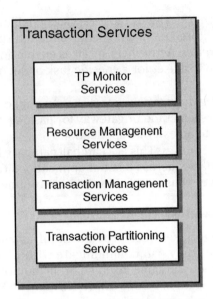

Exhibit 14. Transaction Services

- Transaction management services
- Transaction partitioning services

TP Monitor Services

The TP services are the primary interface through which applications invoke transaction services and receive status and error information. TP services, in conjunction with information access and communication services, provide for load balancing across processors or machines and location transparency for distributed transaction processing.

Resource Management Services

A resource manager provides for concurrency control and integrity for a singular data resource (e.g., a database or a file system). Integrity is guaranteed by ensuring that an update is completed correctly and entirely or not at all. Resource management services use locking, commit, and rollback services and are integrated with transaction management services.

Transaction Management Services

Transaction management services coordinate transactions across one or more resource managers either on a single machine or multiple machines within the network. Transaction management services ensure that all

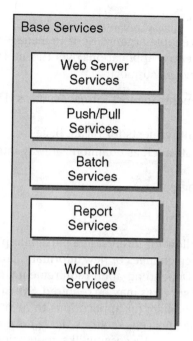

Exhibit 15. Base Services

resources for a transaction are updated or, in the case of an update failure on any one resource, all updates are rolled back. This service allows multiple applications to share data with integrity.

Transaction Partitioning Services

Transaction partitioning services provide support for mapping a single logical transaction in an application into the required multiple physical transactions. For example, in a package- or legacy-rich environment, the single logical transaction of changing a customer address may require the partitioning and coordination of several physical transactions to multiple application systems or databases. Transaction partitioning services provide the application with a simple, single transaction view.

BASE SERVICES

Base services provide support for delivering applications to a wide variety of users over the Internet, intranet, and extranet. Base services include: Web server services, push/pull services, batch services, report services, and workflow services (Exhibit 15).

Web Server Services

Web server services enable organizations to manage and publish information and deploy netcentric applications over the Internet and intranet environments. These services support:

- Managing documents in most formats such as HTML, Microsoft Word, etc.
- Handling of client requests for HTML pages
- Processing scripts such as common gateway interface (CGI) or active server pages (ASP)
- Caching Web pages

Push/Pull Services

Push/pull services allow for interest in a particular piece of information to be registered and then changes or new information to be communicated to the subscriber list. Depending upon requirements, synchronous or asynchronous push/pull services may be required. Synchronous push/pull services provide a mechanism for applications to be notified in real time if a subscribed item changes (e.g., a stock ticker). Asynchronous push/pull services do not require that a session-like connection be present between the subscriber and the information.

Batch Services

Batch processing is used to perform large-scale repetitive processing where no user involvement is required, as well as reporting. Areas for design attention include scheduling, recovery/restart, use of job streams, and high availability (e.g., 24-hour running). In addition, close attention must be paid to performance as batch systems usually must be processed within strict batch windows.

Batch Services are comprised of the following subservices:

- *Driver Services.* These services provide the control structure and framework for batch programs. They are also referred to as "Batch Scheduling Services."
- *Restart/Recovery Services.* These services are used to automatically recover and restart batch programs if they should fail during execution.
- *Batch Balancing Services.* These services support the tracking of run-to-run balances and totals for the batch system.
- *Report Services.* Project reporting tools are used to summarize and communicate information, using either printed paper or online reports.

Report Services

Report services are facilities for simplifying the construction and delivery of reports or generated correspondence. These services help to define reports and to electronically route reports to allow for online review, printing, and archiving. Report services also support the merging of application data with predefined templates to create letters or other printed correspondence. Report services include:

- Driver services
- Report definition services
- Report built services
- Report distribution services

Workflow Services

Workflow services control and coordinate the tasks that must be completed to process a business event. Workflow enables tasks within a business process to be passed to the appropriate participants in the correct sequence, and facilitates their completion within set times and budgets. Task definition includes the actions required as well as work folders containing forms, documents, images, and transactions. It uses business process rules, routing information, role definitions, and queues.

Workflow provides a mechanism to define, monitor, and control the sequence of work electronically. These services are typically provided by the server as they often coordinate activities among multiple users on multiple computers.

Workflow can be further divided into the following components:

- *Role Management Services.* These provide for the assignment of tasks to roles that can then be mapped to individuals.
- *Route Management Services.* These enable the routing of tasks to the next role.
- *Rule Management Services.* Rule management services support the routing of workflow activities by providing the intelligence necessary to determine which routes are appropriate given the state of a given process and knowledge of the organization's workflow processing rules.
- *Queue Management Services.* These services provide access to the workflow queues that are used to schedule work.

BUSINESS LOGIC

Business logic is the core of any application, providing the expression of business rules and procedures (e.g., the steps and rules that govern how a sales order is fulfilled). As such, business logic includes the control structure that specifies the flow for processing business events and user requests.

The execution architecture services described thus far are all generalized services designed to support the application's business logic. How business logic is to be organized is not within the scope of the execution architecture and must be determined based upon the characteristics of the application system to be developed. This section is intended to serve as a reminder of the importance of consciously designing a structure for business logic that helps to isolate the impacts of change, and to point out that the underlying netcentric architecture is particularly well suited for enabling the packaging of business logic as components.

There are many ways in which to organize business logic, including rules-based, object-oriented, components, and structured programming. However, each of these techniques include common concepts, which we can group as interface, application logic, and data abstraction (Exhibit 16).

Interface

Interface logic interprets and maps the actions of users into business logic processing activities. With the assistance of presentation services, interface logic provides the linkage that allows users to control the flow of processing within the application.

Application Logic

Application logic is the expression of business rules and procedures (e.g., the steps and rules that govern how a sales order is fulfilled). As such, application logic includes the control structure that specifies the flow for processing for business events and user requests. The isolation of control logic facilitates change and adaptability of the application to changing business processing flows.

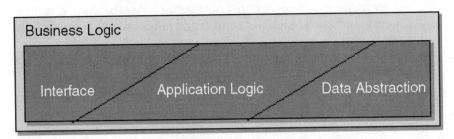

Exhibit 16. Business Logic

Data Abstraction

Information access services isolate business logic from the technical specifics of how information is stored (e.g., location transparency, RDBMS syntax, etc.). Data abstraction provides the application with a more logical view of information, further insulating the application from physical information storage considerations.

The developers of business logic should be shielded from the details and complexity of other architecture services (e.g., information services or component services) and other business logic.

It is important to decide whether the business logic will be separate from the presentation logic and the database access logic. Today, separation of business logic into its own tier is often done using an application server. In this type of an environment, although some business rules such as field validation might still be tightly coupled with the presentation logic, the majority of business logic is separate, usually residing on the server. It is also important to decide whether the business logic should be packaged as components to maximize software reuse and to streamline software distribution.

Another factor to consider is how the business logic is distributed between the client and the server(s) — where the business logic is stored and where the business logic is located when the application is being executed. There are several ways to distribute business logic:

1. Business logic can be stored on the server(s) and executed on the server(s).
2. Business logic can be stored on the server(s) and executed on the client.
3. Business logic can be stored and executed on the client.
4. Some business logic can be stored and executed on the server(s), and some business logic can be stored and executed on the client.

Having the business logic stored on the server enables developers to centrally maintain application code, thereby eliminating the need to distribute software to client machines when changes to the business logic occur. If all the business logic executes on the server, the application on the client will make requests to the server whenever it needs to execute a business function. This could increase network traffic, which may degrade application performance. On the other hand, having the business logic execute on the client may require longer load times when the application is initially launched. However, once the application is loaded, most processing is done on the client until synchronization with the server is needed. This type of an architecture might introduce complexities into the application that deal with the sharing of and reliance on central data across many users.

If the business logic is stored and executed on the client, software distribution options must be considered. Usually the most expensive option is to have a system administrator or the user physically install new applications and update existing applications on each client machine. Another option is to use a tool that performs automatic software distribution functions. However, this option usually requires the software distribution tool to be loaded first on each client machine. Another option is to package the application into ActiveX controls, utilizing the automatic install/update capabilities available with ActiveX controls — if the application is launched from a web browser.

Currently, Internet applications house the majority of the business processing logic on the server, supporting the thin-client model. However, as technology evolves, this balance is beginning to shift, allowing business logic code bundled into components to be either downloaded at runtime or permanently stored on the client machine. Today, client-side business logic is supported through the use of Java applets, JavaBeans, plug-ins and JavaScript from Sun/Netscape, and ActiveX controls and VBScript from Microsoft.

CONCLUSION

To operate optimally in the world of architectures, it is vital to remember a key point: one should not dwell too long at the abstract level. One can get mired in representations, in logical arguments. Pictures are important, but an architecture must be looked at pragmatically. It lives and breathes. It may evolve as the organization evolves. Yet, without the common understandings, common terminology, and common direction provided by architecture frameworks, project teams are putting their entire organizations at risk.

Chapter 5
Information Services
Accenture

"Information" in today's client/server and netcentric environment is much broader and diverse in nature than traditional data, that is, data that were understood as characters. Information, or "knowledge," as we characterized it in the introduction to this book, can consist of many things in today's computing solutions, including graphics, image, voice, and full-motion video. This information is extremely complex and difficult to manage, control, and deliver.

The information challenge of the workplace today is the "feast-or-famine" syndrome: workers often cannot find information when they need it, or they may be confronted by too much information at any given time. Information is of no use unless we know where it is and how to get at it. Information services are where that access is achieved. (Note that although there are many useful distinctions to be made among the words "data," "information," and "knowledge," this chapter will use both the words data and information to refer to the knowledge or content being managed in a netcentric environment.)

In a traditional computing environment, an organization's information is usually centralized in a particular location, or it may be fragmented across multiple locations. In a netcentric environment, however, information is most often distributed because distribution of processors and data is an inherent part of the new styles of netcentric computing.

Exhibit 1 presents an example of how information may be distributed in a netcentric computing environment. In this example from an airline information system, the reservations are centralized in Dallas. Each region has a server to maintain its own flights and maintenance information (horizontally segmented by region), and each workstation at each region maintains replicated airport and plane data. In general, the following may be said about the information within this system:

- Information that is stable or static is often found on all clients.
- Information that is volatile or specific to particular locations or groups is on the server.

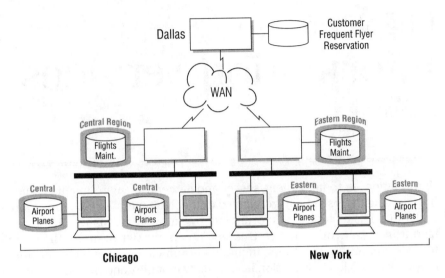

Exhibit 1. Example of Distribution of Information

- Information that is accessed and updated throughout the organization is on the central system or the enterprise system.
- Most information (except, perhaps, for some static codes tables) is stored on the server, although the processing may be distributed across client and server.
- Putting information on a client may require information replication across clients (usually limited to codes tables) and could lead to synchronization and integrity issues.

CHARACTERISTICS OF INFORMATION IN NETCENTRIC COMPUTING

The example in Exhibit 1 illustrates the primary characteristics of information in a client/server and netcentric computing environment.

Information Is Distinct from Processes

The most important characteristic of information is that it is kept distinct from the processes that access and use it. The chief function of the netcentric architecture is to isolate the business logic from the technology itself. Within the information services component of the architecture, this isolation is achieved by maintaining two layers, a logical layer and a physical layer.

- From a logical viewpoint, an application issues a request for information, and elements of that information (e.g., location, formats, and management mechanisms) are transparent to the user. A single information request is all that is necessary to retrieve the information, potentially from multiple sources, to support a business function.

- From a physical viewpoint, the information may actually be stored on, and retrieved from, many different sources that are being managed by many different database managers on many different platforms.

Information Is Usually Distributed

Distributed information can be defined formally as "information that is physically separated between locations or platforms." Netcentric computing does not imply distributed information nor does distributed information imply netcentric computing. However, most client/server and netcentric systems rely on some form of distributed information.

Client/server and netcentric computing implies more processing locations (geographic and platform) with local disk storage capabilities. Because information should reside close to the users who need to access that information, information distribution offers important advantages that will be discussed subsequently.

Information Is Spread across Multiple Environments

Because of the distributed nature of information in a netcentric computing environment, organizations often have to deal with a multivendor environment. This places demands on the networking and communications aspects of the netcentric architecture.

Information Is in Multiple Forms

The graphical environment of today's applications and the ability to send different types of information (e.g., data, graphic, image, voice, or video) directly to the desktop have made the information environment of client/server and netcentric computing much more complex.

Information May Be Replicated or Duplicated

Because information is generally distributed in the netcentric architecture, it often means that information must be replicated across multiple locations. The existence of multiple copies of information means that users must be especially concerned with keeping them synchronized and accurate.

Replication of information implies methods to perform the replication, additional disk resources, possible integrity problems because of multiple copies, and information management and ownership issues. These issues are addressed later in this chapter.

Information Is Often Fragmented or Segmented

Because information accessed by an application is heterogeneous and dispersed, it is often fragmented. The information may be recombined in various ways, and so the information services component of the netcentric architecture must have a way of ensuring the integrity of the information in its various combinations.

ISSUES IN THE DISTRIBUTION OF INFORMATION

The ultimate goal of distributed information processing is to give every user transparent access to dispersed, disparate information. With client/server and netcentric computing, developers seek to isolate applications from knowledge of information location, information access methods, and information management products. At the same time, they seek to ensure that the information is reliable, i.e., that it has integrity.

When to Consider a Distributed Database Strategy

When particular business functions have certain characteristics, distributed information and distributed information processing may be considered:

1. *Geographical distribution.* The business functions are spread over several different sites, making it impractical to support some (or all) of the processing requirements from a central site.
2. *Local decision making and independence.* The organizational structure is distributed and the business has several local sites with the authority to make local decisions as to how to process and act upon its information.
3. *Performance.* The response time at the local site becomes unacceptable due to the transfer of data between the central and local sites.
4. *Scalability.* Business growth has caused the volume of data to expand, the volume of processing to increase, or has resulted in expansion to new sites.

Potential Benefits

The potential benefits for a distributed database strategy apply both to true distributed database management systems and to implementations that incorporate distributed data management strategies.

Organization. A distributed system may better reflect an organization's structure, which often is logically distributed (e.g., into divisions, departments, and projects) as well as physically distributed (e.g., into plants, warehouses, and branch offices).

Ease of Growth. Once installed, a distributed system is able to expand more gracefully than a nondistributed system. For example, if significant business growth has caused the volume of information to expand or the volume of processing to increase, it may be easier to expand the system by adding a new site to an existing distributed system than by replacing or extending an existing centralized system with a larger one.

Lower Costs. It may be less expensive for organizations to add another server or to extend the server than to add or extend a mainframe.

Local Autonomy. Distributing a system allows individual groups within an organization to exercise control over their own information while still being able to access information at remote locations when necessary.

Increased Availability. A distributed system may offer greater availability than a centralized system because it can continue to function (though at a reduced level) even if an individual site or communication link has failed. Also, with the support of replicated information, availability is improved in that a replicated information object remains available as long as at least one copy of that object is available.

Increased Efficiency. Response times can be reduced because information in a distributed system can be stored close to its point of use, enabling most information accesses to be local.

Increased Flexibility. Information can be dynamically moved or replicated, existing copies can be deleted, or new information types can be added to accommodate changes in how the information is used.

Potential Challenges

Although distribution of information throughout a system has many benefits, it must overcome a number of challenges, as well.

Complex Architectural-Level Communications. In these systems, messages containing information, processing requests, and acknowledgments of previous requests are passed continuously among various remote sites. Coordinating this message flow is complex and can be costly.

Complex Update Control. If two users update the same piece of information, a method must be found to mediate conflicts. One way to ensure information integrity is to employ a locking mechanism. However, the locking strategy becomes more challenging as machines are added; network failure must be taken into consideration. Added complexity also arises with distributed transactions where one user updates two data sources simultaneously and both updates must occur in sync.

Network Dependency. When data are distributed across the network, reliable communications between sites are required or processing may be halted. This increased reliability may require expensive duplication of network resources to provide an acceptable amount of system availability for the users.

Complexity of "Location Transparency." In the ideal distributed information environment, the end user or application programmer has access to all required information without having to know where that information is physically located. This feature is known as location transparency and it is supported by some of the database management system (DBMS) products currently available. This places a substantial burden on the architecture and its designers to locate the information efficiently and to transport the information to the application upon request, without excessive processing delays.

Location Transparency also Complicates User Support. A user problem within a single application may originate from any number of remote sites that are transparent to the user, making the problem more difficult to identify and resolve.

Information Synchronization. Maintenance of redundant information over multiple sites and processors increases the complexity of information synchronization routines. Complex time synchronization between separate machines may be required.

Organizations must be aware of what their synchronization requirements are. Timing is one example of a synchronization challenge. When does information need to be synchronized? In real time? Overnight? Several techniques for performing information synchronization efficiently are discussed later.

Changes in Organizational Structure. Changes in the existing organizational structure could invalidate the information design. With distributed information, one must build in flexibility to change as the organization changes.

Security. Managing access to information and preventing unauthorized access are greater challenges in client/server and netcentric computing than in a centralized environment. Complexity here is a result of the distributed nature of system components (hardware, software, and data).

Information Transformation. Because information is on multiple platforms and multiple management environments, the information must be transformed from one format or type to another. Some information types may be supported in one environment and not in another.

Information Management. Distributed information is more difficult to manage, creating challenges for backup and recovery of information and for overall information integrity.

Heterogeneous Environments. Client/server and netcentric information may be on multiple databases, file systems, and hardware platforms connected by multiple network protocols.

Rules for Design

"Location transparency" is a key to successful information design in client/server and netcentric computing. Database expert C.J. Date puts this principle another way: "To a user, a distributed system should look exactly like a nondistributed system. The user or programmer who accesses and manipulates information should be able to do so logically through a single access, as if it were all managed by a single DBMS on a single machine."

From this underlying principle, Date sets forth 12 related rules for distributed data design, or distributed information design. Date's guidelines are helpful in designing overall information access in a netcentric architecture, although it is unlikely that any system will conform to all 12 of these rules. Most organizations focus on the need to achieve local autonomy and the need for information independence.

The 12 rules are:

1. *Local Autonomy.* All operations at any particular site should be controlled by that site and not dependent on another site to function. Each local site owns and manages its own information, and each site is therefore responsible for the accuracy, security, and integrity of that information.
2. *No Reliance on a Central Site.* A corollary of the first rule, this rule is necessary to prevent bottlenecks and the potential vulnerability of relying on a central site.
3. *Continuous Operation.* Planned system shutdowns should never be necessary. Good design means that maintenance, database administration and operations, and upgrades should take place without shutting down the system.
4. *Location Independence.* Users and applications should be able to access remote information as if it were local. This simplifies application design and permits information to be moved around without causing changes to existing applications.
5. *Segmentation Independence.* If an information relation can be separated into segments for physical storage and access, the distributed database design should support storing the segments at the

location where they are used most frequently. Users should be able to access any information logically as if it were not segmented at all.

6. *Replication Independence.* Replication of information should be transparent to the users and to the application. Access proceeds logically as if there is only one copy of the information.

7. *Distributed Query Processing.* Users should be able to make a single query across multiple physical information locations.

8. *Distributed Transaction Management.* The system should provide a single point of entry for the transaction, even if the transaction involves information from multiple sites to complete the business function.

9. *Hardware Independence.* Client/server and netcentric systems include a variety of machines. The system must be able to present a "single-system image" of the database to the user while allowing different hardware systems to participate as partners in the system.

10. *Operating System Independence.* Systems with heterogeneous hardware may use more than one operating system. The information should be able to allow all operating systems to participate in the same distributed system.

11. *Network Independence.* In a client/server or netcentric system, multiple communications systems must be able to operate transparently together to users and application designers.

12. *DBMS Independence.* Many system installations have different types of DBMSs. Thus, it is vital that they all support the same interface and that they can interoperate.

Meeting these challenges of distributed information is the function of the Information Services component of the netcentric architecture.

INFORMATION SERVICES FRAMEWORK

A two-layer approach is useful to keep information distinct from the processes that access and use it: a logical layer and a physical layer. Within the netcentric architecture, the information services component maintains this logical/physical distinction (Exhibit 2).

Logical Layer

The logical layer acts to isolate the physical aspects of information (e.g., location, storage format, and access language) from applications and applications developers. This layer provides all the detail services associated with information and with access to or from that information.

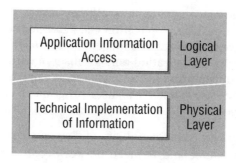

Exhibit 2. Logical and Physical Layers

Physical Layer

The physical layer can be used within a netcentric architecture to isolate the detailed technical implementations of information. This layer insulates an organization and its applications from the rapid pace of change in information management technology. This layer can also be used to position legacy information sources into the netcentric computing environment, independent of migrating applications and implementing new applications.

DATABASE SERVICES

Database services are responsible for providing access to a local or remote database, maintaining integrity of the data within the database, and supporting the ability to store data on either a single physical platform or, in some cases, across multiple platforms. These services are typically provided by DBMS vendors and accessed via embedded or call-level SQL variants and supersets. Depending upon the underlying storage model, non-SQL access methods may be used instead.

Many netcentric applications today are broadcast-type applications designed to market a company's products or publish the company's policies and procedures. Furthermore, there is now a growth of netcentric applications that are transaction-type applications used to process a customer's sales order, maintenance request, etc. Typically, these types of applications require integration with a database manager. Database services include replication/synchronization services, access services, security services, indexing services, and storage services.

Replication/Synchronization Services

Replication services support an environment in which multiple copies of databases must be maintained. For example, if ad hoc reporting queries or operational data stores can work with a replica of the transaction database, these resource-intensive applications will not interfere with mission-critical transaction processing. Replication can be either complete or partial. During complete replication all records are copied from one destination to another; during partial replication only a subset of data is copied as specified by the user or the program. Replication can also be done either real-time or on demand (i.e., initiated by a user, program, or scheduler). The following might be possible if databases are replicated on alternate server(s):

- Better availability or recoverability of distributed applications
- Better performance and reduced network cost, particularly in environments where users are widely geographically dispersed
- Improved access to wider ranges of data as data replicas may be more readily available

The terms "replication" and "synchronization" are used interchangeably, depending on the vendor, article, book, etc. For example, when Lotus Notes refers to Replication it means a combination of replication and synchronization services described previously. When Sybase refers to replication it only means copying data from one source to another.

Access Services

Access services enable an application to retrieve data from a database as well as manipulate (insert, update, and delete) data in a database. SQL is the primary approach for accessing records in today's DBMSs.

Client–server and netcentric systems often require data access from multiple databases offered by different vendors. This is often due to integration of new systems with existing legacy systems. The key architectural concern is in building the application where the multivendor data problem is transparent to the application needing the data. This provides future portability and flexibility, and also makes it easier for application developers to write to a single database access interface. Achieving database access transparency requires the following:

Standards-Based SQL API. This approach uses a single, standards-based set of APIs to access any database and includes the following technologies: Open Database Connectivity (ODBC), Java Database Connectivity (JDBC), and Object Linking and Embedding (OLE BD).

SQL Gateways. These provide a mechanism for clients to transparently access data in a variety of databases (e.g., Oracle, Sybase, or DB2) by translating SQL calls written using the format and protocols of the gateway server or primary server to the format and protocols of the target database. Currently, there are three contending architectures for providing gateway functions.

Distributed Relational Data Access (DRDA). This is a standard promoted by IBM for distributed data access between heterogeneous databases. In this case the conversion of the format and protocols occurs only once. It supports SQL89 and a subset of the SQL92 standard, and is built on top on APPC/APPN and TCP/IP transport stacks.

IBI's EDA/SQL and the Sybase/MDI Open Server. These use SQL to access relational and nonrelational database systems. They use API/SQL or T-SQL, respectively, as the standard interface language. A large number of communication protocols are supported, including NetBIOS, SNA, DecNET, and TCP/IP. The main engine translates the client requests into specific server calls. It handles security, authentication, statistics gathering, and some system management tasks.

Security Services

Security services enforce access control to ensure that records are only visible or editable by authorized people for approved purposes. Most DBMSs provide access control at the database, table, or row level as well as concurrency control. However, there may be severe limitations in the DBMS's ability to pass data needed for security authentication across a network, forcing the architect to build those services into the Security Services layer.

Indexing Services

Indexing services provide a mechanism for speeding up data retrieval. In relational databases, one or more fields can be used to construct the index. Therefore, when a user searches for a specific record, the index is used to find the location of that record, which is faster scanning the whole table sequentially. Revolutionary advances in indexing techniques — such as bitmapped indexing, context indexing, and star indexes — provide rich capabilities for netcentric computing.

Storage Services

Storage services manage the physical storage of data. These services provide a mechanism for saving information so that data will live beyond program execution. Data are often stored in relational format (an RDBMS) but may also be stored in an object-oriented format (OODBMS) or other formats such as IMS or VSAM.

DOCUMENT SERVICES

Document services provide similar structure and control for documents that DBMSs apply to record-oriented data. A document is defined as a collection of objects potentially of different types (e.g., structured data, unstructured data, images, multimedia) a business user deals with. An individual

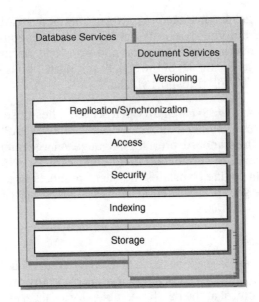

Exhibit 3. Information Services Framework

document might be a table created using a spreadsheet package, a report created using a word processing package, a web page created using an HTML authoring tool, unstructured text, or a combination of these object types. Regardless of the software used to create and maintain the component parts, all parts together constitute the document, which is managed as a single entity.

Netcentric applications that are executed from a browser are particularly well suited for serving up document style information. If the web application consists of more than just a few HTML documents, integration with a document management system should be considered. Document services include replication/synchronization services, access services, indexing services, security services, storage services, and versioning services (see Exhibit 3).

Replication/Synchronization Services

Replication services support an environment in which multiple copies of documents must be maintained. A key objective is that documents be shareable and searchable across the entire organization. Therefore, the architecture needs to *logically* provide a single repository, even though the documents are *physically* stored in different locations. Replicating documents on alternative server(s) may have some benefits: better availability or recoverability of a distributed application, better performance, reduced network cost, or increased information access and availability.

Synchronization services perform the transactions required to make consistent information sources that are intended to mirror each other; they support the needs of intermittently connected users or sites. As with databases, these services are especially valuable for users of remote or mobile devices that need to be able to work locally without a constant network connection and then be able to synchronize with the central server at a given point in time.

Access Services

Access services support document creation, maintenance, and retrieval. These services allow users to capture knowledge or content through the creation of unstructured information, i.e., documents. Access services allow users to effectively retrieve documents they created, and documents that were created by others. Documents can be comprised of many different data types including text, charts, graphics, or even audio and video.

Indexing Services

Locating documents, as well as content within documents, is a more complex problem and involves several alternative methods. The Windows File Manager is a simplistic implementation of a hierarchical organization of files and collections of files. If the user model of where documents should be stored and found can be represented in this way, the use of structure and naming standards can be sufficient. However, a hierarchical document-filing organization is not suitable for many types of document queries (e.g., retrieving all sales order documents for over $1000).

Therefore, most document management products provide index services that support the following methods for searching document repositories:

- *Attribute Search.* Scans short lists (attributes) of important words that are associated with a document and returns documents that match the search criteria. For example, a user may query for documents written by a specific author or created on a particular date. Attribute search brings the capabilities of the SQL-oriented database approach to finding documents by storing in a database the values of specially identified fields within a document and a reference to the document itself. To support Attribute Search, an index maintains document attributes, which it uses to manage, find, and catalog documents. This is the least complicated approach of the searching methods.
- *Full-Text Search.* Searches repository contents for exact words or phrases and returns documents that match the search criteria. To facilitate

Full-Text Search, full-text indexes are constructed by scanning documents once and recording in an index file which words occur in which documents. Leading document management systems have full-text search services built in, which can be integrated directly into applications.

- *Context Search:* Searches repository contents for exact words or phrases. It also searches for related words or phrases by using synonyms and word taxonomies. For example, if the user searches for *auto*, the search engine should look for *car, automobile, motor vehicle*, etc.
- *Boolean Search:* Searches repository contents for words or phases that are joined together using boolean operators (e.g., AND, OR, or NOT). The same types of indexes are used for Boolean Search as for Full-Text Search.

Security Services

Documents should be accessed exclusively through document services. If a document is checked in, checked out, routed, viewed, annotated, archived, or printed, it should be done only by users with the correct security privileges. Those access privileges should be controlled by user, role, and group. Analogous to record locking to prevent two users from editing the same data, document management access control services include check-in/check-out services to limit concurrent editing.

Storage Services

Storage services manage the physical storage of documents. Most document management products store documents as objects that include two basic data types: attributes and content. Document attributes are key fields used to identify the document, such as author name or created date. Document content refers to the actual unstructured information stored within the document. Generally, the documents are stored in a repository using one of the following methods:

- *Proprietary database.* Documents (attributes and contents) are stored in a proprietary database, one that the vendor has specifically developed for use with its product.
- *Industry standard database.* Documents (attributes and contents) are stored in an industry standard database such as Oracle or Sybase. Attributes are stored within traditional database data types (e.g., integer or character); contents are stored in the database's BLOB (Binary Large Objects) data type.
- *Industry standard database and file system.* Documents' attributes are stored in an industry standard database, and documents' contents are usually stored in the file system of the host operating system. Most

document management products use this document storage method today because this approach provides the most flexibility in terms of data distribution and also allows for greater scalability.

Versioning Services

Versioning services maintain a historical record of the changes to a document over time. By maintaining this record, these services allow for the recreation of a document as it looked at any given point in time during its evolution. Additional key versioning features record who made changes and when and why they were made.

DDBMS FRAMEWORK

The rest of this chapter discusses a critical component of managing information in a netcentric application: the distributed DBMS (DDBMS). The DDBMS promises a number of benefits for organizations, including the ability to expand a system more gracefully in an incremental fashion, local autonomy, increased availability and reliability of information, and increased efficiency and flexibility. With a DDBMS, users located in different geographical locations will be able to retrieve and update information from one or more locations in a network transparently and with full integrity and security.

CHARACTERISTICS OF DDBMS IN CLIENT/SERVER AND NETCENTRIC COMPUTING

Client/server and netcentric computing allow information to be kept distinct from the processes that use that information. Any DDBMS product used in a netcentric environment must be able to maintain this distinction. This section discusses a number of crucial characteristics of DDBMS products:

- Stored procedures
- Triggers
- Support for referential integrity
- Two-phase commit
- Support for nontextual or multimedia information
- Information replication
- Information gateways
- Disk mirroring

Stored Procedures

A stored procedure is a set of named SQL statements defined within a function that is compiled within the DDBMS for runtime execution by name.

Essentially, it is information access logic coded into the database server for use by all clients.

Stored procedures can be compared to third-generation language (3GL) routines, but they are executed by DDBMS software and contain SQL statements. At runtime, the stored procedure is accessed through a 3GL or 4GL call.

Advantages of Stored Procedures. Stored procedures have a number of important advantages:

- *Information transfer volume is minimized.* Because the stored procedure can execute all SQL statements and information access logic, only required information is returned to the requesting process.
- *Speeds execution.* Stored procedures are usually compiled into the database engine (not the application) for fast execution, which generally improves DDBMS and information access performance.
- *Decreases lines of code.* Applications can have less code, and they do not need to include, within each application, information integrity or reused information access logic.
- *Eases some maintenance activities.* Applications have less data structure information; therefore, it is easier to change table sizes, column names, and so forth.
- *Promotes code reusability.* Stored procedures can be thought of as object processing for information tables; they modularize and encapsulate information operations into a library-like area. Each stored procedure can be reused when accessed by any application that has permission to use it.
- *Enforces distinctions between information and process.* All information access, location, format, and so forth can be addressed within the stored procedure and therefore removed from the application logic that processes that information.

Potential Drawbacks of Stored Procedures. The use of stored procedures has a number of potential drawbacks:

- *Each DDBMS vendor's implementation is different.* Once an organization chooses a particular DDBMS and uses that vendor's stored procedures, it may be locked in to that vendor or, at a minimum, those stored procedures have to be reimplemented.
- *Changes in a stored procedure can affect many applications.* The balance of application processing between the application and stored procedure must be understood. Like any library routine, changes require a test of all users.
- *System performance may be degraded by the inappropriate use of a stored procedure.* For example, a stored procedure may have to return

multiple information types from multiple sources to respond to a single request.

When to Use Stored Procedures. Stored procedures should be used in the following cases:

- *When a set of SQL calls should be grouped logically for a single business operation.* A logical set of data operations that performs a single business function and is executed frequently (such as "make reservation") provides a good base for a stored procedure.
- *When the same set of SQL calls are used in many applications.* As soon as the same SQL statements are used by more than one application, stored procedures are valuable for avoiding problems in updating several applications when changes are made and for improving the consistency of SQL use within an organization or project.
- *When one wants to decrease information transfer from client to server in complicated information requests.* A stored procedure call is often a smaller information message from a client to a server than a complex SQL statement(s). However, when there is less information transfer, there are more MIPS used on the server.
- *When one wants to maximize processing on a server platform, balancing client processing.* Stored procedures add central processing unit usage on the server and should be balanced against application processing on the client.

Triggers

Triggers are convenient "start" mechanisms to initiate stored procedures or SQL commands. Triggers can be based on either clock events or data events. A clock-based trigger might be, "At 1:00 a.m. each morning, replicate the AIRPORT entity to sites New York, Chicago, and Dulles with the AIRPORT_REP stored procedure." A data-based event might be, "When a new row is inserted into the RESERVATION table, initiate the RESERVATION_ACCOUNTING stored procedure."

Triggers have a number of advantages. They permit applications developers to remove event-based logic from applications or the infrastructure software, and they tie a data-driven event to the actual data that drives the event. However, it is difficult to know what will happen to the database if many triggers cascade on and on. Infinite loops may be possible if designers are not careful and do not conduct thorough testing.

Referential Integrity

Referential integrity is the correctness and consistency of relationships among data tables, and the correctness of information content. These are crucial issues in a relational database environment. The most important question with regard to referential integrity is whether it should be handled by the DDBMS or by the applications.

If the DDBMS enforces the integrity rules, integrity is centralized and not maintained in all application programs; integrity can be changed without modifying applications. However, DDBMS integrity enforcement used indiscriminately generates high overhead. Too much integrity checking slows down the system considerably.

In general, DDBMS-enforced referential integrity should be used when possible. The advantage is that the DDBMS enforces integrity more effectively than application logic. Furthermore, applications do not have to design and code the logic, and the logic can be centralized in the DDBMS. However, applications still have to test it.

There are two reasons to avoid DDBMS-enforced referential integrity:

1. The business rule that needs to be enforced is not a rule available from the DDBMS.
2. Using DDBMS-enforced referential integrity forces awkward constraints on application programs or on database maintenance processes.

It is vital to define all the business rules between tables before deciding how the relationship should be maintained. There are four ways to alter a referential relationship (insert a child, update the primary key of a child, update a foreign key of a parent, and delete a parent), and there are four possible business rules for how to retain referential integrity in each situation, for a total of 16 options. Most DDBMSs offer only six options. When one needs one of the missing options, the application must enforce it.

DDBMS-enforced referential integrity should not make program structures awkward or less maintainable. However, complex links between tables may force difficult management, loading, and unloading scenarios. For example, a credit card company wanted a 24x7 application to allow new credit card products to be defined online, in such a way that the new products were not available to customers until all rules regarding the new product were fully defined. The credit card products had many complex rules, which were to be split across many child tables under the main product table. The simplest way to guarantee that the product could not be used until it was complete was to insert all the children first, and insert the parent only when all the child rows were entered and validated. DDBMS-enforced referential integrity would not permit such a scenario, so application-enforced integrity was used instead.

Similarly, if too many tables are linked together through DDBMS-enforced referential integrity, backup/restore scenarios may become

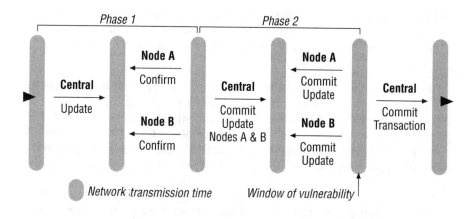

Exhibit 4.   Example of Two-Phase Commit

excessively difficult, so it is wise to keep less than about 15 referentially linked sets of tables.

When bulk-loading information into the database, referential integrity constraints should ensure that the database is consistent and accurate after loading. Some DDBMS products have a "backdoor" load that bypasses integrity constraints.

In general, DDBMS-enforced integrity should be used whenever it is justified by business events. However, the DDBMS should not be used to perform application integrity, for example, to validate codes against code tables. These values usually do not change often, and the constant validation is simply unnecessary overhead. Also, developers should not put more than a manageable number of tables into a single connected referential tree structure that must be maintained by the DDBMS. Developers must understand the characteristics of the specific DDBMS they are working with to determine what that manageable number is.

Two-Phase Commit

Two-phase commit (sometimes abbreviated 2PC) is a protocol used when a logical unit of work updates information in two or more recovery managers or "nodes." 2PC ensures integrity of information between nodes. It has been used for many years to ensure integrity between a transaction monitor and a DBMS running on the same processor.

In a client/server or netcentric environment, distributed 2PC is a technique for guaranteeing integrity across distributed processors. Exhibit 4 shows a timeline of activities associated with two-phase commit.

Phase 1. Phase 1, or the prepare phase, queries all the recovery managers to verify that they are ready to commit, that is, ready for updating. This phase initiates the cleanup tasks of the memory management facilities at each node.

If a participating node (not the coordinating node) is unable to receive the prepare message (and any subsequent rollback), it checks periodically for unreleased locks (or checks when communication/processing is restored) and queries the coordinator about the status of the transaction. The coordinator responds that the transaction was rolled back because all sites could not participate, and the participating site also rolls back, releasing all locks.

Phase 2. Phase 2, or the commit phase, tells each participating node to write a commit log record. If the commit is successful at all the remote nodes involved in the transaction and the originating node receives a successful acknowledgment from each of the remote nodes, the transaction at the originating node is committed. If confirmation is not received from all nodes involved, the transaction is rolled back.

Advantages and Disadvantages. Two-phase commits have several advantages. A 2PC approach can ensure that multiple databases remain synchronous. If some other approach is used to guarantee synchronization, it must incorporate similar synchronization logic and could mean building a custom 2PC architecture.

Two-phase commits are DDBMS supported; the DDBMS product can enforce and control the protocol (e.g., sending the messages, waiting for receipt, confirming, committing, and rolling back). Also, 2PCs are application independent. Because they are controlled by the DDBMS, applications do not need to control the execution of the protocol.

However, the 2PC implementation does leave a window of vulnerability: there are gaps in transmission between the central/coordinating node and the nodes involved in the transaction. If the participating node commits but the initiating node does not receive acknowledgment of the commit, the initiating node does not know whether to commit or to roll back. As a result, the initiating node does not know what to do and data integrity may be lost, defeating the entire objective of 2PC. The probability of this occurring increases with the number and distance of sites involved in the transaction. It works extremely well between CICS and DB2 running on the same mainframe box where the distance between nodes is negligible. However, it is a different matter when the commit message must travel through space to a satellite and back en route between nodes. Two-phase commit can also affect overall system and application performance.

Distributed two-phase commit is a complicated strategy — time consuming and costly. It relies on complex synchronous messaging over the network. Communications failures can have a substantial impact on the practicality of this technique.

In addition, the common approach requires participation and success from all sites involved in the transaction. If one site cannot complete the transaction, the entire transaction fails. Some observers have described 2PC as a protocol that guarantees that failure at one node will be replicated to all nodes.

So, when is two-phase commit appropriate? Developers should avoid two-phase commits by designing applications so that information updated during a single logical unit of work is located within the same node. If they cannot avoid it, designers should use two-phase commits when they need to have some form of synchronization of information between nodes. However, they must remember that inconsistencies in information integrity are still possible, so they must either control the integrity problems with a "data check" program or with regular offline downloads or synchronizations.

Multimedia or Nontextual Information Storage

Support for more complex types of information is an important DDBMS capability to evaluate. This information goes by a number of different names: unstructured information, nontextual information, multimedia, and extended information. By whatever name, this information consists of digital images, graphics, video images, voice, word processing documents, and spreadsheets.

The DDBMS has two primary methods by which it can handle these kinds of information: either defined within the database in data types called binary large objects (BLOBs), or defined outside the database structure with a pointer containing the file name where the information is contained within the DDBMS. The decision to use a BLOB or a file should be reviewed to determine application requirements, data administration requirements, and network impact.

BLOB storage has several advantages. The integrity of information is maintained by the DDBMS. Also, BLOBs are logically equivalent to other data types, which makes retrieval easier. However, a BLOB is a nonstandard SQL data type so the designer must be careful to ensure that the DDBMS supports it. Current performance levels may be poor as a result of the large size of the BLOBs.

An advantage of storing extended data types outside the database is that the file can be accessed independent of the DDBMS, through operating system services. This may lead to better retrieval performance. Disadvantages of this type of storage include the fact that the integrity of the pointer to the file, and of the information itself, must be maintained by the application. Also, backup and restore operations must use both the DDBMS and file procedures.

Information Replication

Information replication is a critical function of most mission-critical distributed information architectures. Replication is the synchronization of a database or subset of a database from one location to another. Replication can occur regularly or irregularly, automatically or manually. Replication works well for information that does not change frequently and for data that needs to be synchronized but not in real time. This is the case most of the time.

Replication provides faster access to information and less transfer of information across the network. However, a challenge to replication is keeping multiple copies of information synchronized. If the DDBMS cannot provide automatic synchronization, additional development time is necessary to provide and maintain this synchronization.

Hands-on experience to date suggests that recovery is very complex. In addition, replication can throw unpredictable loads on the network such that network administration groups are reluctant to allow the feature into the network.

Information Gateways (Middleware)

Information gateways (also referred to as DBMS middleware) are mechanisms that allow applications to access information from a variety of DDBMSs without extensive platform-specific or DDBMS-specific programming.

An information gateway may be a part of the DDBMS or it may be a separate product. The primary functions of the gateway include transparent routing of SQL calls and translating among various dialects of SQL. Gateways are particularly valuable when there is an existing installed base using a variety of DDBMSs.

An information gateway accepts an SQL statement from the client application and translates it into a format understandable by the target DDBMS(s). The gateway then sends the statement to be processed. After processing, the information gateway receives the results, translates them into a form that can be understood by the client, and then returns the information and status to the client.

Gateways allow access to information across multiple database management systems. The applications can use a consistent interface for all information, which saves development time and cost as well as training time for application designers and end users. However, gateways may result in a slower response time to queries because of the time required for formatting, protocol conversion, and other activities of the gateway. Some gateways offer read-only access, so updates must be processed differently. There are also potential information accuracy and integrity issues associated with the use of information gateways.

Disk Mirroring

Disk mirroring is a DDBMS-enforced "hot backup" disk capability within a single platform. It ensures that information is not lost in cases of disk failure. Generally, in a disk failure or disk crash, all information inserted since the last tape backup is lost. With disk mirroring, the backup disk is always up-to-date with respect to the primary disk. Disk mirroring also increases the availability of the DDBMS.

With disk mirroring, the DDBMS automatically transfers to the backup disk if the primary disk fails. It then automatically synchronizes the primary disk after the failure is cleared.

Disk mirroring provides obvious advantages to information security; in addition, it is transparent to applications controlled by the DDBMS. However, more disks are required in disk mirroring, and mirroring cannot be done over a LAN. Also, some minor performance decreases may result from mirroring.

MATCHING FUNCTIONS AND FEATURES

In any particular client/server or netcentric system, some features and functions of DDBMSs may be critical and others may not. When evaluating a DDBMS, it is important to find one appropriate for the specific system and business requirements. A matrix, such as the one in Exhibit 5, is a worksheet for matching functions and features to products under consideration.

CONCLUSION

Maximizing the benefits of client/server and netcentric computing presents some of the greatest challenges to designers and developers. One of the primary business benefits of netcentric computing is that knowledge workers have access to more and better types of information located throughout the enterprise. However, that access requires a methodical approach to enabling applications to access and manipulate information, whether it is stored locally or remotely in files or databases. Even the fact that we refer to this part of the netcentric architecture as information access (rather than its traditional name, data access) reveals an important part of the information challenge of netcentric systems.

In addition, a key technology in client/server and netcentric computing is the DDBMS. Although theoretically a distributed DBMS does not have to

	Product A	Product B	Product C
Stored Procedures			
Triggers			
Two-Phase Commit			
Referential Integrity			
Multimedia			
Replication			
Gateways			
Mirroring			

Exhibit 5.   Matrix of Features

be relational, the relational model provides a simpler and more practical vehicle to support DDBMS functions than hierarchical or network models.

A relational DDBMS also tends to provide better support for the flexible, dynamic information requirements found in most netcentric applications. The major DDBMS products in the marketplace today are built on a relational framework, and the success of relational DBMSs has had a direct impact on spurring the development of DDBMS products. More and more, organizations will see distributed DBMS as a practical technology component that is needed to support their growing business needs.

Chapter 6
Developing an E-Business Architecture

Srinivas Padmanabharao

What is an E-business? All definitions that are floating out there strive to distinguish "E-business" from "E-commerce." The former refers to the process of using the Internet and associated technologies to transform every business process and E-enable all parts of the organization's value chain from acquiring, serving, and retaining customers to interacting with employees, partners, and the world at large. "E-commerce" can safely be considered one vital but small part in the overall E-business architecture.

There are two basic categories of businesses conducted over the Internet. The first category is the Business-to-Consumer (B2C) segment, which includes the popular, Wall Street-friendly businesses like Amazon, E*Trade, etc. The second is the Business-to-Business (B2B) segment, which is increasingly overshadowing the B2C segment and includes such names as Chemtex and AutoExchange. Despite fundamental differences in the business models of these two categories, they share one common key aspect — use of Internet technologies to manage all aspects of the business. This chapter presents an integrated architecture for these Internet technologies so that organizations can effectively implement whichever type of business model they choose.

REQUIREMENTS

An effective E-businesss architecture must satisfy a basic set of requirements. The following sections discuss these requirements.

Multiple Access Channels

While the past decade has seen the use of the Internet as the point of contact with the customer as distinguished from the traditional channels, businesses are increasingly finding that customers are using multiple channels to satisfy their needs. This includes the Internet, handheld devices like Palm Pilots, mobile communication devices like the cell phone, and set-top boxes for cable. A business must be capable of providing the customer the same high level of service irrespective of the channel used by the customer. However, each channel comes with its own unique set of technological challenges and it may not be cost-effective for a business to address each of these individually.

Single View of Customer

Irrespective of the mode of accessing the business, there is only one customer. Businesses need to be able to consolidate all information regarding a customer and develop a holistic view of the customer. This includes having access to all products and services used by the customer to provide opportunities for cross-selling of products and services. In addition, it lets business personalize the entire interaction with the customer by allowing for customer self-care and allowing the customer to dictate the nature of the interaction.

The World Wide Web

In addition to the fact that customers are using multiple access channels, the boundaryless nature of the Internet opens up the entire world as a potential market for one's business. While this is a very attractive proposition, it throws up challenges of the kind few businesses have had to contend with in the past. The obvious issues that come to mind include the multiplicity of languages, customer habits, legal environments, and business practices.

Security and Privacy

One of the fundamental requirements of a successful business is its ability to establish an environment of trust between its customers and itself. The Internet has renewed fears about this traditional issue by creating the impression that the Internet is an unregulated jungle in which evil-minded hackers roam free with the power to tap into information databases and eavesdrop on transactions between the customer and the business. However, businesses need to be prudent regarding issues of security and privacy of customer information and evaluate the level of protection they wish to establish.

Scalability, Availability, Flexibility, and Reliability

It is sometimes said in the Internet world that businesses can die of starvation or die of indigestion — that is, no customers or too many customers. Recent public attention on downtimes at eBay further highlights this point. Most E-businesses start small but, if successful, experience growth rates that have never been seen before; therefore the architecture must provide the ability to start small and grow rapidly to meet business needs. The electronic storefront and the associated channels are the modes of contact with the customer and, hence, reliability of these applications is vital. They have to be 365x24x7.

The Entire Value Chain

While many of the aspects thus far have focused on the interaction between the customer and the enterprise, the remaining interactions between the business and its partners and employees also need to be considered. Its internal operational support systems (appropriate to the specific business), along with e-mail, financial, human resources, and other systems, need to be integrated into the overall architecture.

Integrating the Enterprise

There are very few applications that satisfy all the functional needs of a business. It is most common to adopt a "best-of-breed" approach that utilizes different applications to address specific functional needs. However, this approach creates silos of information within the enterprise and hinders the seamless processing of business functions. In addition, it is necessary to have a unified logical view of the business and customer information to be able to quickly respond to the fast-moving marketplace. Hence, there is a need to integrate all these applications to the fullest possible extent to allow for fast and accurate performance of business functions.

Leveraging the Legacy Applications

While most companies in the news these days are companies that did not exist ten years ago, some of the biggest initiatives in the field of E-business have recently come from old, traditional companies like Ford, GM, and GE. Most of these companies already have billions of dollars invested in their current systems and they would like to leverage this investment as a part of their strategy to move into the E-business space.

A PROPOSED ARCHITECTURE FOR E-BUSINESSS

The proposed architecture is based on a few key concepts, including:

- *A best-of-breed approach* — The proposed architecture does not make any assumptions as to the suitability of any particular application to satisfy specific functional need. It is generic and must be customized to meet the particular needs of an enterprise. Hence, companies are free to adopt a best-of-breed approach to choosing which applications best suit their needs.

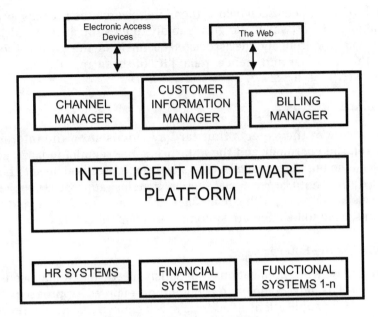

Exhibit 1.   E-Business Architecture

- *The use of middleware* — To meet the requirements of scalability and flexibility, and to be able to best leverage legacy applications, the architecture uses a middleware platform as the central piece. This middleware incorporates business process intelligence as an integral piece of its functioning. This would involve the use of software adapters to connect different applications into this middleware and the middleware will provide the capabilities of information routing and workflow automation.

A high-level view of the proposed architecture is outlined in Exhibit 1. The functions of the various components of the architecture are:

1. *Customer information manager:* This is the application that acts as the single repository of information about all aspects of the customer. A typical example of such a system is a CRM package.

2. *Billing manager:* This system is the invoicing application that stores all information on rates and charges for the various products ordered by the customer and handles all aspects of revenue management, including generating feeds for the General Ledger.

3. *Channel manager:* This system manages all interactions with the external world — especially customers. Either the channel manager or the customer information manager can handle the interface with the Web.

A QUICK SURVEY OF THE MARKETPLACE

This section presents a quick review of the available systems in the marketplace today that can be used to build this architecture.

Channel Manager

One of the companies in the marketplace today that provides a software solution that can function as a channel manager is 724 Solutions. 724 Solutions' software provides financial institutions and other content providers with a device-independent, operating system-independent, and network-independent channel to their own customers. The current applications of 724 Solutions' software solution will evolve to include additional services available on an increased variety of devices, such as set-top boxes, game consoles, and other emerging Internet access devices.

This company has partnered with some of the leading financial institutions of the world (e.g., Bank of America) to provide wireless financial banking capabilities. The banks' customers will be able to access up-to-the-minute account balances and transaction details, conduct real-time fund transfers from one bank account to another, and make bill payments when Bank of America begins piloting its new wireless banking services next year. And they will be able to do this not only from their PCs, but also by simply touching a few buttons on their Web-enabled wireless phones or Palm computing devices.

While the company is currently focused on the financial services industry, the same concept can be adapted to meet the needs of any other industry. The key would be the development of a lightweight, XML-based information framework coupled with a presentation mechanism that is appropriate to the needs of handheld/wireless devices.

Further information on the company can be obtained at http://www.724solutions.com.

Billing Manager

Infranet® from Portal Software, Inc., is one of the leading customer care and billing packages for Internet businesses. It was designed to accelerate the implementation of complex, multi-service Internet business models for IP telephony, wireless data, E-commerce, dial-up and broadband access services, online content and gaming, Web and application hosting, branding, e-mail and unified messaging, and other next-generation communication services.

Infranet delivers a totally integrated real-time solution that enables one to rapidly develop, price, and provision as many new services as one needs to take advantage of the multitude of possible revenue opportunities.

In addition, Infranet's sophisticated rating engine and flexible account administration facilities enable one to more effectively manage customer usage and billing. Some of the features include support for real-time rating and billing, flexible pricing plans, and customizable business policies.

Infranet was designed with the scalability to support millions of customers while also providing secure, reliable service — putting no limits on how large an Internet business can grow. Portal enables service providers to rapidly create and deploy a variety of Internet services, with flexible bundling and pricing options that enable businesses to stay one step ahead of changing market demands. Infranet's architecture is built to be extensible; it enables companies to add new, value-added services to their menu of offerings.

Further information on the company and Infranet can be obtained at http://www.portal.com.

Intelligent Middleware

BusinessWare® from Vitria Technologies. BusinessWare® is an E-business infrastructure software from Vitria Technologies that provides companies with a tool that enables them to integrate various applications across the entire enterprise, potentially spread across the world. In addition to enabling application integration, BusinessWare allows for business process intelligence to be embedded into the integration framework.

The different components of BusinessWare that work together to provide a complete solution include:

1. *Automator:* This tool provides a graphical user interface for businesses to depict business process intelligence into the automation framework.
2. *Communicator:* This tool is the messaging backbone that allows the applications to exchange information. It is built around the publish-and-subscribe mechanism and is designed for high reliablility.
3. *Connectors:* These are pieces of code that are built to provide the connectivity between individual applications and the messaging platform. Each application that needs to be integrated into the end-to-end solution has its own connector.
4. *Analyzer:* This tool enables businesses to monitor and analyze business processes in real-time. The analyzer can be used to gain visibility into key business metrics to enable more efficient management of the overall business.

The following are the steps that need to carried out in order to achieve a full-scale integrated E-businesss solution:

1. Define the information needs
2. Select the individual application
3. Define the information exchange formats
4. Build the connectors
5. Define the process models using Automator
6. Establish the communication framework in Communicator
7. Deploy the individual applicatons, connectors, and the business process models

Further information on Vitria Technologies and the product can be found at http://www.vitria.com.

TIB/Active Enterprise® from TIBCO Software. TIB/ActiveEnterprise® from TIBCO can be used to integrate Internet applications, packaged applications/solutions from a variety of application vendors, and combine it with custom legacy applications to form the required E-business infrastructure. The resulting architecture can support business information flow at the global enterprise scale.

TIB/ActiveEnterprise is a comprehensive suite of products that delivers an Internet and enterprise infrastructure. TIB/ActiveEnterprise has the following major categories of products that work in conjunction to provide a comprehensive business integration platform.

- *TIB/Rendevous, TIB/ETX, TIB/ObjectBus:* These products provide the messaging platform for reliable, guaranteed, and transactional messages.
- *Adapters:* These are used for integration with third-party packaged products such as E-commerce applications and databases.
- *TIB/Integration Manager, TIB/ContentBroker:* These applications provide the basis for business process automation and automated workflow.
- *TIB/Hawk:* This application enables a business to monitor its businesses to achieve 24x7 reliability.

Further information on the company and the products can be found at http://www.tibco.com

CONCLUSION

The business environment is undergoing rapid changes, enabled by the technological changes fostered by the growth of Internet and wireless technologies. Businesses need to adapt their infrastructures to successfully compete in this environment. Firms that adopt an approach that provides them with the flexibility to pick the solutions that best meet their functional needs while managing to achieve enterprise-wide integration for real-time information management, are best positioned to succeed in the next millennium.

Chapter 7

An Information Architecture for the Global Manufacturing Enterprise

Robert L. Sloan
Hal H. Green

The two most important responsibilities of leadership are to establish a vision or strategy for the organization and to put in place the systems, processes, and structures that enable the organization to progressively achieve that vision. One of the structures used by manufacturers to create competitive advantage is integrated information systems. Competitive advantage, including cost and differentiation, can be won or lost by marginal differences in the speed, accuracy, and comprehensive nature of information being delivered to decision-makers.

An organization's competence in timely decision-support capabilities has been given impetus by the total quality movement; the Malcolm Baldrige criteria state that "the ability to access and act on timely, reliable business data is requisite to the achievement of quantitative continual improvement in the delivery of products and services."[1]

Michael Porter has described the importance of horizontal strategy as the interrelationship between business units. Integrated information and control systems support horizontal strategy, enabling independent business units to share key product and process information along the whole supply chain.

0-8493-1149-7/02/$0.00+$1.50
© 2002 by CRC Press LLC

HORIZONTAL BUSINESS INTEGRATION STRATEGY

Manufacturers are providing increased service levels in response to competitive pressure and to create differentiation in product offerings. One trend is toward smaller, custom lot sizes on the part of the process manufacturer and custom product configurations on the part of the discrete component manufacturer.

As manufacturing assumes these higher levels of service, the strategic model of the manufacturing organization is moving toward a professional context, in which the operating work of an organization is dominated by skilled workers who use procedures that, although difficult to learn, are well defined.[2] In this model, empowered workers are given greater decision latitude. In other words, with increased automation of the manufacturing processes, the nature of the work in the plant or factory shifts from manually effecting the independent processes to using information systems in support of customer-driven operating objectives related to production. The empowered worker equipped with business operating objectives makes decisions using information that previously was the purview of manufacturing management. Information systems, integrated with factory automation systems, therefore enable both differentiation and flatter organizational structures.

Compared with the conventional machine concept of the manufacturing organization, empowered or high-performance work teams typify a more people-centered, organic culture. This new manufacturing organization depends on high-speed access to high-quality information. For example,Total Quality Management prescribes the use of statistical quality control (SQC) techniques. Manufacturers use SQC techniques software to help workers process the sheer quantity of data required by the application of SQC principles in manufacturing, further illustrating the affinity between strategy, organization, and information technology.

The IS organization within the global manufacturing enterprise must understand the impact that organizational strategy has on the information technology (IT) infrastructure. Furthermore, it must determine and create the optimum IT architecture to best support a horizontal business integration strategy.

DIFFERENTIATING INFORMATION SYSTEM PRODUCTS AND SERVICES

Historically, IS has delivered custom computer applications to business functions to improve effectiveness and reduce cost. System projects were justified on their stand-alone return on investment. The IS management structure reflected project team independence and aligned applications development teams with their respective customers (i.e., manufacturing, finance, or distribution). This approach to systems development avoided the long-term need to integrate data between applications. Viewed separately, each system met its functional objective. Viewed collectively, they presented a set of conflicting interfaces and incompatible information, thereby constraining a horizontal business integration strategy.

As businesses flatten their organizations, their dependence on integrated information flow across worldwide boundaries increases. The IS organization must find ways to remove the functional and technical incompatibilities of existing computer systems that are barriers to business-centric information access.

Trends in Manufacturing

More business managers recognize that information-related service extensions to their product/service mix can affect their companies' ability to compete favorably in international markets. They are also beginning to recognize that existing computer systems were designed in a way that is inconsistent with the view of information as an asset to be managed by the corporation, which has led to concerns about the return on investment for older systems.

Plant-level information systems, once the domain of process control engineers and production personnel, are being drawn into the scope of the IS function from the standpoint of integrating the operational data in these systems with horizontal supply-chain business strategy. The span of the IS organization's responsibility may expand to include multiple operational (e.g., manufacturing) systems from which enterprise information is collected and delivered. The charter of IS becomes focused on assimilating and combining manufacturing-process data with other forms of business data to enhance the quality of customer service, to support integrated operations objectives, and to provide value-added decision support across the corporation.

QUANTITY OF MANUFACTURING DATA

Information systems are pervasive across the manufacturing supply chain. The entire manufacturing supply chain uses information, but the epicenter of information technology in a modern industrial manufacturing company usually exists at the manufacturing plant site. Here, a variety of systems, using data at different levels of abstraction, are employed to control manufacturing processes, provide decision support to operations, and perform planning functions such as those offered by MRPII (material requirements planning) systems.

The problem of functionally integrating manufacturing software applications is exacerbated by the total volume of data employed in manufacturing. In the case of the process/batch manufacturer who employs process control systems, extensive quantities of process data may exist within the process control applications. Most of that data is needed by other parts of the manufacturing organization. It is common, for example, for a process manufacturing plant to generate eight to ten million pieces of information every 24 hours.

A central concern when manufacturing-process data is integrated into enterprisewide information systems is the requisite changes necessary to derive information from elemental process data. For example, a Fortune 100 diversified chemical company needs to maintain a complete history for each lot or batch of material made, including details of the processes used to make any given batch. A maker of an automobile safety device needs similar detailed information for each discrete component and assembly produced. In addition, the customer, the automotive industry, and proper business practice all specify that the detailed information be maintained indefinitely and be available on demand during the anticipated 20-year life of the product.

NATURE OF MANUFACTURING DATA

The problems outlined in each of these situations can be understood when the nature of manufacturing data itself is examined. Exhibit 1 identifies four categories of data that exist in manufacturing:

1. Derived data needed for longer-term business decision support
2. Transaction-driven, product-oriented data
3. Event-driven, operations-oriented data
4. Real-time, process-oriented data

The columns of Exhibit 1 contrast the key attributes of these different data types. Non-site-specific positioning of derived data is critical to successful horizontal business integration for the multisite manufacturing enterprise.

Process data possesses the lowest level of integration in manufacturing, whereas decision-support data has usually been integrated or summarized to afford the user a basis for broad business and planning decisions. These two extremes can be illustrated by considering the questions the business user of manufacturing data might ask, as compared with those asked by a process engineer concerned about the problem of manufacturing process optimization.

Business users of manufacturing data might want to know about the yield for a given product manufactured at all sites during the previous month. A typical process engineer might inquire about the historical trend of temperature for one or more tag (i.e., input/output) values, related to a particular piece of equipment or process. Both questions have equal relevance

Exhibit 1. Manufacturing Data Framework

Categories of Data	Example Data	Key Attributes of Data			
		Typical Orientation	Typical Use	Integration Scope	Typical Volume
Multisite decision support	Lot/batch quality summary	Subject/table	Multisite read-only	Business	Low
Cross-area integrated operations	Lot/batch quality detail	Subject/table	Transaction driven	Site	Medium
In-area operations	In-area quality	File/field	Event driven	Area	Medium
Process/machine control	Process/quality parameter	Tag or I/O	Real-time	Machine/process	High

and potential merit, but they are fundamentally different, being based on the type of data needed to render a valid response.

The process-related question requires access to manufacturing (i.e., process control) data at its lowest atomic level. The product yield question requires access to data stored at a higher level of abstraction. Process data such as lot/batch yield must be collected and derived uniformly into a value for product yield at each site. This type of query represents a significant change in the level of abstraction and integration of the data across multiple plant sites.

The operations data presented at the middle levels of Exhibit 1 reflects the transformation of data from process (tag) to subject (table). An operations database often provides a repository for manufacturing data that is clearly outside the process domain but is still necessary for manufacturing. Operating conditions, procedures, recipes, and specifications, organized by product, equipment/cell/area, or manufacturing team, are often candidates for operations data. If material requirements planning (MRP) is employed, the operations information database is also often used to provide the MRP system order-operations as they are completed by product, line, or plant.

DATA-DRIVEN MANUFACTURING APPLICATION FRAMEWORK

Past efforts to computerize manufacturing focused on the automation of isolated process steps or organizational functions. The success of the global manufacturing enterprise depends on new application architectures, predicated on data integration, and the availability of derived production data for use in multisite business decision support. Using the categories of manufacturing data from Exhibit 1, a data-driven application framework can be constructed for a typical manufacturing site (see Exhibit 2). This framework takes advantage of the existing differences in data, provides for the horizontal separation of multiple manufacturing process steps, and recognizes the need for operational integration. The upper level in this manufacturing site application framework supports the business need for horizontally integrated, multisite production information access.

Adoption of a consistent manufacturing site application framework both enables multisite integration and presents a major cost-reduction opportunity. The lack of a consistent framework for site applications all too often results in unique site applications requiring expensive life-cycle support. Use of a consistent framework enhances the prospects of multisite applications development (or commercial purchase), which significantly lowers life-cycle support costs.

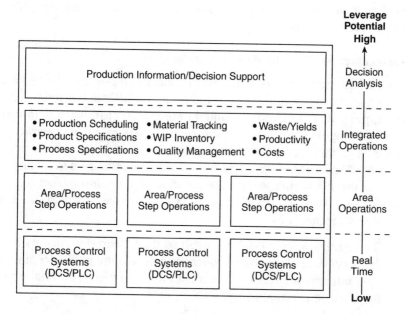

Exhibit 2. Data-Driven Manufacturing Application Framework

EFFECTIVE INFORMATION DELIVERY

In view of the strategic use of IT and the vast quantity of manufacturing data now available, what should be the product of the IS organization? What should be the role of IS in the world-class manufacturing organization?

The manufacturing IS organization is required to reduce total cost of ownership of software systems, reduce lead times, increase flexibility of developed applications, deliver integrated (i.e., customer, supplier, and internal manufacturing) information to a wide variety of users across the enterprise, and develop and acquire applications suitable for multiple sites. The manner in which these conventional business objectives and their implied information needs are provided must improve for the manufacturer seeking integrated information and control systems.

Information collection and delivery is replacing applications development as the IS organization's prime responsibility. The advent of consistent manufacturing site application frameworks and the growing availability of commercial applications to satisfy operational needs can reduce, over time, the IS role in the development and support of operational applications. As a result, IS can focus on the development and support of a new infrastructural layer of decision data services and networks built above the existing base of manufacturing site and centralized order entry/product distribution systems.

Infrastructure for Worldwide Decision Support

This infrastructural layer is designed to collect and position the requisite information for horizontal supply-chain integration and worldwide decision support. William Inmon's unified data architecture with data warehouses holding decision-support information separate from operational systems is gaining acceptance in manufacturing and nonmanufacturing industries alike.[3] The IS organization's prime responsibility is to implement and maintain this secure worldwide decision-support infrastructure (see Exhibits 3 and 4) and to provide business with effective information access and delivery mechanisms.

The IS organizational model has evolved thus far to optimize its traditional primary product: custom applications development. To accomplish worldwide information delivery, IS must adopt an organizational model that reflects its new primary product.

As the IS organization changes from a custom manufacturer to a product distributor, with enterprise information as its essential product, the central focus of IS becomes information supply, inventory, regional warehouses, and business delivery mechanisms. The responsibility for this nonoperational data storage, structure, and content must be separated from applications development and controlled centrally or regionally, driven by the need for data integration, end-user data access, and enterprisewide data integrity (see Exhibit 5). Distributed information storage and access mechanisms, predicated on the use of client/server technologies, can be implemented to insulate both the business users and decision-support system developers from the incompatibilities of existing operational applications.

New or reengineered operational systems are required to pass selected data from manufacturing sites and centralized order entry/product distribution operational systems to the infrastructure layer, thereby taking advantage of the infrastructure's ability to provide data to decision-support applications. New operational systems can be downsized and optimized to best meet the immediate operational tasks. History, nonoperational analysis, and reporting could be accomplished as extensions of the infrastructure layer using commercially available analysis tools. Such a strategy allows users to select analysis tools according to their own business needs, with IS ensuring the integrity of the data managed within the infrastructure layer.

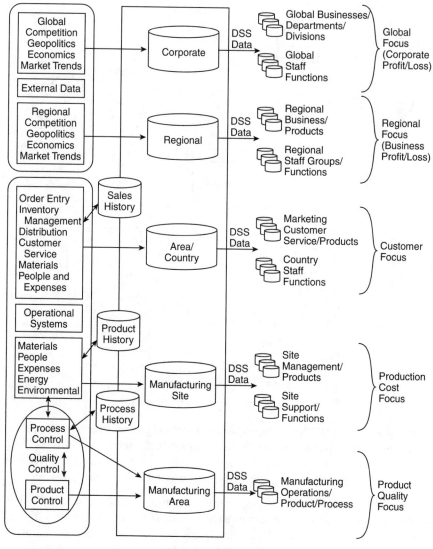

Exhibit 3.   Data Delivery Architecture

Delivery Teams

A consistent set of development policies, principles, methods, and tools is needed to govern the secure development and delivery of information products and services. Online metrics relating to the performance of the infrastructure layer need to be made available to determine who is using information, as well as when, why, and where information is being used. A

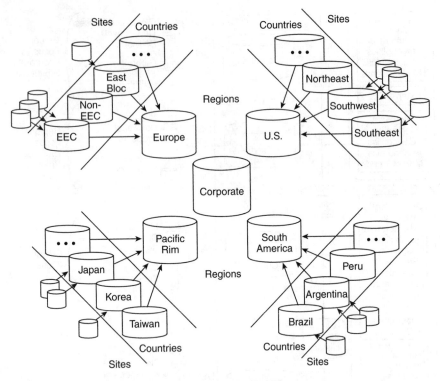

Exhibit 4. Global Scope

single (i.e., logical) decision-support environment can provide insulation from underlying hardware and operating system incompatibilities. Decision-support applications can be accomplished as a unified effort by IS or others, independent of the facilities or physical location of the developer.

A new IS business-focused organizational model emerges in which internal technical support teams assume the responsibility to design, build, and support the infrastructure layer. Radiating from the core are information delivery teams working directly with the businesses to identify information needs and ensure information delivery. Exhibit 6 details the relationships among the different members of the business-focused information delivery team. Exhibit 7 shows the overall organizational model for optimizing information delivery.

RECOMMENDED COURSE OF ACTION

The actual steps required to move an IS organization toward the described information delivery paradigm depend on current IS business practice and how quickly the IS and business cultures can accept change. Although the

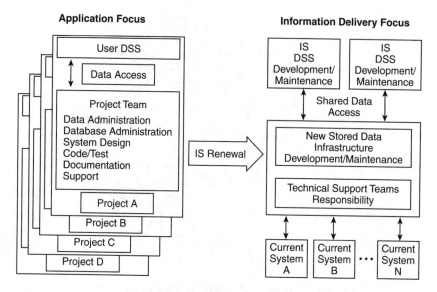

Exhibit 5. The Path to IS Renewal

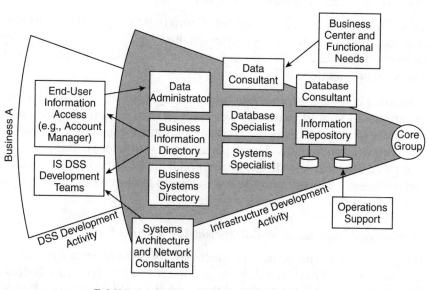

Exhibit 6. Business-Focused Delivery Team

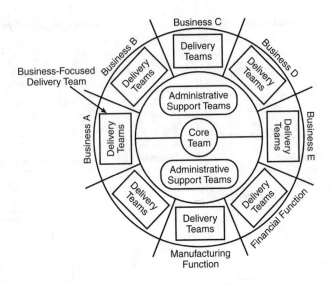

Exhibit 7. Business-Focused Organizational Model

individual paths forward will differ, the overall goal is to establish sustainable change in both the IS technology and the people processes.

Organize Around Information Delivery

If the IS function is to be a provider of information as opposed to a provider of automation, then change is a prerequisite. The IS culture can begin by defining its purpose as that of empowering its user community through access to information.

Existing IS organizational structures that optimize custom applications development should gradually be replaced with structures promoting cross-application integration. Decision-support capability should be removed as a task of individual applications development teams and organized as an enterprisewide infrastructural activity. Employee recognition and reward mechanisms must be redesigned to reinforce and sustain these new IS directions.

Develop and Implement an Enterprisewide Architecture

The plant sites of the global manufacturer are often littered with locally optimized IT solutions that defy integration into a multisite supply-chain strategy. The stand-alone nature of these solutions reflects the fact that no shared business rules or IT framework exist to provide the technical integration ground rules.

An essential IS path forward is the establishment of the architectural framework that provides a consistent technical context for horizontal business integration strategy. This framework should provide specific guidance for both existing and proposed applications, technology, and data. Data is not only a valid architectural consideration, it is fundamental to establishing integrated information delivery mechanisms. The data models resulting from data architecture development become the product catalogs for the IS function's information delivery business.

Information strategic planning (ISP) offers a valid approach to designing the overall enterprise architecture. The deficiency in information engineering has been a lack of recognition of the fundamental differences and uses in manufacturing data at different levels in the architecture. Exhibits 1 and 2 reflect these differences and their implications for manufacturing systems. Exhibits 3 and 4 reflect the logical placement of the data warehouses in the global manufacturing architecture. The use of a computer-aided software engineering (CASE) tool is strongly recommended in the development of the enterprisewide architecture. The distributed nature of this tool allows IS to both automate and share reusable software assets while teaming across geographical boundaries.

Notes

1. Malcolm Balrige National Quality Award, U.S. Department of Commerce and the National Institute of Standards and Technology, Gaithersburg, MD 20899.
2. H. Mintzberg and J.B. Quinn, *The Strategy Process,* Englewood Cliffs, NJ: Prentice Hall, 1991.
3. W.H. Inmon, *Building the Data Warehouse,* Wellesley, MA: QED Information Sciences, 1992.

Chapter 8
Server-Based Computing Architecture

Bosco Cheung

The advent of the computer revolution greatly expanded the universe of information and processing power available to the end user. The once simple stand-alone computer and the software that ran on it grew in complexity, creating a whole new set of problems for enterprise computing.

Faced with an ever-changing computing environment, IT professionals must improve the efficiency of business-critical application deployment. In order to reduce the total cost of computing ownership for their organizations, they must also leverage everything in their current computing infrastructure hardware, applications, networks, and training. And all of this must be accomplished along with:

- Managing and supporting users in a timely and cost-effective manner
- Extending access to business-critical applications to dispersed users, regardless of connection, location, or device
- Ensuring exceptional application performance
- Providing tight security for enterprise-level computing

These challenges have made enterprisewide application deployment even more daunting because the products developed to this point have only addressed one, or possibly two, of the obstacles discussed in this section.

Management

From a management perspective, traditional enterprise application deployment is often time-consuming, expensive, and difficult to maintain. Not only do administrators have to physically distribute applications to every client, but they also have to deal with version control issues, remote support, multiple system configurations, and data replication. When confronted with thousands of users, the cost of application ownership can quickly spiral out of control.

Access

Today's corporate computing landscape comprises a heterogeneous mix of desktop devices, network connectivity, and operating systems. Access to vital Windows-based applications is difficult—or, in the case of Internet/Intranet computing, nonexistent—and often involves costly upgrades, problematic emulation software, and complete application rewrites.

Performance

Most corporate applications today are designed for high bandwidth networks and powerful desktop computers. This type of application design puts tremendous strain on congested corporate networks and yields poor performance over lower bandwidth, remote connections. Because of this, many users simply avoid using the vital applications and data to get their work done. When this happens, redundant work and significant decreases in productivity are often the result.

Security

Security is also a challenge because in traditional client/server architectures, business-critical applications and data live on both the server and the client desktops spread throughout the world. Not only does this increase the risk of unauthorized access, but it also increases the risk of lost or stolen information.

A BETTER APPROACH: SERVER-BASED COMPUTING

Server-based computing is a model in which applications are deployed, managed, supported, and executed 100 percent on a server. It uses a multiuser operating system and a method for distributing the presentation of an application's interface to a client device.

With server-based computing, client devices, whether "fat" or "thin," have instant access to business-critical applications via the server without application rewrites or downloads. This means improved efficiency when deploying business-critical applications. In addition, server-based computing works within the current computing infrastructure and current computing standards, and with the current and future family of Windows-based offerings. This means improved returns on computing investments— desktops, networks, applications, and training. The end result: server-based computing is rapidly becoming the most reliable way to reduce the complexity and total costs associated with enterprise computing.

How Does Server-Based Computing Work?

The server-based computing model employs three critical components. The first is a multiuser operating system that enables multiple concurrent users to log on and run applications in separate, protected sessions on a single server. The second is a highly efficient computing technology that separates the application's logic from its user interface, so only keystrokes, mouse clicks, and screen updates travel the network. As a result, application performance is bandwidth-independent. The third key component, centralized application and client management, enables large computing environments to overcome the critical application deployment challenges of management, access, performance, and security.

Server-based computing is made possible by two Citrix technologies: Citrix Independent Computing Architecture (ICA®) and Citrix MultiWin. A de facto standard for server-based computing, the ICA protocol shifts application processing from the client device to the server. MultiWin, the technology licensed by Citrix to Microsoft to jointly create Terminal Server, enables multiple users to simultaneously access applications running on a server.

WHAT IS INDEPENDENT COMPUTING ARCHITECTURE (ICA)?

Independent Computing Architecture (ICA) is a Windows presentation services protocol from Citrix that provides the foundation for turning any client device—thin or fat— into the ultimate thin client. The ICA technology includes a server software component, a network protocol component, and a client software component.

On the server, ICA has the unique ability to separate the application's logic from the user interface at the server and transport it to the client over standard network protocols—IPX, SPX, NetBEUI, TCP/IP, and PPP—and over popular network connections—asynchronous, dialup, ISDN, Frame Relay, and ATM. On the client, users see and work with the application's interface but 100 percent of the application logic executes on the server.

The ICA protocol transports keystrokes, mouse clicks, and screen updates over standard protocols to the client, consuming less than 20 kilobits per second of network bandwidth.

Role of ICA

ICA is highly efficient; it allows only keystrokes, mouse clicks, and screen updates to travel the network. As a result, applications consume just a fraction of the network bandwidth usually required. This efficiency enables the latest, most powerful 32-bit applications to be accessed with exceptional performance from existing computers, Windows-based terminals, network computers, and a new generation of business and personal information appliances.

With over two million ports in use worldwide, Citrix ICA is a mature, reliable technology and is fast becoming a de facto industry standard for server-based computing.

Server-Based Computing Compared to Network Computing and Traditional Client/Server Computing

While all three computing models have a valid role in today's enterprises, it is important to note the differences between them. In traditional client/server architecture, processing is centered around local execution using fat, powerful hardware components. In the network computing architecture as defined by Sun, Oracle, Netscape, IBM, and Apple, components are dynamically downloaded from the network into the client device for execution by the client. But with the Citrix server-based computing approach, users are able to access business-critical applications—including the latest 32-bit Windows-based and Java™ applications—without requiring them to be downloaded to the client. This approach also provides considerable total cost of application ownership savings since these applications are centrally managed and can be accessed by users without having to rewrite them.

Basically, the server-based computing approach delivers all the benefits of both host computing and personal computing as follows:

- Host computing benefits
  - Single-point management
  - Physically and technically secure
  - Predictable ownership costs
  - Mission-critical reliability
  - Bandwidth-independent performance
  - Universal application access
- Personal computing benefits
  - Thousands of off-the-shelf applications
  - Low-cost and fast-cycle application development
  - Standards-based
  - Graphical, rich data and easy to use
  - Wide choice of device types and suppliers

WHAT IS A WINDOWS-BASED TERMINAL?

A Windows-based terminal (WBT) is a thin client hardware device that connects to Citrix server-based system software. Because the applications it accesses are installed on the server, a Windows-based terminal is not the equivalent of a computer with its operating system and array of local applications. It is also not nterchangeable with a network computer or NetPC because these devices download and run applications off the network.

The key criterion that distinguishes Windows-based terminals from other thin client devices, such as NCs or NetPCs, is that there is no downloading of the operating system or applications, and there is no local processing of applications at the client. All execution of the application logic occurs on the server.

Defining Characteristics of a Windows-Based Terminal

Windows-based terminals have the following characteristics:

- An embedded operating system such as DOS, Windows, or any real-time operating system
- Citrix/ICA or Microsoft Remote Desktop Protocol (RDP) presentation services protocol to transport keystrokes, mouse clicks, and screen updates between the client and server
- 100 percent server-based execution of application logic
- No local execution of application logic at the client device
- A Windows-based terminal may incorporate third-party emulation software such as X, 3270, and 5250 for connection to other host systems

Fitting the Windows-Based Terminal within the Enterprise

The "thinness" of a Windows-based terminal and the many benefits of server-based computing make these thin clients ideal for certain types of workers and market segments. For example, task-based employees who primarily work with line-of-business applications such as order entry would be ideal candidates for a Windows-based terminal. Retail organizations operating point-of-sale terminals and branch locations of banks and stores are markets that are also rapidly adopting these thin clients. Windows-based terminals are also well suited for existing "green screen" terminal users moving to a Windows environment.

SERVER-BASED COMPUTING KEY FEATURES AND BENEFITS

While other approaches for deploying, managing, and supporting business-critical applications across the extended enterprise have been introduced, only the server-based computing model developed by Citrix provides today's growing enterprises with the tools and capabilities they need to be successful. This innovative software enables enterprises to:

- Bring server-based computing to heterogeneous computing environments, providing access to Windows-based applications regardless of client hardware, operating platform, network connection, or LAN protocol
- Offer enterprise-scale management tools to allow IT professionals to scale, deploy, manage, and support applications from a single location
- Provide seamless desktop integration of the user's local and remote resources and applications with exceptional performance

MIS rarely has the luxury of deploying mission-critical applications in a homogeneous environment, let alone from a centralized location. Instead, the enterprise network usually includes a wide variety of servers, client workstations, operating systems, and connections. The user base can include from dozens to thousands of local, remote, and mobile users.

Heterogeneous Computing Environments

Heterogeneous computing environments are a fact of life in the enterprise, comprising an installed base of many client devices, operating systems, LAN protocols, and network connections. However, for the enterprise interested in making Windows-based applications available to all users, server-based computing enables an organization to leverage its existing infrastructure yet still provide the best application fit for both users and the enterprise. This type of approach supports all types of hardware, operating platforms, network connections, and LAN protocols. As a result, organizations can deliver the same set of applications to virtually any client device anywhere with exceptional performance.

Enterprise-Scale Management Tools

Organizations building application deployment systems will want the added benefits of server-based computing system software to gain robust management tools that help scale systems and support applications and users enterprisewide. With these tools, administrators will be able to significantly reduce the costs and complexities of deploying, managing, and supporting business applications across the extended enterprise.

Seamless Desktop Integration

With server-based computing, end users of both Windows and non-Windows desktops gain an enhanced computing experience through broadened application access with exceptional performance that is bandwidth-independent, as well as complete access to local system resources—even though applications are running remotely from the server.

SERVER-BASED COMPUTING SOLUTION SCENARIOS

With server-based computing, customers can increase productivity and develop a competitive advantage by gaining universal access to the business-critical applications they need to operate successfully, regardless of the connection, location, or operating systems they may be using.

The following solution scenarios demonstrate how server-based computing can help customers overcome the challenges of enterprise-wide application deployment.

Branch Office Computing

For manageable, secure application deployment and access over corporate WANs.

Problem. To better serve and support customers, many enterprises are opening branch offices. However, this is creating many difficulties for administrators who do not have the resources to adequately staff these new offices. One such problem is database replication. Many times, individual LANs are built for each branch office. Configuring and managing these branch office LANs and the information on them creates numerous management challenges. Another problem is application performance. Since most branch offices are connected by WANs to headquarters, vital data and applications must travel back and forth across the network. This type of setup creates numerous user delays and unacceptable application response. Previously, the only option was a bigger WAN connection which meant increasing costs, not just once but on an ongoing basis.

Solution. Server-based computing is a better solution because it minimizes network traffic, even for Windows-based, 32-bit applications. This approach allows applications to be deployed, supported, and managed from a central location.

Cross-Platform Computing

For Windows-based application deployment to non-Windows desktop users.

Problem. In today's era of global consolidation, many enterprises are buying and/or merging new companies into their organizations, as well as adding their own new employees and locations around the world. Typically, this has resulted in a widely diverse set of client devices, operating systems, processing power, and connectivity options across the enterprise.

For IT professionals, trying to leverage existing technology investments while deploying business-critical applications—especially the latest 32-bit Windows-based applications—to all users has become more and more difficult. As a result, organizations have had to resort to using problematic emulation software, purchasing additional hardware, or investing in costly application rewrites.

Solution. Server-based computing is a better, more cost-effective solution because it enables virtually any existing device in the enterprise to access Windows-based applications without special emulation software, changes in system configuration, or application rewrites. This means that enterprises can maximize their investments in existing technology and allow users to work in their preferred computing environments.

Web Computing

Web computing allows remote users to access full-function, Windows-based applications from Web pages.

Problem. Web computing is taking off. But to deploy interactive applications on an intranet or the Internet, application development is required. The Java applet "download-and-run" model is not an extension of any current computing technology. New software, and often new hardware, is required to successfully deploy these solutions. Every time the application changes, the Web-based application needs to change as well.

Solution. Server-based computing enables administrators to launch and embed corporate Windows-based applications into HTML pages without rewriting a single line of code. Plus, it eliminates the need to manage and maintain two separate sets of code.

Remote Computing

To give high-performance, secure access to business-critical applications over remote, dial-up connections.

Problem. The changing work environment is allowing more and more employees to work away from the office—at home, hotels, customer locations, etc. This means that a wide variety of network connections is being used to access corporate applications. Unfortunately, the lower the bandwidth, the lower the application performance. Because of this, many remote users are avoiding corporate applications altogether, as they would rather work than wait.

Another factor is application management and support for remote users. Administrators are forced to spend excessive amounts of time trying to diagnose and correct problems over the phone. Unfortunately, the problems are usually not resolved the first time.

Solution. Server-based computing works better for remote users because it keeps all application processing on the server, meaning less traffic is sent across the network. Plus, it's optimized for low-bandwidth connections so users can get LAN-like performance over analog or ISDN modems, WANs, wireless LANs, and even the Internet. By eliminating the need for on-site staff, server-based computing also makes it easier for administrators.

Thin Client Device Computing

Vital, Windows-based applications can be extended to newer, low-cost devices.

Problem. Traditional mini- and mainframe computing deliver some of the same "centralized computing" benefits as server-based computing. The problem is that these types of machines weren't designed for the thousands of GUI-based Windows applications that are available today. Furthermore, users of these types of machines are familiar with the text-based interface and are typically slow to adopt new operating systems.

Also, many of today's new devices—like Windows-based terminals, PDAs, wireless tablets, and information appliances—are not compatible with the Windows-based, business-critical applications being used in the enterprise unless rewrites are performed.

Solution. With server-based computing, the latest Windows-based programs can be extended to these thin devices without application rewrites. This enables users to work in their preferred environments and still access the Windows-based applications they need to work successfully. Plus, organizations can reap the benefits resulting from reduced overhead, lower acquisition costs, and fewer moving parts.

CONCLUSION

The server-based computing architecture model offers any size organization an alternative enterprise computing solution that reduces the total cost of computing ownership, leverages components of their current computing environment, and reduces the development and support hardships normally associated with implementing an enterprise solution.

Section III
Enabling Technologies

Chapter 9
Bridging Legacy Data with XML

Frank Cullen

Extensible Markup Language (XML) is currently being championed as the language of the future for greasing the wheels of the drive toward E-commerce over the "Net." Already, thousands of new "dot.coms" have started from scratch to specifically take advantage of the booming Web-based business world. Light on their feet and already relying on modern relational database management systems (RDBMS), they are readily equipped to switch over to XML.

However, what about the long-established businesses whose database systems harken back to the days of "big iron?" These behemoths also recognize the need to migrate toward a Web-based commerce, and their long track records often endow them with the financial means to make the leap past HTML-prepared data, directly to XML. However, this feat is much easier said than done.

The necessary tagging — or assigning of a data type definition (DTD) — to pre-relational legacy database systems is fraught with unexpected pitfalls for the unwary. Quick solutions are hard to come by. Yet, understanding how to use data-cleansing tools to first untangle, and then migrate, data from older data structures can help immeasurably.

But first, a review of some of the common structures found in legacy databases will help uncover some of the problems often encountered in "untangling" or porting this data to more modern XML.

DIFFICULTIES ENCOUNTERED WITH LEGACY DATA

The major areas of problems/challenges in legacy data management stem from five main categories:

1. Character sets and translations
2. Poor data typing
3. Hierarchical structures: header/trailer record systems

0-8493-1149-7/02/$0.00+$1.50
© 2002 by CRC Press LLC

4. Embedded sub-table structures
5. Departed "legacy programmers"

This chapter takes a brief look of each of these areas and examine the problems, challenges, and solutions that arise as the migration to XML is performed.

Character Sets and Translations. The translation and movement of data between IBM midrange and mainframe systems, for example, introduce a huge potential for faulty translation and data corruption. That is because data stored on computer systems has two main forms: full-character (display) form and packed forms (including signed numeric, packed-decimal, computational, and binary).

Full-character forms are used extensively whenever alphanumeric data is present — in descriptions, names, etc. Conversion here is almost never a problem. However, packed data forms are an entirely different matter. These are reliant not on the 8-bit character as a whole, but rather on the parts (sometimes even the bit configuration) of each character. Translating computational and binary items almost never works and provides a host of examples why character-for-character translations corrupt data irretrievably.

Poor Data Typing. One of the principal contributors to data migration problems in mainframe applications is the lack of strong data typing (and enforcement). Calendar dates are an excellent example of items that are hybrids of data types, but there are countless others.

Fortunately, the development and popularization RDBMSs, such as SQL, has had the wonderful effect of formalizing the idea of rich data types and strict enforcement of data domain rules.

Hierarchical Data Structures. A hierarchical data structure has more than one record type. When a record can belong to, at most, one other record type, the relationship is said to be a "proper hierarchy." Data hierarchies play a crucial role in the philosophy and implementation of XML.

Adding records to the end of a hierarchical data file will usually not cause problems. But when records are added to the middle of the file, all the relative record numbers of the records beyond the point of insertion are bumped down. The idea of using relative record position as an ID generator is valid only for a "one-time" or "cut-and-run" conversion.

Embedded Sub-Table Structures. The popularization of variable-length record techniques brought with it a tremendous savings in mass storage space at a reasonably small price. However, a maximum allowable number of additional fields must be set. Unfortunately, overestimating the number wastes valuable space, while underestimating causes program failure.

Departed Legacy Programmers. Most companies have a "super programmer," who in times of trouble can be the only hope. But super programmers can define hideously complex records with bizarre relationships collapsed into variable length and self-describing attributes. When they leave the organization, their work can be one's worst nightmare. It becomes extremely difficult to clean up after their "legacy."

THE DATA MIGRATION/TRANSFORMATION PROCESS

Preparing flat-plane databases for XML tagging requires a three-step process. Not a single step can be omitted, or the conversion is destined to create more problems than it solves.

1. Analyze current data
2. Clean up current data
3. Transform the data

Analyze Current Data

Having decided to migrate data from one structure to another, the first step is to thoroughly analyze the existing data. This process should focus on domain analysis because it will help set the stage for data type identification.

If the data was analyzed during the Y2K compliance effort, the results of that analysis can be used again for the data transformation effort. This process should have already included the thorough testing of the output.

Clean Up Current Data

The next step is to clean up any bad data revealed during analysis and testing. In many cases, this involves straightforward corrections to field values. What may sound easy at first, is complicated by values that intentionally do not fit the format. Some of these exceptional values carry specific meaning and are commonly referred to as embedded business rules. An example might be XXXX or 9999 to indicate "date unknown" in a field using YYMM format. One may wish to preserve these special rules or replace them with new ones. This can be done with such tools as Data Commander, which analyzes, cleanses, and transforms pre-relational legacy mainframe data and is available from Blackstone & Cullen of Atlanta, Georgia. Its EXCEPTION statements allow one to exempt specified fields from the general conversion (or migration or transformation) process or to convert them in a manner different from the rest of the data fields. Exhibit 1 illustrates some of the processes that are a part of the entire migration effort.

The actual preparation and migration of legacy data from a pre-relational mainframe environment to a clean, consistent relational data store happens in two major places: (1) the host (or mainframe) location, where

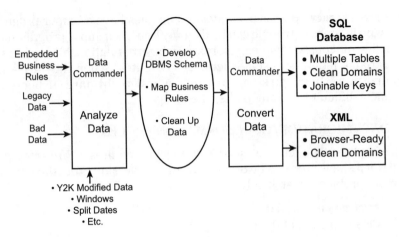

Exhibit 1.   Pre-Relational Data Analysis and Migration Process

---

the main "untangling" takes place and the data is cleaned, reformatted, and scripted; and (2) the server, where the Web client resides. The data untangling is best done on the host, as moving the data *en masse* to a server first might corrupt the packed, binary, and signed data during the conversion of the characters from the host to the server.

Denormalizing Data for XML Output. One of the most important steps of the cleansing process is the denormalization (to 1st Normal Form) of the data. There are two main reasons for this: to avoid making multiple passes through the source data; and to provide data in a single-level hierarchy for an XML table for easier manipulation/access.

This process is also called "flattening" or "spreading" the hierarchy of the data. Exhibit 2 illustrates the general scheme used to both flatten and spread a hierarchy and generate XML output.

Transform the Data

Once the cleansing process is complete, the output data can then be converted directly as XML 1.0 tagged; or even as field-sensitive formats and SQL INSERT syntax (for RDBMS population).

The main benefit of direct output to XML rather than the movement to an intermediate data store (such as a SQL-based Transformation Data Store) is that there is no requirement to have a SQL engine or other RDBMS processor to receive the data and to pass it on; the transfer is direct. Downsides of using XML are similar to those for SQL scripts — mainly that of amazing verbosity. The number of characters it takes to represent (and transmit) data that is

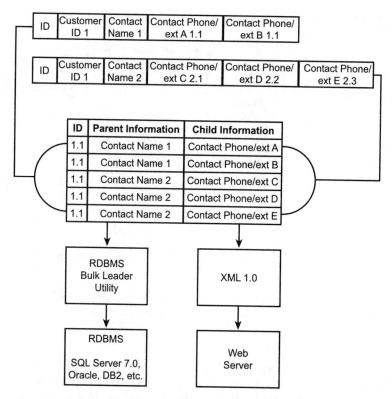

Exhibit 2. Flattening and Spreading Hierarchy Denormalizing for Data Warehouse Bulk Loading and XML Generation

originally in packed or binary form on a mainframe may blow up to 10 to 20 times that amount when all the unpacking and XML field tag insertion is done.

Nevertheless, there are an increasing number of options for receiving and processing XML-encoded data currently available. The ability to publish the legacy as XML data (either spread or not) directly to a Web browser using Data Commander is illustrated in Exhibit 3.

Instead of SQL output, Data Commander can generate XML DTD (data type definition) syntax. This generation is turned on or off in an OPTION statement, so Data Commander can be used to construct DTD-less XML data islands. The combination of the flattening/spreading with the suppression of header record XML syntax and DTD generation provide an easy method to generate XML strings immediately usable for IE5 data islands in live Web pages.

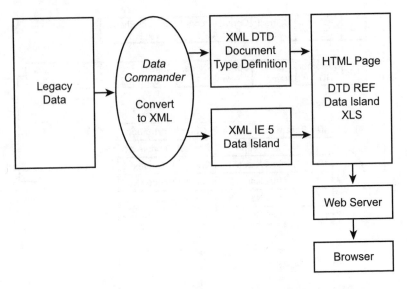

Exhibit 3. Legacy Data to XML with Data Commander

SUMMARY

Legacy data may represent a "Fort Knox" of wealth, but often this data is abandoned solely because it is difficult to access and get into a usable form. But cross-platform tools can extract valuable data from these complex structures, clean it, and generate XML syntax. Established organizations of any size can then take advantage of the golden opportunities afforded by Web commerce.

Chapter 10
Evaluating Object Middleware: DCOM and CORBA

T.M. Rajkumar
Richard J. Lewis, Jr.

Objects in the form of software components are changing the way applications are developed and delivered. Component technology breaks the application into intrinsic components and then glues them together to create the application. Using components, the application is easier to build, more robust, and delivered more quickly. Middleware is used as the object communication bus to enable distribution of these components across heterogeneous networks and operating systems.

The need for reliable distributed computing middleware environments is becoming pressing as three-tier client/server networks become commonplace. Although much of the industry backs the Common Object Request Broker Architecture (CORBA) as the standard object bus, Microsoft is pushing its own Distributed Component Object Model (DCOM). Managers and system architects have to determine what object bus to use in their companies. This chapter reviews the two primary forces in distributed object technology: CORBA and DCOM. It discusses their individual strengths and weaknesses across a wide spectrum of categories, and gives some sensible advice on what technologies might best apply to a system development manager's current projects. Finally, it takes a look into what the future has in store for these architectures.

WHAT IS CORBA?

CORBA is a set of distributed system standards promoted by an industry standards group called the Object Management Group (OMG). The idea behind CORBA is to allow applications to communicate with one another no matter where they are located or who has designed them. The CORBA standard defines the ORB, a mechanism through which distributed software and their clients may interact. It specifies an extensive set of bus-related services for creating and deleting objects, accessing them by name, storing them in persistent store, externalizing their states, and defining ad-hoc relationships between them.

History

The OMG has more than 700 member companies that have been working on the CORBA standard for 8 years. CORBA 1.1 was introduced in 1991 by OMG and defined the Interface Definition Language (IDL) and the Application Programming Interfaces (API) that enable client/server object interaction within a specific implementation of an Object Request Broker (ORB). CORBA 2.0, adopted in December 1994, defines true interoperability by specifying how ORBs from different vendors can interoperate.

Since 1989, the OMG has been working to create standards for object-based component software within the framework of its Object Management Architecture. The key component is the Common Object Request Broker Architecture (CORBA); this specification was adopted in 1991. In 1994, CORBA 2.0 defined interoperability between objects in heterogeneous systems. Since then, the world has seen a growing list of CORBA implementations come to the market. Dozens of vendors have recently announced support for the CORBA Internet Inter-ORB Protocol (IIOP), which guarantees CORBA interoperability over the Internet. Specifications of several generally useful support services now populate the Object Services segment of the architecture, and work is proceeding rapidly in specifying domain-specific technologies in many areas, including finance, health care, and telecommunications.

CORBA Architecture

The five main elements of the object management architecture, shown in Exhibit 1, are:

1. *ORB:* defines the object bus and is the middleware that establishes the client/server relationships between objects. The ORB provides interoperability between applications on different machines in heterogeneous distributed environments and seamlessly interconnects multiple object systems.
2. *Object services:* define the system level object frameworks that extend the bus. These include services such as security, transaction management, and data exchange.
3. *Common facilities:* define horizontal and vertical application frameworks that are used directly by business objects. These deal more with the client than the server.

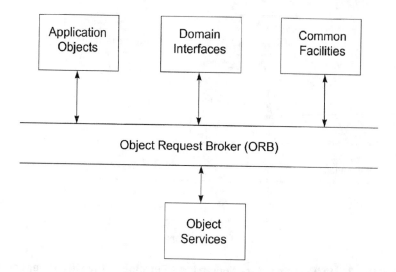

Exhibit 1. The Main Elements of the Object Management Architecture

4. *Domain interfaces:* interfaces like common facilities but are specific to a certain domain, such as manufacturing, medical, telecommunications, etc.
5. *Application interfaces:* objects defined by the developer to solve the business problem. These interfaces are not standardized.

ORB Component and CORBA Structure

Interface definition language (IDL) stubs provide static interfaces to object services. These define how clients invoke corresponding services on the servers. The ORB intercepts the call and is responsible for finding an object that can implement the request, pass it the parameters, invoke its method, and return the results. The client does not have to be aware of where the object is located, its programming language, its operating system, the communication protocol that is used, or any other system aspects that are not part of an object's interface. The CORBA structure shown in Exhibit 2 specifies the workings of the ORB component of the OMG specification.

While IDL stubs are static, dynamic invocations enable the client to find (discover) at run time a service that it wants to invoke, obtain a definition, issue a call, and return a result.

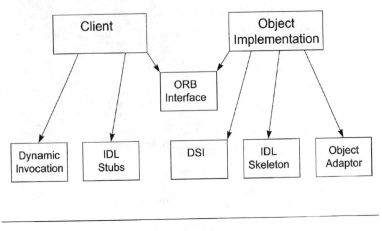

ORB Core

Exhibit 2.   CORBA Structure Specifying Operation of the ORB Component

On the server side, the object implementation does not differentiate between static and dynamic invocations. The ORB locates an object adapter, transmits the parameter, and transfers control to the object implementation via an IDL skeleton or a dynamic skeleton interface (DSI). The IDL skeleton provides support for the IDL-defined methods of a particular object class. The DSI provides a run-time binding mechanism for servers by inspecting the parameters passed by the message to determine the target object and method.

The object adapter accepts the requests for service on behalf of the server objects. If necessary, it starts up server processes, instantiates or activates the server objects, assigns an object ID (object reference), and passes the requests to them. The object adapter also registers the classes it supports and their run-time object instances with the implementation repository. Object adapters are specific to each programming language, and there can be multiple object adapters for every object.

Inter-ORB protocols allow CORBA products to interoperate. CORBA 2.0 specifies direct ORB-to-ORB interoperability mechanisms when the ORBs are resident in the same domain (i.e., they understand the object references, IDL type system, etc.). Bridge-based interoperability is used otherwise. The bridge then maps the ORB-specific information across domains. General Inter-ORB protocol specifies the transfer syntax and a set of standard message formats for ORB interoperation. Internet Inter-ORB Protocol is the implementation of this specification over a TCP/IP network. These systems also support inter-object references to locate and identify an object over the TCP/IP network.

CORBA IN THE REAL WORLD

CORBA has been around for a long time, but differences in early CORBA implementations made application portability and interoperability between implementations difficult. Different CORBA implementations fragmented an already small market, thereby rendering CORBA ineffective. Only recently have issues such as interoperability been addressed.

Other recent events have given rise to the hope that the industry can overcome these early missteps. First, the World Wide Web has created an incentive for a mainstream component architecture. Second, Netscape, Novell, and Oracle have licensed the Visigenic Software ORB, targeting one CORBA implementation, and Netscape has the potential to propagate large numbers of that implementation in its browser, which could create critical mass. Third, IBM, Netscape, Oracle, and Sun have agreed to ensure interoperability between their CORBA and IIOP implementations. Still, these vendors are fighting an uphill battle, and significant interoperability problems remain.

WHAT IS DCOM?

Microsoft's Distributed Component Object Model (DCOM) is object-oriented middleware technology that allows clients and servers in a distributed system to communicate with one another. It extends Microsoft's component object model (COM) technology to work on the network. As is the case with Windows, Microsoft owns DCOM and controls its development. There will be no differing DCOM implementations to fragment the market, and Microsoft has begun shipping DCOM on both Windows NT and Windows 95. In other words, critical mass is quickly building.

COM Architecture

COM is an object-based framework for developing and deploying software components. COM lets developers capture abstractions as component interfaces and then provide binary classes that implement those interfaces. Encapsulation is enforced by COM so that client applications can only invoke functions that are defined on an object's interface.

COM interfaces define a contract between a COM object and client. They define the behavior or capabilities of the software component as a set of methods and properties. COM interfaces are implemented by COM classes. COM classes are bodies of code that implement at least one COM interface. All COM classes implement two functionalities: lifetime management and interface management. COM classes may implement several interfaces. COM clients must explicitly request the interface they need. It also lets clients widen their interface requirement at run time, or query whether a component supports an interface. Lifetime management is accomplished by reference counting.

COM classes reside in a server either as DLLs or EXEs. COM classes implemented as DLLs share the same address space (in process) as their clients. COM classes implemented within EXEs live in different processes (out of process) than their client. Such out-of-process clients are supported via remote procedure calls.

COM classes are like meta classes. They create instances of COM classes, and also store static data for a class interface. For example, if a COM server has four different COM classes inside, that COM server will also have four class objects — one for each kind of COM class within the server.

OLE is a set of system services built on top of COM for constructing compound documents that are also used for supporting components. OLE automation allows a component object to expose its methods through the Idispatch interface, allowing late binding of method calls. OLE controls (OCXs) provide exposure to the interface of an object using method pointer tables called vtables.

COM's binary interoperability standard facilitates independent development of software components and supports deployment of those components in binary form. The result is that software vendors can develop and package reusable building blocks without shipping source code. Corporate application developers can use COM to create new solutions that combine in-house business objects, off-the-shelf objects, and their own custom components.

DCOM Architecture

DCOM, or Distributed Component Object Model, extends COM to the network with remote method calls, security, scalability, and location transparency. With COM, objects may be loaded into the client's process or launched in a separate process on the the same machine. DCOM extends this transparency to include location transparency, allowing objects to exist anywhere on the network. When the client and the object server are on different machines (see Exhibit 3), the remote layer adds a proxy object in the client process space and a stub process in the server process space. The proxy object is then responsible for marshaling the parameters and makes the function call. The stub unmarshals the parameters and makes the actual function call on the component object. The results are then marshaled and sent back to the proxy object, where it is unmarshaled and

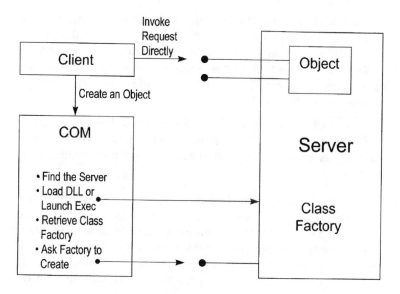

Exhibit 3. A COM Object and an Invocation by a Client

given to the client. The entire process of creating the proxy and stub is invisible to both the client and the server, and they use remote procedure call as the interprocess communication mechanism.

ARCHITECTURE: CORBA VERSUS DCOM

The member companies of the Object Management Group have shared one consistent vision of an architecture for distributed, component-based object computing since OMG's inception in 1989. The architecture is described in the *Object Management Architecture Guide,* first published in 1990, and has been incrementally populated with the specifications of the core inter-object communication component (CORBA), and with common services for handling transactions, security, concurrency control, and other vital support functions for object-based applications. Both the architecture and the individual specifications are vendor neutral, and control of their technical direction and definition is via a public process that ensures broad cross-industry consensus. The specifications are available to all (OMG members or not), and free rights to implement software using the specifications are guaranteed by the terms of the OMG's constitution.

DCOM, a version of Microsoft's COM, has deep roots in the client desktop GUI side as well as the server side. However, CORBA's main focus has always been on the server side. ORB vendors in the past expected the now defunct OpenDoc to compete with Microsoft's COM on the client side.

Today, CORBA has no model specification to compete with desktop COM components for heterogeneous client GUIs. However, Java Beans, a component technology from Sun, is being integrated to support client components with CORBA. This technology is still evolving. Until COM is ported to other platforms, however, Microsoft's client-side advantage exists only on 32-bit Windows platforms.

The CORBA Object Reference differs from DCOM's Interface Reference in several ways. CORBA supports multiple inheritance of object interfaces, while DCOM has a mechanism that allows multiple independent interfaces per object.

Interfaces. Both use the interface mechanism to expose object functionalities. Interfaces contain methods and attributes as common means of placing requests on an object. CORBA uses standard models of inheritance from object-oriented languages. DCOM/ActiveX uses the concept of multiple interfaces supported by a single object. DCOM requires that multiple inheritance be emulated through aggregation and containment of interfaces.

Identity. Another difference is the notion of object identity. CORBA defines the identity of an object in an object reference that is unique and persistent. If the object is not in memory, the reference is used to reconstruct the object. DCOM, in contrast, defines the identity in the interface; the reference to the object itself is transient. This may lead to problems when reconnecting because the previously used object may not be directly accessible.

Reference Counting. Reference counting is also different in both. A DCOM object maintains a reference count of all connected clients. It uses pinging of the clients to ensure that the clients are alive. CORBA does not need to do remote reference because its object reference model allows the recreation of the object if it had been prematurely deleted. CORBA does not attempt to track the number of clients communicating with a particular object. If a client releases the object on the server while another is using it, the object will be destroyed and an error will return to the other client on the next method call. Thus, it is up to the object implementation to provide life-cycle management if such behavior is unacceptable. Without a transaction manager integrated into the distributed system, it is very difficult to implement a reliable life-cycle management system.

APIs. CORBA uses two application protocol interfaces (APIs) and one protocol for object requests. It provides the generated stubs for both static and dynamic invocation. In addition, a dynamic skeleton interface allows changes during run time. DCOM provides two APIs and two protocols. The standard interface is based on a binary interface that uses method pointer tables called vtables. The second API OLE automation is used to support dynamic requests through scripting languages.

PROGRAMMING DCOM AND CORBA

CORBA defines a finite set of primitive data types used for argument passing and structure definitions. CORBA interface definition language (IDL) files are similar in syntax to the C language, but deal only with interface-related details.

Two of the primary differences between COM and CORBA are structure and naming. A COM object consists of one or more categories of interfaces, where each one is named and has its own derivation hierarchy. A CORBA object follows a standard object model; its interface is defined by its class and all the ancestors of that class. In the COM interface definition, the developer provides a universal identifier (UUID) that uniquely identifies the interface and class definitions. The UUID identifies classes instead of a class name so that one can have multiple classes with the same name but different vendors and functionality. CORBA, on the other hand, uses a naming system that includes the class name and an optional module name. Module names are equivalent to the C++ namespace concept, where class names can be scoped (assigned) to a particular module. The COM approach ensures that a collision will not occur. The CORBA version would allow a program to use two or more classes of the same name if their module scopes are different.

Error conditions and the amount of information they return is another difference. CORBA implementations provide an exception mechanism that returns errors as a structure embedded within another object called the environment. A standard system exception structure is defined for system-level and communications errors that can occur during a remote method call. Since CORBA is generally implemented with an object-oriented language, the exception systems of CORBA and the language can be tied together. Thus, in C++, an error that occurs on the server will result in an exception being thrown on the client. In contrast, all methods in COM return an HRESULT integer value that indicates the success or failure of the call. This integer value is split into a number of bit fields that allow the programmer to specify context, facility, severity, and error codes, making error handling more laborious.

The error-handling example is an area that CORBA is better at supporting than DCOM. Although both promote the aspect of location transparency, the reality that object implementations exist in other processes and the complications that can result from this reality are exposed in the way errors are handled. Developers like to know where an object exists when an error occurs. CORBA appears to be better, with its support for reporting system errors separate from application-level errors, which makes it easier for the developer to build appropriate exception-handling code.

Existing Services. To quickly implement distributed object technologies, it is important to have a built-in core set of components that applications can use. While DCOM comes bundled with a few more than CORBA, both suffer from a lack of existing components.

SECURITY

DCOM has a more flexible security implementation than CORBA. DCOM provides multiple levels of security that can be selected by the administrator. DCOM uses access control lists (ACLs) on COM components. Administrators can use ACLs to determine who has access to the objects. DCOM methods can also programmatically control authorization of individual method invocations. By combining NT APIs and registry keys, a method can implement custom security. DCOM's security managers are platform dependent. However, they employ readily available authenticators from third parties.

CORBA object services specify three levels of security. Level 0 specifies the authentication and session encryption using technology similar to that of the secure sockets layer (SSL) on Web servers. This requires that the IIOP be secure, and object servers have to register themselves as secure with the ORB. Levels 1 and 2 are differentiated based on whether the CORBA clients and server objects are aware of the security layer. In level 1, they are not aware; and in Level 2, they are aware of the security layer. Because CORBA's security specification has only recently been completed, ORB vendors have in the past had to come up with their own security implementations, which were incompatible with each other. Most vendors are currently only supporting SSL and Level 0 security.

SCALABILITY

Transaction processing (TP) monitors help with scalability of any application by providing two critical services:

1. Process management: starting server processes, filtering work to them, monitoring their execution, and balancing their workloads.
2. Transaction management: ensures atomicity, consistency, isolation, and durability (ACID) properties for all processes and resources under its control.

Both DCOM and CORBA leverage TP monitors to provide for scalability and robustness.

DCOM is designed to work with the Microsoft Transaction Server, which began shipping in early 1997. Transaction Server is a transaction processing system that enables development, deployment, and management of multi-tier applications composed of COM and DCOM objects. DCOM is used for all object communication among machines. Transaction Server transparently provides transaction support to objects: manages threads, processes, ODBC database connections, and sharing data among concurrently executing objects. Although Transaction Server has a tight integration with SQL Server, it can be used with a wide range of databases. Transaction Server currently does not support failover and load balancing, although it is expected in future releases. In addition, DCOM is scheduled to work with a next-generation Directory Services that is scheduled to ship with Windows NT 5.0. These services will provide a highly scalable store for object references and security information for DCOM.

CORBA has a specification called Object Transaction Services (OTS) that is designed to interoperate with X/Open-compliant transaction monitors. Hence, CORBA OTS is designed to work both with ORB-based and traditional TP transaction processing services. OTS offers the capability of supporting recoverable nested transactions that support ACID and two-phase commit protocols. IDL interfaces can be used to provide a way to remotely access the TP monitor application. Integrating TP monitors within an ORB allows the CORBA components to be wrappers of existing business functionality and to support legacy data.

PLATFORM SUPPORT

DCOM will currently only run on 32-bit Windows platforms. It is currently integrated into Windows NT 4.0, both server and workstation, and is available free for Windows 95. However, cross-platform support for DCOM is coming, with third-party ports coming for Unix, including one for Linux, Digital Unix, HP/UX, and Sun's Solaris, as well as IBM's MVS and DEC's OpenVMS. Microsoft is actively seeking partners to port DCOM to other platforms, although some are concerned that Microsoft will favor its Windows-based implementations over the published DCOM standards. Applications using DCOM running on non-Windows platforms are only able to invoke the services on the Windows platforms, as opposed to allowing applications to be built anywhere.

Among Unix users, there is a driving need to have an easy means to connect the application on the desktop and the server. Software AG, a developer of three DCOM-on-Unix ports, estimates that of the 600,000 Unix servers in production systems worldwide, about 80% need an easier way to bridge the worlds of Unix and Windows.

Critics of DCOM point out that the DCOM component model is not inherently distributed. It must be ported to every platform where it is to be used in order to get portability, which is clumsier than CORBA that was built from the ground up to be distributed.

In order for DCOM to be widely used for creating enterprise applications, cross-platform services such as Transaction Server and Message Queue Server must be in place. Although Microsoft is expected to provide versions of its COM-based messaging and transaction services on other platforms directly or through a third party, no formal commitment has been made.

LANGUAGE SUPPORT

CORBA is well suited for use by object-oriented languages. The code is much cleaner because the bindings fully exploit the features of the host language. DCOM, on the other hand, has done nothing to provide management classes for the method arguments or a way to link error conditions to the C++ exception mechanism. CORBA also has a superior mechanism for handling arrays and sequences and provides an "any" data type for marshaling arguments whose type is not known in advance. For object-oriented languages such as C++, the DCOM interface is cumbersome and requires more low-level code.

On the other hand, because DCOM supports OLE automation, applications can be developed with popular, non-object-oriented languages such as Visual Basic or Delphi. If developing a PC-based application within these environments, DCOM is definitely easier. For those dealing with object-oriented languages and significant object models, the CORBA model is more of a natural fit because of COM's inability to support polymorphism and framework development.

INDUSTRY SUPPORT

Although many key companies such as Netscape, Oracle, and Sun Microsystems have agreed to support the emerging CORBA standards, there is some doubt whether they are fully committed to the standard, or if they will shift to DCOM if it gains considerable market share. DEC has announced it will use more than one technology, and HP has indicated interest in supporting COM on their versions of Unix, but remains uncommitted to DCOM.

Others, such as IBM, seem to be firmly backing CORBA. IBM has introduced a CORBA-based development suite of middleware products, including Component Broker Connector and Component Broker Toolkit, which it plans to offer free with many of its products.

Tools vendors such as Oracle are hoping to find a middle ground in the battle for market share between DCOM and CORBA. Oracle has released a development environment that supports both native COM and CORBA components.

MATURITY

CORBA and DCOM have great potential for creating seamless distributed computing environments, despite the fact that today CORBA is struggling to establish its standards and DCOM has yet to prove it can operate as a cross-platform solution.

A Complete Tool?

Although both architectures can create the structure for enterprise-level applications, neither is capable of generating an actual enterprise-ready application, which requires other services such as transactions, event notification, concurrency control, and naming. Although neither CORBA nor DCOM is a complete solution for network programming, CORBA offers good code for object-oriented languages. DCOM is easy to use with non-object-oriented languages such as Visual Basic.

PERFORMANCE

The network performance of DCOM is comparable to that of CORBA's IIOP, with each accomplishing reasonable request/reply response times. However, a standard method of communicating over an asynchronous transport is needed for both DCOM and CORBA. Currently, because of their highly synchronous operation, these technologies are limited to operating over LANs and server backbones. Internet use, or use over a company WAN, is not practical with the current technologies because of the high rate of synchronous request/reply activity required.

The OMG is in the midst of finalizing the Asynchronous Messaging service. This service extends CORBA's synchronous processes and provides a notion of "store-and-forward" processing with a variety of quality of service guarantees for messaging, reporting, and similar functions.

SUPPORT FOR THE WORLD WIDE WEB

Netscape has declared the IIOP as its standard for communicating between distributed objects and has included object broker technology in Communicator and SuiteSpot. Microsoft continues to position Windows DCOM and ActiveX as its distributed object solution, and Explorer is the only browser to support ActiveX.

Notification services are being provided in conjunction with the asynchronous messaging services in CORBA to enable an object to subscribe and receive notification of changes. This is essential to support the various push technologies emerging on the Web. Along with Event Services, this provides support for publish and subscribe to be effectively supported. Many CORBA vendors have provided support for this technology. However, they are not very scalable because, by their very nature, the Event Services uses a point-to-point connection-oriented approach.

PROTOCOLS SUPPORTED

DCOM supports several protocols, such as TCP/IP, IPX/SPX, and Named Pipes. Although not limited to IIOP, CORBA ORBs only support the TCP/IP-based IIOP or proprietary inter-ORB protocols. DCOM's core network protocol is called Object Remote Procedure Call (ORPC). It is based on DCE RPCs (Distributed Computing Environment Remote Procedure Calls), with extensions such as the addition of a primitive data type to support object references.

EASE OF USE

DCOM has just a few key management tools and has based the transport and security mechanisms on familiar Distributed Computing Environment (DCE) standards. This has made managing distributed components much less of a challenge.

INTEROPERABILITY BETWEEN CORBA AND DCOM

Currently, the IIOP is the OMG-approved method of linking distributed CORBA objects. Microsoft says it has no plans to support IIOP in DCOM, and there is currently no built-in COM support in CORBA. This battle of standards is making the implementation of both CORBA and COM services difficult.

Because most enterprises will have both COM and CORBA environments, it is necessary that the objects in each be able to communicate with each other. OMG published a specification two years ago called "COM/CORBA Interworking" (now part of the CORBA 2.0 specification) that defines standardized mappings between COM and CORBA objects. There are several companies shipping implementations of this specification, including IONA, HP, Digital, and Expersoft. Basically, one of two approaches is used: encapsulation or converter. In the encapsulation approach, a call to the server object system is wrapped in an implementation of the object from the client system. ORB vendors provide generators to create such a bridge from the interface description of the object. In the converter approach, conversation proxies are generated during run time based on the interface description of the object it represents. Both support bidirectional calls to and from either object system.

THE FUTURE

Microsoft's COM+ is designed to simplify the creation and use of software components. It provides a run time and services that are readily used from any programming language or tool. COM+ enables extensive interoperability between components regardless of how they were implemented.

Where COM+ really shines, and where it most affects DCOM, is how COM+ addresses the difficulties inherent in writing component-based distributed applications. COM+ offers an extensibility mechanism called interception, which receives and processes events related to instance creation, calls, returns, errors, and instance deletion. Services that the Microsoft Transaction Server provides today is a part of COM+ and a core part of future Microsoft operating systems.

Similarly, OMG is defining and filling in the services required for most of the service layers, such as directory service, transactions, and security. Vendor implementations of these have appeared. Others such as persistence, concurrency, time, query, trader, collection, and versioning will become more available. In addition, Java Beans technology is being pushed as the client component technology, and Java support for CORBA is growing. This provides additional support for CORBA on the desktop.

CONCLUSION

DCOM is more accessible than CORBA at this stage of the technologies because of Microsoft's experience and focus on the included DCOM management tools. For Microsoft-centric companies, DCOM is a solution that is tightly integrated with the Windows operating system. Customers have the most to lose in the object wars, and interoperability between CORBA and DCOM will likely be an important issue for many years. Where cross-platform capability or access to legacy objects is required, CORBA is currently the clear winner. CORBA provides companies with the highest degree of middleware flexibility through its extensive third-party support. More likely, all enterprises will use a mix of the two technologies, with DCOM at the desktop and CORBA at the enterprise level.

In essence, DCOM and CORBA provide similar enough services that debates of minor technical issues ought to be dismissed in favor of more practical concerns, such as scalability, openness, availability, and maturity. Other important issues to be considered are the operating systems and programming languages used in the current project. Availability of CORBA and DCOM bridges may render the choice moot, and users will not be aware nor care whether it is DCOM or CORBA under the covers because what they will use will be higher services (such as business facilities) built on top of either architecture.

ENABLING TECHNOLOGIES

Recommended Reading

Object Management Group, 1997, "CORBA vs. ActiveX," http://www.omg.org/activex.htm.

Object Management Group, 1997, "What is CORBA?", http://www.omg.org/omg00/wicorba.htm.

T.M. Rajkumar, 1997, "Client Server Development with Components."

InfoWorld, August 4, 1997 v19 n31 p6(1), "HP to Push DCOM as Aart of CORBA," McKay, Niall.

Network Computing, July 15, 1997 v8 n13 p98(5), "Is DCOM Truly the Object of Middleware's Desire?," Frey, Anthony.

Network Computing, July 1, 1997 v8 n12 p101(1), "Three's a Crowd with Object Lessons," Gall, Nick.

InformationWeek, May 26, 1997 n632 p122(1), "Component Software War," Harzog, Bernd.

InfoWorld, May 19, 1997 v19 n20 p51(2), "Microsoft's Cross-Platform DCOM Plans Raise Questions," Bowen, Ted Smalley.

PC Week, May 12, 1997 v14 n19 p8(1), "DCOM-to-Unix Ports on the Way," Leach, Norvin.

PC Week, May 12, 1997 v14 n19 p93(1), "Single Victor Unlikely in Object Protocol War," Lewis, Jamie.

Byte, April 1997 v22 n4 p103(3), "Programming with CORBA and DCOM," Pompeii, John.

DBMS, April 1997 v10 n4 p26(6), "Inside DCOM," Roy, Mark and Ewald, Alan.

Object Management Group, 1997, "IIOP," http://www.omg.org/corba/corbiiop.htm.

Microsoft Corporation, 1997, "COM and DCOM", http://www.microsoft.com/cominfo/.

Byte, April 1997 v22 n4 p93, "Distributing Components," Montgomery, John.

Microsoft Systems Journal, 1997 v12 n11, "Object-Oriented Software Development Made Simple with COM+ Runtime Services," Kirtland, Mary.

Object Magazine, July 1997, p. 68–77. "CORBA/DCOM Interoperability," Kotopoulis, Alexander and Miller, Julia.

DBMS, March 1997, p. 43–50, "CORBA Masterminds Object Management," Kueffel, Warren.

Application Development Trends, Oct. 1997, p. 41–46, "Deeper Inside CORBA," Dolgicer, Max.

Chapter 11
Java-Enabled Data Warehousing
Fred Neufeld

Today's business climate is more competitive and volatile than ever before. Increased competition, evolving global markets, mergers, and acquisitions: these factors and many more have forced enterprises to unlock their collection of market data and use the information to make better decisions faster. Now more than ever, decision support systems, data marts, and data warehouses are not only a component of a competitive advantage, but they are a requirement. They must be easily implemented and able to adapt and scale as the business climate changes.

Sun's Java computing architecture is an implementation framework that uses standard, currently available network protocols and services to deliver the power of Java application to the widest possible base of Java platform-enable devices and users. With this architecture, transactions can be moved transparently to the most cost-effective, appropriate support channel within a network owing to the portable nature of Java application.

There are many areas to consider when Web-enabling a data warehouse. Two of the key areas to address are as follows: hardware (system architecture) and software (tools). There are many hardware considerations to make, including: performance, scalability, high availability, data security, and system and network management. This chapter focuses on the software required for a data warehouse and also answers the following essential question: "How does Java technology enable data warehouses to provide easier access and a more efficient, flexible architecture to meet the end-user requirements of today, tomorrow, and for the unknown requirements of the future?"

0-8493-1149-7/02/$0.00+$1.50
© 2002 by CRC Press LLC

BENEFITS OF A WEB-ENABLED DATA WAREHOUSE

With the evolution of the World Wide Web, the end user is becoming more Web-informed and therefore more sophisticated in its use. More and more corporate officers are becoming the end users of data warehouses. Learning complicated online analytical processing (OLAP) tools is no longer acceptable. A "Web-like" access tool requires little or no training and therefore becomes time-effective and cost-efficient.

The end users of the data warehouses are also more mobile. The standard, local area networks are not as effective in supporting a mobile workforce. The World Wide Web — the Internet — is becoming an inexpensive, effective model for deploying information to thousands of end users.

Maintaining a Web-enabled data warehouse has become easier and more cost-effective, because the application software and the data warehouse data structure can be transmitted over the Web. When the end user accesses the data warehouse, the application can determine if either a software or a data structure update is required and automatically update the application through the Web. This takes the whole maintenance cycle away from the end users — thus resulting in zero-client administration.

Using the Web standard protocols as the data warehouse infrastructure allows for greater end-user collaboration. The end user views and manipulates the data and then forwards the information (via e-mail) to other colleagues. The information can simply be viewed using a Java client — a Web browser; no specific application is required to be loaded onto their machines.

WHY JAVA TECHNOLOGY IS IMPORTANT

There are many features or benefits that make Java technology important to application development and these benefits are extended to data warehouse development. They include:

- The Java language is an object-oriented language that enables faster application development.
- Java applications can be multi-threaded, which will enable them to scale across the enterprise.
- Java virtual machines (JVMs) are now available on all major platforms, allowing applications to be portable across all environments, platform-independent — Write-Once, Run Anywhere.
- Java technology was designed and built using industry standards (i.e., CORBA).
- Java applets are delivered on an as-needed basis, thus reducing the administration cost of upgrading client machines. Security has always been a key factor in developing the Java technology.

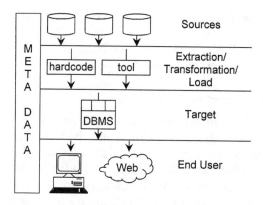

Exhibit 1. Five Logical Layers of a Data Warehouse

- Java applets run in a "sandbox" environment, shielding the end user's machine from unwanted security breaches. Better performance is also available by using the multi-threaded ability of the Java programming language and the just-in-time compilers.

LAYERS OF THE DATA WAREHOUSE

At its most fundamental level, a data warehouse is a staging area for decision-support information. The data warehouse can be divided into five logical layers as shown in Exhibit 1; these layers are:

1. Source layer: the operational data that needs to be extracted, including external sources
2. Extraction, transformation, and loading (ETL) layer
3. Target layer: enterprise data warehouse, operational data stores, and data marts
4. End-user layer: reports, ad hoc queries, OLAP, and data mining
5. Metadata layer: data about data, collected during each stage of the data warehouse process

Sources

The sources are the starting point for the data warehouse. The sources consist of operational systems, current applications, new applications (i.e., ERP), and external data feeds. The data warehouse helps to bridge the data disparity from all operational systems and merges the information from various data types into a consistent format.

Most of the source systems used to feed the data warehouse are legacy systems. During the data warehouse project, there is no need to re-host the sources. Therefore, Java technology has not played a major role in this area of the data warehouse. However, there are significant enhancements to relational database management systems (RDBMS), and these will be highlighted in the Target section of this chapter because most enhancements are related to retrieving data for the endusers.

Extraction/Transformation/Load (ETL)

This layer takes the information from the source operational systems and transforms, merges, and loads the data into the target database. The purpose of this stage is to ensure that the data loaded into the data warehouse is consistent, standardized, and cleansed. The transformation is the process of filtering, selecting, conversion/translation, derivation/summarization, and cleansing of the data from disparate operational systems and external sources. The merged and cleansed data is then loaded into the target data warehouse.

ETL Tools Written in Java

ETL tools developed using Java technology benefit from the object-oriented, fast development, and Write-Once, Run Anywhere. Tool vendors would benefit because they would incur lower development and maintenance costs since only one source code base is required. The benefits for the customers would be the ability to have one ETL tool deployed throughout the organization on multiple platforms. The one tool would reduce the training time of the IT staff and the time required to deploy different tools throughout the organization.

ETL Tools Generating Java Programs

ETL Tools that generate Java code enable the system administrator to optimize system usage. Once the extraction processes are generated, in Java, the processes are portable. This flexibility allows the system administrator to select the best platform to optimize the ETL process. Over a period of time as the requirements for the ETL process evolve and the computing environment changes, the ETL process can be deployed to another platform or even be divided into pieces, which then can be executed on different platforms. The ETL processes will not have to be recompiled or retested, saving both time and resources.

Since the ETL processes are portable, the system administrator has control of the platform where the ETL process executes. The system administrator can optimize the source-to-target workflow and reduce network traffic by moving the ETL process closer to the source data.

By expanding the Java infrastructure with Enterprise Java Beans™ (EJB) technology, the corporation could purchase transformation components (e.g., address verification programs). These components then could be plugged into the current ETL process. This enables the ETL process to grow and expand quickly and easily as the requirements evolve.

Targets

The target layer is where the enterprise data warehouse, operational data store, and data marts are defined and accessed. The information is compiled into a standard, consistent framework for access by the end user. Java technology incorporated into the database engines has many significant benefits for the data warehouse.

One of the key benefits is to add Java technology into the inline procedures. The inline procedures extend the standard SQL, allowing for specialized data types (e.g., voice, video, large binary objects) to be incorporated into the data warehouse.

The inline procedures can also be used for database triggers. These triggers written in Java, and not a database-specific language, are easier to maintain by a development team. The database triggers are then transferable to other Java-enabled databases. Stored procedures become associated with the application and not with the RDBMS.

The object-oriented approach of Java technology enables the business logic to be separated from the database logic, making the data warehouse application easier to maintain. Besides being more maintainable, separating the business and database logic also makes the application more scalable. The more complex procedures can be executed on the database server rather than on the potentially smaller Java client — the Web browser. Performing the majority of the processing on the database server will also reduce network traffic. The client machine formulates the query and passes it to the database server. The server processes the information and returns only the results back to the client, through the network.

Using Java to access the databases (JDBC) also enables the user's application to have a standard interface into the database engines. This builds flexibility into the application, allowing the database engine to be changed without affecting the application code.

The next step would be to incorporate Enterprise Java Beans (EJB), Entity Beans, into the data warehouse structure. This would enable the data warehouse application to access the contents of a database without any knowledge of the underlying database engine. The EJB structure allows the database to be substituted without affecting the application, thereby adding more flexibility to the data warehouse application.

End-User Tools

The end-user layer is the layer that defines the end-user environment. There are many different categories of end-user tools: batch reporting, ad hoc queries, multi-dimensional analysis, and data mining. All categories of tools can benefit from Java technology with multi-platform support and lower maintenance costs. However, the largest benefits are gained when the end-user tools are deployed on the Web. Standard HTML is expanded, using Java technology enabling data-driven reports and graphics to be created and integrated on-the-fly.

WEB INTERFACE

The Web allows the end user to access the data warehouse information through ad hoc queries, or multi-dimensional fashion through their Web browsers. Traditionally, this functionality was only available by loading and maintaining the decision support application on every workstation (fat clients). Java technology removes the requirement for fat clients in the data warehouse architecture. The end users' machines become a zero-client administration, allowing application updates to be distributed through the Web.

Web-based tools created using the Web-like interfaces are easier to understand. The end user does not need to attend a training session or read a complex training manual to understand how to use the tool.

Java technology is based on a distributed computer model. The application logic is passed through the Web and the processing occurs on the end user's machine. Therefore, as end users access the data warehouse, the work is distributed to the client's machines, making the data warehouse more scalable.

Metadata

Metadata is data about data. The metadata repository is a central repository to collect information during the data warehouse process. The end user accesses this information to understand the business rules applied to the data in order to build the data warehouse. All stages of the data warehouse should feed information into the metadata repository. Currently, there are not very many tools in this complex area of data warehousing; however, a number of standards groups are emerging.

Using Java technology in the metadata repository would enable the other tools in the data warehouse architecture to write the appropriate information to the repository using open standards. The metadata repository could use Java inline procedures to validate the information being entered.

A metadata tool, developed using Java technology, would benefit the end users by enabling them to use their browser, over the Web, to access the metadata information. Ideally, the same Java-based tool used to access the data warehouse information should be used to access the metadata repository.

CONCLUSION

A data warehouse is an important application that provides better access to the corporation's information. The structure of the data warehouse is complicated by the fact that information must be extracted from a number of disparate systems and merged into a uniform structure, for access by the end users. The data warehouse structure must be flexible so that it can evolve as the business requirements change.

In the data warehouse infrastructure, the use of Java technology — with its open standards, multi-platform support, and portability — enables data warehouse processes to be easily moved to different platforms when required. Java technology also extends the standard SQL and creates flexible inline procedures and enables a more scalable data warehouse architecture. From a tool's perspective, Java technology allows for a "thin client," easier distribution of software updates, and a browser-like interface that requires less end-user training. Extending the Java architecture to include Enterprise Java Beans allows new or improved data warehouse components to be easily added to the current data warehousing processes.

Leveraging the Java technology enables the IT organization to build and deploy data warehouses using an open-standard, portable architecture that is easily modified as business requirements change.

Chapter 12
JavaBeans and Java Enterprise Server Platform

David Wadsworth

A majority of the world's data resides on mainframe servers. This legacy poses many challenges to the information systems (IS) community as it struggles with the demands of business units for new and innovative solutions to business problems. Organizations need to adopt a flexible, secure, and cost-effective architecture that will enable them to remain competitive and enable breakaway business strategies. Adoption of Java™ computing realizes these benefits by providing key technology enablers.

JAVA TECHNOLOGY REVIEW

The Java programming language was introduced to the public in May 1995. Key features of the language such as platform independence and ease of programming made it an instant success in the software development community. Other features such as safe network delivery and baked-in security have made the language the *de facto* standard for the development and deployment of Web-based applications.

Applications written in the Java programming language are compiled to bytecode that can run wherever the Java platform is present. The Java platform is a software environment composed of the Java Virtual Machine and the Java Core Application Programming Interfaces (APIs). Portability of applications is achieved because there is only one virtual machine specification, which provides a standard, uniform programming interface on any hardware architecture. Developers writing to this base set of functionality can be confident that their applications will run anywhere without the need for additional libraries. Core libraries include functional support for GUI development, I/O, database connectivity, networking, math, components (JavaBeans), multithreading, and many others.

Sun's Java computing architecture is an implementation framework that uses standard, currently available network protocols and services to deliver the power of Java applications to the widest possible base of Java platform-enabled devices and users. With this architecture, transactions can be moved transparently to the most cost-effective, appropriate support channel within a network owing to the portable, Writes Once, Run Anywhere™ nature of Java applications.

JAVA PLATFORM COMPONENT ARCHITECTURES

Designing and developing applications by means of components has been available for many years. The challenge has been to embrace and extend existing technology with new technology. Until recently, such an approach has been proprietary and difficult to deploy. The Java computing environment with JavaBeans, a component technology, and server architecture solution Java Enterprise Server, enables organizations to greatly simplify access to business systems. What follows is a description of the JavaBeans component model and an overview of the Java Enterprise Server platform.

JAVABEANS

A JavaBean is a reusable Java software component that can be visually manipulated and customized in a builder tool. These application building blocks are constructed to communicate easily with each other in a common environment. They also have the ability to store their state on the shelf to be revived at a later date. Because they are written in the Java programming language for deployment on any Java platform, JavaBeans are the platform-independent components for the enterprise network.

JavaBean components can range from simple GUI elements, such as buttons and sliders, to more sophisticated visual software components, such as database viewers. Some JavaBeans may have no GUI appearance of their own, but still can be manipulated in an application builder.

The JavaBean API has been designed to be accessible by builder tools as well as manipulated manually by human programmers. The key APIs, such as property control, event handling, and persistence, can be accessed by both hand-crafted applications and builder tools. In addition to event handling, property control, and persistence, introspection and customization are distinguishing features of all JavaBeans.

Property Control

Property control facilitates the customizing of the JavaBean at both design and runtime. Both the behavior and appearance of a JavaBean can be modified through the property features. For example, a GUI button might have a property named "ButtonLabel," which represents the text displayed in the button. This property can be accessed through its getter and setter methods. Once properties for a bean are configured, their state will be maintained through the persistence mechanism.

Persistence

The attributes and behavior of a bean are known as the state of the bean. The persistence mechanism within the JavaBean API supports storage of this state once the bean is customized. It is this state that is incorporated into the application and available at runtime. This externalization can be in a custom format or the default. A custom external format allows the bean to be stored as another object type such as an Excel document inside a Word document. The default is reserved for those instances where the bean's state needs to be saved without regard to the external format.

Event Handling

Event handling is a simple mechanism that allows components to be connected based on their production of and interest in certain actions. A component or series of components can be sources of events that can be caught and processed by other components or scripting environments. Typical examples of events include mouse movements, field updates, and keyboard actions. Notification of these events generated by a component are delivered to any interested component.

The extensible event-handling mechanism for JavaBeans allows easy implementation of the model in application builder tools. Event types and propagation models can be crafted to accommodate a variety of application types.

Customization

Changing the appearance and behavior of a JavaBean is accomplished through the customization features of the JavaBean's API. Each JavaBean contains a list of exported properties, which an application builder can scan and use to create a GUI property editor sheet. The user can then customize the bean using this dynamically created sheet. This is the simplest form of customization.

Another layer of customization is possible by attaching to the bean a customizer class that acts as a properties wizard. This wizard will have a GUI that can be employed to tailor the properties for the related bean in a guided tour fashion. Such wizards are more likely to be found associated with complex beans such as calculator beans or database connection beans. Once customization is completed the properties will be stored using the persistence mechanism.

Introspection

The properties, methods, and events a JavaBean supports are determined at runtime and in builder environments by means of introspection. Introspection is a prescribed method of querying the bean to discover its inherent characteristics. Introspection is implemented using the Java programming language rather than a separate specification language. Thus, all of the behavior of the bean is specifiable in the Java programming language.

One introspection model supported by the JavaBeans API provides a default view of the methods, events, and properties. This simple mechanism does not require the programmer to do extra work to support introspection. For more sophisticated components, interfaces are available for the developer of the bean to provide specific and detailed control over which methods, events, and properties are to be exposed.

Default, low-level reflection of the bean is used to discover the methods supported by the bean. Design patterns are then applied to these methods to determine the properties, events, and public methods supported by the component. For example, if a pair of methods such as setColor and getColor are discovered during the reflection process, the property color is identified by the application of the get/set design pattern for property discovery.

More complex component analysis can be built into the bean by the use of a BeanInfo class. This class would be used by a builder tool to discover the bean's behavior programmatically.

Security

JavaBeans are governed by the same security model as all other Java applets and applications. If a JavaBean is contained in an untrusted applet, then it will be subject to the same restrictions and will not be allowed to read or write files on the local file system or connect to arbitrary network hosts. As a component in a Java application or trusted applet, a JavaBean will be granted the same access to files and hosts as a normal Java application. Developers are encouraged to design their beans so they can be run as part of untrusted applets.

Runtime versus Design-Time JavaBeans

Each JavaBean must be capable of running in a number of different environments. The two most important are the design time and runtime environments. In the design environment a JavaBean must be able to expose its properties and other design-time information to allow for customization in a builder tool. In some cases wizards contained in the bean may be employed to simplify this process.

Once the application is generated, the bean must be usable at runtime. There is really no need to have the customization or design information available in this environment.

The amount of code required to support the customization and design-time information for a bean could be potentially quite large. For example, a wizard to assist in the modification of bean properties could be considerably larger than the runtime version of the bean. For this reason it is possible to segregate the design-time and runtime aspects of a bean so it can be deployed without the overhead of the design-time features.

JavaBeans Summary

JavaBeans are the component object model for the Java platform. These device-independent components can be customized and assembled quickly and easily to create sophisticated applications.

JAVA ENTERPRISE SERVER PLATFORM

As organizations adopt Internet technologies to enable new business strategies, they are faced with the task of integrating all of their legacy applications, databases, and transaction services with Web-based services. Traditional applications designed in the client/server model do not deploy well in an Internet/extranet environment. Although not new, multitier architectures for application development and deployment are best suited for extending the reach of a company's infrastructure to partners, suppliers, customers, and remote employees. The Java Enterprise server platform provides such an architecture in an open and standards-based environment that incorporates existing infrastructure while extending their reach to intranets, extranets, and even the Internet. An extensible architecture, the Java Enterprise server platform contains the API's products and tools necessary to construct new enterprisewide applications and integrate with existing systems.

Traditional mission-critical applications are written to the APIs of the underlying operating system, thereby tying the application to a single operating system. Porting of the application to a new operating system is both difficult and expensive. These same applications may rely on a service, such as a transaction monitor. Access to this service will be through the software vendor's proprietary APIs creating another platform lock and presenting a barrier to moving to a different service provider.

The Java Enterprise server platform is designed to address these platform-lock issues. It extends the notion of "write once, run anywhere" to include "and integrate with everything." Based on a layer and leverage model, the Java Enterprise server platform can be built on top of existing legacy systems such as transaction monitors, database access, system

Platform Neutral Development							
Enterprise JavaBeans Components Model							
Web Serv.	Nam-ing	Mess.	Dist. Obj.	Secur-ity	Mgt	DB	Trans-action
Java Virtual Machine							
Solaris NT HP-UX AIX MVS IRIX MacOS ... others							
Network Serv. TCP/IP SPX/IPX SNA DECnet LanMgr							
Physical Network							

Exhibit 1.   Java Enterprise Server Platform Architecture

---

management, naming and directory services, and CORBA (Exhibit 1). Interfaces to these services, as well as a component model that provides for application encapsulation and reuse, are integral to the Java Enterprise server platform. The component model includes JavaBeans components for the client, and Enterprise JavaBeans (EJB's) components for the server.

All of the benefits of rapid application development, scalability, robustness, and security of the JavaBeans component architecture are extended to the Java Enterprise server platform. EJBs also have the ability to provide transactional services. Coupled with these benefits is an open architecture capable of providing ease of development, deployment, and management.

Enterprise JavaBeans, an extension of the JavaBeans architecture, provide a distributed component architecture for developing and deploying component-based, multitier applications. Business logic is encapsulated in the Enterprise JavaBeans promoting a high degree of reuse. Access to low-level services such as session management and multithreading is simplified such that developers building applications do not need to deal directly with these functions.

Distributed applications developed with Enterprise JavaBeans can be deployed on any other platform without modifications. Support for transactions and messaging integrate with existing legacy systems and middleware.

The heart of the Enterprise JavaBean platform is the Enterprise JavaBean executive (Exhibit 2). This runtime executive is used to execute the components that provide the services required by an application. Through its components, the executive manages load balancing and handles multithreading,

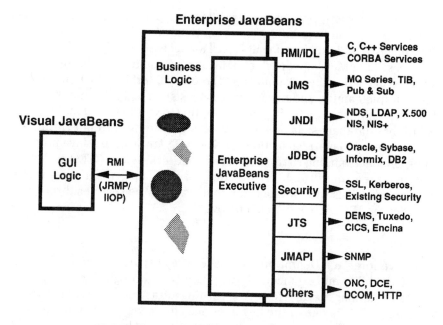

Exhibit 2. Enterprise JavaBeans Framework

transaction management, security, and connection management. This frees programmers to focus on developing the components that contain business logic.

Communication between the client and server in an application does not need to rely on any particular protocol. Both the client and server sides of the application are coded using the Java programming language. At deployment time the underlying communication stubs are generated automatically. The Java programming language introspection of the application class files is used to generate the communication stubs.

Unlike JavaBeans that use the Java event model, Enterprise JavaBeans use the distributed CORBA event model. The event model supported by the Java programming language is well-suited for local, tightly integrated applications, but does not perform as well in a networked environment where high latency and insecure networks are common. Enterprise Java-Bean events are propagated across the network over CORBA's Internet InterORB Protocol (IIOP) to other components.

Enterprise JavaBeans can be configured automatically as CORBA objects, then accessed through IIOP by clients. These client applications do not have to be written in the Java programming language to access the components. EJB's also can function as COM/DCOM objects for Windows clients.

Access to several key services are offered as part of the Enterprise Java-Bean specification (Exhibit 2). These services are offered through specific Java platform APIs such as JavaIDL/RMI for accessing CORBA, DCE, or ONC services; Java Message Service (JMS) for access to messaging systems such as MQ Series; Java Naming and Directory Interface (JNDI) for accessing multiple naming and directory services such as LDAP and NDS; Java Database Connectivity (JDBC) for connecting to various relational and non-relational databases; Java security APIs providing for encryption and authentication; Java Transaction services (JTS) providing a Java programming language binding to the object transaction services (OTS) of CORBA; Java management API (JMAPI) providing for the management of networked resources such as workstations and routers; and Web services through the Java Server API. Each is detailed below.

JavaIDL

The Java Interface Definition Language (IDL) provides standards-based interoperability and connectivity with CORBA. Through these interfaces, Java applications are able to access existing infrastructure written in other languages. This is one of the key interfaces for legacy system integration. JavaIDL is part of the Java platform core API set and is, therefore, available across multiple platforms.

Java Message Service

Java Message Service (JMS) provides an interface to messaging systems that provide publish/subscribe and message queue services. This platform-independent interface also will support the emerging push/pull technologies.

Java Naming and Directory Interface

Many different kinds of naming and directory services exist in today's enterprises. Directory services such as LDAP, NIS, and NDS provide networkwide sharing of information about the users, systems, applications, and resources that exist on an intranet or the Internet. User information can include login IDs, passwords, security access, and electronic mail addresses. System information can include network addresses and machine configurations. The Java Naming and Directory Interface (JNDI) is independent of any specific naming and directory service implementation. Application developers can access multiple namespaces easily through JNDI. A single interface simplifies the access to composite namespaces as well as enabling an application to be portable across different platforms.

Java Database Connectivity

One of the earliest and now core APIs is the Java database connectivity API (JDBC). This is a SQL-based, database-independent API that frees developers from writing database vendor-specific code in their applications. JDBC supports the common database functionality such as remote procedure calls, SQL statements, database connection, and result sets. Because JDBC is implemented via a driver manager, which itself can be implemented in the Java programming language, applets can be delivered to the client with the database connectivity built in. Implementation drivers for all the major RDBMS are already available for JDBC, and a JDBC-to-ODBC bridge is standard in the Java Developer's Kit Version 1.1. JDBC drivers for object-relational DBMSs as well as IBM's IMS are also currently available.

Java Security API

Security is an integral part of the Java Platform and extends to the Java Enterprise Server architecture. There are four key areas that are supported by various security APIs: authentication, authorization, privacy, and integrity.

Authentication is the system's ability to verify or recognize a user. Typically performed at application access or system sign-on, authentication is the first line of defense present in a comprehensive security model. The JavaCard APIs allow smart cards to be employed as secure user authentication devices. These physical cards combined with a secure personal identification number (PIN) enable users to be recognized by the target system. Digital signatures, another authentication method, also are supported through the Java Virtual Machine.

Authorization is the means of determining which data, systems, and services a user can access. The Java Security APIs and access control lists (ACL) are available for managing who can access what. ACLs can be built for each Enterprise JavaBean and consulted whenever the bean is accessed. Based on the user's role, some form of access can be given or denied. Transaction servers installed in the application enforce the ACL at runtime. Because ACLs are not a static structure they can be moved around the network with an EJB object. These embedded ACLs then can be accessed by the application developer.

Privacy concerns are raised in the context of transmission of sensitive data across public networks. To protect data such as credit card numbers, encryption is typically employed. The Java language cryptography APIs provide application or session-level encryption. This interface can support any encryption implementation including DES.

As data passes through a network, be it private or public, there is a chance for malicious or accidental modification. To prevent such actions it is necessary to be able to guarantee the integrity of the transmission. The same mechanisms for insuring privacy can be used for maintaining integrity of network communications, namely session and application encryption.

Java Transaction Services

Java Transaction Services (JTS) within the Enterprise JavaBean framework are a low-level API not meant as an application programmer interface. JTS programming is targeted to the resource managers and TP monitor programmers. Currently available implementations include BEA Systems, Jolt product for Tuxedo access, or IBM's JavaCICS for access to mainframe CICS applications.

Java Management API

The Java Management API (JMAPI) is a set of interfaces for the development of distributed network, system, and application management applications. JMAPI is designed to be incorporated into a variety of devices, across diverse network protocols and numerous operating systems. With support for the Simple Network Management Protocol (SNMP), JMAPI can communicate directly with a variety of existing devices. In the future, device manufacturers will incorporate the JMAPI directly into their products. System administrators using applications developed on this foundation are able to easily manage their network, applications, or other systems from any Java platform located anywhere on the network.

Java Server API

The Java Server API is an extensible framework that can be employed to develop network-centric servers quickly. These servers are capable of providing network-based services, such as Web services, file and print services, proxy services, and mail services. To extend the functionality of a Java server a developer can create servlets using the Java Servlet API. Java servlets are programs that can be local to the server, or downloaded across the network, and then executed on the Java server. These servlets are perfect for processing form data from HTML pages, replacing the platform-dependent CGI-bin scripts in use by many organizations.

SUMMARY

The ability to integrate with legacy systems and extend enterprise services to the network with platform-independent technologies are key benefits of developing a Java Enterprise Server strategy. Enterprise JavaBeans, the component architecture for the Java Enterprise Server, provide a software- and hardware-independent method to access these systems and make them available to business components. These components can easily access services, such as transaction monitors and message systems, DBMSs, and naming services with the assurance of the Java Platform's "write once, run everywhere."

Chapter 13
Web-Enabling a Capacity Database Server

Judith M. Myerson

In the old days, corporate officers used a battery-powered calculator to tally capacity data. The process was too slow to make timely decisions and often contained errors. Today, these officers use Web access tools to automate nearly the same process in much less time, allowing the system to check for errors they might enter via the keyboard. These tools provide these users with a choice of simple actions (retrieving, updating, and other record operations). With additional training, these users can learn more complex actions, such as data analysis, that would help them predict performance problems.

Another benefit is that telecommuters can use laptops for remote access to a centralized capacity database server — from anywhere and at any time. They can employ a variety of remote access technologies to do the following:

- Download files via FTP services (*Note:* FTP software products, such as WS-FTP32, are available)
- Manipulate data and store the results on local disks
- Forward the results to their colleagues via FTP services, attachments to electronic mail messages, and Lotus Notes.
- Collaborate with colleagues via Web-based asynchronous services such as multi-point data conferencing, text chat, whiteboard, and point-to-point audio and video as provided by Microsoft's NetMeeting (*Note:* this software is now part of Windows 2000)

LAYERS OF THE CAPACITY DATABASE SERVER

One of the best ways to explain how the capacity database server works is to divide the server into five logical layers and then elaborate on each:

1. *Source layer:* the operational data that needs to be extracted, including those from disparate sources
2. *Tools layer:* integration, extraction, transformation, and loading (IETL)
3. *Target layer:* capacity database
4. *End-user layer:* reports, queries, analytical tools
5. *Meta-layer:* data about data

Source Layer

As the starting point for the capacity database server, the sources consist of operational systems, applications (current and new), and external data feeds from the legacy systems. Also covered are international database management systems, particularly the relational ones. Not only does the server store these data from diverse sources of operational systems, but also bridges them, transforms them into various types in a consistent, standard format, and eliminates data redundancy via the normalization process.

At the beginning of the capacity database server project, there is no need to re-host the services, as the information about capacity variables can be obtained from system and application documentation of all sorts. Web technologies, such as Java, and Active Server Pages are not considered in this aspect of the project's life cycle. They, however, will be highlighted in the "Target Layer" section of this chapter because they are used in enhancing RDBMs, such as retrieving, searching, adding, updating, and other record options on the database tables.

Tool Layer: Integration/Extraction/Transformation/Loading

This layer takes the information from the source operational systems and transforms, merges, and loads the data into the target database tables according to data formats that have been modified or added. The purpose of this stage is to ensure the data loaded into the tables of a capacity database is consistent, standardized, and cleansed. The transformation is the process of filtering, selecting, converting, translating, normalizing, and integrating the data from diverse operational systems and merging that data into a table in the target database.

Included is data from legacy systems (e.g., COBOL), current database applications, new data to be added for integration with some of the old, and existing data for new applications for capacity database servers.

IETL Tools: Java Servlets, Java Server Pages, and Active Server Pages

This section compares three server tools and briefly discusses why Java-Script is not a server tool.

Java Servlets. When processing HTTP requests, Java servlets are seen as more advantageous than the traditional CGI. One reason is that the chances of overall database performance are very low. Java Servlets permit the Java Virtual Machine to stay up. Each request is handled by a lightweight Java thread — not a heavyweight operating system process. With the CGI, the overhead of starting the process can dominate the execution time even if the CGI does a relatively fast operation.

Another reason is that the servlets contain objects, while the traditional CGI generally does not. This means that Java servlets are portable to various operating systems, while CGI programs need to be changed to fit into a particular operating system. Servlets are supported directly by an application, via plug-ins, or even by some CGI variations on almost every major Web server.

One can probably deal with servlets if one is a regular Java programmer. One can include them in a CGI script if one is also a CGI expert. On the other hand, writing a servlet from scratch can be a bit daunting if one is just a Web-page author with some or very little knowledge of Java.

There is, however, one disadvantage with servlets. Too many servlets on a Web browser can cause problems with lag times when downloading them. This is true when bandwidth is insufficient or network traffic is heavily congested.

Java Server Pages and Active Server Pages. To cut down on the time to produce a servlet and resolve some performance problems, other tools are available. Among them are Java Server Pages (JSP) and Active Server Pages (ASP). JSP allows one to mix static HTML with dynamically generated HTML. In contrast, Web pages that are built by CGI programs are mostly static, with the dynamic part limited to a few locations within these pages.

Similar to JSP is Microsoft's ASP. Both ASP and JSP technologies let developers separate content generation from layout by accessing components from the page. There are, however, some differences.

With JSP, it is more convenient to write and modify regular HTML than having ASP print a million statements that generate the HTML. What this means is that JSP technology enables developers to extend JSP tags to perform repetitious operations on a database and to build custom tag libraries. These custom tag libraries allow page authors to access more functionality using XML-like tags and thus depend less on scripting. The developers can spend more time on better ways of presenting the information to the Web users and prompting them for input to the Web rather than spending endless hours on repeating HTML statements.

Another difference is that ASP supports the COM model, while JSP technology provides components based on JavaBeans technology or JSP tags. ASP interprets JavaScript, VBScript, or PerlScript; JSP compiles Java code.

One can let the server (or a special extension to the server) compile the JSP file into a servlet. If nervous about trying it out on a production server, get a copy of Microsoft's Personal Web Server (free with Windows 98 or downloaded for other versions) and add Allaire's demo version of JRun (also free). One can find a list of JSP add-ons at www.serverpages.com. Even the famous GNU project has a JSP package that works with many popular servlet add-ons (like Jserve for Apache).

The third difference is that JSP is portable to other operating systems and non-Microsoft Web servers, while ASP may be portable only under certain conditions. Originally designed for Microsoft Windows server platforms, the ASP technology is available on other platforms through third-party porting products. There is one catch: the ActiveX objects must be present on the selected platform so that one can access them and interact with other services needed to implement ASP. If not present, a bridge to a platform supporting them is required.

JavaScript. In comparison to JSP, JavaScript is not a server tool. JavaScript can dynamically generate HTML only on the client. This means that the dynamic information is based on the client's environment. With the exception of cookies, HTTP and form submission data to the server are not available to JavaScript. Running only on the client, JavaScript cannot *directly* access server-side resources like databases. Like JavaScript, regular HTML statements cannot contain dynamic information. In contrast, JSP augments HTML pages with the insertion of small amounts of dynamic data.

Target Layer

The target layer is where the enterprise capacity database is defined and accessed. The information is compiled into a standard consistent framework for access by the end user. The choice of Java or ASP technology is contingent on the requirements and specifications as reflected in data models used to build capacity applications from the database.

ASP technology is well-suited for frequent updates and maintaining the capacity database on a server. It enables the user's application to interface with the database engines in a standard, consistent manner. This technology can be used with (but not in) the client-side JavaScript. Although JavaScript cannot directly access the server-side database, it can be used to trigger a form submission to an ASP script. When the user decides to submit the form, the confirm dialog pops up asking for input, for example.

Like the object-oriented approach of Java technology, the ASP technology allows the more complex procedures to be executed on the database server rather than on a Web browser client. Performing the majority of the processing on the database server will also reduce network traffic, provided that:

- The effects of packet jitters are minimized
- The bandwidth is sufficient at peak times
- The quality of service is maintained at acceptable levels

For scalability and reusability across the platform, JSP is the preferred choice, especially when collecting capacity data from diverse sources (as well as updating and maintaining the target databases). Keep in mind that scripting languages, such as ASP, are fine for small applications, but do not scale well to manage large complex applications. Because the Java language is structured, it is easier to build and maintain large modular applications with it.

Many Web hosting providers do not offer JSP. ASP rather than JSP is a standard feature of their offerings to potential users. Their preference for this technology is attributed to the shorter time required for a browser to get a server response to HTTP requests. The server-side HTML requests, in addition, are usually not shown in a client browser's HTML source listing. This is viewed as a form of security protection for the server from the eyes of would-be hackers on the client side. The downloading of an image tagged somewhere in a block of ASP statements is somewhat faster than the same image referenced by JSP tags.

End-User Layer

End users need timely reports to make critical decisions on capacity performance. They must be able to quickly query the database with no or little knowledge of SQL statements. The time factor in obtaining the capacity information is a critical process, especially when the performance is approaching levels above or below the established thresholds.

End users need some sort of tool to allow them to enter capacity parameters on the report screens. Another way is to permit them to select from a list of "standard queries" to produce reports. For those who desire one-time reports, they could enter SQL statements to query the database, but only when they are permitted to do so by system administrators. It is a good idea to create a help file to assist end users in formulating queries, with examples not in the standard list. As a last resort, they can go to a database expert when formulating queries in special situations.

Report examples include:

- Capacity usage
- Capacity performance

- Bandwidth and network traffic
- QoS

Metadata Layer

Metadata is data about when a particular set of data was retrieved, how it was formatted, how it was collected from what source and by whom, and other useful information. There are, however, several metadata types, depending on which viewpoint the end user is taking: business user, system administrator, DSS developer, DDS user, Web master, Web content provider, and corporate manager.

For business users, metadata is data showing where information can be found using site maps, search engine data collection (Web crawling), and other metadata types. The database administrator needs metadata on what methods were used to populate capacity data, how often the database has been maintained, how the software versions are controlled, and when capacity data was not or will not be available.

The metadata of an organization can become the starting point for the person responsible for analyzing the requirements and designing or enhancing data warehousing systems for DSS users. At the corporate level, metadata is a logical collection of data about data from various disparate, enterprisewide sources.

For the purposes of this chapter, Exhibit 1 displays a simple example of how a Web master might place at least four metadata items inside HTML documents to help improve their rankings (on capacity performance and related topics) on search engines. Doing so increases the chance of assisting end users in locating the capacity database sites they want.

```
<head>
<title>Web-Enabled Capacity Database</title>
<meta name="author" content="Judith M. Myerson">
<meta name="description" content="This website focuses on tools to access a Web-enabled Capacity database.">
<meta name="keywords" content="HTML, capacity, performance, network traffic, CRC Press, Auerbach Publishers, servers, servers management, application management, FrontPage2000">
</head>
```

Exhibit 1. Title, Author, Description, and Keywords Metadata Items

CONCLUSION

Capacity databases have been around for a long time, starting with a bygone stand-alone mainframe. Since then, they have gone through several transformations in response to ever-changing technologies in the network world.

The latest challenge is Web-enabling a capacity database server from a variety of template sources — not just the relational databases, but also COBOL legacy systems for integration with capacity variables unique to a distributed system. This server bridges the data from diverse operational systems; transforms this data in a consistent, standard format; and eliminates data redundancy via the normalization process.

Having the information at a moment's notice is important when performance needs to be improved or compared to capacity requirements. With proper analytical, metadata, and search engine tools, an end user can locate a document and pinpoint where capacity needs to be increased or reduced to improve overall performance.

Chapter 14
Application Servers: The Next Wave in Corporate Intranets and Internet Access

Lisa M. Lindgren

A corporation's Web presence typically evolves in three stages. In the first stage, static information is published via Web pages. Information about the company, its products, and its services is made available to the general public via the Internet. In a more secure internal intranet, employees have access to company holiday schedules, personnel policies, company benefits, and employee directories.

While this first step is necessary, it is really only a substitute for other traditional forms of publishing information. The information can become dated, and there is no interaction with the user. Most organizations quickly evolve from the first step to the second — publishing dynamic information and dynamically interacting with the user via new scripts, applications, or applets that are written for the Web server or Web client. An example of this stage of Web presence is a newspaper that offers online news content and classified ad search capabilities. This stage offers realtime information, rather than static "brochureware," and presents the opportunity to carry out electronic commerce transactions. The second stage usually demonstrates to an organization the vast efficiencies and increased customer and employee satisfaction that can result from a well-designed and executed intranet and Internet presence. The challenge many organizations then face is how to rapidly deliver new services over their corporate intranets and the Internet.

In the third stage of Web evolution, the focus is on offering new transactional services that communicate directly with the core IT systems. This allows companies to maintain a competitive edge and meet the unslaked thirst for new and better ways to interact with an organization via the familiar Web interface. The transactional services are offered over the Internet for public use, over business-to-business extranets to allow business partners to more effectively do business, and over internal corporate intranets to offer employees new and better ways to do their jobs. Examples of this third stage of Web presence geared to the public over the Internet include home banking, package tracking, travel booking, stock trading, and the online purchase of consumer goods. Business-to-business examples include online policy sales and updates for insurance agents, manufacturing and delivery schedules for distributors, and direct order entries to suppliers. Intranet examples geared to employees include expense report submission, benefits calculation, and conference room scheduling.

The key emphasis of this third stage of Web presence is its transactional nature. This next level of services can only be achieved by tapping the vast and sophisticated systems and applications that have been built over a period of years. These mission-critical systems and applications represent the "crown jewels" of an IT organization, and include customer records, product availability and pricing, customer service databases, and the transactional applications that literally keep the business running. IT organizations must try to create a unified interface, leveraging a variety of existing systems. The problem is that the existing systems are usually very diverse. They differ in architecture (i.e., client/server versus hierarchical), operating system, programming language, networking protocol, interface (i.e., real-time, batch, programmatic), and access control. The application server is a new breed of product that unifies a variety of different systems and technologies in order to deliver new transactional services to a variety of clients.

OVERVIEW OF A WEB SERVER

To fully understand what an application server does, it is first useful to review the functions of a Web server. A Web server's primary function is to "serve" Web pages to Web clients. The protocol used between the Web client and the Web server is HyperText Transfer Protocol (HTTP). HTTP defines the valid operations between the Web server and the browser. For example, the Get operation is how the browser requests the download of a particular Web page or file. Exhibit 1 illustrates the sequence of events when a Web client requests the download of a particular Web page.

HyperText Markup Language (HTML) defines the contents and structure of the Web page. It is the browser, not the server, that reads and interprets the tags within HTML to format and display a Web page. Extensible Markup Language (XML) is the next-generation Web page content language that allows programmers to define the tags in a page for better programmatic access to the page content. XML separates the definition of content from the presentation of that content.

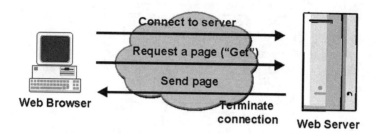

Exhibit 1. Sequence for Download of a Web Page

The Web page can contain text, images, video, and audio. The Web server serves up the files associated with these different types of content. It is the Web browser that must display or play the different data types. As long as the request from the Web browser is valid, the file type is known, and the file exists, the Web server simply downloads whatever is requested.[1] The server behaves differently, however, if the page that the Web browser requests is actually a script.

A script, quite simply, is a program. It can be written in any language and can be compiled or interpreted. A script can be used to access non-Web resources such as databases, to interact with the user via forms, and to construct documents dynamically that are specific to that user or that transaction. The Web server executes the script and the results are returned to the user in the form of a Web page. Scripts interface to the Web server using either a standard or a vendor-proprietary application programming interface, or API2. The base standard API is the Common Gateway Interface (CGI). Some Web server vendors offer proprietary APIs that extend the capability beyond what is possible with CGI. For example, Netscape and Microsoft both defined proprietary extensions in their products (NSAPI and ISAPI, respectively). Microsoft's Active Server Pages (ASP) technology is an alternative scripting technology for Microsoft Web servers.

A Web server, then, serves Web pages to users but also executes business logic in the form of scripts. The scripts can gather data from databases and applications on various systems. The result is returned to a single type of user, the Web browser user.

OVERVIEW OF AN APPLICATION SERVER

An application server is an extension of a Web server running scripts. Like Web servers, application servers execute business logic. The scripts that execute on a Web server can be written to integrate data from other systems, but there are no special tools provided with the Web server to do so.

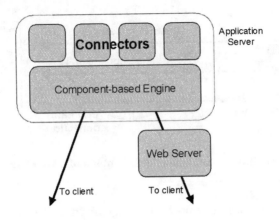

Exhibit 2.   Basic Architecture of an Application Server

In contrast, this integration of other systems is a key focus and integral part of the application server. It includes a set of "back-ends" that handle the job of communicating with, extracting data from, and carrying out transactions with a wide variety of legacy applications and databases. And while a Web server only accommodates a single type of user, an application server can deal with several types of end users, including Web browsers, traditional desktop applications, or new handheld devices.

Some application servers are sold bundled with a Web server. Others are sold independent of a Web server and will communicate with a variety of different Web servers running on the same physical server or across the network to a Web server on a different machine. However, most application servers can function without a Web server. An IT organization could implement an application server that only communicates with in-house PCs over an internal network without using Web servers or Web browsers at all. Nonetheless, the strength of the application server, compared to other types of middleware, is its ability to form a bridge between the existing legacy applications (including traditional client/server applications) and the new, Web-based applications driving what IBM calls "E-business." Exhibit 2 depicts the basic architecture of an application server.

At the core of the application server is the engine that ties all of the other pieces together and sets the stage for application integration. In many application servers, this engine is based on an object-oriented, component-based model like the Common Object Request Broker Architecture (CORBA), Enterprise Java Beans (EJB), or Microsoft's (Distributed) Component Object Model (COM/DCOM). Each of these architectures supports the development, deployment, execution, and management of new, distributed applications.

- CORBA: Defined over a period of years by the Object Management Group (OMG), a vendor consortium of approximately 800 members, CORBA is a component framework that is language-neutral and supported on a wide variety of platforms. At the heart of the CORBA framework is the Object Request Broker (ORB). Communication between objects is achieved with the Internet Inter-ORB Protocol (IIOP).
- Enterprise Java Beans: EJB is a Java-based component framework defined by Sun Microsystems. Once potentially at conflict with CORBA, the two frameworks have begun to complement one another. The EJB specification defined the Remote Method Invocation (RMI) as the method for components to communicate across Java Virtual Machine (JVM) and machine boundaries. RMI-over-IIOP is becoming common as the two frameworks begin to more explicitly support one another.
- COM/DCOM/COM+: The vendor community positions COM/DCOM as yet another Microsoft proprietary architecture meant to lock customers into Microsoft-specific solutions. Microsoft positions it as the most widely implemented component model because COM/DCOM has been an integral part of all Windows systems since the introduction of Windows 95. A number of UNIX system vendors have indicated they will support COM in the future.

The definition of standards and architecture for creating stand-alone components, or objects, allows application developers to combine previously developed components in new ways to create new applications. The developer is then able to focus on the business logic of the problem at hand rather than the details of the objects. With the combination of object technologies and the new visual development tools, new applications are more easily built and more stable than the monolithic, built-from-the-ground-up applications of the past. It is because of this flexibility that most application servers are based on a core component-based engine.

Application servers offer "back-ends" that provide an interface into data and applications on other systems. These back ends are often called connectors, bridges, or integration modules by the vendors. These connectors can interact with an application or system in a variety of different ways and at a variety of different levels. The following connectors are available on some or all of the commercially available application servers:

- Web server interfaces
- Message queuing interfaces for Microsoft's MSMQ and IBM's MQSeries
- Transactional and API interfaces to the IBM CICS or the Microsoft Transaction Server (MTS)
- Structured query database interfaces (e.g., SQL, ODBC, DRDA)

- Component connectors to Java applets and servlets, ActiveX components, CORBA objects, Enterprise Java Beans, and others
- Terminal interfaces to legacy applications on mainframes and midrange systems (e.g., 3270, 5250, VT220, HP, Bull)
- Application-specific interfaces to Enterprise Resource Planning (ERP) applications, such as those from SAP, PeopleSoft, and BAAN
- Custom connectors for custom applications

Downstream from the application server to the client, the protocol can vary, depending on the type of client and the base technology of the application (i.e., CORBA, EJB, COM). A common and basic method of exchanging information with end users will be via standard Web pages using HTTP, HTML, and possibly XML. Another option that involves some local processing on the part of the client is to download Java or ActiveX applets to the client. This thin-client approach is desirable when some local processing is desired but the size of the client program is sufficiently small to make downloading over the network feasible. When a more traditional fat-client approach is required, in which the end user's PC takes on a larger piece of the overall distributed application, a client-side program written in Java, C, C++, or any other language is installed. In this case, the client and the application server will utilize some communication protocol, typically over TCP/IP. In the case of CORBA, the standard IIOP is used. In Java environments, the standard scheme is Remote Method Invocation (RMI). Microsoft's COM/DCOM/COM+ specifies its own protocol and distributed processing scheme. Exhibit 3 illustrates an example of an enterprise that has application servers, multiple back-ends, and multiple client types.

A final but important piece of the application server offering is the support for visual development tools and application programming interfaces (APIs). Because application servers are focused on building new applications that integrate various other systems, the ease with which these new applications are developed is key to the viability and success of the application server. Some application servers are packaged with their own integrated development environment (IDE), complete with a software development kit (SDK), that is modeled after the popular visual development tools. Other vendors simply choose to support the dominant visual development tools, such as the IBM VisualAge, Microsoft's Visual InterDev, or Symantec's Visual Café.

The number of application servers available on the market grows each day. Vendors offering these products come from a wide variety of backgrounds. Some have a solid background in providing client/server integration middleware; others were early adopters of standards-based component technology like CORBA; and still others have evolved from the Web

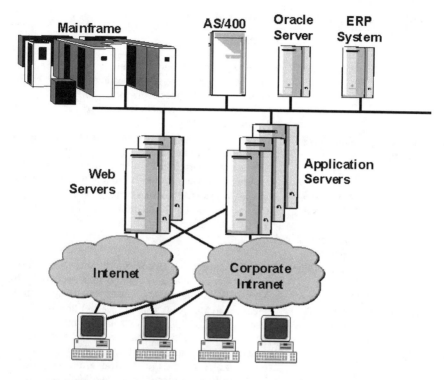

Exhibit 3.   Example of an Enterprise with Application Servers

server space. Exhibit 4 lists some of the application servers available, along with some of the key points of each of the products.

DEPLOYMENT IN THE ENTERPRISE

When deploying application servers in an enterprise environment, there are some very important and key capabilities of the application server that must be considered above and beyond its component architecture, protocols, and back ends. IT organizations that have made it through the first two steps of Web integration and Web presence and are now ready to embark on this third phase realize how quickly Web-based systems become mission critical. Once new services like online catalog ordering, home banking, Web-based trading, and others become available, new users rapidly adopt the services and become reliant on them. If the Web-based systems of a company fail, consumers are likely to go elsewhere and never return. Therefore, it is essential that the application servers be designed and implemented with ample security, scalability, load balancing, fault tolerance, and sophisticated management capabilities.

Exhibit 4. Application Servers Available

Vendor	Product	Key Points
BEA	WebLogic	Family of products offering different levels; based on Java but CORBA support comes in at the high end; built on common base of the BEA TUXEDO transaction monitor; includes support for Microsoft's COM
Bluestone Software	Sapphire/Web	Java-based solution; includes integrated development environment for application development; large number of integration modules for back-end access to systems; state management and load balancing
IBM	WebSphere Application Server Enterprise Edition	Includes Web server; focused on high-volume transactions and high reliability; core technologies are CORBA, EJB, XML; common IIOP infrastructure
Inprise	Application Server	Built upon Inprise's VisiBroker, a dominant ORB in the CORBA market space; integrated solution with Web server, IDE (Jbuilder), and management (AppCenter)
Microsoft	"Babylon" Integration Server	Successor to Microsoft's SNA Server; built around Microsoft's COM/DCOM/COM+ model; integration of UNIX, NetWare, and IBM mainframe and midrange systems; COMTI integrates transaction systems; includes direct access to mainframe/midrange data, DRDA for IBM database access, and MQSeries bridge
Mercator (formerly Novera and then TSI Intl Software)	Novera Integrator (works with Novera Manager)	Integrator includes the Novera Integration Server and the Novera Component Designer allowing the creation of objects that reside in mainframes, relational databases, and applications. Integration Server runs in a Java Virtual Machine. Communication to objects and other servers is based, in part, on the CORBA IIOP

SECURITY

Security is even more critical in an application server environment than in a stand-alone Web server environment. This is because an integral part of the application server is the integration of existing data and applications. Often, these data and applications reside on mission-critical systems like IBM mainframes and midrange systems and high-end UNIX platforms. These are the systems that house the most important and sensitive information in an enterprise, including customer records, historical sales information, and other material that would be valuable to the competition or to the malicious hacker.

An overall security plan and architecture must accomplish three things. First, it must ensure that the data flowing in the network and on the wire is not legible to prying eyes. Second, it must ensure that the identity of the user is verified. Third, it must ensure that a particular user can only access the resources for which the user is authorized.

A number of different technologies and products can be leveraged to accomplish these three goals. For example, Secure Sockets Layer (SSL) is a popular security protocol that accomplishes the first two goals by using encryption on the wire and digital certificates for user authentication. Secure HTTP (HTTPS) is also used to protect Web transactions.

Application-specific user ID/password schemes as well as centralized servers, such as those based on the Lightweight Directory Access Protocol (LDAP) standard, provide user authorization. Application servers must also take into account the notion of session persistence as a facet of security. There is a fundamental mismatch between the Web paradigm of user-to-server interaction when compared to client/server or traditional hierarchical applications. In the Web paradigm, each individual page interaction or request is a stand-alone transaction. The Web server does not maintain state information for each user. Session-state information must be maintained by an application server to prevent the possibility of one user gaining access to an existing, active session. This is a security issue because, without session persistence, user authentication and user authorization security schemes are compromised.

SCALABILITY, LOAD BALANCING, AND FAULT TOLERANCE

Scalability refers to the ability of a system to grow seamlessly to support an increasing number of users. Systems that are scalable are able to add users in such a way that the consumption of resources is linear. The system should not hit a bottleneck point or barrier beyond which the addition of another user dramatically impacts session resources or overall response time. Systems that are scalable can grow to accommodate a particular maximum number of concurrent users in such a way that the response time is roughly equivalent for all users. For many organizations, the design point for scalability will be thousands — or even tens of thousands — of concurrent users.

This level of scalability is usually only achieved by implementing multiple, load-balancing servers. In this design, there are multiple application servers, each supporting the same services and presenting a portion of the total pool of available servers. End users, either fat-client PCs or thin-client Web-based users, should all have a common view to the pool of application servers. That is, one should not have to configure each device or session to use a specific server in the pool. The load-balancing front end (which may be a separate unit or integrated into the application server) should load-balance sessions across all available servers in an intelligent manner based on system capacity, current load, and other metrics.

High availability is provided by the load-balancing front end through its awareness of the availability of the application servers. If a server fails, it obviously should be removed from the pool of servers to which new sessions are allocated. Existing sessions that are active at the time of the failure of an application server will usually be disrupted, although some systems, like the IBM mainframes with Parallel Sysplex, can avoid even session disruption.

MANAGEMENT

Because an application server environment encompasses a variety of different types of users, back ends, and distributed processing technologies, it can be a very complex environment to manage. Most application server vendors provide tools that are supported using one or more of the common management platforms, including IBM TME 10/NetView, CA UniCenter TNG, and HP OpenView.

The management tool should include the ability to manage the pool of application servers as a logical entity. The operator should be able to view and control all of the resources, objects, and sessions from an application viewpoint. A visual display of all elements with current status should be an integral capability. The management tool should be able to assist with the deployment and tracking of new applets and applications. The ability to specify actions based on certain events can help to automate some of the routine management functions. Additional information for capacity planning and modeling is helpful.

CONCLUSION

Application servers allow organizations to evolve to the third phase of Web presence, in which the focus is on providing realtime transaction-based services to both internal and external users. The integration of the wealth of existing data processing systems, applications, and data is essential to the ability to deliver new transactional services quickly and efficiently. Application servers unify the existing systems with the Web-based infrastructure, allowing IT organizations to leverage their vast investment in systems and applications to deliver new services to their employees, business partners, and the public.

Notes

1. Web Server Technology: The Advanced Guide for the World Wide Web Information Providers, Nancy J. Yeager and Robert E. McGrath, Morgan Kaufmann Publishers, Inc., pp. 37–41.
2. Ibid., pp. 58–59.

Section IV
Component-Based Development

Chapter 15
The Economics of Component-Based Development

Richard T. Dué

Component-based development can have major, and possibly unforeseen, positive economic effects on the software development process. Components are standardized building blocks that can be used to assemble, rather that develop, information systems. Software components are encapsulated sets of standardized data and standardized methods of processing data that together provide standardized information services. Software components fall into three categories: presentation, application, and design.

- Presentation components are used by presentation and interface specialists to assemble user or system interfaces for information systems.

- Application components can be thought of as information models of the real world objects in the information system. These objects include the persons, documents, products, resources, and transactions, that are found in the domain of the information system. These application components are used by application specialists who are responsible for providing the information requirements of the application as specified in the requirements documentation.

- Design components are used by systems design specialists to provide resources to meet all of the design constraints of an information system. These design constraints include security, response time, availability, legacy system salvage and reuse, requirements of specific operating systems and computer languages, and the persistent storage or database requirements of the system.

The reuse of these software components and the productivity advantages of the specialization of labor by organizing development teams to

0-8493-1149-7/02/$0.00+$1.50
© 2002 by CRC Press LLC

specialize in presentation, application, or design components, promises economic benefits that have caught the attention of software vendors, consultants, and users of information systems.

Components, however, can be much more that just reusable modules of code. The real power of the component-based approach comes with the understanding that there can also be reusable requirements documentation components; training components; and testing, audit, and quality assurance components.

REUSABLE REQUIREMENTS COMPONENTS

User-centered documentation techniques (e.g., Ivar Jacobson's Use Case or Ian Graham's Task Case) describe the services, responsibilities, and behaviors of a system from the point of view of a typical user of the system. Traditionally, system requirements have been described in terms of features and services from the point of view of the system. In practice, this traditional approach requires redundant and time-consuming activities of documenting the requirements, writing user training manuals, developing testing scenarios, and instituting change management and project management reporting procedures. Traditionally, systems development personnel have spent significant amounts of time trying to analyze and understand the user's current operations in the hope that this will somehow lead to the design of a new system. Users already understand their current operations. What users need is a way to describe their new information system requirements to systems personnel who are experts in implementation. User-centered techniques can be used to produce a single document in the first few hours or days of a project that records the user's system requirements, the user's training manual, the user's test acceptance criteria, the user's change request form, and the user's key vehicle for project management planning and progress reporting (see Exhibit 1). Proper application of user-centered techniques can speed up system development and allows the users of the information system to be 100 percent involved in the specification, development, testing, and maintenance of their own systems. Errors in specification can be caught early in the systems development process when they are easy and relatively inexpensive to correct. Implementation begins immediately, starting with the most significant and most technically challenging of the user-centered. If, in trying to implement these first critical parts of the system, it is indicated that the rest of the system cannot be developed in an economical, efficient, and effective manner, the project can be modified or abandoned before additional resources are wasted.

Each team specializes in presentation, application, or design components. The application team uses application components that are independent of a particular presentation. This means the application components

Exhibit 1. Example of User-Centered Documentation and Team Responsibilities

User Responsibilities	Interface Team Responsibilities	Application Component Team Responsibilities	Design/Implementation Team Responsibilities
User-centered requirements	Environmental filter/interface	Functional requirements	Nonfunctional requirements
Customer Wants to initiate a bankcard transaction	ATM machine Screen displays ATM is ready Customer inserts ATM card in card slot	1. Stimulus User initiates session with the ATM system	Maximum 5-second response time Communication security Session management
	Screen displays message "Enter PIN"	2. Response System requests identification from the user	Maximum 15-second response time

can be reused in conjunction with many different user interfaces. The design team works with components that are independent of any particular application or user interface. This means that the design components can be used in conjunction with many different applications and user interfaces. The details of the application and design implementations are kept hidden from the user. However, the stimulus-response dialogue of the user-centered documentation also becomes the user's training manual and test acceptance criteria. For example, if a user wishes to initiate a bankcard transaction, he or she must first insert the bankcard into an ATM. To test the delivered system, the user must insert a bankcard and observe whether the "Enter PIN" message appears.

SOFTWARE COMPONENTS ARE NOT SUFFICIENT

Reuse of code is not necessarily an appropriate objective. Code will still need to be continually updated and enhanced, even while systems are in operation, as more efficient algorithms and programming languages become available. Instead, effective reuse requires identifying the information services required by the organization's information systems users in terms of previously proven implementations. Traditional approaches to systems development have resulted in the redundant production of billions of lines of code, each line of which has its own unique opportunities for errors. At a higher level of abstraction, however, these billions of lines of application code apparently perform as few as 10 or 20 different basic business information processing functions. Instead of continually embarking on "green field" projects, we need to start the development of new systems with an essential core library of prewritten, tested, proven generic user-centered requirements documents. Systems specification in this case becomes a process of making changes or adding enhancements to these generic user-centered requirements documents. Ideally, these generic user-centered requirements documents will already have been implemented with generic designs and code that in turn will just need to be modified and enhanced instead of developed to produce the new system. If we can identify and reuse the essential requirements of a system, we can reuse the previous implementation of these requirements to speed up the development process, cut costs, and improve quality.

Reuse of Interfaces Instead of Code

An interface is a description of the information services specified in each step of the user-centered requirements documentation. Instead of trying to analyze all of the complex relationships among all of the possible components of an information system, as is typically done in constructing a data-centric entity-relationship model or an object-oriented class diagram, developers using interfaces only specify the information required by the current step of the user-centered requirements. It is possible that one existing component or a collection of existing components will actually provide the services required by this step in the requirements. The allocation of required services to components is be made by examining the contract of the required interface with the contracts of the existing components. Contracts are formal descriptions of the preconditions to using the interface or component, the postconditions or results of using the component, the business rules or constraints that will be in effect during the actual processing of information by the component, and the responses of the component to error conditions. Systems are assembled by matching user-centered requirements contracts with component information services contracts. The results of designing to an interface instead of a particular component implementation are:

- The actual collection of components that provide the services to implement a particular interface may be written in different programming languages, may be running on different operating systems and hardware platforms, and may even be distributed across the Internet.
- The actual components that provide the services to implement a particular interface may be modified, enhanced, or replaced while the system is in operation. As long as the new component has the same contracted interface as the one that it replaces, the substitution will be transparent.

Generic systems can be designed to transform and substitute components to accommodate specialized run-time requirements. For example, systems can be designed to be independent of any particular hardware or software environment. At run-time, when the system is actually being used, the collection of components that provide information services could be dynamically substituted to produce a system that runs on a specific hardware or software platform. In effect, a new system can be assembled during execution of the system to accommodate the user's current information system requirements.

ELIMINATION OF STEPS IN THE TRADITIONAL DEVELOPMENT PROCESS

Component-based development can result, if properly managed, in the elimination of the last insignificant modification of several major steps in the traditional, "waterfall" systems development process.

1. *Analysis.* There is no need to "pull apart" the existing system once we have moved to user-centered documentation (the Use Case or Task Case). Instead, user-centered documentation begins with the specification of how the system the user wants will behave. This behavior specification simultaneously and automatically becomes the

user training manual and the test acceptance criteria. Training the end users can begin the second day of the project! It is much cheaper to change a user case than to rewrite, retest, and redocument code. The relative cost of finding and fixing errors during the initial requirements specification phase is potentially 100 to 1,000 times cheaper than finding and fixing errors during implementation and deployment of the system.

2. *Design.* Component-based development should follow proven patterns that are already tested and documented. Therefore, designs are reused instead of being independently developed. Patterns are descriptions and examples of proven best practices in the development of flexible, robust, and effective information systems. Patterns offer us alternative ways of assembling previously developed and proven components into new information systems. Patterns are a very powerful way to transfer knowledge. The participants in the system development process do not have to be trained in or even be aware of the underlying theory that is the basis for a particular pattern's success. Instead, the participants, no matter at what level of experience, training, or background, only have to be able to recognize the pattern and understand the trade-offs involved in employing the pattern. The quality of a system is audited by judging its design with respect to proven design patterns.

3. *Coding.* Component-based systems are assembled instead of custom coded. This assembly follows proven design patterns. The whole purpose of the component-based development approach is to work at higher levels of abstraction than code. Just as developers in the past moved to higher levels of abstraction from machine language to assembly languages, to compiled languages, and 4GLs, it is now time to continue this migration to the reuse of components.

4. *Testing.* Although it is still controversial, component-based development may make it possible to eliminate integration testing. Since each component is encapsulated and protected with interface contracts, no component can unexpectedly change or produce unexpected results in another. In fact, one-time integration testing is actually made impossible by component-based development, because the user can never be sure which components will actually be used at implementation. The design is about interfaces, not run-time implementations behind the interface.

COMPONENT-BASED DEVELOPMENT HEURISTICS

The philosophy underlying the component-based development approach is that maximum systems development productivity comes from small teams working within the constraints of relatively small time boxes, developing and reusing very specific work products. The component-based development approach should be coupled with some very specific project management guidelines and heuristics that are used to plan and control the activities of these small development teams. Some examples of these combined tasks and heuristics include:

- The entire project will be developed within a three-month time box.
- The Problem Statement (the business reason for undertaking the project, and the standard for the acceptance of all work products) will contain a maximum of three or four paragraphs.
- The Use Case Diagram will be developed in a one-hour time box.
- There will be a maximum of only 50 Use Cases per project. If the project has more than 50 Use Cases, it must be decomposed into two or more projects.
- Use Cases will always be written in a series of stimulus-response sentences. Each of these sentences will be written using a standard grammar of subject, verb, direct object, preposition, and indirect object.
- Each Use Case will fit on one page.

Armed with the component-based development approach and a complete set of project heuristics, each developer, or team of two or three developers, becomes responsible for the development, assembly, enhancement, or acquisition of a relatively small collection of work products and components. In addition, each developer, or development team, becomes responsible for providing the optimistic, typical, and pessimistic estimates associated with each task in the methodology. If the variances for the optimistic or pessimistic estimates are significantly greater than the development team's estimates for previous projects, the team must justify these variances.

AN UNEXPECTED BENEFIT

The unexpected benefit of this method is that the use of standard components within a standard process results in the development of standard project estimates, schedules, and costs. The only real variances in component-based development projects are the variances in aptitudes skills and experience of the actual members of the development team. We can expect that the same team will have the same typical estimates for each task of every project this team works on. The same team may change their optimistic and pessimistic estimates provided that they justify the reasons for the expected variance.

The consequences of reusable estimates and schedules are:

- Management can realistically plan and control component-based development projects. There are now realistic standards that they can manage, negotiate, and compare with other projects, teams, and organizations.

- Quality Assurance and EDP Audit personnel can measure the effectiveness, economy, and efficiency of a particular project against historical standards for each task and each work product.
- Project managers can concentrate on risk minimization and contingency planning for those tasks on the critical path that have especially large variances in their pessimistic estimates from the historical standards.

I believe that generic user-centered requirements documentation, components, patterns, and contracted interfaces must become a part of the information technology infrastructure of our organizations and even our global economy in the new millennium. These approaches must be developed and taught in our schools, taken out and proved in the real world, and then returned to our schools as the teaching medium for the next generation of systems users and developers. Today's redundant training and systems development practices must be abandoned. Instead, training and development must be based on the reuse of proven practices and proven components assembled into proven patterns. The potential positive economic impact of the increased productivity and quality of information systems is simply too great to be ignored.

Chapter 16
Domain Engineering of Components

Dr. Carma McClure

Components lie at the very heart of the future vision of computing. Corporations expect that they soon will be running their businesses using Web-enabled, enterprise business applications composed of predefined, replaceable components that are distributed over networks. Although part of the application may run on a client, part on the middle tier, and another part on a back-end database server, its comprising components, written in different languages and supplied from multiple sources, will be able to work together to perform the application's services.

Such component-based applications offer the advantages of being both easily customized to meet current business needs and easily modified to meet changing business needs in the future. Also, they leverage a corporation's investment in its legacy systems by incorporating valuable existing functionality that has been wrapped into reusable components. These applications are typically composed of an interacting mixture of predeveloped components that preserve core functionality of the business, and new components that take advantage of the newest technologies, such as the Internet.

COMPONENT DEFINITION

A *component* can be thought of as an independent module that provides information about what it does and how to use it through a public interface, while hiding its inner workings. The interface identifies the component, as well as its behaviors and interaction mechanisms. Examples of components include small-grained, desktop-bound visual components (e.g., GUI widgets), as well as large-grained components that capture a complete business function (e.g., a shipping component that includes order entry and shipment functionality).

The idea of components is not new. Rather, earlier software engineering concepts are fundamental to the component concept, such as program

0-8493-1149-7/02/$0.00+$1.50
© 2002 by CRC Press LLC

modularization, structured programming, and information hiding, which were introduced in the 1960s by Edgar Dijkstra, David Parnas, and others.

COMPONENT-BASED DEVELOPMENT

The software development approach used to build a component-based application is called *component-based development* (CBD). This reuse-based, architecture-centric form of software development uses an assembly approach, whereby software products are constructed by assembling components designed to fit into a predefined architecture.

Although CBD may appear to be a simple, obvious approach to software development, it is complicated by its need for standards. To work in practice, CBD demands standardization of the components themselves, as well as the software life cycles by which they are developed, and in which they are used to develop component-based applications. Standards are the only known way to ensure the quality of the components and of the life cycle processes. In particular, process standards that capture proven software practices are considered the best means available to ensure quality.

Recently, the IEEE Computer Society published a process standard applicable to CBD. The *IEEE Std. 1517 — Standard for Information Technology — Software Life Cycle Processes — Reuse Processes* defines the elements of reuse-based software life cycle processes that can be used to define an organization's CBD approach.[1] This standard defines the elements of a software life cycle for developing and maintaining component-based applications, as well as a separate life cycle for identifying, selecting, developing, and maintaining components.

IEEE STANDARD 1517 — REUSE PROCESSES

As the software life cycle process standard for CBD, IEEE Std. 1517 provides the requirements specification for practicing reuse and CBD on an enterprisewide basis. It not only identifies the processes involved in practicing software reuse, but describes at a high level how the processes operate and interact during the software life cycle. As shown in Exhibit 1, this standard organizes the software life cycle processes into a framework that consists of four process categories: primary, supporting, cross-project, and organizational.

The cross-project category is a new category of life cycle process introduced by this standard to define the special life cycle requirements for selecting or building appropriate, high-quality components. As software, components are similar in many ways to software applications. However, a component is different in that it is, by its very nature, a part whose primary function is its use as a building block in multiple software applications. This multi-use characteristic of components places new requirements on

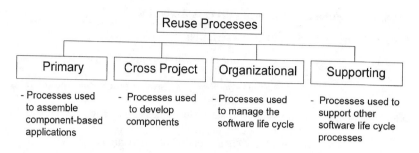

Exhibit 1. Reuse Process Framework

the software life cycle in activities such as planning, analysis, design, and testing. To meet these requirements, the IEEE Std. 1517 defines a software life cycle relevant to components.

As defined in the standard, domain engineering describes the cross-project software life cycle for components. This chapter describes the elements of domain engineering as specified by the standard.

DOMAIN ENGINEERING

Domain engineering is the process of supplying components for use in a particular domain. As the life cycle for components, it is concerned with the analysis, design, selection, development, and maintenance of components belonging to a particular domain. The notion of domain narrows CBD down to a size that is conceptually easier to understand, technically easier to implement, and organizationally easier to manage.

The IEEE Std. 1517 defines a domain as "a problem space," which typically represents one organizational segment that has potential for CBD. The organization determines how to segment itself for CBD, be it by product lines, by business functions, or by technology platforms. According to the standard, a domain should be defined broadly enough to encompass components that may be applied to multiple software applications over a period of time. Since organizations generally practice CBD in multiple domains, the domain engineering process will usually be applied multiple times within an organization.

Supplying Components

Since these components are intended for use by many software projects, the domain engineering process generally takes place higher than the project level. To meet multiple project requirements, components must possess common properties that can be shared and reused by the component-based applications produced. It is because the domain engineering

Exhibit 2. Domain Engineering Process Activities

Activity Name	Activity Description
Process implementation	• Create, document, and execute domain engineering plan • Select representation forms for the domain models and domain architectures
Domain analysis	• Define domain boundaries and relationships with other domains • Identify needs of domain software developers • Build the domain models • Construct the domain vocabulary
Domain design	• Create the domain architectures • Develop component specifications
Asset provision	• Develop the domain components
Asset maintenance	• Maintain the domain components

process exists beyond the boundaries and duration of one project that IEEE Std. 1517 categorizes domain engineering as a cross-project life cycle process.

In the IEEE Std. 1517, domain engineering is defined as follows:

> A reuse-based approach to defining the scope (i.e., domain definition), specifying the structure (i.e., domain architecture), and building components (e.g., requirements, designs, software code, documentation) for a class of systems, subsystems, or applications. Domain engineering may include the following activities: domain definition, domain analysis, developing the domain architecture, and domain implementation.

The standard names the **domain engineer** as the party responsible for performing domain engineering activities, which may be an individual or a group of individuals. In most organizations, a project team will perform the domain engineering function. It will be assembled at the beginning of the project and remain throughout the domain engineering life cycle.

The IEEE Std. 1517 defines the domain engineering process as the set of activities listed in Exhibit 2.

1. Process Implementation

The purpose of the process implementation activity is to formally prepare for domain engineering by creating a plan. This defines the format to be used in representing domain engineering outputs, as well as the technical and management procedures that will take place.

Creating a Domain Engineering Plan. Because the plan should treat domain engineering as a project to be properly managed, it should address such project constraints as budget, schedule, and resources. It should include

Exhibit 3.   Domain Engineering Team Responsibilities

Team Member	Responsibilities
Systems/business analyst	Expert in analysis modeling and data synthesis
Data administrator	Responsible for corporate data dictionary and naming standards
Information architect	Knowledgeable about the information/enterprise architecture for the enterprise or business unit to which this domain belongs
Domain expert	Expert-level knowledge and understanding of the domain
End users and software developers	Knowledgeable about their current and future system needs
Reuse facilitator	Experienced in performing domain analysis

both technical and nontechnical resources needed to perform domain engineering. On the technical side, it should identify tools, methods, and standards. On the nontechnical side, it must define activities, assignments, and responsibilities.

A domain engineering team will have responsibility for the project. The team members should provide the roles and skills listed in Exhibit 3. Because domain experts are a vital source of information about the domain, they are a critical part of the team. IEEE Std. 1517 defines a domain expert as "an individual who is intimately familiar with the domain and can provide detailed information to the domain engineers." Domain experts can include knowledgeable end users and software professionals. The latter should be software system developers and maintainers who are experienced with software products that are similar to those being built for this domain. They should also know which properties are important for future software applications planned for the domain.

The domain engineering plan should also identify the tools to be used in supporting the domain engineering effort. Different types of tools will support analysis, design, and implementation activities. Some tools that are useful for performing domain engineering support the building and analysis of strategic planning models and information architectures, such as entity relationship, data flow, object modeling diagramming tools, and dictionary tools. Others include data synthesis tools, data and process reverse engineering tools, program code analyzers, flow graphing tools, complexity metrics tools, and process logic and data rationalization restructuring tools.

The specific tools that are appropriate for a particular project depend on the types of models and code to be analyzed, and the representation forms chosen for the domain models and architectures. In addition, repositories, browsers, cataloging tools, and configuration management tools are needed to store and manage the domain model, the domain architectures, and other types of domain components.

Defining the Domain Model and Domain Architecture Formats. The next major task in the process implementation activity of a domain engineering project is to define representation forms for the domain models and architectures. In the IEEE Std. 1517, the definitions for a domain model and domain architecture are as follows:

> Domain model: a product of domain analysis that provides a representation of the requirements of the domain. The domain model identifies and describes the structure of data, flow of information, functions, constraints, and controls within the domain that are included in software systems in the domain. The domain model describes the commonalities and variabilities among requirements for software systems in the domain.

> Domain architecture: a generic, organized structure or design for software systems in a domain. The domain architecture contains the designs that are intended to satisfy requirements specified in the domain model. The domain architecture documents design, whereas the domain model documents requirements. A domain architecture: 1) can be adapted to create designs for software systems within a domain, and 2) provides a framework for configuring components with individual software systems.

Thus, the domain model is a generic analysis model, while the domain architecture is a high-level design model. Together, they provide an excellent starting point and guide for building components and component-based applications for the domain.

The representation forms used for the domain models and architectures affect the choice of methods for supplying components, as well as the development tools to be used for CBD projects. Therefore, the representation forms selected should fit the available domain analysis and design approaches and tools. For example, the Features-Oriented Domain Analysis (FODA) approach uses one set of models to represent the domain model, including the entity relationship model, data flow diagram, and state transition diagram and structure diagram. Another set of models represents the domain architecture,[2] including the process interaction model and module structure chart.

In addition, the representation forms should also fit the CBD methodologies and corresponding analysis and design models that will be used to develop component-based applications within this domain. When an organization uses the same kinds of representation forms in both places, there is a reduced learning curve, less need to convert from one representation form to another, and less need to acquire different tools to support domain engineering and CBD.

Organizations should consider a common modeling language such as the Unified Modeling Language (UML) from the Object Management Group for both the model and the architecture representation forms. The UML provides a common notation and semantics to model frameworks, distributed systems, and component-based applications, and to facilitate model interchange across teams and tools.

2. Domain Analysis Activity

Like the traditional software system life cycle, the domain engineering life cycle covers analysis, design, implementation, and maintenance activities. In this case, however, the cycle is applied to domain models, domain architectures, and other types of software parts that are used to assemble component-based systems.

Domain analysis is the analysis phase in the component life cycle. The IEEE Std. 1517 defines domain analysis as follows:

> (A) The analysis of systems within a domain to discover commonalities and differences among them. (B) The process by which information used in developing software systems is identified, captured, and organized so that it can be reused to create new systems, within a domain. (C) The result of the process in (A) and (B).

Domain analysis analyzes, abstracts, and models the characteristics of existing and envisioned component-based applications within a domain to determine what they have in common (their commonality) and how they differ (their diversity). This information is captured in a set of domain models during domain analysis.

The purposes of the domain models are to:

1. Aid in the understanding of the domain's essential common elements and the relationships that exist between these elements
2. Define a domain vocabulary to create a common understanding of the domain
3. Capture the essential common and differentiating features, capabilities, concepts, and functions in the domain.

Defining Domain Boundaries. The IEEE Std. 1517 requires that the domain analysis activity define the boundaries of the domain in which the domain engineering process is being performed, in terms of which functions, features, properties, and capabilities are included in and excluded from the domain. Relationships should also be established, such as when one domain is a subset of another. This "domain definition" is needed to create and, if necessary, redefine the domain models.

The domain boundaries should be iteratively refined by comparison with other domains. Domain boundaries can also be determined from market analysis information, customer requirements, software developers, and domain experts, as well as the enterprise architectures.

A context model, data flow model, or object model can be used to show the boundaries of a domain. A data flow model or structure chart can be used to show relationships between domains. The models showing the domain boundaries should be the same representation forms selected for the domain models and architectures.

Identifying Developers' Needs. The IEEE Std. 1517 also requires that an organization identify the needs of the software developers who assemble the component-based applications, since they will likely be the primary users of the domain engineering outputs. Due to their experience, these developers can best identify the most useful components in performing development. Not only will components that they used in developing previous applications be needed in future versions and implementations of these applications, but these components can be used in new applications with similar features or capabilities. In addition, the components that developers find useful in building current and future component-based applications for the domain can help to define or refine the domain boundaries.

Therefore, the organization should interview the developers of component-based applications for the domain to identify the components that they believe would be most useful in their software projects. Also, the organization should evaluate the reuse experience and expertise of the domain software developers to determine if they have the skills for using components in their work. Based on this information, the organization may need to adjust the domain boundaries to ensure that a particular domain engineering project will identify components that the domain software developers will use in their work.

Building Domain Models. The primary task of domain analysis is building the domain models. Domain analysis is typically performed iteratively, as a combined top-down/bottom-up analysis activity. During the former, the team studies existing systems and models to identify common structures, grouping them for further study. The team identifies both the common and variable aspects of each group in order to create a generic structure that represents the group's properties.

During bottom-up domain analysis, the team identifies common components in the systems and models studied. It also identifies relationships between common components, such as generalization ("is a") and aggregation ("consists of"). The team then maps common components to the generic structure.

Constructing the Domain Vocabulary. The domain vocabulary, constructed during domain analysis, is the foundation for recognizing commonalities between domain components. This vocabulary enables domain engineers and software developers to speak the same language, so they can more easily recognize and understand which components will be the common building blocks in constructing the domain's component-based applications.

The domain vocabulary can be created through discussion with the domain experts. It can also use concepts, keywords, nouns, and verbs contained in the existing software system documentation, analysis, and design models; and in the enterprise and business models that pertain to this domain. The domain vocabulary should be refined during the iterative process in which the domain models are created.

3. Domain Design Activity

The purpose of domain design is to create the domain architecture and the design specifications for domain components.

Building Domain Architectures. The domain architecture offers a common, generalized framework for assembling component-based applications from components. It provides:

1. The general structure for assembling components into a component-based application
2. The impetus to use existing components
3. A guide to selecting or creating new components
4. An aid in understanding the domain's essential common components and the relationships that exist between components

Because domain components are designed to fit with the domain architecture, the latter acts as the "glue" to integrate components into a working application. However, the organization may need to develop more than one domain architecture for the domain if different target environments are required for its component-based applications. Thus, distributed versus host-based applications require different architectures.

To design the domain architecture, the organization should use the knowledge of architecture experts and software developers with experience in building this kind of software architecture. In addition, the domain model should be considered an important input in domain design. The generic structures of the design models are the basis for creating the

Exhibit 4. Ways to Generalize a Domain Architecture

1. Isolate implementation dependencies so they can be easily recognized, and so that implementation (environment) details can be changed to suit the requirements of a particular software application, or to satisfy future environment and technology requirements.
2. Layer the architecture to separate components (e.g., processes and services) that are application specific, operation-system specific, and hardware-platform specific into "layers." In this way, it will be easy to adapt the architecture to the specific requirements of a particular software application in the domain.[2]
3. At each layer, look for common components to use as the basis for specifying components that fit into the architecture. For example, processes and services supporting communications, the user interface, windows management, information management, transaction management, and batch process control should be defined as architecture components. Many of these components are environment dependent and are examples of "horizontal reuse," because they can be used across domains that share the same system environment requirements.

domain architecture. They will either become the domain architecture or a subsystem within the domain architecture.

A domain architecture must be generalized, standardized, and documented so it can be used in building multiple software products. Ways to generalize the domain architecture are listed in Exhibit 4.

Ways for standardizing the domain architecture are listed in Exhibit 5. The organization should validate the usability of the domain architecture, determining if it could have been used as a starter design for this product. It should compare the domain architecture with the design of at least one existing software application that belongs to this domain but was not studied during the domain engineering analysis activity. In addition, a domain expert who is not a member of the domain engineering team should review the domain architecture.

Developing Component Design Specifications. According to the IEEE Std. 1517, another important domain design task is to create design specifications for the domain components. Since a subset of all possible components for use by CBD projects is generally sufficient, organizations would be wise to use a *selective reuse strategy* to focus on the most appropriate domain components. Selective reuse singles out for development or acquisition those components that have the highest reuse potential in the domain, because they:

1. Can be used the most frequently in the domain CBD projects
2. Provide the greatest benefits to the organization (e.g., cost savings, time savings, reducing the risk for CBD project failure, enforcing standards)

Exhibit 5. Ways to Standardize a Domain Architecture

- Standardize the interfaces between components (e.g., standard interface between the application system and the database management system; standard protocol between the application system and the communications software)[2]
- Focus on subsystems (e.g., the communications subsystem) and their interactions
- Use a standardized modeling language such as UML

Exhibit 6. Ways to Identify Highly Reusable Components

1. The potential number of times the component can be used in building software products in the domain
2. The strategic importance of each component-based application in which the component can be used
3. The similarities and differences expected in these component-based applications
4. The impact of these differences on the reuse potential of the component and the reuse benefits of the component
5. The ability to create the component in a way to accommodate expected differences and capture expected similarities over its reuses
6. The ease of certifying the reusability and overall quality of the component
7. The cost to create/reengineer/acquire the component
8. The life expectancy of the component compared against the time to produce/supply the component; and the cost to manage and maintain the component over its lifetime
9. The number of times the component must be used to recover its lifetime cost
10. The business benefits that use of the component may provide (e.g., faster time to market)
11. The ease of fitting the component into the domain architecture

3. Can be used to assemble component-based applications that are of the greatest strategic importance to the organization
4. Have been requested by software developers and maintainers

For ideas on which particular component design specifications to create, organizations should study commonalities (e.g., common features or services) in the domain's software applications that are currently being built or reengineered. They also should ask software developers for their suggestions and contributions, and review components that vendors are currently offering in the marketplace.

Exhibit 6 lists several ways to identify which components have the highest reuse potential in CBD projects.

Exhibit 7 shows the design specification information that should be created when a component is to be used in CBD projects. The design specification is then used to build the component or to help in selecting an existing component.

Exhibit 7. Component Design Specification Information

1. The function performed by the component
2. What the component expects from its client components
3. What the component produces for its client components
4. Performance characteristics of the component
5. The extent of commonality and variability required by the component
6. Assumptions about the target environments of the component
7. Limitations on the use of the component

---

4. Component Acquisition and Development Activity

Components that have been selected as potential CBD building blocks are acquired or developed in this part of the domain engineering process. The general requirements and standard software engineering practices followed when acquiring or developing software also apply to components.

Building Components. Exhibit 8 shows the activities in the IEEE Std. 1517 development process, while Exhibit 9 shows the activities in the standard's acquisition process. An organization should use these activities as a requirements specification to create or select an appropriate CBD approach that can aid in the development of high-quality component-based applications.

Likewise, when creating a component, the organization should follow the IEEE Std. 1517 development process; and, when acquiring a component, it should follow the standard's acquisition process. However, because it may be overkill to apply all of the standard's process activities when creating or acquiring a component, the organization should tailor the processes by eliminating some of the activities. In this way, it can better meet the scope, magnitude, complexity, and criticality of a component-based project, as opposed to an ordinary software application.

Building and Acquiring Reusable Components. Because of its multiple-use capability, a component should be viewed as a special kind of software that has properties over and above those normally expected in a software product such as an application system. For example, since any software product is expected to be of high quality, emphasizing that each component is thoroughly specified, documented, efficient, and tested will help ensure the component's general quality. However, to be reusable, a component must exhibit additional characteristics, such as portability, interoperability, understandability, and maintainability.

If the component is to be developed, then the domain engineer should build into it general quality and reusability characteristics. If the component is to be acquired, then the domain engineer should require general quality and reusability selection criteria.

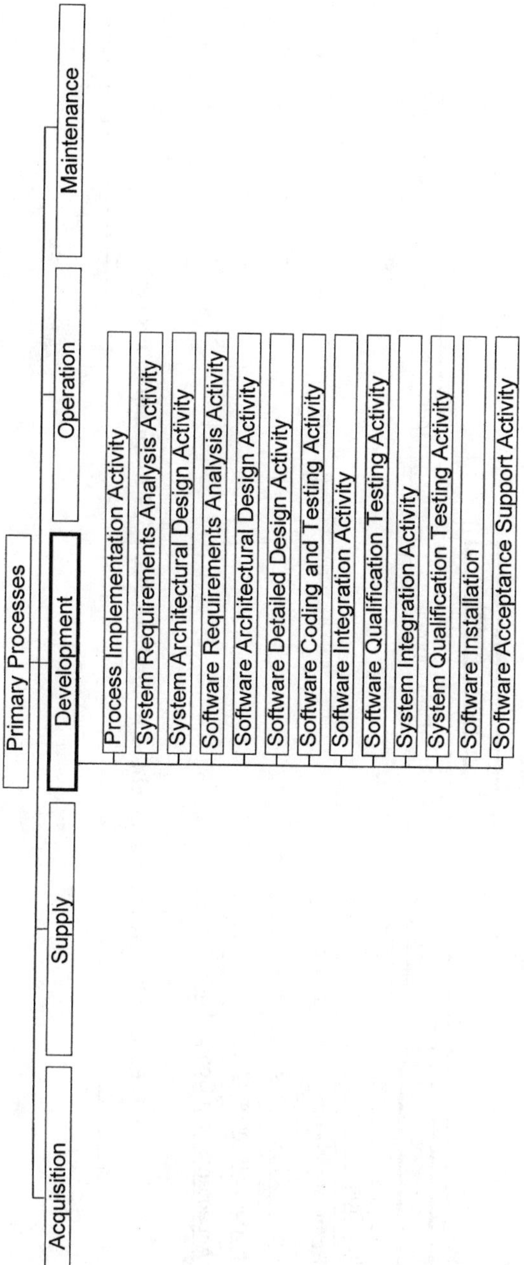

Exhibit 8. Activities Specified in the IEEE Std. 1517 Development Process

Primary Processes

Acquisition
Supply
Development
Operation
Maintenance

Process Implementation Activity
System Requirements Analysis Activity
System Architectural Design Activity
Software Requirements Analysis Activity
Software Architectural Design Activity
Software Detailed Design Activity
Software Coding and Testing Activity
Software Integration Activity
Software Qualification Testing Activity
System Integration Activity
System Qualification Testing Activity
Software Installation
Software Acceptance Support Activity

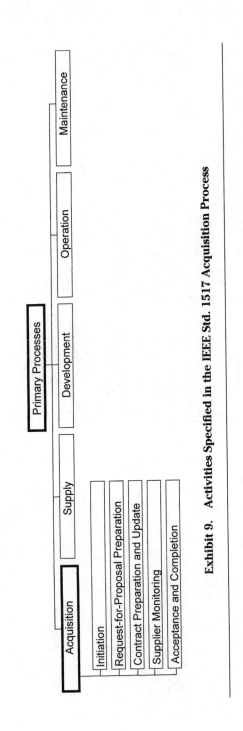

Exhibit 9. Activities Specified in the IEEE Std. 1517 Acquisition Process

The IEEE Std. 1517 defines reusability as follows:

> The degree to which a component can be used in more than one software system, or in building other components. In a reuse library, those characteristics of a component that make it easy to use in different contexts, software systems, or in building components.

Generalizing a Component. Two important characteristics that enable reusability are generalization and standardization. When developing a component, the domain engineer should generalize the component to enable its use in multiple software products. A generalized component captures the common characteristics of the domain, but also allows for expected diversity.

Standardizing a Component. Standardization makes CBD easier. Opportunities for reuse are created by standardizing such software features as menus, GUIs, help functions, and error handling. When components implement features in accordance with the standards, they can be used to enforce the standards. In addition, if a component complies with the organization's documentation, interface design, and testing standards, its reusability is increased because of its better quality and general usefulness.

Exhibit 10 provides some general reusability criteria to follow when selecting a component for acquisition, or developing a new component.

5. Component Maintenance Activity

Like any software product, a component must be maintained over its lifetime. However, because of its multiple-use capability, any change made to a component has broader implications than changes made to a single-use software part. The impact of the change must be considered not only in the context of software products for which the request was made, but to all other current and future software products that use or might use the component.

For example, a change made to a component may compromise its conformance with the domain models and architecture. It may then be difficult to use the component in building future component-based applications in the domain because the modified component no longer fits easily into the domain architecture. In addition, the reusability of a component may be greatly diminished if a change to it adversely affects its generality or adaptability.

An organization should develop component acceptance and certification procedures, using them as the basis for analyzing the appropriateness of a component modification request, and choosing how to satisfy the request. For example, a component modification request should be rejected if this is the only way to preserve the component's reusability, and

Exhibit 10.   Component Reusability Criteria

1. Before building a new component from scratch, make sure that it does not already exist. If it does, make every effort to reuse rather than re-invent the component.
2. Follow the organization's naming conventions.
3. Use a consistent design style and one that is compatible with the design principles that are used in the organization's component acceptance and certification procedures; for example, the GUI design standards.
4. Use templates from the reuse library/catalog to create new components to ensure that the components adhere to a standard format and are complete.
5. Practice information hiding by using object technology. An object encapsulates its data, providing only those operations necessary for manipulating its data.
6. Restrict communication between components, which should be loosely coupled and highly cohesive.
7. Be aware of the organization's component certification criteria, following these criteria as much as possible when creating a component.
8. Make each component development decision or selection decision in a way that satisfies the current known requirements and possible future requirements.
9. Make sure the underlying abstraction for the component is well understood, because abstraction is the basis for reusability. Make the abstraction clean, simple, and amenable to reuse.
10. Make the component as robust as possible so it can handle errors and exception conditions.
11. Make the component as efficient as possible.
12. Follow the organization's programming, user interface, database, testing, and documentation standards.
13. Document the component in a manner so that someone who is not familiar with it can understand the component and the context/domain for which it was originally created.
14. Capture design decisions along with the design to relate the component design to its documentation and implementing code. Provide links to all related components that may be reused along with the component. For example, link the test scripts to their associated use case so that when the use case is reused, its test scripts can also be reused.

to protect the integrity of the component-based applications in which the component has been used.

According to the IEEE Std. 1517, the domain engineer should use the domain engineering life cycle (i.e., the IEEE Std. 1517 domain engineering process) to maintain a component. However, only a subset of the domain engineering activities will be needed to modify an existing component. Therefore, those performing component maintenance should do so by selecting the appropriate domain engineering activities and tasks for a "mini" version of domain engineering.

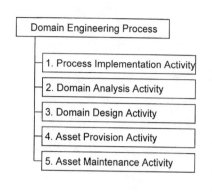

Deliverables

1.1 Domain Engineering Plan
1.2 Domain Model
Representation Form
1.3 Domain Architecture
Representation Form
1.4 Communication Procedures
2.1 Domain Boundaries
2.2 Developers' Needs Document
2.3 Domain Models
2.4 Domain Vocabulary
2.5 Domain Analysis Evaluation Document
3.1 Domain Architecture
3.2 Asset Specifications
3.3 Domain Design Evaluation Document
4.1 Assets
4.2 Asset Evaluation Document
5.1 Asset Modification Implementation Option
5.2 Asset Modification Implementation
Approval
5.3 Asset Manager Notification
5.4 Modified Asset

Exhibit 11.   Domain Engineering Process Activities and Deliverables

SUMMARY

A collection of high-quality, reusable components is a prerequisite for practicing CBD. An organization may create a component inventory by developing and acquiring the components. Since components are intended to be building blocks in developing multiple component-based applications, their life cycle requirements differ from single-use software parts.

A new standard from the IEEE Computer Society has been developed to specify the life cycle requirements for CBD approaches and components. To meet the CBD requirements, the standard modified the specification for the traditional software life cycle by adding activities, tasks, and deliverables to guide the assembly of a software application from predefined components, and adding a new life cycle called domain engineering. Exhibit 11 lists the activities that comprise the IEEE Std. 1517 domain engineering life cycle.

References

1. *IEEE 1517 Standard of Information Technology — Software Life Cycle Processes — Reuse Processes,* Institute of Electrical and Electronic Engineers, Inc., New York, 1999.
2. Kang, K., Cohen, S., Hess, J., Novak, W., and Peterson, A., *Feature-Oriented Domain Analysis Feasibility Study,* Software Engineering Institute Technical Report CMU/SEI-90-TR-21 ESD-90-TR-21, November 1990, Carnegie Mellon University, Pittsburgh, PA.

Chapter 17
Developing and Deploying Server-Side Application with Java

Madison Cloutier

Java's original popularity was its ability to enhance client-side Internet browsers, but developers have discovered that it can bring even greater business benefits to the development and deployment of server-side applications. There is no disputing Java's growing popularity as a server-side programming language and platform. IS shops worldwide are moving to Java for server-side applications because it solves the very real problem of building applications that run across several different operating systems, and Java offers some genuine programming efficiencies which helps with two ever-present issues: development productivity and software quality.

In this chapter we will look at some of the key issues surrounding the development and deployment of server-side Java applications. The focus is on demanding business-critical, server-hosted applications that are driving the Internet, intranet, and extranet sites for E-commerce and Net-business. First we will look at the benefits and some shortcomings of using Java on the server-side application development. We will then review the characteristics and requirements of server-side applications. Next we will look at the development issues and key decisions that will have to be made. Finally, we will look at the deployment issues associated with moving server-side Java applications into enterprise production.

BENEFITS OF USING JAVA FOR SERVER-SIDE APPLICATIONS

While the market hype and platform-independent nature of Java will cause an IS shop to take a closer look at this new programming environment, it is its development efficiencies that is driving its rapid adoption as a server-side application programming language. Some IS shops have reported up to 10 times productivity gains using Java over C++. This is easily understandable in light of the fact that a majority of the problems programmers encountered with C++ deal with memory management, which is automatically taken care of by Java. Java's automatic memory and easy thread management means programmers can create an application faster and with fewer bugs. Because the syntax of Java is similar to C++, programmers can migrate to it with some ease and confidence. Collectively, this makes Java an excellent language for building the new generation of server-side net-enabled applications.

A key benefit of Java is that the language is based on a pure object model which enforces pure object-oriented programming techniques. Unlike C++, which supports object-oriented programming but does not enforce it, Java programmers can develop higher quality software because they cannot circumvent the object model. This makes applications easier to test, debug, and maintain over time. Another benefit of the pure object model is that programmers will find it easier to use existing components and frameworks (which we will talk about shortly) encouraging software reuse which contributes to higher development productivity.

Another aspect of Java that contributes to programming efficiencies is the notion that development and deployment is decoupled (Exhibit 1). This is the fundamental basis for Java's "Write Once, Run Anywhere" benefit. Java source code can be quickly compiled into platform-independent "bytecode" classes and executed immediately, using an interpreter, which can make the edit-compile test cycle very short. Once the program has been functionally tested and is ready for production deployment, the platform-independent bytecode can be easily moved onto the appropriate server platform for execution. This means Java is both a rapid application development (RAD) language and a deployment language. By decoupling development and deployment, programmers can stay focused on the features, functionality, and capabilities of the application during development and, at deployment time, deal with the performance and throughput issues of the application on the targeted server platform.

JAVA SHORTCOMINGS

Even though there are a number of real and tangible benefits to using Java for server-side application development there are some shortcomings that will need to be taken into consideration. Performance is usually the first criticism

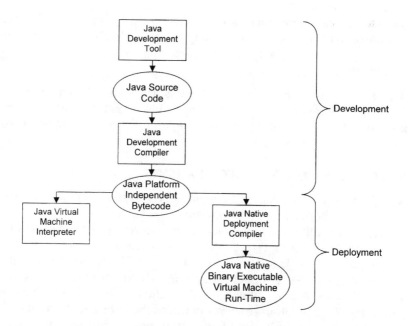

Exhibit 1. Decoupling Development and Deployment

raised against using Java on the server. While it is true that bytecode interpreters cannot deliver the performance necessary for demanding server-side applications, advanced just-in-time compilers and optimizing native Java deployment compilers are becoming available that allow Java applications to execute at the performance levels of C++ applications.

Java standards and its uncertain future are other issues that critics will raise. It is important to remember that there are two elements to Java: Java, the platform, and Java, the language. Where Sun, Microsoft, and others battle over the Java platform especially regarding the desktop, Java, the language, is stable. The idea of 100 percent compatibility across all client platforms may never be truly achieved; however, it is clear that there can be high compatibility of the Java language across server platforms. Using Java as a programming language, along with good object-oriented application design and architecture, will allow for a level of cross-platform compatibility higher than any previous programming language. Because of the industry momentum behind Java, the standards issue will be resolved in time and Java is destined to surpass C++ and Visual Basic in popularity and usage.

Java development tools are currently immature compared to development tools for the more established languages, and the availability of quality components and frameworks are limited today. However, the industry acceptance of Java is strong and many of these shortcomings are being addressed because the language provides long-term benefits for the software industry.

We should note here that Java by itself is not a silver bullet. In order to achieve the full benefits of Java, IS shops must develop competencies in object-oriented design and programming along with other modern software engineering practices.

SERVER-SIDE APPLICATION REQUIREMENTS

Developers who are familiar with client/server systems will already know that the characteristics and requirements of client-side and server-side applications are different. In a typical client/server system, the client handles the graphical user interface (GUI), the server contains the data, and the application logic is spread across the two. The Internet is driving a trend toward multitier client/server systems which introduces the concept of application servers. In a typical multitier client/server system, the client handles the GUI, the database server contains the data, and the application server contains the application logic. An Internet multitier client/server architecture also introduces other types of servers such as HTTP servers and connection servers. We should briefly review the differences between client-side and server-side applications because we will need to consider these differences as we address the Java development and deployment issues.

In client/server environments, the client typically handles the GUI for such things as input forms and information retrieval. In a Java-based system this usually involves the execution of small Java "applets" which are downloaded from a server to the client as needed. Client-side Java applets support a single user on a single computer typically containing a single CPU. Java applets are usually updated "passively," meaning that should an input form or information retrieval display change, a new applet can be downloaded the next time the client accesses the particular application server. The application availability on a single client is not critical because only one user is affected should there be a problem. Because there are an array of different client platforms accessing Internet servers, Java applets need to be represented as bytecode, the platform-independent code that allows the applet to execute on any platform with a Java Virtual Machine (JVM)-enabled browser. The Java promise of "Write Once, Run Anywhere" has not been fully realized on the client side because of the different implementations of JVMs on the different client platforms used on the Internet, especially in the way GUI functions are handled. However, when you are dealing with a known client base as in intranet/extranet environments Java can be highly beneficial for client-side applications.

The servers are the real workhorses of the Internet, intranets, and extranets. This is where the processing logic is executed for business-critical E-commerce and Net-business applications. These are typically sophisticated and demanding applications that must support a large number of users simultaneously. Availability is critical because applications must be accessible 24×7×365. This requires "hot" application updates, or the ability to update an application without having to stop, reload, and restart. Large-scale server applications will typically execute on hardware that contains multiple processors or a cluster of processors. In some cases multiple applications may be running on a single piece of hardware requiring the ability to performance tune and manage them on an application-specific basis. Even though it may be desirable to deploy server-side Java applications as platform-independent bytecode, the need for execution, performance, and manageability will typically overshadow portability once the application is put into production. Because server-side applications usually do not require GUI support, the notion of "Write Once, Run Anywhere" is more realistic, assuming the applications are properly designed and developed.

DEVELOPING SERVER-SIDE APPLICATIONS WITH JAVA

The first major decision will be choosing a server-side development strategy from an array of competing APIs, middleware, and architectural approaches. Because of the object-oriented nature of Java, the notion of acquiring existing frameworks or components as a starting point for custom applications is a realistic approach. Using existing software can provide significant benefits to an IS shop by reducing in-house development efforts and risks while improving application quality and flexibility.

For larger applications the selection of middleware will be critical. The middleware framework will become your strategic infrastructure responsible for connecting clients, databases, application servers, and transaction processors. There are currently three or more major connection models, as shown in Exhibit 2:

1. CORBA (Common Object Request Broker Architecture) — the industry standard for connecting heterogeneous systems.
2. RMI (Remote Method Invocation) — the Java standard for connecting Java-based systems.
3. COM/COM+ (Component Object Model Component Object Model Plus) — the Microsoft standard for connecting Windows-based systems.

There are multiple existing middleware products available that support one or more connection models. In addition, most of the new generation of middleware products also provide database connectivity, transaction processing, security, and other infrastructural support. The supported features

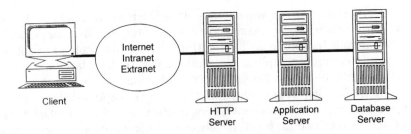

Exhibit 2. Typical Multitier Environment

and capabilities of these middleware products vary considerably and will need to be thoroughly understood to decide which are important to overall strategy and application plans. Some of these products are completely written in Java such as WebLogic's Tanga, Visigenic's Inprise, or Novera Epic. Others such as Progress Apptivity or Netscape's Kiva are primarily written in C/C++ with a Java interface layer. Your ultimate decision should be based on fundamental business reasons such as strategic fit, features and capabilities, support and pricing. However, Java-based frameworks appear to provide better long-term flexibility.

After deciding the middleware infrastructure strategy, application strategy will need to be addressed. As with middleware strategy, existing application components and frameworks should be seriously considered. This will allow acquisition of base capabilities and development of only the specialized capabilities needed. There are currently two major competing component models on which Java frameworks are being built: Enterprise Java Beans (EJB) from Sun and Distributed Component Object Model (DCOM) from Microsoft. Where DCOM has been around somewhat longer and is mature, it currently only works with Microsoft Windows. EJB is gaining industry support and has a good chance of becoming the predominant model for heterogeneous enterprise environments because of its more open nature. Application frameworks provide an environment in which components interact to create a complete application. At some point in the future, components from different vendors may be easily integrated with each other. Currently, most components are part of an existing application framework. The most ambitious application framework to date is the IBM San Francisco project that is building an extensible framework for building and deploying serious enterprise business systems.

A key element of development strategy will be the decision for platform independence versus platform-specific development. Even though Java is touted as a platform-independent development environment, it is possible to design and develop server applications which are not platform independent. If the strategic objective is to maintain platform independence of applications, use caution when using special operating systems services provided by platform vendors because doing so may result in being tied to a specific server platform and loss of future deployment flexibility.

There are a number of Java development tools to choose from. Most include a rapid application development (RAD) environment which allows for the quick development of Java code and components. Currently, the popular tools include: Sun's JavaWork Shop, Inprise JBuilder, Microsoft Visual J++, IBM VisualAge for Java, and Symantec's Visual Cafe. Choice of a development tool should be made after other strategic development issues have been addressed and decided. It will not be uncommon for an IS group to use multiple development tools.

DEPLOYING SERVER-SIDE APPLICATIONS WITH JAVA

Deploying sophisticated server-side applications involve a whole new set of problems in the areas of distribution, updating, testing, performance tuning, and real-time system management, whether they are written in Java or some other language. In the Java world there are two options to executing deployed bytecode; one is based on interpreter technology, the other on native deployment compilation.

The standard Java virtual machine implementation works by interpreting bytecode that is generated off-line by a Java development compiler. The execution speed of the Java Development Kit interpreter correlates closely with the number of bytecode instructions executed. This clearly limits execution performance, making interpreters good for RAD and small applications but unsuitable for deploying demanding server-side applications. Currently, all major server vendors offer a Java interpreter on their platforms.

Just-In-Time (JIT) compilers are a step up from interpreters. They are virtual machine subsystems that convert byte code to native code on the fly during execution. Code optimization is done rapidly and only on a subsection of code at a time. While this can enhance the performance of small applications, the speed-up is limited on larger, more demanding programs. JITs vary in performance and scalability, but even the best ones are slower than comparably coded C++ server applications. Most major server vendors offer a JIT on their platforms.

A step up from JITs are smart interpreters which utilize "dynamic adaptive" techniques that convert only selected portions of the bytecode into optimized native code based on execution patterns. The idea is to begin the execution of bytecode in an interpreted mode, monitoring the execution to find frequently executed code segments or "hotspots," converting these hotspots into optimized native code, and then patching them into the system. Where this approach can, in theory, provide high-performance execution for certain types of Java applications, it is unproven in demanding server-side applications. Because of the monitoring and optimization overhead, this approach requires additional computer resources during application execution, making it unsuitable for CPU-intensive systems. A bigger concern for business-critical systems is that this approach makes it extremely difficult, if not impossible, to fully certify a system or to reproduce the exact circumstances when a bug occurs. This is due to the fact that "on-the-fly" changes are automatically being patched into the system during execution. Sun has been the primary proponent of the "dynamic adaptive" approach via the marketing of its Hot Spot compiler, and currently only a few server platform vendors have announced their intention to offer this type of advanced interpreter.

The interpreter approach and its variations (i.e., JITs and Dynamic Adaptive) are not suitable run-time architectures for the demanding server-side Java applications which will be required to scale for high throughput. This approach also complicates the management of enterprise applications by separating the application from the run-time, thus adding another variable to version control. An alternative approach is to use native compilation that allows the Java Virtual Machine and run-time to be embedded in the applications as part of a self-contained native executable. This approach can significantly enhance execution performance, reliability, and manageability.

There are different flavors of Java native compilers, but in all cases they allow creation of a native executable off-line prior to the application execution. The key advantage of this is the fact that extensive performance optimization can be performed prior to execution, thus enhancing performance and reliability. Also, application-specific performance tuning can be accomplished more easily because the virtual machine run-time is part of the application executable.

Standard native Java compilers will generate binary executables directly from Java source code. If access to all the source code associated with the application is available and platform independence is not an issue, consider this approach. However, it is more likely that all the source code and some level of platform independence will be important. In this situation a "native deployment compiler" will be more appropriate because it will allow generation of binary executables directly from previously generated bytecode.

There is also the notion of "closed" and "opened" native compilers. "Closed" or static native compilers, as they are usually referred to, do not allow the binary executables to be modified once they have been generated. In some cases this is fine, but if performance of "hot updates" is

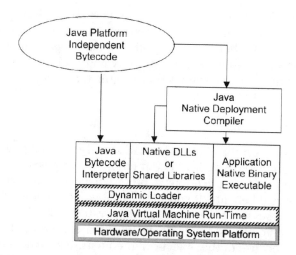

Exhibit 3.   Full "Open" Native Deployment Compiler and Run-Time Architecture

needed for high-availability applications, an "open" native compiler is required. An "open" native compiler allows the generation of native DLLs (or shared libraries for UNIX) from bytecode off-line which can then be dynamically loaded into a running application. This is sometimes referred to as "Ahead-Of-Time" compilation. If required to dynamically update a running application directly with bytecode, the executable will need access to a Java interpreter which a full "open" native compiler and run-time environment support.

The ultimate Java deployment architecture for demanding server-side Java applications is a full "open" native deployment compiler and run-time environment as shown in Exhibit 3. A key benefit of such an architecture is support for "programming in the large," or the ability to rapidly make safe changes to high-availability systems. This allows developers to better manage and evolve sophisticated systems. Using RAD approaches, developers can test new application features and capabilities in bytecode form and safely commit them to the system as native code as they become stable. This approach allows high performance and throughput to be maintained in high-availability enterprise systems during constant modifications. Commercially available full "open" native deployment compilers for Java are available for all the major server platforms.

One final issue to address is that of Java application management. This is likely to become a growing problem for enterprise system administrators as the number of deployed Java applications increases. When evaluating and choosing application deployment options, be sure to consider the application management aspects and how Java applications will be managed within your system management framework. Rapidly changing distributed server-side Internet/intranet/extranet applications, whether written in Java or some other language, will be a challenge to manage. Due to the object-oriented nature of Java, properly engineered Java applications should be easier to manage and it is inevitable that suitable Java management tools will appear over time.

CONCLUSION

There is no question that Java is here to stay. Developing and deploying server-side applications in Java is not completely unlike developing and deploying server-side applications in other languages, however, Java does provide some real benefits. It solves the problem of building applications that run across several different operating systems, and it offers genuine programming efficiencies, which helps development productivity and software quality. Because of the object-oriented nature of Java and its rapidly growing popularity, there will be many opportunities available to acquire existing frameworks and components which will significantly reduce overall development efforts and resource requirements, reduce risks, and improve time to market. As with most new software technologies, use good business sense when planning to use Java for business-critical server-side applications. Java represents a new paradigm for the software industry, so be sure you have appropriate development and deployment strategies in place. A pilot project or two will prove invaluable. Good luck.

Chapter 18
Managing Object Libraries
Polly Perryman Kuver

Software reuse is a concept that has been bounced around in the industry for years and years; still, information systems developers are searching for ways to master its implementation. The principles of object-oriented design and development have shown themselves to be a starting point for developing reusable software. Application of the principles, however, only offers a partial solution since compliance with the principles and the development of objects does not automatically result in reusability. It requires a great deal of planning and effective management of object libraries. This is because until the commonality of the object types is defined and effectively managed, the value of software reuse cannot be realized.

Many companies miss out on valuable opportunities to streamline processes while improving product because they do not have a cohesive plan to implement object library management. Other companies lose out because they think object library management is a practice limited to documented object-oriented design methodologies. Still other companies use clumsy procedures intending to promote software reuse without ever realizing the importance of planning for software reuse, which is itself a form of object library management. When the essential components of object library management are understood and implemented, these missed opportunities can knock again.

One of the biggest mistakes companies make is "throwing" objects into a library without a scheme for making sure the team benefits from them. For example, a company had a practice of telling coders if they develop a routine that others can use, to put it in Library X. This was so everyone could access and use the code. This had a major impact on one project. Several developers faithfully added routines to a common library that indeed saved development time for database access, output, and a number of other common functions. A young fellow we will refer to as Sam contributed a particularly well-used routine. The problem was that while Sam's common object executed beautifully, it was unfortunately a resource hog, and when it was used by other developers it created problems. The impact of modifying the object to correct and improve the performance issues and retest the 50-plus programs using the object was significant. The schedule delay was unacceptable to the customer; funding for the project was withdrawn.

On another project where the "throw-it-in" approach to object library management was used without a master plan, coders duplicated efforts by individually creating their own renditions of routines for common use. The object library became so convoluted with multiple objects for similar types of functions that no one was able to use it. The benefits gained by the concept were preempted entirely by the approach.

So how can object library management be implemented effectively without impinging on the creativity of talented staff? It basically depends on three things to be successful. The first is appointment of a design authority. The designated design authority assumes full responsibility for establishing the highest classification for objects, the characteristics for base objects within the classification, and determining which objects possess commonality to the system for potential reuse within the application, upgrades, and related products. The person who takes on the role of the design authority must communicate beyond the structure of the objects, making certain that the development team understands the standards and methods used to structure, document, build, and subsequently maintain the object library.

The second area for success lies in the effective use of basic configuration management functions such as version control and release management. The implementation of the configuration management functions may use any of the configuration management tools in the market today, such as Rational-Atria ClearCase or Intersolv's PVCS, that have been upgraded to work with large objects. The configuration management functions may also be implemented using internally developed tools and methods when purchase of these tools would strain the budget.

The third area for success is quality control and testing. The quality control and testing that must be performed covers more than the demonstration that the coded object works to specifications. It must also ensure that development personnel are complying with the structure established for object management that allows for improvement in the processes used by development personnel using the object library.

Object library management can and should be practiced regardless of the development methodology being used because it offers direct benefits to developers and customers alike. The most direct benefit of object library management is better product at lower cost. While this may sound like a television commercial for every imaginable product on the market, from baby diapers to automobiles, the positive effects of object library management can demonstrate improved productivity through team-focused procedures and higher quality through uniformity, consistency, and, most importantly, meaningful design controls.

With the components of success identified, it is important to note that as languages, systems, and user applications become increasingly complex to program, the need for object management takes on greater implications in the life of a product. As many companies are finding out, the effects of poor object library management impacts not only initial development of a product but results in spiraling chaos with the maintenance and upgrade of the product.

THE DESIGN AUTHORITY

The design authority is a role rather than a position. The role may be filled by a single individual, such as the engineering manager, the lead design engineer, the system architect, or by a group of people who work together to satisfy the goals of object library management. The critical point is to define the role and fill it. It is important not to confuse the design authority role with the responsibilities of a configuration control board whose function is quite different.

Once the design authority role has been assigned, the work of managing object libraries can begin in earnest. Using input from the users, a rudimentary framework for objects can be set up. It is here that the design authority may elect to use the Unified Modeling Language (UML). Whether UML or some other method is used, it is of particular importance that the system requirements are clearly defined, analyzed, and documented. They are the basis upon which all of the design and system testing are based and they must be clearly understood by all parties. The initial object framework can and probably will be a hodgepodge of objects and classifications both at the highest level and at base levels. The reason for this is that the users will be providing their input at different levels. For instance, one or two of the users may be listing specific types of reports they need to generate on a cyclical basis, while other users may be stating their desire to employ animation and sound without specifying what type of animation or sound. The result is that input will be provided on various levels and the design authority must be able to determine the value to place on the information.

This may be better explained by referring to some of the early discussions about object-oriented programming (see the Recommended Reading list at the end of this chapter) in which a classic shape example was used for clarification. In the example, shapes became the classification for managing objects that performed functions on a shape, such as changing the shape's size or moving it. The type of shapes — circles, squares, and triangles — inherit the capabilities of the objects. This allows functions to be performed on any type of shape, thus setting up the ability for reuse of the functions on shape types added to the system at later dates.

It is the design authority who begins to set up a framework for new and continuing development. Decisions will need to be made as to whether the input falls into the circle/square category, the perform-on category, or the shapes category. If it is a shape category, it will hold objects. If it is an object, it will do something. It is the objects, then, that need to be constructed. It is the classification and management of these objects that takes the design authority to the next critical work effort.

For an object to do something, it needs to possess both the data and function qualities necessary to perform. Peter Coad and Edward Yourdon expressed these qualities as an equation: Object-oriented = Objects + Classification + Inheritance + Communication with Messages.[1] The design authority, in maximizing the potential of solid object library management, must be able to cross-reference and promote the use and reuse of these qualities in the development environment. For instance, objects in an edit classification may include copy, move, and delete. The construction of the object must permit these functions to be performed on any designated text or graphic unit. As such, the design authority can, within the object library management structure, ensure the reuse of these objects from one product to another and from one upgrade to the next. In planning the object libraries, the design authority must also consider those types of objects that will more likely be upgraded in the short and long terms. While the quickness of advancing technology may make this step seem like crystal ball engineering, the design authority will have responsibility for working with management to minimize technological risks and keep development moving in a forward rather than circular direction.

It is not the role of the design authority to determine how the defined object structure is implemented within the configuration system. That function is performed by specialists in configuration management.

CONFIGURATION MANAGEMENT

Configuration management is a function best performed by a specialist who has three principal tasks. The first is making certain the version control mechanisms sustain the object classifications and hierarchy structure laid out by the design authority. The second is ensuring that the version control mechanisms put into place support the application development staff in easy retrieval and storage of objects. The third is tracking the correct object versions and building them into defined releases of the product. Whether your organization has a configuration management tool in place or not, when the decision to implement an object library management plan is made, a serious comparative capability evaluation of the existing tool and those available in today's market must be made.

Most of the recognized configuration management tools available today will, at a minimum, provide version control and support release builds. Nearly all of the tools allow text, graphic, and multimedia object storage. The trick in selecting and using a tool for object library management is in evaluating the available tools in relation to the scope of the efforts it will be supporting and the manpower investment the company is willing to make to ensure the successful implementation of the tool. It is critical that during this evaluation focus is maintained on the design structure and intended reuse capabilities desired. This means it needs to be evaluated not only for what it will do today, but whether it will meet the needs of your organization in terms of future growth. For example, current plans for your product over the next 5 years are to support both Windows and Macintosh users. The tool that best fits the design structure and size requirements for the project only runs in a UNIX environment today. The question as to how the developers will effectively be able to take advantage of the version control features of the tool must be addressed, as does how clean the build feature of the tool really stays.

A similar dilemma presents itself when an organization uses off-site developers for various pieces of the system. One example can be taken from a company whose off-site animation staff developed its product, which was eventually embedded within the company's primary product. It turned out that the operating system used by the off-site developers was not compatible with the configuration management tool being evaluated. A number of work-arounds were drafted and discussed, but the bottom line was that each of them made the version control and build processes cumbersome and less reliable. A lesser known configuration management tool offered the necessary interface for this off-site work and provided all of the other features in a somewhat diminished capacity. The question that had to be asked and answered was which tool was going to best meet the goals of the organization now and in the future. If the organization was willing to fumble through for a while and gamble that the interface for off-site programming was going to be constructed, or the off-site programmers could be transitioned to a different compatible operating system, then perhaps the more well-known tool would be a good choice. If the need for better object management was immediate and the organization was willing to gamble on the eventual expansion of the lesser known tool's capabilities, then the less sophisticated tool would be a good choice.

These examples are merely representative of the types of questions that must be part and parcel of a configuration management tool evaluation. Other important questions include, but are not limited to:

- What support does the vendor supply in configuring the tool in your organization's environment?
- If interfaces are going to be constructed by the tool vendor, will they become part of the configuration management tool product line or stay a customized piece of software your organization will become responsible for maintaining?
- What training is required by your organization's staff to set up and operate the tool effectively?
- How many man-hours must be devoted to maintaining the tool in order to ensure its successful use?

Even when the current in-house tool meets the technical specifications for object library management and object development, there are still set-up factors to be considered in assessing the planned design authority structure in relation to the current configuration of the tool. New areas may need to be prepared and a different hierarchy may need to be defined to support the build features of the tool. This work cannot be overlooked during the evaluation process.

Another stumbling block to successful object library management is in the planning of releases. Here the design authority and configuration management specialists need to work closely to define the contents and status of each release. It is not sufficient for the design authority to send an e-mail that says include x, y, and z. Success is based on knowing not only that x, y, and z are in the release, but also knowing the problem state of x, y, and z within the overall scheme of the object library management plan. In other words, the plan for Release A will include version 2.2 of x, version 2.3 of y, and version 4 of z, and we know that version 2.3 of y includes a few glitches that should be fixed before the release date but will not crash the software if they are not fixed. However, version 4 of z may cause some problems, in which case the fallback plan is to use version 2.8 of z because version 3 of z had to be recalled. This is the type of information that becomes part of the release plan composed by the design authority and the configuration management specialist. This, of course, brings us right to the third component needed for successful object library management, quality control and testing.

QUALITY CONTROL AND TESTING

How did the design authority and configuration management specialist make the decision on which version of z to use if the possible problems with z surfaced during the release build? The answer is that version 2.8 was a thoroughly tested and proven object within the system and it did not have a relationship with either x or y. It would not need to be retested. It could just be used because the quality control supporting solid object library management includes traceability, predictability, and uniformity, which are achieved by testing the design, the constructed objects, the object relationships, and the object system. Keep in mind that objects that have been tested can be used and used and used without having to test and test and test. New development will occur in a more orderly manner because the structure laid out within the object library management plan will lend itself to a clearer and more logical next step. The quality controls are essential in taking the management of objects from basic reuse in the initial product to a viable expanded product vision.

Working with the design authority, quality control personnel complement the object library management plan while imposing and enforcing these controls, because the structure of the objects and the communication from the design authority to the development staff ensures that everyone is working toward the same goal. The quality group does the testing of the object and ensures that it meets the construction and use guidelines established. Quality control accomplishes this by being a part of the development rather than an appendage to development, validating the object structure and conducting walkthroughs where questions and issues can be raised and resolved. The quality group should work closely with the configuration management specialists to ensure the integrity of the released product by validating both the configuration of the tool being used for version control and release management, and verification of the product release plan.

SUMMARY

The goal is to maximize an organization's competitive edge in the marketplace. The components for successful object library management presented in this chapter can be raised to whatever level of sophistication that best fits your organization. The important thing is to plan and manage the objects constructed.

On a small project, the biggest problem may appear to be people resources. Keep in mind that there are three roles that need to be played for success. This may mean that the lead designer is also the design authority, a developer, and the configuration management specialist. The quality control and testing role, however, must be performed by someone other than this person. If necessary, even a nontechnical project manager can perform the quality control and testing role as long as the concepts and goals of the project are clearly stated and the basics of object library management are understood. The greatest benefit to the small project is that communication between the design authority and developers is stronger and the setup of the configuration management tool is generally much easier.

On a large project there are larger problems. There, the design authority may be a team of people for which some protocol and tie-breaking mechanisms need to be laid out from the start in order to keep the design moving. Communication between the design authority and the developers is more difficult to maintain. The setup of the configuration management tool may take several weeks, and training sessions may need to be conducted to ensure that developers fully understand what is expected of them. And quality control and testing is more involved and necessary. The biggest benefit in a large project is the value of being able to gain a greater long-range vision for the application or product, and in being able to cross-train personnel in many areas.

The point is to take action whether the project is the conversion of a legacy system to the new technology or the development of new systems with existing and future technology. Begin by committing in black and white what your organization needs to accomplish. Then establish an organization to assess and plan for that accomplishment. Once the plan is formulated, provide training whether it is vendor-supplied, seminars, or in-house group sessions. Success can be repeated over and over again when there is a plan to implement and an understanding of the technology. Then appoint the design authority, start evaluating configuration management tools, and prepare a testing strategy that will meet your organization's goals for object management.

Notes

1. Coad, Peter and Yourdon, Edward, *Object-oriented Analysis*, Prentice-Hall, Englewood Cliffs, NJ, 1990.

Recommended Reading

Jacobson, Ivar, Griss, Martin, and Jonsson, Patrik, *Software Reuse*, ACM Press, pp 60-61, 117, 356 and 436, 1997.

Entsminger, Gary, *The Tao of Objects, A Beginner's Guide to Object Oriented Programming.* M & T Publishing, Inc., 1990.

Section V
Database Servers in an Integrated Environment

Chapter 19
Designing a Capacity Database Server

Judith M. Myerson

In the old days, performance and capacity reports were run on the much-slower mainframes with smaller memory and bulky storage devices. A data center manager developed the format for a database of eight records of system data for COBOL system programmers. The first part of each record was the same: sort key area of 28 bytes plus the primary part of common areas. Some parameters are still useful, while other parameters have become obsolete. New parameters are needed to better measure the capacity requirements of a system. Network bandwidth, for example, is now an important performance and capacity parameter.

The problem is that the capacity database file designed for a bygone mainframe needs to be updated for today's widely distributed network systems. Another problem is that this database needs to be integrated with current performance databases running on disparate operating systems. Each database comes with a varying set of parameters. The third problem is that the tools for comparing capacity requirements of these systems are generally limited.

WHEN TO INTEGRATE DATA INTO A CAPACITY DATABASE SERVER

The widespread use of performance monitors and application tools for stand-alone PCs in distributed network environments has resulted in many files and databases that are frequently stored on floppy disks or SCSI tape cartridges.

To be useful, data must be available when users need it. This means the capacity data about different systems must be available on a server at all times to all users who are authorized to locate, access, and integrate information. If users are not able to access the data or are not aware of what data they need, they cannot make proper decisions. This results in poor performance for both the individuals and the enterprise as a whole. Capacity data on disparate networks should be integrated into a centralized capacity database server if the cost of poor performance is greater than the expense of integrating all necessary data into a centralized capacity database server.

STEPS IN INTEGRATING DATA FROM DISPARATE SOURCES

The following is one approach to data integration from dissimilar sources and consists of the following steps:

1. *Inventory capacity data.* Source database tables and files to be integrated into a centralized database must be identified. They include flat files, indexed files, hierarchical databases, network databases, and relational databases whether they are current or archived.
2. *Identify capacity values.* Changing technologies largely determine what capacity variables are still useful, which have become obsolete, and what new ones should be identified.
3. *Create database tables.* A COBOL file with its records must be converted into a database table along with its rows.
4. *Normalize databases.* Source database tables and files must be normalized to remove redundant primary keys. This is particularly important when source data is integrated into a relational database.
5. *Model individual files and databases.* The entities and their relationships within each source database and files must be identified. Using the old capacity database to "best-guess" the entities and associated relationships is helpful in determining what should be included or excluded when modeling current databases.
6. *Convert all schemas to relational schemas.* All entities and relationships must be expressed in a common format.
7. *Integrate source schemas into a target schema.* Structural and format inconsistencies among data from disparate databases must be identified and resolved.

MIGRATING TO A SINGLE DATABASE SERVER

The database administrator migrates and integrates source data from the various source databases into a target relational database server. Erroneous and inconsistent data should be identified and resolved. Data elements may be associated with data values, particularly those in COBOL files.

Step 1: Inventory Existing Data

The first step is to identify every source data element that should be integrated into the target centralized data server. Exhibit 1 illustrates an example of a source data element. From this description, the database administrator quickly determines the meaning of the source data element and whether or not it should be included in the centralized database server.

Exhibit 1. Description of a Data Element

English name:	Record types
COBOL name:	Record-identification (table row)
Type:	Short integer
Value:	0 = rates records
	1 = refund records
	2 = task records
	3 = program records
	4 = allocator records
	5 = spool records

Exhibit 2. Description of a Modified Data Element

English name:	Record types
COBOL name:	Record-identification (table row)
Type:	Short integer
Value:	0 = rates
	1 = refund
	2 = task
	3 = program
	4 = allocator*
	5 = spool
	6 = bandwidth
	7 = packet
	8 = hops

Step 2: Identify New Capacity Values

The second step is to identify which values are still useful and which ones are to be added. Exhibit 2 illustrates an example of how a source data element is modified in response to changing technologies. The database administrator marks obsolete terms with an asterisk and underlines the new ones.

Step 3: Create Database Tables

To maintain consistency with relational database management systems, all COBOL files must be reformatted as tables with associated rows (see Exhibits 3 and 4). Information on data elements in COBOL records are found in the Data Division, File Section, under the File Description Header.

Step 4: Normalize Databases

All files and databases should be normalized to remove redundant data and identify which variables should be assigned as primary and foreign

Exhibit 3.   Task Record (COBOL)/Task Table

Account #	User ID	Record ID	Date	Task Seq. #	Time Left in Account	# of Devices Used

Exhibit 4.   Program Record (COBOL)/Program Table

Account #	User ID	Record ID	Date	Program Name	# of Devices Used	Device Information

keys. Without normalization, redundant variables could find their way to a data model, making it a less effective tool for the database administrator to compare files and databases.

Step 5: Model Individual Files and Databases

The database administrator should use the same data model for both source individual files and databases and target database. This would help the administrator to easily locate problems among databases and correct them, and to identify discrepancies.

Popular Data Modeling Techniques

Three types of data models are available: relational data models, entity-relationship data models, and object-oriented data models. It is highly desirable to use a single data model to effectively compare files and databases. Database administrators often debate on what data model to use, elaborating on advantages and disadvantages of each.

Step 6: Convert All Schemas to Relational Schemas

All entities and relationships must be expressed in a common format. They should be clearly and unambiguously understood by all database administrators and data modelers. Some of the same terms used in files and databases in bygone days and today's networking world may have different meanings. This is also true for different data models used to identify what the files and databases are supposed to do.

Step 7: Integrate Source Schema into a Target Schema

One schema integration is to identify the relationship between pairs of source tables, database tables, and files, and then construct the appropriate target table.

Identify Source Tables and Records as Candidates for Integration. Database administrators should use heuristics to identify candidate data elements in source tables and records. One possible heuristic is to consider data elements with the same name, nearly the same name, or names that have the same meanings. Another way is consider source tables and records with several columns with the same name, nearly the same name, or the names that have the same meanings.

Identify New Capacity Variables as Additions to the List of Candidates for Integration. Here, heuristics should be used to identify new capacity names to complete the list of possible candidates. One way is to distinguish these names from those previously identified in database tables. Another way is to consider names that differ from those found in several columns in source tables.

Determine the Name Relationship of the Rows of Source Tables as Pairs. Database administrators should determine the relationships among data elements in source tables. Four possible relationships are:

1. *Logical containment.* If each row in A always corresponds to a unique row in B, then B logically contains A. For example, every Smaller System row always corresponds to a row of Larger System. Therefore, Larger System logically contains Smaller System.
2. *Logical equivalence.* If each row in A always corresponds to a unique row in B, and each row in B always corresponds to a unique row in A, then B is logically equivalent to A. For example, every Task Work row always corresponds to a Task Team row, and every Task Group row always corresponds to a Task Team row. Therefore, Task Team is logically equivalent to Task Group.
3. *Logical overlap.* If some of the rows in A correspond to some of the rows in B, and B corresponds to some of the rows in A, then A and B logically overlap. For example, some Truck rows are found in Truck Registration, and some Truck Registration rows are found in Truck. Therefore, Truck and Truck Registration overlap.
4. *Logical disjoint.* If none of the rows in A corresponds to any of the rows in B, and none of the rows in B corresponds to any of the rows in A, then A and B are logically disjoint. For example, no rows of Larger System are found in Truck Registration and no rows of Truck Registration are found in the Larger System table. Therefore, Larger System and Truck Registration are logically disjoint.

Determine the Name Relationship of the Rows of More Than Two Source Tables; Database administrators should determine the relationships among more than two source tables (databases). Following are seven possible relationships for three tables:

1. *Logical containment-equivalent.* If each row in A always corresponds to a unique row in B, then B logically contains A. If each row in C always corresponds to a unique row in B, and each row in B always corresponds to a unique row in C, then C is logically equivalent to A. Combined, A logically is contained by B and is equivalent to C.

2. *Logical containment-overlap.* If each row in A always corresponds to a unique row in B, then B logically contains A. If some of the rows in C correspond to some of the rows in B, and B corresponds to some of the rows in C, then B and C logically overlap. Combined, B logically contains A and overlaps with C.

3. *Logical equivalence-overlap.* If each row in A always corresponds to a unique row in B, and each row in B always corresponds to a unique row in A, then B is logically equivalent to A. If some of the rows in C correspond to some of the rows in B, and B corresponds to some of the rows in A, then B and C logically overlap. Combined, B is logically equivalent to A and overlaps with C.

4. *Logical containment-disjoint.* If each row in A always corresponds to a unique row in B, then B logically contains A. If none of the rows in C correspond to any of the rows in B, and none of the rows in B correspond to any of the rows in C, then B and C are logically disjoint. Combined, B logically contains A and is disjoint from C.

5. *Logical equivalence-disjoint.* If each row in A always corresponds to a unique row in B, and each row in B always corresponds to a unique row in A, then B is logically equivalent to A. If none of the rows in C correspond to any of the rows in B, and none of the rows in B correspond to any of the rows in C, then B and C are logically disjoint. Combined, B is logically equivalent to A and is disjoint from C.

6. *Logical overlap-disjoint.* If some of the rows in A correspond to some of the rows in B, and B corresponds to some of the rows in A, then A and B logically overlap. If none of the rows in C correspond to any of the rows in B, and none of the rows in B correspond to any of the rows in C, then B and C are logically disjoint. Combined, B logically overlaps with A and is disjoint from C.

7. *Logical disjoint-disjoint.* If none of the rows in A correspond to any of the rows in B, and none of the rows in B correspond to any of the rows in A, then A and B are logically disjoint. If none of the rows in C correspond to any of the rows in B, and none of the rows in B correspond to any of the rows in C, then B and C are logically disjoint. Combined, A, B, and C are all logically disjoint.

RECOMMENDED COURSE OF ACTION

If the cost of poor performance is greater than the expense of integrating diverse databases and files into a centralized data, then data should be integrated. The integration process requires five actions that users must perform to obtain meaningful capacity information among disparate operating systems.

1. Convert COBOL files into database tables.
2. Locate relevant data and the computers containing the data.
3. Formulate separate requests to each data source to access the data.
4. Integrate the data into a single capacity database server.
5. Integrate the results of the users' requests into an integrated format for decision-makers.

Chapter 20
Remote Data Subset Synchronization

John R. Vacca

IT automation is the application of computers, software, and other technical components to define and maintain standard IT processes, with the end result being a more efficient and productive IT enterprise. IT automation systems are typically used by enterprises to help IT users and managers better plan, organize, and execute the IT plan. These systems often allow users to analyze sales trends, schedule account calls, process end-user requests, communicate via electronic mail, keep track of end-user and software and hardware product lists, generate price quotes, and plan end-user IT objectives, among many other IT applications. IT automation systems often incorporate portable notebook or handheld computers, remote database synchronization, and highly specialized software. To date, thousands of IT enterprises worldwide have implemented some form of IT automation.

Successful IT automation implementations commonly result in 20 percent productivity gains and often as high as 50 percent or more. IT enterprises have realized significant and documentable cost savings with payback periods of 16 months or less. Falling technology prices, together with technological advances, make IT automation more attractive today than ever before. Total IT automation expenditures by U.S. IT enterprises grew by 50 percent in 1999 and are expected to total almost $700 billion in 2002.

Distributed IT users using laptop or handheld PC-based IT automation systems need access to up-to-date enterprise data. Remote data subset synchronization allows IT users to access the most current PC-based information, whether the data is entered or updated by remote IT users or the enterprise offices.

Successful IT automation implementations depend on an efficient, reliable data subset synchronization framework. For IT users and managers to effectively share end-user notes, activities, objectives, and IT data, the IT automation synchronization routines need to work without fail.

DATA SUBSET SYNCHRONIZATION FRAMEWORK

At the heart of a data subset synchronization technology is ActiveX Data Objects (ADO),[1] the latest data access technology from Microsoft. ADO offers the following major benefits for IT automation subset synchronization:

- *Universal data access.* Most IT enterprises employ multiple client and server database platforms. ADO is flexible enough to support any database platform that exposes an Object Linking and Embedding Data Base (OLE DB)[2] provider or Open DataBase Connectivity (ODBC)[3] driver.
- *Performance.* Because ADO is a thin layer that sits between an application and its data, the performance of ADO is comparable to direct (often proprietary) database access methods.
- *Future considerations.* ADO is an open technology that will continue to evolve as database technologies evolve.

Now consider the following data subset synchronization topics:

1. Steps in the data subset synchronization process
2. Methods for tracking changes on the client and server
3. Generation and transfer of log files
4. IT library documents
5. Log application
6. Conflict resolution
7. Synchronizing data subsets
8. Cascading deletes on client database
9. Restoring a client database
10. Distribution of application and database changes

Steps in the Data Subset Synchronization Process

The following are the high-level steps involved in the data subset synchronization framework:

1. Remote user databases are created as subsets of the master server database.
2. As updates, inserts, and deletes are made to remote client databases and to the central server database, the changes are flagged to be included in log files created during the data subset synchronization process.
3. The remote user initiates an exchange of log files containing incremental data changes and IT library documents between the client and server.
4. After the successful exchange of log files, changes are applied so that each database contains up-to-date PC-based information.

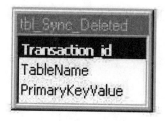
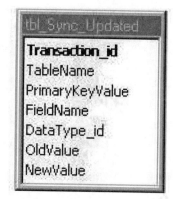

Exhibit 1.   Table Structure to Track Deletes and Field Level Updates as They Occur

Tracking Database Changes in the Client

The client application, for example, uses the table structure (as shown in Exhibit 1) to track deletes and field-level updates as they occur. Each deleted row generates a new record in `tbl_Sync_Deleted` and each updated field generates a new record in `tbl_Sync_Updated`. Optionally, updates for any given table can be handled at the record level. This is often desirable for processing updates on very narrow tables. Both `tbl_Sync_Deleted` and `tbl_Sync_Updated` are later used to generate the log file to be sent to the server.

Inserts to the database are tracked with a simple True/False field in the base table. For example, if a record is added to `tbl_Contacts`, the new row will contain a column indicating that this is a new record. By only tracking a flag in the base table for inserts, the overhead required to copy the transaction to a log table is avoided.

The data subset synchronization framework does not rely on the client computer clock time to track changes. This frees the data subset synchronization process from problems related to unsynchronized clocks and varying time zones.

Tracking Database Changes in the Server

The server database tracks deletes, updates, and inserts in the same structure as the client, as shown in Exhibit 2. The only difference is the method of populating the sync tables. On the server side, it is often desirable to make mass updates to the data using an administrative application or structure query language (as opposed to using the IT application). When mass updates are made, many systems will not be able to track the incre-

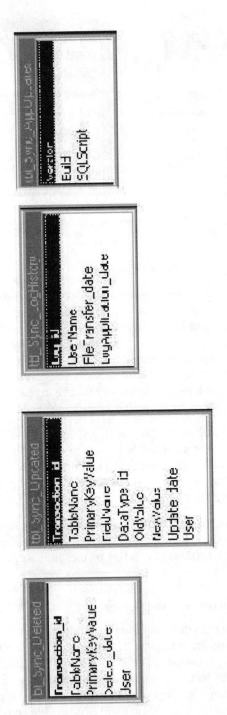

Exhibit 2. The Server Database Tracks Deletes, Updates, and Inserts in the Same Structure as the Client

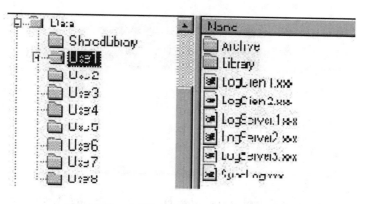

Exhibit 3.   A Client Log File is Generated

mental changes. Because the data subset synchronization framework uses server-side triggers, transaction tables will always be accurate. These database triggers offer extremely high performance and ease of implementation.

Generating and Transferring Log Files for the Client

A client log file is generated each time the user initiates data subset synchronization, as shown in Exhibit 3. The log file contains only incremental changes tracked on the client. The user-initiated process creates the log file and initiates connectivity to the central database server. In the event that the process is interrupted before successfully connecting to the central database and transferring the log file, the log file will remain on the client to be transferred during the subsequent connection. To ensure transactional integrity, each transfer is either committed in its entirety, or backed-out, so that it is as if none of the operations took place.

In the event of an interrupted data subset synchronization process, the user can simply synchronize at a later time. At this point, another log file is created, capturing incremental database changes since the failed attempt. This new log file is saved with a sequenced number appended to the end of the file name. In each data subset synchronization, all waiting sequential sync files are compressed and then transferred once a server connection is established.

Generating and Transferring Log Files for the Server

A server process, which can be scheduled to run automatically at predetermined times, generates client-specific log files that sit on the server until downloaded by the user. The data for this log file is extracted from the server database by pulling out changes made since the time the previous log

Exhibit 4. Data Subset Synchronization Framework Storing IT Library Documents

file was generated. If a user does not synchronize for several days, additional log files are created each time the process is run, with a sequenced number appended to the end of the filename. All log files are compressed after creation, or appended to an existing zip file of logs. All client-specific log files are transferred to the client in a single compressed file when the user initiates synchronization. After the successful transfer of log files between client and server, an entry is made in `synclog.xxx` in the user's data folder, indicating the time of successful transfer (see Exhibit 3).

IT Library Documents

The data subset synchronization framework stores IT library documents in the format shown in Exhibit 4. Documents that are user specific are stored in the path `UserName\Library`. Shared documents, which will be delivered to all users, are placed in `\SharedLibrary`.

When the server process is run, the last modified date for each library document is checked against the `LastModified_date` field in `tbl_Sync_SalesLibrary`. If a document has been modified, it is compressed and added to the `UserName\Library` path for download by the user upon the next data subset synchronization. The date comparison method makes it easy for an administrator to update documents in the library by simply copying the documents to the appropriate directory on the server. All documents are synchronized to the `ClientPath` specified in `tbl_Sync_SalesLibrary`.

Applying Log Files

Log files contain data necessary to process database deletes, inserts, and updates. Deletes are processed first, followed by inserts and updates. All database modification operations occur in a sequence that ensures referential integrity is not violated.

Client. Changes contained in the server log file(s) transferred to the client are applied after the remote connection is terminated. This minimizes potentially expensive connection fees. Before attempting to apply the server log file(s), the sync process checks for a Commit Flag to verify that the file was transferred successfully. Each record that was added, updated, or deleted in the client database as the result of applying the server log is flagged for inclusion in the client application's What's New module the next time the application is opened.

Server. When the scheduled server process is run, all client log files sitting in each of the user directories are applied to the central database server. Each log file applied represents a transaction. If for any reason an error occurs while applying a single log file, all changes are rolled back.

After successful application, the log file is transferred to an archive directory and kept for a specified number of days. The tbl_Sync_LogHistory is updated with user log file transfer and log file application timestamps.

Conflict Resolution

In the data subset synchronization framework, conflicts are resolved at the field level. Conflicts are detected by storing the OldValue and NewValue of a field in tbl_Sync_Updated. For example, if a contact phone number is 111-1111, and the remote user changes it to 222-2222, the client database tbl_Sync_Updated will have a record which has OldValue = '111-1111' and NewValue = '222-2222.' In the meantime, if another user has updated the same phone number field for the same contact to 333-3333, during the data subset synchronization, the client database will see that the current value on the server ('333-3333') is not equal to the OldValue ('111-1111') stored on the client. Because the values are different, a conflict needs to be resolved. This resolution is handled through the server data subset synchronization process.

The default conflict setting applies a last in wins rule. If this rule is not acceptable, the data subset synchronization framework is open enough to allow highly customized conflict rules to be created, such as record owner wins, remote wins, server wins, etc.

Synchronizing Data Subsets

Because rules for partitioning data are seldom exactly the same from one system to another, the data subset synchronization framework defines subsets of the master server database on a per-table basis. For each synchronized

Exhibit 5. The Data Subset Synchronization Framework

---

table, a custom Structured Query Language (SQL)[4] where clause can be implemented so users are given the data that is relevant to them.

This is illustrated using a very simple example that synchronizes tbl_Contacts as shown in Exhibit 5. Implementing the following where clause will partition the data so that each user only receives contacts in his or her region:

```
Where tbl_Contacts.Region_id = tbl_Users.Region_id AND
tbl_Users.UserName = SUSER_NAME()
```

Cascading Deletes on Client Database

It is often necessary to remove large subsets of data from the client database. IT users are often reassigned to different regions, records become outdated, and security access to data changes. If the client database platform does not support cascading deletes, cleaning up a client database can involve specifying individual records for deletion. The data subset synchronization framework includes methods to cascade the deletion of child records on database platforms that do not support cascading deletes.

For example, suppose an IT user is reassigned and will no longer cover IT in France. With cascading deletes, this clean up process only requires an administrative tool to create a single entry in this user's log file that deletes the parent record. All child records will be removed and unneeded data will no longer sit on the client.

Restoring a Client Database

Invariably, there will always be a situation where a hard drive crashes or a database file is inadvertently deleted. When this happens, the client database must be restored from data in the server database. Because the creation of server log files is based on a timestamp parameter, this timestamp simply needs to be reset and a user will receive data to rebuild the client database from scratch. An option can even be given in the client application to perform a complete refresh of data. This allows a user to get up and running in the shortest possible amount of time.

Distribution of Application and Database Changes

A remote application must provide a way to distribute application updates, fixes, new reports, etc. There are two common approaches to updating remote applications: copying new application component files to the client, and packaging program logic and form changes as part of the database. The latter, although an efficient way to distribute changes, often has a negative impact on application performance, especially when processing power on the client is marginal.

A remote application must also provide a way to change the structure of the client database (add fields, tables, relationships, etc.). The data subset synchronization framework handles database structure modifications through transact SQL scripts. SQL scripts make database structure modifications without transferring new database files and rebuilding data.

At the time of data subset synchronization, if a user is running a version older than the version number in tbl_Sync_AppUpdates, new application files and transact SQL script files are transferred to the client. The tbl_Sync_AppUpdates stores version PC-based information and contains a memo field that holds the SQL script required for each update. After the needed files are transferred to the client, an upgrade process is initiated that closes the IT application, copies new application files to their proper locations, runs all SQL scripts against the client database, and reopens the application.

Finally, this is accomplished through the use of a light, secondary application — the application controller — which executes SQL scripts and updates application files. The controller is stored in a location accessible to the IT Library. Should modifications be required to the controller application itself, a new application executable is simply transferred via the standard IT library update process, replacing the original controller application.

CONCLUSION AND SUMMARY

Remote data subset synchronization is the key piece of any remote IT application. It allows IT users to share accurate and up-to-date PC-based information while away from the central office.

Finally, it appears that the data subset synchronization framework is a robust and highly flexible solution for remote IT users. The framework supports a wide range of client and server database platforms and is open enough to allow a high degree of customization.

Notes

1. Short for ActiveX Data Objects, Microsoft's newest high-level interface for data objects. ADO is designed to eventually replace Data Access Objects (DAO) and Remote Data Objects (RDO). Unlike RDO and DAO, which are designed only for accessing relational databases, ADO is more general and can be used to access all sorts of different types of data, including Web pages, spreadsheets, and other types of documents. Together with OLE DB and ODBC, ADO is one of the main components of Microsoft's Universal Data Access (UDA) specification, which is designed to provide a consistent way of accessing data regardless of how the data is structured.
2. Microsoft's OLAP API, effectively the first industry standard for OLAP connectivity. Used to link OLAP clients and servers using a multidimensional language, MDX.
3. A widely adopted Microsoft standard for database connectivity.
4. Abbreviation for Structured Query Language, and pronounced either *see-kwell* or as separate letters. SQL is a standardized query language for requesting information from a database. The original version, called SEQUEL (Structured English Query Language), was designed by an IBM research center in 1974 and 1975. SQL was first introduced as a commercial database system in 1979 by Oracle Corporation. Historically, SQL has been the favorite query language for database management systems running on minicomputers and mainframes. Increasingly, however, SQL is being supported by PC database systems because it supports distributed databases (databases that are spread out over several computer systems). This enables several users on a local area network to access the same database simultaneously. Although there are different dialects of SQL, it is nevertheless the closest thing to a standard query language that currently exists. In 1986, ANSI approved a rudimentary version of SQL as the official standard, but most versions of SQL since then have included many extensions to the ANSI standard. In 1991, ANSI updated the standard. The new standard is known as SAG SQL.

Chapter 21
Using CORBA to Integrate Database Systems

*Bhavani Thuraisingham and
Daniel L. Spar*

Information has become the most critical resource in many organizations, and the rapid growth of networking and database technologies has had a major impact on information processing requirements. Efficient access to information, as well as sharing it, have become urgent needs. As a result, an increasing number of databases in different sites are being interconnected. In order to reconcile the contrasting requirements of the different database management systems (DBMSs), tools that enable users of one system to use another system's data are being developed. Efficient solutions for interconnecting and administering different database systems are also being investigated.

There are two aspects to the object-oriented approach to integrating heterogeneous database systems. In one approach, an object-oriented data model could be used as a generic representation scheme so that the schema transformations between the different database systems could be facilitated. In the other approach, a distributed object management system could be used to interconnect heterogeneous database systems. This chapter explores the distributed object management system approach by focusing on a specific distributed object management system: the object management group's (OMG) Common Object Request Broker Architecture (CORBA).

INTEROPERABILITY ISSUES

Although research on interconnecting different DBMSs has been under way for over a decade, only recently have many of the difficult problems been addressed. Through the evolution of the three-tier approach to client/server,

0-8493-1149-7/02/$0.00+$1.50
© 2002 by CRC Press LLC

the capability of integrating DBMSs has improved significantly. The traditional two-tier client/server approach included the layers of

1. Client
2. Server

For small systems, the two-tier approach works reasonably well. For larger systems with greater numbers of connected clients and servers, and greater levels of complexity and requirements for security, there is a substantial need for three-tier architectures. Two-tier systems are notorious for their development of the "fat client," where excessive amounts of code running business logic are required to be loaded onto the client machine.

The three-tier approach breaks client/server components into the layers of:

1. Client (presentation layer)
2. Middleware (business logic)
3. Server (data and resource management)

The result is much more efficient use of resources, and greater "plug and play" capabilities for both clients and servers. Clients can be superthin browsers running JAVA applets, and servers can be efficiently integrated and load-balanced.

With the advent of web servers, the three-tier model becomes "n-tier" since a web server is often placed between the client and middleware layers.

Schema Heterogeneity. Not all of the databases in a heterogeneous architecture are represented by the same schema (data model). Therefore, the different conceptual schemas have to be integrated. In order to do this, translators that transform the constructs of one schema into those of another are being developed. Integration remains most difficult with the older legacy databases that are prerelational.

Transaction Processing Heterogeneity. Different DBMSs may use different algorithms for transaction processing. Work is being directed toward integrating the various transaction processing mechanisms. Techniques that integrate locking, timestamping, and validation mechanisms are being developed. However, strict serializability may have to be sacrificed in order to create a heterogeneous environment. Independent transaction processing monitor (TP monitor) software is now readily available in the distributed systems marketplace. TP monitor software has been used for years on mainframes, and is now of great assistance in high-volume systems such as Internet commerce. Examples include web-based stock brokerage trading sites.

Query Processing Heterogeneity. Different DBMSs may also use different query processing and optimization strategies. Research is being conducted to develop a global cost model for distributed query optimization.

Query Language Heterogeneity. Query language heterogeneity should also be addressed, even if the DBMSs are based on the relational model. Structured query language (SQL) and relational calculus could be used to achieve heterogeneity. Standardization efforts are under way to develop a uniform interface language.

Constraint Heterogeneity. Different DBMSs enforce different integrity constraints, which are often inconsistent. For example, one DBMS could enforce a constraint that all employees must work at least 40 hours, even though another DBMS may not enforce such a constraint. Moving these business rules over to the application servers on the middle tier and away from the DBMSs on the third tier will also help isolate and correct business rule inconsistencies.

Semantic Heterogeneity. Data may be interpreted differently by different components. For example, the entity address could represent just the country for one component, or it could represent the number, street, city, and country for another component. This problem will be difficult to resolve in older systems that combined multiple domains in a single database field and often assigned cryptic names to tables and fields that do not reveal their content.

THE COMMON OBJECT REQUEST BROKER ARCHITECTURE (CORBA)

CORBA was created to provide an object-based central layer to enable the objectives of three-tier distributed systems, especially in the area of interoperability.

The three major components of CORBA are the object model, the object request broker (ORB) and object adapters, and the interface definition language (IDL).

The Object Model

The object model describes object semantics and object implementation. Object semantics describe the semantics of an object: type, requests, object creation and destruction, interfaces, operations, and attributes. Object implementation describes the execution model and the construction model. In general, the object model of CORBA has the essential constructs of most object models.

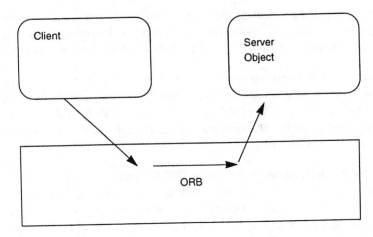

Exhibit 1. Communication through an Object Request Broker (ORB)

The Object Request Broker (ORB)

The ORB essentially enables communication between a client and a server object. A client invokes an operation on the object, and the object implementation provides the code and data needed to implement the object. The ORB provides the necessary mechanisms to find the object implementation for a particular request and enables the object implementation to receive the request. The communication mechanisms necessary to deliver the request are also provided by the ORB.

In addition, the ORB supports the activation and deactivation of objects and their implementation as well as generating and interpreting object references. Although the ORB provides the mechanisms to locate the object and communicate the client's request to the object, the exact location of the object, as well as the details of its implementation, are transparent to the client. Objects use object adapters to access the services provided by the ORB. Communication between a client and a server object using the ORB is illustrated in Exhibit 1.

INTERFACE DEFINITION LANGUAGE (IDL)

IDL is the language used to describe the interfaces that are called by client objects and provided by object implementations. IDL is a declarative language; client and object implementations are not written in IDL. IDL grammar is a subset of ANSI C++ with additional constructs to support the operation invocation mechanism. An IDL binding to the C language has been specified, and other language bindings are being processed. Exhibit 2 illustrates how IDL is used for communication between a client and a server.

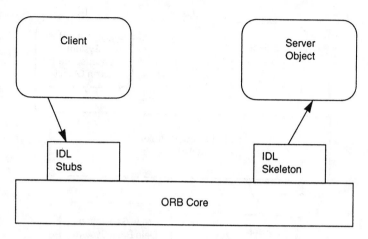

Exhibit 2.   Interface Definition Language (IDL) Interface to Object Request Broker (ORB)

The client's request is passed to the ORB using an IDL stub. An IDL skeleton delivers the request to the server object.

INTEGRATING HETEROGENEOUS DATABASE SYSTEMS

Migrating legacy databases to new generation architectures is difficult. Although it is desirable to migrate such databases and applications to client/server architectures, the costs involved in many cases are enormous. Therefore, the alternative approach is to keep the legacy databases and applications and develop mechanisms to integrate them with new systems. The distributed object management system approach in general, and the CORBA approach in particular, are examples of such mechanisms.

Although the major advantage of the CORBA approach is the ability to encapsulate legacy database systems and databases as objects without having to make any major modifications (see Exhibit 3), techniques for handling the various types of heterogeneity are still necessary. The CORBA approach does not handle problems such as transaction heterogeneity and semantic heterogeneity. However, the procedures used to handle the types of heterogeneity can be encapsulated in the CORBA environment and invoked appropriately.

Handling Client Communications with the Server

A client will need to communicate with the database servers, as shown in Exhibit 4. One method is to encapsulate the database servers as objects. The clients can issue appropriate requests and access the servers through

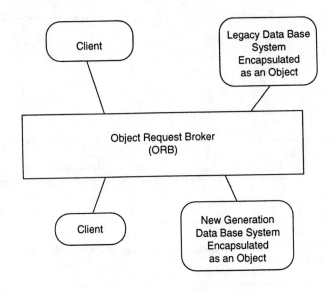

Exhibit 3. Encapsulating Legacy Databases

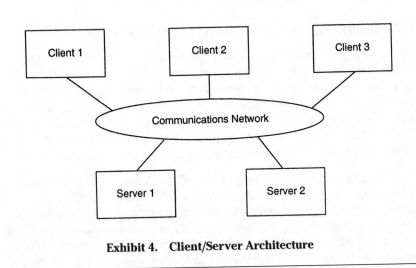

Exhibit 4. Client/Server Architecture

an ORB. If the servers are SQL-based, the entire SQL query/update request could be embedded in the message. When the method associated with the server object gets the message, it can extract the SQL request and pass it to the server. The results from the server objects are then encoded as a message and passed back to the client through the ORB. This approach is illustrated in Exhibit 5.

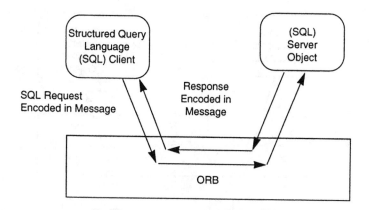

Exhibit 5. **Common Object Request Broker Architecture (CORBA) for Interoperability**

Handling Heterogeneity

Different types of heterogeneity must be handled in different ways. For example, if the client is SQL-based and the server is a legacy database system based on the network model, then the SQL query by the client must be transformed into a language understood by the server. One representation scheme must be transformed into another. The client's request must first be sent to the module that is responsible for performing the transformations. This module, the transformer, could be encapsulated as an object. As illustrated in Exhibit 6, the client's SQL request is sent to the transformer, which transforms the request into a request understood by the server. The transformed request is then sent to the server object. The transformer could directly transform the SQL representation into a network representation, or it could use an intermediate representation to carry out the transformation.

Handling Transformations

The distributed processor could also be used to perform distributed data management functions. The distributed processor is responsible for handling functions such as global query optimization and global transaction management. This module is also encapsulated as an object and handles the global requests and responses. The response assembled by the server is also sent to the transformer to transform into a representation understood by the client. Response delivery is illustrated in Exhibit 7.

Semantic Heterogeneity. If semantic heterogeneity has to be handled, a repository should be maintained to store the different names given to a single object or the different objects represented by a single name. The repository

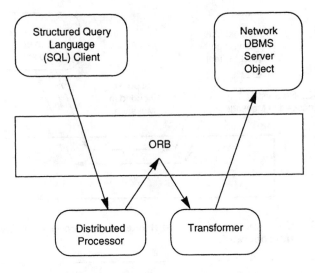

Exhibit 6. Handling Transformations

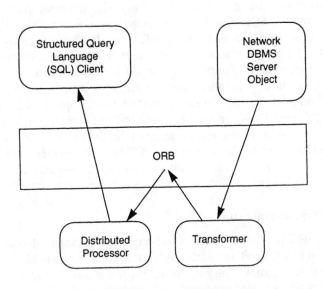

Exhibit 7. Delivering Responses

could be encapsulated as an object that would resolve semantic heterogeneity. For example, a client could request that an object be retrieved from multiple servers. The request is first sent to the repository, which issues multiple requests to the appropriate servers depending on the names used

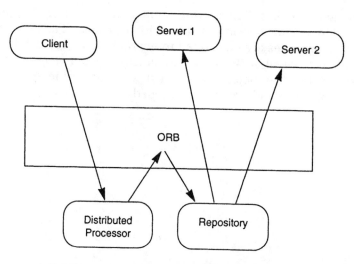

Exhibit 8. Handling Semantic Heterogeneity

to denote the object. This approach is illustrated in Exhibit 8. The response may also be sent to the repository so that it can be presented to the client in an appropriate manner. The repository could be an extension of the transformer illustrated in Exhibit 6. All the communications are carried out through the ORB. This example highlights some of the benefits of separating the business logic from the actual data stored in the DBMS servers.

CONCLUSION

The rapid growth in distributed systems has placed two key demands on IT managers:

1. How can the most efficient and effective design — the three-tier model — best be implemented to manage a very heterogeneous environment?
2. How can the semantic meaning of the legacy data elements be best understood so they can be shared across systems?

The CORBA approach is an excellent means of addressing heterogeneity, especially with respect to queries, languages, transactions, schemas, constraints, and semantics. However, although CORBA is useful for integrating heterogeneous database systems, there are still several issues that need further consideration. For example, should a server be encapsulated as an object? How can databases be encapsulated? Should an entire database be encapsulated as an object or should it consist of multiple objects? Should stored procedures be encapsulated also?

Although there is still much work to be done, the various approaches proposed to handle these issues show a lot of promise. Furthermore, until efficient approaches are developed to migrate the legacy databases and applications to client/server-based architectures, approaches like CORBA and other distributed object management systems for integrating heterogeneous databases and systems are needed.

Chapter 22
Data Dictionary: Data Element Definitions

Judith M. Myerson

A data dictionary, in its simplest form, is only a collection of data element definitions. A more advanced version contains database schema (with reference keys) that allows end users to see certain parts of the tables that interest them the most. It may contain an entity-relationship model of the data elements or objects. This model is useful in determining and constructing relationships among entities for designing a database with a data dictionary in mind.

Database personnel use the dictionary in various ways. Database administrators can look up the dictionary to verify, for example, that a corrupted database has been completely restored to its original tables, forms, queries, and schema. System managers can refer to it when preparing a contingency plan or a disaster recovery plan. Database architects use the entity-relationship model component as background material in building a database system, while programmers customize programs based, in part, on data elements in associated tables as defined in the dictionary. Data dictionaries can be used over the Internet and in distributed applications. The advantage here is that database personnel can use or refer to a data dictionary in a central repository in a consistent manner in all phases of a database system development life cycle in distributed environments.

When designing a database, it is important that data elements are completely free of ambiguities, as English does have some holes into which a careless person can fall. More details are given in the section on ambiguity types in the latter part of this chapter.

0-8493-1149-7/02/$0.00+$1.50
© 2002 by CRC Press LLC

DATA ELEMENT DEFINITIONS

There are two ways of defining data elements: (1) one can create data elements from database specifications; or (2) one can derive them from database textbooks, existing data dictionaries, and practical experience with tools such as Oracle, Ingres, Access, and SQL Server. One gets them after identifying data items and separating the data elements from the files and tables as well as those from COBOL programs (Data Division).

Data element definitions may be independent of table definitions or a part of each table definition. Some are cross-referenced to data elements as defined in other data dictionaries. Others are as a result of consolidating similarly defined data elements from outside sources into common definitions. Because the list of data element definitions can be a bit long, it is more practical to divide them into four arbitrary groups: general, coding, references, and quality control.

General

This category covers the main part of a data dictionary. It includes data element names along with a short description and security classification for each. It also covers how data elements are associated to one another. System administrators may be the only ones who have access to security classification for each element.

- *Data element name:* commonly agreed data element name in, for example, no more than 10 bytes
- *Short description:* description of the element in, for example, no more than 25 words
- *Security classification of the data element:* organization-specific security classification level: privacy data, financial data, confidential, or higher
- *Related data elements:* list of closely related data element names in important relations
- *Cross-referenced data elements:* cross-references of data elements to help users track down a data element
- *Similarly defined data elements:* list of data elements similarly defined from various sources

Coding

This category refers to data elements that the programmers can use to code database specifications into, for example, data entry, query, or report screens. Some examples include field names along with the format and length for each. The programmers rely on validation rules to ensure errors are not introduced when users enter data on the screen.

- *Field names:* the names used for this element in computer programs and database schemas
- *Format:* data type, such as numeric, alphanumeric, date, currency, memo, logic
- *Length:* the size of each data type
- *Null value:* null or non-existing data value may be or may not be allowed for an element (elements with possible null values need special considerations in reports and may cause problems if used as a key)
- *Default value:* may be a variable, such as current date and time of day
- *Intra-element validation:* validation rules for single elements
- *Inter-element validation:* validation rules between this element and other elements in the data dictionary
- *External element validation:* validation rules between elements of one data dictionary and elements in others

References

This category looks at five types of references. They are database table references, and definitions and references. Also included are source, history, and external references.

1. *Database table references:* references to tables and the role of the element in each table; special indication when the data element is the key for the table or a part of the key
2. *Definitions and references:* references to other documents needed to understand the meaning and use of the data element; rules used in calculations are usually written here
3. *Source references:* short description of where the data is coming from
4. *History references:* date when the element was defined in present form, references to superseded elements, etc.
5. *External references:* references to books, other documents, laws, etc.

Configuration Management

Configuration management helps track dictionary updates in a central repository. They include version number and date. Also important are the references to quality control on these updates.

- *Version number:* version number or other indicator of data element; may include formal version control or configuration management references, but such references may be hidden, depending on the system used
- *Version date:* version date for the associated version number
- *Quality control references:* organization-specific quality control endorsements, dates, etc.
- *Data element notes:* short notes not included in above parts

Exhibit 1. Beginning of Data Dictionary

Data Element Name	Data Type	Length
Account_no	Numeric	10
Userid	Alphanumeric	8
Recorded	Alphanumeric	10
Date	Date	6
Idle_now	Logic	1
Task_seq_no	Numeric	8
Time_left_in_acct	Numeric	5
No_harddisks	Numeric	5
Amt_charged	Currency	10

SAMPLE DATA DICTIONARY

A simple data dictionary starts with a data element name, data type, and length as shown in Exhibit 1. This dictionary consists of elements about a capacity database server. Elements in bold make up a primary key.

One may arbitrarily divide the account_no key component into: organizational code (2 bytes), account code (2 bytes), project code (2 bytes), database code (2 bytes), and table code (2 bytes). The advantage of doing so is that one can change the sequence of primary keys by its components. It is not necessary to sort by organization code, account code, and then project code. One can sort the keys by project code and then organization code. Just make sure to have a table of codes with associated names or meanings for each code. One can use this table to print, for example, organizational names in a report.

If one includes null values and default values in the dictionary, one obtains the list shown in Exhibit 2. Do not include them in primary keys, each of which must be unique. This can be further expanded to include a short description, security code, and a field name for each data element, as shown in Exhibit 3. Only the first two rows are filled in. Security is identified by a code, the explanation of which resides in another table that is accessible only by a database or system administrator.

VALIDATION RULES

Some elements require validation rules so that numeric values will not fall out of its range or exceed its size. If a user, for example, enters three digits in lieu of two, an error message will pop up on the screen. To prevent this from happening, one might establish a validation rule for the organizational code component of the account_no data element using Microsoft Access' Expression Builder. This option helps one choose built-in (and customized)

Exhibit 2. Adding Null Values and Default Values

Data Element Name	Data Type	Length	Null Value	Default Value
Account_no	Numeric	10	N	
Userid	Alphanumeric	8	N	
Recorded	Alphanumeric	10	N	Current
Date	Date	6	N	Current
Idle_now	Logic	1	Y	
Task_seq_no	Numeric	8	N	
Time_left_in_acct	Numeric	5	N	
No_harddisks	Numeric	5	N	
Amt_charged	Currency	10	N	

functions, operators, and constants to set up a validation rule for that element.

If the organizational code is valid between 1 and 45, one can enter a simple expression: (0>) And (<45). The expression can be more complex if the organizational code 24 and 45 do not exist. Then one can enter ((0>) And (<45)) And Not (24 or 45). When closing the table in design format, a warning message pops up that

> Data Integrity rules have been changed. Existing data may not be valid for new rules.

After entering the data, one may want to add or change validation rules for the account_no element. Doing so will bring up the following message. This happens when one tries to close the table.

> Existing data violates the new setting for the Validation rule property for account_no.

When one opens the table to enter new data, one may find that some previously entered data does not exist anymore. They violated new validation rules. If incorrect data has been erroneously entered, one will see the following:

> One or more values are probihited by the validation rule ((0>) And (<45)) And Not (24 or 45) for account_no. Enter a value that the expression will accept.

In addition to intra-validation rules as explained above, two other types of rules are important. They are inter-validation rules between elements in the same data dictionary and external validation rules between elements of one data dictionary and elements in other data dictionaries as shown in the capacity account (CA) table in Exhibit 4. This table resides in the capacity server (CS) database.

Exhibit 3. Expanding the Data Dictionary

Data Element Name	Data Type	Length	Null Value	Default Value	Field Name	Security	Description
Account_no	Numeric	10	N		Account Number	23Y	Acct no. assigned to each individual
Userid	Alphanumeric	8	N		User ID	23Y	Userid assigned to each individual
Recorded	Alphanumeric	10	N	Current	Record ID		
Date	Date	6	N	Current	Date		
Idle_now	Logic	1	Y		Idle Now		
Task_seq_no	Numeric	8	N		Task Sequence Number		
Time_left_in_acct	Numeric	5	N		Time Left in Account		
No_harddisks	Numeric	5	N		Number of hard disks currently in use		
Amt_charged	Currency	10	N		Amount charged		

OUTSIDE SOURCES

Now the very interesting part of the design activity: how to record data elements from outside sources for incorporation into an existing data dictionary. The best approach is to create a column for "similarly defined elements." If the element is derived from one or more outside sources, the column should indicate the names of the data dictionaries. This is useful in modifying target data elements or tracking down structural differences (length, data type, etc.) of these elements.

Once done, the next steps are to include related and cross-referenced data elements. A column on "related data elements" should indicate how data elements are associated with one another in OUTER JOIN, INNER JOIN, and other important relations. If a relation is long or complex or there are several separate relations for an element, the column should point to another table. Cross-referenced data elements are helpful to users who need to track down other elements in current and other data dictionaries.

For a complex system, it is important to have configuration management in place. Database or source upgrades can play havoc with the system. More problematic is when the system is distributed over a wide geographic area and a team of system designers, programmers, and administrators are at different locations. Improper communication may mislead a team member to upgrade at the wrong time and wrong location. To handle the challenges of upgrading the system on a wide scale, a separate table should be created on version number, version date, and quality control references for each element — new or modified.

All references on data elements should be treated as memos. They can serve as important information items among others as "input" to discussions on a new system under consideration. This is also true for team efforts on planning changes to an existing system, including the following:

- Database table references
- Definition references
- Source references
- History references
- External references

Of these five, definition references are the most important. They contain references to other documents needed to understand exactly the meaning and use of the data element. Some elements may need to be renamed to avoid ambiguity, even if the meanings are different. If the meanings are similarly defined, structural differences should be included. Rules used in calculations are usually written here.

Exhibit 4. Capacity Account Table

Data Element Name	Data Type	Length	Null Value	Default Value	Field Name	Inter-Valid. Rule	Intra-Valid. Rule	Ext. Valid. Rule
Account_no	Numeric	10	N		Account Number	ca.org: ((0>) And (<45)) And Not (24 or 45)	See ca.org and tab1.org	See cs.ca.org, cs.tab1.org, and es.ea.org
Userid	Alphanumeric	8	N		User ID			
recorded	Alphanumeric	10	N	Current	Record ID			
Date	Date	6	N	Current	Date			
idle_now	Logic	1	Y		Idle Now			
task_seq_no	Numeric	8	N		Task Sequence Number			
time_left_in_acct	Numeric	5	N		Time Left in Account			
no_harddisks	Numeric	5	N		Number of hard disks currently in use			
amt_charged	Currency	10	N		Amount charged			

DATA DICTIONARY REPOSITORY

One can look up a data dictionary from a hard-copy reference book, a local repository on one's client workstation, or a central repository on a host or database server in a distributed network. A Web-enabled central repository may serve as a help file that a user can use with a browser. This file would help the user choose data elements while composing a query on, for example, a capacity database.

The help file could also be used in collaborative efforts over the Internet, such as planning, developing, or enhancing a new or existing database system. It should allow database architects, managers, administrators, and programmers to locate data elements and their associated meanings and references. They can get them by browsing an index or entering data elements in a query.

Also useful is a visual map on the hierarchy of data elements in data dictionaries that are related to one another. This would benefit users who need assistance in finding data elements that they are unable to immediately recall. The system administrator with proper credentials should be the only one permitted to add or change data dictionaries and their associated visual maps.

AMBIGUITY TYPES

All data elements must be very clear on what they mean and what they are used for. If they are not, they are considered ambiguous, meaning that they may have double interpretations, for example. One way of avoiding ambiguity with data elements is to understand what ambiguity types are, such as sentential, anaphora, and join. They are particularly important when users compose SQL queries. One may need to add data elements to help users form an unambiguous query. Well-understood queries must be referenced to correct validation rules and database tables.

Sentential Ambiguity

Data elements, if not clear, can result in ambiguous meaning of both the elements This is also true for a query containing those elements. Ambiguity types include misspelled words, lexical, and structural.

Misspelled Words. This happens when the spelling checker erroneously considers misspelled words as correctly spelled words.This happens in two ways: (1) a user accidentally adds these misspelled words, or (2) the user inadvertently allows the checker to skip them.

Lexical Ambiguity. A grammatically correct query contains words that have several meanings. For example, "Where are Hudson Park hard disks?"

has a double meaning. It may refer to disks sold in Hudson Park or disks sold by the stores in Hudson Park.

Structural Ambiguity. This ambiguity type exists in a sentence with more than one meaning of a word. Selection of a meaning depends on the grammatical relationships of the word to the query. It also depends on how the word is used in relations.

Anaphora Ambiguity

This is a sentential reference in a query to previous queries. Three types of reference must be considered: pronoun, paraphrase, and ellipsis. Suppose a new database table includes data elements for white papers, publication date, and publishing costs. Assume the user enters the query "Which white papers on hard disks for capacity servers were sold last month?" and then follows it with "When were they published?"

The first query is clear. The second query, however, contains a pronoun reference to the first query: "What were our publishing costs at *that time*?" It contains the paraphrase at *that time* for last month.

Ellipsis refers to a query to which the omitted words are intended to be understood from the content of the query. Assume the user enters "What about the month before last?" It is intended to be understood as "Which white papers were published during the month before last?"

Join Ambiguity

This is where a wrong database table is used for a well-understood query. This often happens when the tables are similarly named. Distinct names should be assigned. Relationships among data elements in various tables must be clearly established.

CONCLUSION

Additional data elements may be necessary to record information about their sources and control version changes. The meanings of target data elements must be clear, concise, and concrete. Ambiguity types are presented to help database managers, administrators, architects, and programmers avoid data elements that appear to be unclear or have ambiguous meaning. This is particularly important when designing a large, complex server-side capacity database for distributed applications over the Internet.

Chapter 23
Designing an Integrated Data Server

James A. Larson
Carol L. Larson

An enterprise's information may be scattered across multiple, isolated information islands in a sea of computers and database systems. To use enterprise data, users must locate, access, and integrate data from multiple databases and files that may be located in different data systems on different computers and possibly separated geographically.

The evolution of an enterprise and its databases contributes to the scattering of data. Many companies encourage their enterprise units (i.e., divisions, departments, and subsidiaries) to be independent from each other. Independent enterprise units evolve differently with different data requirements, applications, and systems. Each enterprise unit designs its database to meet its particular needs. Databases of different enterprise units often contain different information used for different purposes.

WHEN SHOULD DATA BE INTEGRATED INTO A DATA SERVER?

The proliferation of PCs has greatly aggravated the data dispersion problem. The widespread use of PCs has resulted in many files and databases that are frequently stored on floppy disks. These off-line databases make it even more difficult to access all of the enterprises's data. To be useful, data must be available when users need it. Furthermore, users may not know what data are available or how to find it.

In such an environment, users must perform three essential actions to obtain meaningful information:

- *Locate information.* Users must determine if relevant data are available somewhere among the computing resources of the enterprise. Then,

0-8493-1149-7/02/$0.00+$1.50
© 2002 by CRC Press LLC

they must locate the appropriate computer containing the relevant data.

- *Access information.* Users must be able to formulate separate requests to access each data source.
- *Integrate information.* Users must integrate the results of their requests into an integrated format so they can review and use the data to make decisions.

If users are not able to access the data they need or are not aware of what data they need, they cannot make the necessary decisions or perform their jobs optimally. This results in poor performance for both the individuals and the enterprise as a whole. Data should be integrated into a centralized server if the cost of poor performance is greater than the expense of integrating the diverse databases and files into a centralized database server.

DATA INTEGRATION FROM MULTIPLE SOURCES

The term *source tables* refers to tables to be integrated. Target tables are the result of the integration. Exhibit 1 illustrates bottom-up and top-down approaches to integrating data from multiple sources. The bottom-up approach consists of four steps:

1. *Inventorying existing data.* Source database tables and files to be integrated into a target centralized database server must be identified.
2. *Modeling individual databases.* The entities and their relationships within each source database must be identified.
3. *Converting all schemas to relational schemas.* All entities and relationships must be expressed in a common format.
4. *Integrating source schemas into a target schema.* Structural and format inconsistencies among data from different source databases must be identified and resolved.

The top-down approach consists of two steps:

- *Designing the target schema.* Data elements needed in the target schema must be determined.
- *Constructing cross-references.* Cross-references are essential from each source schema to the target schema. Mappings between the source and target schemas must be defined.

After using the bottom-up approach, the top-down approach, or a combination of these approaches, the database administrator migrates and integrates source data from the various source databases into a target relational database server. Erroneous and inconsistent data should be identified and resolved.

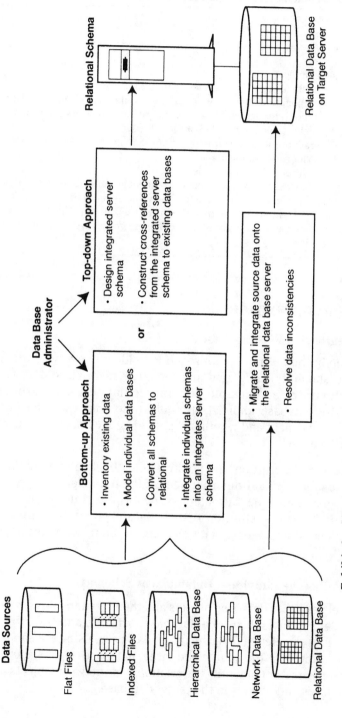

Exhibit 1. Migrating Data from One or More Databases to a Single-Server Database

Exhibit 2. Description of a Data Element

English name:	class
COBOL name:	class
Fortran name:	class
C name:	class
Type:	short integer
Values:	1 = freshman (student with fewer than 45 hours)
	2 = sophomore (student with 45 or more hours and with less than 90 hours)
	3 = junior (student with 90 or more hours and with less than 135 hours)
	4 = senior (student with 135 or more hours)
	5 = graduate student (formally admitted to graduate school)
	6 = other (none of the above)
Source:	student record in student file
Calculation:	automatically calculated from the student's transcript record on the second week of each semester. The value includes the number of hours the student actually earned the previous semester. This field is not updated automatically when incomplete grades are changed to final grades.

THE BOTTOM-UP APPROACH

Step 1: Inventorying Existing Data

The first step in the bottom-up approach is to identify every source data element that should be integrated into the target centralized data server. Exhibit 2 illustrates an example of a source data element. From this description, the database administrator quickly determines the meaning of the source data element and whether it should be included in the centralized database server.

If data element descriptions are not available, the database administrator must examine applications that access the data elements to determine their meaning. If the data element descriptions do not exist, the database administrator should create a data element description for each data element and form a data element dictionary for future reference.

Step 2: Modeling the Individual Databases as Schemas

A data model describes database objects and their relationships, as well as each data element in each source database or file. In addition, the data model describes the elements of the target database. Using the same data model to describe both the source and target database objects allows the database administrator to identify the relationships between objects in the source databases and objects in the target database.

Popular Data-Modeling Techniques. Popular data models include the relational data model, entity-relationship data models, and object-oriented data models. To facilitate a comparison of objects in different databases, it is desirable to use a single data model to describe all databases and files. Database administrators differ in their choice of data models and often argue the advantages and disadvantages of the various data models. Here, the relational data model is used because it is the data model used by the target database management system.

Step 3: Integrating Schemas into an Integrated Server Schema

One strategy for schema integration is to identify the relationship between pairs of source tables and then construct the appropriate target table. The bottom-up approach uses the following four steps to define a target schema:

Identify Pairs of Source Tables as Candidates for Integration. Database administrators should use heuristics to identify candidate pairs of source tables. One possible heuristic is to consider only pairs of source tables that have the same name, nearly the same names, or names that are synonyms. Another possible heuristic is to consider pairs of source tables that have several columns with the same name, nearly the same name, or names that are synonyms.

Determine the Relationship of the Rows of the Source Tables. Database administrators should determine the relationships between pairs of source tables. The five tables in Exhibit 3 describe each of the four possible relationships — logical containment, logical equivalence, logical overlap, and logically disjoint — between any pair of source tables, referred to as tables A and B. These relationships are defined as follows:

- *Logical containment.* If each row in A always corresponds to a unique row in B, then B logically contains A. For example, every SmallAircraft row always corresponds to a row of Aircraft. Therefore, Aircraft logically contains SmallAircraft.
- *Logical equivalence.* If each row in A always corresponds to a unique row in B and each row in B always corresponds to a unique row in A, then B is logically equivalent to A. For example, every CarValue row always corresponds to a CarRegistration row and every CarRegistration row always corresponds to a CarValue row. Therefore, CarValue is logically equivalent to CarRegistration.
- *Logical overlap.* If some of the rows in A correspond to some of the rows in B and some of the rows in B correspond to some of the rows in A, then A and B logically overlap. For example, some Truck rows are found in CarRegistration, and some CarRegistration rows are found in Truck. Therefore, CarRegistration and Truck logically overlap.

Exhibit 3. Sample Source Tables

Aircraft (Source Table)

Owner	RegNumber	Flight Rating Level
Able	14	2
Baker	23	1
Gilbert	67	3

Small Aircraft (Source Table)

Owner	RegNumber	Flight Rating Level	Range
Able	14	2	600
Baker	23	1	800

Car Value (Source Table)

RegNumber	Year	Manufacturer	Model	Price
37	95	Plymouth	Voyager	15000
42	92	Ford	Taurus	7000
54	95	Jeep	Cherokee	17000

Car Registration (Source Table)

Owner	RegNumber	Year	Manufacturer	Model
Carson	37	95	Plymouth	Voyager
Davis	42	92	Ford	Taurus
Elgin	54	95	Jeep	Cherokee

Truck (Source Table)

Owner	RegNumber	Load Limit	Year	Manufacturer	Model
Able	14	2000	94	Dodge	Ram
Elgin	54	1000	95	Jeep	Cherokee

- *Logically disjoint.* If none of the rows in A corresponds to any of the rows in B and none of the rows in B corresponds to any of the rows in A, then A and B are logically disjoint. For example, no rows of Aircraft are found in CarRegistration, and no rows of CarRegistration are found in the Aircraft table. Therefore, Aircraft and CarRegistration are logically disjoint.

The database administrator must determine which of the candidate pairs of source tables to integrate. Two source tables may be integrated if they are logically equivalent, one logically contains the other, or they logically overlap. If two source tables are disjoint, they should only be integrated if the database administrator determines that they represent the same type of entity. For example, the Aircraft and CarValue tables should not be integrated based on logical analysis alone.

Create the Integrated Tables. For each pair of source tables to be integrated, the database administrator must determine how many target tables to create as a result of the integration. There are three general approaches.

No-Table Approach. The database administrator should not integrate the two source tables. For example, because Aircraft and CarRegistration (see Exhibit 3) are logically disjoint, they should not be integrated into a single table. However, these tables may be integrated if the database administrator determines that several applications will access both tables for the same purpose.

Single-Table Approach. A single target table should be created to replace a pair of source tables to be integrated. The single target table contains the union of the columns from the two source tables with columns suitably renamed. Some rows of the target table may contain nulls in the columns that are not common to both of the source tables.

An example of the single-table approach is CarValue's logical equivalence to CarRegistration. The database administrator should create a single-target table, Car, to replace CarRegistration and CarValue by constructing the columns of the Car table to be the union of the columns of CarValue and CarRegistration. The Car target table should appear as shown in Exhibit 4.

Exhibit 4. Car (Target Table)

Owner	RegNumber	Year	Manufacturer	Model	Price
Carson	37	95	Plymouth	Voyager	15000
Davis	42	92	Ford	Taurus	7000
Elgin	54	95	Jeep	Cherokee	17000

As another example, the Aircraft table (see Exhibit 3) logically contains the SmallAircraft table. The database administrator should construct the columns of the target table, Airplane, to be the union of the columns of the source tables, Aircraft and SmallAircraft. The Airplane target table appears in Exhibit 5.

Exhibit 5. Airplane (Target Table)

Owner	RegNumber	Flight Rating Level	Range
Able	14	2	600
Baker	23	1	800
Gilbert	67	3	(null)

There is no value in the Range column for the airplane with RegNumber 67 because it is not a small aircraft and the Range column is not common to both source tables. Some database administrators dislike the single-table approach because a missing value implies additional semantics; in this case, Airplane 67 is a small aircraft.

Multiple-Table Approach. Multiple target tables should be created to replace the two source tables to be integrated. One target table contains the columns and the rows common to both source tables being integrated. Each of two additional target tables contains the key from the source table and the columns from the source table not common to the two source tables to be integrated. In the multiple-table approach, the extra target tables represent rows that are in one but not the other source table.

For example, the Truck and CarRegistration source tables logically overlap. Three target tables can be constructed from the source tables CarRegistration and Truck. The Vehicle target table contains the common columns of the Truck and CarRegistration source tables, as shown in Exhibit 6.

Exhibit 6.   Vehicle (Target Table)

Owner	RegNumber	Year	Manufacturer	Model
Carson	37	95	Plymouth	Voyager
Davis	42	92	Ford	Taurus
Elgin	54	95	Jeep	Cherokee

The Truck target table contains the columns of the source Truck table minus the columns of the Vehicle target table; as shown in Exhibit 7. The Car target table contains the columns of the CarRegistration source table minus the columns of the Vehicle target table, as shown in Exhibit 8.

Exhibit 7.   Truck (TargetTable)

RegNumber	Load Limit
14	2000
54	1000

Exhibit 8.   Car (Target Table)

RegNumber	Price
37	15000
42	7000
54	17000

Some database administrators dislike the multiple-table approach because they feel the target tables are overnormalized or broken into too many tables, which may result in complex operations. For example, the Vehicle, Car, and Truck tables must be joined to access all the data associated with a vehicle. When a vehicle is removed from the database, rows of multiple tables must be deleted.

The choice between the single-table and multiple-table approaches must be made by the database administrator based on the anticipated use of the resulting tables. Generally, the single-table approach is used if the primary usage will be retrieval; the multiple-table approach is used if the primary use will be update.

TOP-DOWN APPROACH

Step 1: Designing the Target Schema

The database administrator designs a centralized database, such as the following two source tables:

- Aircraft (which contains Owner, RegNumber, FlightRatingLevel, and Range).
- Vehicle (which contains Owner, RegNumber, Year, Manufacturer, Model, Price, and LoadLimit).

Step 2: Constructing Cross-References Between the Integrated Server Schema to Existing Databases

This step requires that the database administrator define the mappings between the source and target schemas. For each column in a source table, the corresponding column in a target table must be identified. In Exhibit 9, these correspondences are illustrated by arrows. The database administrator should review the mappings and check for the following situations:

- *New value.* If a data element in a target table has no mapping, then there will be no way for it to contain any values. The database administrator can either specify the manual process for supplying values to this data element or delete it from the schema.
- *Potential inconsistent value.* If a column in a target table has two or more mappings, then it will receive data from two or more source tables. There is a possibility of inconsistencies when data is obtained from the two source tables. These inconsistencies must be detected and resolved by the database administrator.
- *Missing data element.* If a data element in a source table is not mapped to a data element in any target table, the database administrator should verify that the missing data element will not be used by applications accessing the source database. If an application does access

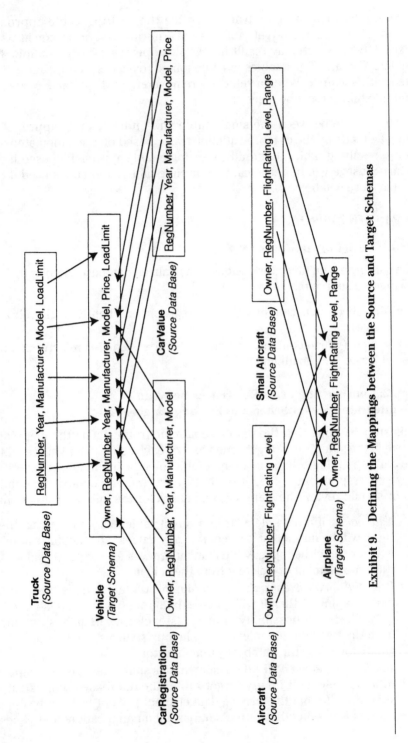

Exhibit 9.   Defining the Mappings between the Source and Target Schemas

the data element, then the missing data element should be inserted in the appropriate target table.

CENTRALIZED DATABASE SERVER POPULATION AND INCONSISTENT DATA RESOLUTION

After using a combination of the bottom-up and top-down approaches, the structural relationships between the source and target data elements should be identified. The database administrator should identify and resolve structural inconsistencies such as naming issues, differing levels of abstractions, inconsistent coding structures, and inconsistent data formats. If a target data element has multiple source elements, value inconsistencies should be detected and resolved.

RECOMMENDED COURSE OF ACTION

Users must perform three essential actions to obtain meaningful information:

1. Locate relevant data and the computer that contains the data
2. Formulate separate requests to each data source to access the data
3. Integrate the results of the users' requests into an integrated format that users review and use to make decisions

Data should be integrated into a centralized server if the cost of poor performance is greater than the expense of integrating the diverse databases and files into a centralized database server.

The bottom-up approach for schema integration creates an inventory of existing data and identifies the local databases and files to be integrated into a centralized database server, models individual databases, converts all schemas to relational schemas, and integrates source schemas into an integrated target schema.

The alternative top-down approach first designs the target schema and then defines the mappings from the source schemas to the target schema. Most practitioners use a combination of the top-down and bottom-up approaches.

Chapter 24
Rule-Driven Databases and Applications: The Automatic Generation of Schema and Software

James A. Larson
Carol L. Larson

Traditional data modeling techniques capture the structure of data but not the procedures and practices for using data. Business rules, which describe these procedures and practices, are buried within a schema and application software and are not available to most enterprise employees. Employees need to review these rules to learn how the business operates, and to review and modify the business rules to make the business more efficient.

WHAT ARE BUSINESS RULES AND WHY SHOULD ONE CARE?

In their seminal book on data models, Tsichritzes and Lochovsky[1] identify the three major components of data modeling as data definition, data manipulation, and constraints. Using the relational data model as an example, a database administrator (DBA) applies the **create** command to define data in terms of relations (tables), domains (columns), and tuples (rows). For data manipulation, the **select** command defines queries, and the **insert**, **update**, and **delete** commands specify updates to the database. The constraints,

0-8493-1149-7/02/$0.00+$1.50
© 2002 by CRC Press LLC

which are specified using a data modeling technique, are referred to as *structured business rules* because they relate directly to the structure of the enterprise's data in the database. Examples of structured business rules include domain constraints, entity integrity, and referential integrity. However, as originally implemented, relational databases were weak in constraint specification and supported only *domain constraints* (the value of a column must be an integer, floating point, or character string) and the *entity integrity constraint* (each row of a table must have a unique value for its primary key). Later implementations were extended to support the *referential integrity constraint* (the value of a foreign key must exist as a value of primary key of some row of the "foreign" table).

Database management systems (DBMS) also enforce additional business rules called *operational business rules,* using triggers to apply predefined SQL commands and stored procedures to apply algorithms before or after updating a table. Operational rules describe the semantics of data in the database, as well as how data should be processed as applications and how employees should perform related business activities. When listening to conversations among enterprise employees, many examples of operational business rules can be heard. A business rule describes how an enterprise defines its policies, procedures, and practices and specifies business and application requirements. Examples include:

- *Enterprise policies:* Do not extend credit to anyone who has less than $20,000 annual income.
- *Pricing:* The price of an Ajax polo shirt is $9.98 each, or three for $27.99.
- *Product configuration:* The Ajax toy truck requires three AAA batteries.
- *Procedures:* A late payment fee of $3.00 is added to a customer's account if payment is not received by the end of the first week of each month.

Other types of business rules can be enforced by stored procedures and include the following rules expressed in English:

- Anyone placing an order with us is a customer.
- If a customer has more than $500,000 in his or her portfolio or has done at least 50 trades in the last year, then the customer is a "platinum" customer.
- If the customer has "platinum" status, then offer the Executive Financial Planning Seminar.
- If the customer is a nonsmoker, then allow a life insurance premium discount of $50 per month.

In order to be competitive, enterprise employees must understand and follow the enterprise's business rules. Software systems and applications must support and enforce operational business rules, and the DBMS must enforce structured business rules.

CLASSIFICATION OF BUSINESS RULES

Business rules can be quite varied and diverse. Barbara von Halle,[2] a leading proponent of business rules, has categorized business rules into the following categories:

- Terms and definitions
  - a customer is defined as...
  - an order is defined as...

- Facts
  - a customer can place an order
  - an order is delivered via a shipment

- Derivations
  - the total dollar amount for an order is calculated as...

- Constraints
  - the total dollar amount for an order must not exceed the customer's credit limit

- Inferences
  - a customer with an order totaling more than $50,000 is automatically considered a preferred customer

- Action enablers
  - if a preferred customer places three orders within one day, then automatically send the customer a free gift
  - if product quantity-on-hand dips below the reorder point, then automatically place an order for it

For a complete description of business rules, see Ron Ross' book, *The Business Rule Book: Classifying, Defining and Modeling Rules, Version 4.0.*[3]

CHARACTERISTICS OF WELL-DEFINED BUSINESS RULES

Because business rules are so important, each enterprise should carefully define its rules. David Plotkin[4] defines seven characteristics of well-defined business rules. They are:

1. *Declarative:* This definition explains the "what," and not "how," of the business rule. How the rule is enforced is not part of this characteristic.
2. *Precise:* A business rule can be interpreted only one way.
3. *Atomic:* A business rule contains a single complete thought, but not more than one.

4. *Consistent:* No business rule may conflict with another business rule.
5. *Nonredundant:* Two business rules may not say the same thing in different ways.
6. *Business-oriented:* The rules are stated in terms the enterprise's employees can understand.
7. *Business-owned:* Business rules are created by business managers, and only they can modify or delete the rule when it is no longer valid.

Note that the criteria for well-defined business rules are very similar to the criteria for well-defined software specifications. Systems analysts and others who define applications will find the concept of business rules quite familiar. Just as software specifications should be reviewed by users, business rules should be reviewed by the enterprise employees. Furthermore, the specification and management of business rules should be the responsibility of business managers, assisted by the system analyst in formatting business rules into a formal language that can be entered into a business rule database.

SPECIFYING BUSINESS RULES

Usually, business rules are specified as either structured business rules or operational business rules.

Structured Business Rules

Database administrators usually represent structured business rules using one of the following languages:

- *English or other natural languages* are textual languages that the DBA and intended database users have in common. An example of structured business rules specified in English is presented in Exhibit 1.
- *Entity-relationship diagrams* are a collection of graphical notations for describing conceptual schemas. First proposed by Peter Chen in 1976, entity-relationship diagrams have become popular with many DBAs. A variation, called IDEF1X, was standardized by the military and is especially popular with defense contractors. Exhibit 2 illustrates the business rules of Exhibit 1 expressed using entity-relationship diagrams.
- *SQL* is a formal computer language for creating and accessing a relational database. Exhibit 3 presents the SQL CREATE TABLE statements used to create a database that corresponds to the rules defined in Exhibit 1.
- *Relational diagrams* are a graphical notation that represents the objects and relationships expressed by SQL CREATE TABLE statements. DBAs create relational diagrams using GUIs to define conceptual schemas for a relational database. Exhibit 4 shows the graphical notation describing the business rules of Exhibit 3 expressed as SQL.

Exhibit 1. Conceptual Database Design Using English Rules

Every department has a name and budget.
No two departments have the same name.

Every employee has an employee identification, employee name, address, and social
 security number.
No two employees may have the same employee identification.
No two employees may have the same social security number.
Every employee must work in exactly one department.
Several employees may work in the same department.

Every project has a name, start date, and end date.
No two projects may have the same name.

Zero, one, or more employees may be assigned to a project.
An employee must be assigned to zero, one, or more projects.
An employee assigned to a project has a role.

Every dependent has a name and birthdate.
For a given employee, no two dependents may have the same name.
Some employees may have a policy that covers zero, one, or more dependents.
Each dependent must be covered by a policy of the employee for which they are listed
 as a dependent.

Every manager is also an employee.
Each manager has a bonus.

These languages can be understood by the enterprise's employees.
Relational diagrams and some entity-relationship diagrams have the added
benefit that software can use the diagrams to automatically generate database schemas for use by the DBMS. For an evaluation of these four languages, see the article by Larson and Larson,[5] "Evaluation of Four Languages for Specifying Conceptual Database Designs."

Operational Business Rules

DBAs can specify operational business rules using a variety of techniques,
including:

- *English or other national languages:* A programmer must convert this
  notation into a programming language if the rule is to be enforced by
  the computer system.
- *Programming languages, such as Java, C++, C, or COBOL:* While programmers understand program code, it is difficult for non-programming em-

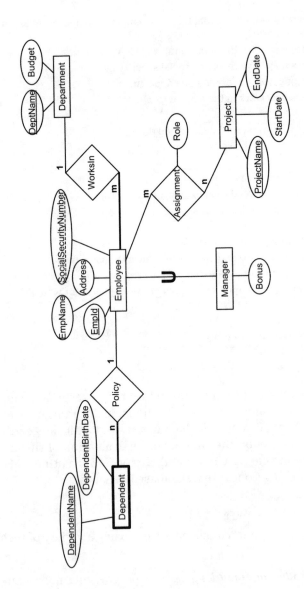

Exhibit 2. Conceptual Database Design Using Entity-Relationship Diagrams

Exhibit 3. Conceptual Database Design Using SQL Syntax

```
CREATE TABLE Department
      (DeptName                              INTEGER,
      Budget                                 INTEGER,
      PRIMARY KEY (DeptName))

CREATE TABLE Employee
      (EmpId                                 INTEGER,
      EmpName                                CHAR(20),
      Address                                CHAR(40),
      SocialSecurityNumber                   INTEGER,
      DeptName                               INTEGER,
      FOREIGN KEY (DeptName)
      REFERENCES Department,
      PRIMARY KEY (EmpId),
      UNIQUE (SocialSecurityNumber))

CREATE TABLE Project
      (ProjectName                           CHAR(20),
      StartDate                              DATE,
      EndDate                                DATE,
      PRIMARY KEY (ProjectName))

CREATE TABLE Assignment
      (EmpId                                 INTEGER,
      ProjectName                            CHAR(20),
      Role                                   CHAR(20),
      PRIMARY KEY (EmpId, ProjectName),
      FOREIGN KEY (EmpId)
      REFERENCES Employee,
      FOREIGN KEY (ProjectName)
      REFERENCES Project))

CREATE TABLE Dependent
      (EmpId                                 CHAR (20),
      DependentName                          CHAR (20),
      DependentBirthDate                     DATE,
      PRIMARY KEY (DependentName, EmpId),
      FOREIGN KEY (EmpId)
      REFERENCES Employee))

CREATE TABLE Manager
      (EmpId                                 INTEGER,
      Bonus                                  INTEGER,
      PRIMARY KEY (EmpId),
      FOREIGN KEY (EmpId)
      REFERENCES Employee))
```

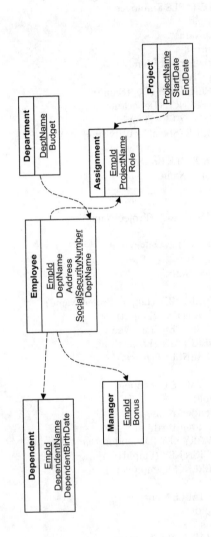

Exhibit 4.   Conceptual Database Design Using Relationship Diagrams

ployees to extract and review business rules expressed as programming languages.

- *Graphical editors that produce flow diagrams:* An example business rule specified using Interlinq's *FlowMan®* rule definition tool [http://www.interlinq.com] is illustrated in Exhibit 5. DBAs drag and drop icons that represent conditions and actions. Enterprise employees extract and review flow diagrams to familiarize themselves with the business rules and improve employee performance. Some systems automatically generate programming code from flow diagrams. Other business rule diagramming editors include JADE Developer Studio (from Vision Software [http://www.vision-soft.com]) and Blaze Advisor (from Blaze Software [http://www.blazesoft.com]).

Operational business rules can be generated from legacy applications using data profilers. Tools, such as *Migration Architect* (from Evoke Software [http://www.evokesoft.com]) uses a combination of automated discovery and interactive analysis to provide DBAs with structured business rules expressed as relational schemas.

BUSINESS RULE DATABASE

Rather than leave business rules scattered inside applications and database schemas, some DBAs prefer to create a *rule base* for enterprise rules. Employees can refer to the rule base at any time to refresh their memories of business rules, procedures, and practices. Business rule owners can also modify them as the business enterprise evolves or change the business rules to make the enterprise more efficient.

Rather than assign a single person to the difficult task of writing down all of the rules, the DBA or systems analyst can conduct several facilitated sessions, each involving several enterprise employees. This spreads the burden among several rule owners. Each participant should describe each business rule using the terms and phrases that relate directly to the names of objects in the enterprise's data model.

For each business rule, the DBA should capture several attributes, including the following:

- Rule name
- Status (whether the rule is proposed, approved, or archived)
- Effective and expiration dates
- Rule owner
- Rule purpose
- Rule definition (which consists of one or more conditions and a sequence of one or more actions)

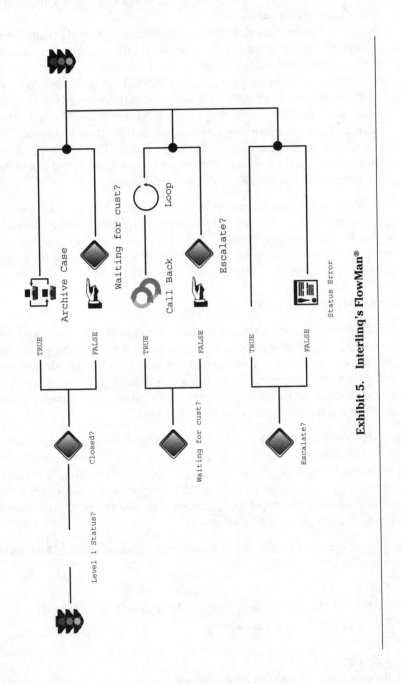

Exhibit 5. Interlinq's FlowMan®

Just as it is possible to generate a relational schema from a set of structured business rules, in some cases it is possible to generate an application or system from a set of structured and operational rules. One approach is to modify an existing application to conform to the rule base. If software developers design parameterized software, then they may change parameters when business rules change.

Another approach is to generate the software directly from business rules. Currently, several rule-driven application generators are commercially available. They include:

- Usoft Developer [http://www.usoft.com]
- Versata's Versata Studio [www.versata.com]
- Brokat Technologies' Brokat Expert [www.brokat.com]

GETTING STARTED WITH BUSINESS RULES

An incremental approach to business rules enables an enterprise to learn, introduce, and experience business rule capture and automation. Barbara von Halle[6] suggests the following five steps:

1. Invest one to four hours to understand the benefits of the approach. DBAs, systems analysts, and lead users should get their feet wet by attending a conference or presentation on the subject.
2. Invest one to five days to learn the fundamental characteristics of the approach. Attend a one-day business rules overview course; a longer, more detailed course; or invite a business rule vendor(s) to the enterprise for an explanation and demonstration presentation.
3. Invest one month to put these principles into practice. Pick a reasonable target application and specify its business rules.
4. Invest three months to develop a production application. Deliver a production application derived from business rules. Measure the savings in time and effort to create and maintain this application.
5. Put business rules into the organizational culture. Prioritize applications that would benefit from the business rules approach.

A business enterprise functions best when its rules for conducting business are specified and available to employees. Business software can also benefit from business rules if the rules are encoded in a format that can be integrated into software applications. In turn, the software applications capture business rules used by both employees and software systems, which enables the employees and the software systems to work together consistently and efficiently.

DBAs should capture structural business rules, while both DBAs and systems analysts should capture operational business rules and construct business applications that use both structural and operational business rules. Periodically, enterprise managers should review all rules and make changes to reflect the changes in how business is conducted. Changes in the business rules should be reflected in both software applications and employee work procedures, which will enable consistency and efficiency in the business enterprise.

NOTES

1. Tsichritzes, D. and Lochovsky, F., *Data Models,* Upper Saddle River, NJ: Prentice-Hall, 1982. Out of print.
2. von Halle, B., The Business Rule Roadmap, *Intelligent Enterprises Database Programming & Design On Line,* 1997.
3. Ross, R., *The Business Rule Book: Classifying, Defining and Modeling Rules, Version 4.0,* 2nd edition, Houston, TX: Business Rule Solutions, Inc., 1997.
4. Plotkin, D., Business Rules Everywhere, *Intelligent Enterprise,* 2 (4), 37 (1), 1999.
5. Larson, J. and Larson, C., Evaluation of Four Languages for Specifying Conceptual Database Designs, *Data Base Management,* 21-01-01, 1999, Auerbach.
6. von Halle, B., How Smart Is Your Enterprise? *Intelligent Enterprises Database Programming & Design On Line,* 1997.

Chapter 25

Mobile Database Interoperability: Architecture and Functionality

Antonio Si

Wireless networks and mobile computing have opened up new possibilities for information access and sharing. The need to interoperate multiple heterogeneous, autonomous databases is no longer confined to a conventional federated environment.

A mobile environment is usually composed of a collection of static servers and a collection of mobile clients. Each server is responsible for disseminating information over one or more wireless channels to a collection of mobile clients. The geographical area within which all mobile clients could be serviced by a particular server is called a cell of that server.

In this mobile environment, databases managed by database servers of different cells might be autonomous. Information maintained in a database will usually be most useful to clients within its geographical cell. In this respect, information maintained by databases of different cells might be disjointed or might be related. A mobile client, when migrating from one wireless cell to another, might want to access information maintained in the database server and relate it to the information maintained in its own database. Such an environment is termed a mobile federation, to distinguish it from a conventional federated environment. The database managed by a mobile client is termed a mobile database, while the database managed by the server is a server database. Using similar terminology, the database system managed by a mobile client is referred to as a mobile component and the database system managed by a server is referred to as a server component.

0-8493-1149-7/02/$0.00+$1.50

It is not clear if existing techniques can address interoperability in this newly evolved computing environment. This chapter presents a reference architecture for a conventional federated environment, proposes a set of functional requirements that a federated environment should support, and examines existing techniques for a federated environment with respect to each functional requirement in the context of the newly evolved mobile federation.

A WORKING SCENARIO

A tourist would like to discover information about attractions and accommodations within a certain area. With a portable computer equipped with a wireless communication interface, each mobile client (tourist) can receive travel information from the server over a wireless channel. Such an application might be called an Advanced Traveler Information System (ATIS).

In practice, each server database would maintain traveler information restricted to its own cell. For example, a server database serving the city of Los Angeles might provide vacancy information for all hotels within the Los Angeles area, such as the Holiday Inn near the Hollywood Freeway. A user might query the server database to obtain all hotels that have vacancies. Information maintained by different server databases might, to a large extent, be disjoint in this application domain, but there might still be some information overlap among different server databases.

For example, a Holiday Inn within the Los Angeles region might decide to maintain partial information on Holiday Inns in other regions, such as Pasadena. It is also important to note that different server databases will, in general, be autonomous, each employing different database management tools and even different data models to manage its own information. Exhibit 1 illustrates a snapshot of the information maintained in different server databases and a mobile client who accesses information via a wireless channel.

It would be useful to have a high-level capability that allows structured units of information to be identified from a server database and incorporated into a local database managed by a mobile client. For example, a client might want to maintain information on all hotels in Cell 1 and Cell 2, since he or she travels to these two areas the most. A client visiting Cell 1 (as shown in Exhibit 1) might issue a query to obtain all hotel information. When the client visits Cell 2, the hotel information incorporated into his or her database will have to be interoperated with the existing information that the client previously incorporated from the server database in Cell 1. This allows a mobile client to query the information using his or her own

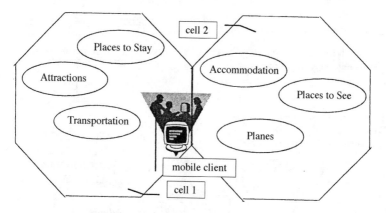

Exhibit 1.   Snapshot of ATIS Databases

familiar database management tools. These various server databases, together with the local database of the mobile client, form a mobile federation. It is interesting to note that the local database maintained in a mobile client is, in effect, a data warehouse since its data is constructed by integrating data from various data sources.

The objective of a mobile federation is similar to a conventional federated database environment. Both environments are trying to share information among multiple autonomous databases. In a mobile federation, the sharing of information is implicit; the information is shared within the context of a mobile client. In a conventional federated system, the information is shared among the databases themselves. Obviously, the server databases of various cells could also share information among themselves, in which case the server databases form a conventional federated environment as well.

FEDERATED ENVIRONMENT ARCHITECTURE

Exhibit 2 illustrates a typical federated environment. As the exhibit shows, a collection of independent database components is interconnected via a communication network. Each component consists of a database and a schema. A database is a repository of data structured or modeled according to the definition of the schema, which can be regarded as a collection of conceptual entity types. (The implementation of an entity type, of course, depends on the database model employed by the component; it may be a relation in a relational model, or it can be an object class, if an object-oriented model is employed.)

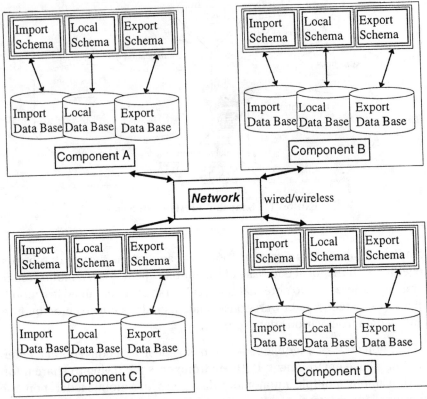

Exhibit 2. Reference Architecture for a Federated Environment

---

Information-Sharing Techniques

Sharing of database information in this federated environment could be achieved at three different levels of granularity and abstraction:

1. Entity types belonging to the schema of individual components could be shared such that modeled real-world concepts could be reused.
2. Data instances stored in individual components' databases (the implementation of which also depends on the database model employed) could be shared such that information of modeled real-world entities could be reused.
3. Applications developed on a component's database could be shared among any other components. For example, if the server database in Cell 1 in Exhibit 1 develops a pathfinder application that allows a mobile client to search for the shortest route to a destination, it could be reused by a mobile client in searching paths within Cell 2 as well.

The simplest way to achieve information sharing in a database federation is for a component to simply browse through the content of a nonlocal (i.e., remote) component's database. In this respect, an explorer should be provided. Alternatively, a component could integrate remote information into its local database. The newly integrated information could be reused by the component in the future. To support such reuse of information, the database of a component, say X, is logically partitioned into three different subsets, as shown in Exhibit 2:

1. *Local database.* The local database refers to the set of data instances originally created by X.

2. *Import database.* The import database refers to the set of remote data instances that X retrieves from the export databases of remote components.

3. *Export database.* The export database is a subset of the union of the local database and import database, which represents the set of data instances the component is willing to share with other components. In other words, a component should be able to export its imported data instances if the access privilege constraints specified on the imported instances are not violated.

Similarly, from the reference architecture in Exhibit 1, the schema of a component X is also partitioned into three different subsets. The local schema refers to the entity types originally created by X and is used to model the local database. The import schema, which refers to the entity types X retrieves from the export schema of remote components, is used to model the import database. Finally, the export schema, which is the subset of the union of the local schema and the import schema, is used to model the export database.

Integrating a remote application belonging to a remote component, say Y, into X's local system is difficult because X's local computer system might be different from that of Y. One possibility (proposed by D. Fang et al.) is to integrate the signature of the remote application into X's local system. To execute the application, X's local data is passed to component Y; the application is run on the remote component using X's data and the results are returned back to X. The Java virtual machine could make application sharing easier.

CHARACTERISTICS OF A FEDERATED DATABASE ENVIRONMENT

Each component within a federation is usually heterogeneous and autonomous in nature. Heterogeneity is a natural consequence of the independent creation and evolution of autonomous databases; it refers to the variations in which information is specified and structured in different components.

Autonomy means each component is under separate and independent control.

Heterogeneity

In general, a spectrum of heterogeneities of different levels of abstraction could be classified.

Database Model Heterogeneity. Each component may use different database models to describe the structure and constraints of its data.

Conceptual Schema Heterogeneity. Each component may model similar real-world concepts in different ways, such as the different schema used by the different database components of the multiple ATIS databases depicted in Exhibit 1. This is also referred to as semantic heterogeneity. This conceptual schema heterogeneity could be further divided into three discrepancies, each of which can be explained as follows:

- *Naming mismatch.* Two entity types from different components modeling the same real-world concept might use different naming conventions in representing the attributes. In the ATIS database in Exhibit 1, the ranking of a hotel might be modeled by an attribute called "rank" of Places to Stay in component A, while the same information might be modeled by an attribute called "number of stars" of Accommodation in component B.
- *Domain mismatch.* The same attribute of two entity types from different components might be represented in different domains. For example, both Attractions and Places to See of components A and B, respectively, in Exhibit 1 might have an attribute "zip code." However, component A might represent the attribute as an integer, while component B might represent it as a string.
- *Schematic discrepancy.* Data in one database might be represented as entity types in another database. In Exhibit 1, entity type Planes of component B might be represented as an attribute of Attractions in component A.
- *Data specification heterogeneity.* Each component may model similar real-world entities in different units of measure. One component might represent the distance of an attraction in meters, while another component might represent it in miles.
- *Update heterogeneity.* Since each component is under separate and independent control, data instances modeling the same real-world entity in different databases might be updated asynchronously. When the daily rate of a hotel is updated, databases A and B in Exhibit 1 might be updated at different times.

- *Database tools heterogeneity.* Each component may use different tools to manipulate its own database. For example, different components might use different query languages.

Types of Autonomy

Orthogonally, each component can exhibit several different types of autonomy.

Design Autonomy. This refers to the ability of a component to choose its own design on the data being managed, the representation of the data instances, the constraints of the data, and the implementation of the component's database system.

Association Autonomy. This refers to the ability of a component to decide to what extent the component would like to participate in the interoperability activity. A component is free to share its schema, data, or applications with other components; a component can even decide not to participate in the sharing activity at all.

Control Autonomy. This refers to the ability of a component to control the access privileges of any remote component on each of its exported information units (entity types or instances). In general, four types of access control privilege could be granted by a component to a remote component on each of its exported information units:

1. Read (R) access to the database instances
2. Read definition (RD) access to entity types
3. Write (W) access to database instances
4. Generate (G) access for creating database instances

These four access privileges form a partial order such that W > G > RD and W > R > RD. Neither G nor R dominates the other. For instance, if component X grants W access privilege to remote component Y on one of its exported entity types, component Y is allowed to read the instances of the entity type as well. By contrast, if X only grants R access privilege to Y on the entity type, Y is not allowed to modify any instances of the entity type.

If an exported unit of a component, say X, is imported from another component, Y, the capability of X to control the access privileges on the exported unit will depend on whether the unit is imported by copy or imported by reference from Y.

Execution Autonomy. This refers to the ability of a component to execute local operations without interference from external components. For example, component X might run an application on behalf of remote component Y.

This autonomy implies that X can run the application as if it is a local execution (i.e., X can schedule, commit, or abort the application freely).

FUNCTIONAL REQUIREMENTS OF A FEDERATED DATABASE ENVIRONMENT

From the perspective of a component, X, several functional capabilities need to be supported in order to be able to participate in the interoperability activity with other components.

Information Exportation

Component X must be able to specify the information it is willing to share with other components. Such a facility should allow the component to specify the export schema, the export database, or any application that the component would like to be sharable. Furthermore, X should be able to specify the access privileges of each remote component on each of its exported information units.

A mobile federation is comparatively more dynamic than a database federation, connecting and disconnecting from the wireless network frequently. A mobile component also enters and leaves a cell frequently. It is difficult for a server component to keep track of which mobile components are currently residing within the cell under its management. Furthermore, a cell can potentially have many components visiting at any moment. Therefore, it is not possible for a server component to indicate the access privileges of each mobile component. An access control mechanism that is scalable with respect to the number of mobile components is necessary. Due to the dynamic nature of a mobile component, it is not always possible to incorporate information from a mobile component.

Information Discovery

Before component X can access or use any remote information, X must be aware of the existence and availability of the information in which it is interested. A facility must be provided to allow X to discover any remote information of interest at various granularity or abstraction, including schema, data, or applications.

In general, there are two ways information could be discovered by component X. One possibility is that X can formulate a discovery request for its interested information, in which case a facility must be provided to identify the components containing information units that are relevant to the request. Another possibility is for component X to navigate or explore the exported information space of each remote component and look for the interested information. An explorer must then be provided for such a navigation purpose.

Information Importation

Once interested information units from remote components are discovered, component X can import the information units into its local database. Through importation, component X can reuse the discovered information in the future. In general, three importation capabilities are required: schema importation, data importation, and application importation.

Schema Importation. This refers to the process of importing remote export schema into X's local schema. This process is further composed of two activities — heterogeneity resolution and schema integration. Heterogeneity resolution is the process of resolving any conflict that exists between X's local schema and the remote schema.

Since different components might use different database models to specify the data, a facility must be provided to translate the remote schema from the remote database model to the one used in X's local system. Furthermore, since different components might model similar real-world concepts differently, another heterogeneity that must be resolved is to identify the relationship between X's local schema and the remote schema.

Referring back to the ATIS federation in Exhibit 1, two entity types belonging to two different schema might model the same real-world concept, such as the Attractions information of component A and the Places to See information of component B. Alternatively, two entity types might model related information, such as the Transportation information of component A and the Planes information of component B. Finally, two entity types might model different concepts, such as the Attractions information of component A and the Planes information of component B.

Data Importation. Similarly, data importation refers to the process of importing remote export database information into X's local database. This process is composed of two activities: instance identification and data integration.

Instance identification refers to the process of identifying the relationship between the remote database and the local database. Two data instances from different databases might model the same, related, or different real-world entities. This process is complicated because, on the one hand, instances from different databases cannot be expected to bear the same key attributes; on the other hand, merely matching nonkey attributes may lead to unsatisfactory results because data instances modeling different entities may possess the same attribute values. This process is further complicated by possible update heterogeneity that might exist between the two instances.

Once the relationship between the remote database and X's local database is identified, the remote database can be integrated into the local database. Again, the remote database should be integrated such that its relationship with the local database is reflected.

There are two different paradigms for integrating a remote data instance from a remote component, Y, into X's local database: imported by copy and imported by reference.

When a remote instance is imported by copy, the data instance is copied into the local database. The copied data instance becomes part of the local database. Any access to the imported instance is referred to its local copy.

When a remote instance is imported by reference, a reference to the remote instance is maintained in the local database. Any access to the imported data instance requires a network request to Y for up-to-date data value. When a remote data instance is imported by copy, the local component, X, has complete control on the local copy of the imported instance and is allowed to specify the access privileges of other remote components on the local copy of the imported instance. However, when a remote data instance is imported by reference from component Y, Y still maintains its control over the imported instance. Component X is still free to export the imported instance; however, X cannot modify the access privileges specified by Y on this imported data instance.

Application importation can only be achieved to a very limited extent due to the possible differences in the computer systems of the different components. However, with the advent of Java mobility code, this could soon become a reality.

In a mobile federation, communication between a mobile component and a server database is usually over an unreliable wireless channel. It is more efficient for a mobile federation to import an instance by copying since a component does not need to rely on the network to obtain the data value of the instance. A mobile component, in general, has less storage space than a federated component. A mobile component, therefore, might not be able to import all data instances and will have to maintain only those instances that it accesses most frequently.

Information Querying and Transaction Processing. Component X should be able to operate its imported information in its local system. The operation on the imported information should be transparent in the following manner:

- *Functional transparency.* All existing local tools of component X, such as its query language and database management system (DBMS) software, should be operational on the imported information units in the same manner as they operate on the local information units.

- *Location transparency.* Users and tools operating on the imported information units should not be aware of their original locations and remote nature.

Very often, there is a conflict between supporting the described functional capabilities in a component and preserving the autonomy of the component. To preserve the autonomy of a component, modifying any component of the DBMS software is not recommended.

TECHNIQUES FOR DATABASE SHARING

To support database-sharing functional capabilities, data model heterogeneity must be resolved. This is usually addressed by employing a common canonical model, which provides a communication forum among various components. Schema and instances represented in the local data model are required to convert to the canonical model. Most research prototypes use an object model as the canonical model because of its expressive power. Most corporations, however, use relational models. ODBC from Microsoft and JDBC from Sun Microsystems are generally considered the industry standards.

Information Exportation

Information exportation can be easily achieved using database view mechanisms. Exhibit 3 illustrates the management of exported information. A subhierarchy rooted at class Exported-Classes is created under the root of the class hierarchy (i.e., OBJECTS). To export a class, O, a class name E_O is created as a subclass of Exported-Classes. To export an attribute of O, the same named attribute is created for E_O; this allows a component to specify exported information at the granularity of a single attribute.

Each exported instance is handled by a multiple-membership modeling construct of the object model, relating the original class to which the instance belongs to the E_ counterpart. In effect, classes belonging to the subhierarchy rooted at Exported-Classes represent the export schema, and the instances belonging to the subhierarchy represent the export database (depicted by the shaded region in Exhibit 3).

In Exhibit 3, only class Places to Stay is exported because only Places to Stay has a corresponding E_Places to Stay class. All attributes of Places to Stay have the corresponding ones defined on E_Places to Stay. Furthermore, two instances of Places to Stay are exported, relating via a multiple membership construct to E_Places to Stay. A component employing a relational data model could use a similar technique to specify its exporting information units since the export schema and database are, in effect, a view of the database.

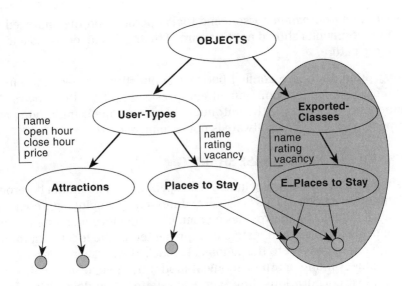

Exhibit 3. Information Exportation via Object View

Access control mechanisms for exported information are limited and especially difficult to achieve in a mobile federation. It is difficult for a server component to keep track of which mobile components are within the cell under its management and specify their individual access privileges. A multilevel access control mechanism is more applicable in this domain.

In a multilevel system, database information units are classified into privilege levels. The privilege levels are arranged in an order such that possessing a privilege level implies possessing all its subordinate levels. For example, a typical multilevel system contains four privilege levels: top secret, secret, confidential, and unclassified. A typical database system could have an arbitrary number of privilege levels. To access an information unit, the user needs to obtain a clearance at least equal to the privilege level of the unit. In a mobile federation, a mobile component could join a privilege level that will inherit the database information units that it could access from the server database.

Information Discovery

Information discovery can be achieved by exploring the exported information of a database component. A typical device that explores the content of several databases is depicted in Exhibit 4. This explorer is implemented on the Netscape Navigator, providing a platform-independent browsing capability because of the availability of Netscape in UNIX workstations, Macintosh computers, and PCs.

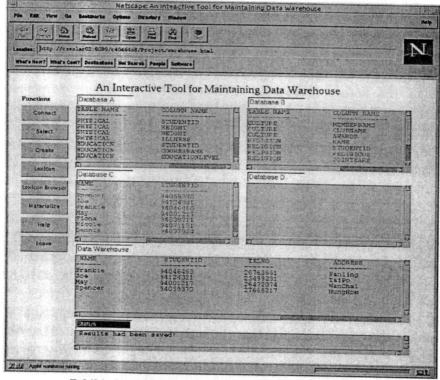

Exhibit 4. A Sample Information Discovery Explorer

The explorer in Exhibit 4 allows a component to explore multiple databases at the same time. It employs a relational model as the canonical model. Exported information units are viewed as relations. The explorer has windows to browse four separate databases of remote components, and a window to the local database of a component.

An alternate approach to discovering remote information units that are interesting to a particular component is to specify the requirements of the interested information units. Remote information units that are relevant to the discovery specification will be identified. Specification could be initiated in an ad hoc manner. Following are three different types of discovery requests:

- A component can request remote entity types (instances) that model the same real-world concept (entity) as a local entity type (instance).
- A component can request remote entity types (instances) that model a complementary view of a local entity type (instance).

- A component can request remote entity types (instances) that model an overlapping view of a local entity type (instance).

To support these three types of discovery requests, one approach is to use a probability model to determine the extent to which two entity types (instances) from different databases modeled the same real-world concept. The probability model is based on two heuristics derived from the common attributes of the two entity types: intraconcept similarity indicator and interconcept dissimilarity indicator.

Intuitively, an intraconcept similarity indicator refers to the probability that the common attributes will be modeled in related entity types. Interconcept dissimilarity indicator refers to the probability that the attributes will be modeled in unrelated entity types. Two entity types from different databases will have a high probability of similarity if their overlapped attributes have a high intraconcept similarity indicator as well as a high interconcept dissimilarity indicator. The use of these heuristics is based on the observation that different databases might model complementary or even disjointed views of the same concept; on the other hand, different databases might model different concepts similarly.

A more general specification could be achieved using first-order logic like language. Each component will thus require a mediator that understands the specification language and identifies information units relevant to the specification.

In a mobile federation, it is not important if a server database returns all information relevant to a discovery request; rather, it is much more important that the returned information units are indeed relevant because of the typically low bandwidth on a wireless channel. One approach to ensure this is to create a profile that captures the interests of each component.

Information Importation

Schema Importation. As mentioned previously, a component, X, can import (partial) remote schema from a remote component, Y, into its local schema by first resolving any heterogeneity between X's local schema and Y's schema.

One common approach to resolve schema heterogeneity between X's local schema and Y's remote schema is through a common knowledge base that contains various real-world concepts. Entity types from different databases are required to match with the concepts in the knowledge base. If both entity types map to the same concept in the knowledge base, they are regarded as modeling the same real-world concept. The knowledge base also provides instructions that define how a remote entity type could be integrated into the schema of a component's local database. The instructions

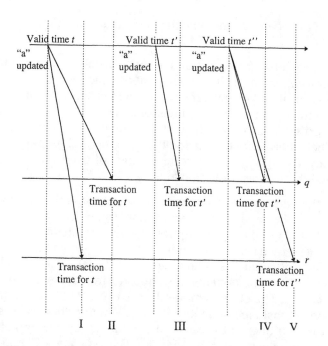

Exhibit 5.   Update Heterogeneity in a Database Federation

could be specified in the form of rules or in a logic-like syntax. The former is easier to understand but is less flexible. The latter is more flexible, but is less user friendly.

In a mobile federation, it is difficult to specify a knowledge base that is applicable to all mobile components because there is a potentially unlimited number of mobile components visiting a wireless cell. It is perhaps more appropriate for a mobile component to provide its own knowledge or its personal profile, containing its own view for integrating remote schema into its own local schema.

Instance Importation. To identify the relationship between instances from two databases, one needs to address the data specification heterogeneity and the update heterogeneity problems. Data specification heterogeneity is usually resolved, again, via a knowledge base, indicating how the representation of a remote instance could be converted into the representation of the local database.

Exhibit 5 illustrates the importance of update heterogeneity in identifying the relationship between instances from various databases. In Exhibit 5, valid time denotes the time in which a fact was true in reality, while the transaction time denotes the time in which a fact was captured in a database.

One approach to addressing update heterogeneity is to use historical update information on the instances to determine their degree of similarity. The historical update patterns of each instance represent the changes of states of the instance since its creation, inherently capturing its behavioral properties. This allows the instance identification to be performed based on behavioral property in addition to structural property, as is done traditionally. The historical update information of an instance could be easily obtained through a transaction log.

As mentioned previously, instance integration could be performed via import by copy or import by reference. Using an object model as a canonical model, it is quite easy to support these two integration paradigms within one general framework. Exhibit 5 illustrates the partial conceptual schema of two components, A and B, of the ATIS databases from Exhibit 1. Instances x and y of component B are imported from class Accommodation of component A. The class Remote-Classes is created in component B to hold the object instance of definitions of the imported instances and the address of components from which the instances are imported (i.e., address of component A in the example). These two types of information are placed in the attributes r_oid and r_host, respectively. A class called R_Accommodation is created in component B as a subclass of Remote-Classes to model the imported instances.

In effect, the subhierarchy rooted at Remote-Classes represents the import schema and the instances belonging to the subhierarchy represent the import database; this is depicted by the shaded region in Exhibit 6. Notice that the structure of the import subhierarchy mirrors that of the export subhierarchy mentioned previously.

Attributes of classes belonging to the Remote-Classes subhierarchy are user-defined methods. To obtain the attribute value for attribute "a" of an imported instance, x, the method "a" will obtain the "r_oid" of x and initiate a remote request to the remote component, whose address is specified in "r_host" of x, to obtain the attribute value for the instance. This achieves the effect of import by reference. To support import by copy, the imported instances are added to a local class via multiple-membership construct. The additional inherited attributes could be used as placeholders for the copied attribute values of the imported instance. This is illustrated in Exhibit 6. The obtained value of an attribute of an instance returned from the corresponding method could be stored in the additional attributes inherited.

In a mobile federation, the connection between a mobile component and the server component could be disconnected at any moment, either due to

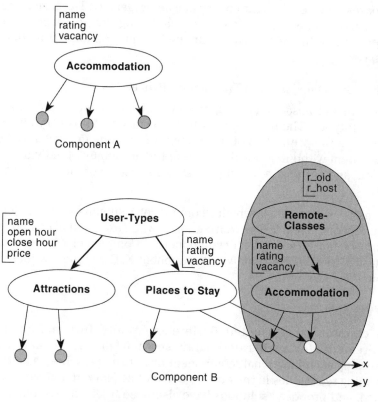

Exhibit 6.   Data Integration

the unreliability of a wireless channel or due to the movement of a mobile component to another cell. It is, thus, more appropriate for a component to import an instance by copy rather than by reference. This also has the effect of caching the instance into the local database of a mobile component. In this respect, one could regard the local database of a mobile component as a data warehouse since the local database is derived from multiple database sources.

Information discovery and importation could be provided within a uniform framework or interface. This allows discovered remote information units to be imported into the local database of a component. The explorer in Exhibit 4 also provides functions for information importation as well. In this particular system, a relational model is employed as a canonical model. The integration of information units from several databases is basically achieved via the "join" operation in this explorer. A component could also create a lexicon containing relationships among attributes of different databases. This resolves the conceptual heterogeneity. This lexicon acts as a localized profile of the component, capturing the perspectives of the component on the relationships among information units from different databases.

Information Querying and Transaction Processing

The notion of transaction is supported weakly in existing database federation prototypes. The reason stems from the fact that it is very difficult to support all the properties of transaction processing in a federated database system without seriously violating the autonomy of individual components and without rewriting the DBMS software of individual components.

Consider a situation in which a component X submits a transaction T to a remote component Y. The transaction T, when executed in component Y, is simply a local transaction of component Y. Component Y is free to abort the transaction without notifying component X. Component X thus might obtain inconsistent data.

CONCLUSION

This chapter has presented a reference architecture and functional requirements for a federated database environment. Techniques for addressing each functional requirement have been presented. Limitations of existing techniques in the domain of a mobile federation have been discussed, and proposed solutions have also been briefly illustrated. Experience with real applications in a mobile federation is necessary to further pinpoint additional problems that require research.

ACKNOWLEDGMENTS

This work is supported in part by the Hong Kong Polytechnic University Central Research Grant Number 351/217. Part of the materials in this chapter are the results of the Remote-Exchange project at the University of Southern California.

Chapter 26
Integrating EDMSs and DBMSs

Charles Banyay

Database management systems (DBMS) have been an integral part of information technology (IT) and the systems development life cycle since the 1960s. The database, especially the relational database, has received ever-increasing visibility during the past decade due to the mass availability of very cost-effective PC-based DBMSs. As a result, the relational database has become ingrained as the natural metaphor for an information repository with most organizations that utilize IT.

With the advent of the electronic document or, to be more precise, the electronic document management system (EDMS) as a significant new metaphor for an information repository, it is useful to juxtapose the two approaches and to explore their relative advantages. First, it is necessary to discuss the traditional process of using a DBMS in managing data. Second, it is necessary to evaluate the unique properties of documents as opposed to structured data and the challenges associated with managing information using this metaphor. Having considered these two, it is possible to discuss how the DBMS can be used cooperatively with the new metaphor for information repositories — the electronic document or EDMS.

THE DATABASE MANAGEMENT SYSTEM

The majority of IT professionals would not consider developing even the most simple of applications without employing some kind of DBMS to manage the data. The traditional approach to utilizing database technology, regardless of the application, involves some form of data analysis. Data analysis generally consists of four stages called by different names, by the various methodologies, but they all involve some form of:

- Data collection and normalization
- Entity-relationship mapping

- Transaction analysis
- Data modeling

At the end of this process, once the type of database management system to be utilized is determined, one has enough information with which to begin a physical and logical database design. The data analysis activities should provide enough information to enable a design which will have a high degree of predictability in terms of data access performance and data storage size.

Data collection and normalization within any organization begins with the analysis of the data as it exists currently. Various methodologies emphasize different approaches to this analysis. Some emphasize beginning with the analysis of source documents, while others advocate analyzing the data as it is presented to the users. For this discussion it is irrelevant where one starts a project; what is important is that a "functional decomposition" process is followed in all instances. Functional decomposition attempts to distill the relevant data from some source (e.g., data collection documents or presentation documents). As recently as one year ago, one could have safely assumed that the documents would have been on paper; today that may not necessarily be so. For the purposes of this discussion, however, the medium is irrelevant.

Once this distillation process or functional decomposition is finished, one proceeds with a truly data-driven approach to analysis. The next step involves grouping the data into logical groups called entities. Using a process called normalization, one then proceeds to remove as much data redundancy as possible from these entities, sometimes producing more entities in the process. There are many good references on data normalization techniques, and, for the purposes of this chapter, there is no requirement to go into any more depth than this.

Once the entities are in their normal form, one generally proceeds to associate each entity with the other entities using some entity-relationship mapping technique. Entity-relationship mapping is, in general, an attempt to reconstitute the data back into something that is meaningful to the business where the data originated. A thorough understanding of the business functions and processes that use the data is crucial for creating meaningful entity-relationship maps. During this mapping process, some form of quantification of the entities also occurs.

The next step in data analysis is the transaction analysis. Transaction analysis involves listing all of the business events that could trigger access to the information within the as yet undesigned database, and mapping the flow of the transaction through the entities as it satisfies its requirement for information. The transaction flow is dependent on the entity relationships. Once all the transactions are mapped in this way and the quantity of each transaction is determined, one has a good idea of how the data should be ordered and indexed.

The final step in the data analysis activity is to construct the data model. Constructing the data model involves quantitative analysis. Using the structure from the relational map and the number of accesses identified in the transactional analysis, one derives a new structure for the model. This new structure may result in new entities that may reduce the number of entities that need to be accessed for certain high-usage transactions. The first data model generally proves to be inadequate. Data analysis is therefore an iterative process. As one proceeds through the iterations, one learns more about the data. The new information may indicate that decisions made earlier in the process may not have been optimal and may need to be revisited.

The ultimate database design will not only depend on the results of the data analysis activity but also on the choice of DBMS. Good design does not just depend on knowledge of the specific data requirements of a particular application or the general information requirements of an organization. These are critical elements of the design, but almost as important is a good understanding of the particular DBMS, its architecture, and its design constraints.

The critical aspect to understand about data analysis for the purposes of this discussion is the process of functional decomposition. Functional decomposition is a process that is extremely important to data analysis. It is the process by which reality or a body of knowledge is decomposed, summarized, or reduced into its most fundamental, elementary components. This decomposition is generally from the one perspective that is important to the particular application being considered. These elementary components are the data items that ultimately make up the database, such as those shown in Exhibit 1.

An important consideration in Exhibit 1 is that any process of reduction or distillation results in a tremendous amount of other "stuff" that does not make it into the final version. This stuff is lost. Consequently, one advantage offered by functional decomposition is that the process reduces reality or a body of information to its elementary components that represent one or at least a very limited perspective on this body of information. This enables the construction of a database. The "bad" aspect of functional decomposition also relates to its strength, namely, that the process reduces reality or a body of information to its elementary components that represent one or at least a very limited perspective on this body of information. Much of the original body of information can be lost in the process.

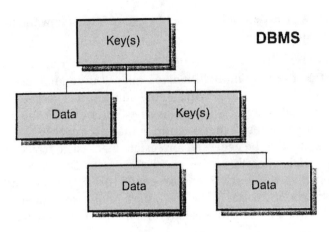

Exhibit 1. Elementary Components

THE ELECTRONIC DOCUMENT

Before comparing the DBMS with the electronic document management system as an information repository, it is useful to build a common understanding of the definition of a "document" in the context of this discussion.

The first thing that most people think of in any discussion of a document is paper. This is due to the fact that most of today's generations have grown up with paper as the most common medium on which documents have resided. A piece of paper or a collection of pieces of paper is usually referred to as a document, especially if it has a collective purpose. Paper, however, is very limiting and is just one method of representing a document. It is certainly not the only way. Even if one disregards the electronic medium for the moment, there is a myriad of ways that documents have existed and do exist. There are stone tablets, scrolls, hieroglyphics, paintings, carvings, and more recently film, just to mention a few. Even the scented letter is a document that is more than just scribbled words on a piece of paper. The scent can convey more information than the words.

If one includes the electronic medium, then a document can be much more than is allowed in the limited paper medium or in anything that has been described above. A document can contain voice-annotated video, graphics, still images, and drawings with backup text. One can imagine the vast information content of a document of this nature.

The second feature that people think of when discussing documents is the concept of a page. This is also due, in all probability, to the association of documents with paper. People, in general, have an optimum quantum of information on which they can focus at any one moment. This is an aspect of what psychologists call bounded rationality. A page is probably an optimum quantum of information. Represented on paper, information could appear in the format that is most familiar; however, in some other form it could be quite different. The concept of a page is useful and will probably evolve as the understanding of documents evolves, and as this understanding moves beyond paper as the common representation of a document. It will suffice for the purposes of this discussion to think of a page as a component of information and of a document as containing one or more pages or one or more quantums of information.

So, in summary, what is a document? The word *document* is both a verb and a noun. To document is to record (e.g., to record an event or to tell a story). It follows that anything that records an event or tells a story can be called a document. A document can and generally does contain many different types of entities. Generally there is either text or an image, but if people expand their horizon beyond paper, a document can contain voice, video, or, in the world of virtual reality, any combination of tactile stimuli. In the most general definition, a document is a representation of reality that can be reproduced and sensed by any combination of the five senses.

The preceding may stretch human creative capabilities somewhat, so for the purposes of this discussion the definition of a document can be limited to a collection of images and textual information types. The information can be coded or uncoded. The essence of the definition of the document, as a representation of reality that can be reproduced and sensed, is really the crucial aspect of the definition that is most germane to this discussion. The representation of reality implies that a document captures information at a quantum level or quantum levels higher than simple data.

The best illustration of this is the well-known "A picture is worth a thousand words." A picture in one entity can represent a thousand data elements or more. An illustration may convey this idea better. Suppose one is creating a document describing an automobile accident report for a property and casualty insurance company. The document would begin with a notice of loss, which could be an electronic form that is created initially by an agent within a call center. The agent would record all relevant information about the accident, including the name and policy number of the policyholder, the date and time of the accident, the date and time of the call, and all particulars of the loss, such as damages to the car and so on.

The agent then sends a compressed version of the document to the adjuster with some comments and instructions. The information to this point is in coded data format and could be through any traditional data system. The new capabilities of a document-based system allow the adjuster, when the document is received, to attach a few still photo shots of the automobile along with further comments and the detailed cost estimates supplied by the body shop. In addition, the adjuster can scan in the police report of the accident and attach it to the document. The claims document now contains a much more complete description of the entire event. This more complete description could produce a very different result by the end of the claims process. This more complete description is not possible through just simple coded data or traditional relational DBMS systems.

It is not necessary to describe the insurance claims process any further. What it illustrates is the wealth of information contained in a document-based approach to information processing. One needs to contrast this to an approach enabled by an application system containing only coded data in a relational format.

FUNCTIONAL DECOMPOSITION AND DATA DISTILLATION

The primary reason that traditional application systems oriented around a DBMS have sometimes failed to meet the expectations of the business community, and the reason that much of the business information today still resides on paper, is the failure of these applications to capture the entirety of the multifaceted information pertaining to an event. That is a real mouthful, but what it says is that if in capturing information electronically a business user only manages to capture the bare essentials focused on a certain perspective and loses most of the other peripheral information which may be central to other perspectives, then the business user will, in general, not be completely satisfied. The business user is forced to keep other, nonelectrical repositories of information and continue to work with information in nonelectrical media. This generally adds up to a lot of paper and a lot of traditional, inefficient, and ineffective business processes.

As discussed at the end of the data analysis activity, in any process of reduction or distillation there is a tremendous amount of other peripheral information that does not make it through the process. Reality is reduced to a very limited perspective based on what is retained. This process may leave out information of interest to other perspectives. The result is a very narrow perspective on the information, general dissatisfaction, and alternative repositories of information within the organization.

THE DBMS AND THE EDMS

So why not just discard DBMSs and rely totally on documents as the new metaphor for an information repository? The above discussion seems to imply that database systems are bad and documents are good — far from the truth. Documents, despite having a tremendous capability of holding a great deal of multifaceted information, have their own weaknesses. Years ago one would have begun the list of these weaknesses with the fact that documents tend to take up vast amounts of storage space, require a great deal of bandwidth for transmission, and generally require expensive equipment for good presentation, such as large, high-resolution monitors and multimedia processors. Today, these weaknesses seem to be fading in importance, although not as quickly as one had hoped and would like. Bandwidth is increasing, storage costs are plummeting, and high-resolution monitors are dropping in cost.

The real weakness of documents, and this has little to do with storage or display technology, is that they are difficult to search. Because most of the information content of a document is uncoded, and because there is very little in the way of search engines for uncoded data, documents are difficult to search. Once stored, they are difficult to find unless they have been indexed with exactly the criteria for which one is searching. Unfortunately, information is of little use if it cannot be found readily when needed.

It seems, then, that there is an impasse. On the one hand, a DBMS is a tool that has tremendous capabilities to search and reproduce information to which it has access, in the combinations that users generally require. The weakness of the DBMS, however, is that it generally has access to only a limited perspective on a small body of information. On the other hand, an EDMS is a tool that can house vast amounts of content about a body of information from a multitude of perspectives. The primary weakness of an EDMS, however, is that once the information is stored it is difficult to find.

Neither one of the tools on its own seems capable of meeting the expectations for comprehensive information management. They do, however, have complementary strengths. With the DBMS, information is relatively easy to find, and, with the EDMS, information content is vast and rich. If one could successfully combine these strengths, then one would have a tool that might better meet the expectations of the business community. The combination might not meet all of the expectations, but would certainly be superior to either tool in stand-alone mode. The whole promises to be greater than the sum of the parts in this case.

The logical question arises, "Why use a DBMS to store data?" Why not use the EDMS to store the information, and use the DBMS to store the data about the EDMS or metadata? This would enable one to search the DBMS for the combination of information that is required to be contained in the EDMS. This is exactly the approach that many leading vendors of document management applications, such as FileNet and Documentum, have taken. Both vendors use a relational database, such as Oracle or Sybase, to store the metadata that points to various data stores, such as magnetic or optical disks, that house the documents.

The DBMS in many of these document management systems has evolved beyond simple metadata which just houses pointers to content

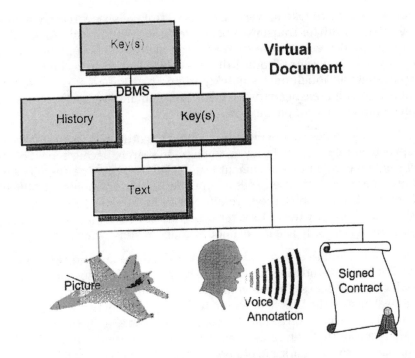

Exhibit 2. The Virtual Document

documents. These second-generation document management systems have developed the concept of the virtual document. The virtual document illustrated in Exhibit 2 is more than a collection of pointers to content documents. The metadata in second-generation document management applications also contains far richer information, such as a comprehensive history of the virtual document. The history may contain work-in-process information or information about each member document, such as the time each was added to the document collection, who entered it, and from which application.

CONCLUSION

The combination of DBMS and EDMS certainly offers advantages over either in stand-alone mode; however, the degree of the advantage can be deceptive. The metadata in the database is just that, data about the document and not about all of the information within the document. Here is the crux of the matter. What is metadata but distillation? If the only way to find a wealth of information is through the limited perspective of its metadata, then the information is not nearly as valuable as if one could find it from the multitude of perspectives contained within the information itself.

The challenge facing most document management application vendors today is how to minimize even this more expanded data distillation. The development of new search engines may be part of the answer. Development of such technologies as pattern-recognition applications, which can scan the uncoded components of documents, may be another part.

Whatever the solution to reducing the effects of data distillation, it is not something that will be totally eliminated within the near future. Combining the strengths of a DBMS and an EDMS, however, definitely provides better access to a larger volume of information than if either one is used alone. The combination is by no means a panacea, but it is a step or a number of steps in the right direction toward solving the information-processing problems that knowledge workers face every day.

As the marriage between the DBMS and the EDMS evolves further, there may be a new dawn for IT. This new dawn will be true electronic information processing rather than electronic data processing. The real payoff in this evolution and in developments of this nature is that it may eventually solve the seeming paradox of information processing in the office environment. This paradox is that, even though there has been a tremendous investment in information technology in the office, office productivity has not risen as dramatically as expected during the past 20 to 30 years.

Chapter 27
Interfacing Legacy Applications with RDBMSs and Middleware
Dan Fobes

Today programmers have a wide range of options when developing applications. There is an endless number of tools and techniques associated with simply writing a program. Hardware advances deliver what used to be the power of a mainframe on a programmer's desktop. Given the pace of software and hardware advances, it should follow that programmer productivity has grown equally as fast. This is not the case, because for many new applications being developed there is one constraint — it must plug into an established world of corporate data and the processes that manage them. For many companies, the processes that manage their enterprise data were written 10 to 15 years ago. These applications are also referred to as legacy systems. Rewriting legacy systems would solve the technology gap experienced today, but the cost and risks are usually too great. This chapter outlines some options available for interfacing legacy systems with the latest technology, enabling a company to continue to compete in a rapidly changing field.

CLIENT/SERVER AND DECENTRALIZED IS

In the 1970s and early 1980s, IBM dominated IS with mainframes, and IS programmers wrote largely in COBOL. All programs were defined by users, then written by IS. As a result, all mission-critical applications were coded by one group and executed on one machine. In the mid to late 1980s, the PC started to replace terminals as companies moved to empower the user with word processors and spreadsheet applications. Nontechnical users could move data from the mainframe to their desktop and do some additional

0-8493-1149-7/02/$0.00+$1.50
© 2002 by CRC Press LLC

client processing within a spreadsheet without the aid of IS. Network operating systems (NOSs) provided a means to connect PCs in a local area network allowing for users to share both the raw mainframe data and PC-processed data, hence the birth of client/server. As a result, companies had distributed their mission-critical data processing from a centralized IS throughout the enterprise.

The Failure of Client/Server

All applications can be broken down into three groups of code (or tiers):

1. Presentation tier — get user information
2. Business tier — process user information
3. Data tier — write processed information

When applications were written by one group and run on one machine, these layers were usually intermixed. It was not uncommon for one programmer to write one program that contained all three. With the advent of modular programming, large programs could be broken down into a collection of shared modules, reducing both the time required to finish an application and the risk of writing entire applications from scratch. Unfortunately, the immediate IS benefit of reusing modules would often come at the expense of large modules with large numbers of parameters instructing them how to behave for different types of invocations. However, modular programming presented the opportunity to separate the presentation tier from the business and data tiers.

With client/server applications, there is a requirement to distinguish among the presentation, business, and data tiers. There are two computers involved in client/server applications — the client and the server. The client application executes on the client PC, with all presentation input being received locally from the user. However, some data are read from and written to the server for the purpose of information sharing. As a result, unlike a mainframe application, a client/server application is separated from some of its data by a network — the slowest part of any computer.

For applications such as simple spreadsheet calculations, the client/server model works fine. However, many corporations, lured by the low cost of client/server technology and a need to standardize, attempted to move all IS applications to a client/server architecture. After investing lots of time and money, many companies found that the tools enabled them to re-create the applications, but the client/server model made it impossible to implement them. No matter how fast the client and server hardware is, the network is a bottleneck. With the business tier executing on the client and saturating the network with file I/O requests, it was not uncommon to see a complex client/server application become unusable when 25 to 50 users began to use it — something a mainframe could handle easily.

SUCCEEDING WITH DISTRIBUTED DATA PROCESSING

The scalability problem that exists with client/server applications has many proposing a return to mainframes and centralized IS. However, given that data is distributed throughout an enterprise and applications exist on various platforms, others would benefit if the data and the processes that manage them can be tied together. Currently available are several options that provide for both types of solutions:

- Relational Database Management Systems
- Remote Procedure Call
- Messaging

As stated above, most legacy mainframe applications contained all three tiers. Clearly the presentation must be rewritten for the PC. For each of the technical solutions above, consider a simple PC application, PCDEPOS, that collects user information such as an account number and amount of money to deposit. The goal is to have PCDEPOS call an existing COBOL program on a mainframe, MFDEPOS, which performs the transaction (i.e., it represents the business and data tiers only).

RDBMS

One solution to the fragmentation of mission-critical data and their processes is to centralize them to one or more relational databases. Data access through a relational engine can be much faster because data contained within files located across various platforms is moved under the control of a technology built to manage it. Files are moved to tables, and selected columns within tables can be indexed. Furthermore, business logic, usually in the form of COBOL programs, can be recoded as SQL-based stored procedures that are compiled and then executed within the RDBMS engine for optimal performance. Additionally, most databases support some form of replication whereby tables from one database can be replicated to others, facilitating information sharing. Finally, Transaction Processing (TP) monitors are available for most RDBMSs. A separate product, TP monitors interface a client application to an RDBMS and increase performance where large numbers of users require data access. It does this by creating a pool of costly connections to the RDBMS and having the application use a connection from the pool only when necessary.

For the example application, PCDEPOS is created to collect information from the user using middleware, called an open database connectivity (or ODBC) driver, supplied by the RDBMS vendor to facilitate communication between the client and the server. Files that MFDEPOS wrote to and read from, or the data tier, must be moved into RDBMS'$ tables. There are two options for MFDEPOS'$ data processing logic (the business tier) — it can be rewritten as a stored procedure within the RDBMS or modified to perform I/O against SQL tables instead of files.

There are two problems with this solution. One, it increases the cost and complexity of applications. An RDBMS requires the purchase of an RDBMS, additional server hardware, and one or more dedicated database administrators (DBAs) to install, design, tune, and maintain it. The other problem is risk. Simple applications may be easy to move to a RDBMS; however, no legacy application is simple. Many companies will be required to spend a large amount of resources normalizing or breaking up the data within records as they move from files to RDBMS tables. This is because an RDBMS table has a limit of 255 columns and no row can exceed 2 kilobytes in size — legacy applications typically exceed this. Also, not all data maps over from a file to a table (e.g., dates), and for each of these, a translation is required. Time and staff must be allocated to not only normalize data and map data types, but also verify that existing data moves cleanly into the RDBMS. Part of the migration to an RDBMS is the modifications to the existing business tier code. In the example application, rewriting the MFDE-POS business tier as a stored procedure introduces significant risk because of the differences between the languages (a form of SQL and COBOL). The alternative of replacing file I/O within the COBOL program with RDBMS I/O is usually not feasible because of the scalability issues (requires the COBOL code to execute on the PC).

An RDBMS solution has many benefits; however, the costs and risks associated with moving the data and recoding the business logic must be weighed.

REMOTE PROCEDURE CALLS

For most, there is a significantly smaller risk in tying together existing systems that work. What is needed is a form of interprocess communication (IPC) to have one process send and receive data to another. One form of IPC is Remote Procedure Call (RPC).

Using RPC, a program calls a procedure that is executed on a different machine. There is always a one-to-one relationship, and the calling program blocks until the called procedure returns. This sounds simple enough, but since the applications are residing in different address spaces, the only data that each share are the parameters they pass, not global variables within the applications. For an RPC across different machines, data mapping must be addressed because not all hardware supports the same byte order (i.e., it stores numbers differently). Finally, either or both machines can crash at any point and recovery must be addressed.

Some vendors of development systems provide proprietary RPC mechanisms that address some of the above issues. There are also standards such as the RPC protocol used by the Open Group's Distributed Computing Environment (DCE). Additionally, third-party vendors provide Object Request Brokers (ORBs) for RPC services. The most common ORB is called CORBA. A standard created by the Object Management Group (OMG), CORBA facilitates RPCs across different machines. Unfortunately, the CORBA standard is just that — a standard. Because CORBA is similar to UNIX, each vendor has a slightly different implementation of that standard, and until very recently different CORBA implementations could communicate with each other. Microsoft has a competing technology called the Distributed Component Object Model (DCOM). Many vendors support both CORBA and DCOM as their RPC mechanism, and although both CORBA and DCOM are complex to program, they are options that should be considered when evaluating distributed processing via RPC.

MESSAGE-ORIENTED MIDDLEWARE

Another form of IPC is messaging. Vendors of message-oriented middleware provide a mechanism to send and receive messages asynchronously from one process to another. A message is simply a string of bytes the user defines. There are two approaches to messaging: message queues and publish/subscribe. In a message queue environment, an application sends messages to and receives messages from queues. In a publish/subscribe model, an application broadcasts and receives messages via a subject. The sender specifies the subject of the message and the receiver specifies the subject(s) it wants to get messages for. There are pros and cons to each; however, both are sufficient for most environments.

As stated above, a message is a user-defined string of bytes — there is no standard that needs to be followed. A typical messaging application sends and receives messages asynchronously across multiple platforms. The messaging subsystem handles the routing with most vendors supporting the concept of guaranteed and assured delivery (i.e., the message will get to the receiver, but only once). One of the strengths of messaging, which differentiates it from RPC, is that the sender need not block or wait until the receiver responds. Another strength is that one message may be delivered to multiple listeners.

For the example application, messages would contain the arguments to the MFDEPOS program. To facilitate messaging, a new server application called MFLISTEN is required, and the client application must be modified to send and receive messages to it. MFLISTEN listens for client messages and calls the server application with the arguments specified in the message. Once completed, MFDEPOS returns control back to MFLISTEN, which sends the arguments back to the client via a message.

**Exhibit 1. Message Containing Parameters with
@@ as a Delimiter for MFDEPOS**

| Parameter 1@@Parameter 2@@Parameter 3@@ ...

Exhibit 2. Simple Message with Segments Supporting Message Versions

| 4 bytes | 2 bytes | 2 bytes | 2 bytes | 2 bytes | ...

| MessageID | Segment Count | SegmentID | Segment Version | Segment Size | Parameter 1...

| SegmentID | Segment Version | Segment Size | Parameter 1...

Since there is no enforced message type, defining one that is flexible becomes a challenge. Different requests for different server applications will likely require a different message, and over time, this may become unmanageable as each request begins to change. There are two ways to solve this problem: message versioning and self-describing messages.

To accomplish the deposit application using message versioning, a message could simply contain the linkage to MFDEPOS with each parameter separated by a delimiter (see Exhibit 1).

Although this works, it requires a dedicated MFLISTEN program for each server program such as MFDEPOS. A more flexible approach would be to break the message into multiple segments and then build a header to contain segment information (see Exhibit 2). Designing messages around segments is not new — a standard called Electronic Data Interchange, or EDI, is also based on segments.

Here, MessageID represents the format of the message, Segment Count is the number of segments in the message, SegmentID is the start of the segment and represents the program name (e.g., 1 for MFDEPOS), Segment Version represents the format of the parameters (number, order, datatypes), and the parameters follow. The parameters can be delimited or fixed length — their layout is defined by SegmentID and Segment Version. The benefit to moving the program name and version down to the segment is that it allows for one MFLISTEN program to serve as an interface to multiple server programs. The only problem with this design is when MFDEPOS'$ linkage changes, the format of the segment changes and the segment version must be incremented. Sending applications such as PCDEPOS would need to be changed to send the new message. Receiving applications such as

Exhibit 3.   Segment Supporting Self Describing Data

| 2 bytes | 2 bytes | 2 bytes | 8 bytes | ? | 8 bytes

| SegmentID | Segment Version | Segment Size | P1 Descriptor | P1 Value | P2 Descriptor | ...

MFLISTEN would need to be modified to verify the new message version and call the updated version of MFDEPOS.

To accomplish the deposit application using self-describing data, the version number within the message is replaced by field descriptors. Specifically, each parameter value in the message is prepended with a field name that defines it (see Exhibit 3).

With self-describing data, the segment remains the same, but each parameter has two components: a descriptor and a value. These two components can be fixed length or delimited (they are fixed length in Exhibit 3). The benefit to this structure is that it automates the process of calling legacy applications. The best case scenario with versioning saw one listener program created to serve multiple server applications. However, the sending applications (PCDEPOS) and the listener application (MFLISTEN) require an update when there is any change to the server application's linkage (MFDEPOS). With self-describing fields, we can reduce this maintenance to a batch scan on the server. An application on the mainframe can be written to scan a COBOL program and extract the linkage to a table that contains each name and type. The sending applications would then use the names in the COBOL linkage to describe their data, followed by the value of that field. The MFLISTEN program, upon receiving a message, can extract the program name and map the linkage in the message to the linkage in the database automatically, then make the call. New versions of MFDEPOS can be scanned and the database updated. No changes are required to MFLISTEN or PCDEPOS in most cases.

Some message systems allow for field mapping within the message. This allows the MFLISTEN application to query the message for fields instead of parsing it directly. This simplifies MFLISTEN and combines with self-describing data, which provides the optimal messaging solution.

Not all is golden with a messaging solution. Although guaranteed delivery insures a message gets to its destination, it may be possible that one transaction is composed of several messages. Additionally, one message may require the execution of multiple listener programs. In either case, a program would have to initiate a transaction locally, send the messages, subscribe to the responses, and roll back if any of them failed. Another possible issue with messaging is security. With messages traveling back and forth on a network, a hacker can easily listen in, make a change, and send messages back out. Here, encryption is required.

RECOMMENDED COURSE OF ACTION

The above technologies are not mutually exclusive, and in fact, it may turn out that a combination of all three is the best solution. For example, a client may communicate with a server using RPC, the server may use messaging to perform IPC with another server, and one or both of these servers may interact with an RDBMS.

In general, all programs should be separated into three tiers and corporate data should be managed by an RDBMS. Business logic should be coded in a high-level language such as COBOL, which calls a minimum number of stored procedures for I/O intensive requests. Finally, the presentation should be coded in a rapid application tool that supports an RDBMS such as Visual Basic. For companies that require a high volume of transactions, middleware in the form of a transaction server or a TP monitor combined with an ORB should be considered.

Migrating an enterprise to this configuration involves many steps and differs for different companies. Avoid the all-or-nothing approach. Risk can be reduced by using a divide-and-conquer approach that targets subsystems. Below are some high-level steps for accomplishing such a migration:

1. Identify a logical subsystem of the enterprise.
2. Form a team composed of programmers who understand the subsystem, and others who understand the target technology.
3. Identify the data of the subsystem.
4. Identify existing applications that manage the data, then tie them together using messaging. This will uncover redundant data and data processing within the subsystem.
5. Design the RDBMS solution (tables, stored procedures, etc.).
6. Create a listener program that listens to the messages created in Step 4 and performs the requests on the RDBMS.
7. Once the RDBMS can service all of the messages of Step 4, it can be phased in.
8. Go to Step 1.

Some applications may span subsystems. Messaging supports this requirement well and should be used. Although most RDBMSs support replication, this usually requires one server to stream over tables of information to another server at scheduled intervals. Not only does this introduce a delay across servers, it does not scale for large databases — messaging the updates as they happen addresses both shortcomings.

When the RDBMS phase-in is complete, new applications should go directly against the RDBMS. Most new technology being introduced provides for access to RDBMSs. The legacy applications can continue using messaging, be modified for direct RDBMS access, or be rewritten.

Section VI
Data Warehousing

Chapter 28

The Data Warehouse: If You Build It with the Users, They Will Come

John van den Hoven

A data warehouse can provide a cohesive view of a company's operations, but to succeed, it must do so for all users, not just senior executives. This chapter describes what various user groups need and how warehouses can be constructed to meet their requirements.

Although the concept of data warehousing is not new, it is only recently that the techniques, methodologies, software tools, database management systems, disk storage, and processor capacity have all advanced far enough to allow developers to deliver effective systems. These advancements in data warehousing technology are being driven by a growing demand from the knowledge worker community for better and faster access to more integrated data at their desktop. Increasingly, data warehousing is also seen as a key enabler for knowledge management within companies.

DATA WAREHOUSE USERS AND BENEFITS

Many companies find themselves faced with challenges to reshape their current business processes as they continuously adapt to changing market conditions. To remain competitive, companies must, in addition to being "lowest cost" producers, adapt to the paradigm shift from being company- or product-focused to becoming customer-focused. Changing the way companies do business requires that business users access information about the company's business, products, markets, and customers that is not readily available in current business systems. Business users also require new views of the company's internal operational data that reflect a longer time horizon as well as new views of its external data that reflect the external forces that shape the company's future direction.

A data warehouse can provide a cohesive view of the company's operations in a manner that is accessible by many employees rather than a few senior executives. The contents of a data warehouse will be of interest to many users in the company. Data warehouse designers need to understand these users and their specific information needs, because the benefits from a data warehouse are realized only through improved decision making by these business users.

There are several categories of business users, each with different requirements and ways of interacting with the data. Those users that will benefit most from better data access and analysis capabilities are likely to fall into four general categories: executives, analysts, knowledge workers, and front-line staff.

Senior executives determine the business's future direction and make high-impact decisions that will benefit from the improved quality of analyses their analysts can produce from the data stored in the data warehouse. Other executives such as general managers, sales managers, line-of-business managers, and the heads of functional departments will use the data in the data warehouse to conduct analyses of their business areas and as an aid in decision making. Executive users are generally consumers of business information who will view the data in a data warehouse through an Executive Information System, predefined queries and reports, or customized applications.

Analysts use the data access and analysis tools associated with the data warehouse to conduct company, market, competitive, and related analyses. Many of these business analysts have been using tools such as SAS (statistical analysis software from SAS Institute, Inc.) and IFPS (interactive financial planning system) for many years. Their main problem has been in getting access to good quality data from within the company and external to the company. Analysts are primarily creators and providers of business information. They view and work with the data through predefined queries and reports, but also use data access and analysis tools to study trends, investigate problems, and conduct what-if analyses.

Knowledge workers are somewhat like analysts, except that they typically focus on a specific subject area. Examples include buyers who focus on purchasing equipment and parts, or a warehouse supervisor who needs to determine what to stock and how much to stock in the warehouse. Knowledge workers are both creators and consumers of business information. They work with predefined queries and reports but also generate their own ad hoc queries and reports. Knowledge workers are especially interested in historical and usage information.

Some front-line staff (e.g., customer service representatives) also need to access a broad range of data to perform their core business processes more effectively. Front-line staff generally interact with the data warehouse through customized applications developed to support their activities or through predefined queries and reports and personal productivity applications such as spreadsheet software.

The business users in these four general categories typically use the data warehouse to access data (what-is information), manipulate data for analysis (what-means information), and manipulate the data for purposes of modeling and simulation (what-if information). Through these capabilities, the data warehouse improves business effectiveness and efficiency.

Business effectiveness is enhanced as users make quicker and better quality decisions through an improved decision-making process. These improvements in the decision-making process result from improved data access through greater data availability and timeliness, improved data quality, data integration, and access to historical information. The result is a better understanding of the key trends and events that affect business through improved sales metrics, trend visibility, improved cost analysis, and improved monitoring of business initiatives.

Business efficiency is enhanced because the business user no longer has to spend a great deal of effort in identifying what data is available, collecting data, and performing manual analysis, but can now focus on using the information. As a result, users spend less time finding data, and more time analyzing it and working with other company staff members to develop more collaborative decisions and solutions. Greater productivity also results by providing direct access to data without programmer intervention.

INVOLVING BUSINESS USERS IN BUILDING THE DATA WAREHOUSE

In order to realize business benefits from implementing a data warehouse, companies should ensure that it is driven by business needs and that data warehousing systems accommodate key user preferences and are tailored to meet their needs.

Business-Driven

First and foremost, a data warehouse project must be driven by the company's business objectives and must have its scope determined by the project sponsor's perceived benefit. With the key business objectives identified, business managers can define what data their business users need to achieve these objectives and to provide benefit to their business areas.

Some of the areas in a company that have most often shown the greatest business benefits are the financial (including processes such as management reporting and financial analysis), marketing (including processes such as market and customer analysis), and sales areas (including processes such as sales support and customer service) of the business. These are key areas in which users need to see historical trend data to create and adjust business plans. Production (including processes such as production planning and quality control) is another area in which analysts often need to consult historical data to analyze trends and pinpoint or target potential areas for improvement.

The budget from the data warehouse's sponsor is a key determining factor when establishing the feasible scope of the project. The sponsor also prioritizes business needs and assesses the potential value of the data warehouse in meeting these business needs.

It is important to ensure that organizational commitment to the data warehouse project is firm, given the significant cost and effort required for these projects. The ongoing involvement, guidance, and support from the data warehouse's sponsor ensures the link to the business needs and a continued focus on the business needs. The most successful data warehouse projects are viewed as business investments, rather than technology initiatives.

User-Driven

It is important to involve users early and often throughout the design and implementation process, so that the data warehousing team can more accurately and quickly uncover the data requirements for the data warehouse and understand the way in which the users will interact with the data. Another goal for the data warehousing team is to gain user acceptance through the process. When the business users are fully involved, they feel more ownership for its success and will work more closely with the data warehousing team to deal with and be more tolerant of the inevitable problems and glitches.

Business users help define the business requirements, get data into the data warehouse, build the data warehouse, and get information out. Each of these is now described in more detail.

Defining Business Requirements. The information services department generally undertakes building a data warehouse with appropriate assistance from external resources, but defining the requirements is the business users' responsibility. Even if a data warehouse is implemented on time and within budget, it will still be deemed unsuccessful if it does not meet the users' needs. This can happen if the data warehousing team tries to guess what the users' needs are.

Business modeling helps establish the dialog between the data warehousing team and the business users. It uses pictures (diagrams) to provide a simplified description of how the business operates. Business modeling is a process for matching the needs of business users to the available data and is the means for defining the business requirements. Interviewing stakeholders and developing a business model delivers more information faster and allows relationships to be built with the sponsors and potential users of the data warehouse. It helps ensure that decisions about data warehousing are driven primarily by business requirements so the focus remains on what is important for the business, not what data is available.

Business modeling is a very useful means of defining both what the business requirements are and how the data warehouse will be used. It is a valuable technique for describing the business value chain and identifying where value can be added to focus the attention of the data warehousing team on areas of most benefit to the business. When defining the business requirements, it is best to strive to identify the most important 20 percent of the operational data that delivers 80 percent of the business benefit, and then to focus on how that data will be used.

Getting Data In. Through the process of defining business requirements, data needs are identified. The next step is to identify and qualify sources of data for the data warehouse. The business users help identify the sources, locations, and formats of the data needed for the data warehouse.

Before this data can be loaded into the data warehouse, its quality must be verified. Companies should not underestimate the importance of user faith in the integrity of the warehouse data or of the effort required to ensure data quality.

Data integrity problems generally originate in the source systems but can also be introduced during the various steps involved in creating and operating the data warehouse. These data integrity problems must be resolved before integrating data from those systems into the data warehouse. Therefore, data cleansing and validation procedures need to be defined. Business users must be very involved in setting up initial and ongoing checks to validate the accuracy, timeliness, consistency, and completeness of the data and in resolving any issues with the data.

After the data sources have been identified and the quality of data from those sources is verified, they need to be mapped to the data warehouse. All data transformations must be identified and defined. Business users define rules that translate the values of the data used in the source application into the values used in the data warehouse. The process also includes translating cryptic field names and codes in the source system to more recognizable and meaningful names.

Building the Data Warehouse. When building the data warehouse, it is best to do development in increments toward a well-defined goal. Often, this is best done through a rapid prototyping approach. Prototyping allows frequent feedback and improves communication between the data warehousing team and the intended users. This is essential because, unlike traditional systems development projects, not all requirements for a data warehouse project can be identified in advance.

The prototyping should be done rapidly with the first deliverable within a few months. The users should be assessing the deliverables and working with the data warehousing team to iteratively prototype improvements as frequently as feasible. It will be necessary to continue to evolve the data warehouse by revising the data and adding new fields, new data, and new capabilities when applicable.

During the prototyping process, it is best to focus on a half dozen or so key users to make the process manageable yet comprehensive. The prototyping process includes introducing these key users to data warehousing, mapping data needs to their jobs, and helping them learn how to use the data in the data warehouse to deliver business value. It is also best to focus on a few subject areas at a time to keep the scope manageable. This allows the data warehousing team to establish the value of the data warehouse, manage expectations, and expand the data warehouse as business value is delivered.

Getting Information Out. Business users help determine what data is needed and what formats are necessary for them to use the data effectively. The data needs to be put in a form that users can easily understand and use. Therefore, the data warehousing team needs to know what kind of queries will be run, what types of analyses will be done, and which reports will be needed.

Information access tools are the windows into the data warehouse, so selecting the most appropriate tools is an important determinant to the success of the data warehouse. Different types of users will require different tools because they have different needs, requirements, and focuses. Executives will access predefined information through report viewers or an executive information system. Analysts will mostly do ad hoc data access through on-line analytical processing (OLAP) tools, advanced query and report writing tools, and statistical tools to conduct what-if analyses. Knowledge workers will do mostly ad hoc data access through query and report writing tools. Front-line staff will use personal productivity tools as well as view reports and run pre-defined queries. Therefore, a successful data warehousing system will require a suite of tools to meet the varied needs of these business users.

The creation of a directory containing information about the data stored in a data warehouse is another key to establishing user independence. It allows users to understand the data in the data warehouse. A directory describes how the data warehouse is organized, including what information is available, how it is defined, where it is located, and how to access it. To identify what they want from the data warehouse, users can browse through a data catalog in the same way customers might browse through a store catalog.

USING A DATA WAREHOUSE FOR KNOWLEDGE MANAGEMENT

The knowledge in a company is stored in the form of structured data and unstructured data. Data warehousing focuses on helping companies make more effective and efficient use of their structured data. A knowledge management system emerges when data warehousing is successfully coupled with other approaches for managing the unstructured data in companies such as that stored in electronic mail systems, intranet(s), and document management systems. A company portal is often used as the integrating mechanism to provide decision-makers with a broad range of information sources.

Knowledge Management

There are many definitions in use for knowledge management (KM), reflecting the various perspectives on the scope and impact of knowledge in a company. Breaking the term "knowledge management" into its component parts can derive one such definition. We see that the dictionary defines

- Knowledge as the sum or range of what has been perceived, discovered, or learned.
- Management as the professional administration of business concerns.

Knowledge management also connotes professional management of knowledge through its collection, integration, organization, analysis, and distribution. Putting it all together, one can define knowledge management as the professional administration of the sum or range of what has been perceived, discovered, or learned in the company by collecting, integrating, organizing, analyzing, and sharing the knowledge so that it can be drawn on and used effectively by the company.

The rationale is that by quickly understanding the complete picture, better decisions can be made. Knowledge management encompasses both structured and unstructured data, as well as intellectual assets that can be shared through collaboration technologies.

Data Warehousing for Knowledge Management

Data warehousing adds value to a knowledge management system by improving the accessibility, quality, and consistency of structured data and by reducing the time required to find and make effective use of the data. A data warehouse helps identify what has happened, and the unstructured data in a knowledge management system explains why it happened and provides context, competitive intelligence, and overall trends in the business environment.

Structured data is highly organized factual information that is explicit such as transaction data from an enterprise resource planning (ERP) application or reports from a data warehouse. Structured data exists in the databases, data files, and reports of the data warehouse and transaction systems.

Unstructured data is more amorphous subjective information that is stored in various information systems and on the Web. Unstructured data exists in the form of electronic mail, video clips, documents, still images, discussion forums, and audio files. Increasingly, extensible markup language (XML) is being used to bring order to unstructured data.

For structured data, the challenge is to turn raw data into information and knowledge. Data warehousing does this and is a key contributor to successful knowledge management. It helps turn data into knowledge in three primary ways:

1. As a corporate memory containing integrated information about the company's operations
2. By cataloging and organizing the information for easy access
3. Through tools to derive knowledge from the corporate memory

A data warehouse serves as a storage medium for keeping the corporate memory in an accessible form. The data contained in a data warehouse represents a large part of a company's knowledge such as customer, product, and sales information. It provides a cohesive view of company operations and contains all the information and accumulated insights that have been generated over time.

The data warehouse provides the what-is information and serves a complementary role to that of the unstructured data in a knowledge management system. It provides structured data that is primarily data on the internal operations of the company, in the form of "hard" factual data. The other information in a knowledge management system is unstructured data that is primarily external data on the business environment, competition, and other areas of interest, in the form of "soft" subjective data. The knowledge management system links the internal, hard data with the external, soft data to provide business users with an integrated view of the knowledge in the company. For example, the Web's sources of external business insight about customers, suppliers, partners, and competitors can be augmented by the data in a data warehouse, which details current activities with them.

By cataloging and organizing the company's data for access, the data warehouse enables business users to find what information is available, where to find it, and how to access it. It plays a key role in extending the knowledge of the company, because, as Samuel Johnson said, "knowledge is of two kinds: we know a subject ourselves, or we know where we can find information upon it." The catalog ensures that business users know where to find data to supplement their knowledge. It does this by synthesizing and organizing the data according to subjects for easy access.

The catalog also provides what-means information in order to enable a deeper and shared understanding of the data through common definition of the data, details on formulas used, and relationships between data. In doing so, it allows the business users to use data that is clearly laid out and defined to identify patterns and develop insights into the operations of the company in order to create knowledge.

Knowledge is embedded in the company's information systems. Data warehousing provides knowledge discovery tools such as data visualization, data mining, and advanced analytical software to derive knowledge from the corporate memory. These knowledge discovery tools help unlock the knowledge by uncovering visual patterns, creating predictive models, and conducting what-if analyses. These tools allow business users to derive valuable knowledge by finding the embedded meaning in large amounts of data in the data warehouse by making unexpected connections, discovering currently unknown patterns, and developing new and useful insights that can then be incorporated into management's decision-making process.

Portal as a Single Point of Access

Portals are a key component of knowledge management systems. Browser-based, personalized intranet portals are becoming the preferred entry points into the company's knowledge. Portals act as a single point of entry to the diverse business content that is in applications, structured data, and unstructured data throughout the company. Portals are the Web sites that business users go to first when they log onto the Internet or intranet, and come back to regularly. They are often referred to as corporate portals, enterprise portals, or enterprise information portals.

A portal provides an effective mechanism for efficiently and effectively delivering structured data warehousing information correlated with relevant unstructured business intelligence. These unstructured data sources are not easily accessible to data warehouses, but the corporate portal can use metadata and XML to integrate both structured and unstructured data, for easy access throughout the company.

In addition to bringing data together, a portal personalizes the content and extends the use of the data warehouse to new users. The portal can be personalized to provide a single view into the company's knowledge that is relevant to a particular person's role, responsibilities, and interests. This is especially important given the "information glut" that exists in most companies today. The portal also allows the information in the data warehouse to be delivered to a broader range of company users and to selectively share information with customers, suppliers, and partners.

CONCLUSION

Data warehousing offers a good approach to satisfying a company's need for better decision support data and better tools to work with that data. It represents the accumulated knowledge in the decision support area through earlier initiatives, such as executive information systems and information centers, while taking advantage of technology advances such as Web-based computing, database replication, advanced networking, object-oriented computing, and powerful desktop environments.

Increasingly, data warehouses are being linked, through corporate portals, with systems to manage unstructured data sources in order to form comprehensive knowledge management systems. Data warehousing is a key component of these knowledge management systems by allowing companies to derive valuable knowledge from their structured data sources.

"If you build it, they will come," said the disembodied voice in W.P. Kinsella's Field of Dreams. Although this approach works well in the movies, it is best to add the notion of building it "with them" for success in real life. "If you build it with them, they will come" should be the guiding principle for the organization's data warehousing efforts to guarantee a happier ending for all stakeholders — users, developers, and senior executives. To do this, companies should ensure that their data warehousing projects are driven by business needs and tailored to user needs. Only then will data warehousing projects be viewed as business investments, rather than technology initiatives.

Chapter 29
Data Warehouse Administration and Management

Alan Benander
Barbara Benander
Adam Fadlalla
Gregory James

Data Warehouse is a repository of integrated information, culled from any number and variety of data sources, including various databases and legacy data sources. The size of a data warehouse is usually massive and the data warehouse typically stores a wide range of information that has been generated over long periods of time. Data related to business subjects such as products, markets, and customers are all collected, integrated, and housed under the data warehouse umbrella. When this vast wealth of information is interfaced to decision support tools that offer powerful data access and analysis capabilities, the data warehouse can be fully exploited by its users.

There are a number of data warehousing tools and products currently on the market. All of these products provide relatively easy access to the data warehouse, both at the enterprise and the data mart level. All of these tools also provide useful facilities for administering and managing a data warehouse. However, creation, maintenance, and daily administration of data warehouses are still formidable tasks that are far from being fully automated.

The successful administration and management of a data warehouse requires skills and expertise that go beyond those required of a traditional database administrator (DBA). There is a need for the creation of a position that is designated a "data warehouse administrator" (DWA). The tasks of a DWA encompass those of a traditional DBA, but the DWA's job is considerably

Exhibit 1.   Operational Databases versus Warehouse Databases

Characteristic	Operational Databases	Warehouse Databases
Users	All users	Executives, analysts, customer service representatives
Goal	Recordkeeping (OLTP)	Information analysis (OLAP, etc.), decision support, database marketing
Update	Online	Batch
Query level	Atomic, detailed	Aggregated, summarized, integrated
Time horizon	Mainly present	Historical + present + future
Data source	Internal	Internal + external
Orientation	Entity oriented (product, account, customer ...)	Category oriented (Product type, account type, customer segment ...)
Data volumes	Gigabytes	Gigabytes/terabytes
Process	Transaction driven	Analysis driven
Structure	Relatively static	Dynamic

more complex because of the nature of the data warehouse and its position within an enterprise data architecture.

DATA WAREHOUSE DATABASES VERSUS OPERATIONAL DATABASES

In order to better understand the distinction between the roles of a DBA and a DWA, it is imperative to understand the significant differences between an operational database and a data warehouse. They differ not only in their ultimate purposes, but also in the types and amount of data stored in them and the methods by which they are populated, updated, and accessed. Some distinguishing characteristics are summarized in Exhibit 1.

There are three main types of data warehouse: operational data stores (ODS), enterprise data warehouses (EDW), and data marts (DM). Operational data stores are the latest evolution of customer information files (CIF). CIFs were widely deployed in the past to maintain all common customer information in one central location. Updates to this information are entered into the CIF, and then all other systems that share this data are synchronized to it. Name, address, and phone number are good examples of shared customer information. Today's more sophisticated ODS performs the same basic function as the CIF but is also actively used by customer support and sales personnel. It is the nexus for all marketing and sales activities, and it contains information pertaining to current, prospective, and past customers. In addition to the basic customer information, the ODS also tracks all recent customer activity and marketing interactions with the customer. ODSs are commonly deployed by corporations reorganizing away from product-line-oriented structures to customer-oriented structures.

Enterprise data warehouses are distinguished from operational data stores by the scope and quantity of the data they contain. They typically contain product, accounting, and organizational information as well as customer information. Where an ODS may typically contain 12 to 18 months of data, an EDW will store three to five years of data or more. Many EDWs are not accessed directly by end users because of their size and complexity. Their role is to store the integrated, scrubbed, historical information that is used as the standard data repository from which multiple, special purpose data warehouses (i.e., data marts) are populated. These secondary data warehouses are then accessed by end users with decision support and ad hoc query tools.

A data mart is a subject-oriented or department-oriented data warehouse whose scope is much smaller than that of an enterprise data warehouse. Its purpose is to provide decision support for a particular department within an enterprise or about a particular subject within an enterprise. Many companies decide to first implement individual data marts before committing to a full-scale EDW. It has been estimated that a data mart typically requires an order of magnitude (1/10) less effort than that of an EDW. In addition, it takes months, as opposed to years, to build, and costs tens or hundreds of thousands of dollars, versus the millions of dollars needed for an EDW.[7]

All three types of data warehouses represent data in fundamentally different ways than do operational databases. In an operational database that has been designed using traditional relational database design principles, data is represented as tables, whereas in a data warehouse, there are many instances where data is most naturally represented as cross-tabulations. As an example, Exhibit 2 shows how sales data might be represented using a relational database design for an operational database. Exhibit 3 shows a two dimensional representation of the same data. The two dimensions are Product (P1, P2, P3, P4) and Region (E, C, W). Adding a third dimension, such as Time (e.g., 1999, 2000), upgrades the two-dimensional representation to a cube, where a cell of the cube represents "sales of a specific product, in a specific region, for a specific year."

Differences between operational databases and data warehouse databases also manifest themselves sharply in their physical designs. An important goal for an operational database is to provide short update and query transactions. The physical structure of an operational database is designed to ensure update efficiency and data integrity over small sets of related data. On the other hand, data warehouses are typically used to answer analytic questions in a user-friendly, ad hoc query environment. The physical structure of a data warehouse is designed to provide data loading and storage efficiency and fast ad hoc query response times. Special

Exhibit 2.   A Sample Relational Sales Database

Product	Region	Sales
P1	E	20
P1	C	30
P1	W	10
P2	E	30
P2	C	25
P2	W	15
P3	E	60
P3	C	50
P3	W	40
P4	E	10
P4	C	40
P4	W	20

Exhibit 3.   A Possible Data Warehouse Version of Exhibit 2

	E	C	W
P1	20	30	10
P2	30	25	15
P3	60	50	40
P4	10	40	20

indexing techniques (for example, bitmap indexes) and physically partitioned schemas are commonly used in data warehouse implementations.

Because of its enormous size, as well as its inherent nature, a data warehouse requires very close monitoring in order to maintain acceptable efficiency and productivity. As more and more users access the warehouse, the warehouse grows both structurally and in size, causing potential system performance problems. The data structure may need to change over time as additional data is kept for analysis. Some physical structures may grow dramatically as the historical content increases. Unusual business events such as mergers and acquisitions and new product introductions may require large system conversions or enhancements to be implemented. All of these changes require specialized tools and procedures to facilitate version control, monitoring, and system performance tuning.

Many data warehouses are designed using a star schema model. A star schema includes a central "fact" table surrounded by several "dimension" tables. The fact table contains a large number of rows that correspond to observed business events or facts. The dimension tables contain classification and aggregation information about the central fact rows. The dimension tables have a one-to-many relationship with rows in the central fact table. The star schema design provides extremely fast query response time, simplicity, and ease of maintenance for read-only database structures. However, star schemas are not well suited for online update operations. Specialized data warehousing tools have been built to explicitly support star schema architectures. The more recent versions of general-purpose relational systems such as the IBM DB/2, Oracle, and Microsoft's SQL Server now support these structures as well.

It is evident that a DBA who possesses knowledge and skills pertinent to only a traditional operational database will not be able to administer and manage a data warehouse. A person knowledgeable of all the various complexities of a data warehouse (i.e., a DWA), is needed.

DATA WAREHOUSE ADMINISTRATION AND MANAGEMENT TASKS

Traditional database administration methods and techniques for operational database applications performed by the DBA have been developed and refined over 20 years of industrywide use. Robust tools exist to aid in all aspects of the job of a DBA. Data warehousing technology, on the other hand, has only recently moved beyond its initial stages, where most efforts are the first of their kind. Database management systems have been enhanced significantly to enable the creation of large-scale data warehouse databases, and physical data storage systems have been enhanced to handle the extremely large capacities as well. Specialized data warehouse administration tools and techniques are also being developed to handle the unique system requirements of data warehouses.

All of the usual operational database administration tasks apply to a data warehouse environment. However, because of the differences between an operational database and a data warehouse previously mentioned, many of these tasks are performed differently, focus on different objectives, or are more complicated. For example, whereas a DBA is generally concerned with small, frequent, online updates to the database, the DWA considers large, less frequent, batch updates to the database. It is critical to the success of a data warehouse that large, batch updates are accomplished as quickly as possible in order to make the refreshed data warehouse available as soon as possible. In many situations, the currency and availability of the data warehouse provides a significant competitive advantage. For example, a business's ability to react quickly to a sudden shift in consumer behavior may result in significant customer retention or in new customer acquisition. Frequent updates to the data warehouse may be needed to support the decision-making cycle, which may be monthly, weekly, or even daily.

Planning

A DWA must plan for a potentially enormous growth rate of the data warehouse, anticipating growth rates that are much higher than a DBA would experience. In fact, a recent Gartner Group management report stated the following: "It is not unusual for organizations' warehouses to experience a 100 percent growth-rate per year. This is not the typical scenario that DBAs take into account when sizing databases for production. Compound this with the fact that adding even incremental amounts of data increases the usefulness of the overall warehouse. Therefore, moderately small additions may result in a multiplier effect for queries. In the end, what one might experience is a drastic growth in not only the size of the warehouse but also the usage, and necessarily its ongoing administration (security, tuning, etc.)."

Clearly such future expansion must be taken into account by the DWA when planning a data warehouse. Using system architectures to support such volumes of data should be considered; these include SMP (Symmetric Processing) and MPP (Massive Parallel Processing) platforms, which introduce new levels of design complexity (parallelism of database operations and storage). DB2 Universal Database Enterprise-Extended Edition, Informix Extended Parallel Server (XPS), and Oracle Parallel Server offer versions that support parallel operations.[8]

Also as part of the planning stage, the DWA must be involved with data-related issues that pertain to data inconsistencies and data semantics. Source data inconsistencies pose potential serious problems to the integrity and functionality of the data warehouse. For example, even though a particular data field is not essential for all business units, it must be entered properly by all business units for the integrated views within the warehouse to be accurate. As an example, suppose that manufacturing batch numbers are not important to the sales department, but are extremely important for manufacturing and customer service to be able to track down all customers using a particular batch of a product. If the sales department does not enter the batch numbers, or enters them inconsistently in their system, then tracking usage from sales back through the manufacturing process might be impossible.

DWAs also need to deal with issues regarding data semantics. Data and its meaning evolve over time. A preferred customer last year may not be a preferred customer this year by virtue of a change in business policy. Consequently, the DWA must pay special attention to high-level business processes and to their effects upon the database structure (process-enforced integrity versus structure-enforced integrity). Processes that manage and maintain data in all of the source systems need to be examined when they change to ensure that the meaning of the data has not also changed. This could affect the fundamental meaning of the data (as it is defined by its source) or its integrated meaning (as it is defined within the warehouse where many more relationships are maintained).

Another difference in the challenges facing the DWA as opposed to a DBA is in the area of planning ahead for storage management. Whereas a typical corporate database might consume several gigabytes of storage, a data warehouse may require several terabytes. Because of the warehouse's enormous size, parallel processing is the norm when dealing with a data warehouse. To achieve acceptable access rates and minimize data loss, the data in a data warehouse generally is distributed over multiple disks, with concurrent access. Because of these and other considerations, the traditional storage management tasks of a DBA are significantly expanded in a data warehouse environment.

Another issue with which a DWA must be concerned is the inclusion of potentially large volumes of external data. The data in a data warehouse is an information asset that may be augmented, thereby appreciating in its overall value. This is often accomplished by adding external data acquired from outside organizations to enrich the data warehouse. Census information, credit reports, purchasing habits, demographics, and more are all available for purchase. When external data is added to a data warehouse, organizations can begin using the augmented data related not only to their existing customers, but also potential new customers that fall within their marketing profiles. This is an important capability for firms wishing to expand their market share. Thus, to truly leverage the power of a data warehouse, the DWA must plan for the future inclusion of valuable external data.

Design

The design goals for a data warehouse differ from those of an operational database. The major design goal for an operational database is to meet business operational data requirements, while the major design goal for a data warehouse is to meet business analysis informational requirements. Consequently, the DWA cannot simply rely on conventional database design techniques such as E-R diagrams, transaction processing constraints, database normalization, and the like. A design approach for the data warehouse uses the business subject–oriented approach.

Data warehouses move beyond data processing to decision-support and knowledge-based applications. In this mission, the semantic complexity of the underlying database structure becomes even more complex. This additional information requirement often takes the form of more complex relationships among base tables, which in turn require more database keys and indexes. The need to index candidate keys is associated with large tables of the kind that pervade data warehouses. Indeed, multidimensional databases, used to deploy data warehouses, often require more space to store their indexes than they do for their main fact tables. Some warehouse designers implement indexes on columns with large domains as a substitute for commonly executed select operations that are known *a priori* to produce small result sets. In such situations, the overhead of building and maintaining the index is smaller than executing the same "where" clause over and over.

The design of a data warehouse is intended to provide integrated views of business objects such as "Customer." The working set of data values that define "Customer" may not all arrive at the warehouse at one time. Therefore, integrity constraints that might be assumed by the user of the warehouse might not be practically enforced during update. The DWA must be sensitive to the temporal aspects of the data warehouse. For example, with time, the meaning of classifications can change. For example, the classification "Middle Income" in 1979 versus "Middle income" in 1999 is probably different. But an important issue is whether the 1979 or the 1999 data is stored in historical records. If the original data used to derive the classifications is no longer available, then there is no ability to adjust it in the future.

Data warehouse designs must be robust to deal with incompleteness and inconsistency, unlike OLTP and operational database designs. The potential for null values, has a significant impact upon query strategies and adds complexity to the warehouse architecture. Does one impose restrictions on the warehouse and disallow nulls, potentially excluding a significant portion of useful, albeit incomplete, data? Or does one allow null values within the warehouse and deal with the potential incompleteness on the query side? As the number of data sources grows (e.g., multiple operational databases that supply data to the warehouse), the potential for "disintegration" increases. This permits a situation in which the total working set of attributes in the integrated views within the warehouse are not totally populated. Missing values may arise through historical discrepancies (the data was not collected during that time period), through incomplete view integration (inconsistent candidate keys), or nonmandatory values (fields that are important for one application may not be important for another application).

Some argue that the RDBMS design approach can fail to deliver adequate performance as a result of the massive size and complexity of the data warehouse. For example, typical queries against the data warehouse are complex and ad hoc, often submitted by high-level managers in the organization. Answering highly complex business analysis queries may require a large number of joins of huge tables. This creates huge, temporary tables and is very time consuming. Expensive hardware solutions do exist, including parallel database servers. Furthermore, the complexity of the SQL statements would likely be an impediment to the nonsophisticated casual query writer. To solve this problem, the DWA could create canned, optimized queries. This solution, however, is time consuming for the DWA and does not offer maximum flexibility, in terms of range of available queries, to the users.

An alternative design model for a data warehouse is the multidimensional database (MDD). In the MDD model, data is stored in a multidimensional array (hypercube) to allow users to access, aggregate, analyze, and view large amounts of data quickly. MDDs give flexible access to large amounts of data and do it quickly by "pre-digesting" data. Several products exist for creating and accessing MDDs. These include eSSbase, Express, and LightShip Server. MDDs usually keep the data warehouse size to a minimum on the server through data compression and provide client front-end tools. Clearly, the DWA needs to be familiar with the various new technologies for implementing a data warehouse.

Implementation

Once the DWA has planned and designed the data warehouse, an implementation approach must be chosen. It is the authors' opinion that the DWA should use an incremental development approach, rather than an enterprise approach, in creating a successful data warehouse. The size and complexity of an enterprise data warehouse makes an incremental approach the preferred strategy. For example, one successful strategy is to approach each business function (e.g., marketing, sales, finance) that will use the data warehouse and build the data model one function at a time. With this approach, the DWA simply creates data marts for each department. When completed, the enterprise data warehouse will comprise the integration of all the data marts.

Those who argue against the incremental approach cite the inherent problems involved in combining several data marts into a single data warehouse. The integration of these data marts, they maintain, is more difficult than initially creating a single enterprise data warehouse. The authors contend, however, that the complexity and cost involved with the enterprise approach is not worth the risk. With the vast array of new technologies and modeling approaches, it is a judicious approach for a DWA to first become expert at creating a data mart before attempting to create the enterprise data warehouse.

Implementing a data warehouse requires loading of data, which is a far more complex task for a data warehouse as compared with a conventional database. The first major challenge for the DWA is locating all data sources for the data warehouse. As mentioned previously, a data warehouse is created by using a variety of data sources as input. These can include relational databases, hierarchical databases, network databases, conventional files, flat files, news wires, HTML documents, and legacy systems. The tasks of identifying and locating all sources are the responsibility of the DWA. With frequent corporate downsizing and the high turnover rate in some businesses, it may prove quite a challenge for the DWA to identify and locate these important inputs to the data warehouse.

After locating all of the data sources for the data warehouse, the DWA must ascertain the various formats in which the data to be inputted to the data warehouse is to be stored. The heterogeneous nature of the data, originating from multiple production and legacy systems, as well as from external sources, creates another challenge for the DWA. All of the data to be stored in the data warehouse must be reformatted to conform to the chosen data model of the data warehouse. A number of management tools are available to assist in this task, including those from such vendors as Carleton, Platinum Technology, and Prism Solutions.

Data quality is a much greater challenge in a data warehouse setting than in an operational database setting. The authors' experiences have shown that nearly 20 percent of the data is potentially inconsistent for one reason or another. For example, it may happen that address changes are not captured, records belonging to the same customer are not merged properly within the warehouse because of inconsistent candidate keys, or old errors in nonessential fields are replicated into the warehouse without notice. The data quality problem becomes evident on the query side when inconsistent results are returned. One particular example occurred at a company that queried its data warehouse for duplicate Social Security numbers. The system returned one SSN several hundred times. Upon investigation, it was found that a particular business office had entered the SSN of their branch manager, instead of the customers', for all special accounts because a favorite production report was sorted by customer SSN rather than by manager!

There are many other data quality challenges inherent to heterogeneous data. For example, different production systems may represent names differently, use different codes that have the same meaning, and may store the same attribute in different formats (e.g., many formats exist for storing the date field).

Another issue that the DWA must address is the possibility of changes in the information source. Detection of changes in the information source can vary in importance, depending on the nature of the data warehouse. For example, when it is not important for the warehouse to be current and it is acceptable for the data warehouse to be off-line occasionally, then ignoring change detection may be acceptable. However, if currency, efficiency, and continuous access are required, then these changes must be propagated up to the data warehouse. How does the DWA detect changes in the input data sources and propagate them up to the data warehouse? It depends on the nature of the data source. For example, if a source has active database capabilities (such as triggers), then change notification can be programmed automatically. If a data source maintains a log that can be inspected, then inspection of the log can reveal changes. Detection of change in input sources and propagation to the data warehouse is simply an additional function of the DWA, a task not normally required of a traditional DBA.

Another traditional database task that is expanded upon for the DWA is the creation of various views that are appropriate for the variety of users. Whereas the DBA created operationally oriented views, the DWA must create views for managers that are oriented toward business decision making. The DWA must be much more familiar with the business rules and policies than the DBA counterpart. The DWA will be in frequent communication with the business managers and must understand clearly their needs and requirements.

Many standard data warehouse queries specify aggregation values, and many of these aggregations are requested over and over again. In order to minimize the number of full-table scans, the DWA should look for often-used aggregates and store them as permanent values in aggregate tables within the warehouse. These tables are refreshed at the same time the warehouse is updated, which requires more processing during load but, over the long term, eliminates redundant scans to produce the same aggregate values even though the base tables have not changed.

Maintenance

In traditional database administration, the DBA is responsible for ensuring the security and integrity of the database, defining user views, and setting access permissions to the database. The responsibilities of a DBA also include implementing policies and procedures related to database security. For a data warehouse, security issues are even more critical. For example, if a business failure occurred in some aspect, many queries would need to be answered, such as "What was the major contributing factor?" Who should be allowed to ask such queries and obtain the answers? The very survival of the business could well depend on proper security in the data warehouse, provided for by the DWA.

Some organizations are sensitive to internal access. For example, at a large healthcare organization, various medical departments were concerned about physicians from other departments viewing specialized test results, making assumptions about the results' meaning, and coming to erroneous conclusions. There are many situations where the data might imply one thing but in reality means something quite different. In these circumstances, knowledge about the data and how it came into existence is not captured within the warehouse. Special security measures put in place by the DWA are required to mitigate these risks.

The "knowledge about the data," or metadata, is important information that must be administered by the DWA. Metadata, which is the syntactic, semantic, and pragmatic documentation of the data in the data warehouse, is crucial for the success of a data warehouse. The DWA must be familiar with the different aspects of data: (1) syntactics, which defines the structure of the database; (2) semantics, which defines the meaning of the data; and (3) pragmatics, which defines the source and life cycle of the data (effective date, source system, etc.). Business metadata defines relatively static business objects and concepts such as branch office code or product code. This data is typical of commonly used "look-up" tables. Business metadata, for example, would keep track of how many systems maintain their own copies of state codes and how many systems maintain copies of product codes.

Finally, backup and recovery of a database that is the size of a data warehouse requires much more efficient techniques than a DBA would use. Because of the enormous size of a data warehouse and the resulting time that can be consumed in the backup process, the DWA must carefully plan backup strategy during the design phase of the data warehouse. For example, the planned use of read-only tablespaces, the use of a strategic partitioning scheme, and the judicious choice of partition size is critical to the success of efficient backup. In the complex world of a data warehouse, it is especially crucial to perform testing on backup strategies. As far as recovery is concerned, the DWA must have a recovery plan for each possible failure scenario.

The DWA must be familiar with the hardware and software needed to implement backup and recovery strategies. For example, there are a large number of tape backup options on the market, including a variety of tape media, stand-alone tape drives, tape stackers, and tape silos. Of course, given the size of the data warehouse, disk backup is not as feasible as tape backup, but, if so desired, disk technology can be used to accomplish disk-to-disk backup and mirror breaking. Backup software packages include Ominiback II (HP), ADSM (IBM), Alexandria (Sequent), Epoch (Epoch Systems), and Networker (Legato). It is possible to achieve different combinations of backup hardware and software that can yield anywhere from 10 BG per hour to 500 GB per hour.[8] Again, due to the size of the data warehouse, performance of the backup process becomes an important issue. To minimize the backup time, parallelism is used. Exhibit 4 summarizes some of the differences between the tasks of a DBA and those of a DWA.

Exhibit 4. Tasks of DBA versus DWA

Task	Dimension	DBA	DWA
Planning	Future growth in size and usage	Moderate	Drastic
	Data consistency and integration	Transaction level	Aggregation level
	Storage requirements	Less issues	More issues (e.g., disk arrays and parallelism)
Design	Goals	Meet business operational data requirements	Meet business analysis informational requirements
	Methodology	Mainly ER diagrams	Mainly dimension maps
Implementation	Scope	Application oriented	Enterprise oriented
	Approach	Monolithic	Incremental
	Granularity	Transaction-based updates	Bulk updates
	Query type	Many reporting predefined queries	Many analysis ad hoc queries
	Data level	Detailed	Summarized and aggregated
Maintenance	Security	View based	User based
	Security risk	Security breaches have relatively contained impact	Security breaches have relatively far-reaching impact
	Backup and recovery	Backup less time-consuming	Backup more time-consuming; performance more critical

The Organizational Role of a Data Warehouse Administrator

As discussed in the foregoing text, the DWA must be familiar with high-performance software, hardware, and networking technologies. Equally important to the technological expertise of a DWA is the possession of strong business acumen. Data warehouses are dynamic resources used by business managers and decision makers to analyze complex business situations. The DWA must be familiar with the relevant decision-making processes in order to properly design and maintain the data warehouse structure. The more specialized the decision support requirements, the more design tradeoffs the DWA must consider. The DWA should possess knowledge of the business organization itself as well as general business principles for which the data warehouse is being developed. It is especially critical for a DWA to balance the current requirements and capabilities of the data warehouse while providing for the rapid deployment of enhancements.

Finally, the DWA must possess excellent communication skills. This is more critical for a DWA than for a DBA, because the DWA will be closely interacting with the managers in using the data warehouse effectively. The DBA often needs to communicate only with programmers and other technical personnel who act as intermediaries in the specification and design process. This is not usually the case for the DWA, who must participate in the business meetings directly in order to meet the fast development life cycles of a typical data warehouse project. If the DWA cannot communicate in the language of nontechnical people, the data warehouse project will suffer from misunderstanding and delay.

FUTURE TRENDS

Data warehousing has given a competitive edge to a number of enterprises that have, in recent years, employed this technology. Whether the data warehouse is an operational data store, a data mart, or a full-blown enterprise data warehouse, the administration and management requirements of the enormous amount of data in a data warehouse differ significantly from those of a traditional DBA managing an operational database.

Because the characteristics (which are determined by the design goals) of a data warehouse are in many ways very different than those of an operational database, the data warehouse administrator (DWA) must possess knowledge and skills that the DBA counterpart need not have. Differences in requirements show up in all phases of the data warehouse development: planning, designing, implementing, and maintaining. Exhibit 4 summarizes some of these differences.

The success of a data warehouse depends to a large extent on the DWA, who must be very knowledgeable about current data warehouse hardware and software technology. In addition, because of the nature and purpose of a data warehouse, it is equally important for the successful DWA to possess knowledge of the business organization itself as well as general business principles.

Emerging trends in data warehousing offer competitive advantages to organizations poised to take advantage of them. These exciting new technologies also offer new challenges to the data warehouse administrator, whose responsibility it will be to leverage them for the benefit of the organization.

One emerging area facilitated by the use of data warehouse technology is Business Intelligence. New forms of data are being integrated with data warehouses to provide higher forms of information to decision makers. Large blocks of text, graphics, and even sound are being added to traditional data. Many large telemarketing organizations have deployed systems for their call centers that provide customer service representatives with telemarketing scripts. The systems are able to capture typed notes and customer responses on a real-time basis. This "nonstructured" data is stored in an integrated fashion within the data warehouse environment and is then available the next time contact is made with the customer. It is also used to evaluate marketing strategies and tactics to improve business performance. Newer generation data warehouses that include more varied metadata and complex data types require specialized database features. New indexing structures and query capabilities are being provided by DBMSs to support these nontraditional data types. Querying a database for text, color, or sound has become a reality during the past several years.

In addition, Internet/intranet access allows organizations to expose information within their data warehouses to users outside their immediate physical networks. Some organizations have opened up portions of their data warehouses to customers. Federal Express, for example, allows customers to query their parcel tracking system over the Internet to obtain the status of their shipment. A number of banks and investment companies provide secured, online access to customers' accounts. Many more organizations have enabled intranet access within their network firewalls to essentially broadcast data warehouse information to employees regardless of where they work and what kind of PC they may have. Intranet access to data warehouses has also become critical to field sales and support personnel to improve their performance. Web-enabling data warehouses potentially places greater need for online query response and 24×7 availability — requirements not necessarily taken into account when the data warehouse was originally designed.

The use of data warehousing will continue to grow as more and more companies realize the benefits afforded to them by this technology. The role of the DWA will, to a large extent, determine the success or failure of the data warehouse within the organization.

References

1. Anahory, S. and Murray, D., *Date Warehousing in the Real World*, Addison-Wesley, Harlow, England (1997), pp. 205–221.
2. Callaway, Erin, "License To Drive," *Inside Technology Training*, (July/August, 1998), pp. 18–21.
3. Gardner, Stephen R., "Building the Data Warehouse," *Communications of the ACM*, Vol. 41, No. 9, (Sept, 1998), pp. 52–60.
4. Gerdel, Thomas W., "LTV Steel Computer Methods Praised," *The Cleveland Plain Dealer*, (July 7, 1996).
5. Radding, Alan, "Support Decision Makers with a Data Warehouse," *Datamation*, (March 15, 1995), pp. 53–56.
6. Ricciuti Mike, "Multidimensional Analysis: Winning the Competitive Game," *Datamation*, (Feb. 15, 1994), pp. 21–26.
7. van den Hoven, John, "Data Marts: Plan Big, Build Small," *Information Systems Management*, (Winter, 1998), pp. 71–73.
8. Weldon, Jay-Louise, "Warehouse Cornerstones," *Byte*, (Jan., 1997), pp. 85–88.

Chapter 30
Web-Enabled
Data Warehouses

Mary Ayala-Bush
John Jordan
Walter Kuketz

Delivering data warehouse access via web browsers has a variety of benefits. Inside a corporate intranet, web-enabled data warehouses can increase ease of use, decrease some aspects of training time, and potentially cut costs by reducing the number of proprietary clients. Upgrades can also be accelerated given a standard client, and data warehouses can more easily integrate with other applications across a common platform. Extended to corporate trading partners via a so-called extranet (a secure extension of an intranet outside a firewall), the information contained within a data warehouse may be of sufficient value to become a revenue source. While such internal and external benefits may be appealing, they do not come without complicating issues.

In these traditional implementations, data warehouses have been used by a small population of either highly trained or high-ranking employees for decision support. With such a small audience having the warehouse application on their desktop, access control was straightforward: either the end-user could access a given table or not. Once the warehouse begins to be accessed by more people — possibly including some outside of the company — access may need to be restricted based on content. Security concerns also change as the user population increases, with encryption over the public Internet being one likely requirement. Because web-based access to a data warehouse means expanding the community of people who will access the data, the types of queries will most likely be more varied. Better business intelligence may thereby be derived, but once again not without complications.

0-8493-1149-7/02/$0.00+$1.50

In addition to security, performance (and therefore cost) issues become immediately relevant, dictating reconsideration of everything from replication patterns to login requirements. This chapter explores how web-enabled data warehouses change the strategy, architecture, infrastructure, and implementation of traditional versions of these applications

STRATEGY

Business Relationships

The strategy for a web-based data warehouse should answer at least two questions:

- Who is being granted access?
- Why are they being granted access via the web model?

Answering these two questions will supply important information for the cost justification of broader access. Possible justifications might include getting better service from vendors, facilitating better relationships with customers, shortening time of products in the supply chain, and receiving revenues from an internal application. The implications of broader access include having to design an architecture flexible enough to allow for new audiences with needs and requirements that may not be well identified. In addition, going into the information business can distract a company from its core focus: how are pricing levels determined? How does revenue derived from a potentially unexpected external source change payback and ROI models? What are the service level agreements and how are they determined? Who becomes the customer service liaison, especially if the IS organization is already running at full capacity for internal constituencies?

Access Control and Security

Security is a primary consideration when contemplating web access to sensitive corporate information. Authentication can be required at three separate stages, allowing administrators to fine-tune who sees what when, while encryption (typically through the use of the secure sockets layer, or SSL) protects both queries and responses from being compromised in transit. Initially, the web server can require either name and password login or the presence of a certificate issued by the data warehouse administrator. This grants access to the site and triggers the SSL encryption if it is implemented. Once inside the data warehouse, the user might also be required to authenticate himsel or herself at the query server, which allows access to the appropriate databases. This might be a dedicated data mart for a vendor, for example, that precludes Vendor A from seeing anything pertaining to Vendor B, whose information is held in a logically (and possibly physically) separate data mart. Finally, authentication may be required by the database to limit access within a given body of data: a clerk at Vendor A can see only a selected portion of the A data mart, while A's president can see that company's entire data mart.

The logistics of security can be extensive. Maintaining certificates requires dedicated resources, while planning for and executing multitiered logins is a nontrivial task. At the same time, limiting access can imply limiting the value of the data warehouse, so security must be designed to be flexible and as friendly to legitimate users as possible.

New Components

Broader access to a data warehouse introduces a number of new elements into the traditional application model. What happens to the query engine vendor's pricing model as its proprietary desktop clients are no longer required? Where are the skill sets and hardware to implement web servers and connect them to the query engine? How much will data be transformed (and by whom) if it is moved out of a central data warehouse into data marts for security, performance, or other reasons?

ARCHITECTURE

If strategy is concerned with goals and objectives, architecture is the unifying conceptual design or structure. It defines a system's component parts and relationships. Good architectures ensure that the component hardware and software pieces will fit together into an integrated whole.

A web-enabled data warehouse introduces additional components within a system architecture, which must be expanded to include:

- The web server component
- The components that connect the web server to the query engine
- The component that formats the results so they are viewable by a web browser

The system architecture may also need a component for integrating data marts.

Even given these elements, the architecture must be flexible enough to change rapidly, given both the pace of innovation in the Internet arena and the evolving place of data warehouses in contemporary business. The warehouse components may change due to increasing numbers of people using it, changing aggregations based on security or performance requirements, new access paths required by technological or organizational evolution, etc.

New design considerations are introduced by each of the above components. web servers introduce new complications, particularly in regard to scalability issues. Secure transactions over a dial-up connection can be painfully slow, but detuning the security at either the firewall or the web server can expose the corporate network to risk. Middleware between the web server and the query server can dramatically affect performance, particularly if common gateway interface (CGI) scripts are used in place of APIs. Database publishing to HTML is reasonably well advanced, but even here some of the newest tools introduce Java programming into the mix, which may cause implementation problems unless the skills are readily available. Java also presents the architect with new ways to partition the presentation layer and the application logic, with implications (for the network and desktop machines in particular) that are only beginning to be experienced in enterprise computing.

The system architecture must support competing enterprises accessing the data sources. One challenge is to support competing vendors where access control is data dependent. Both vendors can query the same tables; for example, by product, by region, by week. If a given retail outlet sells both vendors' products, and people from the sales outlet are allowed to query the data warehouse, they will need access to both vendors' histories.

A good system architecture must include the facility for access control across the entire web site, from the web server through to the database. If a mobile sales force will be given access while they are on the road, the architecture must have a component to address the types of connections that will be used, whether they are 800 dialup services, local Internet Service Providers (ISPs), or national ISPs such as CompuServe or AOL.

INFRASTRUCTURE

The infrastructure required to support the web-enabled data warehouse expands to include the web site hardware and software, the hardware and software required to interface the web server to the query server, and the software that allows the query server to supply results in HTML. The corporate network may have to be altered to accommodate the additional traffic of the new data warehouse users. This expansion increases the potential complexity of the system, introduces new performance issues, and adds to the costs that must be justified.

The web-enabled warehouse's supporting infrastructure also introduces new system administration skills. Because the warehouse's DBA should not be responsible for the care and feeding of the web site, a new role is required — the web site administrator, often called the webmaster. This term can mean different things to different people, so clarity is needed as the position is defined. Depending on the context, corporate webmasters may or may not be responsible for the following:

- Designing the site's content architecture
- Writing and/or editing the material
- Designing the site's look and feel
- Monitoring traffic
- Configuring and monitoring security
- Writing scripts from the web server to back-end application or database servers
- Project management
- Extracting content from functional departments

The amount of work that may have to be done to prepare for Internet or intranet implementation will vary greatly from company to company. For example, if the warehouse is going to be accessible from the public Internet, then a firewall must be put into place. Knowing the current state of web-based application development is essential: if organizational factors, skills, and infrastructure are not in place and aligned, the data warehouse team may either get pulled from its core technology base into competition for scarce resources or be forced to develop skills largely different from those traditionally associated with database expertise.

Web Site

Web site components include the computer to run the web server on and the web server software, which may include not only the web listener but also a document manager for the reports generated from the warehouse. One of the web protocols, called the Common Gateway Interface, allows the web browser to access objects and data that are not on the web server, thereby allowing the web server to access the data warehouse. The interface used does not access the warehouse directly but will access the query engine to formulate the queries; the query engine will still access the warehouse. The CGI has been identified as a bottleneck in many web site implementations. Because the CGI program must incur the overhead of starting up and stopping with every request to it, in high-volume systems this overhead will become pronounced and result in noticeably slow response times. API access tends to be faster, but it depends on the availability of such interfaces from or in support of different vendors.

Application Query Engine

The infrastructure must support the application query engine, which may run on the same computer as the data warehouse or on a separate computer that is networked to the data warehouse computer. This component must be able to translate the query results into HTML for the server to supply to the browser. Some of the query engines will present the results in graphic as well as tabular form. Traditional warehouses have supported relatively small user communities, so existing query engines will have to be monitored to see how their performance changes when the number of users doubles, triples, or increases by even larger multiples. In addition, the type and complexity of the queries will also have performance implications that must be addressed based on experience.

Data Warehouse

The infrastructure for the data warehouse is not altered simply because web browsers are being used; instead, the expanded number of users and new types of queries that may need to be executed will likely force changes to be made. When a data mart architecture is introduced for performance or security reasons, there may be a need to change where the mart will be located: on the same machine as the warehouse, or on a separate machine. The infrastructure will have to support both the method of replication originally specified and new patterns of replication based on DASD cost considerations, performance factors, or security precautions.

Security

Web Server Access. Access to the web server can be controlled by: (1) requiring the user to log onto the web site by supplying a user name and password, (2) installing client certificates into the browsers of the clients to whom access is granted, or (3) specifying only the IP addresses that are allowed to access the web site. The client certificate requires less interaction on the user's part because they will not have to supply a user name and password to access the system. The client's certificate is sent to the web server, which will validate the certificate and grant the user access to the system. (Part of the process of enabling a secure web site is to install a server certificate. This must be requested from a third party, called a certificate authority, which allows one to transmit certificates authenticating that someone is who they say they are.) A less secure strategy is to configure the web server to allow connection from a selected number of computers, with all others being categorically denied access. This scheme will allow anyone from an authorized computer — as opposed to authorized persons — to access the web site. Because this method is based on IP address, DHCP systems can present difficulties in specifying particular machines as opposed to machines in a particular subnet.

Communication Transport Security. Both the query and especially the information that is sent back to the browser can be of a sensitive nature. To prevent others along the route back to the browser from viewing it, the data must be encrypted, particularly if it leaves the firewall. Encryption is turned on when the web server is configured, typically via the Secure Socket Layer (SSL) protocol.

Query Server Application. To access the query server, the user may be asked to supply a user name and password. The information supplied by the certificate could be carried forward, but not without some custom code. There are various approaches to use for developing the user names and passwords: one can create a unique user name for each of the third parties who will access the system (allowing the login to be performed on any machine), or create a unique user name for each person who will access the warehouse. Each approach has implications for system administration.

Database Access. Database access can be controlled by limiting the tables users and user groups can access. A difficulty arises when there are two competing users who must access a subset of the data within the same table. This security difficulty can be solved by introducing data marts for those users where each data mart will contain only the information that particular user is entitled to see. Data marts introduce an entirely new set of administrative and procedural issues, particularly around the replication scheme to move the data from the warehouse into the data mart. Is data scrubbed, summarized, or otherwise altered in this move, or is replication exact and straightforward? Each approach has advantages and drawbacks.

IMPLEMENTATION

The scope of implementing a web-enabled data warehouse increases because of the additional users and the increased number of system components. The IS organization must be prepared to confront the implications of both the additional hardware and software and of potentially new kinds of users, some of whom may not even work for the company that owns the data in the warehouse.

Intranet

Training will need to cover the mechanics of how to use the query tool, provide the user with an awareness of the levels (and system implications) of different queries, and show how the results set will expand or contract based on what is being asked. The user community for the intranet will be some subset of the employees of the corporation. The logistics involved with training the users will be largely under the company's control; even with broader access, data warehouses are typically decision-support systems and not within the operational purview of most employees.

Implementing security for the intranet site involves sensitizing users to the basics of information security, issuing and tracking authentication information (whether through certificates, passwords, or a combination of the two), and configuring servers and firewalls to balance performance and security. One part of the process for enabling a secure web server is to request a server certificate from a certificate authority. Administratively, a corporation must understand the components — for example, proof of the legal right to use the corporate name — required to satisfy the inquiries from certificate authority and put in place the procedures for yearly certificate renewal.

Monitoring a web-based data warehouse is a high priority because of the number of variables that will need tuning. In addition, broader access will change both the volume and the character of the query base in unpredictable ways.

Intra/Extranet

In addition to the training required for internal users, training is extended to the third parties that will access the warehouse. Coordination of training among the third parties will likely prove to be more difficult: competing third parties will not want to be trained at the same time, and paying customers will have different expectations compared with captive internal users. In addition, the look and feel within the application may need more thorough user interface testing if it is a public, purchased service.

Security gets more complex in extranet implementations simply because of the public nature of the Internet. It is important to keep in mind the human and cultural factors that affect information security and not focus only on the technologies of firewalls, certificates, etc. Different organizations embody different attitudes, and these differences can cause significant misunderstandings when sensitive information (and possibly significant expenditures) are involved.

Monitoring and tuning are largely the same as in an intranet implementation, depending on the profiles of remote users, trading partner access patterns, and the type and volume of queries.

In addition, a serious extranet implementation may introduce the need for a help desk. It must be prepared to handle calls for support from the third parties, and combine customer service readiness with strict screening to keep the focus on questions related to the data warehouse. It is not impossible to imagine a scenario in which the third-party employees will call for help on topics other than the warehouse.

CONCLUSION

Because web browsers have the ability to save whatever appears in the browser, in web-enabled data warehouses, information that appears in the browser can be saved to the desktop. Protecting information from transmission into the wrong hands involves a balancing act between allowing for flexibility of queries and restricting the information that can potentially move outside corporate control. Legal agreements regarding the use of information may need to be put in place, for example, which tend not to be a specialty of the IS organization. Pricing the information can be another tricky area, along with managing expectations on the part of both internal and third-party users.

By their very nature, however, data warehouses have always been more subject to unintended consequences than their operational siblings. With changing ideas about the place and power of information, new organizational shapes and strategies, and tougher customers demanding more while paying less, the data warehouse's potential for business benefit can be increased by extending its reach while making it easier to use. The consequences of more people using data warehouses for new kinds of queries, while sometimes taxing for IS professionals, may well be breakthroughs in business performance. As with any other emerging technology, the results will bear watching.

Chapter 31

Distributed Integration: An Alternative to Data Warehousing

Dan Adler

Data warehousing has, perhaps, been the most costly system development in the history of financial services. The concept of data warehousing grew out of regional and departmental consolidation projects in which large relational databases were used to store relatively large quantities of data and make these data available to standard query tools such as SQL and various SQL-based interfaces. These queries were very useful in helping departments track customer behavior, P&L, and, in combination with applications written in VB, C++, and SQL-PLUS, they helped departments and regional entities within financial institutions track market trends, manage risk, and develop predictions.

Many managers, however, when they saw the success of the special-purpose database, were inspired to take this concept to the next level. "If we can do so much with a relational database in one department, I wonder how much value we could extract by representing our entire firm in a relational database?" went the reasoning. And, for expanding global trading businesses that needed to control the risks associated with numerous local portfolios composed of complex financial instruments, the centralized data warehouse containing "everything" was particularly appealing.

At most financial institutions, however, extending numerous departmental and regional data collection projects to create a "firmwide" data warehouse representing a firm's entire global business just did not work. Wall Street — and retail banking's Main Street — are littered with tales of multiyear, multimillion-dollar data warehousing projects that were killed because they did not produce anything near what their architects promised. Problems include: transforming data stored in numerous formats, ensuring the data is "clean" and correct, developing and maintaining a firmwide data model describing interrelationships between different types of data, managing various types of middleware to transport data from place to place, limited network resources, etc. And, of course, users became frustrated waiting for the "warehouse" and its associated promised functionality.

Still, extracting value from firmwide information and controlling global market risk remain top priorities for financial institutions and their information technology departments, which are struggling to develop alternatives to data warehousing. One of the most promising such developments is Distributed Integration.

Distributed Integration is a new approach to integrating both firmwide data and analytics based on Internet technologies, such as cascaded Internet servers and data caching. The "Distributed" refers to data and analytics that reside in numerous physical locations. The "Integration" refers to users' ability to access these disparate data and analytics through an *analytic browser,* which can be any application residing on any desktop which maintains an active connection to one or more *Distributed Integration servers.*

This chapter will describe how Distributed Integration solves some data integration problems that data warehousing projects do not always successfully address, and show how Distributed Integration leverages existing desktop and intranet technologies to deliver this integrated data (and analytics) to large communities of internal and external users at a very reasonable price point.

THE HISTORY OF DATA WAREHOUSING

The firmwide relational data warehouse has been proposed as a solution to numerous business issues facing financial institutions during the 1980s and 1990s.

First, in wholesale banking, per-trade margins have steadily declined in the mature foreign exchange and interest rate markets as the number of market participants increased and interest rate markets became more liquid. To respond more nimbly to market movements and to identify long-term trends, "data mining" — in which information is collected and analyzed to identify underlying patterns — became extremely popular. The data warehouse has been proposed as means of conveniently storing large quantities of historical and realtime data in order to facilitate the data mining process.

An important subset of the data mining issue for wholesale bankers and money managers is the management of time series data. These are data that are periodically collected and time stamped. This sort of data is very difficult to store in relational formats because time series records — when expressed in tabular format — are very repetitive. Likewise, time series data are collected more or less continuously. Therefore, they tend to rapidly overpopulate relational databases and reduce performance. So, time series records are more often stored in file format for convenience. Blending time series and relational data for data mining purposes has often been an objective of data warehousing initiatives.

Another trend in wholesale banking has been the development of complex derivative instruments in response to the shrinking margins described above. These more complex instruments, often developed by local trading offices in response to specific customer demands, have raised control issues highlighted by a spate of "derivatives losses" stories in the mid 1990s as banks, corporations, and investment managers recognized the importance of, first, understanding their derivatives exposures in the context of their whole portfolios and, second, keeping a close eye on rapidly expanding foreign offices. Indeed, the downside of extreme decentralization was dramatically illustrated by the failure of U.K.-based Barings Bank. In the wake of the Barings scandal, many financial institutions turned to data warehousing as a solution to their "control and security" issues.

In retail banking, the consolidation and acquisition of numerous banks meant fierce competition, and product innovation and sales became ever more critical. Data mining became very popular in the retail deposit and credit card businesses, wherein effectively dissecting the customer's spending and living habits equals better product development and sales.

Finally, both retail and wholesale financial services providers became increasingly concerned with the rapid distribution and analysis of so-called "real time" data. Indeed, the global bull market, while providing satisfying returns across the board, also makes it more difficult for investment managers to differentiate themselves from the pack or from benchmark indices. Data warehousing capable of handling real data, then, became a Holy Grail for many firms.

CHOOSE YOUR WEAPONS

While data warehousing seemed like a sound solution to many of the above-mentioned business challenges at the conceptual level, the actual implementation of data warehousing solutions did not live up to the initial promise. First, this is because of the many difficulties associated with obtaining, converting, and transporting data that effectively limit the scalability of most data warehousing solutions.

Second, if it is possible to get data into a warehouse, it is often challenging to get the data out of the warehouse and into the hands of end users who need it.

For example, traditional relational data warehouses are built in conjunction with implementation of a large, costly "enterprise" system. Such enterprise systems are typically limited to a certain number of high-priority users. Providing general access to such a system is usually too costly due to licensing fees. And, if the enterprise system performs crucial operations functions, analysts and other nonoperations staff may not be allowed to apply query tools to the data warehouse; if they did, they could slow down mission-critical processes. When general queries are permitted against the data warehouse, they are often very slow. In most cases, specialized query tools must be purchased in order to identify, copy, and manipulate the relevant portion of warehoused data.

There are three major types of data warehousing implementations, and each has different benefits and drawbacks; these are listed below. However, while all of these solutions have been successfully implemented at the local level, none has successfully scaled up to the enterprise level.

Options for Data Warehousing

Numerous Interfaces. This is the classic, old-style data warehouse in which numerous "interface" programs are developed to create even more numerous download files which, in turn, may be uploaded to a centralized data warehouse during nightly, weekly, or monthly batch processing. While the interface method does possess a certain conceptual simplicity and, in fact, is sometimes the only option available to handle extremely proprietary — or antiquated — bits of data, it traditionally has a low success rate. This is because the sheer number of interface programs which must be successfully run and kept in sync is usually so large. This creates problems because, first, if something goes wrong in any one of these procedures, the entire data warehouse may become inaccurate. Second, these interfaces are often difficult to fix because they are often proprietary and, wherever there is IT turnover, impenetrable and undocumented.

Replication. Data replication can be used to create both a data warehouse and numerous redundant data sources by periodically copying new records across a suitable WAN. For example, let's say Bank X, headquartered in New York, has a London office and a Singapore office. Let's also say the data warehouse resides in New York. As new trades are entered in London and Singapore, they are both stored in local relational databases and copied or "replicated" and sent through the WAN to the data warehouse in New York. The same replication procedure can be used to populate a backup data warehouse located in, say, London. While this method is straightforward and has worked well for medium-sized and smaller portfolios, it also has distinct scalability problems. This is often due to excessive network traffic created by the constant copying and transmission of each and every transaction. As the network slows down, it becomes difficult to keep the data warehouse up to date, and network failures can result in corrupt, incorrect, or incomplete data.

Middleware. Middleware is a catchall term referring to "plumbing" software that is typically transparent to the user and may function as an engine for any or all of the following: data transformation, data integrity checking, transaction monitoring, data transformation, data distribution, and/or object/application communication. Some financial institutions have attempted to populate large physical data warehouses through the innovative use of multiple forms of middleware. Others have attempted to link together various types of middleware in order to create their own "virtual data warehouse" in which middleware supplies applications with RAM copies of relevant data.

Regardless of which sort of warehouse one is attempting to create, managing numerous forms of middleware has some substantial drawbacks. These include the extensive effort required to ensure that different middleware packages are compatible with each other and with critical data sources, scalability limits associated with various types of middleware (particularly ORBs when used in conjunction with a "virtual" warehouse), maintenance associated with upgrades, etc.

The Data Mart Variation

In response to the limitations of data warehousing, many financial institutions have abandoned multiyear data warehousing projects in favor of what is known as the "data mart" approach. Basically, the data mart approach refers to a data warehousing project that is based on a number of local, regional, or functional implementations. The prime benefit of this approach is that, unlike the traditional "big bang" style of warehouse building, users in specific regional or functional areas can actually see results within a more predictable period of time. And, for this reason, data mart projects have found a friendlier reception in financial institutions than "old style" data warehousing.

However, the final step of a data mart project is generally to combine all the data marts into a data warehouse by periodically copying these local databases in their entirety into a centralized, relational data warehouse. Often, it is easier to create a data warehouse from data marts than to build one from scratch because data marts are usually built with consistent technology, thus avoiding the need for massive data conversions.

However, these data mart-based warehouses do not usually work well for realtime analysis, in which constant data-copying would compromise performance both at the warehouse and data mart levels. And, a data mart-driven warehouse still comes up against the challenge of distributing the contents of the warehouse in a usable format to those who need them.

DISTRIBUTED INTEGRATION: A NEW WAY

Distributed Integration is a new way to integrate global financial data, analytics, and applications, and quickly distribute them to a large community of users. Unlike most traditional data warehousing solutions, this does not require all data to be physically co-located in a single huge database. Instead, the Distributed Integration architecture relies on Internet technologies to create a virtual data warehouse that is optimized for both scalability and the cost-effective delivery of critical data to large user communities.

Data and analytics residing in multiple physical locations behave like a single, integrated virtual environment through web-enabled *Distributed Integration servers.* These servers take advantage of Internet server cluster organization and data caching techniques and thus are configured for extreme scalability.

End users access the distributed integration virtual environment through a *Distributed Integration workstation,* which simply refers to any desktop which has a direct Internet connection to one or more Distributed Integration servers.

Almost any application (such as Excel™) residing on a distributed integration workstation can be enabled to view and manipulate integrated data and analytics; such applications are referred to as *analytic browsers.*

Indeed, for the numerous highly paid analysts at most financial institutions who spend the majority of their time gathering relevant information to feed into their spreadsheets and then verifying that this information is clean, consistent, and correct, the analytic browser is truly a revolutionary concept.

Exhibit 1 provides a quick illustration of distributed integration. It depicts a global financial organization with two or more physical locations separated by a WAN or Internet connection.

The top location, say New York, has an equities group that maintains a database of equities using Sybase. They use a distributed integration server to make the data available to their own clients. They deliver analytics to traders at home through analytic browsers. They also have a group of analysts who write specific analytics and incorporate them into the Distributed

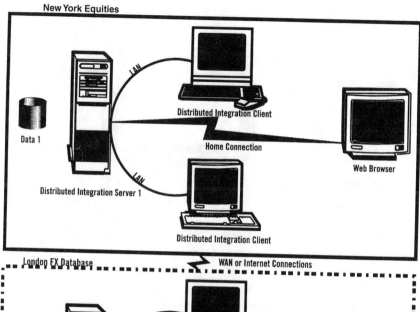

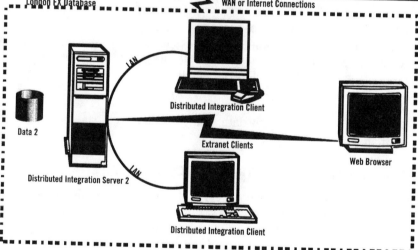

Exhibit 1. A Sample of Distributed Integration Architecture

Integration server, thus making them available to other analysts and to managers for control purposes.

The bottom location, say London, has a number of other groups that maintain an FX database in FAME and a commodities database in ORACLE. They make the data available to their own traders and analysts through their own Distributed Integration server, which also includes proprietary analytics. This group is also servicing some external clients who are connected to them

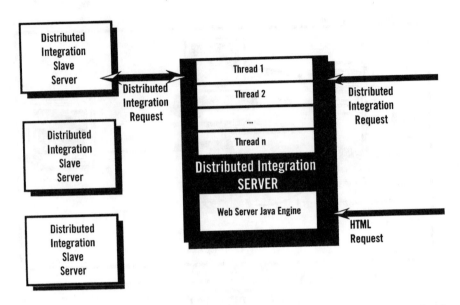

Exhibit 2. Distributed Integration takes advantage of cascaded server technology developed for the Internet to ensure fast and efficient management of Distributed Integration processes.

through the Internet, and get data, analytics, and web-based applications from them.

LEVERAGING INTERNET/INTRANET TECHNOLOGY

Since the Distributed Integration servers in these two locations can be cascaded, as shown in Exhibit 2, each set of end users can see the data in the other location. Moreover, since the Distributed Integration architecture is characterized by transparent caching, the access times for local and remote data are almost identical on average. Data are transparently replicated to the location where they are used without significant IT involvement or administrative overhead; this is a far cry from the various data warehousing techniques described above, which require extensive IT resources to implement. As new locations are added with their own Distributed Integration servers, it is a simple step to make those servers known to the existing ones, thereby creating global multidirectional connectivity.

From an administrative point of view, the data, analytics, and applications are being maintained by the group that originated, and most "cares" about them, and they maintain it in whichever database they have chosen. However, because these data are integrated on the server side, local administration and autonomy does not come at the price of effective controls. This is a critical point for risk managers, HQ treasury managers, and compliance managers, who are often strong advocates of data warehousing initiatives which centralize data and, in theory, enhance controls.

The Distributed Integration server caching will "equalize" the access speed such that the back-end database does not become a bottleneck even if it's a small ACCESS database running on someone's desktop PC. Distributed Integration makes it possible to then selectively share data, analytics, and applications across the entire organization without any additional integration work.

This architecture is highly scalable, since no single point can become a bottleneck as the number of locations increases. Thus, Distributed Integration avoids the scalability pitfalls associated with replication-based data warehousing solutions that tend to "clog up" a company's network.

For optimal scalability, the Distributed Integration server should be configured as a server cluster. This means it is not physically limited to a single process on a single machine. Such a server solution is implemented as a front-end, multithreaded, cluster manager process, with any number of symmetrical back-end servers that share the same configuration. Moreover, such clusters can always be cascaded among themselves, so there truly is no limit to the scalability of the Distributed Integration platform.

THE DISTRIBUTED INTEGRATION SERVER

Distributed Integration servers integrate historical and realtime data, metadata (i.e., data describing data), analytics, and applications. Because the server is capable of handling complex metadata and, by extension, almost any sort of data transformation, Distributed Integration is particularly well suited to address financial institutions' need for integrating time series and relational data.

In order to handle web-based applications naturally and efficiently, Distributed Integration servers must also, by extension, be Internet servers. Indeed, Distributed Integration servers have been built as plug-ins to pre-existing Internet servers. As is consistent with Distributed Integration's reliance on the web and web-related technologies, it is most efficient to organize Distributed Integration servers as server clusters.

These Distributed Integration server clusters are stateless and connectionless, just like most web servers, and should be capable of supporting the HTTP 1.1 keep-alive option for multiple related requests with a single connection for best utilization of network resources. This is also important from a user-functionality perspective; once data have been requested and cached, a user should be able to query that data without recopying it across the network. Likewise, incremental changes should be transmitted without the necessity of replicating the entire data set in which the changes originated.

The server cluster organization is one important reason why Distributed Integration can scale beyond traditional data warehousing solutions. As displayed in Exhibit 2, the front-end Distributed Integration server funnels each request to a number of preconfigured slave servers that actually handle the data and analytical requests.

Scalability is achieved by the fact that any number of slave servers can be added to a cluster, and they are automatically load-balanced by the master server. Fault tolerance is achieved by virtue of the fact that slave servers can be distributed on multiple machines, thereby reducing the chances that a single machine failure will halt the system.

A separate spool of threads handles standard web server requests such as getting HTML pages, downloading Java applets, etc. This integrated architecture means that application, content, and data can be freely mixed to create a powerful application development and deployment model that is web-centric and leverages the currently existing infrastructure.

Distributed Integration, it is important to note, performs best in a reasonably consistent hardware environment in which the server machines may be considered more or less interchangeable, and all the slave servers must have access to all the same data and analytics. This implies a shared configuration, as well as shared metadata and data caches. Thus, the user sees the entire cluster as a single server, with one URL address. And this URL address, then, becomes the user's gateway to the firm's total knowledge base.

The Distributed Integration server cluster architecture delivers:

- Performance — through the use of multiple machines coupled with load balancing
- High availability — through redundancy of slave servers
- Scalability — more processes and machines can be added as the number of users increases

THE GATEWAY TO DISTRIBUTED INTEGRATION

Once one or more Distributed Integration servers have been configured to create a single point of integration for data and analytics, the next critical step is to cost-effectively distribute information to a large community of users. This has, in fact, been a challenge for those traditional data warehousing projects that have managed to get off the ground. A Java interface — or Distributed Integration gateway — can be used to connect desktop machines to integrated data and analytics residing on Distributed Integration servers.

When the gateway is active, a machine becomes a Distributed Integration workstation that is capable of "browsing" through all the information that is part of the Distributed Integration environment. Data and analytics can be accessed through a standard web browser or by building software that connects existing desktop applications to the Distributed Integration environment. Applications that have access to Distributed Integration are called analytic browsers. It is possible to develop Distributed Integration add-ins capable of converting almost any application into an analytic browser.

In the financial services industry, however, one of the most useful applications of the analytic browser will be to connect spreadsheets to the Distributed Integration environment, thus allowing analysts to access integrated data without having to convert files or otherwise participate in the data-cleaning and -collection process. More advanced analytic applications will also become much more powerful when combined with Distributed Integration; indeed, one of the likely benefits of dynamically connecting endusers to an integrated environment is to speed up the pace of financial innovation.

LONG-TERM IMPLICATIONS OF DISTRIBUTED INTEGRATION

Distributed Integration, as it is implemented on a more widespread basis throughout the financial services industry, is likely to have important, even revolutionary, effects on how banks, brokerages, etc. do business in the future. And, as early adopters, the experiences of these financial services firms will serve as a model for other industries. Long-term implications of the Distributed Integration model include the following advantages.

Facilitates Financial Innovation

The desktop PC is synonymous with the modern workplace, and the PC-based spreadsheet application is synonymous with modern finance. However, the demands of today's businesses are straining the practical limits of PC-based spreadsheet analysis. A common illustration of this phenomenon is the fact that numerous highly paid financial analysts spend the majority their time gathering relevant information to feed into their spreadsheets and then verifying that this information is clean, consistent, and correct.

By providing integrated firmwide data and analytics accessible through spreadsheets — such as Excel™ — Distributed Integration frees financial analysts from time-consuming data management duties and allows them to focus on value-added tasks. End users will also benefit from the opportunity to view and use the sum total of their firms' intellectual capital; they may combine this information in new and profitable ways.

Thus, the widespread adoption of Distributed Integration is likely to foster a new period of rapid financial and business innovation as analysts are simultaneously freed from the demands of data gathering and provided with accurate, integrated information.

Encourages a New Form of Corporate Organization: The Internet Management Model

As the number of web-enabled workstations within corporations reach critical mass, organizations will be able to learn from the Internet and adopt new ways of managing themselves that go beyond the traditional trade-offs between centralization and decentralization. The Internet Management Model (IMM) is one such method. It applies the Internet philosophy — that information and services are made globally available by the special interests that cherish them at low or no cost across a system which, to the customer, looks consistent, unified, and available on demand — to the corporate organization.

Distributed Integration, which allows local offices to manage and maintain their own mission-critical information while giving everyone access to the entire firm's intellectual capital, is an ideal vehicle for implementing IMM. Thus, rapid growth is sustained while top managers and business analysts have unprecedented access to the "big picture" presented by their firms' collective data and information systems. Islands of data ownership are eliminated.

By allowing firms to track individual and departmental contributions to firmwide intellectual capital, it becomes possible to identify high- and low-performing areas. Simultaneously, IMM gives individuals and functional units much greater freedom to incorporate new data and analytics into their business activities without obtaining time-consuming approvals from central IT and business planning groups.

Allows Corporations and Financial Institutions to Manage the WHEN Dimension

As businesses' profitability becomes increasingly dependent on the timeliness and quality of the information which serves as the basis for key production, marketing, and strategic decisions, the ability to view, manipulate, and analyze data by time will become a matter of "life and death." Time-centric data, however, is often repetitive and difficult to store in conventional database formats. The Distributed Integration architecture is optimized for the rapid storage, transmission, and analysis of time-centric data as part of an integrated systems environment.

Chapter 32
Online Data Mining
John R. Vacca

Currently, most data warehouses are being used for summarization-based, multidimensional, online analytical processing (OLAP). However, given the recent developments in data warehouse and online analytical processing technology, together with the rapid progress in data mining research, industry analysts anticipate that organizations will soon be using their data warehouses for sophisticated data analysis. As a result, a tremendous amount of data will be integrated, preprocessed, and stored in large data warehouses.

Online analytical mining (OLAM; also called OLAP mining) is among the many different paradigms and architectures for data mining systems. It integrates online analytical processing with data mining and mining knowledge in multidimensional databases. It is a promising direction due to the:

- High quality of data in data warehouses
- Available information-processing infrastructure surrounding data warehouses
- OLAP-based exploratory data analysis
- Online selection of data mining functions

OLAM MINING BENEFITS

Most data mining tools must work on integrated, consistent, and cleaned data. This requires costly preprocessing for data cleaning, data transformation, and data integration. Therefore, a data warehouse constructed by such preprocessing is a valuable source of high-quality data for both OLAP and data mining. Data mining may also serve as a valuable tool for data cleaning and data integration.

Organizations with data warehouses have or will systematically construct comprehensive information processing and data analysis infrastructures surrounding them. The surrounding infrastructures include accessing, integration, consolidation, and transformation of multiple heterogeneous databases; Object-oriented Database Connectivity/Object Linking and

Embedding Database (ODBC/OLEDB) connections; Web-accessing and service facilities; and reporting and OLAP analysis tools. Savvy organizations will make the best use of their available infrastructures, rather than constructing everything from scratch.

Effective data mining requires exploratory data analysis. Users often want to traverse through a database, select portions of relevant data, analyze them at different granularities, and present knowledge/results in different forms. Online analytical mining provides facilities for data mining on different subsets of data and at different levels of abstraction. It does this by drilling, pivoting, filtering, dicing, and slicing on a data cube and on intermediate data mining results. This, together with data/knowledge visualization tools, can greatly enhance the power and flexibility of exploratory data mining.

Users seldom know which kinds of knowledge they wish to mine. By integrating OLAP with multiple data mining functions, online analytical mining provides users with the flexibility to select desired data mining functions, and dynamically swap data mining tasks.

Because data mining functions are usually more computationally expensive than OLAP operations, organizations are challenged to efficiently implement online analytical mining in large data warehouses, and provide fast response. Various implementation methods and ways to perform online analytical mining are discussed below.

OLAM ARCHITECTURE

In a similar manner to how OLAP engine performs online analytical processing, an online analytical mining engine performs analytical mining in data cubes. Therefore, an integrated OLAM and OLAP architecture makes sense, whereby the OLAM and OLAP engines both accept users' online queries (or commands) via a graphical user interface (GUI) application programming interface (API). Work with the data cube in the data analysis is performed through a cube API, and a metadata directory guides the data cube access. The data cube can be constructed by accessing or integrating multiple databases, or by filtering a data warehouse via a database API, which may support OLEDB or ODBC connections.

An OLAM engine can perform multiple data mining tasks, such as concept description, association, classification, prediction, clustering, and time-series analysis. Therefore, it usually consists of multiple, integrated data mining modules, making it more sophisticated than an OLAP engine. There is no fundamental difference between the data cube required for OLAP and that for OLAM, although OLAM analysis might require more powerful data cube construction and accessing tools. This is the case when OLAM involves more dimensions with finer granularities, or involves the discovery-driven exploration of multi-feature aggregations on the data cube, thereby requiring more than OLAP analysis.

Moreover, when exploratory data mining identifies interesting spots, an OLAM engine might need to drill through from the data cube into the corresponding relational databases for detailed analysis of particular portions of data; for example, in time-series analysis. Furthermore, a data mining process might disclose that the dimensions or measures of a constructed cube are not appropriate for data analysis. Here, a refined data cube design could improve the quality of data warehouse construction.

OLAM FEATURES

A well-thought-out design can help an organization to systematically develop OLAM mechanisms in data warehouses. The following features are important for successful online analytical mining:

- The ability to mine anywhere
- Availability and efficient support of multifeature cubes and cubes with complex dimensions and measures
- Cube-based mining methods
- The selection or addition of data mining algorithms
- Interaction among multiple data mining functions
- Fast response and high-performance mining
- Visualization tools
- Extensibility

The OLAM process should be exploratory; that is, mining should be performed at different portions of data at multiple levels of abstraction. When using a multidimensional database and an OLAP engine, it is easy to carve many portions of data sets at multiple levels of abstraction using OLAP operations such as drilling, dicing/slicing, pivoting, and filtering. Such processes can also be performed during data mining, through interaction with OLAP operations.

Moreover, in some data mining processes, at least some of the data may require exploration in great detail. OLAP engines often provide facilities to drill through the data cube down to the primitive/low-level data stored in the database. The interaction of multiple data mining modules with an OLAP engine can ensure that mining is easily performed anywhere in a data warehouse.

Traditional data cube queries compute simple aggregates at multiple granularities. However, many data mining tasks require discovery-driven exploration of multifeature cubes, which are complex subqueries involving multiple dependent queries at multiple granularities. This is the case, for example, when a user studies organizations whose growth rate in certain years in the 1990s was less than 60 percent of their average annual growth rate in that decade. The user could then compare the features associated with the poor performance years versus other years at multiple granularities, finding important associations.

Moreover, traditional data cubes support only dimensions of categorical data and measures of numerical data. In practice, the dimensions of a data cube can be of numerical, spatial, and multimedia data. The measures of a cube can also be of spatial and multimedia aggregations, or collections of them. Support of such nontraditional data cubes will enhance the power of data mining.

Cube-based data mining methods should be the foundation of the online analytical mining mechanism. Although there have been studies of concept description, classification, association, prediction, and clustering in relation to cube-based data mining, more research is needed on efficient cube-based mining algorithms.

Different data mining algorithms can generate dramatically different mining results — unlike relational query processing, which generates the same set of answers to a query with different processing efficiency. Therefore, it is important for organizations to provide alternative mining algorithms for a data mining function, giving users a choice.

Moreover, users might wish to develop their own algorithms in order to experiment with or customize a mining task. If they are given standard APIs and the OLAM system is well modularized, sophisticated users can add or revise data mining algorithms. These user-defined algorithms could make good use of such well-developed system components as data cube accessing, OLAP functionality, and knowledge visualization tools, integrating them with the existing data mining functions.

One OLAM strength is the interaction of multiple data mining and OLAP functions; another is in selecting a set of data mining functions. For example, the steps may be to dice a portion of a cube, to classify the diced portion based on a designated class attribute, to then find association rules for a class of data so classified, and finally to drill down to find association rules at a finer granularity level. In this way, the organization can develop a data mining system that can tour around the selected data space at will, mining knowledge with multiple, integrated mining tools.

Because mining is usually more expensive than OLAP, OLAM may encounter greater challenges for fast response and high-performance processing. While it is highly desirable and productive to interact with the mining process and dynamically explore data spaces, fast response is critical for interactive mining. In fact, miners might choose to trade mining accuracy for fast response, since interactive mining might progressively lead them to focus the search space, and find ever more important patterns. Once users can identify a small search space, they can call up more sophisticated but slower mining algorithms for careful examination.

It is important for organizations to develop a variety of knowledge and data visualization tools, because an OLAM system will integrate OLAP and data mining, and mine various kinds of knowledge from data warehouses. Charts, curves, decision trees, rule graphs, cube views, and box-plot graphs are effective tools to describe data mining results, and can help users interact with the mining process and monitor their data mining progress.

An OLAM system communicates with users and knowledge visualization packages at the top, and data cubes/databases at the bottom. Therefore, it should be carefully designed, systematically developed, and highly modularized.

Moreover, because an OLAM system must integrate with many subsystems, it should be designed with extensibility in mind. For example, an OLAM system might be integrated with a statistical data analysis package, or be extended for spatial data mining, text mining, financial data analysis, multimedia data mining, or Web mining. Modularity allows easy extension into such new domains.

IMPLEMENTATION OF OLAM MECHANISMS

Because the OLAM mechanism requires efficient implementation, special attention should be paid to:

- Modularized design and standard APIs
- Support of online analytical mining by high-performance data cube technology
- Constraint-based online analytical mining
- Progressive refinement of data mining quality
- Layer-shared mining with data cubes
- Bookmarking and backtracking techniques

An OLAM system might well integrate a variety of data mining modules via different kinds of data cubes and visualization tools. Thus, highly modularized design and standard APIs will be important for the systematic development of OLAM systems, and for developing, testing, and sharing data mining modules across multiple platforms and systems.

In this context, OLEDB for OLAP by Microsoft and multi-dimensional API (MDAPI)[1] by the OLAP Council, respectively, could be important initiatives toward standardizing data warehouse APIs for both OLAP and mining in data cubes. Sharable visualization tool packages could also prove useful here — in particular, Java-based, platform-independent knowledge visualization tools.

High-performance data cube technology is critical to online analytical mining in data warehouses. There have been many efficient data cube computation techniques developed in recent years that helped in the efficient construction of large data cubes. However, when a mining system must compute the relationships among many dimensions or examine fine details, it might be necessary to dynamically compute portions of data cubes on-the-fly.

Moreover, effective data mining requires the support of nontraditional data cubes with complex dimensions and measures, in addition to the on-the-fly computation of query-based data cubes and the efficient computation of multifeatured data cubes. This requires further development of data cube technology.

While most data mining requests are query or constraint based, online analytical mining requires fast response to data mining requests. Therefore, the organization must perform mining with a limited scope of data, confined by queries and constraints. In addition, the organization must adopt efficient, constraint-based data mining algorithms. For example, many constraints involving set containments or aggregate functions can be pushed deeply into the association rule mining process. The organization should also explore such constraint-based mining in other data mining tasks.

There is a wide range of data mining algorithms. While some are fast and scalable, higher-quality algorithms generally cost more. Organizations can use a methodology that first applies fast mining algorithms on large data sets to identify the regions/patterns of interest, and then applies costly but more accurate algorithms for detailed analysis of these regions/patterns. For example, in spatial association rule mining, one technique first collects the candidates that *potentially* pass the roughly determined minimum support threshold, and then further examines only those that pass the rough test, using a more expensive spatial computation algorithm.

Each data cube dimension represents an organized layer of concepts. Therefore, data mining can be performing by first examining the high levels of abstraction, and then progressively deepening the mining process toward lower abstraction levels. This saves the organization from indiscriminately examining all the concepts at a low level.

The OLAM paradigm offers the user freedom to explore and discover knowledge by applying any sequence of data mining algorithms with data cube navigation. Users can often choose from many alternatives when traversing from one data mining state to the next. If users set bookmarks when a discover path proves uninteresting, they can return to a previous state and explore other alternatives. Such marking and backtracking mechanisms can protect users from being lost in the OLAM space.

ANALYTICAL MINING METHODS

There are other efficient and effective online analytical mining techniques.[1] These include the design of a data mining language, incremental and distributed mining of association rules, constrained association mining, mining periodic patterns, a wavelet technique for similarity-based time-series analysis, intelligent query answering with data mining techniques, and a multi-layer database model.

A good data mining query language will support ad hoc and interactive data mining. Such a language can serve as the underlying core for different GUIs in a variety of commercial data mining systems, and facilitate the standardization and wide adoption of the technology.

It is best to update data mining results incrementally, rather than mining from scratch on database updates — especially when a database contains huge amounts of data. And, while it is a straightforward process to work out incremental data mining algorithms for concept description, it is non-trivial to incrementally update association rules.

Ad hoc query-based data mining is best when users wish to examine various data portions with different constraints. Constrained association rule mining supports the constraint-based, human-centered exploratory mining of associations. By this process, too, user-specified constraints can be pushed deeply into the association mining process to reduce the search space.

Many patterns are periodic or approximately periodic in nature; for example, seasons change periodically by year, and temperatures change periodically by day. In some cases, while the whole sequence exhibits no periodicity behavior, some particular points or segments in the sequence could be approximately periodic. For example, while someone might watch a particular TV news show from 7:00 to 7:30 a.m. almost every morning, his TV-watching habit is *irregular* at other hours.

Using an OLAP-based technique for mining the periodicity of such patterns in large databases[1] can be explored via two cases: (1) with a given period and (2) with an arbitrary period. For a user-specified given period, such as per day, per week, or per quarter, the organization can aggregate the potential activity patterns for the given period along the time dimension in a data cube. Similar OLAP-based methods apply for mining periodic patterns with arbitrary periods.

Similarity-based time-series analysis is similar to a stock market database. It is used to find similar time-related patterns such as trends and segments in a large, time-series database. In most previous analyses of similarity-based time series, organizations have adopted such traditional trend analysis techniques as Fourier transformation. More recently, wavelet transformation-based similarity mining methods have been used to discover trends or similar curves or curve segments. This method has proven efficient and effective at mining large time-series databases.

Database queries can be answered intelligently using concept hierarchies, data mining results, or online data mining techniques. For example, instead of bulky answers, a summary of answers can be presented, allowing users to manipulate the summary by drilling or dicing. Alternatively, related answers or rules can be presented in the form of associations or correlations, based on association mining results.

The autonomy and semantic heterogeneity among different databases present a major challenge for cooperating multiple databases. Tools to handle this problem use methods for schema analysis, transformation, integration, and mediation. However, because schema level analysis may be too general to solve the problem, the organization should consider data-level analysis, whereby the database contents are analyzed.

The organization can construct a multilayer database model utilizing a common data access API, and using generalization-based data mining to generalize the database contents from a primitive level to multiple higher levels. A multilayer database provides a useful architecture for intelligent query answering, and helps in information exchange and interoperability among heterogeneous databases. This is because the low-level heterogeneous data is transformed into high-level, relatively homogeneous information that can then be used for effective communication and query/information transformation among multiple databases.

OLAM AND COMPLEX DATA TYPES

It is challenging to extend the online analytical mining method to complex types of data. These include complex data objects, spatial data, and text and multimedia data.

Object-oriented and object-relational databases introduce advanced concepts into database systems, including object identity, complex structured objects, methods, and class/subclass hierarchies. A generalization-based data mining method can generalize complex objects, construct a multidimensional object cube, and perform analytical mining in such an object cube.

Here, objects with complex structures can be generalized to high-level data with relatively simple structures. For example, an object identifier can be generalized to the class identifier of the lowest class where the object resides. In addition, an object with a sophisticated structure can be generalized into several dimensions of data that reflect the structure, the generalized value, or other features of the object.

A spatial database stores nonspatial data representing other properties of spatial objects and their nonspatial relationships, as well as spatial data representing points, lines, and regions. A spatial data cube consists of both spatial and nonspatial dimensions and measures, and can be modeled by the star or snowflake schema, resembling its relational counterpart. Spatial data mining can be performed in a spatial database as well as in a spatial data cube.

Text analysis methods and content-based image retrieval techniques play an important role in mining text and multimedia data. By one method of online analytical mining of text and multimedia data, text/multimedia data cubes are built, whereupon the cube-based relational and spatial mining techniques are extended toward mining text and multimedia data.

Organizations can also mine the Web access patterns stored in Web log records. Web log records are preprocessed and cleaned, and multiple dimensions are built, based on such Web access information as page start time, duration, user, server, URL, next page, and page type. The process includes construction of a WebLog, and the performance of time-related, multidimensional data analysis and data mining.

CONCLUSION

The rapid development of data warehouse and OLAP technology has paved the way toward effective online analytical mining. Analysts anticipate that OLAM will become a natural addition to OLAP technology, which enhances data analysis in data warehouses.

Notes

1. The OLAP Council's proposed multidimensional API, now on version 2.0. The earlier, abortive version was called the MD-API (with a hyphen). Very few or no vendors are likely to support even the 2.0 version (which was released in January 1998), and no vendor has even announced a date for supporting it.
2. DBMiner is an intelligent data mining and data warehousing system. This educational release allows university teachers and research institutes to have a comprehensive data mining system to teach students and researchers the concepts and skills of data mining and data warehousing. Its first professional version has been released with enhanced data mining capabilities for professional users.
3. The traditional periodicity detection methods, such as Fast Fourier Transformation, find the periodicity of the whole sequence, but not the periodicity of a particular point/segment in the sequence.

Section VII
Enterprise Resource Planning

Chapter 33
ERP, One Letter at a Time

Bill Jeffery
Jim Morrison

Are you planning to transform your enterprise and supply chain? Better get the business case down, goal markers set up, and everyone on board to make it happen.

When Juan Sanchez took over as CIO of Delphi Automotive Systems Europe in September 1998, the company was in the midst of an ERP project with straightforward targets and a dizzying array of challenges. The European operations are a major component of Delphi Automotive Systems, the world's largest automotive supplier, headquartered in Troy, Michigan. As the project got underway, the stakes for a successful implementation increased. At the end of the day, Sanchez and his team learned that such a project took a lot more than careful planning. It took vigilant monitoring of detailed goals, the committed involvement of both executives and workers, a focus on customer needs, and the careful building of a business case for the endeavor (see Exhibit 1).

At the time, Delphi was organized on a geographic basis with different systems in each European country. Where divisions crossed geographic borders, systems support was not consistent. A major implementation of enterprise resource planning (ERP) software, with a planned expenditure of more than $50 million, had begun more than three years previously when Delphi was still part of General Motors. The project's ambitious goal: to replace dozens of aging — and incompatible — manufacturing and distribution legacy systems scattered throughout the 69 Delphi sites in eight European countries with a single enterprisewide system.

It wasn't simply the technical aspects of the ERP implementation that made the work difficult. It was the complex business scenario at Delphi that made the new system an imperative and heightened the risk of failure. Possible complications included:

Exhibit 1. Diamonds in the Rough

In retrospect, the most interesting part of this experience was that many of the reasons for the project's value couldn't have been articulated at the time the project was jump-started. You could even go so far as to say that Delphi would be a less viable company today if it had not begun putting in the ERP system. Examples of how valuable the project has been to Delphi, a company in transition, include:

- *The ability to serve more customers* — The ability to serve multiple competing customers in an open market, each having unique EDI procedures, forecast requirements, master schedules, and shipping needs. To do that with the old system would have been very difficult and costly, if not impossible.
- *Plants working in sync* — The ability to work in tandem among 69 sites to fill complex orders that spanned multiple customer sites throughout multiple countries. As but one example, plants in Delphi's U.K. operation are now able to share plant resources with plants in Portugal, which was previously difficult to do.
- *A workforce that is technologically up to speed* — Previously, some employees had never touched a PC. According to Sanchez, "The technical education alone was worth it; we pushed the latest technology throughout the entire company."

Delphi has built upon the European experience as it implements its global ERP strategy in North America and beyond.

- *Systems across borders.* The new ERP system needed to cross multiple geographic, cultural, and linguistic boundaries. More than 3,500 employees were going to depend on it to get their daily jobs done. Each country had developed business practices independently, and some could not be reconciled because of the varying legal and regulatory requirements, despite the efforts of the European Union to resolve cross-border inconsistencies.
- *Date-rollovers.* Delphi was using the project to help solve its Year 2000 compliance issues. The project also had to help the company support the new Euro currency; managers wanted the project to provide Delphi's various country locations a single conversion from one system, rather than one conversion for each different system.
- *Changes at the corporate level.* The May 1999 spin-off of Delphi Europe from its parent company, General Motors, occurred in the middle of the project.

More than two years into the project (at the end of 1997) Delphi enlisted A.T. Kearney to ensure ontime/on-budget completion of the project and a tangible ROI, while EDS took responsibility for the technical aspects of the rollout of the new SAP R/3 system.

A.T. Kearney viewed this as an opportunity to drive the implementation from a financial and operational perspective, something we felt other companies implementing ERP projects had not done. You don't have to go far to bump into lots of evidence that shows how ERP software has not delivered on the promises of vendors. Some recent cases where ERP has had publicly disastrous results include Whirlpool, where an ERP implementation crippled the shipping system, leaving appliances stacked on loading docks — and therefore not delivered to paying customers — for a full eight weeks in 1999. Hershey Foods (also in 1999) claimed that a 19 percent drop in earnings was caused by an incompetent ERP implementation that wreaked distribution havoc for one of its traditionally most profitable seasons: Halloween. While these high-profile failures were not top-of-mind when Delphi made its decision to implement ERP, they later served as reminders that such projects can easily go out of control.

Attempting a large-scale ERP implementation (including both implementation and operations) is an expensive proposition for any organization. The total cost of an average system over the course of the project runs approximately $15 million, according to Benchmarking Partners. Our 1998 survey of more than 100 SAP implementations found a whopping average cost per user of $53,000 and a 31-month implementation average.

A recent Meta Group report measuring the net present value of ERP implementation projects found that approximately 60 percent of respondents indicated a negative return on investment. That number climbed as high as 80 percent, depending on the specific software implemented. And because many of these first-generation implementations were internally focused with no associated business case (i.e., emphasizing cost reductions, technology, and process improvements rather than external benefits like extending ERP systems to players in the supply chain), quantifiable benefits were virtually nonexistent.

A HIGHLY STRUCTURED IMPLEMENTATION

The process we employed on Delphi's behalf focused on six major initiatives:

- *Developing a quantifiable business case.* Delphi first established concrete goals for the business processes they wanted to improve, such as increasing service levels, and calculated the expected benefits to be realized from these improvements.
- *Defining best practices.* Functional teams defined best practices, such as standardizing accounting procedures across Europe and standardizing logistics processes. These teams, composed of key Delphi executives from affected areas (in this case, logistics and finance), included representatives from a broad range of nationalities and cultures. These executives identified "key migration points," and the precise type and timing of a change were identified.
- *Planning prior to implementation.* Planning for actual rollout of the new system at each site began very early in the project cycle. An "implementation readiness" assessment was used to determine whether the

necessary IT infrastructure was in place and to make sure each site was capable of handling the transition to the new ERP system.

- *Strict monitoring of implementation schedules and costs.* Once the actual rollout began, a strict deliverable plan was imposed on each local site. All milestones were carefully tracked, measured, and rechecked to ensure that scheduled changes were made on time and on budget.
- *Cross-cultural training.* To make sure that all affected people (targeted users of the new system as well as consultants and managers) were on the same page in terms of goals and priorities, a project "university" was established in a central location (Paris) to provide training to everyone involved in the project.
- *Rigorous tracking of deliverables.* Identifying and then relentlessly tracking the complex web of incremental milestones were critical to the success of the project. The methods used were grounded in A.T. Kearney's deliverables philosophy and capitalized on the company's strength and experience in managing large-scale programs.

LESSONS LEARNED

After Delphi established its goals and expected benefits when the program was initiated, A.T. Kearney used its benefit assessment framework, *Implementation Value Capture,* to strictly monitor all deliverables and identify additional revenue-generating or cost-cutting opportunities that Delphi could achieve as a result of implementing the new system.

This highly structured implementation plan set the stage for success. Some of the valuable lessons learned along the way included:

- Define the business value goal, such as reduction in lead times, in concrete and easily measurable terms.
- Set up regular review measures to make sure goals are achieved.
- Don't underestimate the art of "change management." Establishing a training hub (e.g., Delphi's "university" in Paris) helps ensure that all participants in the project — no matter where they are or what language they speak — understand the goals of the project.
- When more than one company is involved, make sure that each one has "skin in the game," sharing in the risk of the venture. In the case of Delphi, both consulting partners — A.T. Kearney and EDS — agreed to share in the risk that the project might not succeed by adhering to a fixed time frame at a fixed price. Any cost or time overruns would thus be the responsibility of the consulting partners, not Delphi. A.T. Kearney had to excel at planning the program, managing risk, and delivering results.
- Don't lose sight of the impact on the customer. During any major transformation of a company's core business processes, all changes must

be absolutely "transparent" to customers. In Delphi's case, with a technically sophisticated clientele such as GM,

Ford, Volkswagen, DaimlerChrysler, BMW, among others — the slightest hiccup in manufacturing plans could have had an enormous financial impact on a customer's business. Notes Sanchez, "We not only had to make many more changes than we had originally planned but also had to change how we had originally planned them."

Conventional wisdom says that business is changing so fast that a single Internet year is worth four calendar years; this means that the formerly standard five-year corporate strategic plan needs to take into account the equivalent of 20 years of radical change in a given industry. It's the challenge that many companies face these days. Although the business case for Delphi's ERP project was originally completed in 1996, Delphi's earlier decision to implement SAP clearly helped the company achieve specific strategic objectives such as establishing common systems and standardized internal processes; creating fast, accurate information flows across the supply chain that are customer-driven and supplier-supported; enabling the swift integration of any acquisitions; improving productivity of the finance function and working capital utilization; and reducing the cost of legacy systems by more than 30 percent.

About the decisions made so long ago, in a different business climate, Sanchez agrees it was the right thing to do at the right time. "The team made a number of very wise decisions early on in the process. We are a completely different company now," he says.

Chapter 34
Is Supply Chain Management the Same as ERP?

Jim Ayers

Innovation in the supply chain puts new demands on information systems and the people who develop and manage them. Making information systems work to improve supply chains is an important SCM skill. But, putting technology ahead of strategic design and operational requirements is a frequent shortcoming. Consequently much effort is wasted or even counterproductive.

Systems issues present some monumental challenges to senior managers. The reasons are many. Senior managers "may not have a clue" about their need for systems, the capabilities of information technologies, or how to implement the technology. They have only a hazy awareness of how computers work and what infrastructure capability, like networks, provides. Consequently, these managers are often at the mercy of their technical departments and software marketers. Or, their lack of knowledge leads to indecision.

Another influential factor is the constant barrage of stories of computer projects run amuck. Many war stories recount foul-ups costing tens of millions of dollars. In fact, some companies implement high-cost systems only to "unplug" them when they don't work. The Wall Street Journal recounted a flurry of such horror stories brought to light through lawsuits and visible corporate miscues.[1] Among the incidents reported in a single article were the following:

- Whirlpool, the appliance maker, having troubles shipping product due to high demand and conversion to SAP software
- W.L. Gore & Associates, the water-resistant fabric maker, suing Peoplesoft, Deloitte Consulting, and others over a botched installation of new systems

- A quickly implemented SAP ERP system keeping candy maker Hershey from delivering its products to meet the peak Halloween demand — despite having plenty of inventory
- Allied Waste Management, a service company, pulling the plug after spending $45 million on a $250 million SAP system

Of course, many organizations have completed large systems projects with better success than described above, and often the fault is as much that of the craftsmen as it is of the tools.

The examples cite the application category called ERP. ERP systems automate "back office" operations. The back office consists of the many transactions fundamental to the business. Examples are personnel records, booking sales, and ordering materials. In the late 1990s, the need to address "Y2K" risks motivated many of these efforts. Older "legacy" systems built around the needs of individual departments were not ready for the new millennium.

We predict the next "drivers" for systems improvements will be getting strategic value out of systems to improve the supply chain. Those who have implemented new systems will look for ways to capitalize on their investments and exploit technology for competitive reasons. Frequently cited examples include E-commerce capability, electronic links along the supply chain, reducing inventory, exploiting databases for customer information, and otherwise increasing the role of technology in customer interfaces.

This column describes the wide and fragmented supply chain information landscape. We do it lightly, acknowledging that there are multiple sources for more detailed information. This is also a landscape with "blurry" boundaries between categories of applications. Hardly a week passes without notice of a new acronym or "revolutionary" tool in the domain of supply chain systems. Unless one closely follows the technology, one can be excused for being confused. Describing each and every application category would require more space than available, so descriptions will be confined to what we believe are the major categories.

SUPPLY CHAIN APPLICATIONS

The Council of Logistics Management (CLM), in conjunction with Andersen Consulting, maintains an "inventory" of supply chain applications. Its list of software in a CD format describes over 1200 application packages.[2] To find the right fit, the business user can select from the many categories shown in Exhibit 1.

Typically, any listed package will include several of the functions shown in Exhibit 1. Indeed, some packages claim to have them all. Herein lies a problem. One has to decide which features are most important to the busi-

Exhibit 1. CLM Software Categories

Order processing	Stock/pallet location	Vehicle maintenance
Inventory control	Labor performance	Physical distribution system modeling
Inventory planning & forecasting	Material handling	Electronic data interchange
Distribution requirements planning	Transportation analysis	Warehouse management
Materials requirements planning	Traffic routing & scheduling	Promotions & deals
Purchasing	Freight rate maintenance & audit	Other functions

ness and then has to decide how well each candidate package supports the need. Packages will undoubtedly be stronger or weaker in an area. If a great traffic routing and scheduling capability is needed, for example, look closely at each candidate package that provides this function. Some claiming to possess the functionality may, in fact, have it, but do it poorly.

When presented with a "short list" of candidate packages for implementation, we find that some clients — knowing there is an abundance of options — are uneasy with only a few alternatives. They realize that a software package selection could be a commitment for a decade or more. There's a suspicion that there might be a better solution out there beyond the shortlist presented. If the project doesn't go well, the selection team will shoulder the blame. To cover one's risk, they may believe, one must rummage through all 1200, or at least several hundred, to make sure the "right" choice is made. Of course, evaluating a single package is a time-consuming job, taking from one to three weeks for a diligent review. Imagine doing this for hundreds.

When it comes to the supply chain, this list — as comprehensive as it seems to be — is far from complete! Additional categories used by software suppliers, many of which have coalesced with the rise of SCM. They include SCM itself (Supply Chain Management), ERP (Enterprise Resource Planning), CRM (Customer Relationship Management), PDM (Product Data Management), CRP (Capacity Requirements Planning), MES (Manufacturing Execution Systems), and APS (Advanced Planning & Scheduling).

Also, one must consider the possibility of what are called "bolt-ons." These are combinations of packages to cover a user's requirements. They are often developed when two cooperating package purveyors "integrate" their offerings. For example, the Hershey example above included ERP (by SAP AG of Germany), APS (by Manugistics, Inc. of the United States), and CRM (by Siebel Systems of the United States) applications. Another party, IBM, managed the

Exhibit 2. Claims by Information Technology Providers

Source	Excerpt
A ERP system marketer	"[Company] offers integrated Flow Manufacturing that enables dramatic benefits such as a 90 per cent reduction in cycle time, 50-90 per cent reduction in inventory and a dollar for dollar increase in working capital. These are all available with a low risk transition strategy"
B Two software companies	"[Company 1] and [Company 2] have extended their relationship to offer customers a closed loop supply chain solution."
C E-commerce provider	"[Company] is the leading provider of electronic commerce solutions that dynamically link buying and supplying organizations into real-time trading communities."
D Supply chain software provider	"[Company] unveiled [product name], a new approach for demand-driven fulfillment that enables companies to anticipate and meet customer delivery expectations the first time, every time."
E System integrator	"[Company] is a leader in industrial strength, e-business solutions for system and application response performance."
F ERP systems provider	[Product name] allows people to harness the power of the Internet to work smarter, better and faster by optimizing supply chains, managing strategic relationships, reducing time to market, sharing virtual information, and increasing productivity and shareholder value."
G Consulting firm	"[Company's] insight into the global consumer products complex from consumer to retailer to supplier, helps companies develop and implement winning strategies. The firm's thought leadership among retailers and consumer products companies has led to the transformation of entire industry sectors."
H IT consulting firm	"[Company] is one of the most successful and fastest-growing IT consulting firms nationwide. [Company] is differentiated by its tradition of unsurpassed technology expertise; its strong track record of delivering; and its experienced, enthusiastic people — the best in the business."

effort. A trend is the consolidation of bolt-on package functionality — in the Hershey case, the CRM and APS — into core ERP systems.

In addition to applications, supply chain systems include the means of communicating among partners. Many supply chain partners, for example, use Electronic Data Interchange, or EDI. The Internet is the emerging technology of choice, and packages are in varying states of "Internet-readiness." Another application category of software is EAI (Enterprise Application Integration) or "middleware." This category enables different applications to "talk to each other." This can be important both inside an organization and in managing a supply chain. Deploying middleware can bypass or delay investments in new applications.

We've indicated that understanding the benefits and risks of technology is a challenge for many. One would hope that system marketers would be helpful in this regard. Unfortunately, so called "solution providers" seldom emphasize clarity in their communications.

One might be excused if concluding that this industry tends toward hyperbole. These companies have a large investment in product development, and each sale increases the return on that investment. So claims are often extraordinary. Descriptions of the results are vaguely worded superlatives replete with fuzzy multisyllable terms, like "transformation" or "integration."

However, there is no doubt that systems solve real problems. The claims made by Company A in Exhibit 2 are very similar to those made for TQM and JIT just a few years ago. In fact, the changes needed to achieve the benefits probably require both the software and non-software disciplines to gain the most from the system. Often, the preparation for the system is as important as the system itself. Cleaning up the data is a necessary prerequisite to successful system use. Company B reflects a trend among many software suppliers — that of combining forces to offer a "new" product from two or more old ones. Some computer publications caution that many of these alliances are marketing ploys; buyers beware![3]

References

1. Boudette, Neal E., Europe's SAP scrambles to stem big glitches, *The Wall Street Journal*, November 4, 1999, p. A25.
2. Haverly, Richard C. and Whelan, James F., *Logistics Software*: 1998 Edition, Volume 1, Council of Logistics Management. (Compact Disc format)
3. Slater, Derek, The ties that bolt, *CIO Magazine*, April 15, 1999.

Chapter 35
Choosing an ERP Implementation Strategy

Marie Karakanian

The intense recent activity involving ERP (enterprise resource planning) implementations has been driven by a number of factors. These include the need and interest to achieve a single corporate resource for corporate information, to capture the same data item only once, and to integrate business systems into a single platform wherever possible. One overriding factor, of course, has been to develop the ability to face the 21st century with confidence — that is, Y2K-compliance systems. Today, most major organizations have implemented or are implementing at least one of the leading ERP packages, such as SAP, Oracle, or PeopleSoft, somewhere within their organizations.

Although this chapter focuses on experiences derived from PeopleSoft ERP implementations, most of the discussion also applies to all of the preceding packages. As organizations have come to realize, ERP implementations cannot be taken lightly and categorized as another project that has arbitrary resources that have nothing better to do. Experience has shown that no planning will be too much for such an undertaking and this planning needs to revolve around a strategy defined right at the beginning of the project when all the elements of the scope of the project are being identified, specified, and understood by all stakeholders. Organizations should not allow the traumatic experience of the package selection process to lessen their enthusiasm in taking the time to appropriately plan and strategize for the project.

ELEMENTS OF AN ERP IMPLEMENTATION STRATEGY

The enterprise resource planning (ERP) project interfaces with all aspects of an organization: people, process, technology, systems, structure, skills, culture, and — definitely — available technology funds. Executives responsible for such projects must develop a very clear understanding of the tasks they are about to undertake and ensure that all the relevant variables are accounted for in the planning process and that time and effort are dedicated to them during and after the implementation. To be more specific, the strategy should focus on the following aspects of the project:

1. Drivers
2. Resources
3. Visibility and profile
4. Components of the ERP technology to be implemented
5. Package functionality business fit
6. Existing technology platforms, systems, and data
7. Users
8. Implementation logistics
9. Budget and available funds

It is noteworthy to mention that although ERP implementations are categorized as projects, a one-time set of activities with a defined beginning and end, finite resources and deliverables, in reality, they have become perpetual jobs in the current state of affairs. This is because of ongoing technology upgrades, technology change dependencies, mergers and acquisitions, de-mergers, and of course, recycling of people from one project to another. Holding people down to one job they have learned to become good at has become a very difficult task to surmount in today's ERP labor marketplace. Thus, an implementation strategy should also take project staff resourcing and retention strategy into account.

Project Drivers

What instigated the project to start with? A proper understanding of the project, the reasons behind it, and the demands on the organization must be understood very clearly by those who sponsor and run the project long before they initiate it. During the last four to five years, the following were among typical drivers for ERP projects:

- Lack of business systems integration
- Multiple technologies requiring multiple sets of tools, skill sets, and vendors to deal with
- Lack of shared corporate information
- Inconsistency of data
- Strategic information to executives
- Data duplication and "multiplication"

- Lack of Year 2000 compliance of existing systems
- Business globalization
- Centralization of corporate data
- Decentralization of regional or business unit data

A large number of organizations still believe the demand for useful strategic information is greater than ever before in some business processes (e.g., Human Resources). A recent survey conducted by Deloitte & Touche and Lawson Software discovered that 67 percent of the surveyed HR executives believed that the demand for HR to provide useful strategic information is greater than ever before. Previously downplayed corporate disciples of such disciplines continue to try hard to play the strategic partner game with their corporate board members. Their challenge is to convert the value of a not so easily definable asset — human resources — into palatable figures by the means of technology. The journey has been long; however, it continues.

While most of the previous drivers still hold true for a number of organizations, more recent drivers — such as shared services, employee self-service and electronic commerce — also impact ERP projects or the systems that build upon them.

The nature of the driver will impact the formulation of the implementation strategy. For example, the need for Y2K compliance by the year 2000 can overrule a fundamental business process redesign that can be undertaken at a later date.

Resourcing

One key decision at the start of the implementation process involves project resourcing. The choice is between the acquisition of external consulting resources that have the required experience, skill sets, and the know-how, versus internal resources that do not necessarily have the required expertise but do have the promise of learning and internalizing a knowledge base that will remain within the organization following the conclusion of the project. Usually, resource selection is driven by the availability of project budgets, criticality of deadlines, and the promise of knowledge transfer.

Recent experience that organizations have had vary significantly due to what appears to be high expectations from specialized consulting partners. The lack of true expertise is quickly revealed, and some organizations have had the sour taste of providing a learning platform to consultants who have professed prior expertise in a given ERP package implementation. For this reason, organizations should conduct proper research and interviews before hiring consulting partners.

An additional challenge that organizations have faced and are still facing is the loss of their own staff to better-paid jobs once the accumulation of new knowledge is at a level that is sought after in the labor market. In some cases, organizations have rehired their own staff at much higher costs after they have defected into ERP consulting. Thus, the "internalization" of the new knowledge base has proven to be very shaky. Project executives should try to develop retention strategies that the organization can deal with which hopefully also have a certain level of internal equity.

Visibility and Profile

The ERP project needs to have its place among hundreds of concurrent projects it is competing with for executive attention. In smaller organizations, the champions of such projects are the executives themselves. The project manager should make sure that the appropriate communication plans and change management mechanisms are put in place right from the start of the project. Also, the project manager should ensure that time and budget are allocated to such activities within each phase of the project as the intensity for visibility heightens throughout the life cycle of the project.

In large organizations, most executives, although accountable at the end, are detached from such projects until disaster time comes along. To prevent such occurrences, appropriate links and status reporting procedures should be established with at least the line executives to keep them informed of project progress, impact, risks, and challenges. Executive management should also be informed of the various alternative solutions and be part of the decision-making process for the adoption of preferred solutions — especially those that have critical impact on the operations of the organization.

Components of an ERP Package

Before developing an implementation strategy, one focal area on which to concentrate is the package itself and its components. Simplistically speaking, this can involve the following three areas at a minimum:

1. Various application modules included in the package, such as Financials, Distribution, Human Resources, and Payroll
2. Various tools, such as reporting, importing data, and upgrades
3. Various APIs that help integrate the package to various platforms of potentially different technologies, such as scanners and interactive voice response systems

The strategy should address the potential modularity of the implementation. Considering the number and variety of business processes that these applications enable, as well as the legacy data conversion and legacy systems integration, it may simply be impossible to come up with a true "big-bang" approach and attempt to implement all components concurrently. Normally, such implementations are staged based on a number of considerations, including:

1. The application dependencies within the new technology. Are there any mandatory modules that must be implemented before others?
2. Optimization of the benefits of the new technology right from the beginning. Where can quick hits be identified that can start bringing some return on the technology investment?
3. What currently manual business process can be automated for which manual operation costs the organization highly today?
4. Are there internal resources available to the project to enable the concurrent implementation of some applications, such as General Ledger, Payroll, Distribution, etc.?
5. Is the bundling of the package functionality suitable enough to replace and decommission some of the existing systems right away and stage the rest in a manageable manner? This will facilitate the decommissioning of the existing systems and potentially rid the organization of its maintenance costs.
6. From a package perspective, does it make sense to conduct a proper "proof of concept" of mission-critical modules with a representative group of business units before charging ahead with complete implementation?

Finding and developing the answers to these questions are not necessarily easy and straightforward; however, spending the effort up front will help understand the package and the organizational environment better and therefore contribute to a more informed strategy.

Package Functionality Business Fit

The selection of an off-the-shelf package for an organization implies that this package is a reasonable fit for the organization and its business requirements. However, ERP clients generally come to realize during implementation that the way they do business is somewhat different from the way the package expects them to do business. This creates a conflict that must be addressed in one way or another during the implementation.

One option for addressing this gap is to customize the package to the client's requirements with the assumption that the package vendor also provides the customization tools. Another option would be to change the way the client conducts its business. This is easily said — yet not so easily implemented. Apart from the challenges of managing change in organizations that have done certain things in specific ways for several decades, the potential impact of change can extend to collective agreements and union renegotiations, which can take years to say the least.

Normally, a compromise is reached with some customization and some process change. Some "flexible" ERP packages come bundled with their own proprietary tools that are used to perform the customizations. People-Soft is one good example that provides flexible and user-friendly tools. The customizations, however, must be done with the longer term in view and consider the impact on upgrades and the basic application structure.

Existing Platforms, Systems, and Data

This aspect of the ERP implementation project should never be underestimated. Often, legacy data is not in good shape and requires purification or a clean-up process. With respect to the data, a number of decisions need to be made with a view to the implementation. History conversion is one aspect that needs to be thought of during strategy formulation in order to plan accordingly. The possibility of storing historical information in different ways, as well as converting at a later phase, should be considered with a view toward the business requirements.

Although ERP implementations are expected to replace the existing platforms, it does not necessarily happen in all cases. And when it happens, it does not take place in one shot — meaning that the project needs to integrate the new technology with the old technology and therefore recruit resources to the project that have the right expertise. Projects may find that interfaces are required for various legacy mission-critical systems not addressed by the new ERP. These systems might be in the process of being re-hauled or patched up for Y2K compliance.

Users

As users are on the front line, it is crucial to know their numbers, evaluate their needs, profiles, skill sets, and orientation toward the project and the new technology. They are the targets for the training, communication, and change management strategies of the project. An organization that is going to roll-out an ERP system for the first time to managers as end users will have a different approach than the one that is replacing an existing system from its current users such as Accountants or Payroll Data Entry clerks. A project team considering phased rollout will have a different training strategy than the one targeting for a big bang, one-time implementation approach.

An organization replacing a mainframe system with a client/server, Windows-based system will need to consider training the users in Windows first, if required, before training them in the ERP system. Similarly, at the technical and operational user level, a client/server technology will introduce different challenges to operational staff who will require targeted and specific knowledge transfer plans and intensive sessions from the project team. Some of these training sessions may require one-on-one instruction for long periods of time or actual time done on the project.

Implementation Logistics and Scheduling

This can vary significantly from one organization to another. Usually, multi-location, multi-business unit organizations implement and roll-out in a phased fashion. This might mean phased system hand-over to the user community or phased functionality roll-out. This strategy will support organizations that may have pretty decentralized and independent operations from each other, so that the phasing of the functionality and the roll-out schedule are negotiated and well coordinated with other business unit-specific projects.

If it happens that different units within an organization have different requirements in common areas such as payroll, then the system design and configuration timeline can be developed in coordination with the roll-out strategy.

The timing and scheduling of the implementation should take into account not only the readiness of the project team and the user community, but also the other corporate projects. The high profile of the project should not be stained with problems arising from inadequate scheduling of concurrent projects. Decisions and agreements should be reached at the executive level to ensure a smooth implementation where the focus of all parties involved can be directed toward the ERP project, at least for a temporary period of time.

Budget and Available Funds

The ERP project is one of the few winners among those competing for rare corporate resources. The size of the budget is a reflection of the expectations made from the project and its results. Therefore, it must be handled with extreme care and control.

The project manager should establish right from the start a budget-monitoring process and a project reserve fund. Different budget buckets should be established, including those for the consulting partner, independent contractors, implementation specific tools, project space, and team-building activities. The project manager should make sure that the return on financial investment meets expectations, and that budget gaps are highlighted and brought forward to executive attention on a timely basis.

CONCLUSION

As a last word, it is a good strategy to monitor and review the implementation strategy at each milestone of the project. Unfortunately, projects hardly ever finish as started. Changes occur constantly; project sponsors get reassigned; consulting partners move on; project resources depart; corporate priorities shift; and technology performance does not meet expectations. Therefore, a strategy review process should be built into the project plan, especially for longer-term ERP projects.

Chapter 36
Critical Issues Affecting an ERP Implementation

Prasad Bingi
Maneesh K. Sharma
Jayanth K. Godla

The Enterprise resource planning (ERP) software market is one of the fastest growing markets in the software industry. It has seen a rocky start with several project failures and a huge shortage of skilled and experienced workers. The ERP market is predicted to grow from a current $15 billion to a gigantic $50 billion in the next five years. The estimated long-term growth rates for ERP solutions are a stratospheric 36 to 40 percent. Some estimates put the eventual size of this market at $1 trillion. Recently major ERP vendors such as SAP AG, Baan, and Oracle have reported significant financial results. Contributing to this phenomenal growth is the estimation that 70 percent of the Fortune 1000 firms have or will soon install ERP systems and the initiatives by ERP vendors to move into medium to small tier industries with gross revenues less than $250 million. ERP vendors are aggressively cutting deals with these industries to make their products more affordable. For example, SAP, one of the leading ERP vendors, recently started selling its products to customers in the $150 million to $400 million revenue range.

Companies could spend hundreds of millions of dollars and many years implementing ERP solutions in their organizations. Once an ERP system is implemented, going back is extremely difficult; it is too expensive to undo the changes ERP brings into a company. There are several failed ERP attempts, and companies lost not only the capital invested in ERP packages and millions paid to outside consultants, but also a major portion of their business. Recently Unisource Worldwide, Inc., a $7 billion distributor of paper products, wrote off $168 million in costs related to an abandoned nationwide implementation of SAP software.[12] FoxMeyer Drug, a former $5 billion drug distributor, went bankrupt in 1996 and has filed a $500 million lawsuit against SAP. FoxMeyer charged the ERP giant that its package was a "significant factor" that led the firm into financial ruin.[14] Dell Computer Corp. has recently abandoned a much-publicized SAP implementation following months of delay and cost overruns. Dow Chemical, after spending half a billion dollars over seven years of implementing SAP R/2, the mainframe version, now has decided to start all over again on the new client/server version (R/3). Implementing an ERP system is a careful exercise in strategic thinking, precision planning, and negotiations with departments and divisions. It is important for companies to be aware of certain critical issues before implementing any ERP package. Careful consideration of these factors will ensure a smooth rollout and realization of full benefits of the ERP solution.

ERP SOLUTIONS

An ERP system can be thought of as a companywide information system that integrates all aspects of a business. It promises one database, one application, and a unified interface across the entire enterprise. An entire company under one application roof means everything from human resources, accounting, sales, manufacturing, distribution, and supply-chain management are tightly integrated. This integration benefits companies in many ways: quick reaction to competitive pressures and market opportunities, more flexible product configurations, reduced inventory, and tightened supply-chain links. The Earthgrains Co. implemented SAP R/3 and reports that its operating margins improved from 2.4 to 3.9 percent and pushed its on-time product delivery rate to 99 percent in 1997.[13] The company also reports better management information and happier customers. Similarly, at Par Industries in Moline, IL, an ERP system allowed management to base production on current customer orders rather than forecasts of future orders. The delivery performance improved from 60 percent on time to more than 95 percent, lead times to customers reduced from six weeks to two weeks, repair parts reduced from two weeks to two days, work-in-process inventory dropped almost 60 percent, and the life of a shop order dropped from weeks to mere hours.[1] IBM Storage Systems division, after implementing an ERP system, was able to reprice all of its products in five minutes compared with five days prior to the implementation. It also reduced the time to ship a replacement part from 22 days to three days, and the time to perform a credit check from 20 minutes to three seconds.[2]

The first tier players in the ERP market are SAP, Baan, Oracle, and PeopleSoft, while the second tier players are vendors such as J.D. Edwards, Lawson, and QAD. SAP, a German company, holds about one-third of the market share and is the leading vendor of ERP products. SAP's ERP product is R/3 and the current commercial version is release 4.0 b. Worldwide there are more than 16,500 SAP R/3 installations. The product has a strong international appeal with capabilities to support multiple currencies, automatic handling of country-specific import/export, tax, and legal and language needs. The complete suite of SAP R/3 applications is available in 24 languages, including Japanese (Kanji) and other double-byte character languages.

The current ERP systems have an open client/server architecture and are real-time in nature, i.e., clients can process information remotely and the results of a new "input" will "ripple" through the whole "supply-chain" process. The appeal of such systems for businesses is that all employees of a company will have access to the same information almost instantaneously through one unified user interface. ERP systems such as SAP/R3 include not just the functional modules that "crunch" the numbers but also the most advanced technologies and methodologies. Implementing such a system results in benefits from the "integrated" nature of the system as well as from the "reengineering" of the business practices and the entire "culture" of the business, all at the same time.

The popularity of ERP programs can be attributed to an increasing trend towards globalization, mergers and acquisitions, short product life cycles, and the fear of looming disasters from aging legacy systems that could not handle dates beyond the year 2000. To be successful, a global enterprise must have accurate real-time information to control and coordinate far-flung resources. ERP systems have the capability to integrate far-flung outposts of a company along with the supply-chain activities. This integration allows sharing of information in a standard format across many departments in the home country as well as across the national borders regardless of language and currency differences. In this era of global competition and uncertain markets, companies are merging for competitive advantage. In the United States, the past couple of years have seen about $1 trillion in mergers annually, many of which involved overseas firms. These newly formed corporations often have very little in common other than a corporate logo. To achieve synergy across national boundaries and product lines, these businesses must implement a set of standard business applications and consistent data definitions across all business units. ERP packages are extremely useful in integrating a global company and providing a "common language" throughout the company. Digital Equipment Corp. is implementing PeopleSoft's human resources system across its 44 locations worldwide. Digital is not only implementing a standardized human resources application but is also moving to a common architecture and infrastructure. For many companies, a global software rollout is a good time to do some serious housecleaning and consolidation of their IT infrastructure around the world. Digital is expecting a return on investment of

27 percent from this global rollout.[5] If the merging companies have already implemented the same ERP solution, then they will save a tremendous amount in cost and time when integrating their systems. Recently, Daimler-Benz AG and Chrysler Corp. merged to form Daimler Chrysler AG. The new company could dodge five to ten years of integration work because the companies use the same computer-aided design systems and SAP financial applications.[15]

Companies are also finding that the ERP solutions help them get rid of their legacy systems. Sometimes it costs less for companies to replace their dinosaur systems than fix them. AlliedSignal Turbocharging Systems, a California-based turbocharger manufacturer, had more than 120 legacy systems, and the average age of the company's legacy systems was 18 years. In addition to these legacy systems, the company had several home-grown applications that had little or no source code documentation. These systems were so disparate and inefficient that running them not only drove IT costs up but also increased the time to fill customer orders. AlliedSignal implemented SAP R/3 to replace its 120 legacy systems in 15 of the company's 17 facilities worldwide. Company officials estimated a full payback on the $25 million project in a little more than two years. It was able to reduce the order fulfillment process to just a day from its previous weekly procedure.[8]

CRITICAL IMPLEMENTATION CONCERNS

Even in a single site, implementing ERP means "Early Retirement Probably." An ERP package is so complex and vast that it takes several years and millions of dollars to roll it out. It also requires many far-flung outposts of a company to follow exactly the same business processes. In fact, implementing any integrated ERP solution is not as much a technological exercise but an "organizational revolution." Extensive preparation before implementation is the key to success. Implementations carried out without patience and careful planning will turn out to be corporate root canals, not competitive advantage. Several issues must be addressed when dealing with a vast ERP system, and the following sections discuss each of them in detail.

Top Management Commitment

The IT literature has clearly demonstrated that for IT projects to succeed top management support is critical.[4] This also applies to ERP implementations. Implementing an ERP system is not a matter of changing software systems, rather it is a matter of repositioning the company and transforming the business practices. Due to enormous impact on the competitive advantage of the company, top management must consider the strategic implications of implementing an ERP solution.[2] Management must ask several questions before embarking on the project. Does the ERP system strengthen the company's competitive position? How might it erode the company's competitive position? How does ERP affect the organizational structure and the culture? What is the scope of the ERP implementation — only a few functional units or the entire organization? Are there any alternatives that meet the company's needs better than an ERP system? If it is a multinational corporation, the management should be concerned about whether it would be better to roll the system out globally or restrict it to certain regional units. Management must be involved in every step of the ERP implementation. Some companies make the grave mistake of handing over the responsibility of ERP implementation to the technology department. This would risk the entire company's survival because of the ERP system's profound business implications.

It is often said that ERP implementation is about people, not processes or technology. An organization goes through a major transformation, and the management of this change must be carefully planned (from a strategic viewpoint) and meticulously implemented. Many parts of the business that used to work in silos now have to be tightly integrated for ERP to work effectively. Cutting corners in planning and implementation is detrimental to a company. The top management must not only fund the project but also take an active role in leading the change. A review of successful ERP implementations has shown that the key to a smooth rollout is the effectiveness of change management from the top. Intervention from management is often necessary to resolve conflicts and bring everybody to the same thinking, and to build cooperation among the diverse groups in the organization, often across the national borders. Top management needs to constantly monitor the progress of the project and provide direction to the implementation teams. The success of a major project like an ERP implementation completely hinges on the strong, sustained commitment of top management. This commitment when percolated down through the organizational levels results in an overall organizational commitment. An overall organizational commitment that is very visible, well defined, and felt is a sure way to ensure a successful implementation.

Reengineering

Implementing an ERP system involves reengineering the existing business processes to the best business process standard. ERP systems are built on best practices that are followed in the industry. One major benefit of ERP comes from reengineering the company's existing way of doing business. All the processes in a company must conform to the ERP model. The cost and benefits of aligning with an ERP model could be very high. This is especially true if the company plans to roll out the system worldwide. It is not very easy to get everyone to agree to the same process. Sometimes business processes are so unique that they need to be preserved, and appropriate steps need to be taken to customize those business processes. Hydro Agri North America, Inc. implemented SAP R/3 in 1994, and since then the company is fighting against the integration SAP provides because some of the company's processes are very unique. Trying to fit the SAP mold resulted in a lot of pain and fewer benefits. Now Hydro Agri will either build a different front-end application or use a different package whenever their processes clash with that of the SAP.[7]

The companies also face a question as to whether to implement the ERP software "as is" and adopt the ERP system's built-in procedure or customize the product to the specific needs of the company. Research shows that even a best-application package can meet only 70 percent of the organizational needs. What happens to the rest? An organization has to change its processes to conform to the ERP package, customize the software to suit its needs, or not be concerned about meeting the 30 percent balance. If the package cannot adapt to the organization, then the organization has to adapt to the package and change its procedures. When an organization customizes the software to suit its needs, the total cost of implementation rises. The more the customization, the greater the implementation costs. Companies should keep their systems "as is" as much as possible to reduce the costs of customization and future maintenance and upgrade expenses.

Integration

There is a strong trend toward a single ERP solution for an entire company. Most companies feel that having a single vendor means a "common view" necessary to serve their customers efficiently and the ease of maintaining the system in future. Unfortunately, no single application can do everything a company needs. Companies may have to use other specialized software products that best meet their unique needs. These products have to be integrated along with all the homegrown systems with the ERP suite. In this case, ERP serves as a backbone, and all the different software are bolted onto the ERP software.

There are third-party software applications, called middleware, which can be used to integrate software applications from several vendors to the ERP backbone. Unfortunately, middleware is not available for all the different software products that are available in the market. Middleware vendors concentrate only on the most popular packaged applications and tend to focus on the technical aspects of application interoperability rather than linking business processes.

Many times, organizations have to develop their own interfaces for commercial software applications and homegrown applications. Integration software also poses other kinds of problems when it comes to maintenance. It is a nightmare for IS personnel to manage this software whenever there are changes and upgrades to either ERP software or other software that is integrated with the ERP system. For every change, the IT department will be concerned about which link is going to fail this time. Integration problems would be severe if the middleware links the ERP package of a company to its vendor companies in the supply chain. Maintaining the integration patchwork requires an inordinate and ongoing expenditure of resources. Organizations spend up to 50 percent of their IT budgets on application integration.[9] It is also estimated that the integration market (products and services) equals the size of the entire ERP market.[3] When companies choose bolt-on systems, it is advisable to contact the ERP vendor for a list of certified third-party vendors. Each year, all the major ERP vendors publish a list of certified third-party vendors. There are several advantages to choosing this option, including continuous maintenance and upgrade support.

One of the major benefits of ERP solutions is the integration they bring into an organization. Organizations need to understand the nature of integration and how it affects the entire business. Before integration, the functional departments worked in silos and were slow to experience the consequences of the mistakes other departments committed. The information flow was rather slow, and the departments that made the mistakes had ample time to correct them before the errors started affecting the other departments. However, with tight integration, the ripple effect of mistakes made in one part of the business unit pass onto the other departments in real time. Also, the original mistakes get magnified as they flow through the value chain of the company. For example, the errors that the production department of a company made in its bill of materials could affect not only the operations in the production department but also the inventory department, accounting department, and others. The impact of these errors could be detrimental to a company. For example, price errors on purchase orders could mislead financial analysts by giving a distorted view of how much the company is spending on materials. Companies must be aware of the potential risks of the errors and take proper steps, such as monitoring the transactions and taking immediate steps to rectify the problems should they occur. They must also have a formal plan of action describing the steps to be taken if an error is detected. A proper means to communicate to all the parties who are victims of the errors as soon as the errors are detected is extremely important.

Consider the recent example of a manufacturing company that implemented an ERP package. It suddenly started experiencing a shortage of manufacturing materials. Production workers noticed that it was due to incorrect bills of materials, and they made necessary adjustments because they knew the correct number of parts needed to manufacturer. However, the company did not have any procedures to notify others in case any errors were found in the data. The domino effect of the errors started affecting other areas of the business. Inventory managers thought the company had more material than was on the shelves, and material shortages occurred. Now the company has mandatory training classes to educate employees about how transactions flow through the system and how errors affect the activities in a value chain. It took almost eight weeks to clean up the incorrect bills of materials in the database.

Companies implementing electronic supply chains face different kinds of problems with integration of information across the supply-chain companies. The major challenge is the impact automation has on the business process. Automation changes the way companies deal with one another, from planning to purchasing to paying. Sharing and control of information seem to be major concerns. Companies are concerned about how much information they need to share with their customers and suppliers and how to control the information. Suppliers do not want their competitors to see their prices or order volumes. The general fear is that sharing too much information hurts their business. Regarding controlling information, companies are aware that it is difficult to control what they own let alone control what they do not own. Companies need to trust their partners and must coordinate with each other in the chain. The whole chain suffers if one link is slow to provide information or access. The management also must be concerned about the stress an automated supply chain brings within each organization. For instance, a sales department may be unhappy that electronic ordering has cut it out of the loop, while manufacturing may have to adjust to getting one week's notice to order changes and accommodate those changes into its production orders.

ERP Consultants

Because the ERP market has grown so big so fast, there has been a shortage of competent consultants. The skill shortage is so deep that it cannot be filled immediately. Finding the right people and keeping them through the implementation is a major challenge. ERP implementation demands multiple skills — functional, technical, and interpersonal skills. Again, consultants with specific industry knowledge are fewer in number. There are not many consultants with all the required skills.

Since the ERP market in the United States started approximately five years ago (and is growing at an astronomical rate), there are not many consultants with three or more years of experience. This has sent the compensation for skilled SAP consultants through the roof. One year's experience brings in $70,000 to $80,000 annually. Three to five years' experience could command up to $200,000 annually. One might find a consultant with a stellar reputation in some areas, but he may lack expertise in the specific area a company is looking for. Hiring a consultant is just the tip of the iceberg. Managing a consulting firm and its employees is even more challenging. The success or failure of the project depends on how well you meet this challenge.[10]

Implementation Time

ERP systems come in modular fashion and do not have to be entirely implemented at once. Several companies follow a phase-in approach in which one module is implemented at a time. For example, SAP R/3 is composed of several "complete" modules that could be chosen and implemented, depending on an organization's needs. Some of the most commonly installed modules are sales and distribution (SD), materials management (MM), production and planning, (PP), and finance and controlling (FI) modules.

The average length of time for a "typical" implementation is about 14 months and can take as many as 150 consultants. Corning, Inc. plans to roll out ERP in ten of its diversified manufacturing divisions, and it expects the rollout to last five to eight years.[11] The length of implementation is affected to a great extent by the number of modules being implemented, the scope of the implementation (different functional units or across multiple units spread out globally), the extent of customization, and the number of interfaces with other applications. The greater the number of units, the longer the total implementation time. Also, as the scope of implementation grows from a single business unit to multiple units spread out globally, the duration of implementation increases. A global implementation team has to be formed to prepare common requirements that do not violate the individual unit's specific requirements. This involves extensive travel and increases the length of implementation time.

The problem with ERP packages is that they are very general and need to be configured to a specific type of business. This customization takes a long time, depending on the specific requirements of the business. For example, SAP is so complex and general that there are nearly 8000 switches that need to be set properly to make it handle the business processes in the way a company needs. The extent of customization determines the length of the implementation. The more customization needed, the longer it will take to roll the software out and the more it will cost to keep it up to date. The length of time could be cut down by keeping the system "plain vanilla" and reducing the number of bolt-on application packages that require custom interfaces with the ERP system. The downside to this "plain vanilla" approach is conforming to the system's mold, which may or may not completely match the requirements of the business.

For small companies, SAP recently launched Ready-to-Run, a scaled-down suite of R/3 programs preloaded on a computer server. SAP has also introduced AcceleratedSAP (ASAP) to reduce implementation time. ERP vendors are now offering industry-specific applications to cut the implementation down time. SAP has recently outlined a comprehensive plan to offer 17 industry-specific solutions, including chemical, aerospace and defense, insurance, retail, media, and utilities industries. Even though these specific solutions would substantially reduce the time to implement an application, organizations still have to customize the product for their specific requirements.

Implementation Costs

Even though the price of prewritten software is cheap compared with in-house development, the total cost of implementation could be three to five times the purchase price of the software. The implementation costs would increase as the degree of customization increases. The cost of hiring consultants and all that goes with it can consume up to 30 percent of the overall budget for the implementation.

According to Gartner Group, total cost of an outside SAP consultant is around $1600 per day. Going for in-house SAP-trained technologists creates its own worries. Once the selected employees are trained and after investing a huge sum of money, it is a challenge to retain them, especially in a market that is hungry for skilled SAP consultants. Employees could double or triple their salaries by accepting other positions. Retention strategies such as bonus programs, company perks, salary increases, continual training and education, and appeals to company loyalty could work. Other intangible strategies such as flexible work hours, telecommuting options, and opportunities to work with leading-edge technologies are also being used.

Many companies simply strive to complete the projects quickly for fear of poaching by head-hunting agencies and other companies.

ERP Vendors

As there are about 500 ERP applications available and there is some company consolidation going on, it is all the more important that the software partner be financially well off. Selecting a suitable product is extremely important. Top management input is very important when selecting a suitable vendor.

Management needs to ask questions about the vendor, such as its market focus (for example, midsize or large organization), track record with customers, vision of the future, and with whom the vendor is strategically aligned. For a global ERP rollout, companies need to be concerned about if the ERP software is designed to work in different countries. Also, the management must make sure the ERP vendor has the same version of the software available in all the countries in which the company is implementing the system. Vendor claims regarding global readiness may not be true, and the implementation team may need to cross-check with subsidiary representatives regarding the availability of the software. Vendors also may not have substantial presence in the subsidiary countries. It is important to evaluate if the vendor staffers in these countries are knowledgeable and available. If there is a shortage of skilled staff, bringing people from outside could solve the problem, but it would increase the costs of implementation.

Selecting the Right Employees

Companies intending to implement an ERP system must be willing to dedicate some of their best employees to the project for a successful implementation. Often companies do not realize the impact of choosing the internal employees with the right skill set.

The importance of this aspect cannot be overemphasized. Internal resources of a company should not only be experts in the company's processes but also be aware of the best business practices in the industry. Internal resources on the project should exhibit the ability to understand the overall needs of the company and should play an important role in guiding the project efforts in the right direction.

Most consulting organizations do provide comprehensive guidelines for selecting internal resources for the project. Companies should take this exercise seriously and make the right choices. Lack of proper understanding of the project needs and the inability to provide leadership and guidance to the project by the company's internal resources is a major reason for the failure of ERP projects. Because of the complexities involved in the day-to-day running of an organization, it is not uncommon to find functional departments unwilling to sacrifice their best resources toward ERP project needs. However, considering that ERP system implementation can be a critical step in forging an organization's future, companies are better off dedicating their best internal resources to the project.

Training Employees

Training and updating employees on ERP is a major challenge. People are one of the hidden costs of ERP implementation. Without proper training, about 30 to 40 percent of front-line workers will not be able to handle the demands of the new system.[6] The people at the keyboard are now making important decisions about buying and selling — important commitments of the company. They need to understand how their data affects the rest of company. Some of the decisions front-line people make with an ERP system were the responsibility of a manager earlier. It is important for managers to understand this change in their job and encourage the front-line people to be able to make those decisions themselves.

Training employees on ERP is not as simple as Excel training in which you give them a few weeks of training, put them on the job, and they blunder their way through. ERP systems are extremely complex and demand rigorous training. It is difficult for trainers or consultants to pass on the knowledge to the employees in a short period of time. This "knowledge transfer" gets hard if the employees lack computer literacy or have computer phobia. In addition to being taught ERP technology, the employees now have to be taught their new responsibilities. With ERP systems you are continuously being trained. Companies should provide opportunities to enhance the skills of the employees by providing training opportunities on a continuous basis to meet the changing needs of the business and employees.

Employee Morale

Employees working on an ERP implementation project put in long hours (as much as 20 hours per day) including seven-day weeks and even holidays. Even though the experience is valuable for their career growth, the stress of implementation coupled with regular job duties (many times employees still spend 25 to 50 percent of their time on regular job duties) could decrease their morale rapidly. Leadership from upper management and support and caring acts of project leaders would certainly boost the morale of the team members. Other strategies, such as taking the employees on field trips, could help reduce the stress and improve the morale.

CONCLUSION

ERP solutions are revolutionizing the way companies produce goods and services. They are a dream come true in integrating different parts of a company and ensuring smooth flow of information across the enterprise quickly. ERP systems bring many benefits to organizations by tightly integrating various departments. Even though ERP solutions have been popular in Europe for some time, North American companies have been using them for only five to six years. Some of the factors that have contributed to ERP growth are the trend toward globalization, and mergers and acquisitions.

ERP systems are very large and complex and warrant careful planning and execution of their implementation. They are not mere software systems; they affect how a business conducts itself. How a company implements an ERP system determines whether it creates a competitive advantage or becomes a corporate headache. The top contributor for a successful ERP implementation is a strong commitment from upper management, as an implementation involves significant alterations to existing business practices as well as an outlay of huge capital investments. The other important factors are the issues related to reengineering the business processes and integrating the other business applications to the ERP backbone. Upper management plays a key role in managing the change an ERP brings into an organization. Organizational commitment is paramount due to possible lengthy implementation and huge costs involved. Once implemented, an ERP system is difficult and expensive to undo. Since no single ERP solution can satisfy all the business needs, organizations may have to implement custom applications in addition to the ERP software. Integrating different software packages poses a serious challenge, and the integration patchwork is expensive and difficult to maintain.

Selecting and managing consultants pose a continuous challenge due to the shortage of skilled consultants in the market. ERP vendors are bringing out industry-specific solutions and newer methodologies to cut the length and costs of implementation. Organizations could reduce the total cost of implementation if they reduce customization by adapting to the ERP's built-in best practices as much as possible. Selecting the right employees to participate in the implementation process and motivating them is critical for the implementation's success. Finally, it is important to train the employees to use the system to ensure the proper working of the system.

References

1. Appleton, E., "How to Survive ERP," *Datamation*, October 9, 1998.
2. Davenport, T., "Putting the Enterprise into the Enterprise System," *Harvard Business Review*, July August 1998, Vol. 76, No. 4, pp. 121–131.
3. Edwards, J., "Expanding the Boundaries of ERP," *CIO*, July 1, 1998.
4. Johnson, J., "Chaos: The Dollar Drain of IT Project Failures," *Application Development Trends*, January 1995, pp. 41–48.
5. Horwitt, E., "Enduring a Global Rollout — and Living to Tell About It," *Computerworld*, Vol. 32, No. 14, March 1998, pp. S8–S12.
6. Koch, C., "Surprise, Surprise," *CIO*, June 15, 1996.
7. Melymuka, K., "ERP is Growing from Being Just an Efficiency Tool to One That Can Also Help a Company Grow," *Computerworld*, September 1998.
8. Needleman, T., "AlliedSignal Turbocharges its Systems," *Beyondcomputing*, September 1998.
9. Radding, A., "The Push to Integrate — Packaged Applications Promise to Speed Integration and Cut Costs," *InformationWeek*, No. 671, March 2, 1998.
10. Schwartz, K., "Putting Consultants on Your Team," *Beyondcomputing*, Vol. 7, No. 6, August 1998.
11. Stedman, C., "Global ERP Rollouts Present Cross-Border Problems," *Computerworld*, Vol. 32, No. 47, November 1998, p. 10.
12. Stein, T., "SAP Installation Scuttled — Unisource Cites Internal Problems for $168 M Write-off, *InformationWeek*, January 26, 1998.
13. Sweat, J., "ERP — Enterprise Application Suites are Becoming a Focal Point of Business and Technology Planning, *InformationWeek*, No. 704, October 26, 1998.

14. Tiazkun, S., "SAP Sued for $500 Million," *Computer Reseller News*, August 26, 1998.
15. Wallace, B., "Now it's Cost-Cutting Time," *Computerworld*, Vol. 32, No. 47, November 1998, pp. 1 and 82.

Chapter 37
Risk Management Skills Needed in a Packaged Software Environment

Janet Butler

Traditional, customized development has, in many cases, become too expensive, and protracted development times may cause organizations to miss business windows of opportunity. The purchase of packages and off-the-shelf components, as well as contracted development, can greatly reduce costs and speed delivery. Due to the competition in every quarter, organizations would be far more vulnerable to major business risk if they did not seek alternatives to traditional development. But the new approaches pose many dangers.

WHY PACKAGES?

There is little doubt that organizations are increasingly moving to packaged software for major applications. The term coined for packages in industry is enterprise resource planning (ERP) software; in government it is commercial off-the-shelf (COTS) software, which may, however, simply refer to purchased components.

A recent study reported an equal number of applications bought versus those built in-house. Those conducting the study predict an imminent change to a ratio of 3:1 in favor of purchased software.[1]

Government Computer News also recently conducted a survey of 127 managers, who agreed that commercial software is the wave of the present and the future. Of the respondents, 58.3 percent said they use commercial software for one or more of these purposes: financial accounting, human resources, procurement, and electronic commerce. In addition, 85.7 per-

0-8493-1149-7/02/$0.00+$1.50
© 2002 by CRC Press LLC

cent of 42 respondents said customizing commercial software has saved them money.[2]

Packages allow an organization to deliver a complex system in a relatively short time. In addition, common applications are available in many languages and for many platforms. There is also a large installed base of users, accompanied by a proven track record of success. And purchased software provides extensive documentation.

Furthermore, once the purchased software is installed, the organization spends far less money, time, and effort for ongoing maintenance than it would for in-house-developed software, and the organization need not redefine requirements for legal or other new requirements. Instead, it is the vendor's job.

The benefits of purchased software derive largely from economies of scale. The vendor need only develop the software once and can then distribute the cost of development and ongoing maintenance over a large installed base.

But there are downsides to purchased software. For one, it is just as difficult for a software supplier to develop software as it is for an in-house organization. In addition, commercial software is generally developed for the most widely accepted/installed technology, so it might not run efficiently on a particular computer or operating system. In fact, commercial software might use obsolete technology.

Furthermore, purchased software is slow to evolve. It is very expensive for a vendor to make major functional changes to commercial software. By a kind of "reverse economy of scale," as the cost of development and maintenance decreases because it is spread across a large installed base, the cost of implementing major improvements increases.

Another negative of purchased software is the use of multiple programming languages. To reduce maintenance and improve flexibility, vendors tend to write all or part of their software using homegrown report writers or fourth-generation languages (4GL). This might work well for the first package an organization buys, but it becomes a linguistic nightmare with subsequent purchases.

Say each vendor provides at least one language that may, however, differ from package to package, and the in-house development group purchases one or more general-purpose 4GLs. The multiple languages generally do not talk to one another. The languages present a major headache, given their learning curves, requirements for cross-training, and dependence on trained personnel.

Databases have also become an issue when an organization purchases software. Since packages are seldom designed for a specific database management system, an organization might have to choose software based either on functionality or database compatibility. It therefore becomes difficult for an organization purchasing software to have a single-image corporate database of information. In turn, this limits the organization's ability to fit its software to the business's changing requirements.

Risks associated with purchased software also include such vendor-related issues as vendor stability, mergers, acquisitions, and nonperformance. Organizational issues include software modifications, training requirements, budgeting considerations, and installation standards.

Despite its downsides, purchased software is hailed as being one of the few viable solutions to meeting an organization's market needs. Given its productivity benefits, packaged software enables companies to deliver complex systems in a relatively short time.

A new skill for the development function, then, is the effective selection of purchased software. This means the organization must thoroughly understand its requirements, both functional and technical.

HOW TO DEFINE REQUIREMENTS-PLUS

The traditional software development life cycle consists of requirements analysis, software design, code, test/implementation, and maintenance/enhancement. Of these phases, the first and last — requirements and maintenance — respectively, are the stages most relevant to the purchase of packaged software, but the concerns are somewhat different than with in-house software.

As noted above, the key to successful software selection is establishing requirements. Although the requirements definition has always been a critical phase in the software development life cycle, the steps must be expanded. Of course, functionality remains number one on an organization's checklist of requirements, whether it is developing its own software, buying a packaged application, or contracting with a supplier to have a custom system built. However, an organization purchasing a package must not only determine its functional requirements, but it must also analyze available software and compare and weigh the functional characteristics of each product to the requirements.

In this process, similar requirements can be grouped into these general classifications:

- *Product capabilities* — functional requirements for the type of software required, be it operating system or application software

- *Technical support information* — including product documentation and operating systems supported
- *Implementation information* — including report set-up, hardware requirements, software prerequisites, implementation effort, and complexity to change
- *Miscellaneous* — including pricing and maintenance schedules, discounts, the installed base of users, vendor information, and user group information[4]

As many companies are well aware, the major software vendors are formidable negotiators, so software purchasers must understand both their opponents' and their own requirements. They must know, for example, the type of software they need, how it will be used, how many users will access it, and how frequently. They must also know whether the software will be deployed locally or globally, how soon it might be migrated to a different hardware platform, and if an outsourcer will at some point take charge of the software.

To date, few companies have much experience in replacing applications developed in-house with integrated commercial packages, so they rarely agree on the percentage of requirements that must be met out of the box.

However, if users customize commercial software to a great degree, they will suffer the consequences when they upgrade to the vendor's next release. Customization should never be undertaken lightly, because customized functions might no longer work after a patch or a new system release.

In addition, those purchasing software must realize that choosing a package involves many compromises. Some required functions might be only partially met, while others will be missing entirely.

Unfortunately, software purchasers often do not understand their own requirements, so they select software based on specifications presented by a single vendor.

HOW TO NEGOTIATE A SOFTWARE LICENSE

Compared with those who bought technology in the past, today's software purchasers are far more sophisticated, possessing both financial and legal knowledge about software licensing issues. In addition, software is now becoming more of a buyer's than a seller's market, due to the competitive nature of the software market and the growing rate of technology change.

Information technology buyers must still anticipate difficult negotiations with vendors, however, due to the growing complexity of the marketplace. When mainframes and minicomputers were the only existing platforms, applications were licensed based on the box and/or terminals.

While this changed dramatically with client/server computing, traditional licensing models completely broke down with the advent of World Wide Web-based computing.

Software is generally licensed rather than sold, since the product consists of intellectual property, plus the media it is printed on. Because the developing vendor technically retains ownership of the application, it negotiates a license governing its use with the purchaser.

When IBM unbundled software from computer hardware in 1969, it became common practice for software vendors to explicitly price software licenses. However, both maintenance costs and license prices were based primarily on vendor experience with computer hardware maintenance or the cost of the original software development.

By the 1980s, the major software pricing method had become tiered pricing, which was done in two ways. In the first, users paid a fixed price to start and a monthly or annual maintenance fee for license renewal and support, usually between 5 and 10 percent annually of the original fee. With the second tiered-pricing method, users paid a fixed initial fee for a specified term of use and a subsequent monthly or annual maintenance fee for support.

Support in tiered pricing usually referred to corrections or bug fixes as well as upgrades. These new versions included perfective and adaptive changes. If little or no maintenance fee was charged, bug fixes were generally free; installable patches and upgrades were handled separately. Installation of the upgraded or corrected software was seldom included.

Beginning in the early 1990s, the primary software licensing model became 99-year or perpetual right-to-use licenses for a user or organization. However, there are many types of software licensing plans in use today. While software is sometimes licensed for use by a particular user, client/server applications that operate on a network might be priced based on the number of PCs that have access.

Purchasers might pay for software based on concurrent or named users or on site-specific or global use. Alternatively, licenses might be based on servers, networks, or even on the customer's annual revenue. In general, organizations use a transaction-oriented approach when buying software licenses.[5]

Software buyers will have an edge if they know the vendor's motivations and the industry environment in which it competes. Such an understanding can prevent miscommunications and misunderstandings. In addition, buyers can attempt to leverage volume by licensing software on a corporatewide basis, rather than by divisions or business units.

In purchasing software, buyers would be wise to do the following:

1. Obtain competitive bids from several vendors. This helps determine a market price to use in negotiations.
2. Deal with a vendor executive.
3. Understand the vendor's business model.
4. Use a professional arbitrator.
5. Demand clauses for maintenance and support.
6. Try to use their own standard contract.
7. Create a standard licensing process within their organization.

Although obtaining the best price for software is important for the purchasing organization, flexibility should take precedence. After all, there are many organizational changes taking place that might in turn change the way the software is used. For example, the organization might undergo a merger, an acquisition, data center consolidation, or centralization.

When such an organizational change takes place, users might have to buy a new license, unless the contract specifies otherwise. In fact, some analysts have estimated a 70 percent probability that corporations that do not so specify will have to re-purchase their software license within three years.[1]

In addition, an initial software license fee may account for only 10 to 15 percent of the total cost of ownership of software over five years, so the purchasing organization might have opportunities for savings in usage rights, audit clauses, maintenance, and the rights to new versions.

In selling or licensing software, vendors initially try to sell the product for the highest price; they then attempt to earn more money on the sale over time. Because it gains them the most money, they try to make the license as restrictive as possible, giving them more control. Conversely, it is the purchasing organization's goal to obtain a less restrictive license.

The software license is the first product the vendor sells, but software maintenance is often a separate issue. Thus, in software maintenance, as in new development, there are classic choices of "do" or "buy." The choices might apply differently, depending if the maintenance is corrective, perfective, or adaptive. Most vendors offer a contract for maintenance or service or a warranty. In this way, maintenance can become a marketable product and a source of revenue.[5]

HOW TO MANAGE SOFTWARE MAINTENANCE

Maintenance contracts specify how a buyer will receive software upgrades and provide terms for warranty and bug-fix remedies. With such contracts, vendors can profitably lock in customers for the long term. In fact, one major trend in software purchasing is software vendors' continuing, increased dependence upon maintenance revenue. Therefore, organizations would be wise to negotiate software maintenance terms as part of the initial license agreement.

It might surprise buyers that maintenance contracts can be more expensive than software licenses in the long run. If, as is usual, maintenance contracts cost 12 to 20 percent of the initial license fee per year, a contract with a 15 percent annual fee for a $100,000 license will exceed the software's original cost after six years.

Software buyers have better leverage if they negotiate the first maintenance contract at the same time as the initial license. It also helps with long-range planning if the organization knows the total life cycle costs.

In negotiating maintenance, organizations should clearly define the meanings of "upgrade" and "new product." Otherwise, vendors might call a software release a "new product," which is not covered by the maintenance agreement.[1]

Sometimes customer and vendor needs can give rise to a win–win situation. For example, software tool vendor Cadence Design Systems Inc. modified its licensing focus from selling software to contributing to users' productivity. In moving from traditional licensing and maintenance fee practices to the "flexible access model," the vendor changed its software maintenance model.

Thus, in some instances, Cadence now amortizes the fee for software maintenance services over the licensing period. The customer's right to receive software updates (perfective and adaptive modifications), bug fixes (corrections), and help desk support is negotiated as part of the initial license. No longer is software maintenance dependent upon or paid for through the maintenance fee. Instead, vendor updates, corrections, and help desk support depend on the terms of the contract.

While the traditional maintenance goal is to maximize usage, with the new model, it now enhances productivity. Whereas maintenance was formerly licensed per unit, the contract now covers all users. The monthly maintenance fee was generally 1 to 1.5 percent of the initial fee, but it now depends on particular features. As a result, customers gain flexibility, while the vendor has a multiyear financial commitment for maintenance.[5]

Of course, purchase and maintenance of individual software products differs considerably from that of COTS or ERP systems. In purchasing the latter, organizations must determine if the components will adapt to future needs, and, if so, how and by whom that adaptation will occur.

An organization that depends heavily on COTS component or ERP functionality may be at high risk. If the software functionality is not precisely what the organization needs over time, it can be expensive to have the vendor customize the product. If the organization creates "wrappers" or patches as substitutes for real source-code-based maintenance, this can produce instability in the system quality.

Furthermore, the vendor might drop the product. Therefore, organizations would be wise to get a guarantee from the supplier that if the product is dropped, the organization will gain rights to the source code. Even in this case, however, the organization must maintain software not written in-house, and it might have to hire developers who are expert in that code.

Organizations should make some key management decisions related to software maintenance before they opt for COTS or ERP software. They should determine if they can afford the dependency on the vendor, and they should decide if they can accept the risk.[7]

If maintaining COTS or ERP software is risky, some find it hard, at best, to envision. They cite IS' traditional 50 to 80 cost percentage in maintenance, with 60 percent of those costs in enhancement. Finally, they state, "Enhancement of a standardized, generalized product is both undesirable and nearly impossible."[8]

HOW TO EVALUATE SOFTWARE VENDORS

Mergers, competition, and falling software prices are corroding standard software support and services. In this marketplace, purchasing organizations should add new requirements when evaluating software vendors. They should consider the following:

- *Human factors* — Before purchasing packages, organizations should judge the vendor's quality of interaction with human beings for software support and customer service. They might even call the technical support line, timing how long it takes to get through and assessing how difficult questions are handled.
- *Corporate structure* — Purchasing organizations should determine if the vendor is a publicly or privately held corporation. If the former, the vendor might aim at maximizing shareholders' investments. If the latter, its goal might be customer satisfaction. In addition, the buyer should determine if the software being evaluated is the vendor's primary offering or only one of many products, how much the vendor has invested in development, how often it issues new releases, how committed it is to the product, and what the effect would be if support were lost.
- *Size in relation to customer focus* — Smaller companies tend to place more emphasis on customer care than larger ones.
- *User input into product development* — If the software is strategic to the purchaser's business, the buying organization should determine what

impact it can have on future product development. For example, it should find out how the vendor responds to customer input, if the organization can take part in beta programs, and how the vendor handles customer feedback on enhancements and improvements. After all, the buying organization can best protect its software investment if it can influence product development.[6]

CONCLUSION

For whatever reason, users are buying packaged software. The fact remains that commercial software has great and growing appeal. There are several trends in software purchasing that call for action on the part of purchasing organizations.

For starters, ERP package solutions will continue to replace user-developed applications, so buyers should develop flexible enterprise agreements to meet their business needs. In addition, software vendors are increasingly dependent on maintenance revenue, so buyers should see it as a strategic imperative to negotiate maintenance terms as part of the initial license agreement.

Furthermore, buyers should be wary of the increased risk in software contracts resulting from the continued consolidation of vendors. Enterprises should also seek multinational software agreements to address global requirements. Finally, with the Internet accelerating the rate of change in technology, purchasers should aim at increased flexibility in their software license agreements.[1]

Packaged applications are becoming strategic to many businesses. Therefore, software buyers should attempt to form strategic relationships with these types of suppliers versus those who sell commodity-type products, such as Netscape Communications Corp. and Microsoft Corp. It pays dividends for an organization to have a good rapport with a package supplier, since the buyer depends on the vendor for products.

In short, today's software development environment has new skill requirements, including the selection of computer software, the negotiation of licenses, and the choice of and partnership with vendors. Savvy developers would be wise to buff up and enhance their skills to deal with these new needs posed by package acquisition, deployment, customization, and maintenance.

To ensure job security in a changing environment, developers would be wise to take immediate action. Since requirements are so critical in successful package and vendor selection, developers' first step should be to **become proficient at establishing requirements.** In this effort, a spreadsheet could be helpful in spelling out the functional requirements, listing the available software, and comparing and weighing the functional characteristics of each product in terms of requirements.

Next, because license negotiation is so critical, developers should **learn negotiation skills.** To this end, developers can take a class in negotiation given by a business school, an adult education provider, or a private organization.

For the best outcome in negotiations, developers should also **develop a standard contract** for their company, which includes a maintenance clause. Finally, because so much effort is generally involved in "reinventing the wheel," they should help **create a standard licensing process** within their organization.

References

1. "Don't be a licensing lightweight!" Rick Whiting, *Software Magazine*, January 1998, p. 20.
2. "Agencies want their apps off the shelf, survey reveals," Florence Olsen, *Government Computer News*, September 29, 1997, p. 1, 8.
3. "ERP more than a 2000 fix," Craig Stedman, *Computerworld*, August 3, 1998, p. 1, 84.
4. "Selecting computer center software," Howard Miller, *Enterprise Management Issues*, September/October 1997, pp. 19–21.
5. "Software licensing models amid market turbulence," Cris Wendt and Nicholas Imparato, *Journal of Software Maintenance*, 9, 1997, pp. 271–280.
6. "Does size really matter?" John Lipsey, *AS/400*, February 1998, pp. 19–20.
7. "COTS software: The economical choice?" Jeffrey Voas, *IEEE Software*, March/April 1998, pp. 16–19.
8. "SAP — Aligning IS with the enterprise takes on a whole new meaning!" Robert L. Glass, *Managing System Development*, April 1997, pp. 10–11.

Chapter 38
Application Service Providers

Dawna Travis Dewire

The latest trend in the use of technology has spawned a new breed of companies called application service providers. An application service provider (ASP) provides a contractual software-based service for hosting, managing, and providing access to an application from a centrally managed facility. Customer companies have remote Web access to applications that are live on the ASP-provided servers.

ASPs provide business solutions to small, medium-sized, and large companies on a ren-tal basis. Customers of ASPs are seeing cost savings in total cost of ownership and improved time to deployment. ASPs, referred to as outsourcing companies by some, are often restructured software companies or strategic partnerships between consulting groups and infrastructure providers. ASPs provide organizations an alternative to the high fixed costs associated with software projects as well as the impact of these projects being over budget and past deadline.

Traditional applications such as enterprise resource planning (ERP), commerce, and call centers are natural markets for the ASP model. The trend is actually extending the model to include vertical as well as horizontal applications. ASPs are looking at applications within banking, retail, sales management, medical imaging, and groupware, as well as the oil and gas industries.

International Data Corp. (IDC) describes an ASP scenario as "an end user accesses an application resident on a server, just as he or she would on a LAN or in the enterprise data center. However, the server resides at the ASP's third-party data center and is reached via a dedicated line or the Internet (or extranet). The applications can range from low-end, productivity programs (e.g., word processing) to high-end ERP modules. The service is provided on a subscription basis and can bundle a full range of hosted application services."

Compare the process of leasing a car. Not much upfront money is required, consumers get something they might not be able to buy outright, they pay for it monthly and, at the end of the lease, they decide what to do with the car. By just licensing a few seats from an ASP, organizations get a full-functioning application that might be something more powerful and sophisticated than they could buy outright. They have access to the application without having to pay for hardware, software, or installation. Organizations can realize financial cost savings, reduce capital investments, and lower IT management requirements. Such an option also allows organizations to focus on their core businesses and react quickly to changes in the marketplace — both opportunities and threats.

Packaged software developers can use the ASP model to convert the infrequent buyer into a steady revenue stream customer. Usually, a customer buys version 4.2 of a software product and then elects not to upgrade for two or three generations. Under the ASP model, an ASP customer is provided with the latest version of a software package and pays a monthly fee to use that software, thereby generating a steady stream of revenue for the software package developer.

The software vendor upgrades only the master copies on licensed ASP servers. The software vendor is not required to maintain old code or support multiple versions of a product. If customers do not like the upgrade, they cannot go back to a prior version.

Customers of ASPs usually pay a flat fee to sign up and from then on a monthly fee. For that monthly fee, the customer gets all upgrades automatically as soon as they are released — all the new drivers, the new features, everything. However, because the ASP is monitoring the customer's payments, if the customer stops paying, it no longer gets the use of the software. It is as simple as that.

IDC estimates that the ASP market will be $7.7 billion by 2004, and Forrester Research estimates $6.7 billion by 2002. The year-old Wakefield, Massachusetts-based ASP Industry Consortium (www.aspindustry.org) has gone from 25 members to more than 300. The Information Technology Association of America (ITAA) did a survey of more than 1,500 IT executives. Nearly one-fifth were already using ASPs. Nearly 24 percent were planning to evaluate their use over the next year, and 19 percent expected that they would be using ASPs before the end of the year.

An ASP service is not the timesharing of the 1960s or the outsourcing of the 1980s. The ASP model is much more than the rental of a slice of time. The model allows an organization to decide the location of the computing capability based on economic and financial grounds. It provides an option for sharing information and conducting transactions. The ASP model uses client/server architecture and relies on secure, cost-effective data communications. The IT staff does not need to have expertise in the application or the infrastructure that is being handled by the ASP. ASPs can be used to fill gaps in an application portfolio. So, the focus is on saving time as well as cost, and time and cost are two major variables of any IT project.

In traditional outsourcing arrangements, the entire business process is handed off to the outsourcing company — operations, the legacy application itself, the infrastructure it was built on, and some of the internal IT staff to support it. Today, every level of the IT infrastructure (network, data, messaging, system management) can be selectively outsourced. With the ASP model, the software and its required infrastructure (including support) are provided by the application service provider, but the actual business process operations are still handled by the organization. If an insurance company outsources its claims processing, the outsourcer receives the claims and processes the claims on its hardware using its software and its staff. With the ASP model, the insurance company's staff receives the claims and processes the claims on the ASP's hardware using the ASP's software and infrastructure.

ASP BUSINESS MODEL

ASPs provide access to and management of an application. An ASP owns the software or has a contractual agreement with the software vendor to license it. Customers gain access to the environment without making investments in application license fees, hardware, and staff. The application is managed from a central location (the ASP site) rather than the customer's sites. Customers access the application via the Internet or leased lines. The ASP is responsible for delivering on the customer's contract regardless of its structure — sole provider or partnered. If a problem arises, the ASP is responsible for resolving the issue. Service guarantees usually address availability, security, networked storage, and management and are spelled out in service-level agreements (SLAs). ASPs enforce these guarantees by closely monitoring the server environments and often add proprietary modifications to ensure performance uptime and security.

An ASP provides the application service as its primary business. The service may be delivered from beginning to end by a single vendor or via partnerships among several vendors. A single-source vendor controls everything from implementation to ongoing operations and maintenance of the application. The customer deals with only one vendor, and that vendor has complete control over the process. Oracle Corp. is offering ASP services using this model. Under this model, the vendor must have expertise in a variety of areas, maintain a data center infrastructure, and have high capital requirements.

In the best-of-breed model, the company partners with other organizations to leverage expertise. In effect, the ASP has its own supply chain. One partner might be providing data storage, another the Web hosting services, and another the application itself. Two successful ASPs use this model. USinternetworking (USi), recently listed on the NASDAQ, has partnered with Cisco to supply networking infrastructure and operates its own data centers. USi currently has four data centers around the world. Corio has a partnership with Sun Microsystems to supply infrastructure and partnerships with Exodus Communications and Concentric for storage of data. With this model, a customer has many players to deal with but should, ideally by contract, have only one interface point — to the ASP itself.

DRIVING FORCES

The growth of the ASP market can be attributed to a variety of factors. On one hand, it reduces the risk associated with buying software — no huge consulting fees, no huge capital investment in hardware, no huge software cost (ERP package software alone can cost $100,000), just a monthly fee. It also reduces the technology complexities involved in installing such software — the hardware, the network, the support. It allows an organization to focus on selecting a business solution.

Growth of this market is also fueled by reduced network costs, the growing capabilities of communication bandwidth, and improved security on the network. As the cost of connectivity declines as predicted by Moore's law, its capabilities will increase. The ASP market is positioned to take advantage of this trend. Deloitte Research predicts a range of "xSP" companies. BSPs (backbone) will provide high-capacity, long-haul connectivity. ISPs (Internet) will provide access to the Internet gateways and the BSPs. SSPs (storage) will provide remote data storage locations. CSPs (commerce) will provide delivery, Web design, and ISP service. ASPs (application) will rent software via the Internet to any user with a Web browser.

The negative perceptions of outsourcing and off-the-shelf software are changing. Cost/benefit analysis is being used to determine the best alternative. Organizations are weighing the option of off-the-shelf software rather than custom-developed applications, of in-house production versus purchased services. The ASP model provides perpetual maintenance and the latest versions of software, unlike internal efforts; typically, when an application is finally tested and released, the organization has to immediately start planning for the next version, which is already on the horizon.

The business climate is changing quickly with mergers and acquisitions and the rapid growth of E-business. Organizations need to find flexible solutions while still focusing on their core competencies. IT departments are already busy maintaining existing applications and lack the resources to respond in a timely fashion. ASPs allow an organization to respond to changes and opportunities in a user-friendly Internet-based environment. An E-commerce site can be up and running within a short time.

IT talent is harder and harder to find and retain. Using an ASP frees IT from supporting commodity applications and allows companies to use their scarce IT resources for strategic projects. Using an ASP eliminates the need to hold up implementing critical software while trying to find IT talent such as experienced E-commerce people.

Mid-sized companies are turning to ASPs to implement high-end applications. Such companies typically do not have the IT talent or resources to deploy such software or the capital required to license the software and implement it; in some cases, implementation costs can run three to five times as much as the license fee. ASPs give these mid-sized organizations access to these high-end applications at a reasonable price, at lower risk, and more quickly.

CATEGORIES OF ASPS

Currently, application service providers fall into one of four categories based on the types of applications they offer.

Enterprise

These ASPs offer high-end applications that require customization. This category of ASP is offering ERP, customer relationship management (CRM), supply chain management (SCM), or workflow and imaging software services. The software vendors include SAP, Baan (now wholly owned by Invensys), PeopleSoft, Oracle, and Siebel. ASPs in this market segment also offer professional services for design, implementation, systems integration, and ongoing operations management.

General Business

These ASPs are targeting the small to mid-sized companies that need general business applications that require little or no customization. These are relatively simple applications. Templates are used by the user to configure the application to its specifications.

Specialist

These ASPs are focused on a particular type of application such as human resources.

Vertical

These ASPs provide packaged or specialized applications for a vertical market segment such as medical practice management software for medical practices and claims processing for insurance companies.

Application Software Architecture	
Hosting Platform Architecture	Computing Architecture
Network Infrastructure Architecture	

Exhibit 1.   ASP Architectures

ASPs may also offer various levels of service. Core services include the basic level of services: managing the application environment, monitoring the application, network support, and providing upgrades, as they are available. Managed services enhance the core services by offering additional services and guarantees related to security, application performance, and data redundancy. Finally, extended services further enhance the managed services by satisfying demands for strategic planning, application configuration, and training.

ARCHITECTURE

The keys to an ASP's successful delivery of an application are reliable, remote data access and network management. The technology requires four different architectures to work together efficiently and effectively as shown in Exhibit 1.

The applications being delivered use client/server architecture. Client/server architectures consume large amounts of bandwidth between PCs and servers. To provide a high level of quality network service, ASPs typically partner with telecommunications providers. The choice of the network platform ultimately determines the level of service that the ASP can actually deliver.

Hosted application environments require a different architecture from internally hosted environments, because the external environment cannot rely on the high bandwidth of the internal LAN. Internet connections can vary from dial-up to T1 lines. Internet connectivity directly affects the way an ASP can provide access to the hosted application.

The network platform drives the architecture choices for the computing architecture as well as the choices for hosting the application itself. The computing architecture must support the management of the software as if it resided locally. It must also support remote management of the application and desktops.

For organizations with high bandwidth, an ASP can use regular PC clients and traditional client/server software architecture to deliver the application over the high band-width, corporate connections. Users access the application via their browsers using a portal site. The ASP manages the browser application and the individual desktops.

If the network is a limiting factor, an ASP has to consider alternative computing architectures: Java applications or thin client architectures. With Java, an ASP can simplify the Web-based environment. The application is downloaded and run transparently on the user's machine. However, Java downloads work best with high bandwidth and may not perform as well as thin client/server architectures.

Thin client architectures can be used with low bandwidth, including dial-in. The application is run within the data center. Users run the application remotely with the network transporting only keystrokes and screen updates. The ASP administers and manages the desktops from the data center. Thin client architecture is also viewed as the best way to provide the level of reliability and security required by the ASPs.

SERVICE-LEVEL AGREEMENTS

As mentioned earlier, SLAs spell out the customer's expectations for service, which might range from expected response times to minimum bandwidth. Some ASPs include guarantees such as 99.9 percent uptime and disaster recovery. ASPs will add security to an already secure platform (e.g., Windows NT/2000 or .Net) to guarantee security levels.

An SLA details the day-to-day expected service. There should be means to award exceeded minimum requirements that can be offset against days that failed to meet expectations. The SLA might also include provisions for days when the ASP's servers are offline for maintenance. An SLA should also include a clause that allows the customer to terminate the contract without penalty if it receives poor service. A customer should also make sure that it can get out of the deal with whatever it needs to bring a new ASP on board — data, customized software, and the like.

Customers, should keep the contract term as short as possible — no more than three years. It is difficult to know what hosting will look like in five years. Make sure that the performance penalties truly motivate the ASP to address the organization's issues (remember, the ASP has other customers) and that penalties escalate each time the problem occurs. Establish metrics that truly measure growth. Choose two simple ones, and agree on a firm price for the service as usage grows. Furthermore, customers should not try to trade reduced service for lower monthly fees. The only way for an ASP to lower the orgnization's costs is to cut service levels. The quality of the service is key to the customer's successful use of, and therefore its derived benefit from, the ASP.

CHALLENGES AND RISKS

The ASP market is still in its infancy. In order to reach its projected revenue levels, the market has many challenges to overcome and risks to manage.

ASPs need to gain customer acceptance as well as IT acceptance. The selling focus is usually to business management — pitching a business solution or business service. The focus is on value added. The IT organization often comes into the discussions to address security and network issues. IT needs to view the ASP as an alternative, not an interloper. IT needs to become advisors, not turf protectors.

Potential customers must be convinced that their application and its data will be available to them 24×7 but yet secure from outsiders. As Internet traffic continues to grow, potential customers must also be convinced that their access will not slow down. As mobile use escalates, ASPs need to deal with the needs of employees out of the office and the security requirements mobile access demands.

How well the market grows will also depend on how well ASPs can deliver on promised service levels. Can they meet or exceed customer expectations? Since USinter-networking had its successful IPO, ASPs have been springing up seemingly overnight, fueled by venture capital money. Some will not make it. GartnerGroup estimates that of the 300 or so current ASPs, more than 80 percent will disappear before the end of 2001 because of poor service or market consolidation.

WHOSE CUSTOMER IS IT?

An interesting question that remains to be answered is Who owns the customer — the end user? Is it the software vendor of the application itself or the ASP or some combination? Software agreements might give the ASP a master license that can be leveraged across multiple customers, or might give the ASP a discounted license fee and the ability to resell the application directly to the end customer. However, as software vendors are beginning to realize the potential of the ASP market, agreements are being restructured.

The initial agreement between Siebel and USi was as a reseller. The agreement has since been restructured so that Siebel's salesforce is the main distribution point for its ASP offering. Under the new agreement, USi fulfills the back-end hosting role. Oracle decided to maintain complete control over its ASP offerings from software sale to implementation and hosting. This way, Oracle maintains full control over the customer.

The ownership issue will be an interesting one to watch. It is expected that most software vendors will enter this market by partnering with an ASP that wishes to leverage its existing data center infrastructure. Consequently, the two organizations must work together to balance customer ownership. However, if the customer's point of interface is the ASP (predictably, because the ASP is implementing and hosting the application) and not the software vendor, the ASP will have ownership tipped in its favor.

NEW PLAYERS TO WATCH

As the ASP market matures and proves itself, more players will try to join in. There will continue to be ASPs that focus solely on the ASP market. Traditional systems integrators will begin to enter the ASP market using their integration expertise as their strength. IBM Global Services and EDS have already announced that they are adding application hosting to their service portfolios. EDS has a partnership with SAP. Qwest Communications and KPMG have a joint venture named Qwest Cyber Solutions. Qwest provides the data network infrastructure, and KPMG provides nearly 500 application developers and integrators.

However, systems integrators are not noted for their ability to change gears quickly. ASPs are smaller organizations and more agile. The systems integrators are also used to long projects, not the mindset of an ASP turnkey service. The entry of systems integrators into the ASP market could be viewed as validation of the concept rather than a threat.

Web hosting companies will need to improve their professional service capabilities before they become major players in the ASP market. Many will find their way into the market by partnering with other ASPs as back-end data center providers. The same holds true for telecommunications companies. The ASP market would help them leverage their large infrastructure investments. To enter the ASP market, they will have to improve both their value-added capabilities and their service capabilities. Telecomm companies will also most likely end up as partners in the ASP marketplace.

SUMMARY

An application service provider offers organizations business solutions. The ASP delivers the service, handling all aspects of the service: the hosting environment, the network infrastructure, the data center, and the application itself. Organizations typically pay a monthly fee to use the service. Using an ASP allows an organization to reduce capital costs and implement applications in a timely fashion.

As outlined in Exhibit 2, there are many reasons why an organization should consider an ASP for its commodity applications. The prevailing economy forces organizations to focus on what they do best and hire others to do the rest. That is exactly what the ASP model allows an organization to do.

Exhibit 2.   When to Consider an ASP

- The organization is a start-up and doesn't have the capital resources to make significant IT investments
- The organization is undergoing rapid growth and needs to scale its IT infrastructure quickly.
- The organization is undergoing mergers and acquisitions and needs a flexible IT infrastructure.
- The organization can't afford a huge IT capital outlay at the time.
- The organization needs to be able to switch environments in the future.
- The organization needs to deploy applications rapidly.
- The organization is finding it difficult to attract and retain IT staff.
- IT isn't a core competency.

Certainly the trick is picking the right application and the right supplier — in this case an ASP, but isn't it always? So if you saw your own organization as you read the statements in Exhibit 2, start researching which application service providers can supply your needs. Don't wait for the competition to pass you by.

References

1. Application Hosting Market, August 2, 1999, Legg Mason Equity Research — Technology Group.
2. "Application Service Providers," http://www.stardock.net/media/asp_primer.html.
3. "ASP & Ye Shall Receive", *CIO*, May 1, 2000
4. "ASP: Market Hype or a Real Option for Your Business?" an IDC White Paper, *Computerworld*.
5. Butler, Michelle, "Supply Chain Management: Eliminating the Weak Links," June 5, 2000, http://www.aspstreet.com/archive/ditaf/w,s/id, 969.
6. Carter, Todd, "Beginner's Guide to ASP: SLA," May 23, 2000, http://www.aspstreet.com/resources/archive/default.taf/what,show/id,865.
7. "How ASPs Deliver Value: Next Generation Portals for Business Applications," May 3, 1999, http://www.trginternational.com/HTML/giotto.htm.
8. McPherson, Amanda, "Application Service Providers — A New Software Distribution Model," May 13, 1999, http://www.greatconnect.com/transform/projframes_s99.htm. amcpherson_project.html.
9. "Monster in a Box?" *CIO*, May 1, 2000.
10. Rutherford, Emelie, ASP Primer, *CIO*, http://www.cio.com/forums/asp/.
11. Seymour, Jim, "How Application Service Providers Will Change Your Life," http://www.thestreet.com/comment/techsavy/759956.html.
12. The Internet-Based ASP Marketplace, Deloitte Consulting and Deloitte & Touche.
13. Wainewright, Phil, "ASP Insider: An Application Service Primer," ASPnews.com, http://www.aspnews.com/news/article/0,,4191_373981,00.html.

Chapter 39
Host Integration Servers

Lisa M. Lindgren

Research firms and experts estimate that approximately 70 percent of mission-critical data still reside on "legacy" computing systems today. By legacy system, the experts are referring to traditional data processing platforms typically found in data centers and maintained, around the clock, by IT staff. These systems are IBM-style mainframes, IBM midrange systems, and other platforms sold by a variety of vendors (DEC (now part of Compaq), HP, Bull, Unisys, etc.) that support mission-critical applications.

One of the outcomes of the client/server computing revolution was going to be the elimination of these expensive, proprietary, dated platforms by a new generation of low-cost servers based on industry standards or *de facto* standards. Client/server never achieved this lofty promise. In large part, this failure was due to the lack of a solid business case for porting the legacy applications to new platforms. The legacy platforms provided fault tolerance and 24×7 operation that were unavailable on new servers. In addition, the cost of the legacy platforms began to fall and the platforms became much more adept at supporting the new open technologies. The cost of the IBM mainframe in terms of dollar per MIP, for example, has fallen drastically in the past decade, and the standard mainframe operating system now includes support for TCP/IP as a no-charge feature.

The applications and the data that still reside on the legacy platforms are truly the lifeblood of many enterprises. This is where customer records, billing, manufacturing resource planning, and other critical systems are located. The major issue facing IT organizations today is tapping that data and those applications to build new E-commerce capabilities that allow more efficient communication with their trading partners and end customers.

0-8493-1149-7/02/$0.00+$1.50
© 2002 by CRC Press LLC

Many legacy applications are built on a character-based interface that assumes that an end user is communicating to it through a display terminal or software emulating a display terminal. In these applications, the business logic is intertwined and interconnected with the user interface. One cannot access the data that is a part of the application (e.g., the customer billing data) without stepping through the transaction-oriented terminal interface. Some legacy applications, however, are batch or programmatic rather than transaction based. The applications are program-to-program, with an "intelligent" client or server communicating with the legacy host. A prime example of this type of interaction is a middle-tier relational database server that supports a newer, client/server-based program that queries data from a legacy mainframe database. Some large enterprises will have a wide variety of different types of legacy applications, each with its own unique interface.

A host integration server is a relatively new category of products that will allow organizations building a Web-to-host environment to easily tap a variety of types of legacy applications without requiring any change to the legacy applications. It differs from other types of Web-to-host solutions in that it is a server-centric solution that is focused on integrating host data into Web-style applications, rather than providing a general-purpose platform and toolkit for Web application development and deployment.

THIN CLIENTS VERSUS SERVER-CENTRIC SOLUTIONS

The Web-to-host market began in 1996 with a few products that were geared to provide access from a Web browser to an IBM mainframe. Early on, there were two camps as to how that access should be provided and, therefore, two very different types of products. The two basic product types were thin-client emulator applets and server-centric Web-to-host gateways.

Before Web-to-host solutions, users who wanted to access legacy applications usually installed special-purpose terminal emulation software on their desktop PCs. As the name implies, this software emulates the functions of a fixed-function display terminal that provides character-based access to transactional applications on legacy systems. Like so many other PC applications, the emulator software grew in size over time, and enterprise IT staffs spend a lot of money and effort performing the desktop software distribution and maintenance tasks for these emulators.

The thin-client approach to Web-to-host access is based on the premise that these traditional "fat-client" emulators can be replaced with thinner equivalents. Java and ActiveX, Web-oriented technologies that allow for the dynamic download of client software, were the key to eliminating the software distribution and maintenance tasks associated with traditional client-based software. Initially, the thin-client Web-to-host products simply replaced the functions of the fat-client emulator and continued to provide the same, "green-on-black" user interface common to the emulator environment. Over time, however, thin-client Web-to-host products have grown in sophistication. Now, many leading solutions provide one or more means of rejuvenating the user interface so that thin-client solutions can provide users with a more pleasing Web-style interface. The commonality of the thin-client solutions is that an applet is downloaded from a Web server to the client. It is the applet that contains the logic that allows the client to connect to and establish a session with the host.

The second camp for early Web-to-host solutions was established based on the premise that the client software should have a "zero footprint." In other words, all host access processing should be performed on a middle-tier "gateway" server, and the client should only be required to have a standard Web browser. The communication between the client and this host access server is performed only with standard HTML. It is the server that is responsible for containing the logic to connect to and establish a session with the host. Early forms of server-centric products were 3270-to-HTML converters. This class of server-centric product provides on-the-fly conversion between the standard data stream utilized by IBM mainframes (the 3270 data stream) and HTML. The host and the application are not changed, and the client simply needs a browser. Because the 3270 data stream is converted to HTML, there is automatically some level of rejuvenation of the user interface inherent in these products, even if that rejuvenation simply provides a pleasing background, radio buttons for PF key assignments, or other simple enhancements of the user interface.

Initially, the vendors providing these different solutions each claimed that their approaches were suitable for two very different types of audiences:

1. *Intranet/extranet users:* These users are the traditional users of terminal emulator fat-client software. They typically require regular access to one or more legacy applications, perhaps as a major part of their job. Internal to the organization, these may be data entry or customer service representatives who need to access customer records, billing applications, etc. Extranet users may be dealers or distributors who need access to order entry and order status information. To these users, Web-to-host solutions are a *replacement* for their current host access solution.

2. *Internet users:* These are users who have never before seen or interacted directly with the legacy applications. Examples include consumers doing home banking, Internet-based shopping, and package tracking. Business-to-business examples might include insurance agents who used to have to call an insurance company's call center, but now gain direct pricing and policy information over the Internet.

> Web-to-host solutions provide an *extension* of the traditional legacy host access user base.

However, the needs of these very different user bases are quite different, as is the way in which they access legacy systems. Intranet/extranet users often requires many of the features and functions of the traditional emulator because they have built up training, scripts, and tools over the years to accomplish the host access task more efficiently. These users typically have a need to communicate more consistently with the host throughout the workday. And for some of these users (e.g., data entry workers), rejuvenating the application will only impede productivity rather than enhance it. Internet-based users, on the other hand, typically only require a simple, single transaction with the host application. These users do not want to learn how to navigate the legacy application, and therefore rejuvenation of the user interface is a must. These users also count speed and responsiveness as key requirements. Therefore, the time to download even a thin-client applet may diminish the appeal of an applet-based solution.

Because of these differences, the market has more or less naturally segmented itself by user base. The thin-client solutions are more appropriate to the fat-client replacement market, while server-centric solutions are better suited to the extension market, in which new users access the host application. Many vendors now accept and embrace this market segmentation, and currently offer a family of products that includes both thin-client solutions and server-centric solutions. The balance of this chapter focuses on server-centric solutions in general and, more specifically, focuses on the class of server-centric solutions known as host integration servers.

HOST INTEGRATION SERVERS

A host integration server is a server-centric Web-to-host integration solution that has the following characteristics:

- It runs on either a middle-tier server or the destination host server and may support one or more different server operating systems, including perhaps NT, UNIX, NetWare, OS/390, OS/400, or Linux.
- It supports "zero-footprint" clients, sending standard HTML (and perhaps XML) to the clients.
- It communicates upstream with a variety of legacy host applications through a variety or transaction, batch, and programmatic interfaces (e.g., 3270 data stream, 5250 data stream, VT, ODBC/JDBC, MQSeries, CICS API(s)).

- It includes the means to utilize a visual development tool to easily integrate the host data and applications into new Web pages; it may or may not provide on-the-fly conversion for host data streams.
- It may include security, scalability, and fault tolerance features such as SSL, load balancing, and hot server standby.
- It interoperates with Web servers and possibly with new application servers.

By this definition, 3270-to-HTML conversion products are very basic host integration servers that only support a single type of host application interface — the 3270 data stream (which, granted, has the largest installed base and therefore the largest target market). The 3270-to-HTML converter products almost always provide an on-the-fly conversion capability, allowing these products to be installed and up and running with no programming, scripting, or customization.

Modern host integration servers offer much more capability than basic 3270-to-HTML converters. One obvious and apparent difference is in the support for different types of host applications and different data sources. With a host integration server, one can build Web pages that integrate data from a variety of different legacy host applications. For example, a home banking Web page may include the customer's name and address from a mainframe CICS application, current account activity from a Sybase database located on a Tandem system, and special promotions that the customer can take advantage of from an AS/400 back-office system. In contrast, a 3270-to-HTML converter can only communicate with mainframe applications that support the 3270 data stream.

Another difference between the early 3270-to-HTML products and true host integration servers is in the assumed amount of scripting and customization. Modern host integration servers presume that the new user interface will not simply be a one-to-one correlation between the host screen and HTML-based Web page. Therefore, host integration servers are focused on providing customization studios (or interfaces to standard customization studios) that allow programmers to easily design brand-new Web-style interfaces that incorporate host data. On the other hand, 3270-to-HTML products are geared to providing quick and easy access to host applications with some level of rejuvenation. The on-the-fly conversion capability is usually counted on to do the majority of the user interface rejuvenation. Most 3270-to-HTML converters also support some level of scripting or programming to allow more sophisticated rejuvenation, but the simplicity of the on-the-fly conversion is the real selling point of these products.

So, with its sophisticated user interface redesign capabilities, how does a host integration server compare to a new application server? Application servers have many of the characteristics listed above for host integration servers. The major differences between the two is that the application server:

- Is targeted to the development of new business logic rather than the access of existing legacy business logic
- Is built upon an object-oriented base, supporting some combination of CORBA, Enterprise JavaBeans, or Microsoft's DCOM
- Contains connectors to legacy data and applications, but the list may not be as complete as those provided with host integration servers

An application server (or Web application server) is a platform for the development of new applications. Therefore, host integration servers and application servers are complementary products rather than competing products, particularly if they can communicate and share data. For example, a host integration server may create objects containing legacy application access that can be utilized by an application server.

Host integration servers are the new generation of server-centric products that are focused on integrating the wide variety of legacy applications with the new Web environment. Exhibit 1 offers a list of some commercially available host integration servers, along with some of the salient points about the product.

A GOOD FIT FOR HOST INTEGRATION SERVERS

With the plethora of different types of solutions available for providing legacy host system access from Web browsers, it is important for enterprise IT staffs to select only those solutions most appropriate to their specific environments. Host integration servers are a relatively new category of product that can solve some specific needs better than other types of solutions. An enterprise organization that has most or all of the following characteristics should evaluate host integration servers:

- The organization needs to extend current legacy host access to new users who have no experience with the legacy systems.
- The IT department cannot control or dictate the level of browser or type of operating system that the user is running.
- Users need to access data and applications from a variety of different types of host systems.
- It is desirable to redesign the way in which users interact with the legacy host, so there is no longer a one-to-one correlation between host screen and Web page.
- The organization will move to application servers for new business logic in the future, but are not yet ready to deploy this object-oriented framework.
- Fault tolerance, security, and scalability are important factors.

Exhibit 1. Host Integration Servers

Vendor	Product Name	Key Points
IBM	Host Publisher	Written in Java and supported on NT, UNIX OS/390; comes bundled with IBM WebSphere (Web application server platform); multiple legacy data sources (3270, 5250, VT, Java, databases); includes SSL and DES for security and load balancing and hot standby with Network Dispatcher; includes Host Publisher Studio for user interface design
epicRealm (InfoSpinner)	ForeSite Application Server (now offering Content Delivery service)	NT-based solution; co-resides with Web server and interfaces via CGI, NSAPI, ISAPI; supports a variety of data sources (3270, 5250, DB2, ODBC, Java, ActiveX); includes Integrator component, which allows development of HTML templates for user interface design
Microsoft	"Babylon" Integration Server	Windows 2000 only; follow-on to Microsoft SNA Server gateway; based on Microsoft's COM/DCOM object model; supports a variety of IBM mainframe and AS/400 sources as well as UNIX and NetWare
WRQ	Verastream Host Integrator 4.0 (formerly Apptrieve)	NT, solaris, IBM AIX and Linux support; supports host systems (3270, 5250, HP 700/92 and VT 52, VT 100, VT 200 and VT 400); terminal-oriented and database (JDBC) legacy applications; supports Enterprise Java Beans, Java Native Interface, XML and CORBA adapters for VisiBroker on Unix platforms; design tools builds an object that represents how the host data is accessed; standard integrated development environment tools that integrate these objects

An organization whose users are mostly internal users or business partners who are already familiar with the legacy systems may actually find that thin-client solutions are a better fit than host integration solutions, because the thin-client applets are a more complete replacement for their existing desktops. An organization that is more interested in deploying new business logic, with some integration of legacy host data, may find that a full-blown application server (many of which include connectors for legacy data) should be the first step. However, the relatively large number of organizations that fit the characteristics described above are ripe for a host integration server solution.

CONCLUSION

Research indicates that 70 percent of the mission-critical data still resides on legacy host systems. However, the applications that reside on these systems are varied. Early Web-to-host solutions focused on supporting certain types of hosts and certain types of application interfaces. Early solutions also tried to meet the needs of both "expert" host system users and a new population of casual users.

The host integration server is a new category of server-centric solution that excels at allowing IT organizations to build a new interface into a broad base of existing legacy applications. This category of product is a natural fit for organizations that need to extend the vast data locked up in their varied, mission-critical legacy systems to a new population of end users. The host integration server is also a complementary solution to the full-blown application server, which is the modern platform for the development and deployment of new business logic based on object-oriented models.

Chapter 40
ERP Packages: What's Next?

Conghua Li

In the past decade, companies from all around the world have spent tens of billions of dollars in licensing, customizing, installing, maintaining, and upgrading enterprise resource planning systems. These systems have been applied in all conceivable industries, from banks and insurance companies to airlines and telecommunication companies, from manufacturing and utility companies to retail and hotel chains, from health care organizations and media companies to universities and government organizations, etc.

ERP packages, including those from SAP AG, PeopleSoft, Oracle, and Baan, have made a tremendous contribution to the world of business. They have made a wide range of businesses more efficient by providing them with much information they need. This information includes sales figures, financial results, information on the customer/client of the company, information on the suppliers of the company, inventory levels, distribution flow, production volumes, procurement volumes, and much more. This information gives businesses worldwide a clear overview and detailed understanding about their current performances almost any time and anywhere. This information enables the management at all levels, from CEO to the lowest operational units, to make business and operational decisions efficiently and effectively.

However, this information is limited only to "internal information." It does not cover "the other half" of most businesses. It does not include information about the market, the competitors, the industry, the clients of the segment, the customers of the segment, and the distribution channels, for example. Is this information not important to the success of a business? The answer is clearly, "Yes, it is critical!" Why is it not included in the scope of the existing ERP/data warehousing initiative that has cost companies around the world tens, if not hundreds, of billions of dollars to date? Because, historically, it has always been this way.

The past decade has been an area of process reengineering. Emphasis has been on the internal efficiency and effectiveness of a business. As a result, the ERP wave caught the interest and attention of businesses worldwide. CIOs have been required to play a key role in improving the internal efficiency. On the other hand, the millennium was rapidly approaching. The information systems developed in the early days could not survive without significant restructuring and debugging.

But now that most of the businesses in the advanced world have already implemented ERP systems, or are at least in the process of implementing one, the question inevitably turns to "What is next?"

WHAT IS NEXT?

The "next" will need to be "external focus." It will be IT functions taking on the role of a Corporate Antenna. The intrinsic characteristic of doing business is like conducting warfare. In military operations, information technology has been applied not only to facilitate the internal communication and control but also, more important, to gather and process external information — like the antenna of an army. No army can win any battle or war if its information system is applied only to internal efficiency, e.g., to accurately indicate how much ammunition is available or how fast its troops can move. To win any battle or war, the army must accurately and timely understand the move of its opponents, the environment of the battle field, and many other categories of external information.

Unfortunately, in the corporate world, IT has been mainly applied only for internal data gathering and processing. Due to the development of technologies, including information technology and the changing order of the global economy, today's industry and market is changing at an unparalleled rate of high speed. This requires businesses to continually monitor and make decisions against the changes in the industry and the marketplace. Historical approaches to strategic planning, which took place once every year or every couple of years, are dead. To enable businesses to compete effectively in the future, the interests and attention of CIOs of businesses around the globe will need and will be forced to shift from an internal focus to an external focus. The "next" may be called Total Information Solutions (TISs) or External Information Management (EIM).

Today's businesses need to understand, monitor, process, and apply information on their industry, their competitors, their customers, and a large amount of other information on an ongoing basis. The era is long gone in which strategic adjustments were done once every one to five years only by the senior management, and external information is collected, analyzed, and kept only by some strategists and senior management members.

The rise and fall of great companies is now proceeding at an unprecedented rate in corporate history. These ups and downs have hardly been due to how well companies have managed their internal information. Instead they are mostly due to how well they have managed and reacted to the changes in their external conditions. No effort purely focused on internal efficiency can save an organization; the efforts to adapt to external conditions can. Peter Drucker, a father of modern management, recently said: "The forces that most influence organizations come from outside the organization, not from within." Today's businesses have to collect, process, and apply the external information on the fly. Otherwise, a great business will go down in no time.

As a result, today's business management is like flying a jet fighter. The jet fighter, with its complex internal operations controlled by its sophisticated systems, needs to actively search, collect, and process external conditions and information on the flight. In fact, the information that is shown on the instrument panel about the external conditions is so important that pilots need to operate based only on what their instruments tell them instead of what their intuition or feeling tell them. Although managing a business is not exactly flying a jet fighter, the importance of collecting, processing, and using external information has increased to a level of no previous comparison.

In the past, many companies made significant efforts in developing customer and supplier databases, but the companies were mainly focused on their direct customers and suppliers. Although these databases have contributed considerably, they limited those companies to a tunnel vision of their external interfaces.

The TISs will enable businesses to systematically monitor and collect data about broadly ranged external business conditions, integrate the external data with the internal data, and build or extract business intelligence for all adequate levels of management of a business.

The external data will cover, but will not be limited to, such data as the following:

- Consumer or customer trends of the target markets and their relevant segments
  - their changing preferences
  - their changing demand
  - their changing composition
  - their changing distribution

- Trends of the relevant industries
  - technology adaptation — "The technologies likely to have the greatest impact on a company and its industry are technologies outside of its own field."
  - industry economics
  - best practices
  - changing landscape of supply and distribution systems and mechanisms
- Competitors
  - key competitors
  - their market position
  - their competitive approaches
  - their competitive results
- Competitive product or services
  - product or service innovations
  - the benefit of these innovations to the customers
  - their competitive positions
  - the potential threat of these innovations to the company

Traditionally this information was collected and processed by such corporate functions as strategic planning and marketing. By providing ongoing data collection and processing, the contribution and involvement of IT will bring a revolution to the ways in which external data is collected and processed as well as to the ways in which business decision-making processes are organized.

WHO NEEDS THE EXTERNAL INFORMATION?

As in a military operation, almost every one in the army will need to access information and intelligence about the external conditions. In the past many companies prospered with only a small group of elite having access to some fragmented and discontinued external information, but businesses of the future will wonder how they can even conduct the most basic tasks without understanding the external context.

Although almost everyone in any business entity in the future will need to access external information and intelligence on an ongoing basis, the following are some of the most critical areas of people who need to have efficient and effective access to this information and intelligence:

- Strategy management
- Product development
- Product management
- Marketing
- Advertising
- Public relations
- Branding

- Distribution
- Sales
- Customer services

The wide range of people who need the external information will pose a great challenge to the data integration, distribution, and intelligence extraction. Covering external data will be far more challenging than covering internal data. TIS may well make "intelligent enterprise" come true, but of course, "intelligent enterprise" decisions will still be made by human beings instead of computers.

For IT to take on some major responsibilities of collecting, processing, and distributing external information, it should not undermine the importance of corporate planning function. In fact, it is to reinforce the effectiveness of this function by providing a corporate antenna — the ongoing data collection, processing, and distribution.

WHAT ARE THE CRITICAL ISSUES IN DEVELOPING CORPORATE ANTENNA?

The critical issues of dealing with external data will focus on the following key areas:

- What data to collect
- Where and how to collect the data
- How to process the data
- To whom and how to distribute the data
- What are the organizational or process implications

What Data to Collect

The first and foremost critical issue will be identifying the relevant data that is needed by the enterprise. This will be determined by the industry and the company. All information necessary to "fly the jet fighter" will need to be collected. Of course, 20 percent of information will fulfill 80 percent of the need. The key will be to identify the 20 percent of relevant information, particularly in today's environment of over supply of information.

It is vital to understand that IT is not to completely take over the role of collecting external data from the functions that have traditionally borne the responsibilities, such as planning, marketing, etc. IT will focus on the data that can be effectively collected on an ongoing basis.

Where and How to Collect

Companies need to identify suitable sources and determine effective ways to collect the key information. There will be many sources possible for data collection, such as the following:

- Employees
- Customers
- Distributors
- Suppliers
- Strategic partners such as among Star Airline members
- Business information reporters such as Bloomberg, Reuters, Dow Jones
- Online information providers such as Yahoo Finance, E-Trade
- Business analyses from banks, brokerage houses, stock exchanges
- Business studies from associations, government organizations, and research institutes

While in most areas of today's business world team effort and partnerships are highly developed, the area of external information collection and processing team work and partnership approaches are still in the dark age. Team efforts and partnerships will be the keys for effectively establishing corporate antenna functions in the future.

It is also important to realize that collection and process of external data must be continuous and systematic. A jet fighter cannot fly without continuous collection of external data. Any interval in external monitoring may lead to a catastrophe. Only structured data can be effectively integrated with the relevant internal data. And only effective integration of internal and external data can generate business intelligence that an enterprise needs to survive and grow.

How to Process?

Integration of external and internal data will be the key. While an over-supply of data and information exists, a short supply of intelligence persists in today's business world. It is critical to extract intelligence out of the combination of the external and internal data. The speed of processing needs to be high. Results need to be clear. Intelligence needs to be effective. It will not fulfill the mission to simply put information on an intranet. The Internet phenomenon, in which people get billions of bits of data but can hardly find a relevant one, must be avoided.

As with data collection, the processing must be on an ongoing basis. Purpose-oriented processing needs to be emphasized. Miles Au Yeung, an IT expert with Deloitte Consulting, pointed out "Despite some companies collecting external data today, they cannot turn data in real time into decision-making support. External data is not fed into operational systems for real-time adjustments. It still involves a lot of human effort in separating noise from useful data and processing the data into information."

Whom and How to Distribute?

It will be a significant challenge to determine what information will be accessible by whom and how intelligence will be extracted. Virtually every department, operational unit, and individual will need to extract intelligence from a wide range of information. The scope will be far larger than the context of the internal information. Also, the intelligence to be extracted will be far broader than the intelligence that has been extracted from the internal data only. But this will be the price a business will have to pay if it wants to survive in the next millennium.

Data distribution will be increasingly important. Only with effective data distribution can business intelligence be effectively extracted where and when it is needed.

What Are the Organizational or Process Implications?

In today's knowledge economy, information processes drive the organizational structure. As the ways in which external information is collected and processed and, as the ways in which business decision making shift, the organizational structures will be forced to change. This may well represent a new wave of worldwide corporate restructuring. This restructuring will go far beyond the simple change of IT organizational structures. It will cover most of the entire corporate organizations.

The change will be big. Challenges will be daunting. However, companies will have no other choice than to go through it, as this process will select the future winners and determine the future losers.

WHAT WILL BE THE ROLE OF CIOS?

Although CIOs will need and will be forced to shift their interests, attentions, and roles, the process will not be smooth.

CIOs will not only need to be more business oriented in their future approach, but they will also need to help the company transit to new ways of doing business. They will need to assist the next wave of process reengineering and corporate restructuring. This wave of process reengineering and corporate restructuring will be focusing on building "intelligent enterprises." Like any other significant change that happened in the corporate history before, tremendous resistance will occur.

Are today's CIOs prepared to take on these challenges? How much do they understand about strategic positioning? How much do they understand about business processes? How much do they understand about corporate organizational structures? How much do they understand about change management?

What do they need to do if they are not yet equipped with the capabilities to take on these future challenges? Time will be of the essence. The challenges are already approaching. CIOs do not have much time left to get ready.

While accountants' and chief financial officers' roles have matured, the true role of CIOs is just about to be born.

CONCLUSION

With the burden of the year 2000, ERP, and data warehousing out of the way, and with the new landscape of global competition, companies will have the resources and will be forced to start to deal with external information processing issues. "Growth and survival both now depend on getting the organization in touch with the outside world," warned Peter Drucker. What is after ERP will be external data focused. It might be TIS, EIM, or any other fancy term.

The corporate world has been talking about strategic IT for a long time. Now IT is going to put a conclusion on the strategic importance of IT for the first time in history by developing Corporate Antenna, transforming decision-making processes and, hence, establishing Intelligent Enterprises.

Chapter 41
Enhancing Manufacturing Performance with ERP Systems

Rajagopal Palaniswamy
Tyler Frank

The current dynamic global business environment, which is characterized by customer-driven markets, shorter product life cycles, and narrow niches, requires the manufacturing function to play an active role in an organization in coordination with other functional units for the organization as a whole to gain competitive benefits. Recent increases in international competition are awakening U.S. manufacturing companies to realize the need to use manufacturing as a competitive weapon and to enhance manufacturing performance. One of the tools to enhance manufacturing performance is advanced information technologies (IT) implementation.

Manufacturing processes are changing, becoming intellectually stimulating and challenging rather than physically exhausting. The various advanced technologies used in manufacturing, collectively known as advanced manufacturing technology (AMT), would not have been possible without rapid applications of IT. These computer-based AMTs allow firms to produce a variety of parts and end products of even small volumes by changing the software instead of replacing the hardware.

As much as technology has enabled improvements in manufacturing, such as higher productivity, it has also made the process of manufacturing highly complex because of the many different computer software systems used within manufacturing and in other functions. Within local manufacturing facilities, there are discrepancies encountered in fully integrating the automated equipment. Without integration, a plant may have various "islands of automation," and such isolation results in lack of integration and coordination, preventing firms from utilizing the full potential of technology and equipment. Under such circumstances, the investments made in automation may not be fully justified (Vonderembse et al., 1996 and Oliff et al., 1996).

Beatty and Gordon (1988) in discussing the barriers to implementing CAD/CAM systems mention that one of the barriers to the implementation of these AMTs is incompatible systems. Computers in the manufacturing division use different software packages that are incompatible; hence, communication among the systems is not possible. They mention that much time and effort are wasted in reentering the same data many times, data that could have been transferred automatically had the systems been compatible. Beatty (1992) contends that the final aim of factory automation is to integrate the entire database, including CAD, CAM, and bill of materials (BOM).

At the global level, the effort required to integrate the various production facilities is higher, owing to differences in technology in various countries. Many manufacturers depend on technology to assist in their efforts to cope with the increasing demands for product innovation, faster delivery, and better quality. As a result, production and manufacturing operations have become more complex, automated, and geographically dispersed in recent years (Gillenwater et al., 1995). Such geographical dispersion and related complexities need better planning to coordinate and control. Decision making involves different time horizons and different geographical dispersions. Sometimes, decisions must be made concurrently, involving different facilities from different geographical locations from both local and foreign sites. For example, to meet customer demands in an Asian country, production capacity at an Australian subsidiary may have to be increased, which may depend on receiving materials supplied from countries in Europe or Canada. Sometimes, there may be machine breakdowns or other such major incidents that may stop or reduce production capacity in one facility and, in order to fulfill customer demand, production capacity in another facility in another location may need to be changed. Such changes in plan may require quick changes in decisions regarding materials flow, logistics, and production schedule that will affect the global production network of a firm. If the manufacturing systems are not well integrated, much time and effort will be wasted in obtaining information and there will not be an optimum performance.

To overcome problems associated with incompatible and nonuniform systems in an organization, especially in the manufacturing function, many companies have been implementing enterprise resource planning (ERP) systems in recent years. The ERP systems, by providing end-to-end connectivity, have enabled these companies to enhance their manufacturing performance.

Based on case analysis carried out in five manufacturing firms located in Ohio, Michigan, Wisconsin, and Illinois, this study aims to understand and explain the enhanced manufacturing performance due to ERP implementation and explain how ERP implementation has enabled organizations overcome the problems associated with using disparate systems.

PROBLEMS WITH DISPARATE SYSTEMS OR ANTECEDENTS FOR AN INTEGRATED SYSTEM

Rockart and Short (1994) mention that in the current global economy, in order to capture global levels of manufacturing efficiency, to innovate for global markets, and to understand international marketing and world markets, a firm requires increased knowledge and coordination of the firm's operations throughout the geographically dispersed subunits. But integration and coordination of information technology across the national and cultural borders is not an easy task because of many inherent problems pertaining to the technological differences and other issues in various countries. Kerr (1988) reports about the "islands of automation" with reference to various individual units and their respective headquarters, each having a different platform of information systems. A standard of protocol and platforms would alleviate such problems and enable the smooth transfer of data among various units. Gullo (1988), based on interviews with executives from RJR Nabisco, stresses that even if a company's businesses are not centralized, the IS department needs to move to a view of data that is as global as possible to attain competitive advantage. Nearly half of the 75,000-person workforce of RJR Nabisco work outside the United States. If various units use different types of computer hardware and software systems, managers will have only a partial view of data and net information gain will be less. With such lack of accurate information, the decision-making process will not gain significantly from the tremendous investments made in building the information technology.

Alavi and Keen (1991) mention that the higher the communication and interaction among the various team members, the higher will be the performance of the team. In carrying out a project, the members of the product design team should communicate and coordinate with the product engineers, process engineers, and the marketing professionals as well as the suppliers. At a global level, integrated information technology can enable them to interact and make appropriate decisions in bringing out products to various countries; thus, such integrated IT becomes a critical success factor.

If a company uses different kinds of computers in different countries, transmitting information among these disparate systems often requires expensive interfaces, and most of the time, organizational members waste time and effort in duplication of data entry. In addition, as the organization grows and expands, the number of different computer hardware and software systems increases exponentially. Since the 1980s, the business environment has seen many mergers and acquisitions, and such activities have given rise to fragmented information systems within an organization. Rockart and Short (1994) define time to market as the firm's ability to develop new products quickly and to deliver existing products effectively. These authors contend that reducing the time to market necessitates increasing coordination among various functional units in an organization, such as design, engineering, manufacturing, purchasing, distribution, and service. As organizations reorganize to work as teams in charge of projects rather than as individual functional units, information must be disseminated across the entire organization, making sure that each individual unit or division is able to capture the information needed and is able to provide that information to the others in the organization who need it. The various database types must be able to communicate with one another so that there is no redundancy in information retrieval and manipulation.

Gumaer (1996) quotes Rybeck, president of Benchmarking Partners Group (now Surgency) from Massachusetts: "In the present customer driven markets, manufacturers must be able to continuously revise their schedules based upon unplanned events. To accomplish this, their process and data models, information systems and communication infrastructure must operate seamlessly in real time." To bring about such compatibility among the systems, firms are implementing integrated systems that ensure smooth data flow. Such integrated systems, collectively known as enterprise resource planning (ERP) systems, are enabling organizations to enhance their performance, manufacturing performance in particular.

ENTERPRISE RESOURCE PLANNING SYSTEMS — AN IT INNOVATION TO INTEGRATE DISPARATE SYSTEMS

Davenport and Short (1991) explained how business processes were developed before modern computers and communications even existed; whenever technology was applied in the organizations, it was to automate or to just speed up the isolated components of the existing process. Such IT application enabled organizations to achieve higher productivity, but it did not give them sustainable competitive advantage of any kind. There were "islands of fragmented automation," which did not allow the organization as a whole to perform better. The emergence of ERP systems has been changing this situation by providing a mechanism for the organizations to achieve "end-to-end connectivity," thus making the various computer systems compatible with one another.

An enterprise resource planning (ERP) system is an enterprisewide management system made possible by information technology. Organizations have been implementing ERP packages for integrating the business processes in various functions. ERP has been helping companies to automate their entire business processes within the organization as a whole instead of just in some functional units. From the shop-floor activities to performance monitoring in the headquarters, a seamless integration has been achieved through ERP implementation, which makes the various computer hardware and software platforms compatible with one another. Through their case analysis, the authors found that ERP systems help organizations to reduce cycle time, reduce inventories, and share information seamlessly across the organization. Companies that have implemented ERP have made improvements in cross-functional coordination and business performance at various levels.

ERP software is the backbone of the manufacturing systems for production scheduling, materials management, and logistics planning (Saccomano, 1998). Sales of ERP systems were expected to be around $20 billion by year 2001 and to reach around $1 trillion by 2010 (Bingi, 1999). Such demand is due to the following features of ERP (Saccomano, 1998):

- Less emphasis on functional silos
- Emergence of a new class of user and a new meaning of decision support
- Real-time integration of transactional, analytical, and knowledge-based applications
- New paradigms for business simulation and optimization
- Increased importance of knowledge and computer-based applications that connect directly to the customer.

EVOLUTION OF ERP SYSTEMS

ERP evolved from the famous material requirements planning (MRP) systems. The MRP systems evolved into Manufacturing Resource Planning (MRP II) by incorporating a few important aspects of business. MRP II is a sequential technique that is used for converting the master production schedule (MPS) of the end products into a detailed schedule for raw materials and components. It starts with sales and operation planning and demand management and ends with a detailed schedule for components to be made in-house as well as purchased from vendors. MRP II is a tool for planning the engineering, operational, and financial resources of an organization. The vital part of MRP II is the MRP system; around this MRP system other resources are planned and controlled. MRP II deals with sales, production, inventory, schedules, and cash flows, which are the fundamentals of planning and controlling the manufacturing or distribution process.

MRP II systems are the predecessors of today's ERP systems and generally include fewer enterprisewide functions than ERP packages. MRP II systems often run on proprietary midrange platforms. The ERP system is an advanced IT that overcomes the limitations of the MRP II; in other words, ERP systems are capable of integrating the data from all of the functional units, thus improving manufacturing performance. The marketplace has been changing continuously during the past decade. An integrated system such as ERP is necessary given current market conditions because customers, having more choices, are becoming more demanding and product life cycles have become shorter. New technologies are changing the way organizations are organized and business processes are designed. A manufacturing planning and control system such as MRP II is becoming less relevant in today's context because of the following important changes:

- Manufacturing is moving toward a "make-to-order" environment rather than a "make-to-stock" environment. The various products sold are customized rather than standardized thus making the planning process complex.
- Quality and cost have become qualifiers or minimum requirements for the firms who wish to compete in the marketplace. Competition is now based on delivery, lead times, flexibility, greater integration with the customers and suppliers, and higher levels of product differentiation.

Gumaer (1996) has written about MRP II and how ERP has overcome the drawbacks of the MRP II systems. MRP systems focus only on the materials requirements using an infinite capacity-planning model, and these are not in real time. In the current market environment, there is a need to plan and direct manufacturing processes in real time, taking into account various environmental and organizational issues that affect the business and the process of manufacturing. The MRP II systems overcame only some of the drawbacks of the original MRP systems through applying Finite Capacity scheduling and manufacturing execution systems (MES), and the ERP systems have overcome the drawbacks of the MRP II systems by providing an organizationwide integration.

The ERP applications encompass the philosophy of MES and, at the same time, provide organizationwide information that touches all of the functions. In other words, ERP systems affect everything in an organization from order capturing to accounting and procurement to warehousing. Such systems are especially useful when an organization has discrete manufacturing environments and there is a need to plan, coordinate, and manage these facilities to achieve optimal sourcing and production (Laughlin, 1999).

Laughlin also mentions that as companies integrate business units through consolidation, shared services, or global operations, their information technology's ability to support these changes is often stretched, but because of the ERP applications' broad functionality, a company typically can replace much of its legacy systems (*Omnibus Lexicon* defines "legacy systems" as technically obsolescent components of the infrastructure) systems, thus providing better support for these new business structures and strategies.

Davenport (1998) states that an organization collects, generates, and stores vast amounts of data and these data are spread across the entire organization stored in dozens or even hundreds of different computer systems, and each of these systems is housed in various offices, factories, or divisions. Each of these is based on legacy mainframe systems and may provide automation and enable a particular functional unit to perform more efficiently, but in combination, these individual units only impede an organization's ability to grow and expand. Dhar and Stein (1998) discuss the benefits of integrating various computer hardware and software systems in order to bring out the latent information hidden in various functions of the organization. Davenport (1998) explains that if the company's sales and ordering systems cannot talk with its production scheduling systems, then its manufacturing productivity and customer responsiveness will suffer. Similarly, if the sales and marketing systems are incompatible with the financial reporting systems, then management is left to make important decisions by instinct rather than according to a detailed understanding of product and customer profitability.

At Owens Corning, a leading manufacturer of fiberglass-based housing materials and composites where the authors conducted their case study, there were about 200 different systems running on the legacy systems, and all of these were working in isolation from one another. Such a fragmented IT infrastructure impeded the organization in its growth and expansion. The IT structure it had prior to ERP implementation did not fit its business strategy — that is, it would not enable the company to realize the vision of its CEO.

Eastman Kodak Company is another example of IT architecture characterized by multiple fragmented information systems. There were 2,600 different software applications, more than 4,000 system interfaces, and about 100 different programming languages, and they all ran on aging mainframe-based computers before the company switched to an enterprise resource planning system (Stevens, 1997). During the business process reengineering, Kodak found that information systems presented not just an opportunity but also an obstacle if not designed properly. In the words of Davenport (1998) "if the systems are fragmented in an organization then the business is fragmented." When the business is fragmented, an organization is unable to achieve success in the marketplace.

RESEARCH METHODOLOGY

In order to understand the enhanced manufacturing performance of an ERP system and its potential to overcome the drawbacks of fragmented systems, the authors carried out a case analysis in five manufacturing firms. A case study was used because of its inherent advantages in providing information. Because there exists no sound theory base yet in this area, case analysis is a strong means for conducting descriptive research and helps to gain insights into areas that have not been explored previously in the literature. As put forth by Glaser and Strauss (1967), grounded theory development should start with observation, and the theory can be built only after initial observations. Theory building is an inductive process that needs a series of observations, modification of received ideas after each observation, and finally concluding with a sound theory.

Benbasat, Goldstein, and Mead (1987) mention that case-type research is the most appropriate research tool to use when the research and theory are in their early and formative stages. The research context is rife with challenging and practice-based problems, in which the experiences of the actors are important, and the context of action is critical. Chen and Small (1994) mention that the case study approach also helps in situations in which the practitioners have significantly higher levels of knowledge about the subject and the researchers need to gather information from them in their natural setting to build theories. For ERP, research case analysis seemed fitting because it is a recent IT innovation that required elaborate research and understanding before using quantitative techniques based on a large-scale survey.

Open-ended questions were asked, and the responses of the IS executives were audiotaped, thus improving the reliability of the study. To ensure validity, more than one researcher was present during all of the interviews. The written manuscripts were submitted to the respondents for their review and approval, thus alleviating any misinterpretation of the responses. This further increased validity. The interviews were conducted with the MIS directors or chief information officers or ERP implementation project leaders, because these individuals have a comprehensive overview of both the technical and business aspects of the system.

RESULTS AND DISCUSSION

Exhibit 1 details some of the salient features of the companies that were studied in order to understand the enhanced manufacturing performance resulting from implementation of ERP systems. Owens Corning and Viskase use SAP as their ERP system; Valenite and Diebold have Baan and Leeson has Oracle as ERP systems. The reasons for choosing a particular type of ERP are also given in the table. SAP Company most often preferred to offer its products and services to larger firms, and some of the modules of Baan systems (e.g., Product Configurator) made it the system of choice for global companies such as Diebold. The Oracle ERP was chosen by Leeson because of its ability to meet its needs and because of the Web-based network computing architecture (NCA) of Oracle. All of the companies prior to ERP implementation had legacy mainframes, and all of these firms realized that such disparate legacy systems would not enable them to achieve competitive superiority in the coming years. The details of the case studies of each of the companies are reported elsewhere (Rajagopal et al., 1999a and Tyler and Rajagopal, 1999).

Problems with Disparate Systems

There was a common problem found in all of the firms studied — incompatibility among the systems and the corresponding poor manufacturing performance. Various work processes and transfer and access of information among the functional units and divisions were a time-consuming process prior to ERP implementation. For example, at Owens Corning order processing and the subsequent dispatch of materials used to take three days. The paperwork associated with the order-taking process was voluminous, and various documents were circulated from office to office. In every office, copies of the same documents were made and filed.

Diebold had problems in manufacturing automated teller machines (ATMs) for its global customers that required incorporating differences in currency, language, and technology in various countries. Diebold also had problems in coordinating its internal supply chain in order to practice JIT. Leeson wanted to get rid of its obsolete legacy systems and enhance manufacturing performance.

At Viskase, there was no integration of any sort among the production facilities, resulting in poor manufacturing practices. Valenite realized the need to change from aging mainframe-based systems to new systems to cope with the changing business environment.

All of the respondents agreed that they cannot progress and go anywhere with their existing legacy systems, and it was more than inevitable for them to switch to a system such as ERP to obtain an organizationwide integration in order to achieve a smooth flow of information. Especially for internationally active companies, a system such as ERP is necessary to compete in the current and coming years. Exhibit 2 summarizes the antecedents and issues of the ERP implementation process in the five firms studied.

Issues in ERP Implementation

A salient aspect noticed during the interviews and analysis is that ERP implementation requires a business process reengineering (BPR) or some kind of

Exhibit 1. Demographics of the Companies Studied for Their Implementation of ERP Systems

S. No	Salient Points	Valenite	Diebold	Leeson	Owens Corning	Viskase
1	Industry	Metal Cutting	Financial Services	Electric Motors	Fiberglass	Food Packaging
2	Annual Sales	$500 M	$1.2 B	$180 M	$5 B	$800 M
3	Business Description	Valenite offers the metalworking industry a complete line of standardized and special indexable-insert turning, boring, milling, drilling, and high-speed steel products.	Manufactures ATMs and other products for the financial industry. Diebold is a leading global supplier of ATMs, and holds the primary market position in many other countries.	Maker of variety of electric motors. Leeson motors can be found on material-handling equipment, pumps, fans and blowers, machine tools, power transmission products, agricultural applications, treadmills, and other commercial products.	Maker of fiberglass-based building materials and composites. Active in sales in 30 countries around the world and have production facilities in approximately 20 countries. The top three foreign sales areas are the U.K., Germany, and France.	Products used by companies such as Sara Lee. Viskase is a holding company with subsidiaries that produce cellulosic casings used in preparing and packaging processed meat products; heat shrinkable, oxygen barrier plastic bags; specialty films for packaging food products; polyvinyl chloride films and related products.
4	Systems Before ERP	Mainframe based	Mainframe based	Mainframe based	Mainframe based	Mainframe based
5	Problems	Incompatibility Nonuniformity	Incompatibility Global product configuration	Incompatibility	Incompatibility Impeding growth	Incompatibility Poor manufacturing
6	Type of ERP Application	Baan	Baan	Oracle	SAP	SAP
	Reason for choosing this system	SAP mentioned that the company was not large enough for them. Oracle did not have some of the modules required.	Needed a good global product configurator.	SAP mentioned that the company's ERP budget was not large enough. Oracle was found to be most suitable. Network computing architecture (NCA) which is Web based.	SAP was found to be the best ERP. SAP was found to be ideal for this large organization.	SAP was found to be ideal to solve the manufacturing problems.

Exhibit 2. Summary of the Case Findings

S. No	Company	Description
1	Owens Corning	The CEO wanted a system that would help the company better compete because of the expected growth in sales. The information system was expected not to be an impediment in the growth and development of the organization. The MIS department was required to integrate the disparate systems and bring about uniformity in the computer hardware and software platforms. Through SAP implementation, the company has reduced the number of different systems from 211 to about 12 resulting in savings that amount to millions of dollars because of integrated IT.
2	Viskase	To overcome the problems in manufacturing and in various other areas such as sales, senior management wanted to reengineer the business processes. SAP was chosen to integrate computer hardware and software. The company is able to better perform, especially in manufacturing, owing to the implementation of SAP.
3	Valenite	This company in the machine tool industry wanted to make changes in its organizations to cope with changes in the business environment. The Baan system was pilot-tested in their facility located in Canada. They realized better performance in this facility because of Baan implementation. The performance is far superior to their other facilities in the United States. The integrated information system is enabling them to retrieve and disseminate data in real-time.
4	Diebold, Inc.	This company in the banking industry is positioned to grow and expand in global markets. It wanted a system that would enable it to manufacture products for international customers, taking into consideration differences in language and currency.
5	Leeson Electric	This company is one of the world leaders in manufacturing electric motors. To cope with the changes in the business environment, it wanted an IS that would perform better in the current and coming years. The company implemented Oracle ERP and is realizing the benefits of the system. The salient point to note here in this company is that it uses NCA or Network Computing Architecture that allows it to use the Internet to access its databases, thus resulting in high scalability.

discovery process before implementing the system. Such an understanding of the existing process enables the organizations to redesign their organizational processes in order to get the most out of the ERP implementation. Unless the various business processes are redesigned to suit the design of the modules of ERP, the system implementation may not yield the expected success. ERP is not just an office automation software that can be bought off the shelf and installed, but a business transformation process that requires some fundamental changes in the way various business processes are designed and conducted. In addition, the organization's members need to have a good understanding of how the system works before actually putting it into use. Valenite, for example, conducted several simulation studies before putting the systems to use in its Canadian facility. Since data entered in one place connects with many areas or databases of an organization, an error made in one place is multiplied and, if left unnoticed, will result in catastrophe, which may take much time and effort to reconcile. Bingi (1999) provides examples of such situations.

An issue of concern in implementing ERP is employee turnover. Because personnel with ERP experience is much sought after in the market, many companies experienced employee turnover through and after ERP implementation. The companies also needed to revamp their IT architectures in order to implement an ERP system. Most of the companies switched to client/server architecture from mainframe-based systems to implement an ERP system. Dow Chemicals, after investing $500M in implementing mainframe-based SAP R/2 system, started over to implement a client/server-based SAP R/3 system.

Enhanced Manufacturing Performance of ERP Systems

All the companies studied realized enhanced manufacturing performance from the implementation of ERP systems. At Owens Corning, an executive from the corporate headquarters in Ohio can monitor and affect the production planning and logistics activities of a plant in the U.K., if so desired, with no delay other than the milliseconds of transmittal time.

Thus, there is a centralized coordination of activities across various functions, divisions, and countries. The production managers in various factories do not have to worry about order taking from the customers, tracking logistics, or after-sales service. While the production managers focus on getting the best output from their facilities, the corporate headquarters office takes the responsibility for the remainder of the process from advertising to after-the-sale customer service.

The implementation has demonstrated significant contributions to cost savings and performance measures at Owens Corning. Inventory levels have been reduced significantly. Lot sizes and machine allocations have become efficient. Inter-facility coordination has grown significantly. Rather than physical assets being stored as inventory, it is information access and dissemination that is the vital source of production planning and control that can now be accomplished globally and optimally because of the uniformity of systems.

Before the integration of functions and divisions accomplished through ERP, the data collection process was slow and repetitive. Now, the customer can call one location to place an order — unlike the previous system which made it necessary to call two or more different locations. Information about product availability can be retrieved from any linked terminal in the organization, because the system is standardized and uniform across the entire organization.

The manufacturing executives of Owens Corning, during this interview, acknowledged that the SAP systems have significantly improved the performance of the manufacturing function, and the chief information officer mentioned that without ERP, the company would not be able to compete in the global arena. (This discussion about the enhanced manufacturing performance is also reported by the same author in detail elsewhere, Rajagopal and Tyler, 1999a.) Exhibit 3 details the enhanced performance due to SAP implementation at Owens Corning and Viskase.

At Viskase, another firm with SAP, some of the salient benefits realized through implementing SAP include reductions in lead time and inventory, enhanced visibility in inventory planning, reduction in head count, and an integration of information. In any manufacturing organization, the forecast and actual sales orders are converted into plant orders, which are changed into production orders. Prior to SAP implementation, this process was apparent to only a few persons, and only these few were able to comprehend the information and develop plans for production and purchasing. Through SAP implementation, such complex business processes have become available to others in the organization, thus not only connecting the entire organization end to end but also providing related functions with information that they require to work efficiently. Production-based decisions are tied to sales-based decisions in a more timely and efficient manner, and the various complex factory-level processes are becoming transparent to others in the organization. Decision-making times are therefore reduced significantly, and the organization is better enabled to meet customer demands.

At Valenite, the profitability of the Canadian facility definitely increased after the Baan implementation, but actual dollar figures were not provided. The increase was primarily attributed to lower levels of inventory and improved customer satisfaction. Prior to the Baan implementation, order-taking was a time-consuming and tedious process in which the customer service representatives first wrote the information on paper and then keyed it into the system. With the Baan system in place, this task is accomplished without the translation errors involved in moving from paper to digital mode. The data is entered directly onto the screen and, once such data has been entered, the system is automatically updated and current. The users of the system know that the changes and the actions relating to them have been taken. The statistical and daily updates are automatically and immediately made, and the financial and inventory books are always current. When the month-end closings occur, the U.S. facilities, which still have legacy mainframe systems in their facilities, take four days to retrieve

Exhibit 3. Summary of SAP Implementation and Performance in the Sample Firms

	Owens Corning	Viskase
Driving Forces	1. Needed a system to cope with increasing sales 2. Needed a system to enable it perform better rather than being an impediment to growth and expansion	1. Needed change 2. Needed to enhance manufacturing performance
Issues in Implementation	1. Outsourced maintenance of previous system to H-P 2. Employee turnover	1. Employee turnover 2. Resistance to change because some modules of the previous systems were better than ERP
Performance	1. Reduction in inventory 2. Centralized coordination among various functions, divisions, and countries 3. Efficient lot sizes and machine allocation	1. Enhanced manufacturing performance 2. Better coordination among the various facilities 3. Enhanced ability to serve the customers.
Cost	$ 100 M	$ 15 M
Modules Used	Manufacturing	Manufacturing
Consulting Services	SAP	SAP and PricewaterhouseCoopers
Number of SAP Users	1200	35
Technology Profile	Sun Solaris server Microsoft Office products WAN connecting the various facilities	The data center has been outsourced to IBM Global Services. AT&T manages the Wide Area Networks. Switched from the AS 400 to a RISC 6000 with 14 servers, a number of LANs, routers, back-office tools, and MS Office products

the appropriate data and make the required entries. In the Canadian facilities with Baan ERP in place, the bookkeeping, journal-entry, and other such financial and accounting processes are automatic and the information is available in real time. Month-end closings take hours to accomplish, not days. Exhibit 4 details the enhanced manufacturing performance due to Baan implementation at Valenite and Diebold Incorporated.

Prior to ERP implementation, Diebold was operating in batch mode, in which the databases were updated nightly. The desired data was available, but the "age" of the data made its reliability questionable. Now the data is in real time across the entire organization. Before Baan implementation, Diebold had some proprietary interfaces between the various modules to transfer data from the disparate database types. These interfaces were minimal, and there existed no organizationwide level of integration. Since

Exhibit 4. Summary of Baan Implementation and Performance in the Sample Firms

	Valenite	Diebold, Inc.
Driving Forces	1. Need to change the IT for competitive reasons 2. Need to enhance manufacturing performance	1. Need for a better product configurator 2. Need to enhance performance of manufacturing function 3. The old system based on mainframe was not useful for the changed environment
Issues in Implementation	1. Need to change all of the old systems into Baan 2. Need to shift to client/server environment 3. Increased workload in order entry	1. Loss of staff 2. Overrun of estimated budget 3. Increased workload in order entry function 4. Need to convert the various processes into Baan
Performance	1. Low inventory 2. Increased availability of information 3. Information diffusion across the firm 4. Increased profitability	1. Better manufacturing cycles 2. Reduced inventory 3. Information diffusion across the entire organization 4. Better global positioning using the Baan Product Configurator 5. Better internal supply chain management
Cost	$2.5 M	$ 34 M
Modules Used	Manufacturing, Finance, and Sales	Manufacturing, Sales, Finance, and Product Configurator
Consulting Services	Baan only	Arthur Andersen and Baan
Number of Baan Users	35	350

Baan implementation, there are integrated interfaces between all of the modules and data entered in one place automatically triggers changes in all the related databases. Diebold has an internal supply chain, in which the end product from one facility becomes the subassembly for the next facility. The coordination of the facilities thus reduces stockpiling and ensures supplies. Any lack of subassemblies in the process will have an effect on the downstream production processes and profitability. The coordination among the facilities in Diebold thus becomes vital for continued success. With Diebold's size and complexity, an ERP system is required to alleviate problems in coordinating and controlling their manufacturing processes. Baan enables Diebold to more readily do product configuration for the global customers. Given Diebold's expected growth in international markets, a system such as Baan is more than essential to meet customer expectations. (The enhanced manufacturing performance at Valenite and Diebold is discussed in detail in Tyler and Rajagopal, 1999.)

Exhibit 5. Summary of Oracle Implementation and Performance in the Sample Firms

Leeson Electric Company	
Driving Forces	1. Need to change 2. Utilize internet capabilities 3. Increasing functionalities
Issues in Implementation	1. Data translation 2. Beta testing 3. User resistance 4. Employee training
Performance	1. Integration 2. Connectivity 3. Less paperwork 4. Less manual work 5. Organizational visibility 6. Reduction in inventory
Cost	$ 3.5 M
Modules Used	Oracle Manufacturing, Oracle Financials, and Oracle Human Resources (only to some extent)
Consulting Services	None
Number of Oracle Users	300
Hardware	Sun Enterprise 6000 and 3000 Servers running on Sun Solaris
Facilities Connected	31 product warehouses, 6 manufacturing facilities and 1,700 authorized service centers worldwide.

At Leeson, after implementing Oracle, the number of phone calls and paperwork related to order processing has been greatly reduced. Order processing is streamlined and smooth. With Oracle, there is greater coordination, and the organization as a whole works together — unlike earlier times, when departments were working in functional silos independent of one another. Order levels and inventory, which were done manually before, are all automated. Before Oracle implementation, the field officers used to fax orders that generated a lot of paperwork; with Oracle in place, they do it automatically and directly into the system and various order forms are available in the Oracle system. The order process itself is automatic, all the databases in manufacturing are kept current, and the data is available in real time. Exhibit 5 shows the changes in manufacturing performance due to Oracle implementation at Leeson.

Before Oracle, when MRP II was used, only a few were able to see the various business processes. More often than not, various functional staff were calling others and the MIS department for data and reports, but the Oracle systems have opened up the information in the company and put the information needed to the end users in a readily accessible form. The finance, inventory, and transactions are all clean, and the information is available to the decision-makers without limitation.

On the factory floors, large packets of paper used to go around that contained special instructions and product revisions. By putting more PCs on the shop floor and using Oracle Front Page, such paper-based instructions were eliminated. The Front Page has all the needed information in it; previously that information circulated manually. Of all the IT innovations seen so far, the respondent agreed that the Oracle ERP systems have made the greatest impact in the organization. It is the authors' belief that E-commerce or conducting business over the Internet will be another IT innovation that is capable of impinging upon many functions of an organization.

As can be seen from Exhibit 6, various criteria to measure performance, especially in manufacturing, such as global optimal procurement, coordination in manufacturing, manufacturing knowledge about the markets, marketing knowledge about manufacturing, customer satisfaction, paperwork associated with order processing, time to process order and deliver, information availability for logistics for optimization, uniformity of the systems in various production units, forecasting accuracy, positioning for global markets, supply chain management activities, and monitoring of performance in various subsidiaries are all enhanced to some or a great extent as a result of the implementation of ERP systems. This shows the wide variety of advantages the manufacturing function is able to achieve from ERP implementation. So far there has been no single IT innovation comparable to ERP systems for simultaneously affecting the various functional units of an organization, resulting in enhanced manufacturing performance.

CONCLUSION

Many organizations have successfully automated their business processes by implementing many different kinds of computer hardware and software systems during the past few decades. What appeared to be making the various business processes easy and simple ended up making them complex and difficult to handle because of the wide variety of systems that were accumulating in individual functional units and divisions in the organizations over the years. With the increasing intense international competition, shorter product life cycles in the market and ever-increasing niches, there is a need for the organizations to be able to digest the vast amount of information from the environment and make fast decisions to respond to dynamic and changing global markets. There is also a need for the organization as a whole to work together and sometimes to work with other organizations as a virtual corporation to make strategic decisions and achieve competitive gains. Toward integrating organizations to reach these goals,

Exhibit 6. Comparison of Performance Before and After Implementation of ERP Systems

Performance Measures	Owens Corning Before[a]	Owens Corning After	Viskase Before	Viskase After	Valenite Before	Valenite After	Diebold Before	Diebold After	Leeson Before	Leeson After
1 Number of different computer systems	211	1	3	1	N/A	N/A	40	20	1	1
2 Degree of Incompatibility among the systems	Very High	Low	High	Low	High	Low	High	Low	N/A	N/A
3 End-to-end connectivity	None	High	Low	High	Low	High	Low	Very High	Avg	High
4 Global optimal procurement	Very Low	High	Low	Avg	None	Avg	Low	High	Avg	High
5 Coordination in manufacturing	Low	Very High	Above Avg	High	Avg	High	Above Avg	Very High	Avg	High
6 Manufacturing knowledge about markets	Low	Very High	Above Avg	High	Avg	Above Avg	Avg	High	Low	Above Avg
7 Marketing knowledge about manufacturing	Low	High	Low	Above Avg	Above Avg	Same	Avg	High	Low	Above Avg
8 Customer satisfaction	Avg	High	Above Avg	Same	Low	High	High	Same	Avg	High
9 Paperwork associated with order processing	High	Low	High	Above Avg	High	Low	Very High	Above Avg	Very High	Low
10 Time to process order and deliver	High	Low	High	Above Avg	Avg	Same	Avg	Same	High	Low
11 Information availability for logistics for optimization	Low	Very High	Low	High	N/A	N/A	High	Same	Above Avg	High
12 Uniformity of systems in various production units	Low	High	Avg	High	Low	High	High	Very High	Avg	High
13 Forecasting accuracy	Low	High	Low	Same	Very Low	High	Above Avg	Same	N/A	N/A
14 Information availability for decision making	Low	Very High	Above Avg	High	Low	High	High	Same	Avg	Very High
15 Y2K problems	Many	None	Yes	No	Many	None	Very High	Avg	Yes	None
16 Positioning for global competition	Low	Very High	Avg	Above Avg	Very Low	High	Low	Very High	Avg	Very High
17 Supply chain management	Low	Very High	Low	Above Avg	Low	High	Avg	High	N/A	N/A
18 Monitoring of performance in subsidiaries	Poor	Very Good	Avg	Same	Low	High	Above Avg	High	Avg	High

[a] Before and after refer to the manufacturing characteristics before and after implementation of ERP systems.

information technology has once again proved to be a vital tool by providing "end-to-end" connectivity in an organization through implementation of ERP systems.

This chapter has shown the benefits of implementing an ERP system in enhancing the performance of an organization — manufacturing performance in particular. For global organizations, an ERP system may prove to be a vital tool for coordinating the production at a global level, thus achieving optimal production and sales. With many vendors entering the ERP industry, it will be definitely be interesting to see the various types of future information technology integration systems and their capabilities. With such systems providing information at the fingertips of the decision-makers at the right time and right place, the competitive tool in an organization will be the ability of the personnel to focus and develop core capabilities and conceive high degrees of innovation to achieve competitive gains.

As much as ERP systems integrate information technology, they are also making organizations understand their core capabilities, reengineer their business processes, and make any changes needed in the business processes to be a market leader. Organizations may take the process of implementation of ERP systems as an opportunity to reengineer their business activities, and revamp their entire IS/IT structures to compete for the future. The cost associated with ERP implementation is meager compared with the benefits offered by the integration; at the same time, ERP is proving to be a vital tool for future survival in the global marketplace.

ACKNOWLEDGEMENT

The authors wish to thank the Information Systems and Operations Management Department of The College of Business Administration at The University of Toledo for providing financial support through an Academic Challenge Grant, and the respondents from Owens Corning, Valenite, Leeson, Diebold, and Viskase for giving hours of their valuable time to explain their ERP systems.

References

1. Alavi, M. and Keen, P., 1989, "Business Teams in the Information Age," *Information Society*, v. 4, p. 179.
2. Beatty, C. and Gordon, J., 1988, "Barriers to the Implementation of CAD/CAM Systems," *Sloan Management Review*, Summer, v. 29(4), p. 25.
3. Beatty, C., 1992, "Implementing Advanced Manufacturing Technologies: Rules of the Road," *Sloan Management Review*, Summer, p. 49.
4. Benbasat, I., Goldstein, D. K., and Mead, M., The Case Research Strategy in Studies of Information Systems, *MIS Quarterly*, 11(3), Sep., 1987, p. 369.

5. Chen, I. J. and Small, M.H., Implementing Advanced Manufacturing Technology: An Integrated Planning Model, *OMEGA, International Journal of Management Science*, 22 (1), 1994, p. 91.
6. Davenport, T., Putting the Enterprise into the Enterprise System, *Harvard Business Review*, July/August, 1998, pp. 121–131.
7. Gillenwater, et al, 1995, "Distributed Manufacturing Support Systems: The Integration of Distributed Group Support Systems with Manufacturing Support Systems, OMEGA, v. 23(6), Dec, p. 653.
8. Glaser, B. and Strauss, A., 1967, *The Discovery of Grounded Theory: Strategies in Qualitative Theory*, Wiedenfeld and Nicholson, London.
9. Gullo, K., 1988, "SQL: The New Universal Language," *Datamation*, Mar. 1, p. 60
10. Green, J. and Kiran, A., 1996, "Manufacturers Meet Global Market Demands with FCS Software," *IIE Solutions*. v. 28n8, Aug 1996. p. 26.
11. Kerr, S., 1988, "Islands of Automation: Networks Emerge to Connect Them," *Datamation*, Mar. 1, p. 57.
12. Kogut, B., 1984, "International Value Added Chain and Strategic Groups," *Journal of International Business Studies*, v. 15(2), p. 151.
13. Meredith, J.R. and McCutcheon, D., 1989, "Conducting Case Study Research in Operations Management," *Journal of Operations Management*, v. 11 (3), Sep, p. 239.
14. Rajagopal, P. and Tyler, F., "A Comparative Case Analysis of Enterprise Resource Planning Systems Implementation and Performance — SAP," Submitted to *OMEGA, The International Journal of Management Science*.
15. Rockart, J.F. and Short, F.E., "Information Technology in the 1990s: Managing Organizational Interdependence," Ch. 16 in *Strategic Information Management*, Edited by Galliers, R.D. and Baker, B.S.H., Butterworth-Heinemann Ltd., Oxford, 1994.
16. Saccomano, A., "More than Manufacturing," *Traffic World*, v. 256, no. 5, Nov. 2, 1998, p. 46.
17. Tyler, F. and Rajagopal, P., "A Comparative Case Analysis of Enterprise Resource Planning Systems Implementation and Performance — SAP," Submitted to *Information Systems Management*.
18. Vonderembse, M., Raghunathan, T.S., and Rao, S., 1996, "A Post Industrial Paradigm: To Integrate and Automate Manufacturing," *International Journal of Production Resources*, v. 35 (9), p. 2579.

Section VIII
Enterprise Networking

Chapter 42

The Essentials of Enterprise Networking

Keith G. Knightson

Enterprise networks and enterprise networking are buzz-phrases on every salesperson's lips, together, of course, with "open" and "open systems." Many products are glowingly described with these phrases. Creating an enterprise network, however, requires more than just a knowledge of the buzzwords. This chapter explains the basic subtleties of an enterprise network and the challenges of establishing one.

THE NEXT GENERATION OF ENTERPRISES

An enterprise is nothing more than a fancy name for a given company or organization. It conveys, however, the notion of a geographically dispersed, multifaceted organization, an organization comprising many branches, departments, and disciplines (e.g., marketing, manufacturing, finance, administration).

In the past, the networking and information technologies deployed in an enterprise were many and disjointed. In some cases, this was because of local departmental or workgroup autonomy, or simply because of ignorance among different parts of the enterprise as to what information systems were being used, or it was an artifact of historical equipment acquisition procedures.

The allegiance of specific departments to particular vendors was also a factor. When acquisition of capital equipment is performed gradually (rather than implemented all at once, across the board), it is difficult to make sure that all equipment is mutually compatible. Finally, the lack of an enterprisewide view, strategy, or policy with respect to networking and information technology — and the possible convergence solutions — are contributing considerations.

0-8493-1149-7/02/$0.00+$1.50
© 2002 by CRC Press LLC

Consolidating the Network

In the same sense that the word "enterprise" conveys the totality of an organization's operations, the phrase "enterprise network" means combining all the networking and information technology and applications within a given enterprise into a single, seamless, consolidated, integrated network. The degree of integration and consolidation may vary; total integration and consolidation may not be always achievable.

For example, an organization may have an SNA network from IBM Corp. and a DECnet from Digital Equipment Corp. (now part of Compaq). In all probability, these two networks have their own communications components; there might be one set of leased lines serving the SNA network and another completely independent set of leased lines serving the DECnet.

It would be useful if all the IBM users could intercommunicate with all DEC users, but a first and evolutionary step might be to have both the SNA network and DECnet share the same leased lines. Now, only one physical network has to be managed instead of two separate ones, and more efficient and cost-effective sharing of the physical communications plant can be achieved.

A second step might be to interconnect the mail systems of the two networks to achieve at least the appearance of a single enterprisewide electronic-mail system.

A third step might be to unify the data and information and its representation as used within the organization. This would enable basic forms of data to be operated by many applications.

The challenges of building an enterprise network fall into two distinct categories: getting the data (i.e., information) from A to B, and enabling B to understand the data when it receives it from A. These two categories are referred to in this chapter as the "networking challenge" and "beyond the networking challenge." In this context, the network is used as it is in the Open Systems Interconnection (OSI) reference model — that is, Layer 3 and below.

THE NETWORKING CHALLENGE

The networking part of the problem has three major components:

1. Choosing from and integrating the many network technologies
2. Selecting from the many vendor solutions
3. Moving information from a local to a global environment

Integrating Network Technologies

The first basic problem with networks is that there are so many of them. In this context, networks are taken to mean the raw network technologies —

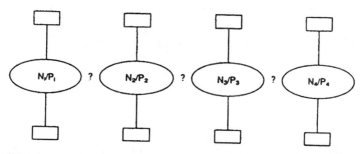

Notes:
• For every (sub)network N$_i$, there is a network-specific protocol P$_i$.
• All P$_i$'s are different and thus not directly interconnectable.
• A way to make all the different networks look the same must be found, if the enterprise network is to appear as a single seamless network.

Exhibit 1.   The Interoperability Problem

---

leased lines (i.e., T_1 and T_3), X.25, DSL, ISDN, frame relay, asynchronous transfer mode (ATM), and the many and various LAN access methods.

If all the users in an enterprise are connected to the same network technology, there is no problem. Unfortunately, this is not always the case. Communication between users on dissimilar networks (e.g., two different LANs) is where the problem occurs.

Each network technology has its own characteristics and inherent protocols. From an enterprise viewpoint, this is bad news. For example, users connected to an X.25 network cannot easily be connected to those already connected to a LAN. For example, how would the X.25 user indicate the destination's media access control (MAC) address, and vice versa? X.25 networks understand only X.25 addresses and LANs understand only MAC addresses. The differences between network technologies and native protocols almost invariably prevent their direct interconnection.

Differences in addressing schemes present another difficulty. Addressing considerations alone usually dictate the use of a network interconnection device (NID) at the point at which two network technologies come together.

Exhibit 1 illustrates several network technologies, represented by N_1, N_2, N_3, N_4. Each of these technologies has its own native protocol (i.e., P_1, P_2, P_3, P_4). A way must be found to integrate all these disparate technologies into a single supernetwork, with globally uniform and globally understood characteristics and a single addressing scheme.

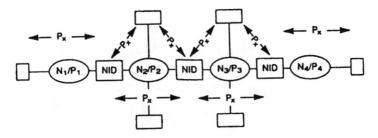

Exhibit 2. The Interoperability Solution

This is achieved by operating an integrating, unifying protocol (shown in Exhibit 2 as Px), sometimes known as an Internet protocol, over the top of all the possible basic communications networks. The Internet protocol (IP) of TCP/IP is one such protocol. The connectionless network layer protocol (CNLP) specified in the OSI International Standard 8473 is another. Proprietary systems have their own Internet protocols — for example, Novell uses its Internetwork Packet Exchange (IPX) and Banyan uses Vines.

From the architectural standpoint, the technical term for such an Internet protocol is subnetwork independent convergence protocol (SNICP). The protocols used on real-world communications networks (e.g., leased lines, X.25, frame relay, LANs) are known as subnetwork access control protocols (SNACP). The basic internetworking architecture is shown in Exhibit 3.

Unification does not mean simplification. Two protocols operating over a given subnetwork still require two address schemes. Routing tables are then needed in the network interconnection device to map the global enterprise address to the address to be used by the network interconnection device for the next link in the composite path. Exhibit 4 is a simplification of how the two addresses are used. In practice, the "next" address may be more complex, depending on the internetworking protocols under consideration. A network interconnection device of this type is called a router.

Selecting Vendor Solutions

The second basic problem is that each system vendor has a vendor-specific idea of how to build the supernetwork — the type of supernetwork protocol, the global addressing scheme, and the internal routing protocols

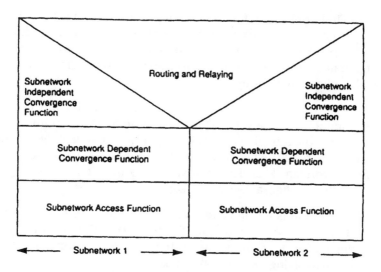

Exhibit 3. Network Layer Architecture

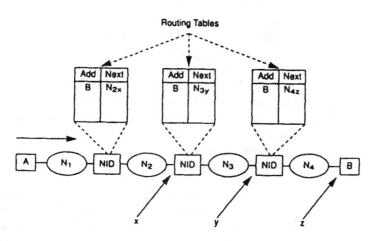

Exhibit 4. Simplified View of Addressing

to be used. At worst, this leads to a multiprotocol network, which amounts to several separate internets operating in parallel over the same physical communications plant.

Dealing with Multiple Protocols. An alternative to the multiprotocol network is to choose a single protocol for the entire enterprise supernetwork.

This inevitably requires finding techniques to accommodate the systems that do not inherently operate this chosen protocol. Techniques include encapsulation (sometimes called tunneling) at the edges of the single-protocol network, or other techniques such as transport service interfaces and application gateways.

However, even with a single protocol, tunneling permits only the coexistence of incompatible systems; there can be little or no interaction between each of the tunneled applications. The major advantage of tunneling is that the core of the network is unified, optimizing network management and networking skills. The disadvantage is the effort required to set up the tunneling configurations at the edges.

The best solution is for all vendors to use the same Internet protocol. Increasingly, the protocol of choice for this purpose is TCP/IP. Although not a networking panacea, TCP/IP is the protocol of choice for most networking challenges involving multiple protocols.

Going Global

Many LAN-based systems include internal protocols that advertise the existence of various LAN-based servers. Such a protocol is sometimes known as a service advertising protocol (SAP). Protocol exchanges, frequently broadcast over the LAN, ensure that the availability and addresses of various servers are known throughout the LAN user community. This is useful when the geographic area is confined to a work group or a floor of a building; for example, the knowledge of a set of available printers is useful only in the area that has ready access to one of them. Thus, local messages must be constrained to local environments by putting adequate filtering at the point of access to the wide area portion of the enterprise network. There is no point in telling a user on a LAN in New York that there is a printer available on a LAN in Seattle.

WAN Transit Delays. Another global problem relates to the extra transit delay involved in transport over a WAN, especially for nonroutable protocols. Many protocol stacks used in local environments do not contain a network layer protocol — in other words, they have no routing layer. Such protocols cannot be routed directly in a router-based enterprise network. Where it is necessary for such an application to be networked outside a particular local environment, the local protocol stack must be encapsulated within an internetworking protocol. Then it can be launched onto the wide area part of the enterprise network.

Many of the local or nonroutable protocols are designed for very rapid acknowledgment. The transfer of these types of protocols across a wide area may cause problems; applications may prematurely time-out or suffer

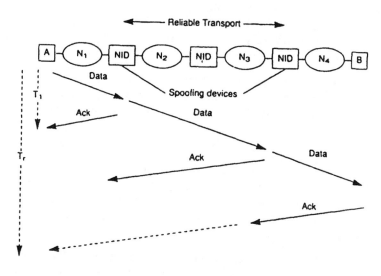

Exhibit 5. Spoofing

poor throughput because of the lack of a windowing mechanism adequate for the wide area transit delay.

To accommodate such applications, it is necessary to "spoof" the acknowledgments. This means that acknowledgments must be generated by the local encapsulation device. This requires the extra complication of adding a reliable transport protocol on top of the internetworking protocol across the wide area portion of the enterprise network. Once a local acknowledgment has been given, the originator will discard the original so it is no longer available for retransmission. Having given the local acknowledgment, the spoofing device must ensure reliable delivery to the remote end by employing a transport protocol of some sort (e.g., TCP or OSI Transport Class 4). The scheme, shown in Exhibit 5, avoids the end-to-end round trip delay T_r for every packet of data by providing an acknowledgment at time T_1.

Addressing. Going global also poses some challenges in the area of network layer addressing, particularly with regard to achieving enterprisewide uniqueness and structuring addresses for scalability and ease of routing.

Usually, addresses of stations within a local workgroup are allocated locally. This can present problems when, subsequently, the local workgroups must be integrated into a single enterprisewide address scheme. If several workgroup addresses — or parts of an address (e.g., an area or server name) — are the same, some changes will have to be made. From an operational perspective, changing addresses is not a trivial matter. It is best to avoid address allocation clashes right from the outset by having an enterprisewide address registration authority set up within the organization.

Some addressing schemes do have some hierarchy associated with them that can be used to avoid address encoding clashes by ensuring that local addresses are only the low-order part of the total address. Even in this case, however, an enterprisewide perspective is necessary to avoid clashes in the high-order part of the address.

Some vendors achieve uniqueness by allocating unique addresses when the equipment is shipped. However, this usually results in a flat, random address space that makes routing considerably more complex because there is no structure in the address to help "scale" the enterprise network from the routing perspective.

If the enterprise is to be permanently connected to the Internet (as opposed to using a dialup connection), IP addresses must be obtained from an appropriate addressing authority. Until recently, all addresses were dispensed directly from the Internet Network Information Center (InterNIC). More recently, in response to a number of problems associated with addressing practices in the past, IP addresses have begun to take on a more hierarchical form. As such, the enterprise may need to obtain a block of addresses from its Internet Service Provider (ISP), in effect obtaining a subset of the addresses that ISP has obtained from the InterNIC.

This practice ensures that the appropriate hierarchical relationships are maintained, allowing improved routing, and it has the added benefit of more efficiently allocating the available addresses. The primary drawback from the perspective of the enterprise is that addresses obtained in this fashion are no longer considered permanent. That is, if the enterprise changes ISPs, the addresses may also have to be changed.

Hierarchical Schemes. The most widely documented and hierarchically administered address available today is the OSI address space available for OSI Network Service Access Point (NSAP) addresses. A more recently developed scheme is the next generation of IP, now known as IP version 6 (IPv6), described in RFCs 1883-1886. NSAP addresses can consist of up to 40 digits, and IPv6 addresses can be up to 128 bits, either of which allows good scaling potential and simplified routing.

The reason that a hierarchical (i.e., scaled) address scheme is so important has to do with the way that routers operate and the size of the associated routing tables. If addresses were allocated completely randomly but uniquely from a large address space, every router would need a table with every address in it. Not only would the table be extremely large, but the time needed to find an entry could also be a problem. Routing is thus better arranged on the basis of hierarchical distinctions that are implicit in the address scheme.

To service a local workgroup or other limited geographical area, a local router must know only whether the destination address is internal or external. If it is internal, the router knows how to get the message to the destination; if it is external, the router can pass it on to the next-level router. This leads to the concept of areas, groups of areas, domains, and countries being components of a hierarchical address.

When legacy systems must be accommodated with conflicting address schemes and reallocation of addresses is impossible, tunneling may have to be employed merely to avoid interaction between the conflicting addresses. Because conflicting networks are divided into separate virtual private networks, the protocol under consideration cannot be routed natively even if the backbone routers are capable of doing so.

Routing Protocols. To reduce the amount of time devoted to setting up routing tables manually, and to allow dynamic rerouting and a degree of self-healing, routing protocols are often employed to distribute routing information throughout the enterprise network. These protocols are in addition to the internetworking protocol itself, but are related to it.

For every internetwork protocol routed in a multiprotocol network, there may be a specific routing protocol (or set of protocols). This also means in general that there will also be a separate routing table for each internetworking protocol. The situation in which several routing protocols are used simultaneously, but independently, is sometimes known as a "ships in the night" situation, because sets of routing information pass each other and are seemingly oblivious to each other even though there is only one physical network.

Some router manufacturers operate a single proprietary routing protocol between their own routers and convert to individual protocols at the edges of the network. There have been some attempts to define a single standard routing protocol based on the International Standards Organization's intermediate system to intermediate system (IS-IS) standard.

In an enterprise network, end systems (e.g., terminals, workstations, mainframes) usually announce their presence and their own addresses to the nearest local router. The local routers record all the local addresses within their area and inform all neighboring higher-level routers of their own area address. In this way, a router at the next and higher level in the hierarchy only needs to know about areas. Recursive application of these principles to a hierarchical configuration can lead to efficient routing by minimizing the amount of routing information to be transmitted and by keeping the size of routing tables small.

As the process of promulgating routing information proceeds across the network, every router in the enterprise network will obtain a table of reachability that it can then use for choosing optimum routes. Route optimality may be based on a number of independent metrics (e.g., transmit delay, throughput, monetary cost). Invariably, a shortest path first (SPF) algorithm is used to determine the optimal route for any particular metric chosen as the basis for routing. Both the Internet and OSI routing protocols use an SPF algorithm.

ROUTERS

Routers are the key interconnection devices in the enterprise network; subsequently, the router market has been one of the key growth areas during this decade. Some router vendors have grown from small $10 million companies to $1 billion companies.

In most cases, routers are purpose-built communications processor platforms with hardware architectures specifically designed for high-speed switching. Several possible pitfalls await the unwary purchaser of routers. Such a purchase involves four important considerations:

1. The capacity and architecture in terms of the number of ports accommodated and throughput achievable
2. Internetwork protocols supported and their associated routing protocols
3. Support of technologies for the connected subnetworks
4. Interoperability between different vendors

Capacity and Architecture

The number of ports required determines to a large extent the size of the router required, which in turn affects the architecture and throughput of the router. Physical size of circuit boards dictates how many ports can be placed on a single board. The greater the number of ports, the greater the number of boards required and the more critical the architecture.

Routing between ports on the same board is usually faster than routing between ports on different boards, assuming that there are on-board routing functions. Boards are usually interconnected by means of some kind of backplane. Backplane speeds can vary greatly between vendors. Routing functions and tables may be distributed across all boards or may be centralized. The bottom line is that the architecture affects the performance, and performance figures are sometimes slanted toward some particular facet of the architecture. Thus, some routers may be optimal for certain configurations and not so good for others.

Many of the router manufacturers make several sizes of router, which could be referred to as small, medium, and large. All of one vendor's routers may, regardless of size, offer the same functions, but the circuit boards may not be interchangeable between the different models. This can make a big difference when it comes to stocking an inventory of spare parts. There may also be differences in network management capabilities.

When making comparisons, the data communications manager must carefully analyze vendor throughput and transit delay figures. Although worst cases are helpful for the user and network designer, some vendors specify either the best cases or averages. Other metrics involved in measurement may also be different (e.g., packet size assumed, particular internetwork protocol, particular subnetwork).

Other architectural considerations include extensibility and reliability. For example, is hot-swapping of boards possible? If the router must be powered down and reconfigured to change or add new boards, the disruption to a live network can have severe ripple effects elsewhere in the network. Can additional routing horsepower be added easily as loads increase by simply inserting an additional routing processor?

The question of using stand-alone or hub-based routers may also be relevant. This is a difficult problem because of the traditional split between the hub and router manufacturers. Hub vendors tend not to be routing specialists, and router vendors tend not to be experts at hub design. Alliances between some vendors have been made, but the difference in form factors (of circuit boards) can result in some baroque architectures and poor performance. Except in the simple, low-end cases, purpose-built stand-alone routers usually perform better and are more easily integrated with the rest of the network.

Some stand-alone routers can directly handle the multiplexed input streams from T1 and T3 links, making voice and data integration possible. This is unlikely to be the case for a hub that has been designed mainly for operation in a LAN.

Internetwork Protocols Supported

Most router vendors claim that they support a large number of internetworking protocols. In some cases, however, there may be restrictions on the number of protocols that can be supported simultaneously. There may also be restrictions on the use of multiple protocols over certain network technologies, or hidden subnetwork requirements. An example of the latter might be the need for a separate X.25 permanent virtual circuit (PVC) for every individual protocol, as opposed to operating all the protocols over a single PVC.

Some vendors may also use a proprietary routing protocol scheme for internal routing, only making the standard protocols available at the periphery of the network. This makes it difficult to mix different vendors' router products on the same backbone or within a single routing domain.

Network Technologies Supported

Most manufacturers provide interfaces to a large number of network technologies (e.g., X.25 ISDN, frame relay, T1, T3, Ethernet, Token Ring). The method of support may also vary. For example, in the case of leased circuits, it may or may not be possible to directly connect the carrier's line to the router. Some routers may accept the carrier's framing mechanism directly; others may require an external converter to provide a simple serial interface (e.g., V.35) before connection can be achieved. Buyers should remember that the interaction between these interfaces and the multiple internetwork protocols may not be clearly reported by the vendor.

Interoperability

In the not too distant past, there was little interoperability between routers from different vendors. The reason most often cited was lack of standards for operating multiple protocols over a given subnetwork topology. Fortunately, the Internet community has made substantial progress subsequent to its definition of the Point-to-Point Protocol (PPP), which originally defined encapsulation and discrimination methods for multiprotocol operation over leased circuits. More recently, the utility of PPP has been extended with numerous enhancements. For example, it can now be used over switched services, including dialup, ISDN, and Frame Relay, and it can be used in a multilink configuration. It can operate with or without authentication, and with or without compression.

This plethora of options has led to the widespread support for PPP, both in terms of the number of protocols standardized for use with PPP, and in terms of the number of vendors building compatible routers. As such, interoperability among routers of different vendors is much more common than it was just a few years ago.

Network Management

It is extremely unlikely that a common set of management features will apply to all vendors' routers. Thus, if several manufacturers' routers are deployed in a given enterprise network, several management systems probably will be required. In the best case, these systems can be run on the

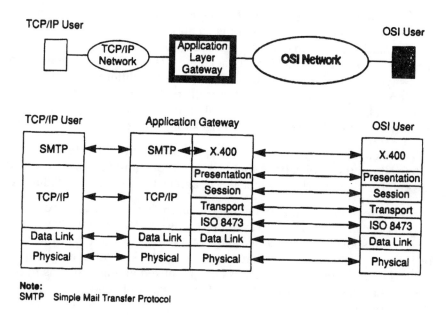

Exhibit 6. Mail Application Gateway

same hardware platform. In the worst case, different hardware platforms may be required.

Filtering

The degree of filtering that can be applied — to prevent local traffic uselessly flooding the enterprise network — may vary with the manufacturer. Various parameters can be used as the basis for filtering — for example, source address, destination address, protocol type, and security codes. The disadvantage of using filtering is the labor involved in setting up the filter tables in all the routers.

BEYOND THE NETWORKING CHALLENGE — THE APPLICATIONS

Gateways, Tunneling, and Transport Service Interfaces. All the considerations discussed so far apply to the internetworking protocols. Multiprotocol networks serve only to share bandwidth; they do not allow applications to interoperate. Where that is necessary, with completely different stacks of protocols, an application gateway must be used. Exhibit 6 shows an OSI-based mail (X.400) application interoperating with a TCP/IP- based mail application over an application gateway.

Such gateways may be sited either centrally or locally. The use of local gateways makes it possible to deploy an application backbone with a single standard application operating over the wide area portion of the enterprise network (e.g., an X.400 mail backbone). This reduces the number of gateways needed for conversion between all the different applications. Only one conversion is necessary for each application (i.e., to the one used on the backbone). A considerable number of different local systems could interoperate through the "standard" backbone application.

The encapsulation technique already mentioned in the context of IP tunneling allows the applications that can be so configured to operate across the enterprise network. A tunneled SNA application is shown in Exhibit 7.

Another solution that may help in the future is the availability of transport service interfaces for end systems (e.g., workstations, terminals, servers). A transport server interface allows a given application to be operated over any underlying communications protocol stack. In other words, applications and communications stacks can be mixed and matched as necessary. The so-called open operating systems (e.g., POSIX and X/Open) adopt this approach.

The transport layer is a fundamental dividing line in the system architecture. Network-related functions are separate from application-related functions so that applications work with many communications protocols. Exhibit 8 shows an end system containing both an open OSI/TCP/IP stack (shaded) and a proprietary stack (unshaded). Within an end system, protocol stacks can generally be separated into the communications-specific lower-layer parts and the application-specific upper-layer parts. The two stacks communicate through a transport-layer interface (TLI).

SUMMARY

In practice, legacy systems or other requirements result in the existence of a variety of heterogeneous systems. Several techniques can be applied to at least make the heterogeneous systems networkable over a single physical network. Varying degrees of interoperability between them may also be possible.

TCP/IP is the single common protocol that has made the most tremendous advances toward this objective. With the continued progress in developing Internet protocols, coupled with the impending migration to IPv6, the multivendor networking situation will only improve.

Nonetheless, developing an enterprise network architecture continues to pose significant challenges. An overall plan for the network minimizes confusion and puts in place a timed migration strategy toward a completely integrated network. Central control has fallen into disrepute, but

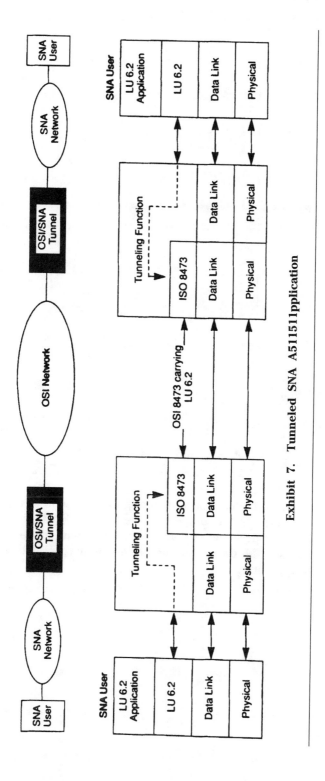

Exhibit 7. Tunneled SNA A511511pplication

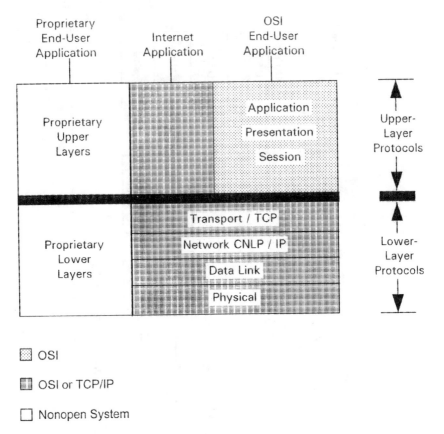

Exhibit 8. Transport Layer Interface

without some control over how networking is to be achieved, all the real benefits of an enterprise network will not be realized. Finally, it is probably fair to say that enterprise networking is still something of a black art and is bound to present all data communications managers with some surprises and disappointments.

Chapter 43

Planning, Designing, and Optimization of Enterprise Networks

Roshan L. Sharma

Network planning, design, and optimization are important components of the network management process. Traditionally, these functions have been performed through the use of powerful mainframe computers. Because these computers required the use of large tariff-related databases, a great deal of time was spent entering input data and interpreting the output data that invariably came in the form of a thick stack of computer printouts. No graphics were available to illustrate the network topologies. Furthermore, the user was always kept out of the design process. However, advances in very large scale integration (VLSI) technology have made powerful PCs available, which has opened the door to the development of better network planning and design tools.

The network planning and design effort can be broken into the following distinct tasks:

- Creating an enterprisewide database of dumb terminals (e.g., telephones), intelligent workstations, customer premise equipment (CPE), such as private automatic branch exchange (PABX) or data LANs, and communications facilities serving those locations.
- Modeling all types of end-to-end multi-hour traffic flows between all locations.
- Modeling traffic growth during a life cycle of the network system.
- Defining end-to-end performance requirements for all forms of communications.
- Designing strategic and tactical network alternatives using available technologies.

0-8493-1149-7/02/$0.00+$1.50
© 2002 by CRC Press LLC

- Selecting the best alternative network based on cost, cutover, and performance.
- Testing the performance of a post-cutover network implementation.
- Updating the analytical tools and preparing for the next design cycle.
- Documenting the results.

THE ENTERPRISE DATABASE (EDB)

Creating the enterprise database is by far the most time-consuming of all network design tasks. An enterprise database (EDB) should at least list:

- All vendors' exact mailing addresses
- All vendors' ten-digit telephone numbers
- All pieces of CPE with vendor's name, date of installation, and single point-of-contact for maintenance
- The usage level of each CPE
- The type and number of communication facilities serving each location; associated point-of-presence (POP) central offices of local exchange carriers (LECs); and interexchange carriers (IECs) with their vertical and horizontal coordinates

The list can grow into a very large one when the database must also classify the users at each location and their communications needs. However, the tasks involved in network planning, design, and optimization are impossible without the availability of an EDB. The table that appears later in this chapter illustrates a sample EDB.

TRAFFIC ENGINEERING TECHNIQUES AND TOOLS

The next three network planning tasks demand a capability for traffic modeling and analysis. Before defining the traffic engineering efforts, some basic traffic-related concepts should be introduced.

There are two types of traffic encountered in enterprise networks:

1. Well-behaved voice and video traffic
2. Bursty data traffic

It is always assumed that connection-oriented voice traffic behaves in a predictable fashion, which implies that:

- The call-holding times can be expressed by at least two moments (i.e., an average and a variance).
- The finer structures of traffic flows do not require rapid changes in network resource deployment.

A close observation of speech energy over the duration of a conversation will show that there are many pauses. Furthermore, two of the four-wire access lines (ALs) and trunks are always idle since only one party can talk at a time. These facts have helped long-distance carriers send more calls over expensive ocean cables than are possible over available trunks using pure circuit-switching by using the time-asynchronous speech interpolator (TASI) technology. Such a technology was never cost effective over cheaper land-based leased lines. With the availability of asynchronous transfer mode (ATM) and Broadband Integrated Services Digital Networks (B-ISDN), users can get the same benefit through the use of variable bit rate (VBR) capability.

The data traffic between two CPEs is always bursty because of the complex rules of data communication protocols. Very small control messages may be involved in both directions before user information can flow. Although a full-duplex connection can be maintained, shared transmission lines in a packet-switched network can carry variable-length packets from many sources concurrently, thus muddying the picture. The faster the transmission lines, the burstier the transmission will appear.

Circuit-Switched Voice and Video Traffic. Circuit-switched voice and video traffic intensity is measured in erlangs, which is equal to the average number of circuits busy during a "busy hour" between two network nodes. For example, if 15.5 conversations are observed concurrently between two network nodes (e.g., between a PABX and a voice switch or over an access line bundle) during a busy hour, then the voice traffic intensity is 15.5 erlangs.

Packet-Switched Data Traffic. Packet-switched data traffic intensity can be measured as the traffic rate in bits per second (bps) during a busy hour. Only the data rate in bps can describe the bursty nature of data traffic. Experienced network specialists have been using the concept of data erlangs for many years in defining the average data traffic intensity between two network nodes. This is obtained by dividing the observed busy hour data rate (R) by the capacity (C) of each separate transmission line. For example, if the busy hour data rate between two nodes is 392,000 bps and the capacity of a transmission line is 56,000 bps, then the data traffic intensity is 7 erlangs.

MODELING TRAFFIC FLOWS IN A BRAND NEW ENTERPRISE NETWORK

It is sometimes difficult to model traffic flows for a brand-new system. Many approximate methods have been devised for predicting traffic intensities (TIs) between all major CPEs. For example, a voice LAN (or PABX) generates about 0.1 * Ns erlangs of busy-hour traffic, where Ns is the number of active subscribers served by the PABX.

A breakdown of these traffic expressions into intranodal and internodal traffic should be determined by the known pattern observed at each enterprise. Some network designers use the 70/30 breakdown — 70 percent of the traffic remains within the site (voice/data LAN) and 30% of the traffic goes to other CPEs as internodal flows. These TI values can then be entered into an input file that defines each site ID, the related vertical and horizontal coordinates, and the total traffic intensity handled by the site.

The next task is to model the internodal traffic flows (i.e., exact traffic intensities handled by all the nodes and links in the path of a CPE-CPE connection). These computations are generally performed by the network design software for each assumed network topology (i.e., number of network switches and the link types employed at each network hierarchy). Some tools use critical design parameters to determine the fraction of traffic handled by access lines (connecting CPE and a switch) and trunks (connecting two switches). Eventually, the tool provides the total traffic intensity handled by each resource (node or link) of each network topology considered during a typical busy hour.

MODELING TRAFFIC FLOWS IN AN EXISTING ENTERPRISE NETWORK

Exact traffic flows can be modeled using the detailed traffic data gathered by intelligent network nodes (e.g., PABX or LAN). The source ID, destination ID, call originating time, and call duration for each connection is recorded in station message data recording (SMDR) tapes of the voice network. Similar data is recorded by the data LAN for the packetized traffic. Simple traffic analysis packages are obtainable for analyzing the exact internodal traffic patterns between all pairs of CPEs. Such data can then be entered in a from-to data file (FTF) to define CPE traffic as simple vectors (i.e., From-Node ID, To-Node ID, and the BHR traffic intensity) for each CPE-nodal pair.

This effort eventually provides actual traffic flows (i.e., the actual traffic intensity handled by all resource, nodes, and links) of each network topology studied during a typical busy hour.

Modeling Time-Consistent Averages (TCAs) of Traffic Flows

Choosing a "busy" hour is an important task. Networks are not cost effective when they are operating during the hour with the highest traffic. A network may provide the required grade-of-service (GOS) during the busiest hour, but at all other hours of the day (especially during the evening and night hours), the GoS level would be overkill. No organization can afford such a network. Network managers who select an hour with the least traffic during the day will hear complaints all day long. Therefore, a proven methodology is needed to select the average traffic intensity for network design. There are two methodologies — one used in North America and one used in all other countries.

The first methodology requires the selection of a typical month and the creation of a matrix (30 × 24) of traffic intensities (TIs) for each network resource for that month. Next, the average traffic intensity for each hour of the day over all 30 days of the month is computed. This process is repeated for each hour of the next 24. The TCA traffic is the maximum value of all 24 TCA values. This value determines the size of the resource (i.e., number of AL and trunks in the bundle connecting two nodes or the computing power of an intelligent node). It is helpful to have a software package for computing TCA traffic intensity (TI) values.

The second methodology requires that the 36 highest TI values be observed over an entire year and then the average computed to get a TCA value. This must be done for all resources.

Both of these methodologies result in more economical networks. However, no single methodology can predict an exact traffic pattern. Traffic values behave like the stock market. A single catastrophe, such as an earthquake, can also change the traffic patterns drastically. The objective of an effective traffic engineering practice is to synthesize an economical enterprise network using a consistent approach.

Modeling Traffic Growth During the System Life Cycle

To estimate the total costs incurred during the life cycle of a network system, the traffic intensities for each year of the life cycle should be modeled. The Delphi approach often works best. In this method, all general managers are interviewed and realistic models of traffic growth during every year of the life cycle can be built. Some divisions may disappear through divestiture or attrition. The data from all of the interviews must be collected, weighed, and processed to create a meaningful model.

PERFORMANCE ISSUES

Before performance requirements for all the communication needs of an enterprise can be defined, network managers must first study the available concepts of performance and identify the exact enterprise needs in each business area.

Network System Performance

Many network systems are implemented without any regard to performance. As long as they satisfy the basic needs for communications, everyone is happy. Often, no effort is expended in:

- Predicting or measuring the actual performance of the system
- Making any measured systemwide improvements after the system is operational

The lack of any concerted effort in defining and measuring performance of network systems may lie in an ignorance of certain system performance concepts. The performance of a network system can be defined in four ways:

1. Total system costs computed on a monthly basis
2. System throughputs in terms of all types of transactions handled during a unit time
3. Systemwide quality-of-service (QOS)
4. Systemwide grade-of-service (GOS)

Total Monthly Costs. Transmission facilities determine the majority of the total monthly cost of MANs and WANs paid to the local exchange carrier (LEC), interexchange carriers (IECs), and other common carriers. The other major costs are for hardware and the recurring price of network management and control (NMC). Financing the hardware can turn a large one-time cost into an affordable monthly cost. The NMC costs related to spares can be handled just like one-time hardware costs. Some companies hire in-house NMC specialists; others prefer to outsource.

System Throughput. System throughput is measured by the rate at which the various types of transactions are handled per unit time (usually second or minute). Throughput is defined by the number of call attempts or calls completed per second for a voice network. In a data network, throughput is defined by the number of packets or bits handled per second. The throughput capability of each node is generally defined by the equipment vendor. The challenge lies in measuring the system throughput. System throughput can be estimated by enumerating the exact paths of each transaction.

System Quality-of-Service (QOS). Performance aspects dealing with transmission quality, perceived voice quality, error-free seconds, data security, and network reliability (mean time between system failures) fall into the QOS criterion. Most of these parameters are very hard to compute for the entire system. Performance aspects of a critical resource can be estimated to get a feel for the quality of service of the entire system.

System Grade-of-Service (GOS). The GOS criterion deals with end-to-end blocking for a voice network and average response time (measured as the elapsed time between the moment the send key is pressed and the moment the return reply is discerned by the user) for data communications. Analytical tools are available for estimating GOS parameters for voice, data, and integrated networks.

Defining Enterprise Performance Goals

Performance goals for enterprise networks are generally developed by corporate strategic planners. A typical strategic planning cycle lasts several years and entails:

- Continuous evaluation of the needs of the enterprise and its competitors. This activity defines the relationship of system response times to user productivity for each transaction.
- Study of evolving new technologies, CPE, and networking standards. The most effective way of deploying these new technologies should also be investigated. This study should establish the cost and performance attributes of new hardware (e.g., ATM and LAN switches).

A network planning group should work closely with the IT department. It is better not to outsource strategic planning because an outside group cannot fully understand the close synergy between the demands of the marketplace, corporate IT, user productivity, and network operations.

Network managers today have to deal with ever-increasing demands for:

- Voice, video, image, and data communications.
- Multiplexing of digitized voice, image, and video signals with regular data traffic at all hierarchies of enterprise locations through switches (e.g., ATM switches).
- Unscheduled or varying demands for digital bandwidth at all hours of a day on a dynamic basis.

To design an integrated enterprise network, the strategic planning group needs a user-friendly tool for quickly evaluating solutions that take user demands into account. The right tool should help the strategic planning group reach solutions iteratively and interactively.

MAJOR NETWORK DESIGN ISSUES

No single approach to network design is ideally suited for all enterprises. Network design is basically concerned with two issues:

1. Topological optimization, which determines the way network nodes are connected to one another (including the type of connections) while satisfying a set of critical design and performance constraints.
2. System performance dealing with end-to-end response times, path congestion, and availabilities. Recurring network cost is generally the most important performance criterion and it is mainly determined by its topology. Network topology also determines the remaining performance issues such as response times and availability. Each network design package analyzes these performance issues in only an approximate manner.

Previous Network Design Technology

Many older network design tools handled only voice or multidrop data networks. Some of the tools that came later handled only interconnections of data LANs to achieve an enterprise data WAN. Furthermore, most of these tools required mainframes. The use of a mainframe introduced an unnecessary curtain between the network designer and the host processor. The network design jobs were entered invariably via the "batch" approach, and the outputs came in the form of large printouts after a good deal of delay. Each change of a design parameter or study of a new technology required a new non-interactive delay. The absence of network-related graphics from outputs caused additional delays in interpreting the significance of results.

The old design technology also required the use of an extensive database of tariffs. The complexity of the tariff database was probably the main reason behind the need for mainframes. If such a database were incorporated into a desktop minicomputer or a PC-based workstation, users would experience significant processing delays.

Because network topologies do not change with perturbations in any given tariff (they change only with varying design parameters and technologies), using a simplified set of existing or new tariffs is sufficient for designing an optimized network. These topologies can be studied for a detailed cost analysis using one of the many available PC-Line Pricer (PCLP) units. This two-step approach should create a separation between the network design algorithms and the ever-changing tariffs. There should be no need to update the network design package just because a tariff changed slightly.

Simulation Tools. Some vendors market software packages based on computer simulation for evaluating system performance. LANs (voice or data) and WANs consisting of interconnected data LANs can be evaluated for performance through computer simulation. A good deal of time must be spent on:

- Writing the simulation program based on the exact network topology and the underlying communication protocols
- Debugging the software before one can evaluate all of the performance metrics such as throughput and end-to-end response times

Because typical enterprise networks require exorbitant run-times, a simulation tool is no longer an ideal way for synthesizing an optimum network topology. A network topology optimization package based on analytical tools is always the best approach. The resulting topology can be evaluated for studying detailed system response times and availabilities using an expensive simulation tool.

NEW NETWORK DESIGN TECHNOLOGY

New network design tools are user-friendly, interactive, and can optimize network topology in an iterative fashion while quickly varying the values of critical design parameters. Many of these tools provide special menus for computing end-to-end response times for unusual operational conditions. Some packages even provide special tools for analyzing subsystem security and reliability.

Many new tools based on the graphical user interface (GUI) can evaluate any mix of CPEs, transmission facilities, and network topologies very rapidly in an intuitive manner. Today's design tools also allow the entry of approximate tariffs, but in no way can this new technology eliminate the need for an expert network designer or an architect. Because the expert designer is always involved with "what-if" type analyses, the potential solutions are meaningful only if the network design tool provides them quickly.

ONE EXAMPLE: THE ECONETS NETWORK PLANNING AND DESIGN PACKAGE

Inputs into this network design package are in the form of flat, sequential files. Results are provided in the form of:

- Graphics illustrating a network topology with summary costs of communications facilities and response times
- Output files containing detailed cost distributions and critical performance data

The most important input file, the VHD file, lists the site/node ID, vertical and horizontal coordinates, and total busy hour, time-consistent traffic intensities in bits per second (for data) or millierlangs (for voice) for each location of the enterprise. A from-to data file can also be used to represent exact traffic flows. Another file called the daily traffic profile relates the busy-hour intensities to the other 23 hours of the day for computing the costs on a daily or monthly basis. For an enterprise with many time zones, several busy-hour models can be used.

The second most important input file, the link file, defines the link type that serves each location. Another important input file, the NLT file, defines the link type, capacity, allowed maximum data rate, multiplexing factor, corresponding tariff number, and the multiplying factor for a privately owned facility, if applicable. Up to ten link types and corresponding capacities, allowed maximum data rates, multiplexing factors, corresponding tariff numbers, and multiplying factors can be defined by the NLT file. The tariff file can define up to ten manually entered tariffs, each modeled on 17 parameters. Several link, NLT, and tariff files can be prepared to model many combinations of links and tariffs at all levels of the network hierarchy.

The system design file defines the busy hour, from-to traffic for all significant pairs, if such data is known. Other input files are also used for modeling/designing ACD networks using a mix of virtual facilities and leased FX lines.

The File menu allows the creation, viewing, and updating of all input/output files. The Networking menu allows the modeling/design of multilevel voice, data, and IV/D networks using the appropriate star data, directed link, and multidrop data network topologies and voice networks based on star topologies. Network managers can also model, design, and optimize backbone networks in an iterative manner.

The Networking menu also allows the designer to find optimum locations for concentrators/switches by starting with effective solutions and improving these through a fast interative process. By specifying the design parameters, network managers can model and design data networks based on IBM's SNA, packet-switched networks based on CCITT's X.25 standard, and fast packet-switched networks based on frame relay and ATM technology.

By specifying the design parameters, hybrid voice networks can be modeled using all types of leased and virtual facilities with or without multiplexing. Network managers can also optimize a backbone network topology and model any given topology (for cost and routes).

The Analysis menu allows the designer to model/analyze any point-to-point and several multilink paths for congestion/queuing delays, LAN performance, and reliability. Another Analysis menu item allows the computation of the equivalent monthly cost of hardware and payoff periods for privately owned hardware and transmission facilities. The following section outlines a case study of an EcoNets implementation.

AN ENTERPRISE NETWORK PLANNING AND DESIGN CASE STUDY — ECONETS

The enterprise in this case study manufactures, distributes, markets, and maintains highly specialized intelligent workstations. It has 17 sites scattered across the U.S., with headquarters in Las Colinas, TX. Two separate networks serve the enterprise. A voice network connects all 17 locations (or PABXs) to a voice switch located at Las Colinas with leased voice-grade lines (VGLs). A separate data network connects workstations located at all of its locations to a host using the SNA-BSC protocol and 9600-bps lines. The newly appointed network manager wants to study the feasibility of a new network architecture, so a consultant is engaged to study the problem.

A database (a subset of the EDB) for network design was created and is outlined in Exhibit 1.

Exhibit 1.   Enterprise Database (EDB) for a 17-Node Network Design (Voice/Data Applications)

*************** **NODAL DEFINITION DATA** ***************

N#	-V-	-H-	LOAD (BPS/MEs)	LATA	LINK	NAME
1	8438	4061	40000	552	0	LCLNTX
2	8436	4034	5000	552	0	DALLTX
3	8296	1094	1300	952	0	SRSTFL
4	8360	906	1300	939	0	FTMYFL
5	6421	8907	1300	674	0	TACMWA
6	6336	8596	1300	676	0	BELVWA
7	4410	1248	1400	128	0	DANVMA
8	6479	2598	1300	466	0	VERSKY
9	9258	7896	1300	730	0	TOAKCA
10	9233	7841	1400	730	0	NORWCA
11	9210	7885	1400	730	0	WLAXCA
12	7292	5925	1400	656	0	DENVCO
13	7731	4025	1300	538	0	TULSOK
14	7235	2069	1300	438	0	NORCGA
15	5972	2555	2500	324	0	COLMOH
16	9228	7920	2500	730	0	STMNCA
17	8173	1147	2500	952	0	TMPAFL
Tot. BHR Traffic =			68500			

************* **Node(N)Link(L)Type(T) [NLT] FILE PRINTOUT** *************

***** **LEGEND** *****

{ C=Link Cap.: MaxR=Max. Allwd. Rate(Wm): MF=VMpxg.Fact.: FPF=Priv.Fac. Fact.}

LType	LinkC	MaxLinkR	MF	Tariff#	FPF
1	9600	6300	1	1	1
2	56000	48000	8	2	1
3	1544000	1440000	24	3	1
4	45000000	40000000	672	4	1

**************** **TARIFF DATA PRINTOUT** ******************

TARIFF #=1 AVG. LOCAL LOOPS CHARGES ($)=294 MILEAGE BANDS:

50	100	500	1000	10000
FIXED COSTS ($):				
72.98	149.28	229.28	324.24	324.24
COST PER MILE ($):				
2.84	1.31	0.51	0.32	0.32

TARIFF #=2 AVG. LOCAL LOOPS CHARGES ($)=492 MILEAGE BANDS:

50	100	500	1000	10000
FIXED COSTS ($):				
232	435	571	1081	1081
COST PER MILE ($):				
7.74	3.68	2.32	1.3	1.3

Exhibit 1.   Enterprise Database (EDB) for a 17-Node Network Design (Voice/Data Applications) (continued)

TARIFF #=3 AVG. LOCAL LOOPS CHARGES ($)=2800 MILEAGE BANDS:

50	100	10000	10000	10000
FIXED COSTS ($):				
1770	1808	2008	2500	2500
COST PER MILE ($):				
10	9.25	7.25	7.25	7.25

TARIFF #=4 AVG. LOCAL LOOPS CHARGES ($)=8000 MILEAGE BANDS:

10000	10000	10000	10000	10000
FIXED COSTS ($):				
16600	16600	16600	16600	16600
COST PER MILE ($):				
47	47	47	47	47

* * * * * * * * * * * * * * * SYSTEM DESIGN PARAMETERS * * * * * * * * * * * * * * *

=0

ATP/D=3	UPR/D=56000	HPR/D=56000	IML/D=28	RML/D=300
Ncu/D=4	Rmph/D=100	HTT/D=0.001	Fopt/D=0	Tnp/D=10
Thm/D=4	Kpg/D=0.01	BKL/D=64	ICPB/D=56	TGF/C=1
Flk/C=0	Fnn/C=1	Flt/C=1	Fftd/C=0	NA =0
ALT/V/D=1	NA =0	Bal/V/A=0.1	ECC/V=13.33	ECD/V/A=300
DREQ/A=60	PEXD/A=0.15	Clbr/A=23	Frst/A=1	ACDT/A=2
TKLT/V/D=1	NA =0	Btk/V=0.1	Ffdx/D=1	MTKU/D=0.8
BBTF/C=2	Vmin/C=3000	Vmax/C=10000	Hmin/C=0	Hmax/C=10000
Fvc0/C=0	Fvc1/C=0	Fvc2/C=0	Fvc3/C=0	Fvc4/C=0
Fvc5/C=1	Fvc6/C=30	Fvc7/C=0	Fsh/D=0	Fnp/C=1
DPM/A=30	Fdis/C=1	NA =0	TFXC/A=1	NDEC/C=7
DECT/C=1	/A=ACD=0	/C=Common=0	/D=Data=0	

* * * * * * * * * * * * * * NAMES OF INPUT FILES * * * * * * * * * * * * * * *

VHD17* LINK17* MAPusa* NLT* TARIFF* SDF* NAME17* FTF1* LATA17*
FILES.TXT* CSABDS* UTBL* WUTBL* MUTBL* RSTBL* DTP8* Swf2*

* * * * * * * * * * * * * * DAILY TRAFFIC PROFILE * * * * * * * * * * * * * * *

Hour Numbers & Corresponding Fractions of Daily Traffic are as follows:

1	0	2	0	3	0	4	0	5	0	6	0
7	0.05	8	0.1	9	0.1	10	0.1	11	0.1	12	0.1
13	0.1	14	0.1	15	0.1	16	0.1	17	0.05	18	0
19	0	20	0	21	0	22	0	23	0	24	0

* * * * * * * Switch File Definition * * * * * * *

Number of Switches =2 @ 11, 1.

Networking Menu Item No. Employed= 6

-END OF DATABASE

The 17 sites, their vertical and horizontal coordinates, and busy-hour TCA of traffic intensities are shown for both voice (in millierlangs) and data (in bps). Also shown are their names according to a six-symbol city-state (CCCCST) code. Next, an NLT file is defined for these link types. The various design parameters are defined in the SDF. The design parameters for the voice network define the access link type, desired blocking on access lines, trunk line type, and desired blocking on trunks. The major design parameters for the data network are ATP (analysis type is equal to 3 for response time modeling for an SNA-BSC network), user port rate, host port rate, nodal processing time in ms for each transaction, and half-modem time in ms spent in going through the modem in one direction.

The consultant first modeled the existing voice and data networks. The monthly costs for these two separate networks were $60,930 and $10,017, respectively. The EcoNets tool was then used to study various topologies consisting of switches and three link types for voice and only the 9600-bps line for data (higher-speed lines resulted in no improvements). The results are shown in Exhibit 2. The optimum voice network topology (see Exhibit 3) consisted of two switches (as determined by the EcoNet's center-of-gravity finding item on the Networking menu) and 56K-bps lines, each of which carries eight digitally encoded voice conversations.

The one-time cost of 17 special hardware boxes that perform voice encoding and multiplexing in the same box did not influence the optimum network topology. The optimum data network topology (see Exhibit 4) consisted of the same two switches as used for the voice network and 9600-bps lines. The costs of these optimum networks were $37,546 and $9147, respectively. This represented a monthly savings of $23,254 (or about 32.8 percent of existing costs). No matter how the figure is examined, it amounts to a substantial savings.

Additional savings can be achieved by computing the total data rate (in bps) of voice conversations from each site and adding the regular data traffic and constructing a new VHD file. An optimum star-data topology consisting of two switches and 56K-bps lines can be achieved. The topology is identical to that of the optimum voice network (see Exhibit 3) and the monthly cost is about the same. The cost of the separate data network disappears completely. The new monthly savings of $33,392 represent 47.1 percent of existing costs. These additional savings resulted from the fact that the 56K-bps line used in the integrated voice/data network had enough excess capacity to handle the data traffic. Such a phenomenon is similar to the one experienced by network managers working with larger T1 networks in the 1980s. Those networks had enough excess capacities in the T1 trunks to handle the data traffic. The broadband data networks of the future should have enough excess capacity to handle voice traffic.

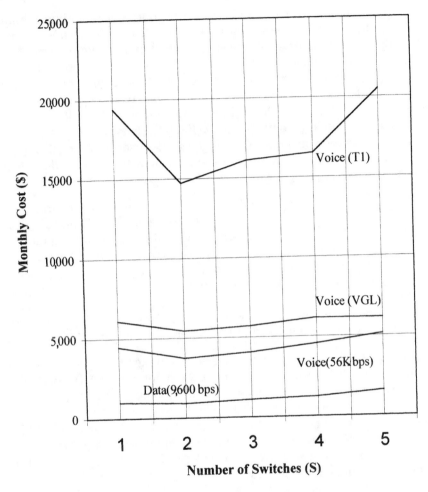

Exhibit 2.   Costs Versus Number of Switches and Link Types

This example illustrates only a small enterprise network. Bigger savings can be achieved through optimization of larger enterprise networks. Savings result because: integrated networks make use of excess capacity, and aggregation of many separate applications allows the deployment of transmission facilities with higher capacities that generally cost less on a pertransaction basis. These types of network planning and design tools provide network managers with many more opportunities for providing a cost-effective, integrated network to the enterprise.

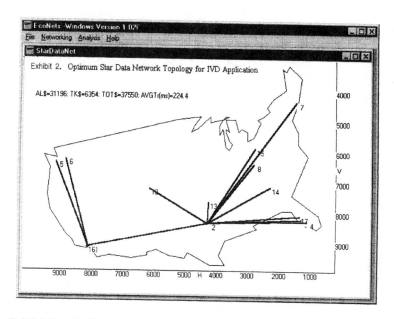

Exhibit 3.   Optimum Star Data Network Topology for IVD Application

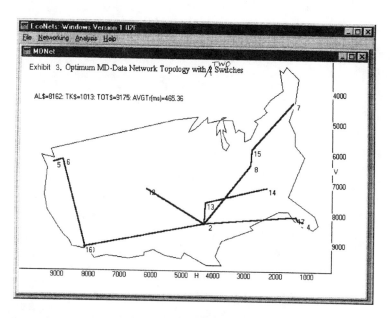

Exhibit 4.   Optimum MD-Data Network Topology with Two Switches

Chapter 44
Enterprise Network Monitoring and Analysis

Colin Wynd

Users are starting to expect error-free network connectivity with guaranteed uptime and response time. Users are also expecting that network services are delivered regardless of the underlying technology. Business end users also expect that data transmission will be secure. This increase in reliance on client/server applications as a fundamental part of conducting business means that end users need to rely on the network as much as the phone. Thus, whether the IT department is ready or not, the network is expected to be as reliable as the phone system.

The Changing Face of the Business Environment:

Corporations are more geographically dispersed, and entities that once were autonomous are working closely together. The network has become a critical method of communicating among these various groups. Applications are now client/server rather than on a central mainframe, meaning that the network must be operational for the end users to perform.

As the use of the network increases, more groups can be geographically dispersed. The increased focus on work/life balance has increased the number of work-at-home participants. The side-effect is that the amount of traffic on the network also increases.

This chapter discusses the role that network monitoring and analysis takes in administrating networks. We start by explaining network monitoring and where it fits into the IT management arena before showing the range of functionality that network monitoring brings to the IT manager's arsenal.

0-8493-1149-7/02/$0.00+$1.50
© 2002 by CRC Press LLC

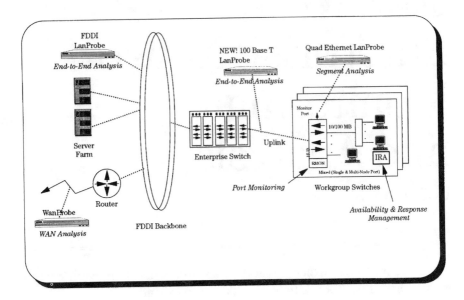

Exhibit 1. Remote Monitoring Agents Installed on a Large Enterprise Network

NETWORK MONITORING AND ANALYSIS DEFINED

Distributed network monitoring is the ability to view a remote network and perform monitoring and analysis on that remote network as if it were local. In the past, portable devices were carried out to remote sites and placed onto the network when problems were occurring on that segment. Having a network monitoring device on a segment only when there are problems means that the segment is not being monitored 99 percent of the time. Monitoring devices permanently placed on mission-critical segments can constantly monitor traffic. This means that analysis can be performed over and above fault management.

Exhibit 1 shows an example of remote monitoring agents installed on a large enterprise network with a variety of media types such as WANs, switches, FDDI, and ethernet.

The agents or "probes" reside on the remote segments and collect information of the traffic that it sees. The segments can be of any media type from various LAN media types such as ethernet, FDDI, Token Ring, or some WAN protocol such as Frame Relay. The segments can be geographically dispersed, but in general must be interconnected. The network management console contains a suite of applications that collect the network information from these remote agents and interpret it using power graphical user interfaces. Interestingly, the network management console communicates with agents using the same network that the agents are monitoring (out-of-band communication between the manager and agents is also possible).

With this configuration, network administrators can use monitoring tools to manage the whole network. Some functions that the network administrator can perform are as follows:

- *Network Performance Management:* The ability to continuously monitor certain network statistics to ensure adherence to the service level agreement; setting network thresholds to identify anomalies and the creation of baselines to aid in determining "normal" network performance.
- *Network Security Monitoring:* Ensuring that only authorized users are accessing the network. This includes both monitoring the effectiveness of firewalls as well as internal security monitoring.
- *Fault Management and Availability:* Being able to troubleshoot network problems in a timely fashion and monitor the availability of servers from the end users' perspective.
- *Capacity Planning:* Traffic profile modeling allows the network manager to do a quick "what if" analysis before reconfiguring network resources. Having the appropriate data of past network trends determines what changes need to be made in the future to handle the ever-growing network.

NETWORK MONITORING AND ANALYSIS
IN THE IT ENVIRONMENT

The IT management environment covers the whole scope of devices that reside on the network, as well as the network itself, that enable business end users to function. We can break this down into four components:

1. *Systems Management* is concerned with the performance of the computers on the network, and usually deals with issues like database performance and disk use on file servers.
2. *Element Management* is concerned with managing the various networking devices, like bridges, routers, and hubs. Typical management issues deal with configuration tables, throughput, link states, and port partitioning. A device management application usually shows a picture of the device on your screen, complete with installed cards and indicator lights.
3. *Desktop Management* is concerned with the end user workstations and PCs. The management issues are PC config files, disk use, application support, etc.
4. *Network Monitoring and Analysis* is primarily concerned with the activity on the wire itself. It is looking at the flow of data across the net-

work in an effort to understand network performance and capacity, and to resolve problems related to networking protocols.

Service level management (SLM) is the strategy of defining, controlling, and maintaining the desired levels of IT service for the business end user. Business end users define with the IT department the level of service that is needed to support them. The level of service is turned into a set of objectives that the IT department can then monitor.

Network monitoring and analysis allows the IT department to manage one part of the end-to-end management picture. System, database, and application management issues are not discussed in this chapter.

STANDARDS OVERVIEW

Network monitoring has benefited from several standards. The main standard currently in use for network monitoring is the RMON standard which defines a method of monitoring traffic up to the DataLink layer (Layer 2) in the OSI stack. The RMON2 standard defines how to monitor traffic at the network layer (OSI Layer 3) and some portions of the application layer (Layer 7):

Simple Network Management Protocol (SNMP)
Simple Network Management Protocol version 2 (SNMPv2)
Remote Monitoring (RMON) standard
Remote Monitoring version 2 (RMON2) standard

Why Perform Network Monitoring?

As part of an IT department's Service Level Agreement (SLA) with its business end users, IT must maintain a certain level of network service. To be able to do this, the network must be monitored to ensure error-free connectivity, responsiveness, and level of throughput. If the network is not monitored then it would be impossible for the IT department to guarantee any level of service.

In today's competitive environment, new client-server applications are quickly appearing in business environments; some examples are the WWW, Lotus Notes, and network Doom. If the network is not being monitored, then the effect of adding one of these network-intensive applications is unknown, and eventually one will bring the network to its knees. If the environment is being monitored, then network bandwidth can be monitored and traffic trends analyzed to ensure that network bandwidth will always exceed future growth.

The ability to monitor trends changes the IT from being reactive — waiting until something breaks before resolving the problem; to being proactive — resolving potential issues before they break. The IT department should now blend into the background allowing business end users to focus on their own functions.

Who Does Network Monitoring?

Since there are many areas to network monitoring, many people are involved. Here are some generic descriptions:

- *Network Manager.* Responsible for long-term strategic decisions regarding the network, involved in looking at new technologies such as 100Base-X or ATM, and deciding where and when to modify bandwidth, this person tends to look at network trends, performing forecasting and capacity planning.
- *Network Engineer.* Responsible for day-to-day operations of the network, upgrades network devices, adds capacity, and also acts as a second line of support for problems that the operations center engineer cannot resolve.
- *Operations Center Engineer.* Most large corporations have a centralized monitoring center staffed with "level 1" engineers who attempt basic troubleshooting of problems. These engineers monitor for events that are triggered by servers, workstations, or network devices that can alert the operations center on potential problems. These engineers are the first line of support and are constantly in reactive mode.

What Data Is Provided?

Monitoring the network means that information on every single packet on every single segment can be gathered. Network monitoring really means deciding which data are important and should be gathered, and which data are redundant. Corporations with a large number of segments need to decide on only a few critical pieces of information, otherwise they are inundated with data. The cost of analyzing the network would exceed the actual cost of the network! Some of the most critical measurements that should be gathered are:

- *Utilization.* Segment utilization information should be gathered to generate trends for capacity planning purposes, baselining purposes, and performance information.
- *Error rates.* Total error rate information can give performance indicators, baselining the error rate of the network, correlated with utilization it can give indicators of physical layer network problems.
- *Protocol distribution.* This can generate trends for changing application mixes, monitoring the usage of new applications and the effect of new applications on the network.
- *Performance.* These top talkers can give indications on the performance of the network, performance of machines, and load of appli-

cations and services on the network. Top talkers can also indicate potential new applications that are unknown to the network department (new Internet applications such as PointCast have been discovered using this method).

- *Latency measurements.* They are echo tests leading to trends in performance.

How Does Network Monitoring Work?

Network monitoring is a large subject and there are many proprietary protocols that are involved. We will only cover standards-based protocols, plus the most widespread proprietary protocols.

The Simple Network Management Protocol (SNMP)

The Simple Network Management Protocol (SNMP) was a draft standard in 1988 and finally ratified in April 1989. SNMP is described by Request For Comments (RFC) 1098. SNMP has three basic components:

1. *Agent.* A software program that resides in a managed element of the network such as a hub, router, or specialized device.
2. *Manager.* Communicates with the agent using the SNMP commands
3. *Management Information Base (MIB).* A database that resides with the agent and holds relevant management information.

The diagram in Exhibit 2 shows the relationship among the three components (agent, MIB, and manager).

There are five types of SNMP commands called protocol data units (PDU's):

1. *Get request.* A manager requests (from the agent) the value of a variable stored in the MIB.
2. *Get-Next request.* Used by the manager to request information on multiple variables. Used to reduce network traffic. If one variable is not available, no values are returned. Also used to retrieve unknown rows, if available.
3. *Set request.* The manager instructs the agent to set an MIB variable to the desired value.
4. *Get-Response.* Sent by the Agent as a response to a SET or Get-Next command as either an error or identical to the SET to show it was accepted, or to a Get-Next with the value portions of the request filled in. The Manager checks its list of previously sent requests to locate the one that matches this response and, if none is found, the response is discarded; otherwise it is handled.
5. *Trap.* One of two unsolicited messages sent from the agent to the manager, often used for event notification.

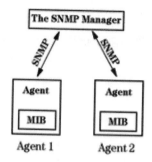

Exhibit 2. Relationship between Agent, MIB, and Manager

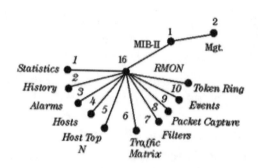

Exhibit 3. The Hierarchical Nature of MIBs

THE MANAGEMENT INFORMATION BASE TREE

MIBs are hierarchical in nature (Exhibit 3); this allows unique identifiers for each MIB variable (or Object). Some MIBs of interest are:

RFC1213 — MIBII — basic system information and basic level statistics
RFC1757 — RMON (Remote Monitoring)
RFC1513 — RMON (Remote Monitoring) extension for Token Ring

There are several advantages that network management applications have with SNMP:

- The protocol is easy to implement.
- The protocol requires few resources to operate.
- The protocol is mature, stable, and well understood.
- The protocol is widely available (on most computers) and most network devices have some form of agent/MIB embedded within them.

However, as networks have grown and the need for network management has become more imperative, several disadvantages with SNMP have become apparent. Some of these disadvantages are:

- Limited security
- Lack of a block transfer
- Polling-based protocol
- Trap limitations

SNMPv2

SNMPv2 is a proposed standard that is attempting to address these issues. Some of the proposed extensions to the standard include:

- Manager-to-manager communication capability.
- Additional SNMP commands (PDU's):
  — Get BulkRequest for getting whole tables
  — InformRequest, Manager-to-Manager PDU
- Reliable traps

The last area of contention with SNMPv2 is security. Currently, there are two proposed drafts that are attempting to address the security issue.

The Remote Monitoring Protocol (RMON)

The RMON standard is a specific standard for performing remote monitoring on networks. The RMON standard is defined by two standards: RFC 1757 and RFC 1513. The standard defines a MIB that is broken down into ten groups; the first nine define monitoring of ethernet networks and the tenth defines extensions for Token Ring. There are currently no standards for monitoring FDDI, 100Base-X, or WAN networks. RMON vendors have added their own proprietary extensions for these additional media types. RMON is limited as it only gives visibility up to the DataLink Layer (Layer 2) in the OSI stack.

Statistics Group. This group contains many segment statistics in 32-bit counters such as packets, dropped packets, broadcasts, and multicasts. These are just counters and not studies.

History Group. This group contains segment history statistics for various counters such as broadcasts, errors, multicasts, packets, and octets. These numbers are for certain time periods. RMON defines two default time periods: — five seconds and 1800 seconds.

This means:

Alarms Group. This covers threshold monitoring and trap generation when that threshold has been reached. Allows alarms to be set of various counters and patch match. Traps can start and stop packet capture.

Host Group. This contains host table and traffic statistic counters, plus a time table of discovery.

Host Top N. This contains studies for X time and X hosts, listing top talker for the study group.

Traffic Matrix Group. Thiscontains matrix of MAC layer (Layer 2) conversations. Information such as error, packets, and octets sorted by MAC address.

Packet Capture/Filter Group. These two groups are used together. Packet capture group contains the packets that have been captured. Multiple instances can be created.

Token Ring Group. This contains specific information about Token Ring such as ring order, ring station table, and packet size distribution for history studies.

Remote Monitoring Version 2 (RMON2) Protocol

The RMON standard brought many benefits to the network monitoring community, but also left out many features. The RMON2 standard is trying to address this. RMON2 attempts to address these issues by allowing the monitoring of Layer 3 (Network Layer) information as well as protocol distribution up to Layer 7 (Application Layer).

NETWORK PERFORMANCE MANAGEMENT

Performance management means being able to monitor segment activity as well as intrasegment traffic analysis. Network managers must be able to examine traffic patterns by source, destination, conversations, protocol/application type, and segment statistics such as utilization and error rates. Network managers must define the performance goals and how notification of performance problems should happen, and with what tolerances. Some objectives that network managers are faced with are:

- *Baselining and network trending.* How to determine the true operating envelope for the network by defining certain measurements (such as segment utilization, error rate, network latency) to check service level objectives and out-of-norm conditions which, if left unchecked, may have drastic consequences on networked business users' productivity.

- *Application usage and analysis.* Helps managers answer questions such as, "What is the overall load of WWW traffic?" and "What times of the day do certain applications load the network?" This allows network managers to discover important performance information (either realtime or historic) that will help define performance service level objectives for applications in the client/server environment.

- *Internetwork perspective.* Is traffic between remote sites and interconnect devices critical to business? With Internetwork perspective capabilities, discover traffic rates between subnets and find out which nodes are using WAN links to communicate. It can also help define "typical" rates between interconnect devices. Internetwork perspective can show how certain applications use the critical interconnect paths and define "normal" WAN use for applications.
- *Data correlation.* Allows selection of peak network usage points throughout the day and discovery of which nodes were contributing to the network load at that peak point in time; which nodes they were sending traffic to; and which applications were running between them.

The diagram (Exhibit 4) shows an example of traffic flow between several segments. The thickness of the line (and the color) indicates the volume of traffic. With this information, it is easy to identify potential WAN bottlenecks.

The second diagram (Exhibit 5) shows clients and servers correlated with a time graph. Being able to determine how much one particular server affects the network can help in the positioning of that server and, again, improve performance.

NETWORK SECURITY MONITORING

Security management encompasses a broad set of access control policies that span network hosts, network elements, and network access points (firewalls). Consistent policies are the key here; the objective is to support access and connectivity that is appropriate to the business need while restricting clearly inappropriate network-based access. As in other activities, constant monitoring for specific violations is critical, as is a notification mechanism. For certain conditions, immediate, automatic action may be required (i.e., "Shut down this connection," or "Shut down the firewall"). Monitoring should include both passive and active monitoring (probing).

Access level monitoring ensures that the controls and security that are in place are actually performing to expectations. Monitoring the traffic flow to a firewall, for instance, ensures that no intruders are accessing internally. Access level monitoring polices the "police" and ensures that nothing has been overlooked by the security.

FAULT MANAGEMENT AND AVAILABILITY

Fault management is the continuous monitoring of the network and its elements, and the detection of failures within the network environment. When a failure is detected, then notification of the failure must occur in a timely fashion. The failure must be qualified with respect to other failures and prioritized.

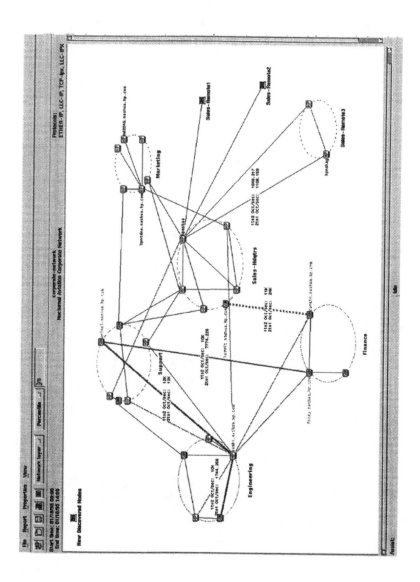

Exhibit 4. Traffic Flow between Several Segments

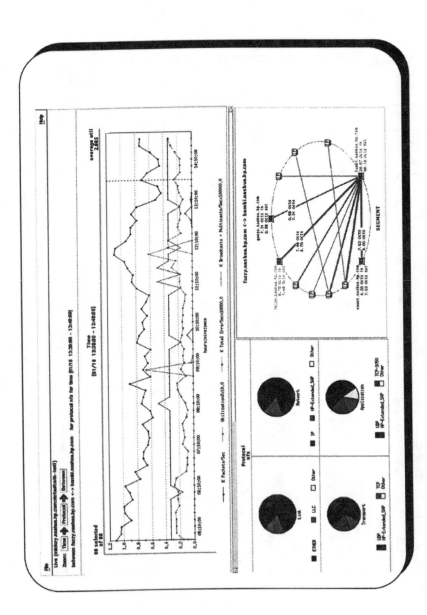

Exhibit 5. Clients and Servers Correlated with a Time Graph

Fault management systems include software bundles to detect and notify a centralized system of these failures. The centralized system normally includes some form of discover and mapping software that allows the network manager to have a graphical view of the network. These notifications must be correlated so that event storms are eliminated. A trouble ticketing system can also be incorporated so that a document trail is kept of the problem and allows a mechanism to communicate the status of the problem to the end users.

Another aspect to fault management is availability. This is the monitoring of servers from business end users' perspective to ensure that the machine is available to the end user. Tracking and notification of any interruption of client/server access is a critical part of the IT department's function.

CAPACITY PLANNING

Network demand is growing at unprecedented rates. New applications such as SAP and the World Wide Web (WWW) are encouraging extensive use of the network. Graphics are now sent regularly over the network (either through a corporation's Intranet or over the Internet). As network managers increase bandwidth, new applications for the network (such as Voice-over-IP or multimedia) become viable. This causes another spurt of demand for the network.

Capacity planning allows the network manager to look forward by looking at the past, and helps the manager to forecast what the demand will be. This means that the IT department can keep one step ahead of demand.

NETWORK REPORTING

Part of the IT department's function is to demonstrate that it is performing its function to the prescribed level. Being able to document that the network is running at the level agreed to in the service level agreement is an important justification tool.

It is critical that any reports are generated automatically; otherwise, reports will not be generated or the effort to generate them will be too substantial to make it worthwhile.

LIMITATIONS OF NETWORK MONITORING AND ANALYSIS

Monitoring the network with the RMON standard means that only DataLink layer (Layer 2) information is collected. This is not high enough in the OSI stack to gather information about traffic trends of client-server applications.

The RMON2 standard defines a method of monitoring up to Layer 7 at certain times. RMON2 does not define continuous monitoring of all Layer 7 traffic, nor does RMON2 define any metrics for performance management.

ENTERPRISE NETWORKING

SUMMARY

Enterprise network monitoring and analysis is a fast-changing environment. From the early days just a few years ago of monitoring the physical layer of the networks to the future of application layer service level management, the whole arena is helping IT management take control of the distributed environment that it spans.

Network monitoring and analysis will always have several aspects that have been described in this chapter, and the tools for implementing service level agreements between business end users and IT departments are quickly maturing.

However, network monitoring is only part of the total end-to-end solution that must include the whole environment that business end users operate. This means that systems, databases, and application monitoring tools must be deployed in conjunction with the network monitoring tools so that the whole environment can be viewed. Some tools, such as HP's PerfView product, that for the first time seamlessly integrate database, application, network, and system information on a single pane of glass for the end-to-end view that is necessary in this complex environment in which IT must now work, are just being released.

References

Peter Phaal. *Lan Traffic Management*, Prentice Hall, ISBN: 0-13-124207-5.
Dah Ming Chiu and Ram Sudama. *Network Monitoring Explained*, Ellis Horwood, ISBN 0-13-614-710-0.
Nathan Muller. *Focus On OpenView*, CBM Books, ISBN 1-878956-48-5.
Marshall T. Rose. *The Simple Book*, Prentice Hall, ISBN 0-13-812611-9.

Chapter 45
Troubleshooting and Analyzing Network Problems

Greg Kilmartin

Network analyzers probe into the wire where network communication takes place to understand what is occurring over that medium. Without such tools, network engineers would be left in the lurch as to when, how, and what is traversing the network. Analyzers are also responsible for decoding the bits and bytes of data communication into useful information used by network engineers, hardware/software developers, and others. Without these tools, it would be nearly impossible to troubleshoot communication errors, hardware failures, network design errors, and a farrago of other network problems.

Network analyzers take many forms, but they can be divided into a few distinct categories and they have a basic set of features and functions. The categories of network analyzers are as follows: protocol analyzers, traffic generators, and a combination of both. Although each category presents considerable strengths and weaknesses over the other, having the mix of both is the best choice if dollars permit. However, the cost of these devices ranges from a few hundred dollars to several thousands, even up to the tens of thousands, and cost is usually the defining factor in choosing one. Nevertheless, the absolute defining factor is what the network analyzer will be used for. To begin, look at network analyzers from the most basic level.

PROTOCOL ANALYZER

The first type of network analyzer is the protocol analyzer, and it provides an analysis of network protocols. Network analyzers have two distinct modes of operation, depending upon which technology is being used. The two modes are in-line (typically used for wide-area network (WAN) technologies such as T1, T3, Integrated Services Digital Network (ISDN), etc.) and

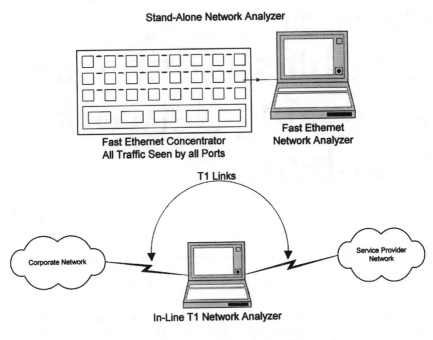

Exhibit 1. The Stand-Alone Mode of Operation

stand-alone (used for local-area network (LAN) technologies such as Ethernet, Token Ring, Flow Distributed Data Interface (FDDI), etc.). In-line analyzers provide two interfaces that allow the traffic to pass through one interface and be captured by the analyzer. They then pass the packets/frames back out of the second interface.

In-line analyzers are required to capture and analyze full-duplex traffic, such as Gigabit Ethernet, although some companies have made Gigabit Ethernet concentrators where stand-alone analyzers can be used. The stand-alone mode of operation typically has one interface and is usually used in a shared media environment such as a Fast Ethernet concentrator or a Token Ring media access unit (MAU) (see Exhibit 1).

However, with more network devices providing port mirroring capabilities and management ports (which when enabled, all traffic gets retransmitted to) the stand-alone network analyzer can be used more often.

Protocol Decodes

No matter what the mode of operation is, all network analyzers provide the user with protocol decodes, a hardware interface or interfaces, and a software (controller) interface. Decodes are the transformation of the bits and bytes into the information used by the operator whether they be a network engineer, an application developer, a research and development specialist, or a multitude of others. Decodes provide information about the network traffic they capture. This leads to another concept: the network capture. To capture traffic means that an analyzer has received some traffic on its interface and stored it either on disk or in RAM for processing later.

A network capture consists of stored frames and is referred to as a "trace." These are frames that have traversed the network and have been captured by the network analyzer. They have also been saved to disk. Decodes provide the user with information such as network addresses, protocol numbers, sequence numbers, protocol type information, frame size, layer statistics, and port numbers. An important note is some analyzers (usually WAN-based) provide only hexadecimal dumps of decodes, and before they can be used, they have to be converted either manually or through the use of another application.

Analyzer Platform

Another important difference in protocol analyzers is the platform used. The most common are software- or hardware-based. The first type, software-based, also can be placed into two distinct categories: hardware-independent or hardware-dependent. Software-based protocol analyzers that are hardware-independent usually require a particular operating system and are not truly independent because they tend to support only devices from particular network vendors. Software protocol analyzers that are hardware-dependent may require a particular operating system and may come packaged with some proprietary networking hardware, but they can be used only with that hardware. However, hardware-dependant protocol analyzers tend to provide better performance but at a higher price.

Although software-independent protocol analyzers are more portable and less expensive, they usually provide performance based on the speed of the computer, amount of RAM, and other system settings. As with any software application, systems requirements vary from product to product, so be sure to check these things when choosing one. Also, keep in mind that not all software-independent protocol analyzers support every network adapter or technology on the market, which is another important thing to be aware of before making a selection.

Hardware-based protocol analyzers are usually dedicated to a particular network topology but are not limited to that technology through the use of expansion modules. These types of protocol analyzers have an interface for the supported network topology and are very similar to a laptop computer in the sense that they provide a display screen, mouse, and keyboard on a portable platform. Expansion modules are analogous to computer-based expansion slots. They allow additional interfaces of the same or different network topology, increased RAM, a pass-through module, and other system upgrades. Again, as with software-based analyzers, they support only network topologies that the software package allows.

To illustrate this point, an analyzer may have an expansion module for a Token Ring interface; however, if the software that controls the analyzer does not have support for Token Ring decodes, it cannot be fully utilized until the software is upgraded. One main advantage of a dedicated hardware-based protocol analyzer is that it provides better performance and usually more functionality than a software-based composite. As is usually the case, though, dedicated hardware-based analyzers tend to be expensive and only some provide expansion modules for other network topologies.

A Limitation

One limitation of any hardware protocol analyzer is that it can decode traffic only for that particular hardware protocol. For example, an Ethernet analyzer can decode only Ethernet traffic, not Token Ring, FDDI, asynchronous transfer mode (ATM), and an Ethernet network adapter cannot be used on an ISDN network. However, the same is true for software-based protocol analyzers whether they are hardware-dependent or not. Another limitation of protocol analyzers is that they must support the software-based protocol they are to decode. Most analyzers support a wide range of protocols, but it is important to consider this before purchasing one. To illustrate, to decode Internet packet exchange (IPX) network traffic on a Token Ring network, one must have a Token Ring hardware interface for the analyzer that supports the IPX software decodes. Decoding an ISDN Basic Rate Interface (BRI) requires the appropriate analyzer with the correct hardware and software support.

Protocol analyzers have several uses for a variety of industries and objectives. From network application development to application functional verification, network communication troubleshooting, physical layer error detection to hardware-based troubleshooting, without protocol analyzers the networking industry would not be where it is today. This recalls the proverbial question — which came first, the chicken or the egg? Or, in this case, the network analyzer or the technology? The following paragraphs describe some of the more advanced features that analyzer vendors have added to their products.

More advanced protocol analyzers today provide a much wider variety of features and functions that have not always been available. Some software packages bundled with hardware-based protocol analyzers provide physical layer error statistics, illegal frame errors (frame size violations, dribble bits, alignment errors, checksum and frame check sequence errors are just a few), retransmission notifications, broadcast counts, and connection resets. Some products allow a user to specify thresholds, such as five broadcast packets in a given interval of time and, if this threshold is reached or exceeded, the analyzer fires off an e-mail message or sends a numerical or text page to notify the network manager of the condition.

Some of the advanced broadcast features include the ability to check a server's network connection at defined intervals and, if the server does not respond, the network manager is alerted. However, repeated retransmissions can indicate that a network device is either malfunctioning or traffic is being disrupted on its path. Other tools allow for the verification of service-level agreements (SLAs) to make sure the allotted and paid-for bandwidth is available at defined times — once-a-day, every hour, every minute, or whatever is desired. Keep in mind that newer and better software packages come out every few months, and these are not necessarily the most advanced features these devices support.

Network Probes

Network analyzers do not have to be used in a single locale of a network, and some can be deployed much like any other network equipment. Some analyzers allow network probes to be placed in remote areas of a network, which is extremely useful in large enterprise networks. A master unit that collects all of the information gathered by the probes for centralized network analysis must be defined. The only requirement is that each probe must have a path to the master controller to exchange information. To illustrate this point, consider an office building that has three floors and requires network analysis on all levels.

Without probes, network captures would have to be obtained and then transferred to a single location, each one individually reviewed, analyzed, and combined if needed. Then corrective action can be taken. However, with the addition of probes, all required information is sent to one unit and reviewed at one time, and corrective measures can be implemented where needed. Another advantage to this solution is that each individual probe can be configured from the master instead of having to travel to the analyzer. Network probes cost more, but they are less than duplicate analyzers and are easier to manage. But not all analyzer vendors support distributed network analysis.

Although network analyzers have many uses, here are a couple scenarios where they can be used. Take, for example, a typical database query between a server and a client where it seems like the server is not responding to the client's requests. One would think the server is causing the problem. However, once a protocol analyzer is introduced to the situation, it captures the exchange of information between the client and server and one can soon see how it may not be the server. After capturing the network traffic and examining the trace, one sees that the client's requests are never transmitted over the network, and the problem is soon diagnosed as either a network adapter or cable failure in the client machine, not the server.

Another common situation where protocol analyzers can be used to troubleshoot a network communication problem is between two computers on the same Ethernet segment running Transmission Control Protocol/Internet Protocol (TCP/IP) that for some reason cannot exchange information. Once a network capture has been taken and the trace is reviewed, it is revealed that one of the computers was configured with the wrong TCP/IP network address and therefore communication did not occur. Although this is an oversimplified example that could have been diagnosed through a system configuration inspection, a protocol analyzer is still an extremely useful tool for network communication troubleshooting.

Other Features

Other features of protocol analyzers worthy of mention include capture buffer playback, capture packet adjusting, frame/packet crafting, display and capture filtering, and network analysis. Capture buffer playback is the ability of a protocol analyzer to retransmit onto the network what it has captured, whether or not it is on the same network on which it was captured. In addition, some analyzers allow a single packet to be retransmitted out of a trace or a selection of packets and even send a single packet X times. This is useful when a particular packet acts as a trigger for a network device, such as Wake-On-LAN (WOL). Capture packet adjustment is the ability to alter a captured packet to be retransmitted later.

A good use for this feature is sequence checking. When a network application requires packets to be received in sequence, one packet can be altered to verify proper operation in the face of an erred sequence number. Frame/packet creation allows a user to create a packet from scratch. Although this is not a feature for a novice, network engineers who work with proprietary or beta protocols can take advantage of such features. Display and capture filters allow the user to limit what packets the analyzer displays or captures, for example, in an Ethernet hub where all traffic is seen by all devices on that hub, but just the transaction between two computers is needed. A capture or display filter can be configured to show only packets from the appropriate machines' hardware MAC addresses, IP addresses, or whatever is supported by the protocol analyzer.

RMON Monitoring (RMON)

Another subject related to network analyzers but not covered in detail in this section is RMON monitoring tools. RMON probes can complete network captures, but few tools have actually implemented this support. That is probably because they have steep system requirements. In addition, other devices are available to provide this service. However, they do collect network statistics and are useful to network managers, but not many uses for a network engineer. Although these tools provide some of the same statistics as network protocol analyzers, they do not have many of the advanced functions. For down-and-dirty network analysis, protocol analyzers are the way to go, as they are at the lowest level of network communication.

TRAFFIC GENERATOR

The next type of network analyzer is the traffic generator. Just as protocol analyzers are responsible for capturing and decoding the traffic on the wire, traffic generators are responsible for transmitting traffic on that wire. Not only do they transmit traffic, but they also receive it. They have to be able to compare the transmitted traffic to the received to test the performance of network equipment. But, testing network devices for performance is not their only use.

Almost anyone can use a protocol analyzer and use it well; however, one needs to have a basic understanding of networking to use a traffic generator. It is easy to plug in an analyzer and look at the traffic it has captured and read decodes without fully understanding all of the details involved in network communication. This is not the case for configuring traffic on a generator. One needs to understand protocol numbers, interframe gaps, burst sizes, stream control, MAC addresses, Layer 3 addressing, bridging, the purpose of the test, the device or feature that is being tested, frame types, and many more of the gory details involved in network communication.

Transmission/Receive Ports

Traffic generators do not simply have transmission ports; they also need to have receive ports. That is because network communication always involves devices participating in a conversation. One transmits while the other receives and vice-versa. Hence, a traffic generator needs two ports: one to transmit a predetermined number of packets and the other to receive that number of packets. Some generators do both at the same time (transmit and receive, full-duplex communication). Moreover, in the case of testing an application, one port can be used to transmit requests and receive responses all together. Exhibit 2 illustrates a typical use of a traffic generator.

Traffic generators are not completely different from analyzers; they both share some features. The most important common feature to both protocol analyzers and traffic generators is the hardware and software interface. The generator needs a connection to the network just like a protocol analyzer. There also needs to be some way to control the generator, thus it must have a software interface. Some generators require the use of a whole

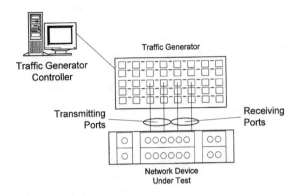

Exhibit 2.   Typical Use of a Traffic Generator

PC to control it, whereas others come bundled with a controller. Just like some analyzers, traffic generators can have a mix of network topologies in a single device. However, generators tend to have more ports and cost more.

Craft Custom Frames

Some protocol analyzers can transmit either traffic that was created by the user or traffic that had been previously captured, and some traffic generators can capture traffic and retransmit it much in the same way. Some generators do not provide the granularity in the decodes that are present in analyzers. Another common function between some analyzers and traffic generators is the ability to craft custom frames from scratch to test proprietary or non-standardized protocols and to capture traffic. However, most generators offer predefined protocol types and can be used as a base. Not all packets have to be created from scratch.

Traffic generators allow a user to transmit packets at the absolute maximum rate the network medium can support, regardless of the frame size, protocol, or whatever. Some generators let a user violate interframe gaps and transmit packets at a rate faster than what is supported for the purpose of testing a network device in an erred environment. Generators also usually allow a user to transmit packets with errors, such as frames too large or small, dribble bit errors, alignment errors, runt frames, and jabber frames for the same reason.

It is important to remember that some protocol analyzers generate traffic at wire speed; however, they are not designed for testing large numbers of ports, do not allow the flexibility inherent to traffic generators, and do not provide a user with a good means of recording results. A good example of this is a four-port full-mesh test where one port transmits to the other three in a round-robin fashion. This type of configuration is fairly simple with a traffic generator, but it is nearly impossible to do with an analyzer. However, if that traffic can be captured, it could be retransmitted. Nevertheless, protocol analyzers do not provide the received packets counters on a per-port basis, which would have to be done manually by examining the trace.

Higher Port Densities

Traffic generators provide higher port densities and cleaner interfaces for using them. Traffic generators are more than single-purpose devices made for simply testing the maximum number of packets that a network device can remit. They can be used to test a wider variety of features to quantify the performance of network devices, such as latency measurements, packet loss, congestion handling, flow control support, and traffic shaping verification. Traffic generators are definitely not single-purpose devices.

For instance, latency testing involves transmitting packets with time stamps on one interface and receiving those packets on another interface to calculate the total transmission time. Packet loss testing involves transmitting packets on one interface and receiving them on another, while comparing the total number of transmitted packets to the total number received. It then calculates loss, if there is any (a wire-speed device may not produce packet loss). Congestion handling tests involve two ports transmitting to a single output port, while oversubscribing the output port on purpose to determine how the network device operates in these situations.

This is useful when attempting to verify a congestion notification algorithm that notifies the transmitter to "slow down" because it is flooding that particular port. The previous test is the same for flow control verification, as a port needs to be oversubscribed for such mechanism to trigger. Traffic shaping is a network concept that grants a percentage of network traffic to a particular profile, MAC address, IP address, or some notifying characteristic over another. Again, two streams of traffic would be required and directed to the same output port and a receiving port on that particular output port to verify that the appropriate percentage of traffic was let through. These are only a few of the functions that can be tested with a traffic generator.

Performance Testing

Traffic generators are designed specifically for testing network devices for performance and have interfaces designed to do just that. Some vendors in the traffic generator market have added automated scripts for testing wire-speed performance and include results-recording mechanisms that can export results directly into spreadsheet file formats for easy and quick analysis. Again, performance is not the only automated test script. Some include latency measurements, head of line blocking, and those previously mentioned.

HYBRID DEVICE

The final type of network analyzer is a hybrid between a protocol analyzer and traffic generator. Although the industry has a few such devices, some vendors are seizing upon this as a market opportunity and providing customers with the mix of the two. After describing the two other types one can determine the pros and cons of this mixture. One important fact, however, is that the hybrid may provide the decodes of a network analyzer and the performance of a traffic generator. One thing missing is the port density provided by a true traffic generator not to mention the ability to easily save, record, and transfer test results. Eventually some vendors will see this and create a proper hybrid combination.

CONCLUSION

As network technologies change and newer protocols are added, the need for analysis equipment to support these new technologies and protocol also changes. Without network analysis equipment, researchers and developers would have no means of verifying their latest and greatest communications breakthroughs. Network analysis is as ever changing as the networking communication industry.

The emergence of new technologies creates the need for equipment to test and verify these technologies. As long as there is data communications, there will be network analyzers.

Section IX
Enterprise Messaging

Chapter 46
Jurisdictional Issues in Global Transmissions

Ralph Spencer Poore

In the information age where teleconferences replace in-person meetings, where telecommuting replaces going to the office, and where international networks facilitate global transmissions with the apparent ease of calling one's next-door neighbor, valuable assets change ownership at the speed of light. Louis Jionet, Secretary-General of the French Commission on Data Processing and Liberties stated: "Information is power and economic information is economic power." Customs officials and border patrols cannot control the movement of these assets. But does this mean companies can transmit the data that either represents or is the valuable asset without regard to the legal jurisdictions through which they pass? To adequately address this question, both the legal issues and the practical issues involved in transnational border data flows are discussed in this chapter.

LEGAL ISSUES

All legally incorporated enterprises have Official Books of Record. Whether in manual or automated form, these are the records that governmental authorities turn to when determining the status of an enterprise. The ability to enforce a subpoena or court order for these records reflects the effective sovereignty of the nation in which the enterprise operates. Most countries require enterprises incorporated, created, or registered in their jurisdiction to physically maintain Official Books of Record within their borders. For example, a company relying on a service bureau in another country for data processing services may cause the official records to exist only in that other country. This could occur if the printouts reflected only a historic position of the company, perhaps month-end conditions, where the

0-8493-1149-7/02/$0.00+$1.50
© 2002 by CRC Press LLC

current position of the company — the position on which management relies — exists only through online access to the company's executive information system. From a nation's perspective, two issues of sovereignty arise:

1. The other country might exercise its rights and take custody of the company's records — possibly forcing it out of business — for actions alleged against the company that the company's "home" nation considers legal.
2. The company's "home" nation may be unable to enforce its access rights.

Another, usually overriding factor, is a nation's ability to enforce its tax laws. Many nations have value-added taxes (VATs) or taxes on publications, computer software, and services. An organization's data may qualify as a publication, as computer software, or even as services in some jurisdictions. Thus, many nations have an interest in the data that flows across their borders because it may qualify for taxation. In some cases, the tax is a tariff intended to discourage the importation of computer software or publications in order to protect the nation's own emerging businesses. More so than when the tax is solely for revenue generation, protective tariffs may carry heavy fines and be more difficult to negotiate around. With the advent of Internet businesses, determining a business' nexus for tax purposes has become even more complex. Such business may have income, franchise, and inventory or property tax issues in addition to sales tax, excise tax, and import or export duties. Business taxes, registration or license fees, and even reporting requirements depend on the applicability of a given jurisdiction.

National security interests can include controlling the import and export of information. State secrecy laws exist for almost all nations. The United States, for example, restricts government classified data (e.g., Confidential, Secret, Top Secret), but also restricts some information even if it is not classified (e.g., technical data about nuclear munitions, some biological research, some advanced computer technology, and — to varing degrees — cryptography).

Among those nations concerned with an individual's privacy rights, the laws vary greatly. Laws like the United State's Privacy Act of 1974 (5 USC 552a) have limited applicability (generally applying only to government agencies and their contractors). The United Kingdom's Data Protection Act of 1984 (1984 c 35 [*Halsbury's Statutes,* 4th Edition, Butterworths, London, 1992, Vol. 6, pp. 899–949]), however, applies to the commercial sector, as does the 1981 Council of Europe's Convention for the Protection of Individuals with Regard to Automatic Processing of Personal Data (an excellent discussion of this can be found in Anne W. Brandscomb's *Toward a Law of*

Global Communications Networks, The Science and Technology section of the American Bar Association, Longman, New York, 1986). Privacy laws generally have at least the following three characteristics:

1. They provide notice to the subject of the existence of a database containing the subject's personal data (usually by requiring registration of the database).
2. They provide a process for the subject to inspect and to correct the personal data.
3. They provide a requirement for maintaining an audit trail of accessors to the private data.

The granularity of privacy law requirements also varies greatly. Some laws (e.g., the U.S. Fair Credit Reporting Act of 1970 [see 15 USC 1681 *et seq.*]), require only the name of the company that requested the information. Other laws require accountability to a specific office or individual. Because the granularity of accountability can differ from jurisdiction to jurisdiction, organizations may need to develop their applications to meet the most stringent requirements (i.e., individual accountability). In this author's experience, few electronic data interchange (EDI) systems support this level of accountability (UNCID Uniform Rules of Conduct for Interchange of Trade Data by Teletransmission, ICC Publishing Corporation, New York, 1988; all protective measures and audit measures are described as options, with granularity left to the discretion of the parties).

To further complicate data transfer issues, patent, copyright, and trade secret laws are not uniform. Although international conventions exist (e.g., General Agreement on Tariffs and Trade [GATT]), not all nations subscribe to these conventions, and the conventions often allow for substantial differences among signatories. Rights one might have and can enforce in one jurisdiction might not exist (or might not be enforceable) in another. In some cases, the rights one has in one jurisdiction constitute an infringement in another jurisdiction. For example, one may hold a United States registered trademark on a product. A trademark is a design (often a stylized name or monogram) showing the origin or ownership of merchandise and reserved to the owner's exclusive use. The Trade-Mark Act of 1946 (see 15 USC 1124) provides that no article shall be imported that copies or simulates a trademark registered under United States laws. A similar law protecting, for example, trademarks registered in India might prevent one from using the trademark in India if a similar or identical trademark is already registered there.

Disclosure of information not in accordance with the laws of the jurisdictions involved may subject the parties to criminal penalties. For example, the United Kingdom's Official Secrets Act of 1989 clearly defines areas wherein disclosure of government secrets is a criminal offense. Most nations have similar laws (of varying specificity), making the disclosure of state secrets a crime. However, technical information considered public in one jurisdiction might be considered a state secret in another. Similarly, biographical information on a national leader may be mere background information for a news story in one country, but be viewed as espionage by another country. These areas are particularly difficult since most governments will not advise one in advance as to what constitutes a state secret (as this might compromise the secret). Unless an organization has a presence in each jurisdiction sensitive to these political and legal issues to whom one can turn for guidance, competent legal advice should be sought before transmitting text or textual database materials containing information about individuals or organizations.

From a business perspective, civil law rather than criminal law may take center stage. Although the United States probably has the dubious distinction as the nation in which it is easiest to initiate litigation, lawsuits are possible in most jurisdictions worldwide. No company wants to become entangled in litigation, especially in foreign jurisdictions. However, when information is transmitted from one nation to another, the rules can change significantly. For example, what are the implied warranties in the receiving jurisdiction? What constitutes profanity, defamation, libel, or similar actionable content? What contract terms are unenforceable (e.g., can one enforce a nondisclosure agreement of ten years' duration)?

In some jurisdictions, ecclesiastical courts may have jurisdiction for offenses against a state-supported religion. Circumstances viewed in one jurisdiction as standard business practice (e.g., gifts) may be viewed in another jurisdiction as unethical or illegal. Even whether or not an organization has standing (i.e., may be represented in court) varies among nations. An organization's rights to defend itself, for example, vary from excellent to nil in jurisdictions ranging from Canada to Iran, respectively.

Fortunately, companies can generally choose the jurisdictions in which they will hold assets. Most countries enforce their laws (and the actions of their courts) against corporations by threat of asset seizure. A company with no seizable assets (and no desire to conduct future business) in a country is effectively judgment-proof. The reverse can also be true; that is, a company may be unable to enforce a contract (or legal judgment) because the other party has no assets within a jurisdiction willing to enforce the contract or judgment. When contracting with a company to develop software, for example, and that company exists solely in a foreign country, one's organization should research the enforceability of any contract and, if there is any doubt, require a bond be posted in one's jurisdiction to ensure at least bond forfeiture as recourse.

Specific and General Jurisdiction

In September 1997, in Bensusan Restaurant Corp. *v.* King (1997 U.S. App. Lexis 23742 (2d Cir. Sept. 10, 1997)), the 2d U.S. Circuit Court of Appeals held that a Missouri resident's Web site, accessed in New York, did not give rise to jurisdiction under New York's long arm statute. The court ruled there was no jurisdiction because the defendant was not physically in New York when he created the offending Web page. However, a similar case in California with a similar ruling was reversed on appeal (Hall *v.* LaRonde, 1997 Cal. App. Lexis 633 (Aug. 7, 1997)). Citing the changing "role that electronic communications plays in business transactions," the court decided that jurisdiction should not be determined by whether the defendant's communications were made physically within the state, instead concluding that "[t]here is no reason why the requisite minimum contacts cannot be electronic."

To comply with due process, the exercise of specific jurisdiction generally requires that the defendant intentionally took advantage of the benefits of the jurisdiction, and thus could have expected to be hauled into court in that jurisdiction. The nature of electronic communications and their growing role in commerce have contributed to findings that defendants' Internet communications constitute "purposeful availment" (legalese for intentionally taking advantage of the benefits) and establish jurisdiction. For example, in California Software Inc. *v.* Reliability Research Inc. (631 F. Supp. 1356 (C.D. Cal. 1986)), the court held that a nonresident's defamatory e-mail to a resident was sufficient to establish specific jurisdiction. The court noted that, as modern technology makes nationwide commercial transactions more feasible, it broadens the scope of jurisdiction.

Courts have also pointed out the distinguishing features of the Internet when holding that a Web site gives rise to specific jurisdiction for infringement claims arising out of the site's content. In Maritz Inc. *v.* Cybergold Inc. (947 F. Supp. 1328, 1332, 1334 (E.D. Mo. 1996)), the court suggested that Web site advertising more likely amounts to purposeful availment than advertising by direct mail or an "800" telephone number, noting the "different nature" of electronic communications.

Conceivably, a Web site could reflect contacts with a state's residents that were sufficiently continuous and systematic to establish general jurisdiction over the site owner. Courts have held, however, that the mere creation of a Web site does not create general jurisdiction. See, for example, McDonough *v.* Fallon McElligott, Inc. (1996 U.S. Dist. Lexis 15139 (S.D. Cal. Aug. 6, 1996)). Further, courts have held in more traditional contexts that merely placing advertisements in nationally distributed periodicals, or communicating through a national computer-based information system, does not subject a nonresident to jurisdiction. See, for example, Federal Rural Elec. Ins. Corp. *v.* Kootenai Elec. Corp. (17 F.3d 1302, 1305 (10th Cir. 1994)).

This area of law is evolving rapidly, with many jurisdictions asserting what amounts to extraterritorial jurisdiction on the basis of electronic transactions into, through, or out of their territory. The Council of Europe's Convention for the Protection of Individuals with Regard to Automatic Processing of Personal Data is but one of many examples. The entire area of cryptography, for example, is another. In January 1999, France dramatically eased its long-standing restriction on the use of cryptography within its jurisdiction. This announcement came only six weeks after France joined with 32 other countries signing an update of a document known as the Wassenaar Agreement. Signatories to this agreement promised to tighten restrictions on the import or export of cryptography. The so-called "long arm" provisions of many laws and the lack of concensus among nations on important issues — including privacy, intellectual property rights, communications security, and taxes — will challenge (or plague) us for the foreseeable future.

TECHNICAL ISSUES

Any nation wishing to enforce its laws with regard to data transmitted within or across its borders must have the ability (1) to monitor/intercept the data, and (2) to interpret/understand the data. Almost all nations can intercept wire (i.e., telephone/telegraph) communications. Most can intercept radio, microwave, and satellite transmissions. Unless an organization uses exotic technologies (e.g., point-to-point laser, extremely low frequency (ELF), super high frequency, spread spectrum), interception remains likely.

The second requirement, however, is another matter. Even simple messages encoded in accordance with international standards may have meaning only in a specific context or template not inherent in the message itself. For example, "142667456043052" could be a phone number (e.g., 1-426-674-5604 x3052), or a social security number and birthday (e.g., 142-66-7456 04/30/52), or dollar amounts ($14,266.74 $560,430.52), or inventory counts by part number (PN) (e.g., PN 142667 Quantity 45, PN 604305 Quantity 2), or zip codes (e.g., 41266, 74560, 43052). Almost limitless possibilities exist even without using codes or ciphers. And this example used human-readable digits. Many transmissions may be graphic images, object code, or compressed text files completely unintelligible to a human "reading" the data on a datascope.

From the preceding, one might conclude that interception and interpretation by even a technologically advanced nation is too great a challenge. This is, however, far from true. Every "kind" of data has a signature or set of attributes that, when known, permits its detection and identification. This includes encrypted data, where the fact of encryption is determinable. Where transmitting or receiving encrypted messages is a crime, a company using encryption risks detection. Once the "kind" of data is determined, applying the correct application is often a trivial exercise. Some examples of such strong typing of data include:

- Rich-text format (RTF) documents and most word processing documents
- SQL transactions
- Spreadsheets (e.g., Lotus 1-2-3, Microsoft Excel)
- DOS, Windows, UNIX, and other operating system executables
- Standardized EDI messages
- ASCII vs. EBCDIC

If this were not the case, sending data from one computer to another would require extensive advanced planning at the receiving computer — severely impacting data portability and interoperability, two attributes widely sought in business transactions.

Countries with sufficient technology to intercept and interpret an organization's data can pose an additional problem beyond their law enforcement: that of government-sponsored industrial espionage. Many countries have engaged in espionage with the specific objective of obtaining technical or financial information of benefit to that country's businesses. A search of news accounts of industrial espionage resulted in a list that included the following countries: Argentina, Cuba, France, Germany, Greece, India, Iran, Iraq, Israel, Japan, North Korea, Peoples Republic of China, Russia, South Korea, and Turkey. Most of these countries have public policies against such espionage, and countries like the United States find it awkward to accuse allies of such activities (both because the technical means of catching them at it may be a state secret and, because what one nation views as counter-espionage, another nation might view as espionage).

Protective Technologies

For most businesses, the integrity of transmitted data is more important than its privacy. Cryptographic techniques a business might otherwise be unable to use because of import or export restrictions associated with the cryptographic process or the use of a privacy-protected message, can be used in some applications for data integrity. For example, the Data Encryption Standard (DES), when used for message authentication in accordance with the American National Standard X9.9 for the protection of electronic funds transfers between financial institutions, may be approved by the U.S. Department of the Treasury without having to meet the requirements of the International Trade in Arms Regulations (ITAR).

(Note that technological advances can also impact this; for example, the key space exhaustion attack in January 1999 of a DES Challenge was successful in 22.25 hours. Both the U.S. and French governments made policy changes that permit stronger cryptography for export and import than had previously been permitted.)

Integrity measures generally address one or both of the following problems:

- Unauthorized (including accidental) modification or substitution of the message
- Falsification of identity or repudiation of message

The techniques used to address the first problem are generally called message authentication techniques. Those addressing the second class of problems are generally called digital signature techniques.

Message authentication works by applying a cryptographic algorithm to a message in such a way as to produce a resulting message authentication code (MAC) that has a very high probability of being affected by a change to any bit or bits in the message. The receiving party recalculates the MAC and compares it to the transmitted MAC. If they match, the message is considered authentic (i.e., received as sent); otherwise, the message is rejected.

Because international standards include standards for message authentication (e.g., ISO 9797), an enterprise wanting to protect the integrity of its messages can find suitable algorithms that should be (and historically have been) acceptable to most jurisdictions worldwide. With some exceptions, even the Data Encryption Algorithm (DEA), also known as the Data Encryption Standard (DES), can be used in hardware implementations of message authentication. For digital signature, this may also be true, although several excellent implementations (both public key and secret key) rely on algorithms with import/export restrictions. The data protected by digital signature or message authentication, however, is not the problem, as both message authentication and digital signature leave the message in plaintext. Objections to their use center primarily on access to the cryptographic security hardware or software needed to support these services. If the cryptographic hardware or software can be obtained legally within a given jurisdiction without violating export restrictions, then using these services rarely poses any problems.

Digital signature techniques exist for both public key and secret key algorithm systems (also known respectively as asymmetric and symmetric key systems). The purpose of the digital signature is to authenticate the sender's identity and to prevent repudiation (where an alleged sender

Exhibit 1. Sample Codebook

Code	Meaning
RED SUN	Highest authorized bid is
BLUE MOON	Stall, we aren't ready
WHITE FLOWER	Kill the deal; we aren't interested
JUNE	1
APRIL	2
JULY	3
DECEMBER	4
AUGUST	5
JANUARY	6
MARCH	7
SEPTEMBER	8
NOVEMBER	9
MAY	0

claims not to have sent the message). The digital signature implementation may or may not also authenticate the contents of the signed message.

Privacy measures address the concern for unauthorized disclosure of a message in transit. Cipher systems (e.g., DEA) transform data into what appear to be random streams of bits. Some ciphers (e.g., a Vernam cipher with a key stream equal to or longer than the message stream) provide almost unbreakable privacy. As such, the better cipher systems almost always run afoul of export or import restrictions. The United States is currently working on the Advanced Encryption Standard (AES) to replace DES. One of the policy issues with the AES will be its exportability, as it will allow 128, 192, and 256 bit encryption keys. (The National Institute of Standards and Technology expects AES to be available by 2003.)

In some cases, the use of codes is practical and less likely to run into restrictions. As long as the "codebook" containing the interpretations of the codes is kept secret, an organization could send very sensitive messages without risk of disclosure if intercepted en route. For example, an oil company preparing its bid for an offshore property might arrange a set of codes as shown in Exhibit 1. The message "RED SUN NOVEMBER MAY MAY" would make little sense to an eavesdropper, but would tell the company representative that the maximum authorized bid is 900 (the units would be prearranged, so this could mean $900,000).

Other privacy techniques that do not rely on secret codes or ciphers include:

- Continuous stream messages (the good message is hidden in a continuous stream of otherwise meaningless text). For example,

  THVSTOPREAXZTRECEEBNKLLWSYAINNTHELAUNCHGBMEAZY

  contains the message "STOP THE LAUNCH." When short messages are sent as part of a continuous binary stream, this technique (one of a class known as steganography) can be effective. This technique is often combined with cipher techniques when very high levels of message security are needed.
- Split knowledge routing (a bit pattern is sent along a route independent of another route on which a second bit pattern is sent; the two bit streams are exclusive-OR ed together by the receiving party to form the original message). For example, if the bit pattern of the message one wishes to send is 0011 1001 1101 0110, a random pattern of equal length would be exclusive-OR ed with the message 1001 1110 0101 0010, to make a new message 1010 0111 1000 0100. The random pattern would be sent along one telecommunication path and the new message would be sent along another, independent telecommunication path. The recipient would exclusively OR the two messages back together, resulting in the original message. Since no cryptographic key management is required and because the exclusive-OR operation is very fast, this is an attractive technique where the requirement of independent routing can be met.
- The use of templates (which must remain secret) that permit the receiver to retrieve the important values and ignore others in the same message. For example, in the string used above,

  THVSTOPREAXZTRECEEBNKLLWSYAINNTHELAUNCHGBMEAZY

  used with the following template

  XXXXXXXNNXXXNNNXXXXXXXXXXXXNXXXNXXXXXXXXXXXXXXX

  where only the letters at the places marked with "N" are used, reveals a different message, RETREAT.

The first technique can also be effective against traffic analysis. The second technique requires the ability to ensure independent telecommunication routes (often infeasible). The third technique has roughly the same distribution problems that codebook systems have; that is, the templates must be delivered to the receiver in advance of the transmission and in a secure manner. These techniques do, however, avoid the import and export problems associated with cryptographic systems.

In addition to cryptographic systems, most industrialized nations restrict the export of specific technologies, including those with a direct military use (or police use) and those advanced technologies easily misused by other nations to suppress human rights, improve intelligence gathering, or counter security measures. Thus, an efficient relational database product might be restricted from export because oppressive third-world nations might use it to maintain data on their citizens (e.g., "subversive activities lists"). Restrictions on software export can sometimes be averted by finding a nation in which the desired product is sold legally without the export restriction. (Note: check with legal counsel in your enterprise's official jurisdiction as this work-around may be illegal — some countries claim extraterritorial jurisdiction or claim that their laws take precedence for legal entities residing within their borders.) For example, the Foreign Corrupt Practices Act (see 15 USC 78) of the United States prohibits giving gifts (i.e., paying graft or bribes) by U.S. corporations even if such practice is legal and traditional in a country within which that U.S. corporation is doing business. Similarly, if the People's Republic of China produces clones of hardware and software that violate intellectual property laws of other countries but that are not viewed by China as a punishable offense, using such a product to permit processing between the United States and China would doubtlessly be viewed by U.S. authorities as unacceptable.

THE LONG VIEW

New technologies (e.g., Software Defined Digital Network [SDDN] and Frame Relay) will make networks increasingly intelligent, capable of enforcing complex compliance rules and allowing each enterprise to carefully craft the jurisdictions from which, through which, and into which its data will flow. North America, the European community, Japan, and similar "information-age" countries will see these technologies before the turn of the century. But many nations will not have these capabilities for decades.

Most jurisdictions will acquire the ability to detect cryptographic messages and process cleartext messages even before they acquire the networking technologies that would honor an enterprise's routing requests. The result may be a long period of risk for those organizations determined to send and receive whatever data they deem necessary through whatever jurisdictions happen to provide the most expeditious routing.

The use of public key infrastructures (PKIs) and the reliance on certificate authorities (CAs) for electronic commerce will force many changes in international law. The jurisdictional location of a registration authority (RA), for example, may dictate whose personal data can be captured for registration. In a ruling by the EC Privacy Council early in 1999 with regard to IP addresses, it was determined that a static IP address constituted privacy-protected data, just as a name and mailing address would. The existence of a CA in a jurisdiction might constitute a nexus for an assertion of general jurisdiction or for taxation if the certificates signed by this CA are used for commercial purposes. Although this technology promises solutions to many problems — including restricting access to data on a selective basis that could bind jurisdictions — it also introduces rapid change and complexity with which societies (and legal systems) are already struggling.

SUMMARY

Data flows daily from jurisdiction to jurisdiction, with most organizations unaware of the obligations they may incur. As nations become more sophisticated in detecting data traffic transiting their borders, organizations will face more effective enforcement of laws, treaties, and regulations — ranging from privacy to state secrets, and from tax law to intellectual property rights. The risk of state-sponsored industrial espionage will also increase. Because organizations value the information transferred electronically, more and more organizations will turn to cryptography to protect their information. Cryptography, however, has import and export implications in many jurisdictions worldwide. The technology required to intelligently control the routing of communications is increasingly available, but will not solve the problems in the short term. Rather, the advancing technology will complicate matters further in two ways:

1. Where the controls become available, it will make indefensible their non-use
2. Where the controls are used, it will make the jurisdictions intentional, thereby strengthing the state's case that it has jurisdiction

With more legal entities asserting jurisdiction, conflict of laws cases will increase. Implicit contracts will become extremely hazardous (e.g., an e-mail message might be sufficient to constitute a contract, but what are its default terms?). Ultimately, the need for effective commerce will prevail and jurisdictional issues will be resolved. But for the near term, jurisdictional issues in global transmissions remains a growth industry for legal professionals, politicians, lobbyists, tax accountants, and electronic commerce consultants.

Companies will need to exercise care when they place their data on open networks, the routings of which they cannot control. They will need to understand the jurisdictions in which and through which their global information infrastructure operates. The information security professional will want to have competent legal assistance and stay well-informed. The effectiveness of the enterprise's information security program is now irreversibly intertwined with the jurisdictional issues of global electronic commerce.

Chapter 47
Messaging Gateways
Peter M. Beck

Gateways are a necessary evil in today's world of diverse electronic messaging systems and networks. They serve the important function of linking together users of different environments which, without a gateway, would not be able to exchange messages effectively.

This chapter explores the many facets of gateway technology. The topic is timely and vast, but also somewhat confusing as a result of a lack of standardization, unique jargon, and a moving-target quality.

ASSESSING THE MESSAGING ENVIRONMENT'S COMPLEXITY AND COSTS

At first glance, the concept of an electronic messaging gateway seems straightforward, particularly to the nontechnical observer. Upon closer examination, however, gateway issues can be quite complex, controversial, and even costly if mishandled.

The fact is that a very wide range of different messaging environments exist today inside and around the fringes of almost any large organization. These varieties of messaging can range from legacy mainframe systems to local area network (LAN)-based packages to extremely rich value-added networks (VANs) and the Internet. On the horizon in many organizations is new or increased use of groupware and a shift to client/server products for messaging. The protocols, addressing methods, data formats, and capabilities in each of these environments are very different.

In a perfect world, gateways would be unnecessary. Users would simply standardize on one messaging type and discontinue the use of everything else. Unfortunately, it is not quite that simple. An example helps illustrate the point (see Exhibit 1).

A large, multinational corporation uses several types of electronic messaging systems internally. The firm's U.S. headquarters is using IBM's Professional Office System (PROFS) product on a centralized mainframe. Alternatively, the corporation's engineering and production divisions recently deployed a large new network and began using Microsoft Mail. Because of

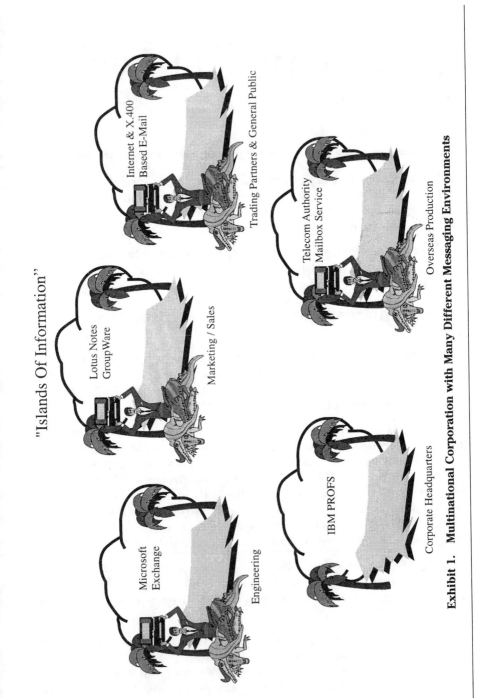

Exhibit 1. Multinational Corporation with Many Different Messaging Environments

an acquisition, many factories have been added overseas in a country where the local communications authority provides an e-mail service.

Each of the groups is fairly satisfied as long as they stay on their island of information. Users cannot easily exchange messages with users in other divisions, however, because the systems essentially speak different languages. To make matters more complicated, employees must exchange messages with external trading partners and the general public by way of several different types of public networks, including the Internet. Finally, senior management would like to see fax, groupware, and possibly electronic commerce considered in any long-term solution.

Although this scenario sounds like enough to perplex even the most savvy data communications experts, it is quite typical in today's fast-moving world. Several high-level questions come to mind immediately, including:

- How can gateway technology be used to link all of these messaging environments together?
- In what particular areas are careful analysis and planning especially important before starting a project?
- How much will this sort of connectivity cost to put into service, and how can these costs be recovered or justified?
- What level of expertise is required to put gateway technology to work successfully?
- What sorts of products, facilities or features, and services are available?
- What are some of the issues, pitfalls, and long-term hidden costs?

BASIC GATEWAY FUNCTIONS

Before embarking into the more detailed aspects of gateways, it is important to discuss functions in somewhat simple terms. In other words, what does a gateway system really do?

At the most basic level, a gateway must be able to act as a middle man, facilitating the exchange of messages between the two (or more) different environments it links together. As shown in Exhibit 2, each message received by the gateway from Environment A must be evaluated in terms of its sender, format, content, and intended destinations.

Next, the gateway must perform a translation. This essentially renders the message suitable for the destination, shown as Environment B. The degree to which the message remains intact as it traverses the gateway depends on many factors, most of which will be touched on later in this chapter.

Finally, the message must be sent by the gateway into Environment B for subsequent delivery to the intended recipients. During message handling, several additional functions are often performed by a gateway. These

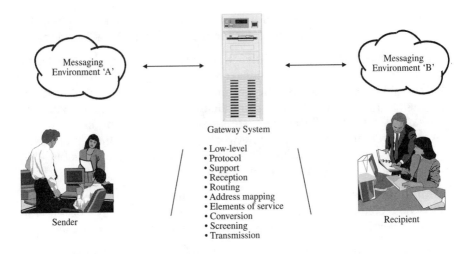

Exhibit 2. Basic Gateway Functions Linking Messaging Type A to Type B

---

might include creating log entries for tracing purposes, archiving the message itself, and updating statistical-billing counts.

The process just described is, of course, oversimplified for the sake of illustration. Each electronic messaging environment has its own special characteristics that make it unique. Despite this, it is useful to break things down further into a set of generic functions that practically all gateway systems must provide to some degree. These functions include the following:

- Message reception processing
- Routing-address mapping
- Element of service handling
- Screening
- Message transmission processing

Message Reception Processing

As with any technical issue, it helps to divide things into steps. The first step to consider for a gateway is the initial transfer of a message into the gateway system for processing. This is referred to as *reception*.

Externally, message reception usually works as follows. First, the sender submits a message addressed to a recipient in another environment. One of the components of the recipient's address, typically the post office or domain name, results in the message being forwarded into the gateway system for handling.

570

The internal mechanisms actually required for reception might vary greatly depending on the situation at hand. It could range from relatively simple transfers of formatted ASCII text over a modem-telephone line connection to very complex communications protocol handshaking over a dedicated high-speed link.

When interfacing with a LAN-based messaging system, a gateway usually achieves *message exchange* by a combination of file server access and an applications programming interface (API). APIs are important for several reasons, which will be discussed later. In any case, as part of this step a gateway typically checks the message for errors, creates a log entry indicating the reception, and stores the message in preparation for the next step.

Routing and Address Mapping

Once a message has been successfully received, the next step is to determine where the message should be sent. This is referred to as *message routing*.

Routing can be accomplished in a variety of ways. Some low-cost gateway products do not really perform routing at all. They simply force all messages received from one environment into another environment serviced by the gateway. Other more flexible products use a combination of predefined routing rules or a directory to decide where to send a particular message.

The difference between routing and address mapping is subtle, and the two are often confused. Actually, they are two separate functions. Routing is the process of deciding where to send a message. Address mapping refers to the rendering of the recipient (and sender) addresses on transfer out of the gateway. Both are certainly among the most important functions a gateway provides.

In a simple example of address mapping in a gateway, to reach an external trading partner named John Smith (who works in the accounting department at a fictional company called ACME), a user of Lotus cc:Mail might send a message to the following address: JOHN SMITH at GATEWAY. When processing the message, the gateway system might need to render, or map, this address into the recipient's true Internet electronic mail address, which could be: SMITHJ@ACCOUNTING.ACME.COM.

Like message routing, address mapping functions can be accomplished in many different ways. These include the use of predefined rules, the use of a directory, or a combination of the two. When implemented correctly in a gateway product, the end results should always adhere to the following two basic rules: the sender should be able to easily address a message to a recipient in another environment using a familiar addressing method, and the recipient of a message should be able to easily identify and reply to the sender.

Element of Service Handling

The term *element of service* is electronic messaging jargon for a feature offered to users. For example, the sender's ability to designate a message for high-priority delivery is an element of service.

As might be expected, it is very important for a gateway to handle each element of service in a consistent, meaningful fashion when transferring a message from one environment into another. Sometimes this involves a rather straightforward conversion or mapping; such is usually the case when handling message priority.

Often, however, the element of service is trickier. For example, some modern messaging environments allow users to request return of content in case an error condition prevents delivery to the intended recipient. This amounts to something like requesting a package be returned by the postal service when the mailman cannot deliver it. Electronically performing a conversion of this element of service in a gateway can be fairly involved. To illustrate, the following are some of the steps a gateway might perform:

- Recognize the reception of a nondelivery type notification message containing returned content
- Extract the returned content section from the notification
- Perform a correlation to determine which recipient could not receive the message
- Translate the often cryptic nondelivery reason code into a plain English text that the sender will hopefully understand (e.g., recipient's address incorrect)
- Render the returned content, recipient address, and the reason text into a notification message appropriate for the sender's environment
- Transmit this notification back to the sender

Element of service handling is where the bulk of all difficult message processing is performed in a gateway. It is therefore the one area where especially careful analysis and planning pay off, particularly when older legacy systems are involved.

Every important element of service offered in each environment linked by the gateway should be thought of in terms of how it will be handled. This is because there are often gaps or, even worse, subtle differences in the way elements of service work in one product or environment versus another. The return of content feature is a perfect example. Some products or environments support it wonderfully, but many do not.

Screening

What happens if a user in one environment unknowingly attempts to send a very long message by way of a gateway to a user in another environment that only supports very short messages? Ideally, the message should be gracefully discarded by the destination environment and the sender should be notified. At worst, the message might cause a serious problem in the destination network. In any case, gateways are usually required to screen messages for conditions like this and take corrective action. The action taken depends on the type of error condition. For example, when detecting an overlong message, a gateway might prevent transfer or perhaps perform a splitting operation.

Other conditions gateways usually check to prevent problems include invalid content or data, illegal file attachment, too many recipients, or a missing or invalid sender's address. How well a gateway performs this type of screening often dictates how successful an implementation will be over the course of time. A poorly designed gateway can cause problems if it allows "bad" messages to enter into an environment not expecting to have to deal with these sorts of error conditions.

Transmission Processing

The final step in handling any message is its transfer into the recipient's system or network, referred to as *message transmission processing*. Much like reception processing, the actual functions required can vary greatly. Most important is that the gateway adheres to the rules of the destination environment and provides for safe, reliable transfer of the message. Upon completion of this step, the gateway has fulfilled its main responsibility for the message.

GATEWAY COMPONENTS

Now that basic functions have been examined, it is appropriate to take a look at the main components that comprise a gateway system. Without focusing on a single product or scenario, this discussion must be left at a high level — but it is interesting nevertheless. The typical gateway system can be broken down into both hardware and software components. Hardware is more concrete, so it is an appropriate place to start.

Hardware Components

Generally, the minimum hardware needed for a gateway is a computer, generous amounts of main memory, and some sort of mass storage device (e.g., a hard disk). This might range from a PC with a small hard drive to a multiprocessor server with huge amounts of storage. The exact system required will depend on such factors as the operating system selected, throughput desired, fault tolerance needs, communications protocols used, and message archiving and logging requirements.

It is worth mentioning that many gateway products are what is termed *hardware model independent*. In other words, the vendor really supplies only software. If this is the case, the vendor usually indicates minimum hardware requirements and leaves it up to the person deploying the gateway to decide on details (e.g., what exact model of computer to buy). Beyond the basic computer and its storage device, hardware components are very specific to the situation. Perhaps the most frequently used is a network interface card (NIC). The two basic types of cards are Ethernet and Token Ring among others.

When a gateway must be connected to a public network (e.g., the Internet or a VAN), it is common to have a communications hardware device in the configuration. This might take the form of an X.25 adaptor card, a multiport asynchronous controller board, or modems. High-end gateway systems often use additional equipment (e.g., a CD unit or magnetic tape drive). A CD unit is essential for loading and installing software components. A tape drive is often useful for backing up the system hard drive, archiving messages, and saving billing and statistical information.

Software Components

Gateway software components fall into one of the following three categories: operating system software, gateway applications software, and third-party support software.

Operating System Software. The operating system is the fundamental, general-purpose software running on the computer. It allows reading and writing to a disk, allocating memory resources, and a user interface mechanism. Examples of operating systems software supported by gateway product suppliers include UNIX, Novell NetWare, Windows, and MS/DOS.

Applications Software. Applications software is the set of programs that perform the actual message handling in the gateway. This might be as simple as one single program/file or as complex as a whole directory structure filled with dozens of software modules, each performing a special function.

Third-Party Software. Typically a certain number of third-party software components are necessary in a gateway system. Examples of this are device drivers, communications protocol stack components, and tape archive and backup packages.

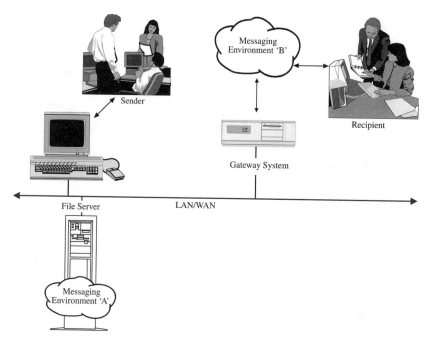

Exhibit 3. Stand-Alone (Dedicated Machine) Gateway Model

GATEWAY CONFIGURATION MODELS

Individual hardware and software components must be put together in a certain way to make things work. This is referred to as a *configuration*. Gateway configuration models fall into three categories: stand-alone or dedicated, colocated, and distributed processing.

Stand-Alone or Dedicated Model

The stand-alone configuration model (see Exhibit 3) is typical in today's environments. For this, a separate computer is dedicated to performing the gateway functions. All hardware and software components reside in this type of single box system. In one sense, this is the easiest gateway configuration to understand and explain because messages enter the box in one form and come out in another.

This model has several other advantages. First, all or most of the computer's resources can be allocated to the job at hand. Second, very little — if any — change is required in the environments being linked together by the gateway. When considering this model, one important question to ask is, how will the gateway system be managed? This is particularly true if a

575

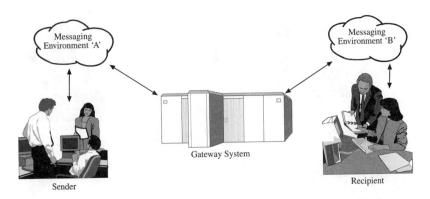

Exhibit 4.   Colocated Gateway Model

number of gateway systems will be deployed across a wide geographical area.

Colocated Model

Colocating the gateway components in the same main computer system where one or more of the electronic messaging environments to be linked resides is also possible (see Exhibit 4). The disadvantage with this model is that gateway functions, which are often resource-intensive, will steal power from the main computer system. In addition, it may be necessary to add hardware and software components into a system that has been in operation and running unchanged for quite some time — something generally frowned upon.

Sometimes management advantages are associated with using this model. Often an already familiar set of commands, reports, and alarms can be used to manage the gateway.

Distributed Processing Model

As shown in Exhibit 5, one of the newer and more interesting configurations now available from some product suppliers actually allows gateway functions to be distributed across multiple computers. In this model, clever software design allows for a high-speed exchange of information between dispersed gateway components. Typically, a file server acts as a central, common repository for information. This effectively forms one logical gateway system out of pieces running on several computers.

With the availability of hardware as a relatively cheap commodity (due to reduced hardware prices) today, this configuration model is worth

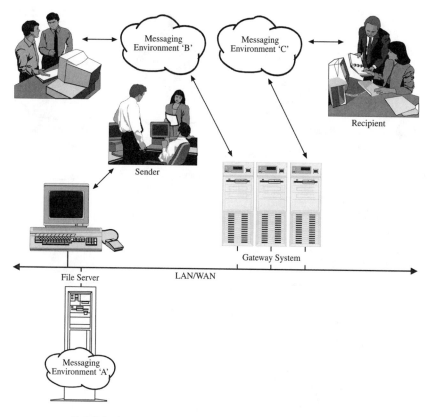

Exhibit 5. Distributed Architecture Gateway Model

examining. For large-scale gateways, it offers advantages in the area of scalability, load sharing, and fault tolerance.

GATEWAY SCENARIOS

This section offers a brief summary of three fictional but realistic scenarios in which gateway technology is used. Most actual situations will match or at least have much in common with one of these scenarios.

Scenario One: Linking LAN Messaging to the Outside World through a Network Service Provider

This scenario is very typical today for a large organization that has deployed any one of the very popular and powerful LAN-based e-mail packages available (e.g., Lotus cc:Mail, Microsoft Exchange, or a Novell MHS-compliant product). Inevitably, users start to ask how they can exchange messages with external trading partners. Some discover on their own that

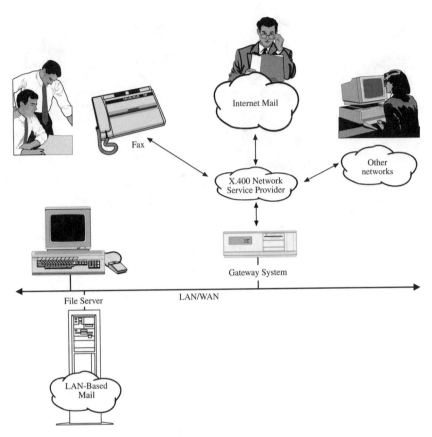

Exhibit 6. **Scenario One: X.400 Gateway Used to Communicate with the Outside World**

if they use a somewhat crazed mix of packages, network access subscriptions, and a modem, they can communicate individually. But this gets messy, expensive, hard to control, and is a bad long-term solution for any organization.

The best answer for business-quality messaging is to deploy what is known as an X.400 gateway (see Exhibit 6). This essentially links the LAN-based e-mail environment to the outside world via a network service provider. In the U.S., the more well-known service providers include MCI, AT&T, Sprint, GE Information Services, and IBM Advantis.

X.400 Implementations. Gateways can exchange messages with the network service provider by way of X.400. This is a very flexible, rich, and open set of standards or protocols for messaging. Lower-level communication protocols (e.g., X.25, TCP/IP, and OSI transport/session) are used to ensure the reliable exchange of data.

Also important is that in this configuration the gateway forms what in X.400 terminology is referred to as a *private management domain* (PRMD) for the organization. To send a message to anyone in an organization, external trading partners must specify this PRMD by name in the address. Many network service providers offer enormous capabilities, including international access points, links to other carriers, Internet mail access, EDI capabilities, fax delivery, and detailed billing. In other words, they provide immediate connectivity and huge potential. Of course, this is not free. There is normally a charge for the communications link and for each message sent through or stored on the service.

Benefits to Users and Administrators. So what does having a setup like this mean to users in the organization? Now they can exchange messages with external trading partners by way of their normal desktop e-mail application. They only have one mailbox to deal with and do not have to be trained to use several packages or understand different addressing schemes. The payback in large organizations can be enormous.

What are some of the administrative advantages when using a gateway in this scenario? First, all messages exchanged with external trading partners can be logged and archived in one central point — the gateway. This is much neater, easier to manage, and more economical to the organization than allowing users to send, receive, and store correspondence in a chaotic fashion.

Second, the network service provider and gateway, to a certain degree, act as a security firewall between the outside world and the organization's private network.

Finally, it can be said that these companies are professionally staffed, 24-hour operations that will lend a hand with some of the issues pertaining to providing business-quality communications.

[*Author's Note:* An increasingly popular and in most cases more economical solution is to deploy an Internet mail gateway. Again, this can link one's local environment to the outside world via an Internet service provider (ISP) such as UUNET, AOL, or Sprint. Direct Internet gateways present additional issues such as security, reliability of the Internet as a transport network, and, as of this writing, the lack of certain value-added features such as delivery confirmation. For example, it is usually necessary to deploy a separate firewall system to protect one's local network from unauthorized access. However, because of the rapid growth of Internet e-mail as the *de facto* standard for messaging, a direct Internet mail gateway should be part of any large organization's strategy.]

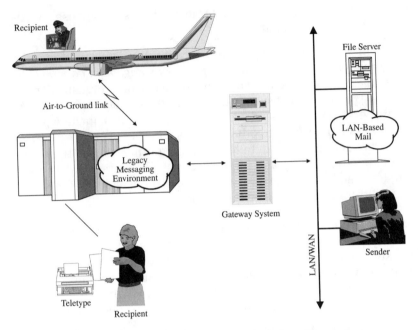

Exhibit 7. **Scenario Two: Tying Legacy and Modern Messaging Environments Together**

Scenario Two: Tying Together Legacy and Modern Messaging Environments

This scenario is also quite common as an attempt is made to tie a legacy messaging environment together with one of the newer messaging environments by gateway technology. Often a very large investment in money, personnel, and political chips has been made in the legacy network. Examples include messaging running on older mainframe hosts, specialized networks for civil aviation and banking, and government or military systems.

Sometimes gateways are required for a very long transition period as the legacy environment is phased out. Other times, the investment in the legacy network is so large that there is no end in sight. The gateway becomes a permanent fixture, allowing for a modern user interface to an older or very specialized environment (see Exhibit 7). Gateway issues are sometimes difficult in this type of scenario and often require some degree of customization. This is because of the large difference in capabilities offered in the legacy environment versus the modern environment.

The legacy environment may have specialized features that do not convert unambiguously into an element of service used in the new environment. On occasion, it is even a challenge to determine enough about how a long-ago-deployed environment functions to effectively set up a gateway. Address space restrictions can also be an issue in this scenario.

For example, many older legacy networks use a simple seven- or eight-character addressing format. Given a fixed number of possible character combinations, it simply is not possible to allocate a separate address in the legacy network for each potential recipient when linking to a huge new environment (e.g., Internet mail). In cases like this, it is necessary to work with a gateway product provider to make special provisions.

Scenario Three: The Electronic Mail Hub

This scenario, in which several different noncompatible packages are being used inside a single large organization, exists frequently. It is usually the result of a merger or acquisition, a high degree of decentralization, business-unit autonomy, or just poor planning. In addition, during the past several years some organizations have stumbled into this scenario as a result of deploying groupware at the departmental or division level and beginning a slow shift toward using its built-in e-mail capabilities for forms, workflow, and electronic commerce.

Whatever the cause, multiple gateways are sometimes configured together into a master, hub-like system (see Exhibit 8) used to link all of the environments together. If this approach is used, gateway issues take on a new dimension of importance and complexity. The master system becomes mission-critical. For example, should this single central system break down entirely, all of the messaging environments are disconnected from each other. In many situations, a failure like this can be very costly to an organization.

A master, hub-like system can also be far more complex to run than a simple two-way gateway. It is not uncommon for administrators to request the use of an outside professional service organization to perform the initial design, installation, and testing of such a system.

GATEWAY FACILITIES AND FEATURES

This is where gateway products differentiate themselves. Low-end products typically offer a minimum set of facilities and features — just enough to get the job done. On the other hand, more expensive high-end products deployed by large organizations generally supply a comprehensive set of facilities and features. These usually allow for a much better level of service. The facilities and features can be broken down into the following two categories: message handling-related facilities and features, and management or administration facilities and features.

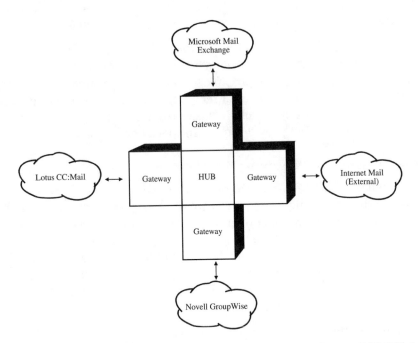

Exhibit 8. Scenario Three: Multiple Gateways Configured as an E-Mail Hub

Message Handling Facilities and Features

Message handling-related facilities and features dictate how well a particular gateway performs its main job of reliably moving messages from one environment to another. Although usually not directly visible to users, they are the "meat and potatoes" of any gateway. What follows here is a short definition of some of the more important messaging handling facilities and features. Administrators should look for these in any products being considered and discuss them with gateway vendors/integrators.

Support for Lower-Level Communications Protocol Layers. Much like a river with barges floating downstream, a lower-level communications protocol provides a means of reliably transporting information, such as messages, from point A to point B. Examples include Ethernet, TCP/IP, X.25, IPX/SPX, Appletalk, and OSI Transport/Session.

Even today, the world of lower-level protocols can sometimes be complex. With regard to gateways, message reception and transmission functions essentially ride on top of these types of transport protocols. In other words, these functions cannot work without lower-level connectivity. This means a gateway product must include top-quality support for the particular flavors being used by the environments to be linked together.

Prioritized Message Handling. This is an important feature, especially in environments where messages contain extremely vital, time-sensitive information. Ideally, a gateway should handle messages according to a first-in, first-out (FIFO) order within priority grade. This means, for example, that a message marked as high priority will be forwarded by the gateway before a message marked as low priority.

There is a big difference between a gateway product that simply converts the priority field from one format to another versus one that actually handles messages internally based on priority. In the case of the former, an administrator might have to explain to the CEO why the junk e-mail got through the network before an urgent message to all vice-presidents.

Delivery Notifications. During the past decade, all sorts of mechanisms have sprung up in an effort to make electronic messaging more reliable and generally useful for commerce. One such mechanism is delivery notifications.

Essentially, this is an element of service that allows the sender to request a confirmation be returned by the destination system or network indicating successful delivery of a message. The delivery notification is the equivalent of requesting that the postal service return a receipt when a package is delivered by a mailman.

It is extremely important that a gateway be able to handle the delivery notification element of service. This usually refers to several capabilities, including forwarding a sender's request for delivery notification into the destination network (typically as part of the message envelope or header), processing or translating any delivery notifications returned by the destination system or network and relaying information back to the sender, and issuing delivery notifications when appropriate.

A word of caution about notifications: Not all gateways handle this element of service correctly or consistently. Some gateways issue a delivery notification immediately upon successful reception of a message. This is premature and can be very misleading to the sender. Also, some gateways issue a delivery notification when transferring a message into a legacy or proprietary network, again, potentially misleading to the sender. Administrators should be aware of these issues and, at a minimum, alert users to the fact that there may be inconsistencies.

Directory Facility. It is fair to say that no two system or network managers ever agreed on the best way to handle electronic messaging directories. This holds especially true in the case of gateways. In any event, many gateway systems use some type of local directory facility. This directory is typically used for routing messages, mapping addresses, and sometimes even to define lower-level communications protocol-related information.

To save work for administrators and make things consistent, gateway product providers have come up with some ingenious ways to automatically populate and maintain a gateway's local directory. These include features known as directory synchronization and auto-registration.

Arguably, the best place to not have a local directory facility is within a gateway. This is because of management concerns. A large, enterprisewide messaging network with dozens of different gateways — each with its own local directory to populate, maintain, synchronize, and backup — is easy to imagine. Even with some degree of automation this can be a nightmare. The use of a local directory facility can be one of the first difficult issues encountered during a gateway project. Methods and technologies are available to minimize the use of local directories in gateways; however, they require the right planning, product, and people factors.

Automatic Registration. Automatic registration is a useful feature in some situations. To avoid the administrative work of what otherwise might amount to defining thousands of entries in a gateway local directory, a clever technique is used. Users essentially define themselves in the directory by way of messaging.

When a user sends a message through a gateway for the first time, his or her address is automatically registered in the directory. Upon responding, the recipient's address is registered. Slowly but surely, the gateway's local directory is populated as needed, allowing users to communicate easily and take advantage of advanced messaging features (e.g., replying and forwarding).

Directory Synchronization. When tying different messaging environments together with gateway technology, the consistency of directories is almost always a challenge. Each time a user is added or deleted from one environment, the user should also be added or deleted in a gateway's local directory, and in the directory of the other environments as well. This process is called *directory synchronization.*

Most gateway product providers either include automatic directory synchronization as a feature or sell it as a separate add-on facility. Many organizations (including the U.S. Department of Defense) are looking to X.500 technology to help solve directory- and security-related issues. X.500 is actually a set of open standards that provide for defining, distributing, and accessing directory information. Many experts feel that using an X.500-based directory, in combination with synchronization tools, is an effective long-term strategy when linking diverse messaging environments.

Big Time Toy Store
Bob J. Jones Manager

Tel: 609/665-6800 • Fax: 609/665-6672
E-mail: Bob_Jones@TOYSRGOOD.COM

To: Bob_Jones@TOYSRGOOD.COM at IGATEWAY

Sender

**Exhibit 9.   Sender Uses Public E-Mail Address Taken from Business Card
(via Wild Addressing)**

Wild Addressing. Wild addressing is sometimes referred to as *in-line* or *native addressing*. It is a feature that allows users to easily send a message to an external trading partner using a public electronic mail address specified in its original format (e.g., taken right from a business card).

For wild addressing to work, the gateway must be capable of accepting and using a public electronic mail address encapsulated within a normal environment-specific recipient address. The intended recipient does not have to be registered in the gateway's directory, hence the name wild addressing.

Wild addressing is most valuable in situations where much ad hoc communicating with external trading partners is required and it is impractical or cumbersome to register them in the gateway's directory. Because this is an increasingly important feature to look for in a gateway, an example is appropriate. Exhibit 9 represents a typical business card for Bob Jones, a manager of a toy store chain. Bob Jones's public e-mail address is shown as: BOB_JONES@TOYSRGOOD.COM.

The president of another company, Sally Roberts, wishes to send Bob a thank-you message for the order he placed for 30,000 model airplanes. For this example, it is assumed that Sally's firm uses Lotus cc:Mail on a LAN and has an Internet mail type gateway. At the cc:Mail TO: prompt, Sally might look at Bob's business card and set the address for him as follows: BOB_JONES@TOYSRGOOD.COM at IGATEWAY.

The gateway would receive the message from the cc:Mail network as a result of Sally specifying "at IGATEWAY." Next, the gateway would perform the necessary message translation into Internet format. It would include the recipient address exactly as entered by Sally, but with the "at IGATE-WAY" stripped off. The gateway in this case would not require a directory entry be defined for Bob, nor would it perform any validation (other than perhaps basic syntax checks) on the address.

Error Handling and Message Repair. What happens when a message is received by a gateway system with an error? Perhaps the address of the recipient is misspelled or the message is not in the expected format.

For cases like this, it is quite important that the gateway recognize the error and handle it gracefully. Sometimes it is appropriate for the gateway to automatically issue a negative notification response back to the sender. In many circumstances, however, this is not possible or not desired. The message might be from a far-away international location and contain vital, time-sensitive information. For this, a repair-correction facility in the gateway is very useful. It allows the administrator to view the message, correct it, and resubmit it for delivery.

Transmission Retry. Every network administrator understands Murphy's law and plans accordingly. The administrator tries to shield users from equipment failure, communications line outages, and software bugs.

Transmission retry is a gateway feature network administrators will therefore appreciate. It provides for the automatic retry by the gateway of a failed transmission attempt into the destination network. An additional capability allows the administrator to adjust the maximum number of retries, and the wait period between retries should be included as part of this feature.

File Attachment Support. Most newer messaging environments allow users to attach a file (e.g., a word processing document) to a message being sent. Some of the more sophisticated packages even allow for the launching of a particular application (e.g., a word processor) to view or edit a file attachment. It is therefore quite reasonable for users to expect a gateway to allow for the transfer of a message containing a file attachment from one environment into another. In fact, most gateways do allow for this.

Unfortunately, however, a few interesting pitfalls must be considered when it comes to file attachments. For example, one of the environments being linked together by a gateway may not even support file attachments. In this case, the gateway should detect any message containing an attachment, prevent its transfer into the destination network, and inform the sender.

Another fact of life is that there is often a loss of functional ability when a message traverses a gateway. For example, the file name, creation date, and access privileges are usually dropped as the message passes through a gateway into another environment. This situation has attracted much attention in recent years and may be improved in next-generation standards and products. For now, the bottom line is to use caution when planning to mix file attachments and gateways.

Applications Programming Interface (API) Support. An API is actually a standardized mechanism gateway that software developers use to interface with a compliant messaging environment. Examples of well-known APIs include vendor-independent messaging (VIM), the messaging applications programming interface (MAPI), common messaging calls (CMCs), and the X.400 applications programming interface (XAPI).

What do all these names and acronyms really mean in the context of gateways? First, if a gateway software product uses one of these standard mechanisms to access a messaging environment it services (versus a homemade interface), it helps ensure future compatibility. If the environment changes (e.g., a version upgrade), the gateway itself will be minimally affected. This can be very important in today's world of constant new product releases.

For example, gateway software written to use VIM for interfacing with Lotus Notes Mail generally will not be affected when a new version of Notes is released. The second reason support for an API is desirable is that larger organizations with special needs sometimes must customize or enhance a gateway product themselves. This can be much easier if a standard API has been used versus another access method.

Management and Administration Facilities and Features

These facilities and features allow the administrator of a gateway system to ensure a high quality of service to users. Over the long haul they are invaluable, especially in high-traffic volume situations and when message accountability is of the utmost importance.

While on the topic of management, it should be noted that this is also an area of much activity in the messaging industry. As of this writing, product vendors, network service providers, and users are working together to formulate standards for better messaging management.

These efforts promise to bring about increased compatibility across different hardware and software platforms, and are certainly worth watching in the context of gateways.

Alarms and Reports. Many gateway products have become sophisticated enough to automatically detect problems and alert an administrator before users are affected. This might take the form of a visual/audible alarm or perhaps a report printout. In any case, the ability to detect events such as an excessive backlog of messages awaiting transfer, a failed software component, or a communications link outage is very important.

Billing and Statistics. A billing or statistical facility is essential in most large-scale settings. Regardless of how well a gateway is functioning and how happy users are, the issue of cost justification and recovery usually arises. In some organizations, a so-called chargeback policy that allows the cost of a gateway service to be paid for by the specific departments most frequently using the service is put in place. For this, very detailed usage information (often in the form of counts) must be generated by the facility on a weekly or monthly basis.

Also, if the gateway is used as a link to a network provider, billing and statistical information can be used to prove that overcharging is not taking place. Finally, should there be a need to expand or enhance the gateway service, the information provided by a billing or statistical facility can help justify the cost. It is always easier to advocate something with the numbers to back it up in hand.

Message Tracing. Message tracing is a feature that offers the administrator the ability to determine exactly when a message was received and transmitted by a gateway. This feature is usually accomplished via the automatic generation of some sort of log entries (usually written to disk). Often, the log entries contain detailed information (e.g., the sender, the recipients, the time of reception, the time of transmission, and the message priority level).

This is a feature found in all better gateway products. It is certainly a requirement for any project involving business-quality communications.

Message Archiving. As its name indicates, archiving refers to the short- or long-term storage of messages handled by the gateway. Short-term storage is usually on disk; long-term storage is typically performed using tape.

Archiving can be considered a high-end facility, but not necessary in all gateway situations. This is because archiving often takes place outside the gateway in the environments being linked together.

Despite this, there are instances when this feature proves useful. For example, in a gateway used to link a private network to a public electronic messaging environment, archiving might be used to record all messages sent outside the organization.

Message Retrieval or Resend. This feature provides the retrieval and viewing of selected messages by the administrator from an archive. An administrator can typically pick a certain message or range of messages to be retrieved from the archive. This is done by specifying a date-time range, a particular sender, or a particular recipient.

Associated with retrieval is the ability of the administrator to actually resend a message. This is useful in environments where messages are sometimes garbled or lost on their way to an endpoint.

Alternate Routing. Once found only in very large-scale backbone message switching systems, alternate routing is a feature now finding its way into some gateway products. It allows the administrator to redirect messages from one destination to another during vacation periods, equipment outages, office closures, or temporary personnel shifts. Some very high-end gateway products even offer an automatic alternate routing feature, which is activated without any manual intervention when there is some sort of component failure.

Hold and Release. This feature is simply a way in which the administrator can instruct the gateway to temporarily stop sending messages to a particular destination environment. Messages queue up in the gateway until the administrator issues a release command.

Remote Management. This facility allows the administrator to manage a single gateway system or perhaps a whole network of gateway systems from a single location. In its simplest form, this feature is sometimes offered by a so-called remote control software package. This essentially allows an administrator to take control of a system from a remote location by a telephone line or a network connection. Video display, mouse, and keyboard information is exchanged across the connection, giving the effect that the administrator is actually on-site. Almost all of the features normally provided locally can then be used remotely.

More sophisticated (and expensive) management solutions are now becoming available for gateways. These go beyond simple remote control in that they provide a single console facility for monitoring, controlling, and troubleshooting multiple gateways dispersed across a network. Graphical displays, showing overall status as well as actual or potential trouble spots, are often included in such packages.

Security. One item sometimes overlooked by those tasked with putting an electronic messaging gateway in service is security. Perhaps this is because a messaging-only gateway, unlike a general-purpose access unit allowing file transfers and real-time login sessions, is viewed as somewhat less dangerous.

Many issues must be considered when deploying a gateway, particularly if one (or more) of the environments being linked together is considered secure. Should a particular sender be allowed to access the destination network by way of the gateway? Are messages containing file attachments screened for viruses as they transit the gateway? Is there password protection when connecting to a public network? These are all important questions that must be asked before putting an electronic messaging gateway into service.

QUALITIES TO LOOK FOR IN A GATEWAY PRODUCT

Everyone, from managers to administrators to users, desires quality, especially in something that is eventually used by the entire organization. What should administrators look for when deciding on a gateway product? The answer, of course, varies depending on the type of organization, messaging environments to be linked together, and the budget available.

Certain points should be ensured before even beginning. The hardware and operating system platforms should be reliable, up-to-date, well-supported by vendors and third-party suppliers, and, if possible, fit the organization's overall information technology strategy. Beyond these basics, many additional gateway-specific qualities must be checked.

Ease of Installation and Configuration

Nothing is more frustrating than starting a project with a product that is difficult to install and configure. Gateways by their nature are not simple desktop applications — they are data communications systems, and often complex ones at that. Some vendors have done a better job than others at designing and documenting installation and configuration procedures. This is usually a positive sign when considering a product.

Documentation

Administration manuals, utilities reference guides, cookbook-type procedures, and even release notes fall into the category of documentation. Administrators should ask to see these ahead of time to avoid any unpleasant surprises during the first month of a project.

Reliability

Even if the installation goes well and the documentation is perfect, over the long term perhaps nothing matters as much as the reliability of the system. Design problems, not-ready-for-prime-time early product releases, and nasty software bugs can be the downfall of even a carefully planned endeavor.

Administrators should check with other users of the gateway product. If not many can be found or they will not discuss their experiences, it is a bad sign. Some product suppliers can be enticed to actually help set up an evaluation system at little or no cost to allow an organization to test drive a gateway.

Flexibility

Administrators should look for a gateway product that offers maximum flexibility in terms of its message handling and management facilities. After the gateway is in service, it should be possible to add an interface to another messaging environment, perform version upgrades, and perform maintenance easily. Is it possible to do these things while the system is running or is a complete shutdown required?

Throughput

Some gateway systems perform incredibly poorly in this category. Message throughput rates of one message per minute are not unheard of when complex translations, protocols, and routing decisions are necessary.

In low-end situations this may not be an issue worth spending much time and money on, but in many cases it is. Unfortunately, vendors are traditionally averse to handing out performance statistics because it involves them in a numbers game that is difficult to win. Even when they do, the numbers should be taken with a grain of salt and should be proven firsthand if possible.

Scalabilty and Ease of Expansion

It is rare for a single, standard issue gateway system to be deployed across an entire large organization. In one location, only a small-capacity gateway might be needed. In another location, a high-capacity gateway might be necessary. If the same basic gateway product can be used in both instances, perhaps by adding more powerful software or hardware components where they are needed, the gateway can be considered scalable and easy to expand.

Fault Tolerance

In some messaging environments any downtime is totally unacceptable. Such is the case when messaging is used to facilitate point-of-sale transactions, air transportation, or military operations. For networks like this, gateways must be just as bulletproof as all of the other components in the network. This is referred to as fault tolerance.

Solutions that provide hardware fault tolerance include specially designed casings, redundant storage devices, and even the use of a complete backup (hot-standby) system. On the software side, some gateways include a mechanism designed to restart components automatically in the event of a failure. Features like this are usually rather expensive, but can be vital.

Value

Getting the most for the organization's money is always important. In general, a low- to medium-end gateway software product used to link two commonly found environments (e.g., Microsoft Mail and Internet mail) can be obtained for $5000 to $10,000. This price can be deceiving, however. In larger organizations, the true cost of a project is usually in manpower (e.g., analysis, installation, configuration, testing, trial service, and support).

If the situation calling for a gateway requires customization, fault tolerance, high throughput, or special message accountability-archiving, deploying a gateway may amount to a much more significant investment. High-end products start at approximately $40,000 for the basic software license, with hardware and software options often increasing the cost well beyond this figure. The payback point in terms of increased productivity can be difficult to measure and prove. Most experts believe that in a large organization, where e-mail has become business-critical, it is reached quite quickly.

STEPS TO DEPLOYING A GATEWAY

The following sections detail the actual steps involved in selecting, deploying, and running an electronic messaging gateway.

Up-Front Analysis and Planning

During this step, which might last anywhere from several days to several months, the functional requirements for the gateway are considered, confirmed, and documented.

In a small-scale, low-budget scenario, the resulting document might amount to just a few pages of bulleted requirements. For a very large organization with complex issues, this document might be quite long. In this case, it usually serves as part of a request for proposal (RFP) sent to gateway product vendors.

The rule of thumb is that the more precise the functional specification document, the better a vendor will understand the organization's true needs and, hence, the less chance of any misunderstandings.

Picking a Vendor or Product

In today's business climate, giving advice on how to pick a vendor is difficult. Some household names in the computing industry seem to be doing poorly these days, while new, upstart firms blossom almost overnight (and sometimes disappear just as quickly).

It is important to know that most of the larger, more well-known messaging product vendors have, in fact, formed relationships with smaller firms to supply gateway technology. This is a win-win situation for the partnering firms, with the larger company rounding out its offerings and the smaller company receiving royalties. At least in theory, this makes it less risky for the buyer because the large company stands behind the gateway product.

One idea when trying to select a gateway vendor is to check the Electronic Messaging Association's (EMA) Products Service Guide. Published annually, it lists dozens of gateway providers. A few of the larger, more well-known names include Control Data Corp., Digital Equipment Corp., Infonet, Lotus, Microsoft, Novell, and Worldtalk Corp.

Many smaller, less-known companies have good products. When considering these vendors, regular attendance and participation in organizations (e.g., the EMA) usually indicate a healthy company with a commitment to the messaging industry, as well as a desire to listen to the needs of the user community.

Do-It-Yourself versus Outsourcing

Installing, configuring, and putting in service a business-quality gateway system is often a task an organization can handle on its own. There are times to call in an expert, however, especially if the project involves customization, a legacy system no one on staff understands, links to a public network, unusual time constraints, or complicated lower-level protocol issues.

Often, even large organizations with big IS departments will rely on the product vendor, an expert consulting firm-integrator, or a network provider to supply at least a few months of planning, training, and support. Some large organizations have even gone the route of completely outsourcing the selection, deployment, administration, and maintenance of their entire messaging infrastructure, including gateways. For those wanting to focus on their core business, such companies as CSC, Control Data, Infonet, EDS, Lockheed Martin Federal Systems, and a host of smaller firms are more than willing to give birth to, rear, and even babysit an organization's messaging environment — for a hefty price.

Initial Testing

Once the gateway is installed and configured, a period of initial testing begins. During this period, the administrator checks to make sure that all the basics work well. Messages and notifications (if applicable) are exchanged, facilities and features are tried, and overall reliability is confirmed. This is an appropriate time to torture-test the gateway. Examples of "tests" to try include large messages, messages with multiple recipients, messages with file attachments, and high-priority messages. Not to be forgotten is a duration or high-load test.

Larger organizations will go so far as to write an acceptance test plan (ATP). Often a payment schedule milestone is associated with successful completion of this ATP. Then, if everything seems acceptable, it is time to begin trial operation.

Trial Service and User Feedback

No matter how much testing has been done, trial service is always interesting. This is a chance to see how well the gateway performs in a live environment with a small, select group of users exchanging messages by way of the gateway.

Before the trial service begins, administrators must make sure of a few things. First, users should be given some advance notice, explaining why the gateway is being put in place and how it will affect them. Second, all of the parties involved (technical and nontechnical) must be sure of the role they are to play. Gateways, because of their nature of tying together different messaging turfs, are often a "political hot potato" in an organization. One single person or group must clearly be in charge of administering the gateway during the trial operation.

Another thing to carefully consider is the selection of users. It is helpful to find a small group of users who meet the following criteria:

- Users who have an interest in seeing the gateway project succeed (perhaps the department needing to exchange messages with an important external trading partner)
- Users who are somewhat computer literate
- Users who seem willing (and have the time) to offer constructive feedback

A department under unusual workload pressure or a group of users who will in any way feel threatened by the new gateway capabilities should be avoided.

Live Service and Maintenance

Assuming that the trial service went well, the gateway is ready to be cut-over into full-scale operation. During this step, message traffic levels will typically escalate steadily until all users are aware of the gateway and are actively using it to communicate. It is during this step that administrators must reckon with the cost of providing help to users and quickly trouble-shoot any problems.

For example, one or two users might discover that the gateway allows them to transport huge amounts of information to a remote database system by way of messaging — something they always wanted to do but found difficult. This may be fine and, in fact, help prove the gateway useful, but perhaps it will have to be restricted to off-peak hours.

Maintenance issues become very important at this point. These include regularly scheduled hardware housekeeping and careful backup of software, configuration information, and perhaps directory facility files. In some cases, messages must be archived to tape on a periodic basis.

SUMMARY

Gateways are complicated beasts. In the likely continued absence of widespread standardization, however, there is often no choice but to use them to link together different messaging environments. The important steps to go through during a gateway project include an analysis phase, product selection, installation and configuration, initial testing, trial operation, and live service.

During the analysis phase, many important issues must be considered. Depending on the particular situation, these might include hardware-software choices, configurations, message routing, address mapping, directory use, element of service handling, lower-level communications protocols, and systems management.

When examining different products, certain qualities are desirable. Reliability, high throughput rates, flexibility, fault tolerance, scalability, and ease of administration fall into this category.

Gateways come in various grades, from low-end products that just get the job done to high-end systems with advanced facilities and features. Keeping in mind that the initial cost of a product can range from a few thousand to a few hundred thousand dollars, administrators should strive for the best range of features and facilities possible within their budgets.

The key to success with gateways is a common-sense recipe. Ingredients include effective planning, selecting the right products, successfully dealing with integrators and network service providers, as well as a healthy dash of sheer hard work. When these are mixed together correctly, electronic messaging gateway technology can be useful and rewarding to an organization.

Chapter 48
Enterprise Directory Services

Martin Schleiff

Many consulting organizations, trade associations, and vendors are touting directory services as the center of the communications universe. They believe that enterprises will benefit as they put increasing efforts and resources into their directory services. Application directory services (e.g., the address books in today's e-mail packages) are devoted to enhancing the functional ability of a particular product, service, or application to its user community. Even though e-mail address books are capable of displaying and possibly administering some information about e-mail users, they are not geared to manage corporate-critical information and deliver it to other applications, users, and services. The predicted benefits are not realized until a company embraces the concept of an enterprise directory service.

APPLICATION VERSUS ENTERPRISE DIRECTORY SERVICES

Perhaps the simplest way to contrast application and enterprise directory services is to consider the community, or user base, being served. Application directory services typically have a well-defined user base. This may consist of the users of a particular calendaring or scheduling system, or an electronic messaging system. Where multiple, disparate e-mail systems are deployed, the community may consist of the users of all interconnected messaging systems, and the application directory service may include processes that synchronize directory information between each system.

Enterprise directory services focus on providing a core set of fundamental services that can be used by many environments and customer communities. The prime objective is to leverage the efforts of few to the benefit of many (see Exhibit 1).

The enterprise directory service provides an enabling infrastructure on which other technologies, applications, products, and services can build. It is

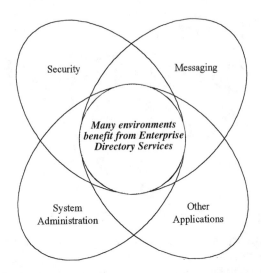

Exhibit 1. Enterprise Directory Services Environment

wise to establish this infrastructure even before receiving hard requirements from specific customer environments. Two symptoms of companies that lack enterprise directory services are hindered deployment of new technologies and applications, and redundant processes that have been built by each environment to meet its own needs.

Another way to contrast application and enterprise directory services is to consider how they evaluate the merit of a potential new service. Providers of enterprise directory services will consider the potential for their efforts to eventually be leveraged across multiple user communities. If only one community will ever use the new service, little advantage is associated with hosting that service at the enterprise level. It might be more appropriate to encourage that community to build its own service and offer to support its efforts with managed directory information. For example, if an organization wishes to track the activities of its employees on various projects, an enterprise directory service would likely decline the request to track activities, but offer to support the project by providing access to the appropriate employee information.

WHAT GOES ON IN AN ENTERPRISE DIRECTORY SERVICE?

In a nutshell, any directory service consists of activities and processes to collect and publish information. Many directory services also add value by integrating various types and sources of information into commonly usable formats.

Services that are likely candidates to be provided as part of an enterprise directory service include the following: information solicitation, registration, naming, authentication, directory synchronization, and coordination of publication infrastructure. Each of these services is briefly described in the following paragraphs. Consideration is given to some of the issues and challenges facing the providers of directory services.

Information Solicitation Services

Providers of enterprise directory services can be characterized as data hungry; they realize that empty directories are worthless. They continually seek new and better sources of information to include in their directories. Frequently, these information sources are less than enthralled about expending any efforts and resources that do not directly benefit their own causes.

For example, the human resources department of a subsidiary may not see the benefit of including subsidiary employee information in the directories of the parent company. Likewise, a payroll organization may not fully appreciate that the information they maintain about who is authorized to sign an employee's time card could also be used to approximate the company's management hierarchy. Presenting this information in a directory provides visibility of the company's dynamic organizational structure.

Enterprise directory service providers tend to accept information in any way they can get it. Data submitted by e-mail, file transfer protocol (FTP), floppies, facsimile, phone calls, and even yellow sticky notes are readily accepted in any format. A service provider would rather bend over backward than impose the service's conventions on a hesitant supplier and risk losing their willingness to provide information. In fact, the most critical task in providing enterprise directory services is to build and maintain relationships with data providers.

Service providers also realize that directories with misleading information are worse than worthless. They therefore fret continually about the condition of the data they receive and publish.

At the system level, service-level agreements normally provide some level of confidence about the availability of systems and the quality of hardware and software support. The challenge for enterprise directory service providers is to expand this concept to include information.

Agreements with information sources help identify the quality and availability of the information that will appear in the directory. Information does not need to be perfect to be meaningful and useful, as long as the quality characteristics of the information are made known to users so they can make value judgments about how to use the information appropriately.

Registration Services

Whenever possible, enterprise directory service providers attempt to acquire directory content from other sources — they prefer to be information publishers rather than information owners. Sometimes, however, no managed source for a particular type of information can be identified. In such cases, building a registration service to collect the desired information may be considered. The following list offers examples of registration activities that may be included in an enterprise directory service:

- *Collection of workstation e-mail addresses.* In most messaging environments, e-mail address information can be collected from a well-defined group of administrators. Unfortunately, where UNIX and other workstations are abundant, administration tends to be much less defined and coordinated. In such areas, each workstation may have its own messaging system, and each user may be responsible for administration of his or her own system. There is probably not a single source from which to obtain address information for a large company's workstation community.

- *Primary address designation.* Many people have more than one e-mail mailbox. For example, engineers may prefer to use their UNIX systems for messaging, yet their managers may require them to maintain an account on the same mainframe used by all the managers. Individuals may require the flexibility to work with binary attachments offered by a LAN messaging system and still maintain a mainframe account to use a calendaring system that scales to enterprise levels. With frequent migrations from one messaging system to another, large groups of people may have multiple mailboxes for several weeks while they gain familiarity with the new system and transfer information from the old system. All these cases breed confusion among senders when it is not apparent which system holds the intended recipient's preferred mailbox. Registration services may be established to let individuals designate their preferred mailbox (or preferred document type or preferred spreadsheet type).

- *Information about nonemployees.* The human resources department is an obvious source of employee information to be included in a directory. The HR department, however, probably does not track information about nonemployees who may require access to a company's computing resources, and who may have e-mail accounts on the company's systems. A service to register, maintain, and publish information about contractors, service personnel, and trading partners may be considered.

- *Information about nonpeople.* Other entities that may be appropriate to display in a directory include distribution lists, bulletin boards, helpdesks, list servers, applications, conference rooms, and other nonpeople entities.

Caution is advised when considering to offer registration services, because such services frequently require extensive manual effort and will significantly increase the labor required to run the enterprise directory service. Also, the enterprise directory service then becomes a data owner and can no longer defer data inconsistencies to some other responsible party. Even though resources are consumed in providing such services, the benefits can far outweigh the costs of uncoordinated, inconsistent, absent, or redundant registration activities.

Naming/Identification Services

A naming service simply provides alternate names, or identifiers, for such entities as people, network devices, and resources. A prime example is domain name service (DNS), which provides a user-friendly identifier (i.e., host.domain) for a networked resource and maps it to a very unfriendly network address (e.g., 130.42.14.165).

Another popular service is to provide identifiers for people in a format that can be used as login IDs or e-mail addresses, and which can be mapped back to the owners. LAN-based messaging systems frequently identify and track users by full name instead of by user ID, assuming that people's names are unique across that particular messaging system. This is one of the major hurdles in scaling LAN-based messaging systems beyond the workgroup level. A naming service could manage and provide distinct full names and alleviate a major scaling problem.

Naming services should adhere to the following principles when defining identifiers.

1. *Stable and meaningless.* Identifiers, or names, are like gossip; once they become known, they are difficult to change, recall, and correct. Inherent meanings (e.g., organizational affiliation or physical location) should not be embedded in an identifier because these values change frequently, rendering the identifier inaccurate or out of date.
2. *Uniqueness.* Identifiers must be unique within a naming context.
3. *Traceable back to an individual.* To effectively manage a system, knowledge about the system's users is required.
4. *Extensible to many environments.* Many companies are striving to minimize the number of user IDs an individual must remember to gain access to myriad accounts. Others hope to eventually implement a single logon by which their users can access any computing resource.

5. *User friendly.* Identifiers should be easy to convey, easy to type in, and easy to remember.

6. *Easy to maintain.* Algorithmically derived identifiers (e.g., surname followed by first initial) are easy to generate, but such algorithms may cause duplicate identifiers to be generated if they are not checked against some registry of previously assigned identifiers.

Some of the principles are in contention with each other, so enterprise directory service providers must identify a practical balance of desirable characteristics. A hybrid approach might incorporate some of the following rules:

- Algorithmically assign identifiers (ease of generation)
- Include a maximum of eight characters (extensible to many environments)
- Base identifiers on people's real names (semi-stable and user friendly)
- Use numbers as needed in the rightmost bytes to distinguish between similar names (uniqueness)
- Register the identifiers in a database (traceable back to owner and guaranteed uniqueness)
- Allow individuals to override the generated identifier with self-chosen vanity plate values (user friendly)

Naming an entity should occur as soon as that entity is known (e.g., on or before an employee's hire date), and the identifier should immediately be published by the enterprise directory service. Then, when system administrators establish user accounts for an entity, they can find the entity's identifier in the directory and use that identifier as the user ID. Thereafter, the identifier can be used to query the directory for a user's updated contact and status information. This approach enables system administrators to focus on managing user accounts instead of employee information.

Authentication/Confidentiality Services

The swelling interest in electronic commerce has brought much attention to the need for encryption and electronic signature capabilities. The most promising technologies are referred to as public-key cryptographic systems (PKCS), which provide two keys for an individual — one a private key and the other a public key (see Exhibit 2). A private key must remain known only to its owner. An individual's public key must be widely published and made easily available to the community with which that person does business.

Information encrypted with an individual's public key can only be decrypted with the associated private key. Therefore, information can be sent confidentially to its recipient. Information encrypted with an individual's

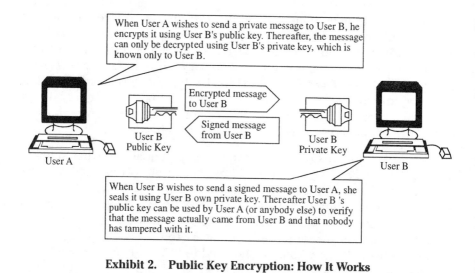

When User A wishes to send a private message to User B, he encrypts it using User B's public key. Thereafter, the message can only be decrypted using User B's private key, which is known only to User B.

Encrypted message to User B

Signed message from User B

User B Public Key

User B Private Key

User A

User B

When User B wishes to send a signed message to User A, she seals it using User B own private key. Thereafter User B 's public key can be used by User A (or anybody else) to verify that the message actually came from User B and that nobody has tampered with it.

Exhibit 2.   Public Key Encryption: How It Works

private key can only be decrypted with the associated public key. Therefore, a recipient can authenticate the origin of the information.

Companies are now grappling with such PKCS deployment issues as which organization will manage keys, which algorithms will be used to generate keys, if private keys will be held in escrow, and whether employees will be allowed to use company-generated keysets for personal use. The one issue that seems clear is that public keys should be published in a directory service. Soon, enterprise directory service providers will be grappling with their own issues (e.g., when the directory should actually begin to carry public keys, how to encourage vendors to build products that can query a directory for somebody's public key, how many keys should be carried for an individual, and how to make those keys accessible to trading partners and other areas beyond corporate boundaries).

Directory Synchronization Services

The press routinely represents cross-platform directory synchronization as the most difficult task in a directory service. Depending on the approach taken, this situation may be true. Several messaging system vendors provide products that can synchronize non-native address books into their own. If a company attempts to use such products to synchronize address books from more than two vendors, a true mess will result.

A much more effective method is to synchronize each address book with a central (probably vendor neutral), bidirectional synchronization service. The central synchronization service can pool the addresses from all participating messaging communities, translate between native and common address formats, and finally make the pooled addresses available to each community in its respective native format. The advantages of a central service over two-way address book synchronizers can be likened to the advantages of providing a messaging backbone service instead of two-way e-mail gateways. Large companies taking the centralized approach have been able to provide cross-platform synchronization services with minimal resources (e.g., one allocated headcount).

Directory standards (e.g., X.500) have the potential to further simplify cross-platform directory synchronization. If vendors ever half-embrace the standard to the point that their products actually query an X.500 service instead of (or in addition to) their local address books, directory synchronization can become a unidirectional process. Each messaging community would still submit the addresses of its users to the enterprise directory service. However, there would be no need to bring other addresses back into their local address book. If vendors ever fully embrace the standard to the point that their products actually manage their own address information right in an X.500 directory, processes for cross-platform directory synchronization will be unnecessary. Enterprise directory service providers ought to encourage their vendors to include these capabilities in their products.

With growing interest in electronic commerce, enterprise directory service providers are being asked to carry trading partner information in local directories. In response to such requests, and in the absence of better solutions, service providers commonly exchange files containing address information with trading partner companies and then incorporate the address information into their own processes.

A better approach would be to link the directories of the trading partner companies so that each company is responsible for its own information; there would be no need for a company to obtain a file of trading partner addresses and manage the information locally. This is yet another area where directory standards provide hope for a better future. The X.500 standards specify the technologies and protocols required for such an interenterprise directory. Before participating in an interenterprise X.500 directory, service providers will need to evaluate their company policies on external publication of directories, access control to sensitive information, and the readiness of trading partners to participate.

What Is X.500?

X.500 is a set of international standards, jointly developed by the International Telecommunications Union-Telecommunications Standards Sector (ITU-TSS) and the International Standards Organization (ISO), that specifies standards-based directory components and protocols. Some of the major components and protocols include the following:

- *Directory System Agent (DSA)*. This is where information resides. Multiple DSAs can replicate and distribute information among themselves. They can communicate among themselves to resolve directory queries.
- *Directory User Agent (DUA)*. This enables a user (or application) to access information stored in DSAs. DUAs may be stand-alone programs or incorporated into other applications (e.g., an e-mail user agent).
- *Directory System Protocol (DSP)*. This protocol is used by DSAs to communicate among themselves to resolve queries.
- *Directory Access Protocol (DAP)*. This protocol is used to communicate between DUAs and DSAs. A Lightweight Directory Access Protocol (LDAP) has been defined that is less bulky than DAP and is appropriate for desktop devices.

X.500 Infrastructure Coordination Services

Various approaches can be taken for deployment of X.500 technology. Frequently, X.500 is included as a component of some other product the company wishes to deploy. For example, a company may purchase a new message transfer agent (MTA) that includes an X.500 DSA to manage message routing information; a company can also acquire a public-key crypto system product that includes X.500 to publish public keys, or a company may use X.500 as a distributed computing environment (DCE) global directory.

Another approach is for a company to first deploy a stand-alone X.500-based directory service, and then tie in messaging, security, and other products as they are acquired. In a large company, some combination of these approaches may occur simultaneously. Setting up X.500 for a particular application is much easier than setting up a general X.500 infrastructure, but it is not the preferred approach.

It is likely that various computing communities will acquire their own X.500 directory system agents to meet their own special needs. Unless the efforts of these groups are coordinated, conflicting definitions, incompatibilities, and redundant efforts and data will emerge — foiling the potential for the efforts of the few to be leveraged to the benefit of the many.

Even though the enterprise directory service may not own all the directory components, it is the best place to organize the activities of these components. Coordination activities include acting as the company's registration authority, managing the root DSA within the company, providing a map of the company's directory information tree, registration of new DSAs, schema management, registration of object classes and attribute types, controlling where new information is incorporated into the directory, and managing replication agreements.

A SERVICE PROVIDER'S PERSPECTIVE ON X.500

These days, technologists promote technologies as directory services, vendors market products as directory services, and standards bodies represent specifications as directory services. Enterprise directory service providers must remember that all these are just tools by which to provide a directory service, and it is their responsibility to select the appropriate tools to best deliver their services. They must discern between what works in theory, what works in principle, and what works in practice.

X.500 technology is sound, but until vendors actually deliver products that use the technology, it will remain difficult to justify a serious investment in establishing X.500 infrastructure. Home-grown applications are driving X.500 deployment in some companies, but even in these companies a stronger vendor commitment would ease the burden of justification.

Information Management Issues

X.500 is frequently cast as a panacea for directory services. This is not true; the biggest challenges for enterprise directory service providers are information management issues.

X.500's strength is in information publication, not information management. In some companies, X.500 receives more attention from the security and systems administration communities than from messaging organizations. These communities have much more stringent requirements for timely and accurate data; service providers will need to revamp processes and clean up content to meet these requirements. Remembering that directories with bad information are worse than worthless, service providers will need to give as much attention to information processes and relationships with data providers as they do to X.500 technologies.

Database Issues

X.500 is often described as a type of distributed DBMS. This can be misleading, and some applications that began building on X.500 have had to back off and use conventional database products. X.500 is well suited for information that is structured, frequently accessed by a heterogeneous community, primarily read only, and latency tolerant. X.500, however, lacks database capabilities (e.g., referential integrity or the ability to update groups of information in a single operation). A common debate concerns whether data should be managed in X.500, or if it should be managed in a database and then published in X.500.

Directory Information Tree Structure

Most literature suggests that there are only two basic models to follow when designing the X.500 directory information tree (DIT): the DIT should reflect either a company's organizational structure or its geographical structure.

In fact, both the organizational and geographical approaches violate the first principle of naming (stable and meaningless identifiers). Frequent reorganizations and relocations will cause frequent changes to distinguished names (DNs) if either the organizational or the geographical model is followed. When designing a DIT, sources of information must be considered. For example, in companies where all employee data are managed by a central human resources organization, it may not make sense to artificially divide the information so that it fits a distributed model.

These observations are not intended to discourage use of X.500-based directory services; rather, they are intended to encourage cautious deployment. Reckless and inappropriate activities with X.500 will likely damage its chances for eventual success in a company, and this technology has far too much potential to be carelessly squandered. The previously lamented lack of vendor products that use X.500 can also be taken as a window of opportunity for companies to gain X.500 experience in a controlled manner before some critical application demands knee-jerk deployment. An ideal way to start (assuming that the information is already available) is to build an inexpensive and low-risk "White Pages" directory service using the following components:

- *A single DSA and LDAP server.* Inexpensive products are available today; a desktop system can provide good response for thousands of White Pages users. Worries about replication agreements and getting different vendors' directory system agents to interoperate can be postponed until the service grows beyond the capabilities of a single DSA.
- *A simple Windows DUA.* Vendor-provided directory user agents can be purchased. Unfortunately, many vendor products tend to be so full-featured that they risk becoming overly complex. An in-house-developed DUA can provide basic functions, can be easily enhanced, can be optimized for the company's directory information tree, and can be freely distributed. Freeware Macintosh DUAs are also available.
- *A Web-to-X.500 gateway.* Freeware software is available.
- *A White Pages Home Page that resolves queries through the Web-to-X.500 gateway.* This brings the service to a large heterogeneous user community.

A precautionary note about deploying such a service is that users will consider it a production service even if it is intended only as a pilot or prototype. Support and backup capabilities may be demanded earlier than expected.

ROLES AND RESPONSIBILITIES

As companies attempt to categorize enterprise directory services, especially those that include X.500, they begin to realize the difficulty in identifying a service provider organization. An enterprise directory service is as much a networking technology as it is an information management service, or a communications enabler, or a foundation for security services. One cannot definitely predict that messaging will be the biggest customer of the service or that HR information and e-mail addresses will be the most important information handled by the service. Possibly the best approach is to create a new organization to provide the enterprise directory service.

To build and provide effective directory services, service providers must be intimately familiar with the data so they can witness the changing characteristics of the information, recognize anomalies, and appropriately relate various types of data. Rather than assign an individual to a single role, it is preferable to assign each individual to multiple roles so that nobody is too far removed from the data, and so that no role is left without a backup.

Roles and responsibilities fall into the following categories: operations management, product management, project management, and service management.

Operations Management. Directory operations management focuses on quality and availability of directory data as specified in service-level agreements. Responsibilities include the following:

1. Operate day-to-day directory processes and provide on-time availability of deliverables.
2. Ensure that the directory service is accessible by supported user agents.
3. Register information that is not available from other sources.
4. Interface with existing data suppliers to resolve inaccurate information.
5. Validate data, report exceptions, and track trends.
6. Staff a user support help desk.

Product Management. Directory product management focuses on the type of products and services offered to directory customers, as well as tools and processes to best provide the services. Responsibilities include the following:

1. Acquire, build, and maintain tools that enable or improve day-to-day operation of directory processes. Appropriate skills include database development, programming in various environments, and familiarity with the company's heterogeneous computing environment.

2. Establish and administer service-level agreements with information providers and customers. Negotiate formats, schedules, and methods of information exchange between the directory service and its suppliers and customers.
3. Provide and maintain approved directory user agents to the user community.
4. Promote current capabilities of directory services to potential customers.
5. Build directory products to meet customer needs.

Project Management. Directory project management focuses on the near-term future of directory services. Responsibilities include the following:

1. Conduct proof-of-concept projects to explore new uses of directory services.
2. Coordinate activities to put new uses of directory services into production.
3. Conduct proof-of-concept projects to explore the use of new technologies in providing directory services.
4. Coordinate activities to deploy new directory technologies into production.
5. Consult and assist customer environments in incorporating directory services into their applications and services (e.g., assist with LDAP coding, assemble toolkits to ease coding against directories, train application developers in use of toolkits, and provide orientation to the enterprise directory service).
6. Ascertain which projects are most needed. Possible projects include interenterprise directories, participation in global directories, authentication and access control, public keys in directories, electronic Yellow Pages, combining disparate registration services, achieving DNS functional ability with X.500, explore the use of whois++ and finger as directory user agents, partner with other groups to achieve synergy with WWW and other technologies, and assist corporate communications organizations to optimize electronic distribution of information bulletins.
7. Participate with appropriate forums to define and establish international standards.

Service Management. Directory service management focuses on the soundness of current and future directory services. Responsibilities include the following:

1. Coordinate project management, product management, and operations management efforts.
2. Author and maintain service descriptions.
3. Run change boards and advisory boards.

4. Coordinate X.500 infrastructure (registration point for DSAs, object classes, and attributes).
5. Develop and gain consensus on position statements and direction statements.
6. Formulate business plans and justify required resources.
7. Act as focal point for major customer communities; collect requirements, assess customer satisfaction, and gain consensus on direction statements.
8. Represent the company's interests at external forums and to vendors.

SUMMARY

It is important to have realistic expectations of a directory service. Some who expect that a directory will provide huge payback as a single data repository and source of all corporate information may be disappointed. Others who consider directories to be of limited use beyond messaging will reap only a portion of directory benefits. It is difficult to predict which visionary ideas will become practical applications in the near future.

Probably the most vital point to consider when planning for an enterprise directory service is flexibility. In light of dynamic customer demands, new sources and types of information, increasingly stringent requirements for quality data, and emerging technologies, many service providers have elected to use a database to manage directory information (exploiting its data management capabilities) and a directory to publish managed data (capitalizing on its publication strengths).

As buzzwords proliferate, it is easy to get caught up in the glitter and pomp of new technologies. Wise service providers will realize that the important part of directory services is service, and that the role of new technologies is simply to better enable the providing of a service.

Chapter 49
Enterprise Messaging Migration
David Nelson

The goal of this chapter is to discuss large enterprise messaging migration projects and help the information technology professional avoid many of the common pitfalls associated with these types of projects. Messaging migration is the process of moving users from one or more source e-mail systems to one or more destination e-mail systems. Large enterprise projects are those involving anywhere from a few thousand to over 100,000 users.

The checklists and methodology in this chapter can save frustration, time, and money. For example, what does it cost an organization if enterprise e-mail directories are corrupted and e-mail is down for hours or days due to a migration? What happens in the middle of a messaging migration project if the gateways cannot handle the traffic load and e-mail is terminally slow? What's the impact if stored messages are lost? How about personal address books? What's the benefit of completing the migration sooner than planned?

E-mail, or messaging, is necessary for people to do their jobs. It is no longer a "nice to have" form of communication — it is mission-critical. A recent Pitney-Bowes study found that the average office worker sends and receives more than 190 messages per day.[1] Even though much of this e-mail is superfluous, many messages concern important meetings, projects, and other information necessary to do one's job. Messaging is indeed a valuable resource and changing e-mail systems should be treated with care.

WHY MIGRATE?

There are many reasons why organizations are migrating to new messaging systems. New systems have more capabilities and attractive features. Older systems have become difficult to maintain. An environment of 6, 12, or more different e-mail systems, which is common in large enterprises, is difficult and costly to manage. The basic idea behind messaging migration is to simplify, consolidate, and lay a foundation for future applications.

Current E-Mail Systems

Over the years, large enterprises have "collected" many different e-mail systems. They may have started out using mainframe computers and implemented e-mail systems like IBM's PROFS, Fischer's TAO or EMC2, or H&W's SYSM. Engineering or manufacturing divisions may have used DEC VAX computers and implemented VMSmail or ALL-IN-1. Later on, sales and marketing groups may have implemented PC LANs with Microsoft Exchange, Lotus Notes, or a number of other PC-based e-mail systems.

Each different computing environment carries with it a proprietary e-mail system. Each e-mail system has its own method of addressing users and storing messages. Enterprises have overcome these differences with gateways, message switches, and directory synchronization products. Over time, many have discovered that a complex environment of many different messaging systems is not ideal.

Some of the problems associated with multiple e-mail systems include the following:

- Lost messages
- Long delivery times
- Complex addressing
- Corrupted e-mail attachments
- Inability to communicate with Internet mail users

Future Outlook

Which e-mail systems will enterprises migrate to? It's important to note that many enterprises will never be able to migrate to a single e-mail system. Mergers and acquisitions, different business division needs, and new technology will invariably introduce different e-mail systems over time. There is, however, a benefit in reducing the number of messaging systems and having the processes and technology in place to perform messaging migrations. In their report on messaging migration, Ferris Research stated, "Migration is a fact of life and is going to remain a fact of life."[2]

Internet mail has had a tremendous impact on today's messaging environment. The ability to communicate with millions of people on the Internet is of great benefit. The Internet mail standard of RFC-822 addressing and SMTP/MIME format (simple mail transport protocol/multipurpose Internet mail extensions) has also become the *de facto* corporate e-mail standard.

New client/server messaging systems support SMTP/MIME and also add new functionality such as:

- Group scheduling and calendaring
- Public bulletin boards
- Shared documents and databases
- Collaborative groupware applications
- Application development environments

Some of the leading client/server messaging systems include the following:

- Microsoft Exchange
- Lotus Notes and Domino
- Novell GroupWise and Internet Messaging System
- Netscape Messaging Server

PROJECT SPONSOR(S)

Politics play a very large role in the success of enterprise messaging migration projects. A successful project requires a sponsor that can ensure a timely decision on the company's new e-mail standard and the process that will be followed to get there.

The main concern is that the new e-mail system has to be agreed upon by all of the key decision makers in the organization and the migration process cannot disrupt the business. Each business unit will have its own unique requirements and seasonality. While the CEO may not have time to sponsor the messaging migration project, it is important that leadership and support are provided for the project. Business unit managers are also key members of the leadership team. Some organizations go the other direction, forming "grass-roots" committees that span all the different business units so that consensus can be formed. Whatever the approach, it's critical to gain buy-in from the entire organization.

Do not underestimate the time that will be required to gain consensus for a messaging migration project. In some large enterprises, this first step can take months. Look at other large IT projects that have touched all business units within an enterprise to gauge what the consensus forming stage will be like.

USE CONSULTANTS

There are many reasons to bring consultants in on a messaging migration project. First of all, they have been involved in enterprise messaging migration projects thereby providing benefit from their experience. Second, they can augment current resources so that the staff can stay focused on other critical projects. Finally, they are viewed as having an objective opinion that can help gain consensus across different business units.

Each of the messaging vendors (Microsoft, Lotus, Novell, Netscape, etc.) has its own consulting services organization. Some of the independent consulting organizations that specialize in messaging migration include:

1. Wingra Technologies
   1-608-238-4454
   http://www.wingra.com
   info@wingra.com
2. Control Data Systems (now Syntegra (USA), Inc.)
   1-888-742-5864
   http://www.cdc.com or www.us.syntegra.com
   info.us@syntegra.com
3. Digital Equipment Corp (now part of Compaq)
   1-800-888-5858/0220
   http://www.compaq.com/comments.html
      then click Webmaster
4. Hewlett-Packard
   1-800-752-0900
   http://www.hp.com
   http://www.hp.com/country/us/eng/contact_us.htm

DEVELOP A MIGRATION PLAN

A well thought-out migration plan is the cornerstone of a successful enterprise messaging migration project. If a consulting organization has been hired, migration planning will be one of their services. They will work closely to define what is important for your organization. The checklist in Exhibit 1 shows the basics that should be included in a messaging migration plan.

Define the Current Environment

The first step in the planning process is to define your current messaging environment. One of the best ways to start is to develop a network diagram. This diagram should show the e-mail systems in your enterprise and how they're connected. A simplistic diagram is given in Exhibit 2 to illustrate what a messaging network diagram should look like.

The description of your messaging environment should include:

• Names and vendors of existing messaging systems
• Number of users on each e-mail system
• Geographic locations of existing e-mail systems
• Names and vendors of existing gateways and/or message switch
• Current Internet address standard

Exhibit 1. Migration Plan Checklist

- Executive overview
- Project goals
- Current messaging environment
- New messaging environment
- Migration infrastructure
- Message switch
- Directory synchronization
- Migration technology
- Migration timing
- Migration policies
- Date range of stored messages
- Message and attachment size restrictions
- Personal address books
- Messaging-enabled applications
- Distribution lists
- Bulletin boards
- Service levels
- Delivery times
- Functionality
- Risk analysis
- Gantt chart/timeline
- Budget

- Message traffic volume within systems, between systems, and external to the Internet or other networks
- Average message size
- Average message store size — number of messages and size in megabytes
- Network bandwidth between systems and different geographic locations
- Names and contact information for the people who manage each of the current messaging systems, gateways or message switch, and networks.

Choose the Destination System

The choice of destination system will depend on a number of things. Sometimes it's simply a matter of sticking with a preferred vendor. Other times the decision is driven by a particular application or fit with existing standards. Some of the market-leading client/server messaging systems and their relative strengths are listed below:

- Microsoft Exchange 2000
  - Good integration with Microsoft Office 2000 and Microsoft Outlook 2000

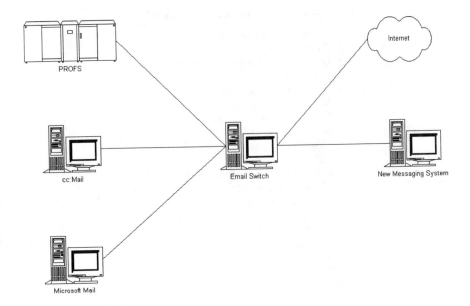

Exhibit 2. Simple Enterprise Messaging Network Diagram

   — Good solution where the main need is for e-mail
- Lotus Domino
   — Wealth of third-party applications
   — Strong collaborative functionality and mobile sevices
- Novell GroupWise
   — Strong integration with Novell network servers
- Netscape Messaging Server
   — Pure Internet standards

New System Requirements

Once the destination system has been chosen, define the requirements for that system. Some of the decisions should include the following:

- Standard messaging server configurations
- Standard desktop client configurations
- User training required
- Number of messaging servers required
- Geographic locations of messaging servers
- Network bandwidth requirements between servers

Migration Infrastructure

The messaging migration infrastructure includes technology to provide the following:

- E-mail gateway services
- Enterprise directory services, including directory synchronization
- Internet mail routing
- Message store migration

For enterprises with more than two different e-mail systems, an e-mail switch is required. The e-mail switch should be scalable so that it can handle the peak load when half the enterprise is on the old e-mail systems and half are on the new system. One large enterprise with more than 100,000 users found that they needed six to ten message switches to handle their peak loads. Several message switch vendors are listed below:

1. Wingra Technologies
   1-608-238-4454
   http://www.wingra.com
   info@wingra.com
2. Control Data Systems (now Syntegra (USA), Inc.)
   1-888-742-5864
   http://www.cdc.com or www.us.syntegra.com
   info.us@syntegra.com
3. Lotus Development Corp.
   1-617-577-8500
   http://www.lotus.com
   www.lotus.com/home.nsf/welcome/corporate
     then click webmaster.mail

Migration technology should work with the message switch to ensure that addresses are translated correctly as message stores are migrated. Migration and integration, or coexistence, technology will also need to work together so that e-mail routing is updated as users switch to their new e-mail system. Migration technology should also make it easy to select a group of users to migrate, move their message stores and personal address books, create accounts on the new messaging system, and update the enterprise directory. It is also useful if message store migration can occur in a two-step process so that the bulk of stored messages can be moved two to three weeks ahead of the time and the remainder can be moved the weekend prior to the cutover date. This is an elegant way to deal with the large size of message stores, often measured in gigabytes.

Migration Timing

In this section of the migration plan, define which groups of users will be moved when. Usually it makes sense to approach migration on a business unit basis. Since 80 percent of e-mail is within a functional group, it makes sense to move each group at the same time. This approach will also allow taking into account the seasonality of different business units. A retail operation, for example, will not want any system changes to occur during their peak selling season, often around Christmas time. Other business units may want to avoid changes around the time leading up to the end of their fiscal years. Migration timing will be negotiated with each business unit. Date ranges will need to be laid out for each business unit for installing new messaging servers and desktop hardware and software, training users, migrating message stores, and cutting over to the new system.

Migration Policies

There are several different philosophical approaches to messaging migration. One approach, often referred to as the "brute-force" method, advocates moving everyone at the same time and disregarding stored messages and personal address books. Another philosophy is to view messaging migration as a process and message stores as the knowledge of the enterprise.

Messaging migration technology is available to perform format and address translations between the old and new systems, preserve folder structures, and move personal address books and distribution lists. As mentioned earlier, it is critical that the migration technology chosen be integrated very tightly with the message switch and directory synchronization infrastructure. This integration will allow addresses to be translated properly so that stored messages can be replied to. Also, it is important that the migration technology feed into directory synchronization and message routing processes so that e-mail will continue to flow properly as users are moved to the new messaging system.

Assuming the organization would like to retain the valuable information contained in stored messages and personal address books, the next step is to define migration policies. Migration policies will need to cover the following areas:

- Personal folders and stored messages — what will be migrated?
  — Restrictions on dates
  — Restrictions on message or attachment sizes
  — Preservation of status flags, i.e., read or unread
- International characters — for users in France, Quebec, Asia, or other parts of the world, will their folder names, message subjects, and e-mail addresses contain the same characters as they do in their current e-mail systems?

- Address translation as messages are migrated — will users be able to reply to stored messages from within the new e-mail system?
- Archives and laptops — will these message stores need to be moved to a server before they can be migrated?
- Internet mail addresses — will they change as users are migrated? What will the new standard be?
  — Personal address books
  — Distribution lists
  — Bulletin boards
- Personal calendars — is there a way to move appointments to the new system?
- Mail-enabled applications — often these have to be rewritten to work with the new messaging system
- Service-level agreements — what can users expect in terms of availability and e-mail delivery times during the migration?

Risk Analysis

The risk analysis section of the migration plan will define which elements of the migration process are reversible and what the backout plans are. If moving a group of users results in the corruption of all the e-mail directories in the enterprise, how will you those changes back out so that e-mail can continue to flow properly? Have current message stores and directories been backed up properly? What is the impact if the project timeline slips? These are some of the questions that need to be addressed in the risk analysis section of the migration plan.

Project Timeline

A project timeline is useful both as a means of communication and as a way to manage the overall project. The timeline should, at a glance, show the steps involved, their interdependencies, and the resources required to achieve objectives. A high-level timeline is given in Exhibit 3 to illustrate the basic structure.

COMMUNICATE THE PLAN

The migration plan will not have much meaning unless communicated within the organization and support gained for it. Communicate the following to management:

- Why enterprise is migrating
- What the new messaging standard will be
- When the migration will take place
- Benefits of migrating

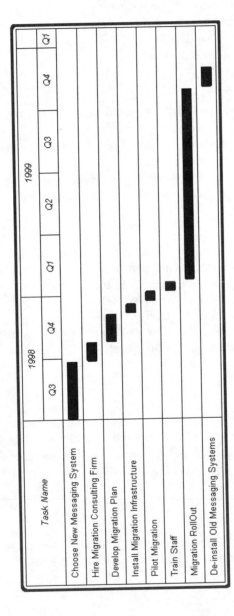

Exhibit 3. Sample Migration Timeline

Management in this case has a very broad meaning. Executive staff, business unit managers, and functional managers will all need to know about the messaging migration plan. Methods for communicating the plan include e-mail, formal meetings, or interoffice memos.

Of course, the rest of the organization will also need to know what's going to happen. E-mail users should receive information telling them:

- High-level view of the reasons the enterprise is migrating
- What the new e-mail standard will be
- When new hardware or software will be installed on their desktops
- Their new account name and initial password
- Training schedule
- What will happen to their stored e-mail, folders, and personal address books
- What their external Internet mail address will be
- When they should begin using their new e-mail system
- Who to contact with questions or issues

Because of the need to communicate individual account names and passwords, user communication will probably take the form of e-mail or interoffice memos with some form of mail-merge capability. For some of the more general information, consider developing a brochure or flyer describing the project and its benefits.

EXECUTE THE PLAN

A decision will need to be made of who is going to perform messaging migration. Will it be internal IT staff, a migration consultant, or another third party? The key considerations are whether the resources are available and whether those resources should be devoted to messaging migration.

The first step in testing a migration plan is to perform a migration pilot. Set up a test lab that includes primary e-mail systems, messaging integration and migration technology, and the destination e-mail system. It is very important that this pilot be performed in a test lab environment. This is the stage where problems with the messaging migration plan will be discovered, thereby preventing introduction into the production mail environment. Go through all of the steps of the migration plan and document results. Change the plan as required.

The next step is to migrate the first business unit on the schedule. Communicate with the users what will be happening and how it will affect them. Again, document the results and adjust the migration plan accordingly.

For the remainder of the project, which can often last 12 to 24 months, the migration process will be repeated on a business unit basis. Standard project management practices should be followed to set milestones and make sure the process stays on track. Once complete, shut down and deinstall old e-mail systems and wait for the next migration opportunity.

SUMMARY

The goal of this chapter was to describe enterprise messaging migrations and help the IT professional avoid many common pitfalls. The critical success factors for an enterprise messaging migration project include the following:

- Consensus and leadership
- Use of consultants
- Detailed planning
- Tightly integrated messaging migration and coexistence technology
- Communication with management and users
- Project management

Messaging migration is a complex process, but with careful planning an enterprise can deploy new e-mail systems on time and within budget.

References

1. *Pitney Bowes' Workplace Communications in the 21st Century*, May 18, 1998, Institute of the Future, 1 Elmcroft Road, 6309, Stamford, CT 06926-0700, http://www.pitneybowes.com
2. *Migration of E-mail Systems*, February 1998, Jonathan Penn, Ferris Research, 408 Columbus Avenue No. 1, San Francisco, CA 94133, telephone 415-986-1414, http://www.ferris.com

Chapter 50
Selecting and Deploying E-Mail Migration Tools and Utilities

Sven James

During the past three years, a revolution within the corporate world has taken place. Companies started implementing Lotus Notes and Microsoft Exchange. Due to the sheer market share that these two products have captured, new companies have been born, or reinvented, and have dedicated themselves to creating products and services specifically geared toward automating the process of migrating from any other e-mail system to Notes or Exchange. This chapter discusses customer requirements for e-mail migration tools and utilities and goes on to describe features and functionality of products currently available on the market.

The marketplace for e-mail migration tools and utilities is young even compared to today's quickly evolving e-mail systems. E-mail migration tools have only been around a couple of years; however, these tools are having an impact far beyond what has, up to this point, been the definition of tools and utilities. E-mail migration has seen the birth of full-blown migration and coexistence applications that can be integrated into today's most popular messaging systems.

CUSTOMER REQUIREMENTS FOR MIGRATION AND COEXISTENCE

Customer requirements for migration and coexistence are simple: "Move the user data, synchronize directories and data, allow everyone to send and receive from and to all other systems, and automate it so that it requires no additional personnel or resources."

0-8493-1149-7/02/$0.00+$1.50
© 2002 by CRC Press LLC

Migration tools and utilities can be configured to do all of the above. However, before starting to think about the tool, it is very important to consider what you want to do and the order in which you want to do it. Small shops (less than 1,000 users) may be in the position of being able to migrate their mail over a weekend. However, the rest of the corporate world must function with "e-mail system coexistence." Coexistence is the act of two or more e-mail systems exchanging data in a manner seamless to the user. Since most shops will be in coexistence mode, this chapter is written for them. Users that have the luxury of a straight migration can ignore all the coexistence steps and just move their users. Aren't they lucky!

MIGRATION AND COEXISTENCE PLANNING — BEFORE THE TOOLS AND UTILITIES

Before describing the various data types, functions, and features of migration tools and utilities, it is very important that the company has a migration and coexistence plan. Other chapter(s) and entire books are becoming available on enterprise migration planning, and the reason is simple. Migration and coexistence need to be carefully planned and implemented.

The following is an overview of just some of the issues and answers that should be addressed prior to actually implementing the migration and coexistence process:

- Create a messaging topology that reflects the current e-mail system
  — Today — as it really exists today
  — Tomorrow — a picture of the e-mail environment to which the company is migrating
  — Reality/Interim — a picture of what the e-mail environment will really look like during the coexistence period
- Moving the data is a necessity: would one really move offices without taking the filing cabinet?
- Prepare for user migration and use migration as a training aid.
- Who is going to move? In what order? Who moves first?
- Determine the data-types that are business critical (i.e., directory, in-baskets, file folders, archives, bulletin boards, etc.).
- Determine what data can be migrated and what data must be synchronized.
- Determine migration schedule.
- Determine which tools and utilities can automate the process to fulfill the plan.

THE DIRECTORY

The prerequisite for any migration tool or utility is the directory. A directory must exist on the legacy e-mail system, and a directory must be created or synchronized with on the new e-mail system.

The company will be in one of two positions:

1. It will either have a messaging switch (hub) with directory synchronization already in place, which means a great head start on the rest of the corporate world, or
2. The directory will need to be built on the new e-mail system.

An issue to consider when looking for tools is the ability to build names for the new e-mail system based on their rules, yet at the same time using the legacy e-mail addresses as the source for the new directory. It is important to have a reliable cross-reference of names in each e-mail system. In addition, match a unique identifier on names across the e-mail systems and the ability of the directory synchronization process to run automatically without manual intervention. Other useful tools include the ability to do a "one-way load" and the ability to load mailing lists from the legacy system into the new e-mail system.

Heads Up! Resolve Duplicate IDs Today!

The number one issue in migrating the directory from the legacy system to Notes or Exchange is resolving duplicate IDs. If there are duplicates now, stop creating them. Go to management, get their buy-in on this as soon as possible. If there is the people-power, start resolving duplicate IDs today and build toward a new corporate directory in the future. Suffice it to say, this one paragraph cannot even begin to resolve all directory issues; however, for migration purposes, most tools and utilities on the market, not to mention the help desk, will have a much easier time if this issue is resolved.

Directory synchronization tools are generally available for migration to Lotus Notes, Microsoft Exchange, and Novell GroupWise from the following legacy e-mail systems. A complete list of migration vendors is contained in Exhibit 1.

- OV/400
- OV/VM
- OV/MVS
- Emc2/TAO
- MEMO
- SYSM
- Netscape
- Exchange
- Notes
- CC: Mail
- MS Mail
- All-In-1

Exhibit 1. Chart of Migration Tool and Utility Vendors

Company/URL	Legacy E-mail Systems	Destination E-mail System
Altis Limited www.altisltd.com	All-In-1	Notes
Binary Tree www.binarytree.com	MS Mail, Exchange, cc:mail, Schedule+, Organizer	Notes
CompuSven, Inc. www.compusven.com	Emc2/TAO, SYSM, MEMO	Notes, Exchange
www.iga.com	All-In-1	Notes, Exchange
Lotus Development Corp. www.lotus.com	OV/VM, OV/400	Notes
Microsoft Corp. www.microsoft.com	MEMO, AlL-In-1, Group-Wise, OV/VM, CC:mail	Exchange
Toronto Business Systems www.tbssoft.com	OV/MVS	Notes, Exchange

PRIVATE AND PUBLIC MAIL MIGRATION AND COEXISTENCE

Private mail is usually defined by an individual's inbasket and file folders. Public mail is usually defined as letters in bulletin boards, conferences, and newsgroups.

Private data is usually migrated and public data can both be migrated and then synchronized if the tool or utility is up to the task.

When evaluating e-mail migration tools, look for applications that can be easily integrated into a company's directory synchronization and administrative processes. The reason for this is that one should be able to let the e-mail system know that one wants to migrate a user in a single location. From specifying this in one location, the process should run from there. Lotus Notes R5 has done a superlative job of integrating the migration process in with the administrative interface. Other tools interface with Exchange so that one can define various levels of migration.

Levels of migration might include the ability to migrate mail once a user has his forwarding address changed in the new e-mail system, or it may mean that a user has his mail migrated to the new e-mail system, but still has the ability to log on and use the legacy e-mail system.

Private data features and functions to look for should include:

* Retain "from address":
  — This ensures that recipients can reply to migrated mail.
  — This is the major advantage of using a migration tool over each user manually forwarding mail.
* Retain original date/time stamp.

• Migration filter (do not migrate) mail older than a specified date. This allows for e-mail system cleanup.

Public data migration is very similar to private data migration, with the only difference being that public data is usually migrated to public databases in Notes, or public folders in Exchange. Again, look for the same features and functions as for private mail.

Public data synchronization can be the key to making migration and coexistence a success. Public data synchronization allows one to migrate a bulletin board, conference, or newsgroup and then keeps them all synchronized. If a user adds a letter to the legacy system, it is automatically (and, ideally, realtime) copied to the new e-mail system. Conversely, should a message be added to a Notes database or Exchange public folder, then that message should be copied to the legacy e-mail system.

One of the world's largest banks uses a legacy e-mail system bulletin board to post daily foreign currency exchange rates. In order for management to buy-in to user migration, they had to get beyond the real business issue of providing the functionality of the new e-mail system without removing access to the data on the legacy system.

GATEWAYS BETWEEN E-MAIL SYSTEMS

One of the very basic needs of coexistence is for mail to flow from the legacy system to Notes, Exchange, the Internet, GroupWise, etc. The past year has seen vendor-specific gateways move from old SNADS-based addressing to open standard SMTP-based gateways. Another phenomenon is the availability of a new type of gateway called a Point-to-Point Gateway.

Gateways do more than just deliver mail from one system to another. They also determine addressing standards and ease of addressing mail from the local e-mail system. For example, e-mail systems that support SMTP addresses may have the SMTP address of firstname.lastname, wherein the firstname.lastname corresponds to a specific Notes Address Book (NAB) or Exchange Global Address List (GAL) entry.

Look for a gateway that will satisfy specific needs. Gateways typically interface with specific e-mail systems and then interface to SMTP, SNADS, or directly to Notes or Exchange. Notes and Exchange now have the ability to become the Messaging Switch. This enhancement (or set of enhancements) will allow customers to move from the older Softwswitch Central, LMS, Linkage, and legacy Exchange type of solutions to gateways that connect directly from one e-mail system to another. This then allows Notes and Exchange to become the hub and the central directory.

Another very important component of a gateway for coexistence is performance. A company may have an e-mail policy or specific service level agreements in place that the gateway needs to meet.

Finally, a gateway, more than any other application, will determine the success or failure of the migration and coexistence process. A migration for a user can be re-run. However, a gateway is an important part of an e-mail system and must be dependable and robust. The support organization behind the vendor is often the key for a gateway's stability since gateways usually have a number of points of failure and the ability, or the support organizations ability, to reduce the points of failure can often make the difference.

FORMS MIGRATION AND CROSS-PLATFORM DISTRIBUTION

Forms migration products come in many shapes and sizes. Most migration products base their ability on what the legacy system forms supported. For those e-mail systems (3270 — green screen) that support limited functionality forms, one will end up with forms that look more like legacy forms rather than the forms in the new e-mail system. The good news here is that there are migration and coexistence utilities that allow cross-platform forms distribution; however, do not expect forms to look exactly as they did in the legacy system. One may find utilities that convert 90 percent of forms. However, forms may require manual updates once they have been migrated.

Look for products that provide the company with the ability to find the forms, convert the forms, distribute forms cross platform, and maintain the basic look and feel of each form.

Forms migration applications are usually limited to flat forms and do not support intelligent workflow style forms. The reason for this is that most intelligent forms contain proprietary (or interpretive) language that would really require a compiler converter, much like converting an application from COBOL to "C."

MIGRATION IS NOT JUST FOR USERS! DO NOT FORGET MAIL-ENABLED APPLICATIONS OR APPLICATION PROGRAM INTERFACE (API)

Once one has moved the users, set up directory and data synchronization, and has the gateways working, then one will be on the way to a complete migration. Once the last user is moved, turn off directory synchronization, some of the gateways, and then … Wait … Are there any applications that send mail or access the legacy e-mail systems? If not, go ahead and turn off the legacy e-mail system. Otherwise, look at tools and applications that either re-route the legacy API programs, can be substituted for the legacy

Exhibit 2. Legacy and Current E-Mail Systems

	Legacy						
	OV/400	**OV/VM**	**OV/MVS**	**Emc2**	**SYSM**	**Exchange**	**Notes**
New: Notes	X	X	X	X		X	
New: Exchange			X	X			X

API programs, or have the legacy API programs manually moved from the legacy platform to the new e-mail platform.

Look to the large migration product vendors for this type of product. A prerequisite for this type of application is a good cross-reference of legacy mail IDs and mail IDs in your new e-mail system. Then, depending on the platform (MVS, for example), one can find specific vendors who have the ability to help either re-route the mail from the legacy e-mail system to the new one, or have the ability to actually port the entire application from the legacy platform to the new one.

CALENDAR MIGRATION AND COEXISTENCE

A number of utilities are available for migration and limited cross-platform scheduling. However, of all the data-types, calendaring migration tools have been the last to be developed. There are some migration tools available; however, functionality is limited. Exhibit 2 contains a chart of known, generally available calendar migration and cross-platform scheduling products and a list of legacy and new e-mail systems.

PUTTING IT ALL TOGETHER

Once one has identified all the data-types and components that are required for the company, one is ready to start the migration. There are tools and utilities available that "do it all" and are completely integrated, with service offerings and end-to-end message system expertise. The ideal coexistence application is one that has directory synchronization, a gateway, built-in migration tools, built-in data synchronization, and cross-platform forms ability. Such an application will allow one to install one application and provide a single point of administration. If running more than two or three legacy e-mail systems, one may have to run multiple migration tools and utilities from various vendors.

Chapter 51
Integrating Electronic Messaging Systems and Infrastructures

Dale Cohen

As a company grows and changes computing systems, the job of implementing a messaging system turns from installing and maintaining software to integrating, fine-tuning, and measuring a series of systems — in other words, managing an ongoing project. For organizations integrating multiple e-mail systems, this chapter discusses the goals of a rollout and gives sample implementation scenarios.

PROBLEMS ADDRESSED

Implementing a messaging system infrastructure requires taking small steps while keeping the big picture in mind. The complexity of the endeavor is directly affected by the scope of the project.

If implementing messaging for a single department or a small single enterprise, a vendor solution can probably be used. All users will have the same desktop application with one message server or post office from that same application vendor.

In contrast, integrating multiple departments may require proprietary software routers for connecting similar systems. When building an infrastructure for a single enterprise, the IT department might incorporate the multiple-department approach for similar systems. Dissimilar systems can be connected using software and hardware gateways.

If the goal is to implement an integrated system for a larger enterprise, multiple departments may need to communicate with their external customers and suppliers. The solution could implement a messaging backbone or central messaging switch. This approach allows the implementers to deploy common points to sort, disperse, and measure the flow of messages.

If an organization already has an infrastructure but needs to distribute it across multiple systems connected by common protocols, the goal may be to make the aggregate system more manageable and gain economies of scale. Implementations can vary widely — from getting something up and running, to reducing the effort and expense of running the current system.

HOW TO ACCOMPLISH ROLLOUT AND MANAGE CONSTRAINTS

Messaging is a unique application because it crosses all the networks, hardware platforms, network operating systems, and application environments in the organization. Plenty of cooperation will be necessary to accomplish a successful rollout. The traditional constraints are time, functionality, and resources, although implementers must also manage user perceptions.

Resource Constraints: Financial

In an international organization of 5000 or more users, it is not unreasonable to spend $200,000 to $500,000 on the backbone services necessary to achieve a solution. The total cost — including network components, new desktop devices, ongoing administration, maintenance, and end-user support — can easily exceed $2500 per user, with incremental costs for the e-mail add-on at $300 to $500 per year.

The initial appeal of offerings from Lotus Development Corp., Novell Inc., and Microsoft Corp. is that a component can be added at a low incremental cost. In reality, the aggregate incremental costs are huge, although most of the purchaser's costs are hidden. For a corporate PC to handle e-mail, the corporatewide and local area networks and support organizations must be industrial-strength.

Although this investment may at first glance seem prohibitively high, it allows for add-ons such as web browsers or client/server applications at a much lower start-up cost. Vendors argue that they make it possible for the buyer to start small and grow. It is more likely that an organization will start small, grow significantly, and grow its application base incrementally. In the long run, the investment pays for itself repeatedly, not only for the benefits e-mail provides, but for the opportunities the foray offers.

Resource Constraints: Expertise

It is easy to underestimate the expertise required to operate an efficient messaging infrastructure. Most IT departments are easily able to handle a single application in a single operating environment. Multiple applications in multiple operating environments are a different story.

Messaging systems must be able to deal with multiple network protocols, various operating systems, and different software applications — all from different vendors. Given these facts, it is difficult to understand why already overburdened LAN administrators would take on the significant systems integration responsibilities of a messaging system rollout.

When confronted with problems during a messaging system integration, the staff must be able to answer the following questions:

- Is it a network problem or an application issue?
- Is it an operating system-configured value or an application bug?
- Can the problem be handled by someone with general expertise, such as a front-line technician or a support desk staff member?

Skill Sets. Individuals performing the rollout must be technically adept, have strong diagnostic skills, and understand how to work in a team environment. They must be adept with multiple operating systems and understand the basics of multiple networks. Ideally, they will understand the difference between a technical answer and one that solves the business issue at large.

Many organizations make the mistake of assigning first-tier support staff to an e-mail project when systems integrators are what is required. The leanest integration team consists of individuals with an understanding of networks and their underlying protocols, operating systems, and two or more e-mail applications. Database knowledge is very useful when dealing with directories and directory synchronization. A knowledge of tool development helps automate manual processes. Application monitoring should occur alongside network monitoring because nothing signals a network error as well as an e-mail service interruption.

Cross-functional Integration Teams. The most efficient way to coordinate a rollout is through cross-functional teams. It is important to incorporate e-mail implementation and support into the goals of the individuals and the teams from which they originate. Many organizations do this informally, but this method is not always effective. A written goal or service level agreement is extremely helpful when conflicting priorities arise and management support is needed.

When creating the core messaging integration team, it is very helpful to include individuals from WAN and LAN networking, systems, operations, and support desk staff, in addition to the individual application experts from each e-mail environment.

Functionality and Scope

At any point in the project, network administrators may find themselves trying to implement an enterprisewide solution, a new departmental system, a corporatewide directory service, or a solution for mobile e-mail users. When building a house, it is commonly understood that the plumbing and waste systems must be installed before hooking up the bath fixtures. This is not the case with messaging.

A messaging system rollout should start with a basic infrastructure "plumbed" for future expansion, and be followed directly with reliable user functionality. Results should be monitored and measured, and original infrastructure issues should be revisited as appropriate. Project success comes with regular reports on what has been delivered, and discussions of incremental improvements in reliability and services.

Supporting Internal and External Customers

No matter how good the features of any product or set of products, if the system is not reliable, people cannot depend on it. If the system is perceived as unreliable, people will use alternative forms of communication.

To satisfy user needs, the IT department should separate internal customers from external customers. Internal customers are those who help provide a service. They may be IT management, support personnel, or networking staff — they could be considered internal suppliers.

Because of the nature of most organizations, internal customers are both customers and suppliers. They need to be provided with the means to supply a service. For example, IT management may need to create step-by-step procedures for the operations staff to carry out. If the IT group cannot satisfy the requirements of internal customers, it probably will not be able to satisfy the needs of external customers.

External customers are the end users. If they are in sales, for example, external customers may include the enterprise's customers from other companies. It is the job of the IT staff to provide external customers with messaging features, functionality, and reliability so they can do their jobs.

IMPLEMENTATION MODELS AND ARCHITECTURES

It is helpful for network managers to know how other enterprises have implemented messaging systems. The next few chapter sections describe the various components of the infrastructure, common deployment architectures, and how to plan future deployments.

Infrastructure versus Interface

Often, messaging systems are sold with the emphasis on what the end user sees. Experienced network managers know that this is the least of their problems. The behind-the-scenes components, which make the individual systems in an organization work as a near-seamless whole, include

- Network services
- Message transfer services

- Directory services
- Management and administration services

Network Services. The network services required for a messaging rollout involve connectivity between:

- Desktop and server
- Server to server
- Server to gateway
- Gateway to foreign environment

It is not unusual to have one network protocol between a desktop device and its server and a second protocol within the backbone server/gateway/router environment. Servers may communicate via WAN protocols such as TCP/IP, OSI, DECnet, or SNA, and the desktops may communicate over a LAN protocol such as IPX or NetBIOS. WAN connections may occur over continuous connections or over asynchronous dial-up methods.

The network administrator's greatest concern is loss of network connectivity. It is important to understand how it happens, why it happens, how it is discovered, and what needs to be done on an application level once connectivity is restored.

If the network goes down, e-mail will be faulted. Weekly incident reports should be issued that cite direct incidents (i.e., an e-mail component failure) and indirect incidents (i.e., a network failure), as well as remote site issues (i.e., a remote site lost power). Such information can help to clarify the real problem.

Message Transfer Services. The message transfer service (also termed the message transport system) is the most visible part of the messaging infrastructure. The message transfer service is responsible for moving a message from point A to point B. This service consists of one or more message transport agents and can be extended to include gateways and routers. The most popular services are the X.400 and SMTP international standards, and IBM's SNA Distributed Services (SNADS) and Novell's Message Handling Service (MHS) proprietary industry standards.

X.400. More widely used in Europe than in North America, X.400 is popular because it:

- Provides universal connectivity
- Has a standard way of mapping features
- Is usually run over commercial WANs so it does not have the security problems associated with the Internet

SMTP. Simple Mail Transfer Protocol's (SMTP) allure is its simplicity. Addressing is easier and access to the Internet is relatively simple compared with establishing an X.400 connection. Because it is simple, there is not much that can go wrong. However, when something does go wrong, it is usually monumental.

Directory Services. The directory service is critical to a company's e-mail systems, but it is also problematic. The problems are a result of the difficulty in keeping directories up-to-date, resolving redundant or obsolete auto-registered entries, and failures of directory synchronization.

The directory serves both users and applications. End users choose potential recipients from a directory. The directory should list sufficient information for a user to distinguish between the George Smith in accounting and the George Smith in engineering. Some companies include in their directory individuals who are customers and suppliers. The ability to distinguish between internal users and external users is even more important in these cases.

Management and Administration Services. Management refers to scheduled maintenance and automated housekeeping procedures that involve system-related tasks such as reconfiguration and file maintenance. The constant I/O on messaging components leads to disk and sometimes memory fragmentation. Regular defragmentation procedures, including repro/reorg, tidy procedures, and checkstat and reclaim, are required. Whatever the environment, such procedures should be done more often than is recommended to prevent problems from occurring.

Alerts and Alarms. Alerts and alarms are extremely helpful because the system can tell the user if there is a potential problem. Alerts generally refer to warnings such as "too many messages in queue awaiting delivery." Alarms are a sign of a more serious problem, such as a "disk-full" condition.

Mail Monitoring. Mail monitoring is typically an administrative function. One way of monitoring a system is to send a probe addressed to an invalid user on a target system. On many systems, the target system will reject the message with a "no such addressee" nondelivery message. When the initiating system receives this message, it indicates that mail flow is active.

Timing the round trip provides a window to overall system performance. A message that does not return in a pre-established timeframe is considered overdue and is cause for further investigation.

Reporting. Reporting is used for capacity planning, measuring throughput and performance, chargeback, and statistical gathering. At initial implementation, network administrators will generally want to report breadth of coverage to demonstrate the reach of the infrastructure. Breadth can be measured by counting users and the number of messaging systems within each messaging environment.

Exhibit 1. Implementation Scenarios

	Enterprise	
	Single	**Multiple**
Single department	One-tier single system	Two-tier similar systems
Multiple departments	Two-tier dissimilar systems	Three-tier cross-enterprise systems

Performance can be measured by reporting the volume — the average number of messages delivered per hour, or messages in each hour over a 24-hour period. This measure can be further divided by indicating the type of message (i.e., text only, single/double attachments, read receipts). This information gives network managers a measurable indication of the kind of features the user community requires.

For network planning purposes, it may be useful to measure volume or "system pressure," ignoring the number of messages sent and focusing on the number of total gigabytes sent per day.

IMPLEMENTATION SCENARIOS: A TIERED APPROACH

Manufacturing environments have long used a tiered approach to messaging for distributing the workload of factory-floor applications. As environments become more complex, the tiered approach offers additional flexibility.

An entire enterprise can be considered a single department, indicating the need for a one-tier system in which clients are tied into a single server or post office. Multiple departments in a single enterprise, or a single department communicating with multiple enterprises, require routers and gateways to communicate with the outside world. When multiple departments need to communicate with each other and with multiple enterprises, a messaging backbone or messaging switch is required.

Exhibit 1 summarizes the implementation scenarios discussed in this chapter.

One-Tier Messaging Model

A single department in a single enterprise will most likely deploy a one-tier messaging model. This model consists of a single messaging server or post office that provides all services. It may be as large as an OfficeVision system on a mainframe or a Higgins PostOffice on a Compaq file server running NetWare. The department need only concern itself with following corporate guidelines for networking and any naming standards.

Caution should be observed when using corporate guidelines. It is often simple to apply mainframe conventions when standardizing PC LAN-based

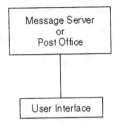

Exhibit 2. One-Tier Model

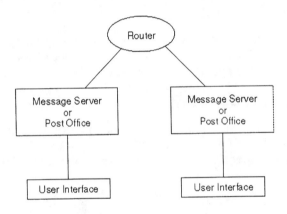

Exhibit 3. Two-Tier Model

applications. Many large organizations tend to forget that the whole reason for deploying desktop computers is to move away from mainframe conventions (e.g., eight-character user IDs) that are nonintuitive for users. Exhibit 2 shows a typical one-tier model within a single department of an enterprise.

Two-Tier Messaging Model: Multiple Servers

As the number of e-mail users grows, or multiple departments need to be connected, an organization will probably deploy multiple servers. This two-tier model can consist of integrating similar messaging systems from the same vendor or from different vendors. Exhibit 3 illustrates a connection between two departments using the same vendor software connected via application routers.

In a typical PC LAN environment using a shared-file system such as cc:Mail or Microsoft Mail, the router acts the same way as the PC. The post

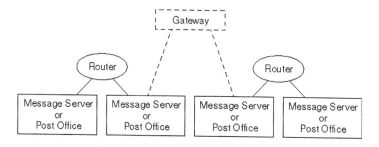

Exhibit 4. Using Application Gateways

office is completely passive. When users send messages, their worksta-tions simply copy the message to the file server as an individual file or as an insertion into a file server database. In either case, the PC workstation actually does the work; the post office simply serves as a shared disk drive. The router is also an active component but has no user-moving messages. It periodically moves messages from one post office to another without user interaction.

Application Gateways for Integrating Dissimilar Systems

Many enterprises have different departments that have chosen their own e-mail systems without a common corporate standard. To integrate dissim-ilar systems, application gateways can bridge the technical incompatibili-ties between the various messaging servers (see Exhibit 4).

A simple gateway can translate e-mail messages to GroupWise. A more complex gateway can bridge networks (e.g., Ethernet to Token Ring), net-work protocols (i.e., NetWare to TCP/IP), and the e-mail applications.

Converting one e-mail message to the format of another requires a sig-nificant amount of translation. Document formats (i.e., DCA RFT to ASCII), addressing formats (i.e., user@workgroup@domain to system:user), and message options (i.e., acknowledgments to read or deliver receipts) must all be translated.

Gateways can emulate routers native to each environment. They per-form message translations internally. The alternative to this approach is to place the gateway between the routers, as opposed to between the post office and the routers. This is not an end-user design; it is merely a function of the vendor software (see Exhibit 5).

If an enterprise is large, network administrators may want to make use of economies of scale to handle common administration, common gateways to X.400, and Internet networks. The network administration staff may simply

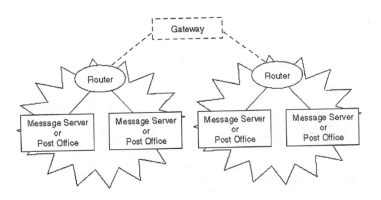

Exhibit 5.   Placing a Gateway between Routers

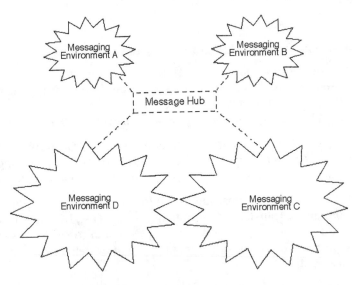

Exhibit 6.   A Central Switching Hub

need points in its network where it can measure progress. Gateways from each environment to every other environment can be provided, but this solution becomes costly and difficult to maintain. A better approach would be to use a central switching hub or a distributed backbone, as shown in Exhibit 6.

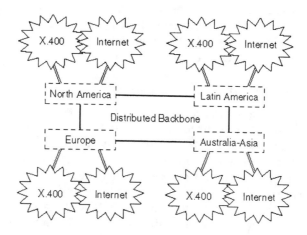

Exhibit 7. Worldwide Distributed Hubs

Distributed Hubs

The central switch or hub allows for a single path for each messaging environment to communicate with all other messaging environments. The central hub, if relatively inexpensive, can be expanded into the distributed model. This is often done as the aggregate system grows and requires additional performance and capacity.

However, this implementation can be taken to an extreme, as seen by the number of companies that have grown PC LAN/shared file systems beyond their original designs. It is inexpensive to grow these systems incrementally, but difficult to provide end-to-end reliability. Most organizations plug the technical gaps in these products with the additional permanent and contract personnel to keep the multitude of routers and shared-file system post offices up and running.

Some organizations have taken this distributed hub approach to the point where they have multiple connections to the Internet and the X.400 world (see Exhibit 7). Some organizations offer the single message switch for their global environment, and their messages are more well-traveled than their administrators. A message sent from Brussels to Paris may stop in Los Angeles on the way because of the central switching mechanism. In addition to local switching, the distributed hub allows for redundancy.

THREE DEPLOYMENT ARCHITECTURES AND OPTIONS

Most companies deploy e-mail systems using variations of three architectures: a common platform in which all e-mail systems are identical; a multiple backbone in which each e-mail environment has its own gateway; or a common backbone in which all systems share common resources. The following chapter sections describe these architectures, along with the advantages and disadvantages of each.

Common Platform Architecture

For years, a major automotive manufacturer delayed PC LAN e-mail deployment in deference to the purported needs of the traveling executive. Senior managers wanted to be able to walk up to any company computer terminal, workstation, or personal computer anywhere in the world and know that they would be able to access their e-mail in the same manner. This implies a common look-and-feel to the application across platforms as well as common network access to the e-mail server. In this company's case, OfficeVision/VM to Notes Mail was accessible through 3270 terminal emulators on various platforms. As long as SNA network access remained available, e-mail appeared the same worldwide. This IBM mainframe shop had few problems implementing this model.

The common platform model is not unique to IBM mainframe environments. Another manufacturer used the same technique with its DEC ALL-IN-1 environment distributed across multiple VAX hosts. As long as a DECnet network or dial-up access was available, users could reach their home systems. The upside of this approach was that an individual's e-mail files are stored centrally, allowing for a single retrieval point. The downside was that the user had to be connected to process e-mail and was unable to work offline.

This strategy is not limited to mainframe and minicomputer models. A number of companies have standardized on Lotus Notes, Microsoft Exchange, or Novell's GroupWise. None of these products are truly ready for large-scale deployment without IT and network staffs having to plug the technical gaps.

Multiple Backbone Model

The multiple backbone model assumes that an organization integrates its e-mail systems as if it were multiple smaller companies. The OfficeVision/VM system can connect via Advantis to reach the Internet and X.400 world. The Lotus Notes WAN may have an SMTP gateway for access to the Internet and an ISOCOR MTA for access to the Message Router/X.400 gateway. All the various e-mail environments may have a "soft switch" gateway for access to the IBM/MVS host so that everyone who needs to can access their OfficeVision/400 systems (see Exhibit 8).

On the surface, this hodgepodge of point-to-point connections might seem a bit unwieldy, but it does have advantages. Users of cc:Mail can

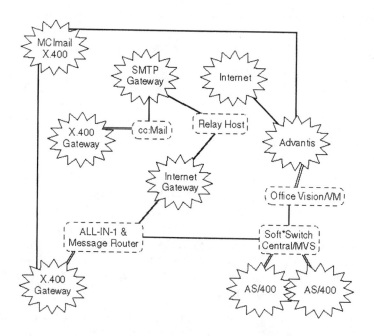

Exhibit 8. The Multiple Backbone Model

address Internet e-mail users by filling out an SMTP template rather than waiting until the Lotus Notes administrator adds recipients to the cc:Mail directory. OfficeVision/VM users can fill out a simple address block within the text of their message to reach an Internet user. AS/400 users can send mail to an application that forwards the message on their behalf.

This architecture may still work. If each e-mail environment had its own gateway, network administration could offer multiple connections to the Internet.

Common Backbone

The common backbone takes two forms:

1. A central e-mail hub or message switch on a single system that serves as the common denominator among all e-mail environments
2. A distributed model in which all backbone components run a common software protocol

The common hub involves a single switch that serves the users' applications, thus serving their needs indirectly. Each e-mail environment has an application gateway that converts its environmental format to that of the

643

common hub. Other systems are attached to this hub in a similar manner. Messages destined for dissimilar environments all pass through this central point to be sorted and delivered to their final destinations.

The distributed backbone takes the central hub and replaces it with two or more systems sharing a common application protocol. This solution offers the ability to deploy two or more less-expensive systems rather than a single, more-expensive system. Any system connected to any point in the backbone can use any other service (e.g., gateway) connected to that same backbone.

Network managers may decide to purchase a single hub and gradually add systems to form a distributed backbone. Should one decide to use a common backbone protocol such as X.400 or SMTP, there is an advantage. Because these protocols are available from a number of vendors, the cc:Mail/X.400 gateway could connect to an X.400 system running in an HP9000, DEC/Alpha, or Intel/Pentium system — all running the same protocols. It is possible to change distributed servers without having to change the gateways to these servers. Exhibit 9 illustrates three-tier flexibility.

A third approach is to use one central server or a distributed backbone of similar systems. In the central server/central hub approach, all e-mail environments use application gateways to connect to the central switch. There they are routed to their target environment.

Two-tier models may seem most convenient because they can use the offerings of a single vendor. One problem is that the system must use that vendor's protocols for a long time. Three tiers allow the layers in the model to be changed, which allows for ease of transition.

Under most application scenarios, changing one component of the messaging environment entails changing all the pieces and parts with which it is associated. It may be necessary to provide adequate support staff and end-user training, or hire consultants to handle the need for temporary staff during the transition — a significant business disruption.

For example, in one environment, users have Microsoft Mail/Exchange Client on their desktops and a traditional MS post office is used, as well as message transfer agents (MTAs), to route mail between post offices. The engineering department uses OpenMail (Hewlett-Packard). The IT group would like to begin consolidating systems. With minor changes to the desktop, IT can retain the Microsoft Mail user interface, remove the back-end infrastructure, and use the same OpenMail system as the OpenMail desktop users by consolidating the second tier and simplifying the support environment. The client changes somewhat because it is using a different directory server and message store, but it appears as a minor upgrade to the users; thus, no significant training is necessary.

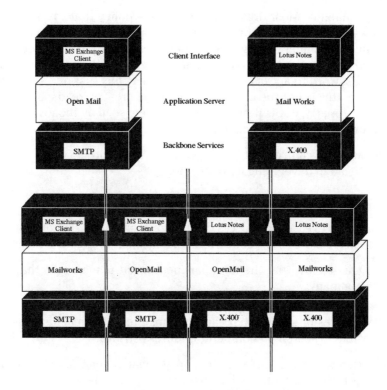

Exhibit 9. Three-Tier Flexibility

Likewise, IT can change the back end and still allow the OpenMail systems to communicate with the Digital Mail Systems such as MAILworks and ALL-IN-1 systems, without locking into a single-vendor solution. This is a feasible option. Today, users can plug an MS Exchange client into a MAILworks or OpenMail server. Note that MS Exchange Connector for Lotus Notes connects an existing Lotus Notes messaging system to a MS Exchange Server.

ESTABLISHING MESSAGING POLICIES AND PROCEDURES

An organization can prevent misunderstandings, conflicts, and even litigation if it publishes its policies and procedures for messaging applications at the outset. Most important are privacy and confidentiality.

Privacy

A privacy policy serves two purposes: (1) to properly inform employees that their messages may not be private, and (2) to protect the organization from legal liability. Most organizations create a policy that cautions users as follows: all electronic data is company property and can be viewed by designated personnel to diagnose problems, monitor performance, or for other purposes as the company deems necessary. While one normally types a password to access one's e-mail and may feel that one's messages are private, this is not the case. The e-mail one creates, reads, or sends is not one's property, nor is it protected from being seen by those other than oneself or one's intended recipients.

Organizations can contact the Open Group EMA Forum (www.ema.org), for a kit to aid in developing a privacy policy.

Proprietary and Confidential Information

E-mail appears to ease the process of intentional or inadvertent disclosure of company secrets. If this is a concern, an organization could try the following:

- Let users know that the IT department logs the messages that leave the company.
- Perform periodic audits.
- Apply rules or scripts that capture e-mail to or from fields, making it possible to search on competitor address strings.

Some systems insert a header on incoming e-mail that says: "WARNING: This message arrived from outside the company's e-mail system. Take care when replying so as not to divulge proprietary or confidential information."

A company can also specify that proprietary information should not be sent to Internet addresses if security measures on the Internet are inadequate for the company's needs. Users may be asked to confirm that only X.400 addresses are used. It is helpful to incorporate any such e-mail ground rules — for example, that the transmission of proprietary information without a proper disclosure agreement is grounds for dismissal — as part of the new employee orientation process.

RECOMMENDED COURSE OF ACTION

One of the most important elements of a successful messaging system roll-out is a staff that is well-versed in the workings of the network, operating system, backup procedures, and applications.

Network Connections

An implementation needs individuals who can set up network connections efficiently. A messaging system needs procedures in place to notify users when a network link is unavailable. If the network goes down, often one of the first applications blamed is e-mail. It is the job of the network staff to diagnose the problem quickly and have the right people remedying the problem.

Operating Systems

Many e-mail groups have their own systems and servers and operate them as their own. Consequently, many successful organizations pair systems programmers or senior software specialists with systems engineers who can provide installation services and upgrade support.

Backup

Most messaging support organizations are not set up to provide 24-hour support. It is important to borrow methodologies from the mainframe support environment and staff an operations center that can answer phone calls, fix problems, and backup and archive applications regularly.

Applications Support

This function demands staff members with:

- Excellent diagnostic skills
- Excellent communication skills
- Database and business graphics experience
- Cross-platform network experience
- A basic understanding of the operating environment of each of the platforms

E-mail integration by its nature involves cross-platform expertise. Most applications are fairly straightforward. In the case of an integrated infrastructure, an organization may need people familiar with NetWare, SNA, TCP/IP, and LAN Manager. They may also need to understand Mac/OS, UNIX, OS/2, and VMS.

When staffing an implementation, the key is to match expertise across the various groups within the company. The team should be application-centric with contributors from across the enterprise. If an implementation is properly staffed, and the implementers keep in mind the big picture as well as the daily objectives, the messaging system rollout is far more likely to be a success.

Section X
Internet Commerce

Chapter 52
Web-Based Testing and Capacity Planning

Trevor Clarke

Every day, more and more companies are entering the E-marketplace by offering their products and services through the Internet. This shift has led to fundamental changes in the product-development life cycle. The challenges facing CIOs and IT managers have increased accordingly as they are expected to deliver complex applications and application environments in less time than traditional client/server applications to meet the more sophisticated demands of customers and to remain competitive. Consequently, a much more rigorous testing process, completed in a shorter timeframe, is required.

Coupled with this new medium of transacting business is a much larger marketplace, which makes it increasingly difficult for IT managers to predict loads and appropriately provision infrastructure. Failure to sufficiently provision the infrastructure will result in performance degradations and ultimately, the loss of customers. This chapter addresses two key challenges facing CIOs and IT managers including Web-based testing and capacity planning in a rapidly changing Internet environment.

THE ADDED COMPLEXITIES

Web-based systems introduce many additional and different complexities over traditional client/server systems and the earlier mainframe environments. As businesses go online, there are many unknowns that could adversely affect the success of their E-business venture. The following list identifies some of the major complexities and unknowns that a testing organization will have to consider to ensure a quality service:

- *Speed:* The increased competition faced by companies doing business on the Internet has resulted in shorter development life cycles. To meet customer expectations, companies have to respond quickly to market demands and continuously improve their site to keep existing customers and attract new customers. Testing must also be completed in much shorter timeframes than experienced with client/server solutions.

- *Scenario Development:* A key challenge with Web-based systems is the development and testing of all possible scenarios of user interaction with the system. For transaction-based-systems, rigorous testing is required to ensure the integrity of transactions as users may willingly or unwillingly be disconnected from the system. Also, transaction integrity must be ensured during peak activity when performance degradations and system time-outs are more likely. Finally, the testing organization must consider that users may freely navigate forward or backward within a Web site and may cause unwanted duplication of transactions.

- *Performance Testing:* Ensuring the performance of one's Web-based system is another key challenge as some components are not under direct control of one's enterprise. The system or the network could cause performance issues in a web-based environment. Keynote, The Internet Performance Authority, indicates that Internet performance problems are generally not server problems.[1] They demonstrated that most performance problems occur out in the Internet infrastructure between the users and Web-servers at network access points (NAPs), routers, or in a Domain Name Server (DNS). Assuring performance could equate to the company's ability to attract and keep customers loyal to one's Web site.

- *Capacity Planning:* Effectively planning the capacity of systems and networks becomes difficult as one's business becomes global when online. Ineffective planning could lead to excessive performance issues that result in loss of customers.

- *Security:* Additional security risks are associated with Web-based systems that operate in a relatively "open" environment and could provide access to the company's confidential systems and data by unauthorized users. Simple bugs in the Web-server could enable users to corrupt or steal data from the system or even render systems unavailable.

- *Multiple Technologies:* A complete testing cycle would include all possible software configurations that users leverage to access with one's site (primarily Netscape™ or Microsoft's Explorer™). Configurations may include various browser versions and service packs.

THE TESTING CYCLE

Utilizing typical client/server testing approaches will not address the many added complexities resulting from a Web-based system. Additionally, the more aggressive time schedules involved in Web site development projects result in a need for an organization to develop a different and effective approach.

Defining Testing Scope

Determining the testing scope is critical to the success of a Web-based testing project. Due to the short timeframe associated with Web site testing, it can become difficult to test all components of the application and network. When possible, testing the complete Web-based environment is ideal. However, when time constraints and budget constraints are incorporated, an organization may need to determine critical requirements and potential high-risk areas and focus testing effort on these areas.

Critical requirements and high-risk areas can be determined by analyzing the requirements to determine the functionality that is most important to the success of the Web site, the areas within the Web site that will draw most customer focus (both positive and negative), and areas of the Web site that pose security threats.

Testing scope may include the complete system environment, including network performance testing. Alternatively, testing scope may be isolated to a particular module of the Web site or system environment (e.g., Web server, application server, database, etc.). Although not every component of the Web-based application or infrastructure may be tested before production, it is recommended that testing continue post-production for components not initially tested.

Test Planning

Based on the testing scope, the testing organization needs to plan the testing phase, including the types and timing of tests to be performed in both the pre- and post-release stages. The following testing types would be executed in a complete testing cycle:

- *Unit Testing:* Unit testing is the process of testing individual application objects or functions in an isolated environment before testing the integration with other tested units. Unit testing is the most efficient and effective phase in terms of defect detection.
- *Integration Testing:* The purpose of integration testing is to verify proper integrated functioning of the modules (objects, functions) that make up a subsystem. The focus of integration testing is on crossfunctional tests rather than on unit tests within one module.

- *End-to-End Testing:* End-to-end testing is a comprehensive test of the integration of subsystems and interfaces that make up the Web site. Typically, end-to-end testing models all scenarios of user or business activity possible on the Web site. Included within this testing phase is the verification of all links to other Web sites, whether internal or external (referred to as link testing). Link testing is a key activity that should be completed on a recurring basis as Web sites tend to change URLs or are discontinued.

- *Security Testing:* Although implemented security measures are considered as part of the end-to-end solution, this testing type is kept separate due to its importance. Security testing involves two key processes. The first is the assurance that unauthorized users are blocked from accessing data and systems not intended for the user population. The second involves the testing of the data encryption techniques employed by the organization.

- *Regression Testing:* Regression testing ensures that code changes made during application testing or post-production have not introduced any additional defects into previously tested code.

- *Usability Testing:* Usability testing ensures the presentation, flow, and general ergonomics of the Web site are accepted by the intended user community. This testing phase is critical as it enables one's organization to measure the effectiveness of the content and design of the Web site, which ultimately leads to the ability to attract and keep customers.

- *Stress Testing:* Stress testing observes the capabilities of production hardware and software to continue to function properly under a predetermined set and volume of test scenarios. The purpose of stress testing is to ensure that the system can maintain throughput and efficient operation under different load conditions. Stress testing enables one's organization to determine what conditions are likely to cause system (hardware or software) failures. This testing phase needs to consider the possible hardware platforms, operating systems, and browsers used by customers. Results from stress testing are also a key component used for capacity planning (capacity planning is discussed later in this chapter).

- *Performance Testing:* Performance testing observes the response times of systems (i.e., Web server, database, etc.) and capabilities of a network to efficiently transmit data under varied load conditions. Performance testing should enable one's organization to determine and resolve bottlenecks within the application and infrastructure. Performance testing should also consider the possible hardware platforms, operating systems, and browsers used by customers.

If testing scope has been limited to a certain aspect of the system and network environment, only a limited set of tests will be completed in the pre-production phase. Based on the priorities set in the scoping phase, the test manager must determine the set of test types and resources required in the pre-production testing phase and those that will be completed in the post-production phase. The minimum testing that needs to occur for code changes is unit and integration testing for the modules affected by the code change.

The requirement for much quicker development and testing cycles has led to the creation of sophisticated software quality tools that automate many of the test types described above. Key competitors in this market-place include Segue Software, Mercury Interactive, RadView Software, and Empirix. The following paragraphs describe the solutions offered by each company:

Segue Software. Segue Software's Silk™ family of E-business testing products automates several threads of the testing process including functional (unit) and regression testing (SilkTest™), load and performance testing (SilkPerformer™), and scenario testing (SilkRealizer™). Segue also provides professional services to help install and configure the Silk products to test company products.

Additional value-added products in the Silk line include SilkMonitor™ (24×7 monitoring and reporting of Web, application, and database servers), SilkObserver™ (end-to-end transaction management and monitoring of CORBA applications), SilkMeter™ (access control and usage metering), and SilkRadar™ (automated defect tracking).

For more information, visit Segue Software's Web site at www.segue.com.

Mercury Interactive. Mercury Interactive provides the Astra™ suite of Web-based testing products. Specific modules include Astra LoadTest™ to test scalability and performance, and Astra Quick Test™ for functional and regression testing. Additional value-added tools include Astra Site Manager™ to manage the Web site and identify problems and user "hotspots."

For more information, visit Mercury Inter-active's Web site at www. mercuryinteractive.com.

Radview Software. Radview's WebLOAD™ product line provides tools for verifying application scalability and integrity. Scalability and integrity refers to load and functional testing. Additional products include Web-LOAD Resource Manager™ to facilitate and coordinate testing and resources in the development lifecycle.

For more information, visit Radview Software's Web site at www.radview.com.

Empirix. Empirix's e-Test™ suite of products provides solutions to test the functionality, scalability and availability of web-based applications. e-Load™ is used for load and scalability testing while e-Test™ is used for functional and regression testing. Additional value-added modules include e-Monitor, which provides 7×24 monitoring of deployed applications. For more information, visit the Empirix Web site at www.empirix.com.

To significantly decrease the time required to perform testing, assessment of the organization's testing requirements and choice of an automated software quality tool to expedite repetitive testing tasks is recommended. Additionally, these test tools will enable one's organization to perform stress testing, which is key to ensuring sufficient network and server resource levels for the production environment.

Capacity Planning

Effective performance testing is difficult without an accurate depiction of future loads. Many companies simply over-engineer hardware and networks at high costs to minimize potential performance issues leading to service degradations or deal with performance issues on a reactive basis. Reacting to performance issues in today's highly competitive marketplace could ultimately lead to the loss of customers during system downtime or periods of poor performance. Planning capacity is a critical step required to ensure the future performance of a Web-based environment. The key components involved are network, server (e.g., memory, CPU, I/O) and storage capacity.

Establishing performance benchmarks and subsequently estimating future growth is critical to planning the capacity of the network and servers. Although benchmarks are published by the Standard Performance Evaluation Corporation for Web servers (www.specbench.org), their uses are limited and do not accurately represent a real-world integrated Web environment. Alternatively, benchmarks can be determined through stress testing and mapping of performance (e.g., response times) to specific network or hardware configurations under varying loads. Modeling tools and techniques can also be used to determine performance characteristics under varying loads.

Once initial benchmarks are established, future production loads can be estimated using historical growth statistics or growth estimated by various Internet-analyst groups (e.g., IDC, Gartner Group, and Forrester Research). Subsequently, the growth forecasts can be put to test to determine the resource and scalability requirements of the network and hardware in the future. Note that peak loads of three to four times average loads should be tested during the stress test phase. Additional stress testing considerations are to model higher-volume loads for cyclical periods. For example, online retailers may have much higher loads during the Christmas period than during the rest of the year. Ensuring performance, especially during these peak periods, will have an impact on Web site success. For this reason, overprovisioning hardware or network components to a certain level is justified.

Although effective capacity planning should enable the systems to handle future growth, monitoring of one's networks and server resources should continue to ensure capacity is within acceptable limits.

CONCLUSIONS

Web-based applications have resulted in many challenges for the testing community. The ability of an organization to effectively prioritize the components requiring testing and to rapidly execute the tests is a requirement in a competitive E-marketplace. Leveraging the tools designed specifically for Web-based testing will enhance the organization's ability to get a quality product to market faster. Finally, proactive capacity planning rather than reactive performance issue resolution will result in greater customer satisfaction and, ultimately, in greater revenue.

Note

1. "Top 10 Discoveries About the Internet," Keynote Systems, Inc., 1998.

Chapter 53
Business-to-Business Integration Using E-Commerce

Ido Gileadi

Now that many of the Fortune 1000 manufacturing companies have implemented ERP systems to streamline their planning and resource allocation as well as integrate their business processes across the enterprise, there is still a need to be integrated with the supply chain.

To reduce inventory levels and lead times, companies must optimize the process of procurement of raw materials and finished goods. Optimization of business processes across multiple organizations includes redefining the way business is conducted, as well as putting in place the systems that will support communication between multiple organizations each having separate systems infrastructure and requirements.

This type of business-to-business electronic integration has been around for some time, in the form of EDI (electronic document interchange). EDI allows organizations to exchange documents (e.g., purchase orders, sales orders, etc.) using a standards such as X.12 or EDIFACT and VANs (value-added networks) for communication. The standards are used to achieve universal agreement on the content and format of documents/messages being exchanged. EDI standards allow software vendors to include functionality in their software that will support EDI and communicate with other applications. The VAN is used as a medium for transferring messages from one organization to the other. It is a global proprietary network that is designed to carry and monitor EDI messages.

The EDI solution has caught on in several market segments but has never presented a complete solution for the following reasons:

- High cost for setup and transactions: smaller organizations cannot afford the cost associated with setup and maintenance of an EDI solution using a VAN.
- EDI messages are a subset of all the types of data that organizations may want to exchange.
- EDI does not facilitate online access to information, which may be required for applications such as self-service.

With the advance of the Internet both in reliability and security and the proliferation of Internet based E-commerce applications, E-commerce has become an obvious place to look for solutions to a better and more flexible way of integrating business-to-business processes.

The remainder of this chapter discusses a real-life example of how internet and E-commerce technologies have been implemented to address the business-to-business integration challenge.

BUSINESS REQUIREMENTS

The business requirements presented to the E-commerce development team can be divided into three general functional area categories:

1. General requirements
2. Communicating demand to the supply chain
3. Providing self-service application to suppliers

General requirements included:

- 100 percent participation by suppliers (the current EDI system was adapted by only 10 percent of suppliers)
- Minimize cost of operation to suppliers and self
- Maintain high level of security both for enterprise systems and for data communicated to external organizations
- Utilize industry standards and off-the-shelf applications wherever possible; minimize custom development
- Supplier access to all systems through a browser interface

Demand requirements included:

- Send EDI standard messages to suppliers
  — 830: Purchase Schedule
  — 850: Purchase Order
  — 860: Purchase Order Change
- Provide advance notice of exceptions to demand through exception reports

Exhibit 1 describes the flow of demand messages (830, 850, 860, exceptions) between the manufacturer and supplier organization. The demand is generated from the manufacturer ERP system (Baan, SAP, etc.). It is then

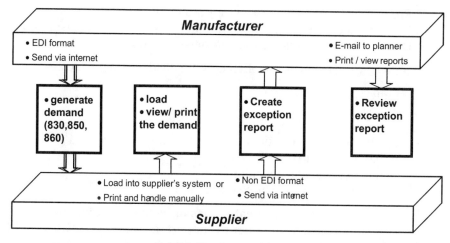

Exhibit 1.   Demand Flow

delivered to the supplier through one of several methods (discussed later). The supplier can load the demand directly into its system or use the supplied software to view and print the demand on a PC. The supplier can then produce an exception report, indicating any exception to the excepted delivery of goods. The exception report is sent back to the manufacturer and routed to the appropriate planner. The planner can view the report and make the necessary adjustments.

Self-service application requirements included:

- Ability for suppliers to update product pricing electronically, thereby ensuring price consistency between manufacturer and supplier
- Provide online access with drill-down capabilities for suppliers to view the following information:
  — Payment details
  — Registered invoices
  — Receipt of goods details
  — Product quality information

TECHNICAL REQUIREMENTS

The technical solution had to address the following:

- Transport EDI messages to suppliers of various levels of computerization
- Provide complete solution for suppliers that have no scheduling application
- Support small and large supplier organizations seamlessly

- Provide batch message processing and online access to data
- Provide security for enterprise systems as well as data transmission
- Utilize industry standards and off-the-shelf products

Once again, the technical requirements are divided into three categories:

1. General requirements:
   a. Low cost
   b. Low maintenance
   c. High level of security
   d. Industry standards
2. Batch message management
3. Online access to enterprise information

In reviewing the three main categories of technical requirements it is apparent that one needs a product to support message management (EDI and non-EDI), and the same or another product to provide online access. The selected products will have to possess all the characteristics listed under general requirements.

E-COMMERCE PRODUCT SELECTION

Selection of E-commerce products to construct a complete solution should take the following into consideration:

- What type of functionality does the product cover (online, batch, etc.)?
- Is the product based on industry standards or is it proprietary?
- Does the product provide a stable and extensible platform to develop future applications?
- How does the product integrate with other product selections?
- What security is available as part of the product?
- What are the skills required to develop using the product, and are these skills readily available?
- What is product cost (server, user licenses, maintenance)?
- Is product innovation and further development necessary?
- What is product base of installation?
- What is product architecture?

The E-commerce team chose the following products:

- **Gentran WebSuite and Server** from Sterling Commerce. This product was selected for handling EDI messages and communication EDI and non-EDI messages through various communication mediums. This product provides the following features:
  — Secure and encrypted file transfer mechanism
  — Support for EDI through VANs, Internet, and FTP
  — Browser operation platform using ActiveX technology

— Simple integration and extendibility through ActiveX forms integration
— Simple and open architecture
— Easy integration with other products
— EDI translation engine

- **Baan Data Navigator Plus (BDNP)** from TopTier (now SAP Portals, Inc.). This product was selected for online access to the ERP and other enterprise applications. The product has the following main features:
  — Direct online access to the Baan ERP database through the application layer
  — Direct online access to other enterprise applications
  — Integration of data from various applications into one integrated view
  — Hyper Relational data technology, allowing the user to drag and relate each item data onto a component thereby creating a new more detailed query providing drill-down capabilities
  — Access to application through a browser interface
  — Easy-to-use development environment

Both products were already released when the project started using them (Summer of 1998). The products were chosen for their features, the reputation of the companies developing the products, and the level of integration the products provided with the ERP system already in place. Note that iBaan portal is now available.

E-COMMERCE SOLUTION

Taking into account the business and technical requirements, a systems architecture that provided a business and technical solution was put together. On the left side of the diagram are the client PCs located in the supplier's environment. These are standard Win NT/95/98 running a browser capable of running ActiveX components. Both the applications (WebSuite and TopTier) are accessed through a browser using HTML and ActiveX technologies. As can be seen in Exhibit 2, some suppliers (typically the larger organizations) have integrated the messages sent by the application into their scheduling system. Their system loads the data and presents it within their integrated environment. Other suppliers (typically smaller organizations) are using the browser-based interface to view and print the data as well as manipulate and create exception reports to be sent back to the server.

Communication is achieved using the following protocols on the Internet:

- HTTP, HTTPS: for delivery of online data
- Sockets (SL), Secure Sockets (SSL): for message transfer

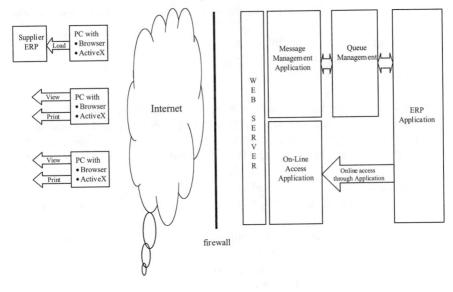

Exhibit 2.   Firewall

All traffic enters the enterprise systems through a firewall for security. Security is discussed in the following section.

On the enterprise side, the client applications first access a Web server. The Web Server handles the HTTP/HTTPS communication and invokes the server-side controls through an ASP page.

The online application (TopTier) intercepts the HTTP/HTTPS communication address to it and interprets the query. It then provides a result set and integrates the result set with an HTML template to be sent back to the client PC as an HTML page. The online access application communicates with the ERP application through the application API or through ODBC.

The message management application (WebSuite) communicates to the message queue using server-side ActiveX controls and FTP to send and receive files between systems. The message management application communicates with the ERP and other enterprise applications using a set of processes that can read and write messages to a shared mounted disk area.

The above system architecture supports a mechanism for transferring messages in a secure and reliable fashion as well as providing online access to data residing in the enterprise systems — all through a browser interface with minimal requirements from the supplier and minimal support requirements.

SECURITY

The are two categories of security that must be handled:

1. Enterprise systems security from outside intrusion
2. Data security for data communicated over the web

Security for the enterprise is intended to prevent unauthorized users from accessing data and potentially damaging enterprise systems and data. This is handled by various methods that are far too many to have a meaningful discussion in this chapter. One can review the steps taken to secure the system on this project; these are by no means the only or the complete set of measures to be taken. In addition each organization may have different security requirements. For this project, the following steps were taken:

- Use of a firewall that provided the following:
  — Limitation on IP and PORT addresses
  — Limitation on protocols allowed (HTTP, HTTPS, IP)
  — User Authentication at the firewall level
  — Abstraction of Server IP address
- Authentication:
  — Front-office application layer
  — Back-office application layer
  — Operating system layer
  — Firewall layer
- Domain settings:
  — The Web server machine is not part of the enterprise domain
  — The Web server machine has IP access to other servers

Data security is required to protect the information that is transferred between supplier and manufacturer over the public domain of the Internet. The intent is to secure the data from unauthorized eavesdropping. There are many methods to protect the data; these methods can be grouped into two main categories:

1. Transferring data through a secure communication channel (SSL, HTTPS). This method utilizes:
   a. authentication
   b. certificates
   c. encryption
2. Encryption of data. This method is typically used in conjunction with the previous method, but can be used on its own. There are various encryption algorithms available. The encryption strength (cipher strength), which can be defined as how difficult it would be to decrypt encrypted data without the keys, can vary and is designated in terms of number of bits (40 bit, 128 bit, etc.). This project employed Microsoft Crypto API, supported both by the Web server (IIS

4) and by the client browser (IE 4). The cipher strength selected was 40 bits to allow non-United States and Canada access to the application; 128-bit cipher strength is not available for browsers used outside of the United States and Canada.

CONCLUSION

Manufacturing organizations striving to reduce inventory levels and lead times must integrate business processes and systems with their supply chain organization. E-commerce applications utilizing the Internet can be used to achieve integration across the supply chain with minimal cost and standard interfaces.

When implementing E-commerce applications, it is recommended to select an application that can be used as an infrastructure to develop future business solutions to address new requirements. Selecting applications that provide technology solutions with a development platform, rather than applications that provide an integrated business solution, will provide a platform for development of future business applications as the use of E-commerce proliferates through the organization.

Chapter 54
XML-Based Business-to-Business E-Commerce

Michael Blank

Most companies have already recognized the benefits of doing business electronically. E-commerce takes many forms and includes supply chain integration, procurement, online banking, and shipping and logistics. Solutions such as Enterprise Resource Planning (ERP), Electronic Data Interchange (EDI), and the Web have formed the foundation for E-commerce today. These applications link groups of departments, divisions, and companies that want to buy, sell, and exchange services and products, and that depend on seamless information access.

However, in order to remain competitive, companies will have to find solutions to extend their electronic trading networks among companies of all sizes. The technological hurdle to overcome is to find ways to access data that may reside in other complex systems, such as legacy databases, ERP, EDI, and the Web.

The goal of this chapter is to explore how XML (Extensible Markup Language) technologies allow businesses to rapidly and easily engage in business-to-business (B2B) E-commerce. It explores how companies can achieve application-to-application integration across highly heterogeneous environments by leveraging existing investments in legacy and Web-based products and technologies.

COMMERCE COMPONENTS

In order to fuel the growth of electronic trading networks beyond the enterprise, three major sources of information must be unlocked — EDI, ERP, and electronic commerce on the Web. A B2B integration solution must allow these disparate systems to communicate with each other, without requiring changes to the systems themselves.

EDI

EDI is based on a set of computerized forms that automate common business transactions such as package orders, invoices, shipping notices, and requests for proposals. EDI lets companies send and receive purchase orders, sales orders, invoices, and electronic payments.

EDI messages consist of agreed-upon data elements that typically appear in commercial business forms: names, addresses, prices, dates, and item numbers. Standardized lists of these data elements comprise forms such as purchase orders, invoices, ship notices, and medical billing forms. Hundreds of these forms have been developed over the past 20 years or so by a committee called X.12 of the American National Standards Institute (ANSI). International EDI standards have been coordinated by a United Nations organization called UN/EDIFACT.

EDI documents are essentially flat text files. They must be translated out of and into trading partners' internal systems, often at great cost. The widespread acceptance of EDI historically has been hampered by the prohibitive development and maintenance costs. Because EDI is a rigid standard, it requires complicated, proprietary translation and integration software. Furthermore, EDI is typically carried over private value-added networks (VANs), which requires expensive hardware as well as transaction- and volume-based subscriber fees.

As such, EDI solutions have been limited to large companies, while excluding any trading partners that may not have the purse to play along. Because EDI is so expensive, cumbersome, and proprietary, Forrester Research estimates that only 2 percent of electronic transactions are done via EDI.

The Internet, with its low cost of entry and ease of use, could change all that; EDI over the Internet currently allows organizations to access a wider range of trading partners. Even though Internet-based EDI would eliminate the need for proprietary VANs, it does not address the need for costly translation software and integration with enterprise applications.

Traditional EDI vendors, such as Sterling Commerce, Harbinger (now part of Peregrine Systems), and GE Information Services (now GE Global eXchange Services), have allowed smaller companies to participate in EDI activities by providing Web-based forms for manual entry of EDI information, which is translated to an EDI format and forwarded to a larger trading partner. Internet-based EDI is still very interactive and allows very little automation in comparison to direct automated VAN access from one company's system to another's. Other forms of Internet-based EDI include sending data through encrypted e-mail.

While Internet-based EDI is offered by several vendors, they are not interoperable, again due to the lack of standards. Large trading companies have coerced EDI standards to conform to their business processes, making it hard for smaller companies to compete. With different standards between trading partners, a company might have to support as many EDI implementations as they have trading partners, making it too costly for smaller companies to participate.

While the Internet expands the network reach of EDI, there is still a market requirement for seamless information exchange among all trading partners that extend the reach of proprietary EDI networks. As we will see, EDI combined with XML-enabled integration solutions holds the promise of leveling the playing field and achieving a high degree of interoperability.

ERP

The Enterprise Resource Planning (ERP) system is another form of electronic commerce. It seeks to automate business processes that span the organization, incorporating functions such as sales and materials planning, production planning, warehouse management, financial accounting, and personnel management into an integrated workflow of business events. ERP applications provide universal access to information across heterogeneous networks and data sources throughout the enterprise.

While automating key internal business processes is an important step towards integration, integrating processes and information with the information systems of key customers and suppliers is a real competitive advantage. Sharing ERP data among business partners can streamline value chain processes, automate purchasing or customer service applications for real-time processing, and reduce the cost of order processing and financial transaction management.

SAP, one of the leading vendors in the ERP space, has already recognized the need to extend R/3, their ERP solution, to address supply chain management. Unlike ERP systems, supply chain systems must cope with the complexity of integrating information from any number of disparate information systems spanning the entire length of the supply chain. In response, SAP has exposed business components within the R/3 system to applications compliant with open standards such as DCOM and CORBA.

Like EDI, ERP installations are not only proprietary but also involve substantial investment, which limits these solutions to larger companies. Because they focus on the enterprise, there are even fewer standards that link the ERP systems of *different* companies. Technologies and standards that bridge the gap between ERP and EDI or Web-based systems are virtually nonexistent.

XML has the promise to extend ERP beyond the bounds of the enterprise to achieve higher levels of intercompany and multivendor interoperability.

THE WEB

The Web has changed the face of business. Advertisements now feature URLs, and many organizations support sales over the Internet. Consumer Web users can browse catalogs, select items, and make purchases from the comfort of their living rooms. But Web-based shopping is only the tip of the electronic commerce iceberg. While much of E-commerce has been consumer oriented, the Internet can also be used to drastically improve efficiency, reduce costs, and increase sales for an organization by automating the business-to-business relationships with suppliers, distributors, and other partners.

Without realizing it, organizations have already established a viable set of services, available on the World Wide Web and addressable by URLs. Existing Web services span the spectrum from package tracking and online banking to procurement and supply chain integration.

Companies have looked to the open standards of the Web as a common means to communicate with their trading partners. Legacy databases, mainframes, and even EDI systems have been exposed via HTTP and HTML. The Web has truly become an integration platform.

However, HTML-based applications assume that a human is interacting with the system through a Web browser, browsing catalogs and placing orders. While this approach is appropriate for a casual shopper, it is not the most efficient design for business process-driven applications such as supply chain management. For greatest efficiency, the intercorporate supply chain should be automated to work without human intervention. For example, as inventory levels are depleted, the ERP system should automatically query suppliers for inventory levels and delivery schedules, and automatically place orders for replacement stock. Although the information and processes to query and place orders might already be integrated with the Web, they are not designed to support external automated interfaces. Therefore, new interfaces need to be created to support Internet-based supply chain automation.

THE NEED FOR BUSINESS-TO-BUSINESS INTEGRATION

Solutions such as EDI and ERP focus only on providing software for automating operations within tightly coupled organizations. For an organization to achieve full benefits from electronic commerce, a solution must automate the operations between trading partners.

An integration solution must cope with the complexity of integrating information from any number of varied information systems, spanning the entire length of the E-commerce continuum. A solution must provide a secure and reliable mechanism to communicate between applications; the message format must be open and flexible enough for different applications to understand, process, and respond to it.

Some users are looking toward XML to solve the problem of business-to-business integration. XML may be the emerging standard that promises to bridge the communication gap between enterprise resource planning, electronic data interchange, and Web-based systems. Its real significance may emerge as a means for making it easier to create, deploy, and manage integration solutions over the Internet.

WHAT IS XML?

XML (eXtensible Markup Language) is a universal standard for data representation that can encode documents, data records, structured records, even data objects and graphical objects. XML documents are ASCII files that contain text as well as tags identifying structures within that text.

This enables XML to contain "meta data" — data about the content in the document, including hierarchical relationships. As such, XML is a standalone data format that is self-describing.

The following example illustrates how a purchase order might be represented using XML.

```
<?xml version="1.0"?>
<PurchaseOrder>
    <OrderNumber>1001</OrderNumber>
    <Status>Pending</Status>
    <Company>The ABC Company</Company>
    <LineItem>
        <SKU>45669</SKU>
        <Description>Modem Cable</Description>
        <Price>9.95</Price>
    </LineItem>
    <LineItem>
        <SKU>35675</SKU>
        <Description>Modem</Description>
        <Price>99.95</Price>
    </LineItem>
</PurchaseOrder>
```

A business application can locate a particular element and extract its value, regardless of the order of the elements within the document, and regardless of whether it recognizes all of the elements.

INTEROPERABILITY WITH XML

XML offers a lot more flexibility and extensibility than traditional messaging. The application that publishes the XML document could add a new attribute to the document, such as "Quantity," to support the requirements of another application. The original applications that used the document would be unaffected by the additional attribute since they may only be interested in the SKU, Description, and Price of the Item.

An XML document may be fully described by a Document Type Definition (DTD). An XML DTD specifies the format for a particular XML document type and identifies what tags must or may appear within the document. An XML document may contain or reference a DTD, in which case the DTD may be used to validate that the document matches a specific format.

DTDs may be utilized to define standard vocabularies, designed for specific communities of interest. For example, the messaging formats for partners along the supply chain could be specified by a common DTD.

XML Alone Is Not Enough

XML is an open standard, which leads us to a Utopian perception of automatic interoperability. However, XML alone does not provide a complete integration solution, but it represents a central piece of the puzzle. Integrating applications with XML actually requires a fair amount of work. Applications have to be able to understand, process, and respond to XML message formats.

Although the two applications do not need to agree on a specific message format, they still must reach consensus on the meaning of the data being passed. The two different applications are very likely to use different DTDs, and they must establish a way to match elements and attributes from one DTD to the entities and attributes in the other DTD.

In most circumstances, it is not enough to simply pass information from one application to another. The sending application has to tell the receiving application what to do with the data. Therefore, the two applications need to agree on a mechanism for specifying what should be done with the data.

A complete B2B solution would supply mechanisms that relate one application's data structures to those of another. And it would provide a mechanism for requesting specific services to act on the information. Combining XML and integration software brings us closer to a B2B integration solution.

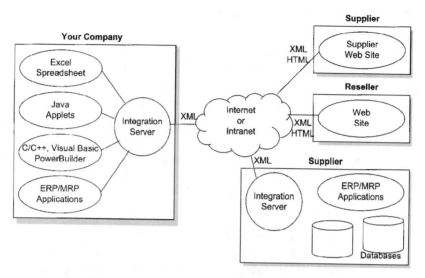

Exhibit 1. Integration server connecting applications to applications and applications to Websites, over the Internet or an extranet, enabling the integration of business processes between trading partners.

AN XML-BASED B2B INTEGRATION SOLUTION

Although it is extremely powerful, XML by itself cannot deliver application integration. Application integration involves much more than self-describing, extensible message formats. The application must be adapted to learn to communicate using XML. It must be able to route requests, manage tasks, and translate between messages conforming to different DTDs.

A complete solution must also provide the integration between other internal or external systems. We refer to the application that implements such a solution as an "integration server." The integration server exposes a collection of integration services to XML-enabled clients. An integration service in the most generic sense is addressable by name, and it has a set of inputs and a set of outputs. The integration server provides the mapping of XML messages in and out of integration services.

Exhibit 1 illustrates how such a solution might support Web and application integration between multiple corporations based on an XML messaging mechanism. The environment provides a central integration point to support XML-enabled client applications and provides access to both internal and external resources.

XML AS THE RPC MESSAGE FORMAT

An application that requests a service of another application must issue a message to the other application. For the purposes of this discussion we refer to such a message as a Remote Procedure Call (RPC). An application issues an RPC by packaging a message, sending the message to the other application, and then waiting for the reply message.

Integration servers can combine the power of RPC middleware with the flexibility of XML to build a highly extensible, intercorporate integration system. XML RPC passes data as self-describing XML documents, unlike traditional RPC middleware systems that use a fixed, predefined message format. Formatting the messages using XML makes all B2B integration solutions highly flexible and extensible.

XML RPC performs all communications over HTTP using standard HTTP get and post operations. The contents of the XML RPC messages are standard Internet traffic: XML documents. XML RPC obviates the need to open firewalls to traditional middleware protocols such as DCOM or IIOP.

MAPPING BETWEEN DIFFERENT DTDS

The integration server must be able to map between different XML data formats, or DTDs. WIDL (Web Interface Definition Language)[1] provides such mapping capabilities and allows applications to communicate with each other via XML, regardless of the DTD they conform to.

WIDL provides document mapping by associating, or binding, certain document elements with application variables. Data bindings may be used to extract some or all of the information in an XML or HTML document. The following example illustrates the use of a WIDL binding with the XML document presented in the earlier example.

```
<OUTPUT-BINDING NAME="PurchaseOrderData">
<VALUE NAME="OrderNumber">doc.OrderNumber[0].text
</VALUE>
<VALUE NAME="SKU" DIM="1">doc.LineItem[].SKU[0].text
</VALUE>
</OUTPUT-BINDING>
```

An application would apply this binding to the XML purchase order document in the first example to map the order number and the list of SKU numbers to the variables OrderNumber and SKU. Only the variables defined by the WIDL binding are exposed to the application.

The variables within a WIDL binding abstract the application from the actual document reference, even from the XML data representation itself.

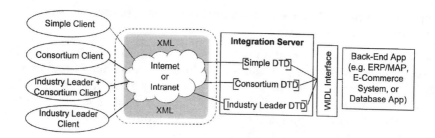

Exhibit 2.   Using WIDL to Make Different XML Messages Interoperable

An integration server would be able to apply similar bindings to a variety of XML formats to achieve the mapping between different DTDs.

Exhibit 2 illustrates the benefits of this capability. Here, industries and businesses have defined a variety of DTDs to which different RPC encodings conform. The interface defined with WIDL captures a superset of the services and data available through the DTDs. Although different client applications speak different XML encodings, the integration server is able to bridge these differences and to make the application universally accessible.

This approach enables different organizations to construct loosely coupled application integration schemes. One organization may want to establish electronic integration among many different partners. Each partner maintains electronic relationships with many other partners. It is extremely difficult for such a loose partnership organization to reach agreement on a single set of message formats. But XML DTD mapping bypasses the need to reach total agreement. Each organization can define its own DTD. An integration server would automatically resolve the differences and deliver information to an organization in the format that the organization requires.

EXPOSING APPLICATION SERVICES

Application services provide access to certain resources, which the integration server exposes to other XML RPC-based applications. The integration server decodes the XML RPC request, identifies the service requested by the RPC, and passes the request on to the service in a data format it understands. It then encodes the output of the service as a properly formatted XML RPC reply that the client is able to understand.

The application service provides the actual integration with internal or external resources, such as the Web, databases, EDI, or ERP systems. The implementation of a service, therefore, is completely abstracted from the message format. XML-based integration solutions actually XML-enable the systems they are integrating.

For example, an integration solution might support the direct integration of different ERP systems across the Internet. A manufacturer running SAP R/3 can integrate its procurement system with the order processing system at a supplier running Baan. The integration solution is implemented separately from the application systems. No modifications are required within the back-end ERP application systems.

In addition to providing a centralized switching system to support intercorporate communications, an integration server might also host business logic modules that tie the entire environment together or that add additional services to the integrated applications.

EXPOSING WEB SERVICES

An integration solution must also be able to leverage the vast quantities of information available on the Internet. It must provide unmanned access to Web resources, without a browser, and allow applications to integrate Web data and services. Programmatic access to the Web may also be referred to as Web Automation.

WIDL enables Web Automation by defining Application Programming Interfaces (APIs) to Web data and services. By using its data bindings, WIDL is able to extract data from fields in an HTML or XML document and map them to program variables. WIDL abstracts the application from the actual document references (that is, where the data being mapped actually exist in a page). Web Automation makes complex interactions with Web servers possible without requiring human intervention.

An integration server exposes Web services as regular integration services. With an XML RPC, client applications are able to invoke a Web service, provide a set of inputs, and receive a set of outputs. The client is abstracted from the actual implementation of the service and is not concerned whether data were derived from a Website, a local database, or remote ERP system.

AN INTEGRATION STRATEGY

Companies must be able to achieve application-to-application integration by leveraging existing investments in legacy and Web-based products and technologies. An integration server provides a transitional strategy for integrating the systems and processes of trading partners into the corporate infrastructure.

Let us look at an example. A manufacturer aims to integrate with a number of suppliers. If a supplier does not yet have a Web presence, it would be free to choose a Web-enabling technology that best suits its environment. By deploying an integration server, the manufacturer can incorporate its suppliers' Web services into its procurement process, for instance. To accomplish even tighter integration, the supplier could expose internal data by adding XML markup to its existing Web offering. The final step in achieving complete application-to-application integration occurs when a supplier also deploys an XML-enabled integration server.

CONCLUSION

Business-to-business integration delivers significant cost savings and operational efficiency through business process automation and just-in-time supply-chain management. Traditional EDI is cost prohibitive for most organizations, so the industry is turning to Internet-based B2B E-commerce. XML is a tremendous enabler. Using XML, applications can implement loosely coupled integration services that are flexible and extensible. But XML by itself will not provide automatic interoperability. Application integration requires infrastructure services to support reliable and secure performance. An integration server provides the infrastructure services that XML lacks.

The growth of electronic trading networks depends on access to diverse data and information sources that reside in various formats in electronic catalogs on the Web, legacy databases, EDI, or ERP systems. Suppliers who can provide solutions which interoperate with multiple and diverse trading networks will become the dominant players in the electronic commerce arena. And their customers will become the earliest winners in the extended enterprise.

Notes

1. In September of 1997, WebMethods, Inc. submitted the original WIDL specification to the World Wide Web Consortium (W3C). In October the W3C acknowledged WIDL for its significance as an IDL and for its significance as a technology for programmatically accessing the Web. The W3C makes the submission available at the URL <http://www.w3.org/Submission/1997/15/Overview.html>.

Chapter 55
Multilingual Web Sites

Deborah Tyroler
Elana Yellin

International World Wide Web usage is on the rise. Between January 1997 and January 1998, the total number of people accessing the Internet worldwide rose from 57 million to 102 million, and that number is expected to top 700 million by 2001.[1] While the United States and Canada currently make up 61 percent of Web users worldwide, the scales were poised to tip by the end of 1999.[2]

Reduced connectivity and hardware costs and improved infrastructure continue to lower barriers to access worldwide. Analysts expected 1 out 10 households in the United Kingdom, Germany, and Denmark to be online, and similar percentage rates were anticipated for Italy and the Netherlands by the year 2000.[3] Nearly 10 percent of the Japanese population accesses the Internet[4] and growth in emerging markets such as Brazil, China, and Korea is taking off. E-commerce is fueling the growth of the global Web, principally in the area of business-to-business commerce. Analysts project E-commerce will reach $327 billion by 2002.[5] By that time, non-U.S. commerce will account for 37 percent of E-commerce worldwide.[6]

Paralleling the growth of the public Internet is the spread of intranets and extranets throughout the global enterprise. Businesses are enabling their information systems, moving mission-critical business applications to powerful private networks based on Web technologies. Systems for order processing, inventory tracking, supply chain management, and invoicing are moving to the Web. Enabling systems to tap the power of the Web offers a key competitive advantage to global companies who need to conduct business across geographies and time zones. In a global marketplace where customers, suppliers, and co-workers are international and located worldwide, multilingual content is integral to effective, efficient, communication.

As Internet technologies permeate the enterprise and the Web continues to evolve into a global mass medium, the profile of the international

0-8493-1149-7/02/$0.00+$1.50
© 2002 by CRC Press LLC

Internet user is rapidly changing. There is a direct correlation between increased international usage and decreased viability of the English-only Web. Illustrating this trend, Brazilian ISP Universo Online (UOL), reported that the percentage of Brazilian Internet users who understood English dropped from 62 percent in 1996 to 58 percent in 1997.[7] Today users are coming online with all levels of technical and linguistic aptitudes, making multilingual content a key ingredient to a successful global Web strategy.

GLOBALIZATION PLAN

Providing multilingual content will augment the benefits and cost savings already derived from a Web site. However, few companies have an unlimited development budget, and innovations and enhancements to a site must be cost justified. To ensure maximum return on localization[8] dollars, the first rule of thumb is fairly obvious: do not create multilingual content that will not be relevant to international users. To assess what is most relevant to international users, the litmus test must be tempered to specificities of one's site as well as to the objectives and mandates of one's organization by determining what will be pertinent in each market as well as what will be possible.

Budgeting constraints generally prescribe a phased approach to localization. Priorities must be set both with respect to content and to target markets, and these will shift over time. The Web is a medium of change and innovation. A Web site is in a constant state of evolution, progressing toward greater usability. Adding multilingual content is an important enhancement in this direction. It helps reach a broader audience and at the same time makes one's site more specialized and personal.

Whether one's Web site is a corporate marketing site, an E-commerce site or an intranet, it is likely to reach out in multiple directions to different audiences. Think through how the various aims of a site — supporting existing customers, global branding, recruiting, linking to suppliers, training employees, tracking orders, transacting sales, attracting investors — relate to each of the targeted language markets. For example, if products and services will vary from market to market, reflect this in the site by customizing the content. Even if the content remains ostensibly the same, local tastes, preferences, and conventions may also influence the position of products or services. The degree to which cultural nuance impacts how contents are handled depends on an assessment of how important cultural differences are to target markets. This will vary greatly depending on whether one's audience is consumer-based, business-to-business, or within one's organization.

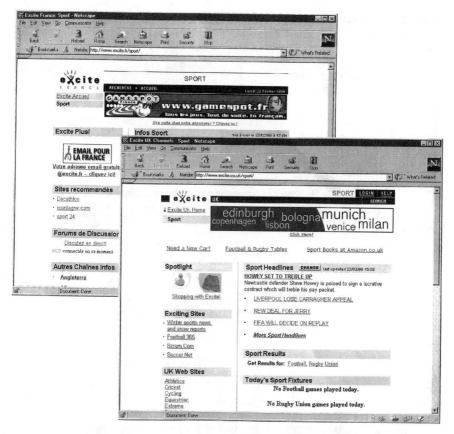

Exhibit 1. Excite's French and British sites illustrate a multilingual/multilocal approach where content has been tailored to local preferences.

CONTENT MANAGEMENT

Multilingual, multilocal sites are Web sites that have country-specific content. These sites often contain content that is uniform across languages as well. A well-managed and well-conceived multilingual, multilocal site will succeed in providing local flavor without forfeiting brand identity. Major search engines such as Yahoo!, Lycos, and Excite offer a good case in point. They all allow for multilingual searching and the content within search categories is tailored to the interests of each market. A sampling of sports categories from Excite's French site (Exhibit 1) include the Tour de France, the French Decathalon, and the World Cup '98. In contrast, Excite U.K. includes cricket, rugby, and equestrian events.

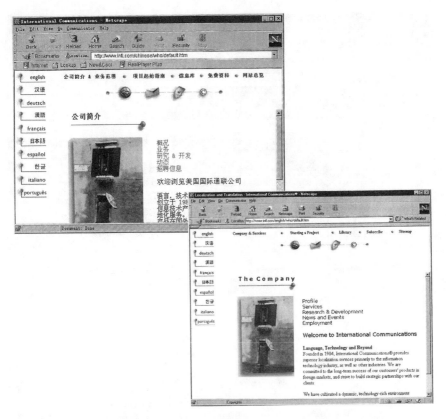

Exhibit 2. Content is presented consistently across language versions of Intl.com satisfying global branding objectives. Multilingual navigation is structured to let visitors change languages at any point.

While the content has been tailored to local tastes, two core elements of the site have been preserved: the features and functionality, and the look and feel. As a result, whether a user is searching Excite in French or in U.K. English, the experience is authentically French or British, and, at the same time, brand identity is promoted.

If global branding is a central aim of an international campaign, then a more uniform treatment of content across language versions of one's site may prove a better approach. International Communications (Exhibit 2) has done this on their site, www.intl.com, which is localized into 10 languages.

The site producers have prioritized key portions of the site to translate based on their target audiences and have chosen to leave other portions in

English. For example, the company's services, profile, and resource information is translated, while job listings and news and events have been left in English. The localized pages maintain the same look and feel across languages. A unique feature of this site is that the language navigation bar appears on every page, allowing visitors to move between languages from any point in the site.

Whatever the configuration of content on the site, one will need to address content management issues. A pivotal decision will be whether to apply a centralized or decentralized model. Corporate mandates will be an important determinant and assessment will be needed where corporate aims and local concerns overlap and where they diverge. The challenge is to determine what must remain uniform for consistency and global branding and what is open to local flavor and interpretation.

The basic architecture of one's site will also impact how one prioritizes what to localize and for which markets. The site may be database-driven, static, application-rich or more likely some hybrid. It may contain frequently updated content posted at predictable intervals, or it may incorporate erratic or constant data streams. One will need to architect a system to manage updates and data streams across languages. For some companies, it makes sense to localize the static portions of a site first and tackle frequently updated content in a later phase. As with other considerations, be sure to weigh the relevance of content to the target before architecting the content management system.

INTERNATIONALIZATION

English is not going to serve effectively in every market the world over; however, it is difficult to cost-justify localization of a Web site into 30-plus languages. To leverage the English version of the site beyond a North American audience, the English Web content can serve multiple purposes. Most obviously, it can target English language markets outside the United States, such as India, Australia, or Singapore. It can be used to target smaller markets such as Norway or Finland, where local language content would be preferable, but English may be acceptable. Additionally, the English language version of the site can provide a short- to mid-term solution for second- or third-tier priority markets one intends to localize at a later date. Ideally, begin to think of the English language version of the site as the "international" version, the foundation upon which the entire site is built.

Creating an internationalized site consists of taking the original language version and looking at it as yet just another language. Considerations generally entail removing cultural references and colloquialisms, enabling time and date functions, and implementing double-byte character support[9] for

Asian languages. Bringing an international perspective to the site helps keep the design and architecture open and flexible enough to accommodate and anticipate new markets. Taking this step ensures that content will be accessible and acceptable to international visitors, allowing them to utilize one's site, while also preparing it for possible localization.

TEXT AND IMAGES

Ad copy and company slogans, common on marketing and E-commerce sites, are notorious for being difficult to introduce into a foreign market, whether or not they are translated. Popular examples of *faux pas* made by large corporations making the foray into the international market include the Pepsi slogan "Come alive with the Pepsi Generation" that was translated for the Taiwan market as "Pepsi will bring your ancestors back from the dead." Salem cigarettes' slogan, "Salem — Feeling Free," was translated for the Japanese market into "When smoking Salem, you feel so refreshed that your mind seems to be free and empty."

When looking at copy and images, remember that specific cultural references may confuse or offend those outside the target market. If later in the game one decides to target a specific market with localized content, add cultural images, references, and slang to create a local flavor (Exhibit 3).

The same holds true for images and color schemes. Although there may not be universal colors or images, there are certainly cultures that identify more closely with some than others. For example, a picture of a woman of Japanese origin on a site targeting U.S. visitors would probably be considered multicultural and open-minded. But if a U.S. company tried to bring their site into the Japanese market with images of stereotypical American-looking people, it would probably be considered inauthentic by Japanese visitors.

TECHNICAL ISSUES

Apart from marketing-related issues such as images and copy, there are also various technical considerations to take into account when providing internationalized content for the Web site visitor. One of the most important considerations is to be aware of how the visitor interacts with the site to find the needed information. If a visitor can fill out a contact form, order items generated by a database, or simply track down an e-mail and phone number, make sure needed information can be gleaned from them, as well as effectively responding to their inquiries.

Providing contact information for one's company or asking visitors to provide various bits of information may seem very straightforward, but

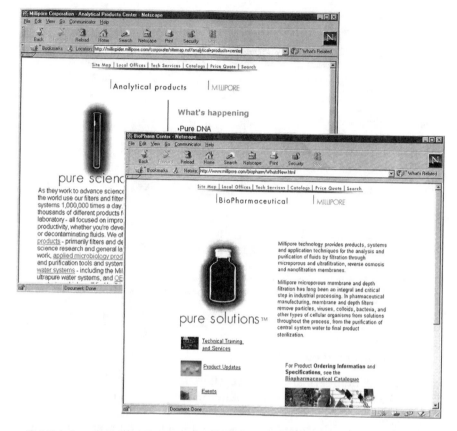

Exhibit 3. **Millipore uses universal images such as eyeglasses, a computer chip, a test tube, and a vial to illustrate their global branding campaign. These images are widely understood, even when copy is not translated.**

there are certain query fields that need to be properly internationalized. Names, addresses, and phone numbers may not follow the same format conventions in other countries as they do in the U.S. For instance, telephone numbers may not be grouped as xxx-xxx-xxxx, "State" may not exist, and a surname may be quite lengthy. Hard-coding form fields to allow only a limited number of characters, or requiring certain fields, can frustrate the international visitor (Exhibit 4).

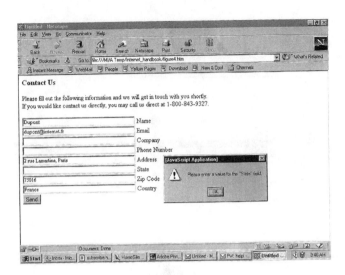

Exhibit 4. **This form prompts the user to enter in a State, where "State" is not valid outside the U.S. A more appropriate field label would be State/Province**

Other considerations include:

- Toll-free numbers are not accessible from outside the United States. Make sure to include an alternate phone number including the country code.
- Time and date formats are generally formatted differently than in the United States. Not everyone knows what PST or EST means. It is helpful to also mention local time in relation to Greenwich Mean Time. Date format can also vary from country to country. For example, the date 1/5/99, understood as January 5, 1999 in the U.S., would be understood in Europe and elsewhere as May 1, 1999. To avoid confusion, it would be more appropriate to show the date as January 5, 1999.
- If targeting a particular market, make sure to be able to effectively answer foreign language e-mail inquiries with an internal employee, a partner office, or a translation partner. To help reduce overall costs, it can be beneficial to build a multilingual FAQ from the inquiries received over a period of time. Visitors can then be encouraged to seek answers on one's Web site, reducing the need for individual tech support.

If the decision is made not to localize the site, there are also backend issues to consider, especially if targeting the Asian market. Unlike English and European languages which are handled by single-byte (8 bits) character sets, Asian languages (Chinese, Korean, Japanese) require double-byte (16 bits) or multibyte character sets. If allowing a Japanese customer to order through an online form using Japanese characters, determine whether the back end is available in double-byte versions or are double-byte enabled.

The database may need to accept double-byte characters, but this does not mean all of the content within will need to be completely localized. For example, a database used for online ordering that stores the sizes, colors, and styles of various shoes, would not require localization. The user interface (where the visitor chooses the items he wishes to purchase) would have to be translated into the target market language, but the items the user is selecting — the items that are being referenced in the database — would remain in English.

BANDWIDTH/DOWNLOAD TIME

Large images, video clips, and Shockwave™ can take an inordinate amount of time to download for any users who are still using a 14.4 or 28.8 kbps modem. In addition to a slow modem, add poor telephone lines and costly Internet access fees, and suddenly there is a very frustrated user. These issues are still real considerations in many countries outside the U.S. Kenyan users have to accept speeds as slow as 9.6 to 14.4 kbps[10] and must pay an average of U.S.$65 per month for Internet access.[11] A recent report showed that 88.9 percent of Internet users in China complained of slow connections and 61.2 percent said online fees were too expensive.[12] Good Web design takes these issues into account, whether creating a site for a domestic or international market (Exhibit 5).

INTERNATIONAL SITE PROMOTION

"If you build it they will come" is a slogan now well known to be inaccurate by savvy Web marketers. Simply building a Web site does not ensure the traffic, and this certainly holds true for multilingual versions as well. Web users will first search for content in their native language and will switch to English (provided they know English) only if they cannot find the information they are seeking.

A recent survey by SiteMetrics[13] examined 31,000 U.S.-based sites run by companies in 14 different industries with annual revenues from $10 million to more than $1 billion. Only 30 percent included the Meta keyword tag used by the largest search engines to catalog Web sites. Only 27 percent of those surveyed included the Meta description tag.

The above statistic is surprising, considering the abundance of promotional information available on the Web. Not only is Meta tag usage[14] important for English pages, but it is also equally important for a translated site. Although every search engine doesn't utilize Meta tags, they can help a site get indexed in the foreign language engines. Additionally, Meta tags may increase the searchability of the site in the English engines by bringing up one's site when users enter in foreign language keywords.

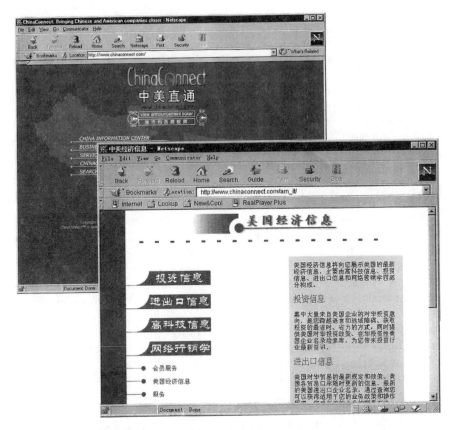

Exhibit 5. **ChinaConnect makes use of graphics with limited colors and complexity to cater to its high percentage of visitors originating from a low-bandwidth market.**

If a site offers goods, services, or information to the foreign market, but isn't yet multilingual, translating some Meta key words within the English pages for target markets can be a cost-effective first step that helps drive foreign language speakers to the site. Make sure your site is internationalized for these visitors to ensure it delivers relevant and useful content, products, or services.

Translating Meta tags is only part of promoting the site to non-English speakers. There are other forms of promotion to consider, whether or not creating a global marketing campaign.

- The search engines need to find out about the multilingual or internationalized versions of one's site. This step involves manually entering URLs and site description into search engines and language directories.

- If traffic to the English version of the site has benefited from reciprocal links for the English version, this can also be an effective form of promotion for multilingual versions.
- One can announce a site to the international press using companies that specialize in distributing online press releases. These companies often have an international module, as in the case of the Internet News Bureau (www.newsbureau.com). They maintain international affiliates while also providing translation services for worldwide press distribution.
- Multilingual banner ad campaigns can be created by an internationally savvy advertising firm, or one's preexisting ads can be localized for each market. LinkExchange (www.linkexchange.com), a popular banner exchange program, recently added an option to categorize a site based on language categories, enabling the exchange of banners with other sites of the same language.

GLOBAL WEB TEAM

When a decision is made to target an international market and one begins to grapple with these many issues, the capability of one's team will become essential to the success of localization strategy for the Web. Draw on expertise from within the organization, supplemented and strengthened by experts external to the company. For example, Web developers with strong internationalization experience will consider issues such as double-byte-enabled databases and optimizing graphics for the Web. A knowledgeable localization partner will use native translators, familiar with the chosen target market's own cultural nuances, as well as technical, project management, and publishing specialists who will be able to republish a site with all the features and functionality of the original kept intact. E-marketing firms will work to develop a successful international E-marketing campaign for a global Website. In addition to the central team of experts, make multilingualism and internationalization a priority within the company so internal staff will view it as a critical and worthwhile step in the overall success of the company.

CONCLUSION

The global nature of the Web has rapidly accelerated the need for well-thought-out international Web strategies. Traditionally, companies introduced their products market by market. Now via the Web, information, products, and services are instantaneously available around the world. The Web provides companies with constant and immediate global exposure, heightening the need for careful attention to global branding and international product marketing. The question is no longer when or whether to go international; it is how to plan and manage the process to derive the greatest benefit from a global Web presence.

When mapping lobal Web strategy, which sections to localize and which language markets to target first will fall into place. Whether opting for a multilingual, multilocal site or a site that is uniform across language versions, multilingual content adds a layer of richness and functionality to the site. By approaching site design with an international mindset, taking structure, aesthetics, and content into account, an architecture that can support any language direction is ensured. The World Wide Web is a global medium and ignoring an international, non-English-speaking audience, will deminish the efficacy of your Web presence. Creating a multilingual Web site for overseas target markets is one of the best ways to transcend linguistic barriers and "speak" the customer's language.

Notes

1. Headcount.com, http://www.headcount.com, June 1998.
2. "Is the World Wide Web Really Worldwide?" *EMarketer,* July, 1998, http://www.emarketer.com.
3. Jupiter Communications, http://www.jup.com, August, 1998.
4. Jupiter Communications, http://www.jup.com, August, 1988.
5. "CEOs Feel Internet's Global Impact," *Internet Week,* May 25, 1998, http://www.internetwk.com.
6. Headcount.com, http://www.headcount.com, January 1998.
7. Brazil Net Use Diversifying, *News.com,* April 3, 1998, http://www.news.com.
8. Localization: the process by which all elements of a product are customized to the local culture and characteristics of a particular target market. This generally includes translating the user interface, altering time/date formats and ensuring images and terms are culturally sensitive and make sense to the end user.
9. Double-byte character enabling (DBCE): Chinese, Japanese, and Korean are written in complex systems of thousands of ideographic and syllabic characters. An advantage of ideograms is that one character may have a single meaning but a different spoken word in another dialect. Other characters may present similar sounds with vastly different meanings. There are so many characters that two bytes are required to specify them in computer operating systems, hence the term "double byte." That is, Roman characters can be easily represented in 128 characters using 7-bit ASCII, while East Asian languages require 16 bits to represent roughly 32,000 double-byte characters. Some programs are not written with these double-byte character sets in mind, and so are not able to handle the input, output, and internal manipulation of words or strings that include double-byte characters. Double-byte enabling is the process in which the program is altered to allow the proper handling of double-byte characters.
10 "Kenya on an Information Dirt Track," Fox News, June 12, 1998, http://www.foxnews.com.
11. "A Picture of Africa," Sagonet, April 15, 1998, http://demiurge.wn.apc.org/.
12. "1.2 Million Chinese Now Online," Techserver, July 13, 1998, http://www.techserver.com/.
13. SiteMetrics, Web Content Survey, April 1998, http://www.sitemetrics.com/contentsurvey/byindustry.htm.
14. Meta tags: A special HTML tag that provides information about a Web page. Unlike normal HTML tags, Meta tags do not affect how a page is displayed. Instead, they can provide a summary, title, and key words for a page, as well as information about the author, how often the page is updated, character encoding, and its audience rating. Many search engines use this information to help build their indexes. For more information on search engine ranking and Meta tag usage, view http://www.searchenginewatch.com/.

Section XI
Project and Systems Management

Chapter 56
Nine Factors for Project Success

John P. Murray

The successful design, development, and implementation of information technology (IT) projects is a very difficult, complex, and, at times, daunting process. However, although developing IT projects can be difficult, the reality is that a relatively small number of factors control the success or failure of every IT project, regardless of its size or complexity. There is nothing esoteric about those factors. The problem is not that the factors are unknown; it is that they seldom form an integral part of the IT development process.

Of course, the recognition and management of these factors does not ensure IT project success. Understanding the factors and the part they play in successful project management is one thing; appropriately managing them is something else. In addition, there is a high potential for project failure in not recognizing the part these factors play, or failing to appropriately manage them.

If these factors are so clearly important and well-known, why do they not form an integral part of every IT project? The short answer is that they should. The issue here is that because they are not used, too high a number of IT projects suffer some degree of failure.

The phrase "IT project failure" often raises a specter of some colossal failure. For example, the project never goes operational, or it is abandoned in midstream after considerable expense. In addition, there are other qualified IT failures, such as projects that exceed their development time and expense estimates, but ultimately become operational. There are also many projects that move to production status, but do not meet the expectations of internal customers as defined in the project specifications. And projects may be considered failures if the applications take too long to process the data, or if they regularly fail in the operational environment.

0-8493-1149-7/02/$0.00+$1.50
© 2002 by CRC Press LLC

In short, many organizations do not have a particularly good track record in IT project success. However, many IT project failures can be eliminated or mitigated by understanding and managing the nine project failure factors described in this chapter. These factors should be recognized for the strength they can bring to every project, and accorded the attention they deserve.

THE NINE FACTORS

The following nine factors can and do make or break IT projects:

1. Appropriate senior management levels of commitment to the project
2. Adequate project funding
3. A well-done set of project requirements and specifications
4. Careful development of a comprehensive project plan that incorporates sufficient time and flexibility to anticipate and deal with unforeseen difficulties as they arise
5. An appropriate commitment of time and attention on the part of those outside the IT department who have requested the project, combined with a willingness to see it through to the end
6. Candid, accurate reporting of the status of the project and of potential difficulties as they arise
7. A critical assessment of the risks inherent in the project, any potential harm associated with those risks, and the ability of the project team to manage those risks
8. The development of appropriate contingency plans that can be employed should the project run into problems
9. An objective assessment of the ability and willingness of the organization to stay the project course

The reader will realize that none of the factors has anything to do with technology. In addition, all the factors are straightforward and can be easily understood by anyone with a business background.

Organizations that recognize and work to appropriately include the nine factors in IT project development are taking an important step in moving to more consistent IT project success. However, they will have to do more than recognize the factors' importance. They must also understand the interlocked nature of the factors, which together form a mosaic of strong project management. If IT project success is to improve, the role and importance of each factor must be understood. A discussion of each of the factors will provide information about how they affect IT projects.

1. SENIOR MANAGEMENT COMMITMENT

When it is clear that a particular IT project has the interest, the support, and the commitment of the organization's senior management, everyone involved in the project will have a sharper focus. Almost all IT projects are expensive. In addition, these projects present opportunities — some of them significant — that foster organizational success. Poorly done projects can hamper the organization's success; some can even put the organization in jeopardy. Therefore, it is imperative that the senior managers responsible for the areas affected by a particular project become and remain involved. If, as often happens, the process is completely left to the IT department, the project is in trouble.

There are numerous examples of IT projects that have considerably benefited an organization. There are also many examples of IT project failures that have seriously disrupted an organization's business. Beyond the issue of total IT project failures, there are IT projects that are not true failures, but are less than successful. Those projects never deliver what was originally promised and are sometimes simply abandoned.

IT projects are sometimes conceived, funded, and built without appropriate senior-level review and involvement. This should not be seen as a failure on the part of senior management to approve a given IT project. In virtually all organizations, senior management approval is mandatory when a project reaches a certain funding level. In the majority of failed IT projects, such approval was undoubtedly granted at a high organizational level. Therefore, the issue is not that IT projects go forward without appropriate approval, but rather that the approval is too often automatic.

All too often, senior management approves IT projects that carry potentially serious consequences for the enterprise, without clearly understanding the organization's exposure or risk. Of course, one can argue that IT management is obliged to properly inform senior management of the project's potential downside. However, in the euphoria of getting the project approved, the project's risks may be ignored or glossed over. In fact, some organizations have a repeated pattern of project proposal and subsequent failure, yet senior management remains aloof.

There is an important distinction between approval of and commitment to an IT project. In IT projects that encounter difficulty, there is usually some point at which members of senior management become involved, and their attention and commitment are in place. However, this often happens at the wrong end of the project.

IT projects beyond a set funding level, which varies by organization, should never be seriously considered without senior management's clear understanding of the project's perceived difficulties, risks, and benefits. Too many IT projects gain approval based upon hype and an unrealistic calculation of the potential benefits. Thus, senior management, with or without an IT background, should probe for the facts. And the project

should be abandoned, or at least halted, until their questions can be satis-
factorily answered.

2. ADEQUATE PROJECT FUNDING

IT projects often require heavy financial investments if they are to be successful. However, ample project funding is not in and of itself a panacea;
access to large sums of money does not ensure IT project success. Conversely, inadequate project funding will lead to delivery of less than promised, if not outright failure.

Organizations must recognize that the time, hardware, software, and
people components that make up an IT project are expensive. They should
therefore devote ample time and attention at the project's beginning to
analyze and apply realistic costs to the components. Although good
project expense analysis may not produce complete figures, the process
should provide a reasonable understanding of the expense associated with
the project. Once a set of realistic figures is produced, the organization
should also build a reasonable amount of contingency funding into the estimated project cost.

IT project funding should be seen as a continuing and flexible process.
While a reasonable estimate of project expense must be made to obtain initial approval, this figure should not be considered the final project cost.
After all, changes will be incorporated into the project plan as it goes forward. These will undoubtedly involve added functionality, which will in
turn translate into increased project cost.

As the project moves forward, its implications will be better understood. As the true scope of the project is revealed, the project manager can
more accurately identify project expenses. Therefore, costs must be recal-
culated at several checkpoints in the project life cycle, and the new figures
communicated to senior management.

Senior management should view the changing project costs in a positive
light, although they are more likely to rise than to fall. This is because a discussion of the changing expense offers senior management an opportunity
to probe why the estimates changed. For example, the project sponsors
might have requested additional functionality, which increased the cost. At
this point, senior management has an opportunity to decide whether or not
they want to fund these additional project expenses or forego the added
functionality. Otherwise, there is often *de facto* approval of increased functionality (and project expense), without senior management involvement.

Without interim project expense reviews, additional functions are often
added, raising project expense, but such additions are not revealed until
the project is completed, if ever. In addition, interim estimates provide an

opportunity to reduce the project scope, if necessary, to bring the cost to a more desirable level. This might entail extending the project's installation date, abandoning parts of the project, or curtailing some of the features. Whatever the result of the project review, it presents an opportunity to make project-expense-related adjustments in a businesslike manner.

3. WELL-DONE REQUIREMENTS AND SPECIFICATIONS

It is absolutely critical to the success of any IT project that the organization develop a clear understanding of what will be delivered and what will not be delivered within the project's scope. In fact, is not unusual for the people who requested the project to raise issues part way through it, about functions that are not to be delivered.

This sparks arguments between the project sponsors and the members of the IT department, who both seek to assign blame for the apparent oversight. It represents poor development work to make assumptions about inclusion or exclusion of items in an IT project, and is bound to create confusion and disappointment, if not serious project disruption.

Even if there are well-thought-out and documented project requirements and specifications, unforeseen events will arise as the project moves forward. Sometimes, minor additions can be made to the applications, requiring little time and expense. However, the lack of inclusion of major items can render the project inoperable. When this happens, there are two unattractive options. The project can be reworked to include what was overlooked, which is likely expensive and time consuming, and shows the IT department in an unfavorable light, even if it was not responsible for the oversight. The other option is to abandon the project.

Not only must the project-related requirements and specifications be complete, they must be carefully reviewed by people familiar with the business issues the project is to support. This review must be careful and thorough, to avoid subsequent IT development difficulties.

All too often, when it is found that additions must be made to the requirements and specifications in the later stages of the project, a workaround is attempted. In addition to the time and expense of such a solution, it often does not work, or does not work well. And, while strong project management requirements and specifications do not ensure project success, they add considerably to the probability that the project will succeed.

4. A COMPREHENSIVE PROJECT PLAN

IT project planning is not a waste of time, although many believe it is. In fact, there is a very strong correlation between the length of time allocated to project planning and the project's ultimate success. Granted, IT planning can be overdone, but IT installations seldom exhibit excessive attention to planning.

There are three benefits to be gained from strong project planning. First, planning allows the planners to present a clear, well-documented, properly focused understanding of the project. Second, the planning process raises questions that would not otherwise be considered. There is often a rush to begin the project without an adequate understanding of what will be done or the ramifications of the work.

The third planning benefit is that it builds confidence in the project and its processes. As a result, when planning is finished, it is easier to confidently begin the project. In a well-done versus a poorly planned project, then, the transition from project concept to delivery will be easier and faster. Appropriate project planning is a function of an organization's strong IT project discipline. To succeed, IT management must make it clear that planning is an important component of project management, and that the required planning must be completed and approved before the project moves forward.

5. COMMITMENT OF STAKEHOLDERS

The track record is poor in organizations where responsibility for IT projects rests with the IT department. In fact, IT projects are, with limited exceptions, developed and operated to meet the organization's business needs and interests, rather than those of IT. The organization is poorly served when people outside the IT department can dissociate themselves from projects in which they have a vested interest.

Sometimes, IT projects of significant size are completed with virtually no internal customer involvement. Their attitude might well be, "Show me the results when the project is done." If and when projects of this type are finally installed, they rarely meet internal customers' needs.

IT department managers should realize that IT has a vested interest in developing a process that ensures strong internal customer involvement in its projects. A lack of customer involvement virtually ensures eventual customer dissatisfaction with some project aspect. If IT managers cannot get customers to share project ownership, they set themselves up for eventual customer criticism.

Therefore, IT should not initiate or install any projects without the complete support, involvement, and attention of the appropriate internal customers. It represents a failure on the part of senior management if internal customers take no project responsibility, yet complain about the project's content and performance once it moves into production.

Because business projects warrant the investment of large sums of IT time, effort, and money, they should warrant a comparable investment on the part of the internal customers who requested the project. It is senior management's responsibility to make certain that everyone affected by a particular IT project has a share in the project's ownership.

It will require fortitude on the part of the IT management team to halt development of an IT project due to a lack of internal customer involvement. However, this is the correct approach; otherwise, IT is exposed to excessive risk.

6. PROJECT STATUS REPORTING

It is not enough to simply provide regular project status updates; these updates must be accurate. In fact, IT project status reports are often overly optimistic. While it might be more comfortable for departments to believe that steady project progress is being made, it is more important that the reported status is realistic. IT projects routinely fall into difficulty. One cause is in the failure to accurately report the real project status in a timely fashion.

IT might provide inaccurate project reporting in the usually mistaken belief that lost ground will be regained as the project moves forward. After all, no one will be the wiser when the lost ground is made up and the project is back on schedule. However, it is almost universally true that once a project falls behind, the situation will only get worse without high-level involvement. And senior management will not provide the needed help as long as it thinks things are going well.

As early in the project as possible, project status reporting should identify adverse issues, as well as recommend how the difficulties can be overcome. Of course, candid project reporting can create tension for both the project team and the customer areas. Some degree of tension is desirable, because it will cause people to consider issues early on which otherwise might not arise until later in the project. And, while dealing with IT project problems and tensions can be difficult, ignoring them will only make them more difficult.

Members of IT projects typically delay the delivery of bad news, such as a delay. When this happens, senior management might be alerted to the problem by some other area, or the project manager might have to reluctantly admit to the project's delayed status. Both scenarios have a negative effect on senior management, on everyone involved in the project, and on the project itself.

7. CRITICAL RISK ASSESSMENT

An organization's senior management should complete and publish a careful analysis of the project's risks before it seriously considers approval. It is not enough to recognize that the project has some risk or to have a vague idea of some of the possible project-related risks. Risk, as it applies to a particular IT project, must be well-understood. More importantly, those who will suffer from the project-related risks must be made as aware of them as promptly as possible.

Identification of project risk falls into two categories: the more usual and obvious risks, and the risks that will be generated based upon the functions and requirements of the particular project.

Usual and obvious project risks include:

- The use of IT software that is new, or at least new to the organization.
- The organization's level of IT skill and knowledge. Obviously, a seasoned, well-trained group of IT professionals will be more likely to master the project development than less experienced people.
- The track record of the IT department in successfully managing IT projects. IT departments that have a strong development track record bring less risk to a project, regardless of its size and complexity, than an organization with a poor development record.
- The size and complexity of the proposed project.
- The willingness of the organization to properly fund the project.
- The level of trust and respect between the IT members of the project team and the internal customers on the team.

Risks associated with the particular project's functions include:

- The perceived importance of the project to the business of the organization. Obviously, an IT project that carries heavy business implications will present a considerably higher risk level than upgrading an existing system.
- The ability and willingness of those outside the IT department who have requested the project to become and remain involved throughout the life of the project. In projects where the assistance of outside vendors is required to bring the project to a successful completion, the level of dependency on that vendor must be calculated and managed. The willingness and ability of the vendor to perform as expected must be seriously considered. In addition, circumstances within vendor organizations change. For example, part way through the project, the vendor might decide to abandon the line of hardware the project is using. Alternatively, a competitor might buy out the vendor, lowering the vendor's level of project support. Finally, the vendor might just go out of business.

- The quality of the project requirements and specifications. The higher the quality of that work, the more probable the project will be a success.
- The possibility of the loss of a key person on the project, either from IT or from the internal customer side. If that person alone has knowledge critical to the project's success, his or her loss could deal the project a fatal blow.

Every IT project presents its own set of risks. A businesslike approach to project management requires carefully considering and addressing these risks with internal customers and senior management as part of the project's approval process. If the risk analysis leads to a decision not to move forward, it is much better for everyone involved that the decision is made sooner, rather than later.

8. PROJECT CONTINGENCY PLANS

As a project moves forward, difficulties might well arise. Although the organization might be highly confident that the project will succeed, it is prudent to consider the possibility of some type of failure. Because such a possibility exists, the organization should put a plan in place to overcome difficult situations if they should arise.

Some examples of IT project contingency planning include:

- Recognition that the planned level of hardware resources to support the project may prove inadequate when it is moved into production. One of the common failings of IT projects, particularly in client/server environments, is disappointing processing performance when the applications move to the production environment. Although the hardware plan might seem adequate, that might not be the case. Therefore, the project plan should have a provision to increase hardware resources should the need arise. In addition, senior management should be advised of this possibility.
- Anticipation of "surprise" additions to the project's functionality as it moves forward. Too often, part way through a project, the project must incorporate items that were overlooked, or changes in the business needs associated with the project. This means schedule delays (with talk of "phase two") and additional project expense. In addition, other projects may be delayed, and business initiatives dependent upon the successful completion of this project may be delayed.

Project surprises are always a possibility, despite a strong set of project requirements and specifications. It should therefore be a mandatory part of the development process to recognize this possibility and raise the issue with the appropriate people.

When an IT project is of paramount importance to an organization, it makes good business sense to consider the possibility of delay. In addition, an attempt should be made to construct a plan to work around this eventuality.

Developing a project contingency plan should be linked to the issues of project planning and project funding, as addressed earlier in this chapter. However, while appropriate planning will identify many of the issues that may arise and that should be built into the project, no amount of planning will anticipate everything that might happen. If funding is flexible, senior management will already realize the possibility of additional expense.

Obviously, the ideal is to generate a plan, the first time around, that is absolutely precise with regard to expense and functions. However, that is virtually impossible in a project of any magnitude. Believing that such a process is viable represents one of the fundamental causes of IT project difficulty.

9. A WILLINGNESS TO STAY THE COURSE

All IT projects face some level of difficulty, and much of it can be mitigated through sound management approaches. However, problems must be anticipated. As they arise, people will try to find ways to reduce the pain associated with the project. At this point, pressure will likely build to modify the project.

Some of the suggestions for doing so include:

- A reduction in the features to be delivered. A phased approach to the project can be introduced, designed to shift parts of the project from the current schedule to some (often poorly defined) future date.
- An approach that proposes that flaws or problems in the system be fixed by some workaround process. This process offers a solution to the current problem, but will often do less than what was specified in the original project plan. The idea is that the problem should be fully and correctly repaired, but there is no time to do that work now. The workaround is usually accompanied by a promise to return to the problem at some later date and make things right. When this occurs, the chance of correcting the problem at some later date will be close to zero.
- A willingness to reduce testing standards and controls to meet project deadlines. Again, the stance is to wait to fix testing-related problems so that the schedule is met.
- Abandonment of the project.

Obviously, if a project is in difficulty, some steps must be taken to correct the situation. These steps, and their ramifications on the entire project, should be carefully thought out and considered. It is important that everyone involved in the project realize that if there are project difficulties, there may be pressure to adjust the original plan. The plan should be flexible enough to allow adjustment, if needed. Organizations must avoid overreacting to problems, and adapting the wrong approach to solving them.

Those responsible for the project's ultimate success within the IT department should ensure the continuing support of the organization's senior management for the project. If the project is of sufficient importance to be initiated, it should be adequately supported if things go wrong. In obtaining senior management support, project managers must be willing to present an accurate picture of the potential difficulties inherent in the project. Insofar as is practical, senior management must be given a realistic assessment of the potential for difficulty and be willing to stay the course if things go wrong.

CONCLUSION

It is impossible to identify and manage all the potential difficulties and ramifications associated with IT development projects. The larger the project, the greater the probability of unforeseen difficulty. In large IT development projects, it can become a massive task to coordinate the various teams working on the project.

If organizations attempted to find and resolve all project difficulties and potential difficulties, it would keep projects from moving forward; this is sometimes referred to as "analysis paralysis." This chapter does not strive for perfection. Rather, it tries to raise the awareness in IT installations and with the internal customer community, that the better prepared everyone is going into a given project, the greater the likelihood of a successful project.

While no one wants to be involved in an IT project that is less than successful, virtually every organization has project failures. If available, methods should be implemented to alleviate some of the difficulties and, as a result, improve the levels of IT service and customer satisfaction.

Of course, the nine factors outlined here create more work. However, this additional workload need not be a burden if the factors are understood and realized. When an organization incorporates the nine factors into the normal IT project development processes, the work required becomes less of a burden. If a relatively small amount of extra time and effort can improve IT projects and increase internal customer satisfaction, it is a small price to pay.

Chapter 57
The Systems Integration Life Cycle
Michael A. Mische

With process reengineering and organizational transformation becoming mainstays for many organizations, the major performance issue for information management and technology (IM&T) executives and professionals is speed — that is, speed defined as the rapid delivery of enabling solutions and responsive and cost-effective IM&T services to an increasingly sophisticated and demanding user community. Providing cost-effective computing solutions has always been a major goal for the IM&T professional; however, with reengineering and systems integration projects taking on increasing importance and megadollar proportions, the issue of rapid development and deployment of integrated solutions and enabling technologies is elevated to a new level of prominence and visibility in the enterprise.

The realities of systems integration, as discussed by several authors in this book, are that these projects are large, complex, and often mission critical to any operational reengineering effort. The advances in technologies combined with the needs created by a less hierarchical organization create a new set of urgencies and priorities for the delivery of systems that bear little resemblance to historical precedents.

Several key factors drive the need for the accelerated delivery of enabling solutions. At one time, technology created competitive advantage; today, however, systems are easily replicated. Therefore, competitive advantage through technology is short-lived and lessening. Organizations cannot wait three, four, and five years for traditional systems development and integration methods to deliver enabling solutions. By the time solutions are fully implemented and available for users, their needs, management sponsors, and technologies have all changed.

Another factor is that technology is advanced and adaptable. At one time, large mainframes, special rooms and environments, and many people were required to support complex programs and interfaces; today, the computing environment has evolved and contains smaller, easier to support, and far friendlier technologies that are rapidly deployable.

Also driving the need for accelerated delivery is improvements in the quality of technology. Historically, some of the more fundamental measures of IM&T success included such criteria as technically correct programs, rapid response times, and 99 percent systems availability. Today, processing accuracy, technically correct applications, and system availability are fundamental "givens": they are prerequisites and no longer the predominant measures of an IM&T organization's effectiveness. Therefore, users and executives have a different set of expectations for IM&T performance that are beyond the traditional technical performance measures.

In addition, organizational transformation and operational reengineering are redefining entirely new applications and data needs. In the process, they are creating new opportunities for using technology and leveraging human resources.

End users are also simply smarter and more comfortable with technology. They understand technology and what is and is not possible. As a consequence, users are far more demanding of the systems provided, and more discriminating of the services, resources, and costs of the IM&T organization. They are holding the IM&T organization and the quality of systems and services delivered to much higher standards.

As a consequence of these changes, there is a need for a more flexible and accelerated approach to systems integration and the deployment of technology-enabling solutions. This chapter explores some of the issues associated with integrating systems in the context of reengineering, and offers an overview of a new life cycle methodology for the systems integration and development processes. This model is called the process-driven integration model (PDIM).

THE PROCESS DRIVEN INTEGRATION MODEL

For the most part, the historical systems development life cycles (SDLCs) were restricted to use by the IM&T department for the development of new systems. In a sense, systems integration projects have relied on the traditional SDLC methodologies, or some derivative of the traditional SDLC, as a guide for developing systems integration work plans and managing the integration process. The classic SDLC provided a formal structure for developing mainframe and mid-range systems, a structure that included a number of phases and work steps. Some methodologies had as few as 4 phases, and some had 12 or more.

Over the course of time, variants to the traditional models were introduced and evolved to include computer-aided systems engineering (CASE) tools and joint user designs to support the systems integration process. Without question, the traditional SDLC methods were relatively effective in aiding the development of classic mainframe-based systems and facilitating the integration of function-specific systems. However, systems integration projects in support of reengineering are proving to be an entirely different matter. Whereas the classical methods benefited from a limited number of mainframe and proprietary technologies and methods, systems integration in support of operational reengineering and organization transformation involves the complete spectrum of technology, applications, data structures, and significant organizational and operational changes to the IM&T organization. Whereas the development process and integration of systems were once restricted to a finite set of applications and related data, integration in the reengineered enterprise requires cross-functionality and portability of technology and applications in support of leaner and more agile operations and organizational structures.

For most organizations attempting to reengineer, the traditional methods for systems development and the development project life cycle are no longer effective models for the management of the system integration processes that are required to support new cross-functional and leaner organizations. They are too slow, rigid, mechanical, and bureaucratic. The needs of reengineering and organizational transformation mandate a more accelerated approach to systems integration and providing enabling technologies to support the systemic changes related to reengineering. Hence, in systems integration and reengineering, there is a need to bridge the gap between traditional SDLCs and contemporary demands for the rapid delivery of integrated solutions.

Readdressing the concepts and principles of the traditional SDLC model in the context of reengineering is fundamental to effective project management and successful integration. A new model must provide for a fast-track integration process that successfully leverages technology to realize and support process reengineering and organizational transformation. To be effective in supporting reengineering, the new systems integration methodology (SIM) must provide for the successful melding of reengineering and systems development.

The following characteristics help to define the SIM for reengineering. This chapter presents a new template for managing and performing the systems integration project in the context of reengineering. The model is composed of a five-phase life cycle. The manager must:

1. Establish the integration environment
2. Assess integration requirements and applications design
3. Assess data requirements and design integrated data warehouses

4. Develop and prototype integrated systems
5. Implement integrated systems

Exhibit 1 provides an illustration of the PDIM's five phases. This approach provides for the management of activities, practices, and progress reporting in a process-driven methodology. The model can be applied to the most complex as well as the simplest of integration efforts. Each of the five phases has a specific purpose, objective, work plan, work products, and level of complexity and risk associated with it. The main objective is to create speed and integration to support reengineering. The model comprises over 125 primary work steps and 35 major work products.

The five-phase model for systems integration provides a number of advantages for the organization performing integration and reengineering. First, it is a convenient method for framing the process and scope. Second, the model can be used to organize the activities and resources assigned. Third, the model provides for easy tracking and reporting of activities and progress. It is designed to be performed concurrently with reengineering and supports a concept called continuous integration.

Integration process acceleration is accomplished through the combination of several techniques that are implicit in the process-driven methodology. The process-driven approach to systems integration achieves the rapid deployment and delivery of integrated systems by using many of the reengineering concepts that are applied to business processes and the principles of concurrent engineering. The major principle is to view the systems integration project as a continuous and harmonious process rather than distinct or separate pieces that somehow must fit together. In this regard, the PDIM has the following key attributes:

- Use of concurrent engineering practices and techniques
- Adoption and adaptation of business process reengineering principles
- Front-loading of critical human resources into the design and assessment stages of the integration process
- Use of quality function deployment (QFD) techniques to ensure that design changes are recognized early in the integration process and are minimized later in the effort to help ensure efficiency

The need for front-end loading of critical customers and resources is important to the PDIM. In the traditional model, resources are gradually increased or ramped-up: resources are at a peak near project completion. In contrast, the PDIM assigns and applies the necessary user, external, and internal resources early in the process. This allows a number of activities to be performed concurrently and facilitates the exchange of knowledge and information that support the design process. Acceleration in the integration process is supported in a number of ways. First, greater emphasis is

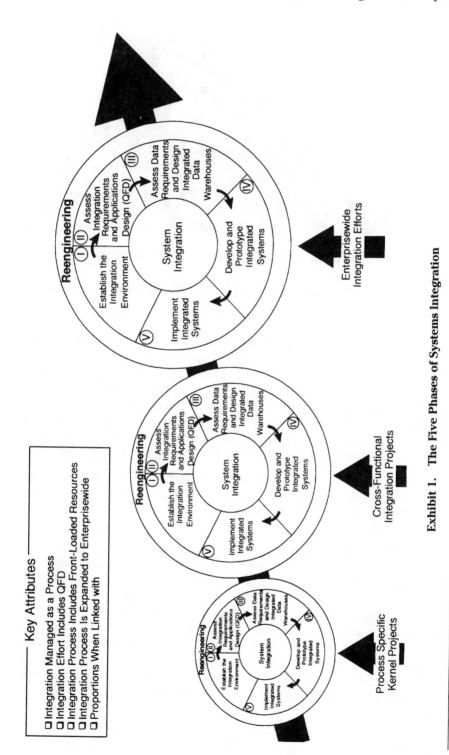

Exhibit 1. The Five Phases of Systems Integration

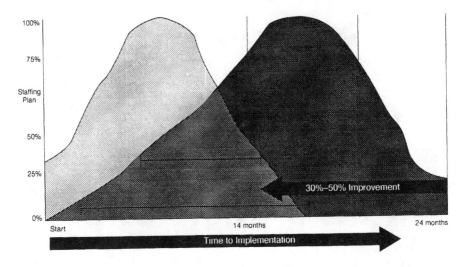

100%

75%

Staffing
Plan

50%

25%

0%

Start

14 months

24 months

30%–50% Improvement

Time to Implementation

Exhibit 2.   The Potential Effects of Front-End-Loaded Integration Projects

placed, during the first two phases, on developing a knowledge of the technical aspects of the integrated environment and developing a robust understanding of the analytical and functional needs of the integration process. A fluent knowledge of the target technical environment and the new to-be processes (i.e., to be supported by the integrated environment) is absolutely essential to the success and efficiency of the integration time line. These phases can be performed concurrently by two different components of the project team with the results converging, as appropriate.

Second, Phase 3 can be performed simultaneously. During this phase, databases and data requirements are commonly identified, defined, and assigned to warehouses and residences in the organization's overall information architecture.

Third, user training, system testing, and performance tuning are all done concurrently in Phase 4. The processes are performed in the context of prototyping, which allows the convergence of users and developers for testing and fine-tuning integrated systems and business processes. Exhibit 2 compares the PDIM and the traditional life cycle methodology in light of the resources and time to completion each requires. In general, the PDIM should help accelerate the integration project by as much as 40 percent when used with effective project management practices and the proper CASE tools. The resources under PDIM are also applied much earlier and in greater numbers than in the traditional methods.

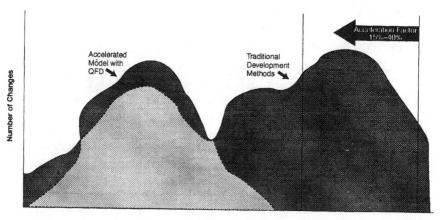

Exhibit 3. The Potential Effect of QFD on Systems Integration

The other major characteristic of this approach is the use of QFD. QFD is integral to any efficient product and process design and can be adapted to the systems integration process. Thus, QFD is primarily a process designed to integrate the "voice of the customer" into the design process. This is critical to accelerating the implementation of systems integration efforts because it can identify changes to the base design of the target environment early in the process. The earlier changes are identified, the better, as early detection limits leapfrogging and scope creep, which can both be fatal to the systems integration process. Exhibit 3 provides an example of QFD's potential impact on the changes and change management process of systems integration as compared to typical methods.

Essential to the QFD process is the creation of cross-functional teams and the front loading of the appropriate resources to the project. The creation of cross-functional teams in QFD, as in business process reengineering and organizational transformation, is fundamental to ensuring that all salient issues and target attributes are visible to the design team. The process ensures that data requirements have been interpreted properly and that relative data is factored into the design. The process also provides for the incorporation of definable measurements and results into the integration process early in the effort. These are important attributes in managing the integration project and ascertaining the project's progress and quality. The combination of these attributes makes QFD an integral component of the accelerated systems integration effort. Some of the other benefits of the QFD process in systems integration include:

- Accelerated design and development times
- Lower project development costs

- Greater stability of product design
- Improved use of resources and higher contribution for those resources
- More complete, visible, and defined target environment and results

The accelerated approach to systems integration requires the melding of the above techniques with the five-phase methodology. In deploying resources and budgeting time, emphasis is placed on techniques designed to ensure that changes are minimized and that long-lead-time activities are identified as early as possible. These activities help ensure that the staffing is adequately applied and that outsourcing long-lead-time activities is given consideration. As a result of using the accelerated approach, the actual implementation of the integrated system becomes a routine activity rather than an event. Implementation and deployment become natural and logical extensions of the overall process and are deemphasized, in contrast to historical approaches. The following distribution of effort is suggested for the five phases of systems integration. The manager must:

1. Establish the integration environment — percent of effort: 10 to 15
2. Assess integration requirements and applications design — percent of effort: 25 to 30
3. Assess data requirements and design integrated data warehouses — percent of effort: 25
4. Develop and prototype integrated systems — percent of effort: 25 to 30
5. Implement integrated systems — percent of effort: 5 to 10

The total distribution of the manager's time should equal 100 percent

PHASE 1: ESTABLISHING THE INTEGRATION ENVIRONMENT

The purpose of this phase is to create the technical environment for systems integration and establish that environment's support and operating structure. The technical environment includes processors, servers, routers, operating systems, personal computers, workstations, memory, controllers and peripheral equipment, database environments, and networks. The technical environment typically involves a three-tier computing architecture and distributed computing environment, which include mainframes or mid-range consolidating processors, local and wide area networks, and workstations in the form of personal computers.

Key Processes

The following key processes are performed in this phase. The staff:

- Conducts initial technical environment orientation and training
- Develops the physical technical environment plan
- Creates the physical technical environment

- Develops the technical environment connectivity and networking plan
- Acquires the technical environment
- Installs the CPU technical environment
- Installs all system software related to the technical environment
- Installs the peripherals
- Conducts the technical environment tests
- Conducts the technical environment connectivity tests
- Conducts all the peripheral tests
- Validates the tests
- Establishes all working areas and partitions as appropriate
- Refines the instruction sets as necessary
- Establishes final configuration of all peripherals
- Readies the production environment
- Certifies the production environment for application readiness

Key Work Products/Results

This phase, upon completion, should produce or demonstrate the following:

- An integration-ready production environment
- A certified operational environment
- Trained operations and support personnel
- Trained applications personnel
- An enabled applications environment

PHASE 2: ASSESSING REQUIREMENTS AND APPLICATION DESIGN AND CAPABILITIES

This phase is designed to develop formal functional requirements and technical specifications for the integration of systems and data. It usually involves the acquisition, design, and installation of software to support reengineered business processes and an integrated systems and data environment. During this phase, a comprehensive assessment is performed to formally document user requirements that enable reengineering. These are linked to immediate needs and new to-be operations and processes.

Once the requirements are documented and new to-be processes defined, a search is performed for enabling software that supports the new processes and end-user requirements. The process usually includes an assessment of both internal software that currently supports a process and external sources that are available from third-party vendors. In performing the assessment, the gaps between the functionality of existing software and the needs of reengineered processes are identified and evaluated in the context of technological feasibility, need, cost-performance, and return on investment. The functional requirements for process reengineering and systems integration are compared and mapped to the specific capabilities of the existing systems that are targets subject to the integration effort. Once mapped, the gaps are assessed and ranked according to priority for severity, and plans are developed to address them.

In performing this phase, the integrator must develop estimates for several key areas, including the number of concurrent users who will be performing functions on the integrated systems, estimates of transaction volumes to be supported by the integrated environment, and data volumes. These are used to direct where, within the overall information technology architecture, the applications and data should reside. This sizing is especially important when considering the use of a client/server integration strategy.

Key Processes

The following key processes are performed in this phase. The staff:

- Develops functional test cases and flows based on to-be process and integration needs
- Develops transaction tests
- Develops flow tests
- Identifies functional linkages
- Develops detailed assessment procedures
- Develops assessment criteria and expected results
- Develops documentation procedures
- Identifies and acquires application software systems and products
- Confirms application software systems and products
- Loads application software products, as needed
- Develops final application software production assessment procedures
- Establishes an application software production testing schedule
- Performs an application software assessment
- Documents performance characteristics
- Assesses the performance compared to standard benchmarks and re-engineering targets
- Documents performance results
- Performs comparative assessment:
  — By function
  — By module
  — By existing system
- Documents assessment results
- Determines interface requirements:
  — To and from flows
  — Timing and frequency
  — Files and data

- Determines enhancement requirements
- Identifies key changes to existing systems and acquired packages
- Evaluates the impact of discrepancies and changes on the project and budget
- Performs retests, as necessary
- Readies the application software environment for integration

Key Work Products/Results

This phase, upon completion, should produce or demonstrate the following:

- Application software products reconciled to contract
- A readied application software system environment
- An initial application software testing and validation
- An integrated application software testing and training environment
- An integrated application software production performance profile
- A comprehensive report on comparative assessment
- Integration and interface requirements
- An application and database enhancement list
- Database requirements
- An economic assessment of changes

PHASE 3: ASSESSING DATA REQUIREMENTS AND DESIGNING INTEGRATED DATA WAREHOUSE ENVIRONMENT

Phase 3 of the SIM is designed to identify, define, redefine, and rationalize data elements necessary for the realization of systems integration. This is perhaps one of the more rigorous processes. It directly involves end users in creating consensus definitions through the comprehensive mapping of existing and to-be data elements to the required and to-be logical and physical structures. The process also requires a normalization of all data definitions and a rationalization of all data elements.

Key Processes

The following key processes are performed in this phase. The staff:

- Establishes data dictionary standards, including:
  - Developing dictionary and definitions
  - Determining logical structures
  - Determining physical structures
  - Identifying logical and physical relationships and dependencies
  - Documenting any unique or unusual data structures, dependencies, uses, and sources
- Identifies all pertinent existing data elements, including
  - Populating data dictionary with definitions
  - Determining logical data structures

- — Determining physical data structures
- — Identifying logical and physical relationships and dependencies
- — Documenting any unique or unusual data structures, dependencies, uses, variants, and sources
- Performs data mapping, including
  - — Identifying common data and equivalents
  - — Identifying data discrepancies
  - — Determining rationalization data requirements
  - — Determining normalization data requirements
  - — Developing discrepancy resolution plan
  - — Developing rationalization and normalization plan
- Performs rationalization and normalization, including:
  - — Determining data normalization rules
  - — Determining data rationalization rules
  - — Developing data rationalizations and normalizations
- Develops an integrated data dictionary
- Develops an initial integration data conversion and population plan

Key Work Products/Results

This phase, upon completion, should produce or demonstrate the following:

- A data map
- Rationalized data
- Normalized data
- A data dictionary
- A database conversion and population plan

PHASE 4: DEVELOPING PROTOTYPE AND INTEGRATED SYSTEMS

Phase 4 of the SIM is designed to develop, test, install, and document integrated systems that support reengineering and new business processes. Systems are developed for the integrated environment and are tested through a prototyping process that links them with new business practices. The prototyping process tests overall systems performance by simulating transaction volumes and the environment that the systems will support.

During Phase 4, a series of comprehensive unit and full-system integration tests are performed on the communications network, applications, and databases.

In developing new applications, the integration process is facilitated by the use of CASE tools, such as PowerBuilder. These tools have capabilities that support systems development through the use of templates, formal rules, and standard presentation techniques. The integration effort also benefits from the use of project management software and database definition and development tools.

Key Processes

The following key processes are performed in this phase. The staff:

- Develops overall integration, programming, and interface specifications
- Develops integration work plans, including:
  — A conceptual overview
  — A program structure
  — Input/output shells
  — Files accessed/generated
  — Frequency/timing
  — Control programs
  — Data structures
- Develops programs, performs integration, and develops:
  — Presentation standards
  — Logic standards
  — Programming specifications
  — Programs and applications
- Documents programs for:
  — System/program
  — User/development
- Performs tests, including
  — Developing test procedures
  — Developing test criteria
  — Performing tests
  — Documenting results
- Resolves all discrepancies
- Validates all programs for production use
- Places validated interfaces in preproduction library
- Finalizes all documentation

Key Work Products/Results

This phase, upon completion, should produce or demonstrate the following:

- Integration and programming specifications
- Final programs
- Production programs and interfaces
- A secure preproduction library
- Formal test plans
- Established criteria
- A formal acceptance
- Substantiated documentation
- Audit trails
- Documented procedures
- A preproduction fine-tuning list

PHASE 5: IMPLEMENTING INTEGRATED SYSTEMS

The objective of this phase of the project is to prepare, convert, and migrate to the integrated application and database environment. The integrated systems environment represents the culmination of the systems integration process. During this phase, enabling solutions are delivered, and users are trained to exploit fully the capabilities of integrated technology and applications.

Key Processes

The following key processes are performed in this phase. The staff:

- Develops formal testing procedures and scenarios, including:
  - Functionality tests
  - Transaction tests
  - Compliance tests
  - Substantive tests
  - Data relationships and validity
  - Access control
  - Interfaces, linkages, and feeds
  - Special tests
- Develops specific transaction loads (i.e., volumes) for performance testing
- Develops testing plan
- Develops documentation procedures, including:
  - Error recording
  - Error resolution
- Establishes performance documentation
- Develops sign-off procedures from:
  - Testing team
  - Project managers
  - Project steering committee
  - End users
  - Quality assurance
- Develops the preproduction fine-tuning list
- Establishes the data conversion schedule
- Develops the data conversion standards and documentation
- Develops a detailed data conversion plan
- Develops the data conversion and testing plan
- Performs data conversion and populates the database structures
- Performs the following tests and validates test results:
  - Transactions tests
  - Validation tests
  - Accuracy tests
  - Read/translation tests
  - Population tests

- Documents test results
- Isolates validated databases for preproduction
- Documents databases
- Develops data administration and management standards

Key Work Products/Results

This phase, upon completion, should produce or demonstrate the following:

- Populated databases
- Validated data
- A documentation trail
- An updated data dictionary
- Populated data repositories
- Completed programs and integrated systems
- A completed multitiered computing environment

SUMMARY

The systems integration process is essential to the reengineering efforts of any process and organization. The approach described above represents an outline for accelerating the systems integration process. The major objective of any integration is the effective melding of technology, applications, and data into a framework that supports cross-functional business processes, accessibility to data, and leaner organizational structures.

However, as in reengineering, speed of delivery is of the essence. The rapid delivery of systems is necessary to support reengineering and to fully exploit the investment in technology. In this regard, the methodology presented must be supported through the use of rapid development techniques and tools and CASE products.

Chapter 58
Salvaging Projects in Trouble

John P. Murray

According to an ancient proverb, "when the ox gets in the ditch, you do what you have to do to get him out." Too often, information technology (IT) application development projects fall into a ditch. When that occurs, organizations must direct every effort toward getting the IT ox out of the ditch.

One reality of managing IT applications projects is the high probability that they will, at some point in their development cycle, fall into difficulty. That difficulty usually comes, or is at least formally recognized, well into the project life cycle. The project team then faces several issues:

1. It must take steps to get the project back on track as quickly as possible.
2. The pressures associated with meeting project deadlines will increase because the issues are being raised late in the project life cycle. Because there will be a push to get the project completed, pressure will grow to remove agreed-upon features and functions. Although in theory these features and functions will simply be "delayed," at least some of them will never be delivered.
3. The project will probably be divided into phases, in an attempt to deliver something by the original deadline. One result is that overall project deadlines will be extended to accommodate the new phases. In many IT installations, because of the new deadlines, one or more planned but not yet started projects for other areas will also be delayed.
4. Organizations will make changes that will negatively affect the project's quality. Examples might include:
   a. Reducing the testing processes and procedures required to ensure high quality. Again, the project team might try to overcome current difficulties by showing some positive results, rationalizing that once the applications are in production, someone can go

    into the applications and conduct the delayed testing. In reality, this will probably not happen.

    b. Attempting to circumvent normal project quality controls. The team might try to avoid strict adherence to development standards, arguing that they are now too time consuming and will delay project progress.

    c. Abandoning project documentation processes, claiming no time to do that work because the project must meet its deadlines. Although documentation will be seen as being delayed rather than abandoned, it is highly unlikely that the documentation will ever be delivered as a completed package.

Beyond the issues related to acknowledging problems late in the development cycle, political concerns will arise. As the intensity to bring the project to completion grows, there will be an effort to place or avoid blame for the project's failure. Given the project team's already high stress level, this will only add to the problem and accomplish nothing concrete. In fact, taking such a tack negatively affects morale and makes people reluctant to identify and present project-related problems from a concern that doing so will jeopardize their careers.

It is far better to direct the time and energy for placing blame toward improving the project. Later, after the project has been salvaged, the team can spend time in assessing the problems' causes and taking corrective action.

THE COST OF QUICK SOLUTIONS

The project team makes a serious mistake when it lowers the project's quality in an attempt to make up lost time. Although the project is behind schedule and must be completed as quickly as possible, taking shortcuts with quality results is a short-term gain at the expense of a long-term loss. While the project might be completed more quickly, the IT product delivered will probably require considerable fine-tuning and general repair in the future to keep it going. In terms of overall project cost, attempting to build in quality after the fact will be more expensive than doing it right the first time around.

Too often, when a project is determined to be facing difficulty, the team moves to a series of "quick fix" solutions. When developers give in to the pressure to meet the project deadline, they will try anything that appears to offer some type of improvement. Usually, applying these "improvements" in an uncontrolled manner, without thinking through all the issues, just makes matters worse, and it becomes more difficult to correct the basic project problems. What happens is that the changes brought about by the improvements add one more layer of confusion to the project problems.

While taking the time to do the work right when the project is facing difficulty will be very frustrating for everyone involved, the frustration will generally last only a short time, and then go away. However, attempting to retrofit quality into the system after it moves to production drags out for a long time, as does the accompanying frustration.

The only way to salvage a troubled project might be to work around normal project development practices. However, there will be costs attached.

- There will be a tendency to rush ahead with changes and adjustments before the team has a clear understanding of the problems' causes. Therefore, time and money will be wasted on problems that have little to do with the real project difficulties.
- The organization will probably see the staffing level as one cause of difficulty, and might therefore add more people to the project. However, this measure requires additional management time and attention to deal with the project's increased communication lines. While bringing on more experienced people might be the right approach, this should be done in a careful, controlled manner. Before adding staff to a project, the decision-maker must have a clear idea of why people need to be added, and their exact roles and responsibilities.
- There will likely be increased senior management attention directed at the troubled project — a mixed blessing. Senior managers can help cut through constraints to move the project forward and provide additional, needed resources. However, they might have little understanding of the issues, yet be ready with quick (usually wrong) solutions.

In dealing with troubled IT projects, the easy answer is to avoid the situation. However, experienced IT project managers know that keeping projects out of difficulty is often beyond the project management team's control. And, although the most pragmatic approach to IT project management is to provide adequate project discipline and control from the onset so the project does not fall into difficulty, the issue being explored here is recognizing when a project is in difficulty and developing approaches that will bring the project back on track.

Many organizations realize that the project will fall into difficulty at some point in the development cycle. When IT projects do come apart, actions must be taken to restore them as quickly and efficiently as possible. The key to successfully restoring troubled IT projects is to determine as early as possible in the development cycle that the project is beginning to deteriorate, and to then move quickly and decisively to take corrective action, assessing and installing the needed correction processes in a disciplined and controlled manner.

RECOGNIZING PROJECT DIFFICULTIES

A difficult aspect of dealing with a failing IT project is to recognize that the project is indeed in trouble; this is all too often an emotional issue. Usually, those managing the project simply deny that the project has begun to slip (possibly in the sincere belief that it is not in trouble). Alternatively, they might admit to some slippage, but state that it will be made up and the project will be brought back on schedule.

When people are just beginning to recognize project difficulties, they will make little attempt to develop a plan to overcome the problems. Instead, they suggest that time (and perhaps additional effort) will help correct the problems. This approach often rests on a false assumption. In reality, management is depending on luck, rather than factually assessing the project's status.

Accurately assessing the project status is also difficult because, early on, project managers may have incorrectly reported the project as being on or ahead of schedule. After reporting favorable project progress, project managers will find it difficult to admit that the project is in trouble. Usually, however, believing that things will work out becomes an untenable position, as the project's failure becomes highly apparent to people outside the project team.

Once the project team recognizes that the project is in trouble, it can begin work on correcting the problems and salvaging the project. However, there must first be a clear understanding of the problems' causes. Unfortunately, when projects fall into difficulty, people tend to jump to an apparent solution without understanding the issues involved; this will only make the problems worse. A more effective approach is to investigate what went wrong and develop a solution that addresses the real problems.

A team that rushes to a solution without clearly understanding the causes of the difficulty usually addresses the problem's symptoms, rather than the problem itself. An example is when application testing uncovers a series of difficulties. The team may well assume that the problem stems from poorly written code, which shows up in testing. The obvious approach to improvement is to go through the code, find the errors, and make the needed corrections. However, while the code seems to be the problem, in fact, the trouble may be tied to the established testing processes.

In this example, rushing to redo the code will not help; it will only make the problem worse. Where the issue is seen as poor coding, the team will waste both time and effort on "correcting" flawed coding (which, in fact, is not flawed at all). When the team discovers that the coding did not cause the problem, the correction work must be backed out, and the changed code re-tested. Thus, moving to an obvious but incorrect solution for expediency is the wrong approach to the problem.

STABILIZING THE ENVIRONMENT

While it is understandable that people want to overcome project problems as quickly as possible, the team should take the time to identify the real problem causes, rather than jump to a quick solution. Once the causes have been identified, the team should verify that the apparent cause is indeed what needs correction. The final step in the process is developing a plan for making the needed corrections.

In salvaging the project, the team should avoid panic. Of course, there will be pressure to correct the problems and get the project back on schedule. And it requires determination and discipline on the part of the project manager to hold off pressure from other areas, while identifying the problem's causes.

An immediate step in bringing the project back on track must be to temporarily stop or freeze all project work. Because the cause of the problems is unknown, doing any work would simply add to the project problems. The idea is to contain damage to the project while looking for workable solutions.

What can project members do while the project is frozen? Of course, some team members will help investigate and verify the causes of project difficulty and help develop the improvement plan. In addition, some project areas can be fine-tuned in the interim. For example, the team can review documentation, bringing it up-to-date and clarifying it. The team can also review testing plans, both technical and business cases, developing and strengthening them. Developers can also examine project specifications and requirements to determine if they are still correct, or if anything should be added. Finally, as a last resort, project team members can be temporarily shifted to other work within the IT department.

Particularly with large IT projects, freezing the project may not be seen as a viable option because there are so many staff members working on the project. Managers might argue that everyone must be kept busy or those people taken off the project temporarily will be permanently lost to the project. In such cases, the project will likely be broken, with predictably unfortunate results. It is a poor reflection on management when it is not an option to freeze a project to discover and correct the problems' causes, although there is a strong case for the freeze.

There may well be defensiveness on the part of those working on the troubled project, and strong pressure to get the project back on track. The stabilization process may involve appointing a new project manager. This can substantially benefit the project because the new person has no connection to the project and can therefore make objective judgments about what he or she is told and observes. In addition, a new project manager can more easily take a firm stance about investigating what has occurred, before making project adjustments. Also, a new manager will not have pre-conceptions or assumptions about what is or is not causing the problems; such prejudgments can otherwise cloud the analysis.

THREE CRITICAL CRITERIA

In dealing with IT applications development projects that have fallen into difficulty, accomplishing anything of substance requires that three criteria be met:

1. The team must admit that the project is in difficulty and corrective action is needed, despite earlier representations to the contrary.
2. The best approach is to shut down the project until there has been an assessment of the project's status and the issues associated with its falling behind schedule.
3. A plan must be developed to begin the correction process so that the project can proceed.

It is exceedingly difficult to begin the correction process unless people accept that the project is in difficulty and understand that steps must be taken to make corrections. People will argue about whether the project is really in trouble, and why it got that way. Such arguing is counterproductive because one argument will simply lead to others. Therefore, someone in authority must declare that the project is in difficulty, that it will be frozen until the problems have been adequately investigated and understood, and that the process of correcting the situation can begin. While this approach is not easy, particularly in light of mounting pressure, it is the right course of action.

Determining what has gone wrong will take patience. The key to success is in asking the right questions, and testing the answers against the project's apparent conditions. Care must be exercised here because the answers will be based on peoples' interpretation of the facts, or their beliefs, which may not be accurate. In addition, the atmosphere will be tense, thus people may be reluctant to admit that their work may have contributed to the difficulty.

For example, someone might state that testing the applications and changes are not part of the problem because the testing schedules have been met. Yet a testing review may reveal poor-quality testing processes. While test plans were developed for both technical and business unit testing and those plans were followed, the testing plans lacked the rigor to test some important conditions. Because the criteria were not sufficient to meet project requirements, portions of the applications are flawed.

If it is accepted that testing is not part of the problem, nothing will be done to verify testing quality, and testing problems will not be identified until later. In addition, considerable time and effort may be spent on other areas of project difficulty before the true testing conditions are identified. The net result will be a delay in making the needed project improvements.

Although it is tedious to question and search for the correct answers to the causes of project difficulty, it must be done before conclusions about corrective action can be made. The first step is in understanding what has actually gone wrong, rather than what appears to have gone wrong. As possible causes are considered, there must be a mechanism to test these assumptions against reality. That mechanism is to ask probing questions and, where appropriate, require concrete proof of the statements being presented.

Once the problems have been identified, they should be prioritized as to their effect on the effort to bring the project back on track. A lengthy list of items will be developed in a short time; all that bear upon the project difficulties should be recorded. Then the items should be analyzed to determine those that must be addressed immediately and those that can be set aside for correction at some later time.

Beyond identifying the problem issues and setting the correction priorities, the linkages between identified items must be analyzed. IT projects' inherent complexity tends to lock many parts of the project together; therefore, there must be assurance that correcting an item in one part of an application will not negatively affect other processes in that application or others. After all, it is possible that correcting one application in a system will disrupt processing connected to that application in some other system. This is another reason why the team should understand what went wrong before starting corrections.

DEVELOPING THE SALVAGE PLAN

Once the project problems have been identified and prioritized, a correction plan must be developed. The team must allow sufficient time for and attention to developing the plan to ensure that what it proposes will work, and that the order of the various correction components is correct. The goal is a logical progression in the order of applying changes to ensure that, as the changes are applied, they do not disrupt either the prior changes or some other area of the system. The team should avoid a process that forces backtracking to other parts of the applications within the project as the result of changes made.

The plan should also appropriately control the changes. Several basic planning rules can assist in this control, to include:

- A member of the project team should be assigned the responsibility of managing the application of changes once they have been identified and prioritized.
- Changes should be applied one at a time.
- Sufficient time (at least one processing cycle) should be set between the introduction of changes.
- Two members of the project team — one representing IT and one representing the business unit — must certify that the changes being applied are working correctly.
- A log should be maintained of all changes in the order in which they have been applied, as a method of tracking change problems should they arise after the changes have been installed.

Once a plan is developed, it should be submitted to all the parties involved to solicit comments about its appropriateness. Consistency in the development and execution of the plan must be maintained, just as a consistent and disciplined approach was required to determine the causes of project failure. When everyone involved has had an opportunity to respond to the plan, it should be published, and copies should be given to all project team members. Everyone should understand that, from this point on, the project will be managed according to the plan.

DEVELOPING A STRONG COMMUNICATION PROCESS

In gaining control of a failing project, a clear communication process is absolutely critical. Communication should be addressed by regular meetings of the project team members and via written status reports that can be distributed among those outside the project team who need to be kept informed of progress.

As part of the communication process, someone on the project must be assigned the task of recording and maintaining the status of all outstanding issues. Those issues will include identified problems, required additions or deletions to the applications within the project, status of the work in process, and identification of all application abnormalities. Each member of the project team should have specific assignments, and each project team meeting should provide an update of the work being done, as well as progress being made or difficulties encountered.

Daily meetings should be held involving all members of the project team, until the project manager decides that the team is making sufficient progress to meet less frequently. There will probably be some resistance; IT people generally see meetings as a waste of time. However, if the meetings are well run, they will provide some real benefits. First, if everyone involved with the project is in the same room at the same time, hearing the same reporting of status and problems, there is an opportunity for people who disagree to voice their opinions. This can be helpful, especially if the person presenting a given solution does not understand its ramifications, and the solution is therefore incorrect.

It is important to carefully maintain the list of outstanding project items. Problems that may arise as people work through solutions to these items must also be recorded, along with the solutions when they are found. In large projects, it might take considerable effort just to maintain an understanding of what each participant is doing. It can prove disconcerting to find out too late that work has not even been started, when it was assumed to be in process, or even completed.

RECOMMENDED COURSE OF ACTION

Virtually all IT projects experience some level of difficulty during their development. If the project's process has been well managed throughout, dealing with the problems that arise and keeping the project on track usually can be handled as part of the normal course of project development. In such cases, although project deadlines might need to be adjusted, the projects move to the production environment within a reasonable timeframe and with acceptable quality.

For those projects that encounter great difficulty, there must be an emphasis on getting the work back on track as rapidly as possible. However, correcting the problems and moving on require an accurate understanding of what has gone wrong, rather than what people might believe has gone wrong. Once the problems have been identified and understood, the salvage process can begin. This process starts with development of the plan to make the needed corrections and to ensure that the plan is being followed.

Salvaging failing IT projects is a difficult process that calls for careful analysis of the problems involved. The critical component of project salvage is in developing an understanding of the causes of failure, and preparing and following a plan that will overcome the problems and put the project back on course. It requires strong management skill and patience to overcome the difficulties posed by a troubled project. The real keys to success are understanding that broken IT projects can be repaired and having the will to make that happen.

Chapter 59
Choosing a Systems Integrator

Michael A. Mische

Selecting a systems integrator can be a perplexing, emotional, and time-consuming process. Not only is the competition among integrators increasing, but the proliferation and rate of change of technology have created countless options and choices. In less than a decade, technology has changed from a field dominated by mainframe computers, rigid applications, and highly complex and intricate interfaces to one that is defined by end-user computing, client/server components, workstations, enterprise-wide networks, and data sharing. There is very little agreement as to what actually constitutes a systems integration project and systems integration services. Integrators themselves disagree about what constitutes systems integration, and few can define it in contractual terms rather than as a substantive service. Whereas once organizations seeking integration consultants had only the Big Four accounting firms, hardware and software vendors, and a few regional and boutique contract programming firms from which to select, today's choices are varied and constantly growing. Thus, the industry has a real need for an effective method to help guide the organization through the choices and options in the systems integration and service provider marketplace.

This chapter provides a perspective on how to evaluate and select a systems integrator. The seven principles discussed here provide a simple and convenient method for the selection process, and have been developed as a result of experience on both sides of the systems integration table.

THE NEED FOR A SYSTEMS INTEGRATOR

Confronted by never-ending technical and business challenges, end users and information management and technology (IM&T) organizations are finding themselves under enormous pressures to improve performance and accelerate the delivery of enabling systems. No longer is it sufficient for the IM&T organization to simply react to users and supply systems and technologies to satisfy yesterday's needs. In the decade of organizational transformation, IM&T organizations must anticipate their users and function as enablers of process and organizational change. To address their needs, many organizations rushed into situational management and development programs, such as total quality management, computer-aided systems engineering, joint application designs, client/server technologies, and a host of others, only to be disappointed by results that fell far short of oversold benefits and inflated expectations. Many found that the costs involved greatly exceeded the benefits derived; still others learned of the "hidden" costs.

Uncertain, understaffed, or lacking the resources necessary to support an integration effort successfully, many organizations are turning to external consultants that provide systems integration and reengineering services. With daily per-person billing rates ranging from several hundred dollars to over $10,000, selecting an integrator can be a confusing and difficult challenge. Systems integrators can contribute much to the process and the organization. Used properly, the systems integrator can assume the majority of the project risk, supplement or supersede internal resources, and deliver turnkey results. Systems integrators can also contribute perspective to their clients' business processes and internal management capabilities. The organization can engage the appropriate integrator and find its money well spent; the organization that chooses the wrong integrator not only wastes its money but finds that its vision and project may never be realized. Thus, there are risks and advantages to using a systems integrator. Some of the more significant benefits are that integrators:

- Bring a fresh perspective and energy to any systems integration project, which can be invigorating and extremely beneficial to the organization and overall integration process
- Have stamina and a clearly defined role; they are not distracted by the everyday business needs or organizational politics
- Have tools and methods that can be brought to the organization in various forms and as the need requires
- Can be held accountable for their performance on a legal, moral, financial, and professional basis. Unlike internal resources, organizations have a legal recourse with integrators.

THE PRINCIPLES OF SELECTING A SYSTEMS INTEGRATOR

In light of the variety and diversity of systems integrators, selecting and effectively using an integrator's services are challenges, even for the most experienced organization. A natural starting point is with any existing relationships that the organization may have with integrators. The buyers of services (i.e., the clients) and providers (i.e., integrators) know one another, their cultures, and their capabilities. Presumably, they have an established rapport and a track record of working together. Nevertheless, each integration situation is different, and the needs for an integrator may be different. The following 12 principles provide a basic framework for evaluating the capabilities of the prospective integrator.

PRINCIPLE NUMBER 1: THERE ARE FIVE TYPES OF SYSTEMS INTEGRATORS

Although the market is undeniably large and varied, one could easily group systems integrators into one of five basic types of systems integration firms:

1. Blue Chip management consulting firms
2. Big Four public accounting firms, many of which have now spun off or become limited liability partnerships for their consulting services
3. Global integrators
4. Proprietary vendors
5. Contractors

Briefly, the Blue Chip firms, which include such pedigree names as A.T. Kearney; McKinsey, Bain & Co.; and Booz, Allen & Hamilton, are known as breeding grounds for extensive intellectual talent and strategic management savvy rather than as technical service providers of information technology. Although the Blue Chip firms are a source for systems integration talent, that is not their major area of internal investment and personnel development. In this regard, Blue Chip firms may not necessarily be the best resource for systems integration services.

The once Big Eight and now the Big Four accounting/consulting firms represent a large pool of systems integration talent. These firms include such stalwarts as Andersen Consulting (now Accenture), Ernst & Young, and PricewaterhouseCoopers. Although Big Four firms are predominantly known for their accounting and tax services, they are also known for their extensive consulting capabilities. With revenues in excess of $1.5 billion, Accenture is one of the largest providers of integration services, and is the dominant force in the Big Four arena. Big Four clients typically include middle- and upper-level managers in both the private sector and government. Billing rates per person for systems integration projects generally range from $1000 per day per person to more than $6000 for certain senior partners. However, Big Four firms have a reputation for discounting their rates, as competition within the peer group is fierce. Discounts of 25 to 50 percent of their standard hourly rates are not unusual, especially for long-duration projects and audit clients. The Big Four represent a tried-and-true source for integration services.

Global integrators are a new breed of firms that are quickly establishing themselves as dominant forces in the marketplace. In a sense, global integrators are a hybrid of the Blue Chip and traditional Big Four firms in that they can bring both highly skilled management consulting services and technical IM&T service providers to their clients. These firms include such organizations as IBM Consulting, CSC, TSC, SHL Systemhouse, and EDS. Many global integrators, such as EDS and TSC, began as technical service providers and evolved into firms that meld technology with business processes. Their rate structures are competitive with the Big Four and Blue Chip firms. Global integrators are quickly becoming some of the best sources for systems integration assistance and general management consulting in the marketplace today.

Proprietary vendors include hardware and software manufacturers and value-added resellers that provide integration and management consulting services. However, their capabilities tend to be restricted to their own product offerings or specialized product line and are usually less extensive with respect to general management consulting issues and services. As captive service providers, proprietary vendor integrators have a distinct orientation toward making their products work and do not necessarily concentrate on making sweeping changes to the organization through reengineering and reinvention. Therefore, the organization runs the risk that vendor integrators can be less dimensional in their approach to integration, which may lead them to miss broader opportunities for radical improvement and competitive advantage through integration and reengineering business processes. Professional management consulting services, at least in the classical context of the Blue Chip, global integrator, and Big Four firms, are not necessarily their main stream of business or source of revenue. Hardware and software vendors make the majority of their money from the sale of software, new releases, and annual maintenance fees, not from hourly rates for systems integration and project management professionals. The rates span the spectrum from several hundred dollars per day per person to over $2000 per day per person. In all but a few situations, the use of vendor integrators may not be as desirable as the alternative sources for systems integration talent.

Finally, the fifth group of systems integrators is composed of the sole practitioner and contract programming firm. Contractors include a growing group of individuals who have a particular industry orientation and specialized technical or application system skill set. Contractors can sell their talents either directly to the organization or to a contract programming firm that brokers them to a needful organization. Contractors are generally used in a specific role and work under the client's direction. The billing rates for the contractor firms are quite low compared with the other types of systems integrators. Some rates range from a low of $35 per hour for a programmer to as much as $125 per hour for an experienced project manager. Contractors can be most effective when the engaging organization is supplementing its own resources and has an extremely strong project management and quality assurance function in place.

PRINCIPLE NUMBER 2: SYSTEMS INTEGRATORS ARE COMMODITY SERVICE PROVIDERS

The services, capabilities, and qualifications among systems integrators are all similar. Core services, which relate to the technical aspects of integration and project management, are fairly uniform among integrators. Virtually all types of systems integrators can provide the same technical resources, similar types of references, and experienced project managers. The issue is understanding what combination of skills and talents is needed by the project and matching them with integrators.

As a starting point for evaluating and selecting a systems integrator, the organization should understand that system integrators have four very important qualities:

1. They possess a number of specialized skills and capabilities.
2. Their marketable products include time and people — and they charge for them.
3. They possess tools, techniques, and information that organizations may lack or can only partially assemble.
4. They can deliver turnkey results while usually assuming the risk of the project.

This is where the subtle differences among integrators can be found, which can help differentiate integrators in a relatively homogeneous marketplace. These differences are primarily the result of structure, management, development of personnel and methodologies, and the transference of project risk to the integrator.

The Big Four, Blue Chip, and global integrators are primarily professional consulting firms. These firms have established standards of work and a well-defined structure of responsibility and accountability. They have the capability to manage, assume the risk of, and perform multimillion-dollar and multiyear projects. They can manage, supply personnel, and deliver completed projects to their clients anywhere at any time. These firms are in the full-time business of providing professional services and are constantly seeking, training, cultivating, and employing highly talented and well-compensated individuals to provide consulting and integration services to their clients. They have extensive infrastructures and organizational arrangements that provide not only a high level of client service but also the structure and management to develop personnel, manage resources, develop intellectual capital, evaluate project status and progress, and assess the quality of work performed. They offer their professionals well-defined career paths, and the internal competition among the employees and partners/officers helps ensure a steady stream of competent and responsive resources.

Most importantly, these firms have two other major operational elements. They measure their consulting performance not only based on client feedback but according to their own standards, which are often more rigorous than those of the client. Also, they have internal methods for managing risk, assuring quality, measuring progress, and generating value for the client. Clients that hire this type of firm generally transfer all or a significant portion of project risk to the integrator.

In contrast, vendor and contractor integrators tend to be less formal in their organizational structure and their work performance. They normally have partial, not complete or significant, responsibility for the project. Similarly, they rarely assume the majority of risk for the entire project. Contract integrators are usually assigned to an internal team and function under the management of the client rather than their sourcing firm. Typically, their standards of work, performance, and quality are those of the client, and their performance is based on client acceptance of their skills.

PRINCIPLE NUMBER 3: THE CLIENT MUST UNDERSTAND THE INTEGRATOR'S FEE STRUCTURE AND BILLING PRACTICES

Systems integrators generate their revenues and earnings based on hourly or daily rates and the mix of staff assigned to a project. In general, the more experienced and advanced in the organization the person is, the higher the billing rate. Typically, the Big Four, Blue Chip, and systems integration firms try to achieve at least a 3.0 multiple between their cost of service for an employee and the employee's billing rate to the client. For example, if a project manager at a Big Four accounting firm were compensated at $100,000 per year, plus benefits and burdens of an additional 35 percent, the total cost of service would be $135,000, or $64.65 per hour, based on a standard of 2088 hours per year. For client billing purposes, the project manager's minimum standard hourly rate would be at least $195 per hour, plus administrative recovery and add-on charges of $10 to $50 or more per hour. Thus, the hourly rate to the client would be anywhere from $205 to $300. Again, discounts should be available for large projects and long-term client commitments. In general, the greater the duration, the greater the discount, especially when Big Four audit clients are involved.

The systems integrator measures project profitability by using a concept called realization, which is computed by multiplying the number of hours or days the person worked by the person's standard billing rate to derive the theoretical total standard revenue generated by that person. This amount plus total expenses serves as the denominator of a profitability equation. The total fee at standard plus expenses is divided into the total amount of cash collections in addition to expenses reimbursed on the project and received from the client. Another method of computing realization is to consider net fees collected divided by total fees at standard. Either method provides a profitability picture of the vendors' economics. For example, if a $300-per-hour Big Four manager worked 100 hours on a project, the total chargeable time would generate a revenue of $30,000, at standard rates. If the Big Four firm billed and collected the entire amount of fees, net of expenses, the realization percentage would be 100 percent, and the firm's profitability would be enormous.

Conversely, if there were a fixed-fee contract, a set budget with not-to-exceed limits, or a dispute about the hours worked or quality produced, profitability could be lower. For example, if $30,000 of chargeable time revenue were generated, but only $15,000, net of expenses, was collected, the realization on the project by the systems integrator would only be a dismal 50 percent — a generally unprofitable figure by the time fully-loaded costs were applied.

In negotiating rates with a systems integration vendor, the concept of realization must be understood and used to negotiate discounts. A client should never pay the standard rates of the systems integrator, as there are numerous alternatives in the marketplace. In negotiating with a potential integrator, the client always should ask the integrator for its standard rates as a basis to negotiate lower rates. As noted, Big Four accounting firms can be aggressive discounters and have significant room to negotiate. As a rule, the more resources supplied by the integrator and the longer the duration of the project, the greater the discount. In general, if the project is extensive, the integrator has higher chargeability per person assigned to the project and can afford to give greater discounts.

Chargeability, the second major element in the integrator's profitability equation, is the lifeblood of any professional services firm, as it represents the percent of time that an employee, partner, or officer actually bills to clients. For example, if a Big Four project manager billed 1535 hours to clients during the firm's fiscal year, the chargeability would be 75.3 percent, based on a 2088-hour year. Considering a standard billing rate of $300 per hour, the firm would expect to generate $750,000 in service revenues from the project manager — measured against a cost of service of $135,000. In general, integrators, especially the Big Six, try to achieve a minimum of 60 percent chargeability per person, depending on the organizational level and the individual's responsibilities.

PRINCIPLE NUMBER 4: THE CLIENT MUST KNOW ITS REQUIREMENTS AND HOW TO USE AN INTEGRATOR

No guidelines, rules, or criteria guide the decision as to when to use a systems integrator. The classic method of using the systems integrator involves securing an integrator's services on a well-defined assignment or project. Generally, organizations that use this traditional approach outsource their integration requirements and risk to the integrator in the form of a stand-alone project. The client must have a well-defined project with tightly defined schedules, deliverables, and performance measurements or it leaves itself open to the discretion of the integrator.

Many organizations agonize over what type of systems integration firm to hire. The larger firms certainly have more assets, bigger payrolls, established practices, and greater overhead than the smaller firms. However, as many organizations learned through their own downsizing efforts, bigger is not necessarily better, quantity does not translate into quality, and having an office in every city does not guarantee a service advantage to the client. For example, many of the Blue Chip and Big Four firms have downsized and closed offices. The pervasive considerations and guiding criteria in selecting a systems integrator are the credentials, capabilities, and commitment of the individuals assigned directly to the project.

The capabilities and personal qualities of the individual consultants combined with the philosophy and operating structure of the firm are the determining factors in rendering exceptional services. Smaller systems integration and contractor firms can provide the same services and the appropriate depth of resources as those of the Big Four, global integrators, or Blue Chip firms. In certain situations, smaller firms may be better positioned to provide higher quality service, more experienced consultants, and lower rates because the pressures of profitability (i.e., realization) and keeping masses of junior and less experienced people busy (i.e., chargeability) are not present. The contractor firms have an ability to staff client needs selectively with the "best of the best" rather than just relying on internally available resources. Because of their operating structures, the large firms rely on personnel leverage; the greater the leverage of junior to senior resources, the more advantageous it is to the larger firm. This relationship, combined with internal performance pressures to maintain high levels of chargeability — which is common to all of the large, professional service firms — may not represent the best situation for the client. Alternatively, the larger firms have instant access to resources. Also, depending on the unique circumstances of the client, using a big-name firm may be desirable when the organization is seeking insurance, expects to be or is in litigation, believes it is advantageous to extend such an existing business relationship to an audit, or needs masses of people to accomplish very controllable and homogeneous tasks.

PRINCIPLE NUMBER 5: THE CLIENT MUST UNDERSTAND WHO WILL DO THE WORK

The relationship of selling integration services to the actual performance of the services is a key concern for many organizations considering the use of a systems integrator. Typically, in the large Blue Chip and Big Four firms, selling is the responsibility of the partners, officers, and a select group of senior managers. A few firms have even tried using professional salespeople. Because of their orientation and emphasis on personnel leverage, the majority of client work is usually performed by less experienced staff and mid-level management personnel rather than the partners or officers. Contractors and sole practitioners generally service their clients with professionals who have extensive industry and consulting experience. Therefore, it is always important to know exactly who will work on the project, when they will work on it, and how much time they will spend on it.

PRINCIPLE NUMBER 6: PROSPECTIVE CUSTOMERS, SHAREHOLDERS, AND CLIENTS DO NOT KNOW OR CARE WHO THE SYSTEMS INTEGRATOR IS

Some clients are sensitive to the stature and name of the systems integrator. Others may look for public relations and advertising value in using a well-known name. However, the use of a systems integrator's name in marketing and advertising provides little, if any, advantage in attracting prospective customers or clients. Most people have no or, at best, only limited knowledge of systems integrators. In the final analysis, customers and clients judge the organization and firm by its performance and services rather than by the name of the consultant used to integrate technology. Customers and clients only care if the system works, and shareholders are only concerned if the integration process failed or was significantly over budget or past due. In the case of failure, they may find greater legal recourse if a larger firm was used.

PRINCIPLE NUMBER 7: THE CLIENT MUST UNDERSTAND VALUE AND GET A GUARANTEE

Judging the quality of an integration firm is difficult, as all firms have positive and negative client experiences and successful and unsuccessful projects. The client must evaluate an integration firm by its consultants and their personal commitment to the organization and its values, not just by its name or technical prowess. All system integrators have experience, methodologies, and credentials, and all claim quality service. All have positive and negative client references. Usually, they have been successful, at least from a technical perspective, in the process of integration, or they simply would not be in business. However, technical competency is not the issue; the process used by the integrator is the most important aspect of the experience. Systems integration firms almost always tout the value of their services and the results of their efforts. However, very few, if any, offer any tangible proof of value or guarantees.

Warranties and guarantees are difficult to craft in professional service industries. Generally, Blue Chip firms do not warrant or guarantee work, the results of their work, or client satisfaction. American Institute of CPA rules prohibit Big Four accounting firms from offering guarantees. Very few contractors can afford the financial implications of a warranty if something goes wrong, and software vendors usually invoke their products' disclaimers. However, most integrators stand behind their work and usually seek to enhance their value to their clients.

Performing a thorough check of the vendor's references is another method of performing due diligence on a prospective systems integrator. However, references can be deceiving, as they are often based on subjective criteria, impressions, and hearsay. When checking an integrator's references, the client should develop a complete perspective of the experience curve, both positive and negative, and develop an understanding of what the integrator did well and where it may have fallen short. When exploring negative experiences, more important than learning what went wrong is understanding how the integrator reacted and responded. References are opinions and should be used only to calibrate thoughts and impressions — not as the basis for the decision.

Even for the most experienced and discriminating of clients, asking the correct questions can greatly improve the prospects of engaging a responsive integrator. Using the following simple but revealing 12 rules to ask the right questions will facilitate the effort and enhance the process.

Ask Specific, Direct, and Detailed Questions. A major portion of the integrator's role and test of competency is communication style and the ability to listen, interpret, and spontaneously respond to changing client demands, attitudes, and concerns. The client should beware of integrators that appear to have strong biases, as their independence and objectivity could be compromised when evaluating needs, direction, and available alternatives.

Understand the Integrator's Background, Experience, and Familiarity with the Issues. A major portion of the integrator's job is to bring perspective to the client's organization. The client should strive to engage integrators that have a broad perspective and demonstrate empathy. The client should avoid integrators that have a narrow perspective or rely on a limited knowledge base, and should be careful of integrators that have "canned" answers for everything or have to do an inordinate level of research.

Understand the Integrator's Approach, Work Plan, Work Products, and Deliverables. The client should relate the consultant's people, process, and work products to the organization's needs and expectations and verify that the integrator is not providing generic methods, standard products, "warmed-over" reports, or a cookbook approach. If senior resources are needed, the client must ensure that the integrator provides them and does not attempt to "bait and switch" the project with less experienced junior people. The client must normalize the integrator's responsibilities and the engaging organization's expectations in a contract and stipulate the work plan, deliverables, time schedules, and all costs in the contract. The client should always reduce the scope, deliverables, and timing to written form.

Assess the Individual Personality and Chemistry of Those Assigned to the Project. The client should evaluate whether the integrator is open and honest and whether it is trying to establish a personal rapport. The client should check for whether the integrator has a personal interest in the success of the project and evaluate the integrator's ability to listen, interpret, restate, and provide feedback. References for both successful and unsuccessful projects are important, as is an understanding of how the integrator responded to clients. The client should seek integrators that will make a personal commitment to the organization.

Match the Integrator's Technical and Managerial Abilities to the Organization's Needs. The organization engaging the systems integrator must be absolutely realistic about and confident of its needs, objectives, and scope of the integration effort and technical requirements. The organization must be honest in the assessment of the need for an integrator, what role the integrator will play, and what type of integrator is needed. Being the world's foremost integrator of mainframe technology probably will not help when the organization is trying to implement client/server components if the mainframe is not the issue. Similarly, engaging a technical integration firm to solve fundamental business and organizational issues will not achieve much either.

Understand the Integrator's Internal Performance Measures and Quality Measures. When selecting a systems integrator, the client should determine how the integrator, in turn, selects and assigns personnel to the project. Determining the average number of years of experience as a consultant and systems integrator and billing rates is also important. The client should determine the basis and criteria used to match consultants to the needs of the project; the client should also address such issues as whether the integration firm stresses chargeable time, pressuring consultants to force more work and additional fees.

The client should challenge the integrator's objectivity on all issues. If the integrator represents or has business relationships with other vendors, the client should find out what those relationships are and how integrity and independence are maintained. Clients should avoid systems integrators that are self-centered or driven by their internal performance measures for personal billing targets, the next sale, or client profitability (i.e., realization), as they may compromise their commitment to the client's best interests.

Develop a Comprehensive Understanding of the Project. The client must stipulate the following in a contract:

- How the work is to be performed, the work plan, and when the work is to be performed
- What deliverables will be produced, what they will be composed of, and what tangible results will be produced
- Who will do the work, staff responsibilities, experience, organization level, and billing rate
- How many personnel days or hours are estimated to complete the project and the basis of the estimate
- Who, in the integrator's organization, is personally accountable for the quality of work, performance of the people assigned, and budget
- How much the total fees are and what the rates are by hour or day for each person assigned to the project

Determine Whether the Integrator Is Considered an Expert or Just Highly Experienced. The client should determine whether the integrator has rendered expert testimony in litigation cases, has been litigated against as a direct result of its performance, or has appeared as an expert before legislative bodies, such as state legislatures or the U.S. Congress.

Determine Whether the Integrator Is a Leader or an Accomplished Journeyman. Several questions should be posed. Does the integrator publish? Does the integrator actively research and develop ideas, concepts, and approaches? What intellectual capital does the integrator contribute that is important, new, or different? What intangible contributions can the integrator make to the project and the engaging organization?

Understand How the Integrator Establishes the Fees and Rates for Its Professionals. Questions that help determine this include: Are fees based on hourly or daily rates? What is the integrator's rationale and justification for the rates? Why does the integrator believe that it is worth the rate charged? What are the integrator's multiples for cost of service and billing rates? What are the chargeability goals of the integrator? What component of the rate is overhead? Are expenses truly out-of-pocket or are there blanket add-on charges for administration?

Develop a Knowledge of the Integrator's Quality Commitment and Client Satisfaction Processes. The client should determine how the integrator measures quality and client satisfaction. If surveys are used, who reviews them and how quickly? Surveys take weeks, and sometimes months, and are usually performed, evaluated, and responded to far too late in the process. What does the integrator believe the client's role to be in the project, quality, and satisfaction?

Determine How Many Other Clients the Integrator Has. The integrator may have many clients that may be doing well; however, its attention to detail and individual situations may be compromised. A key measure of an integrator's success is not growth, number of people, profits, or how many clients a firm has, but how many potential clients the integrator turns away and why.

SUMMARY

There is little doubt that systems integrators can provide valuable service and resources to the organization. However, they must be selected and managed carefully. Above all, the client organization must be realistic and honest in its self-assessment. It must also have a clear and stable understanding of its project, the scope, and major deliverables to be received. In selecting a systems integrator, the decision should be based on value to be received, not prices charged. In the final analysis, the client has choices and controls not only the process but the results.

Chapter 60
Service Level Management Links IT to the Business
Janet Butler

Downtime is becoming unacceptably expensive as businesses increasingly depend on their information technology (IT) services for mission-critical applications. As user availability and response time requirements increase dramatically, service level management (SLM) is becoming the common language of choice for communication between IT and end users. In addition, to foster the growing focus on the user, SLM is moving rapidly into the application arena, turning from its traditional emphasis on system and network resources.

E-BUSINESS DRIVES SERVICE LEVEL MANAGEMENT

Businesses have long viewed IT as an overhead operation and an expense. In addition, when IT was a hidden function dealing with internal customers, it could use ad hoc, temporary solutions to address user service problems.

Now, with electronic commerce gaining importance, IT is becoming highly visible as a front door to the business. However, while Internet visibility can prove highly beneficial and lucrative to businesses, it can also backfire. Amazon, eBay, and Schwab all learned this the hard way when their service failures hit *The Wall Street Journal*'s front page. And few other organizations would like their CEO to read about similar problems.

As such cases illustrate, downtime on mission-critical applications can cost businesses tens of thousands or millions of dollars per day. In the financial industries, for example, downtime can cost $200,000 per minute, according to one industry analyst. And poor end-to-end application response time can be nearly as costly. Not only does it cause serious tension between internal users and IT, but it creates considerable frustration for external users, and the competition may be only a mouse click away.

0-8493-1149-7/02/$0.00+$1.50
© 2002 by CRC Press LLC

With IT now the main entry way to the business, then, businesses cannot afford the perception of less-than-optimal service. They are therefore increasingly adopting service level agreements (SLAs), service level management, and quality of service initiatives. In fact, some organizations have developed SLAs guaranteeing availability levels exceeding 99.9 percent, or aggressive application response times — which depend on optimal end-to-end performance.

SLM DEFINED

Service level management (SLM) is that set of activities required to measure and manage the quality of information services provided by IT. A proactive rather than reactive approach to IT management, SLM manages the IT infrastructure — including networks, systems, and applications — to meet the organization's service objectives. These objectives are specified in the SLA, a formal statement that clearly defines the services that IT will provide over a specified period of time, as well as the quality of service that users can expect to receive.

SLM is a means for the lines of business and IT to set down their explicit, mutual expectations for the content and extent of IT services. It also allows them to determine in advance what steps will be taken if these conditions are not met.

SLM is a dynamic, interactive process that features:

- Definition and implementation of policies
- Collection and monitoring of data
- Analysis of service levels against the agreement
- Reporting in real-time and over longer intervals to gauge the effectiveness of current policies
- Taking action to ensure service stability

To implement service level management, the SLA relates the specific service level metrics and goals of IT systems to business objectives. By linking the end-user and business process experience with what is happening in IT organizations, SLAs offer a common bridge between IT and end users, providing a clear understanding of the services to be delivered, couched in a language that both can understand.

This allows users to compare the service they receive to the business process, and lets IT administrators measure and assess the level of service from end to end. SLAs may specify the scope of services, success and failure metrics, goal and performance levels, costs, penalties, time periods, and reporting requirements.

The use of SLM offers businesses several benefits. It directs management toward clear service objectives, and improves communication between IT and users by enabling responsiveness to user issues. It also simplifies the management of network services, because resource changes are made according to the SLA and are based on accurate user feedback.

Furthermore, SLM clarifies accountability by allowing organizations to analyze service levels and evaluate IT's effectiveness. Finally, by enabling businesses to optimize current resources and make educated decisions about the necessity for upgrades, it saves money and maximizes investments.

FROM SYSTEM TO APPLICATION FOCUS

In the early days of performance evaluation and capacity planning, the emphasis was on system tuning and optimization. The field first took off in the mid-1960s with the introduction of third-generation operating systems. The inefficiency of many of these systems resulted in low throughput levels and poor user response time. So, tuning and optimization were vital.

As time passed, however, the vastly improved price/performance of computer systems began to limit the need for tuning and optimization. Many organizations found it cheaper to simply buy more hardware resource than to try and tune a system into better performance. Still, organizations continued to concentrate on system throughput and resource utilization, while the fulfillment of service obligations to the end user was of relatively low priority.

Enter the PC revolution with its emphasis on end-user requirements. Enter, too, the client/server model to serve users, with its promise of speedy application development and vast amounts of information at users' fingertips, all delivered at rapid response times. Of course, the reality does not always measure up.

Now the Internet and World Wide Web are joining the fray, with their special concepts of speed and user service. Organizations are now attempting to plan according to Web time, whereby some consider a Web year to be 90 days, but WWW may well stand for "world wide wait." So organizations are turning their focus to the user, rather than the information being collected.

The service-desk/helpdesk industry, for example, has long been moving toward user-oriented SLM. In the early 1990s, service desk technology focused on recording and tracking trouble tickets. Later, the technology evolved to include problem-resolution capabilities. Next, the service desk started using technologies and tools that enabled IT to address the underlying issues that kept call volumes high.

Today, organizations are moving toward business-oriented service delivery. IT is being called upon to participate as a partner in the corporate mission — which requires IT to be responsive to users/customers.

Today's SLM requires that IT administrators integrate visibility and control of the entire IT infrastructure, with the ability to seamlessly manage service levels across complex, heterogeneous enterprise environments, using a single management interface. However, many IT organizations currently have monitors and probes in isolated parts of the network, or tools that monitor performance on certain platforms but not others. In addition, they may only receive after-the-fact reports of downtime, without proactive warnings or suggested actions.

SLM requires a single, comprehensive solution whereby every facet of an IT infrastructure is brought into a single, highly automated, managed environment. This enables IT to quickly isolate and resolve problems, and act proactively in the best interest of the end user, rather than merely reacting to network or resource issues. And while comprehensive tools to do this were not available in the past, that situation is changing as the tools evolve.

In this complex new environment, organizations must define IT availability in terms of applications rather than resources and use language that both IT and business users can understand. Thus, in the past, IT's assurance of 98 percent network availability offered little comfort to a salesman who could not book orders. It did not mean the application was running or the response time was good enough for the salesman.

While SLM was formerly viewed as a lot of hot air, today's business SLAs between IT and the line of business define what customers should expect from IT without problems. A subset could be operational.

SLAs Tied to User Experience

Current SLAs, then, are tied to applications in the end-user experience. With their focus on the user, rather than the information being collected — SLAs aim at linking the end user's business process experience with what is happening in the IT organization.

To this end, organizations are demanding end-user response time measurement from their suppliers, and for client/server in addition to mainframe application systems. For example, when one financial organization relocated its customer service center from a private fiber to a remote connection, call service customers were most concerned about response time and reliability. Therefore, they required a tool that provided response time monitoring at the client/server level.

Similarly, a glass and plastics manufacturer sought a system to allow measurement of end-user response time as a critical component of user satisfaction when it underwent a complex migration from legacy to client/server systems. Although legacy performance over time provided sub-second response time, client/server performance has only recently gained importance. To measure and improve response time in client/server environments, organizations must monitor all elements of the response time component.

Application Viewpoint

The application viewpoint offers the best perspective into a company's mosaic of connections, any one of which could slow down the user. This is no news to end-user organizations. According to a 1999 survey of 142 network professionals, for example, conducted by International Network Services, 64 percent measure the availability of applications on the network to define network availability/performance. (INS, Sunnyvale, California, is a global provider of network consulting and software solutions, recently acquired by Lucent.)

For this very complex environment, organizations must do root-cause analysis if users have service problems. When IT organizations were more infrastructure oriented, service problems resulted in much fingerpointing, and organizations wasted valuable time passing the buck around before they found the domain responsible — be it the server, the network, or the connections. Now, however, as IT organizations change from infrastructure providers to service organizations, they are looking at the application level to determine what is consuming the system.

SLM APPROACHES, ACTIVITIES, AND COMPONENTS

While users care most about response time, this has historically been ignored in SLAs. That situation is changing, as organizations try to capture the end-user experience for SLM. As they concentrate on applications, organizations must collect application response time metrics. Some analysts have defined four ways of measuring end-to-end response time: code instrumentation, network X-ray tools, capture/playback tools, and client capture.

Code Instrumentation

By instrumenting the source code in applications, organizations can define the exact start and end of business transactions, capturing the total round-trip response times. This was the approach taken by Hewlett-Packard and Tivoli with their Application Response Measurement (ARM) application programming interface (API) initiative.

For ARM's purposes, application management is defined as end-to-end management of a collection of physical and logical components that interact to support a specified business process. According to the ARM working group draft mission statement, "The purpose of the ARM API is to enable applications to provide information to measure business transactions from an end-user perspective, and the contributing components of response time in distributed applications. This information can be used to support SLAs, and to analyze response time across distributed systems."

However, although the approach is insightful in capturing how end users see business transactions, it is also highly invasive, costly, and difficult, requiring modifications to the application source code as well as maintenance of the modifications. Many users want a nonintrusive system to measure end-user response time. Others need a breakdown by segment rather than a round-trip response time measurement. And, despite the promise, only three to five percent of ERP applications have been ARMed, or instrumented.

Network X-Ray Tools

A second collection approach is via X-ray tools, or network sniffers. An example is Sniffer Network Analyzer from Network Associates, Menlo Park, California. Sniffers use probes spread out in strategic locations across the network to read the packet headers, and calculate response times as seen from that probe point. Although noninvasive, this approach does not address the application layer. Because it does not see transactions in user terms, it does not capture response time from the end-user perspective. And, because the data was not designed for performance purposes, converting it into workload or user transaction-level metrics is not a trivial task. However, while the method might be considered the "hard way" to obtain performance data, it does work.

Capture/Playback Tools

Capture/playback tools use synthetic transactions, simulating user keystrokes and measuring the response times of these "virtual" users. While simulated transactions have a role in testing the applications' potential performance, they do not measure the actual end-user's response time experience. Examples are CAPBAK from Software Research, San Francisco, California, and AutoTester from AutoTester, Inc., Dallas, Texas.

Client Capture

Client capture is the fourth and most promising approach to measuring response time from the user's perspective. Here, intelligent agents sit at the user's desktop, monitoring the transactions of actual end users to capture the response time of business transactions. Client capture technology can complement network and systems management solutions, such as those from Hewlett-Packard, Tivoli, and Computer Associates. Examples of client capture products include the VitalSuite line from INS and FirstSense products from FirstSense Software, Burlington, Massachusetts.

Service level management encompasses at least four distinct activities: planning, delivery, measurement, and calibration. Thus, the IT organization and its customers first plan the nature of the service to be provided. Next, the IT organization delivers according to the plan, taking calls, resolving problems, managing change, monitoring inventory, opening the service desk to end users, and connecting to the network and systems management platforms.

The IT organization then measures its performance to determine its service delivery level based on line of business needs. Finally, IT and the business department continually reassess their agreements to ensure they meet changing business needs.

Delivering service involves many separate disciplines spanning IT functional groups. These include network operations, application development, hardware procurement and deployment, software distribution, and training. SLM also involves problem resolution, asset management, service request and change management, end-user empowerment, and network and systems management. Because all these disciplines and functions must be seamlessly integrated, IT must determine how to manage the performance of applications that cross multiple layers of hardware, software, and middleware.

The following general components constitute SLM, and each contributes to the measurement of service levels:

- *Network availability*: A critical metric in managing the network
- *Customer satisfaction*: Not as easily quantified, customer satisfaction results from end-users' network experience, so IT must manage the network in light of user expectations
- *Network performance*
- *Application availability*: This, along with application response time, is directly related to customer satisfaction

It is difficult to define, negotiate, and measure SLAs. The metrics for network availability and performance include the availability of devices and links connected to the network, the availability of servers, the availability of applications on the network, and application response time.

Furthermore, in order to track any SLA elements, it is necessary to measure and report on each. SLAs can include such elements as network performance, network availability, network throughput, goals and objectives, and quality-of-service metrics (e.g., mean time to repair, and installation time).

Other possible SLA elements include conditions/procedures for updating or renegotiating, assignment of responsibilities and roles, reporting policies and escalation procedures, measurement of technology failures, assumptions and definitions, and trend analyses. SLAs may also include penalties for poor performance, help-desk availability, baseline data, benchmark data, application response time, measurement of process failures, application availability, customer satisfaction metrics, and rewards for above-target performance. But a main objective of SLAs is setting and managing user expectations.

IMPROVING SERVICE LEVEL MANAGEMENT

While the concept of SLM has gained widespread recognition, implementation has been slower, in part due to the complexity of the network environment. In addition, according to the 1999 INS survey findings on SLM, it is a continuing challenge.

The good news is that 63 percent of respondents with SLM capabilities in place were satisfied with those capabilities in 1999 (according to the survey) — a dramatic improvement over the previous year. However, despite the high satisfaction with SLM, improving it was important to more than 90 percent of respondents.

Furthermore, organizational issues presented the greatest challenge to improving SLM for half the respondents, and managerial issues were the top challenge for another third. Also, customer satisfaction was considered an important SLM metric by 81 percent of respondents. Finally, the top barriers to implementing or improving SLM were said to be organizational/process issues, other projects with higher priority, and the difficulty in measuring SLAs.

Despite the fact that SLM and SLAs are moving in the right direction by focusing on applications and end-user response time, the SLA tool market is not yet mature. Instead, SLAs are ahead of the software that is monitoring them. Indeed, 47 percent of the network professionals surveyed by INS in 1999 said that difficulty in measuring SLAs was a significant barrier to implementing or improving SLM.

Although SLA contracts have not been monitorable by software people until recently, that situation is changing. Vendors are starting to automate the monitoring process and trying to keep pace with the moving target of customers' changing needs.

Businesses should also realize that SLAs are a tool for more than defining service levels. Thus, SLAs should also be used to actively solicit the agreement of end users to service levels that meet their needs. Often, the providers and consumers of IT services misunderstand the trade-off between the cost of the delivered service and the business need/benefit. The SLA process can help set more realistic user expectations and can support higher budget requests when user expectations exceed IT's current capabilities.

Businesses can implement SLM for important goals such as improving mission-critical application availability and dependability, and reducing application response time as measured from the user's point of view. In general terms, SLM can also enhance IT organizational efficiency and cost-effectiveness.

To improve their SLM capabilities and meet these objectives, organizations can address the relevant organizational issues, providing processes and procedures that aim at consistent service delivery and associated user satisfaction. In addition, because application performance has become paramount, organizations can implement tools to monitor and measure the behavior of those mission-critical applications that depend on network availability and performance.

TOWARD A BUSINESS-PROCESS FOCUS

As IT continues to be a business driver, some analysts predict that SLM will move toward a focus on the business process, whereby organizations will abstract the state of the business processes that run their companies. In turn, the available data and its abstraction will consolidate into a dashboard reporting system. As organizations move toward a business dashboard, the data will be just a given. Because solution providers are rapidly becoming sophisticated in making data available, this is already happening today — and more rapidly than expected.

Section XII
Appendixes

Appendix 1
ERP Vendors

The following is a list of 17 ERP vendors. All but Baan, Siebel, and Wonderware appear in the ERP Stock Index. Great Plains Software is to be acquired by Microsoft. The first seven are leading industries that offer ERP integration tools, solutions, and applications.

- Baan
- Wonderware
- Infinium Software
- J.D. Edwards
- American Software
- MAPICS
- Oracle
- Deltek Systems
- QAD
- PeopleSoft
- Epicor
- SCT
- SAP
- Frontstep
- Siebel
- Computer Associates
- Great Plains Software

Each has a different way of tailoring ERP systems to organizations' needs. Not all provide their own ASP hosting service. Some vendors offer ASP solutions through a network of authorized ASPs.

One vendor, Oracle, integrates application messaging schemes as part of its ERP offerings, while other vendors need to integrate these schemes into the ERP systems. Several vendors, including Baan and J.D. Edwards, focus on industry-specific ERP solutions, the range of which can be very broad. Baan, now wholly owned by Invensys Software Systems, has partnered with Wonderware to combine their ERP solutions to reach a wider share of the market. SAP frequently appears in the first edition of *Enterprise Systems Integration*. PeopleSoft, Computer Associates, and Wonderware have been around for a while.

For each major vendor, a summary capsule highlights important facts about their ERP products and hosting service. All capsules include information on integration tools, ERP solutions and/or applications, platforms, e-Business, and ASP hosting service, if any. For details, go to the vendor's Web site.

One can run ERP systems within an enterprise or outsource some of them to an ASP when considering the costs of training people to install, customize, maintain, and operate them. Should one's organization decide to outsource them, look at the service of level agreements the ASP may have with ERP and third-party network vendors to guarantee maximum uptime availability. Determine if this ASP has appropriate network tools and fail-over schemes to resolve network traffic problems when they happen.

For our own purpose, this appendix contains two sections: major ERP vendors and other ERP vendors. The latter vendors specialize in applications for certain vertical markets or industries.

MAJOR ERP VENDORS

Of the 17, seven major vendors provide ERP integration tools, solutions, and applications. They are Oracle, Baan, Wonderware, J.D. Edwards, PeopleSoft, SAP, and Computer Associates.

Oracle

Oracle Corporation, 500 Oracle Parkway, Redwood Shores, CA 94065; Tel: (650) 506-7000, Fax: (650) 506-7200, http://www.oracle.com.

Integration tool:	Oracle Applications InterConnect (a CRM integration product)
ERP solutions:	SAP R/3, Oracle Applications, release 10.7, and legacy systems
e-Business suite:	Finance, human resources, and Internet procurement; intelligence and analytics; project management; process manufacturing and business-to-business
ASP hosting service:	Oracle Financials Online, Human Resources/Payroll Online, Internet Procurement Online, Manufacturing Online, Supply Chain Online, Sales Online, Marketing Online, Business Intelligence Online
Platforms:	Windows NT, UNIX, Linux, and Sun Sparc Solaris

Oracle Applications InterConnect integrates ERP solutions with Oracle CRM suite of applications. Included is iStudio, a wizard-based integration specification tool. It allows the product developer, consultant, or IT professional to visually review and modify the process of integration in response to an organization's needs. With this software, a business analyst can set up an integration model — from start to end, including information flows.

The InterConnect architecture is based on an asynchronous messaging model allowing the applications to exchange messages with one another. What this means is that the applications are loosely coupled with one another. These applications can function autonomously as if they were separate modules. When an application becomes unavailable, the system frees up the resources that it needs for other tasks. Doing so maximizes uptime of active applications integrated to one another.

The messaging backbone for this integration tool is supported through the Advanced Queing features of Oracle 9i (or Oracle 8i, release 8.1.6). Oracle Message Broker supports Java Message Services that provide standard APIs for accessing messaging systems on multi-computing platforms.

Baan

Baan, Baron van Nagellstraat 89, 3771 LK Barneveld, P.O. Box 143, 3770 AC Barneveld, The Netherlands; Tel: +31 (0)342 428888, Fax: +31 (0)342 428822, www.baan.com.

Integration tool:	iBaan
ERP software:	iBaanERP
ERP applications:	ERP Financials, ERP Purchasing, ERP Sales, and ERP Project
Industries:	Automative, aerospace, industrial machinery, and electronics; telecommunications, construction, metal, paper, and cable
e-Business suite:	E-Sales, E-Procurement, E-Configuration, E-Collaboration, E-Service, E-Service Remote
ASP hosting service:	Available through a network of certified ASPs worldwide
Platforms:	Windows 2000, Windows NT, IBM iSeries (formerly AS/400 family suite)

On March 22, 2001, Baan and Wonderware announced a new component of the Invensys Software Strategy Integration Policy. With this update, Baan can use its iBaan OpenWorld integration technology to integrate iBaan with Wonderware's FactorySuite 2000 software.

iBaan suite includes a thin-client user interface for iBaanERP applications, an internet portal and software supporting business-to-business collaboration through the Web. iBaan Webtop allows users to access and enter ERP data for ERP applications. All ERP solutions can fail and automatically restart on a second server with minimal or no need for client system restarts.

Although Baan does not provide its own ASP hosting service, it offers ASP solutions through a network of certified ASPs worldwide. Baan focuses on collaborative commerce, or c-Commerce, to stress the importance of timely flow of information among suppliers, partners, customers, and employees in an enterprise setting.

PeopleSoft

PeopleSoft, 4460 Hacienda Drive, Pleasanton, CA 94588-8618; Tel: (800) 380-SOFT, (925) 225-3000, Fax: (925) 694-4444, http://www.peoplesoft.com.

Integration tool:	eCenter
ERP software:	PeopleSoft ERP
ERP applications:	Enterprise Performance Management, Human Resources Management, Financial Management, and Project Management
Industries:	Automative, aerospace, industrial machinery, and electronics, telecommunications, construction, metal, paper and cable, consumer products, financial services, healthcare, higher education, professional services, public sector, retail, utilities, wholesale distribution
e-Business:	Portal, E-procurement
Platforms:	IBM eServer xSeries (NT), IBM's eServer pSeries (AIX)

PeopleSoft's eCenter solution provides an entire suite of e-Business applications, including Portal and eProcurement. Many applications have been leveraged against the PeopleSoft ERP backbone. What this means is that PeopleSoft has developed applications to interface with PeopleSoft ERP, allowing ERP or legacy systems to work with requisitions, purchase orders, or receipts in eProcurement, for example. PeopleSoft also offers Internet Architecture, Internet Collaboration, Portal Solutions, Open Integration Framework, and DB2 Universal Database.

Wonderware

Wonderware, 100 Technology Drive, Irvine, CA 92619; Tel: (949) 727-3200, Fax: (949) 727-3270, http://www.wonderware.com.

Integration tool:	ERP (PRISM/Protean)
ERP solution:	Process ERP
ERP applications:	Protean Customer Order Management, Financials, Inventory Management, Planning and Quick Scheduler, Production, Product Costing, and Production Modeling
Industries:	Gas, food, chemical, pharmaceutical, beverage, and other process industries
Platforms:	Windows 2000, Windows NT, IBM AS/400

ERP Protean is a plant-centric ERP solution for process companies that addresses all aspects of running and managing process operations. The product contains multiple modules that support production, formula management, inventory management, procurement, planning, scheduling, product costing, asset management, customer order management, and financials. These modules link with legacy systems, third-party software, and process control systems.

PRISM is an integrated suite of applications for managing production, logistics, financials, and maintenance. It runs only on the IBM AS/400 with PRISM's Visual WorkPlace graphical user interface. Partners include IBM, Oracle, and PeopleSoft.

Wonderware also offers two programs for developers of third-party software products. They are FactorySuite Partners and WonderTools for integration with FactorySuite 2000. Baan, for example, has combined iBaanERP suite with it.

J.D. Edwards

J.D. Edwards Corporate World Headquarters, One Technology Way, Denver, CO 80237; Tel: (303) 334-4000, (800) 777-3732, Fax: (303) 334-4141, http://www.jdedwards.com.

Integration tool:	WorldVision ERP
ERP applications:	OneWorld Manufacturing, Distribution Logistics, Human Resources, Procurement, Asset Management, Financial, Collaboration
Industries:	**Industrial:** automative, high-tech/electronics, industrial fabrication and assembly, manufacturing/distribution, medical devices
	Services: engineering and construction, entertainment, recreation and hospitality, mining, public services, real estate, professional services
	Consumer: packaged goods, food, beverage, energy, chemical, life sciences
e-Business suite:	ERP applications are Internet-enabled and part of e-Business suite. IBM Websphere Commerce Suite integrates with World Software applications.
ASP hosting service:	Available via offerings with its OneWorld enterprise software
Platforms:	Windows NT, UNIX, IBM AS/400, HP 9000

OneWorld and WorldVision ERP software offer more than 1000 Internet-enabled business applications. OneWorld provides a full range of integrated e-Business, front-office, and supply chain management functionalities. OneWorld and World Software customers can access "self-service" applications through Web-enabled devices, including wireless devices. The industries that the company serves are broad — from engineering to entertainment, from mining to medical devices, from manufacturing to chemical, and from professional services to public services.

OneWorld's configurable Network Computing architecture is an infrastructure for Internet-enabled ERP. It utilizes Java technology, Microsoft Windows client interfaces, and also supports multiple platforms, including UNIX and Windows NT Web servers. J.D. Edwards offers hosted application services and has integrated IBM Websphere Commerce Suite with WorldSoftware applications.

SAP

SAP, Strategic Planning and Support Office, 3999 West Chester Pike, Newton Square, PA 19073; Tel: (610) 661-1000, Fax: (610) 355-3106, http://www.sap.com/usa.

Integration tool:	SAP R/3
ERP applications:	Sales and materials planning, production planning, warehouse management, financial accounting, and human resources management
Industries:	mySAP Aerospace and Defense, Aerospace and Defense, Apparel and Footwear, Automotive, Banking, Consumer Products, Engineering and Construction, Healthcare, Higher Education, High Tech, Insurance, Media, Mill Products, Mining, Oil and Gas, Pharmaceuticals, Public Sector, Retail, Service Provider, Telecommunications, Transportation, Utilities
e-Business:	mySAP E-Procurement, Product Lifecycle Management, Business Intelligence, Financials, Human Resources, Mobile Business
ASP hosting service:	Finance management, business intelligence, human resource management, back-office enterprise applications
Platforms:	Windows NT, AIX, Digital UNIX, HP-UX, Raliant, UNIX (SINIX), Solaris, OS/390

All SAP R/3 applications are modules. They can be used either alone or combined with other solutions and integrated into the workflow of business events and processes across departments and functionality. From a process-oriented perspective, greater integration of applications increases the benefits derived. mySAP.com is built on e-Business standards and technologies such as XML, HTML, HTTP, and Simple Object Access Protocol (SOAP) to ensure openness and interoperability.

SAP offers three levels of mySAP hosted solutions: application hosting, marketplace hosting, and ASP solutions. Application hosting provides hosting packages of any mySAP.com solutions, including infrastructure, implementation, operation, and ongoing support of selected applications. Marketplace hosting runs a meeting place for customers and partners to transact online business in the marketplace. ASP solutions are available for small and mid-sized companies that want to outsource any mySAP applications. EDS and Hewlett Packard are SAP's Preferred Data Center Providers.

Computer Associates

Computer Associates, interBiz Solutions, One Computer Associates Plaza, Islandia, NY 11740; Tel: (800) 225-5224, (516) 342-6000, http://www.ca.com, http://www.interbiz.com.

Integration tools:	eBusiness Platform
ERP software:	interBiz eCommerce Suite (eBusiness Application)
ERP applications:	interBiz Procure
Industries:	Manufacturing, general finance, wholesale distribution, human resource management, and banking
e-Business solutions:	interBiz eCommerce Suite
Platforms:	Windows 2000, Linux, OS/390, OpenVMS

The interBiz eCommerce Suite provides tight integration with interBiz order-processing systems, as well as "off-the-shelf" integration with applications from other ERP vendors. interBiz Procure integrates with ERP and other back-office systems to provide order and receipt status.

BizWorks uses data providers through Jasmine technology to integrate diverse applications. What these providers do is convert and translate data from any application running with the BizWorks infrastructure through data specification provided by the information metadata store. In addition to interBiz's enterprise business applications, Computer Associates has been developing ERP providers for SAP/R3 and PeopleSoft in the first stage and J.D. Edwards's OneWorld in the next stage.

OTHER ERP VENDORS

The remaining ERP vendors specialize in applications for vertical markets and certain industries. They include American Software, Deltek Systems, Epicor, and Frontstep. Also included are Great Plains Software, Infinium Software, MAPICS, QAD, Siebel, and SCT.

American Software

American Software, 470 East Paces Ferry Road, Atlanta, GA 30305; Tel: (800) 726-2946, (404) 264-5296, Fax: (404) 264-5206, http://www.american-software.com.

Integration tools:	Intelliprise & Flow manufacturing
ERP applications:	Procurement, payables, receivables, expenses, store, forms, bid
Industries:	Manufacturing industries
e-Business solutions:	e-intelliprise, e-collaboration, e-applications, e-hosting, e-services
ASP hosting service:	All American Software applications
Platforms:	System/390

Deltek Systems

Deltek Systems, Corporate Headquarters, 8280 Greensboro Drive, McLean, VA 22102; Tel: (703) 734-8606, (800) 456-2009, Fax: (703) 734-1146, http://www.deltek.com.

Integration tools:	Deltek Costpoint
ERP applications:	Accounting, Auditing, Purchasing, Fixed Assets, Travel, Timesheets, Payroll, Human Resources, Consolidations, and Materials Management
Industries:	Architecture, engineering, and construction, biotechnology/pharmaceutical, computer technology and services, business services
e-Business solutions:	e-intelliprise, e-collaboration, e-applications, e-hosting, e-services
Platforms:	Contact Deltek

Epicor

Epicor, 195 Technology Drive, Irvine, CA 92618; Tel: (949) 585-4000 Fax: (949) 585-4021, http://www.epicor.com.

Integration tools:	Advante ERP Software
ERP software:	Advante ERP Software
ERP applications:	Accounting, budgeting, analysis, distribution, and manufacturing
Industries:	Dot.coms, financial services, hospitality and food service, manufacturing, not-for-profits, professional services, retail, software and computer services, sports and recreation, wholesale distributors

e-Business solutions: eCommerce Suite, eFrontOffice, eBackOffice, eManufacturing, eProcurement, ePeople, ePortal, eIntelligence
ASP hosting services: eCenter (full service, subscription, managed service)
Platforms: Windows NT, HP/UX, DG/UX Unix, AIX, Sun OS, Alpha Ultrix, SCO Unix

FrontStep

Frontstep (formerly Symix), 2800 Corporate Exchange Drive, Columbus, OH 43231; Tel: (614) 523-7000, Fax: (614) 895-2504, http://www.front-step.com.

Integration tools: FrontStep ActiveLink
ERP software: ERP Syteline (industrial manufacturers), ERP SyteCentre (consumer manufacturers)
ERP applications: Manufacturing, distribution, financials
Industries: Industrial and consumer manufacturing industries
e-Business solutions: FrontStep Procurement Center, Intelligence
Platforms Contact FrontStep
Note: FrontStep is the originator of Customer Synchronized Resource Planning (CSRP) that extends ERP to incorporate customer needs into manufacturers' central planning processes.

Great Plains Software

Great Plains Software, Inc., P.O. Box 9739, Fargo, ND 58109-9739; Tel: (800) 456-0025, (701) 281-0555, http://www.greatplains.com.

Integration tools: Dynamics Customization and Integration Series
ERP software: Dynamics ERP solution
ERP applications: Dynamics Foundation Series, Financial Series, Purchasing Series, Human Resources Series, Project Series
Industries: Agricultural, analytics, apparel/garment, banking, automative, financial, communication, construction, document imaging, EDI, education, electrical service and repair
e-Business solutions: Dynamics Electronic Business Series
ASP hosting: eEnterprise and Dynamics
Platforms: Contact Great Plains
Special note: Microsoft will acquire the company

Infinium Software

Infinium Software, 25 Communications Way, Hyannis, MA 02601; Tel: (508) 778-2000, Fax: (508) 775-3764, http://www.infinium.com, http://www.infinium.com.

Integration tools:	Web- and server-based Infinium solutions
ERP software:	Web- and server-based Infinium solutions
ERP applications:	Human Resources, Financial Management, Process Manufacturing, Business Intelligence Analytics
Industries:	Transportation, manufacturing, gaming and hospitality, healthcare, retail, financial services, and distribution
e-Business solutions:	Infinium eBusiness
ASP hosting:	Infinium ASP
Platforms:	AS/400, Windows

MAPICS

MAPICS, 1000 Windward Concourse Parkway, Suite 100, Alpharetta, GA 30005: Tel: (678) 319-8000, http://www.mapics.com.

Integration tools:	XA
ERP software:	XA
ERP applications:	Manufacturing, financial, engineering
Industries:	Seven key verticals within the manufacturing industry: heavy-duty transport suppliers, industrial equipment, semiconductors (fabless), fabricated metal products, auto parts suppliers, measuring and controlling devices, and electronic and electrical suppliers
e-Business solutions:	TeamWeRX Connects
Platforms:	AS/400, UNIX, Windows NT

QAD

QAD, 6450 Via Real, Carpinteria, CA 93013; Tel: (805) 684-6614, http://www.qad.com.

Integration tools:	QAD Connects A2A (application-to-application)
ERP software:	MFG/PRO
ERP applications:	Manufacturing, distribution, financials
Industries:	Automotive, consumer products, electronics, food and beverage, industrial products, medical
e-Business solutions:	B2B/B2C/EDI Ecommerce
Platforms:	UNIX, Windows 98/NT

Special notes: QAD Connects A2A solutions integrate QAD applications with legacy systems and ERP from multiple vendors such as SAP and Oracle; QAD has been using IBM's Websphere for its QAS eQ B2B applications

SCT

SCT, 4 Country View Rd., Malvern, PA 19355; Tel: (800) 223-7036 (within U.S.), (610) 647-5930 (outside U.S.), http://www.sct.com.

Integration tools:	Adage ERP
ERP software:	Adage ERP
ERP applications:	Finance, human resources
Industries:	Education, energy, utilities and communications, government and process manufacturing and distribution, food and beverage, chemical, pharmaceutical and consumer packaged goods
e-Business solutions:	iProcess.scr
Platforms:	Multi-platform
Note:	ADAGE is an object-oriented graphical ERP solution

Siebel

Siebel Systems, Inc., 2207 Bridgepointe Parkway, San Mateo, CA 94404; Tel: (800) 647-4300, (650) 295-5000, http://www.siebel.com.

Integration tools:	eConfigurator
ERP software:	eBusiness Applications
ERP applications:	Automotive, public sector, communications, apparel and footwear, energy, finance, insurance, healthcare, pharmacy, portal.
Industries:	Automative, general auction, collectibles and special interest, communication and media, real estate, healthcare/pharmaceutical, construction and machinery, technology, consumer goods, telecommunications and energy, finance and insurance, travel and transportation
e-Business solutions:	eAutomotive, ePublic Sector, eCommunication, eApparel and Footwear, eEnergy, eFinance, eInsurance, eHealthCare, ePhara, eRetail
Platforms:	Multi-platform
Special note:	Available in Personal and MidMarket editions

Appendix 2
Other ERP Resources

This appendix consists of two sections: ERP Web sites and Collaborative Commerce. The first section covers some ERP resources on the Web, while the second section briefly discusses what collaborative commerce is and how useful it may be to multi-enterprises.

ERP WEB SITES

Four parts comprise this section: ERP Research Center, ERP Supersite, ERP World, and IBM's ERP Page. The first part focuses on example resources of interest to CIOs, such as ERP technologies, services, and issues. ERP Supersite, in the next part, gives a list of additional vendors providing ERP solutions, although some may not be categorized as ERP vendors. ERP World provides an online directory that the user can index in different ways, while IBM's ERP Page looks at selecting, implementing, operating, and maintaining ERP Packages.

ERP Research Center, http://www.cio.com/forums/erp/links.html

Among the topics in this Research Center are ERP Front Page, Metrics, Vendors, ERP Articles, and ERP Resources. For this appendix, only the latter two are covered.

ERP Articles. Research Center's ERP articles (as of March 30, 2001) comprise three groups: CIO Articles, Other Source Articles, and Research Reports, some of which might be useful for future reference.

CIO Articles:

- "Can IT Save A&P?" The granddaddy of grocery chains is betting $250 million that the right technology — and the right people to run it — will revive its wilting profits (*CIO,* Feb. 15, 2001).
- "Damned It If You Do." Will integration tools patch the holes left by an unsatisfactory ERP implementation? (*CIO,* Sept. 15, 2000).

- "ERP, One Letter at a Time." Transforming your enterprise and supply chain? Better get the business case down, goal markers set up, and everyone on board to make it happen (*CIO*, Sept. 1, 2000).
- "The Missing Link." Integrating ERP with e-Commerce applications does not have to be a nightmare, but it depends on where you start (*CIO*, June 15, 2000).
- "ERP Training Stinks." As ERP implementations falter and fail, many people think the answer is more training. They are wrong (*CIO*, June 1, 2000).
- "Big Risks for Small Fry." Contractual tips for new entrants in the ERP game. (*CIO*, May 15, 2000).
- "The Vision." Getting to the truly integrated enterprise should not be a piecemeal journey. One must have a vision of where one is going in order to get there (*CIO*, May 15, 2000).
- "The Biggest Gamble Yet." After pledging to annihilate each other's internet e-Commerce exchanges, Ford and General Motors lowered their swords and decided to work together to build the world's biggest online bazaar (*CIO*, April 15, 2000).
- "Talk to Your Plants." Enterprise systems yearn to know what is happening on the factory floor. CIOs, do not be shy (*CIO*, March 15, 2000).
- "Long Live ERP." Reports of the demise of enterprise systems have been greatly exaggerated (*CIO*, March 1, 2000).
- "Does ERP Build a Better Business." In this excerpt from Thomas H. Davenport's new book, one learns how leadership made Earthgrains' ERP investment pay off. (*CIO*, Feb. 15, 2000).
- "Fine Line." A manufacturing process makeover helped Dell change its production line enough to climb to the top in U.S. PC sales (*CIO*, Feb. 1, 2000).
- "Prescription Strength." Pfizer created its own magic pill that brought speedier cycle times and a collaborative spirit to the company (*CIO*, Feb. 1, 2000).
- "The ABC's of ERP." What is ERP? How long will an ERP project take? What are the unforeseen costs of ERP? How does ERP fit with electronic commerce? Find the answers to these questions and more! (*CIO.comvb*, Dec. 22, 1999).

Other Source Articles:

- "Making Change." The U.S. Mint's Philip Diehl found that overseeing an enterprisewide systems project is no easy task — especially when there is a deadline one cannot afford to miss. (*Darwin*, June 1, 2000).
- "On the Front Lines." Optimize decision-making where the customer meets the business (*CIO*, Oct. 15, 1999).
- "Second Wave, New Beginning." Introduction to an ERP white paper from Deloitte Consulting, the full report is available in pdf format.

Research Reports

- "The Bad Things that Happen When ERP Goes Live." Some things to think about before writing the big check for ERP (registration required, with privacy option). (*Ten Go Live Surprises,* 1998).
- "Enterprise Application Integration." With the move to e-Commerce comes the need to change and integrate applications faster than ever (*Meta Group*).
- "Enterprise Application Integration Confronts E-Buiness." There is a ways to go before there are software tools flexible enough to handle the integration needs of e-Business (*Meta Group*).
- "ERP/ERM Strategies: Beyond the Backbone." To provide e-Commerce ROI, ERP needs to link with other applications in the company (*Meta Group*).

ERP Resources. This subpart includes three segments: IT research companies, communities and forums, and ERP information sites.

IT Research Companies. This segment gives a list of the following eight companies that track the progress of ERP and supply-chain software, as well as general IT management.

- Aberdeen Group, One Boston Place, Boston, MA 02108; Tel: (617) 723-7890, Fax: (617) 723 7897, http://www.aberdeen.com
- AMR Research, 2 Oliver Street, Fifth Floor, Boston, MA 02109-4925; Tel: (617) 542-6600, Fax: (617) 542-5670, http://www.amrresearch.com
- Forrester Research, 400 Technology Square, Cambridge, MA 02139; Tel: (617) 497-7090, Fax: (617) 613-5000, http://www.forrester.com
- Gartner Group, 56 Top Gallant Road, P.O. Box 10212, Stamford, CT 06904; Tel: (203) 964-0096, Fax: (203) 324-7901, http://www.gartner.com

  Note: Gartner subsidiary TechRepublic, Inc. (http://www.techrepublic.com) targets at IT professionals by IT professionals
- Giga Information Group, 139 Main Street, 5th Floor, Cambridge, MA 02142; Tel: (617) 949-4900, Fax: (617) 949-4901, http://www.gigaweb.com
- Hurwitz Group, 111 Speen Street, Framingham, MA 01701; Tel: (508) 872-3344, Fax: (508) 672-3355, http://www.hurwitz.com
- Meta Group, 208 Harbor Drive, PO Box 12061, Stamford, CT 06912-0061. (800) 945-META; Tel: (203) 973-6700, http://www.metagroup.com
- The Yankee Group, 31 St. James Avenue, Boston, MA 02116-4114; Tel: (617) 956-5000, Fax: (617) 956-5005, http://www.yankeegroup.com

Communities and Forums. American's SAP User Group, Supply Chain Council, and APICS — The Educational Society for Resource Management are useful to users. Brief information on each is provided below.

- America's SAP User Group (ASUG), 401 N. Michigan Avenue, Chicago, IL 60611-4267; Tel: (312) 321-5142, Fax: (312) 245-1081, http://www.asug.com
  — This user group, independent of SAP, helps IS departments better understand this complex software, mostly through newsgroups and conferences.

- Supply Chain Council, 303 Freeport Road, Pittsburgh, PA 15215; Tel: (412) 781-4101, Fax.(412) 781 2871, http://www.supply-chain.org
  — Spearheaded by research and consulting group AMR (Advanced Manufacturing Research) and a group of manufacturers, the Supply-Chain Council has developed a generic work-in-progress supply-chain model, called the Supply Chain Operations Reference model (SCOR), that is used by council members in different industries. Council members trade supply-chain war stories and decide how to modify SCOR as they go.
  — *Advanced Manufacturing Magazine* is available online.

- APICS — The Educational Society for Resource Management, 5301 Shawnee Road, Alexandria, VA 22312-2317; Tel: (800) 444-APICS (2742) or (703) 354-8851, Fax: (703) 354-8106, http://www.apics.com
  — APICS focuses on "resource management," including ERP and supply chain. An exhaustive online buyers' guide lists all forms of resource management software and the consulting firms that claim to understand it.
  — APICS also publishes a monthly magazine.

ERP Information Sites. These sites focus on informing ERP customers on technologies, systems, and issues.

- TechRepublic's ERP Supersite, http://www.erpsupersite.com
  — An ERP gathering spot, with discussion forums and chat rooms, as well as analyst reports, news, links to other ERP sites.

- SAP FAQ, http://www.sapfaq.com
  — A FAQ page from the SAP newsgroup (news:de.alt.comp.sap-r3)

- SAP Assist, http://www.ittoolbox.com
  — News, white papers, peer publishing, SAP forums, as well as ERP-SELECT mail list.

ERP SuperSite, http://www.erpsupersite.com

Gartner's TechRepublic, an independent subsidiary, presents an ERP SuperSite as part of its larger Enterprise AppFocus category. This site focuses on ERP technologies, vendors, issues, and news. In addition, it lists worldwide ERP solution suites, data collection and analysis, ERP data reporting products, enterprise performance enhancement applications, low-end PC-based ERP and supply-chain automation products, enterprise application integration, storage management, and intelligent output management.

The following are vendors listed on the ERP Solution Suites page as of March 31, 2001.

- ABAS
- Glovia
- ROI Systems, Inc.
- Aspen Technology
- HarrisData
- Ross Systems, Inc.
- AXIS Technology, Inc.
- IAS — Industrial Application Software
- Scala Business Solutions
- CIMA, Inc.
- Gaec Computer Corp
- IFS — Industrial and Financial Systems
- Software 21
- NavisionDambgaard
- Intentia International AB
- Software Engineering
- Demand Solutions
- Integrated Business Systems and Services
- System Software Associates
- Eastern Software Systems Ltd.
- Made2Manage Systems
- Sage Enterprise Solutions
- Evolus (India) Private Limited
- MAI Systems
- TTW, Inc.
- Expandable Software
- PowerCerv
- Visibility
- Qube

ERP World, http://www.erpworld.org

ERP World's Marketplace presents ERP World Directory. One can search it in one of three ways: by vendor, product, and category. The following gives category examples:

- Accounting/Financial
- Client-Server Development Tools
- Communications
- Data Management Tools
- Data Center Management
- Data Warehousing
- Data Mining
- Electronic Commerce
- EDI
- ERP
- Job Scheduling/ Workload Management
- Network Management
- Security
- Systems Management
- Workflow Management

IBM's ERP Page, http://houns54.clearlake.ibm.com/solutions/erp/erppub.nsf/detailcontacts/Home?OpenDocument

IBM offers a range of ERP solutions in an ERP life cycle that emphasizes the importance of integrating ERP into a larger system. This simplistic life cycle was drawn from IBM's experience with initial ERP implementation of SAP R/3 financial modules in its Storage Systems Division. It was later refined when R/3 included procurement, production, fulfillment, and finance. Today, browser users can access R/3 data residing in Web-enabled databases.

Life Cycle Approach. The life cycle begins with a solution inquiry for an ERP strategy approach that will lead to successful implementation. The next step is to select an ERP package that will best meet an organization's needs and minimize customization. The life cycle then moves on to an implementation plan that will effectively deploy ERP across the organization within budget and on time. For the plan to succeed, the project teams must have the tools and support needed to achieve expected financial results and meet project schedules for the remaining components of the life cycle.

The next phase focuses on deploying the ERP that will return expected benefits, minimize disruptions to the customers, and maximize uptime ERP availability. There are different ways of integrating ERP to other applications or systems in an environment of scalable, responsive, and secure IT infrastructure. The life cycle then looks at effective options of operating business systems of which ERP is a significant component.

Enterprise Application Service Approach. This approach comprises three phases: selection, implementation, and operation and optimization.

1. *Selection:* package-enabled business transformation (PEBT), package selection tool
2. *Implementation:* package implementation, SMOOTH — streamlined package implementation, organizational change, training, infrastructure for ERP, network consulting and e-Business integration
3. *Operations and optimization:* application management, performance management and capacity planning, post-ERP implementation, systems management consulting, business continuity and recovery, strategic outsourcing

COLLABORATIVE COMMERCE

The Gartner Group defines collaborative commerce as follows.

> Collaborative commerce (or c-Commerce) involves the collaborative, electronically enabled business interactions among an enterprise's internal personnel, business partners, and customers throughout a trading community. The trading community can be an industry, industry segment, supply chain, or supply chain segment.
>
> —Gartner Research

What this means is that c-Commerce allows some ERP systems to become specific to an industry sector or a particular industry and externally connected via Web-based, open architecture. This reflects that ERP systems are ever evolving in response to changing technologies, needs, and issues and the efforts of an enterprise to collaborate with other enterprises. The original ERP systems evolved from the MRP systems, some of which certain vendors still run.

c-Commerce for ERP systems would be useful in resolving, for example, the energy shortage in California starting in December 2000 and continuing throughout the first quarter of 2001. The utilities' lack of collaboration capabilities worsened the energy shortage and further raised costs to consumers. Multiple plants voluntarily shut down almost at the same time for "scheduled maintenance, emission concerns, and breakdowns" without collaborating with other plants.

According to the California Independent System Operator (CAI-ISO) press release dated December 7, 2000, electricity shortages in California resulted in declaration of a stage-three emergency when operating reserves fell below 1.5 percent of available power. The state requested that residents and businesses of the world's seventh-largest economy voluntarily reduce power consumption to avoid unplanned power outages and shortfalls for electricity in the power grid.

Several ERP vendors are offering or beginning to offer collaborative commerce (or c-Commerce) in addition to e-Commerce. Baan focuses on c-Commerce to stress the importance of timely flow of information among suppliers, partners, customers, and employees in an enterprise setting. Its iBaan product family includes applications with three themes — collaboration, information, and integration. What this means is that the ERP systems are integrated to one another and to non-ERP systems for successful deployment. These systems are supplemented with collaborative efforts of employees, suppliers, partners, and customers who exchange information via the Web.

In addition to Baan, other major vendors such as Oracle, JDE, and PeopleSoft have come out with new releases that signal a change in underlying ERP architecture — database, network, and messaging. Like ASPS, c-Commerce is not for everyone. It depends on the enterprise's requirements and needs and the expected ROIs that ERP systems would generate.

About the Editor

Judith M. Myerson is a System Architect/Engineer. She received a Special Act Award from the U.S. Navy for outstanding systems analysis work and was in charge of a computer/network security program for several years.

Myerson holds a Master of Science in Engineering degree from the University of Pennsylvania. A noted writer with more than 150 articles published, she has authored, edited, and reviewed numerous books.

The author of the upcoming book, *Middleware*, her articles appear in the following Auerbach publications:

- *Server Management Handbook*
- *Enterprise Systems Integration Handbook*
- *Information Security Management Handbook*, 4th Edition, Volume 3
- *Data Communications Management*
- *Data Base Management*

She can be reached at jmyerson@bellatlantic.net.

Index

Index

A

Acceptance test plan (ATP), 594
Accenture, 733
Access
    control lists (ACL), 152, 175
    lines (ALs), 514
    services, 61, 62, 88, 91
Accounting/consulting firms, Big Four, 733
ACL, see Access control lists
Active server pages, 74, 178, 179
ActiveX Data Objects (ADO), 252
Addressing
    in-line, 585
    native, 585
    simplified view of, 501
    wild, 585
Address mapping, 571
Administration manuals, 590
ADO, see ActiveX Data Objects
Advanced Encryption Standard (AES), 563
Advanced manufacturing technology
    (AMT), 475
Advanced planning & scheduling (APS), 413
Advanced Traveler Information System
    (ATIS), 306
Advertising, 470
AES, see Advanced Encryption Standard
Allen & Hamilton, 733
Allied Waste Management, 412
ALs, see Access lines
Altis Limited, 626
Ambiguity types, 279
American National Standards Institute
    (ANSI), 668
American Software, 764
America's SAP User Group, 772
AMT, see Advanced manufacturing
    technology
Analytical mining methods, 399
Anaphora ambiguity, 280
Andersen Consulting, 733
ANSI, see American National Standards
    Institute
AOL, 374, 579
API, see Application programming interface
APICS, 772
Application(s)
    architecture, 44, 45

availability, 751
changes, distribution of, 259
communication between client and
    server in, 173
development environments, 613
device management, 531
E-commerce, 660
enterprise directory services versus,
    597
gateways, for integrating dissimilar
    systems, 639
HTML-based, 670
integration, organization IT budgets for,
    431
line-of-business, 129
logic, 75
mapping, 25
market analysis of commercially
    available, 24
mission-critical, 333
monitoring, 633
packages, bolt-on, 433
programming interface (API), 144, 167,
    571, 587
protocol interfaces, 150
query engine, 375
Response Measurement, 749
selection alternatives, in multibusiness
    unit environments, 28
services, 70
software production
    assessment procedures, 714
    performance profile, 715
tunneled SNA, 511
usage and analysis, 537
Application servers, 185–194
    basic architecture of, 188
    deployment in enterprise, 191
    management, 194
    overview of application server, 187–191
    overview of Web server, 186–187
    scalability, load balancing, and fault
        tolerance, 193–194
    security, 192–193
Application service providers (ASPs),
    449–458
    architecture, 454–455
    ASP business model, 451–452
    categories, 453–454
    enterprise, 453

O

INDEX

visualization, 395
Toronto Business Systems, 626
Total Information Solutions (TISs), 468
TP, see Transaction processing
Trace, 545
Tracking tools, 51
Traffic
  generator, 549, 550
  growth, modeling of during system life
    cycle, 517
  intensities (TIs), 515, 517
Transaction
  analysis, 324
  management
    end-to-end, 655
    services, 72
  partitioning services, 73
  processing (TP), 152, 314, 322
  services, 71
  tests, 714, 718
Transformations, handling, 267, 268
Transmission Control Protocol/Internet
    Protocol (TCP/IP), 459, 502, 548,
    579, 639
Transport
  -layer interface (TLI), 510, 512
  services, 67
Triggers, 95, 365
Tunneling, 502
Two-phase commit, 97, 98
Two-tier model, 638

U

UML, see Unified Modeling Language
Unified Modeling Language (UML), 211, 235
Unisource Worldwide, Inc., 425
Unit testing, 653
Universal identifier (UUID), 151
Universo Online (UOL), 680
UNIX, 189, 462, 574
UOL, see Universo Online
URLs, advertisements featuring, 670
Usability testing, 654
Use Case Diagram, 203
User
  administration, 55
  -centered documentation techniques,
    198, 199
  experience, SLAs tied to, 748
  ID strategies, complexity of, 41
  interface tools, 49
  navigation services, 57, 58, 59

USi, see USinternetworking
USinternetworking (USi), 452, 456
Usoft Developer, 303
Utility(ies)
  reference guides, 590
  vendors, 626
UUID, see Universal identifier
UUNET, 579

V

Valenite, 484, 485
Validation
  external element, 273
  rules, 274
Value chain, 105
Value-added networks (VANs), 567, 574, 659,
    668
Value-added taxes (VATs), 31, 556
Vanilla state, software in, 33
VANs, see Value-added networks
Variable bit rate (VBR), 515
VATs, see Value-added taxes
VAX hosts, 642
VBR, see Variable bit rate
Vendor(s)
  allegiance of specific departments to
    particular, 497
  DBMS, 87
  ERP, 35, 434, 437
  hub, 507
  integrators, 736
  middleware, 430
  ORB, 156
  proprietary, 734
  -provided directory user agents, 607
  selection of, 593
  software, 442
    evaluation of, 446
    offerings, integrated, 7
    upgrades, 450
  solution, selection of, 500
  support, 238
  tool, 162
  UNIX system, 189
  utility, 626
Vernam cipher, 563
Version
  date, 273
  services, 63, 93
  upgrade, 587
Very large scale integration (VLSI)
    technology, 513
VGLs, see Voice-grade lines